THE WILSON YEARS

SOURCES FOR MODERN BRITISH HISTORY

General Editors: Kathleen Burk, John Ramsden, John Turner

THE CRISIS OF BRITISH UNIONISM: The Domestic Political Papers of the Second Earl of Selborne, 1885–1922
Edited by George Boyce. 1987

LABOUR AND THE WARTIME COALITION: From the Diary of James Chuter Ede, 1941–1945
Edited by Kevin Jefferys. 1987

THE MODERNISATION OF CONSERVATIVE POLITICS: The Diaries and Letters of William Bridgeman, 1904–1935
Edited by Philip Williamson. 1988

THE CRISIS OF BRITISH POWER: The Imperial and Naval Papers of the Second Earl of Selborne, 1895–1910
Edited by George Boyce. 1990

PATRICK GORDON WALKER: Political Diaries, 1932-1971
Edited by Robert Pearce. 1991

PARLIAMENT AND POLITICS IN THE AGE OF BALDWIN AND MACDONALD: The Diaries of Sir Cuthbert Headlam, 1924–1935
Edited by Stuart Ball. 1993

DUTY AND CITIZENSHIP: The Correspondence and Papers of Violet Markham, 1896–1953
Edited by Helen Jones. 1994

A LIBERAL CHRONICLE: Journals and Papers of J.A. Pease, 1st Lord Gainford, 1908–1910
Edited by Cameron Hazlehurst and Christine Woodland. 1994

LIBERAL BY PRINCIPLE: The Politics of John Wodehouse, 1st Earl of Kimberley, 1843–1902
Edited by John Powell. 1996

THE WILSON YEARS: A Treasury Diary, 1964–1969
Alec Cairncross. 1997

THE WILSON YEARS

A Treasury Diary

1964–1969

Alec Cairncross

THP

British Library Cataloguing in Publication Data

A copy of the catalogue entry for this publication can be obtained from the British Library

   ISBN 1-872273-06-8

PUBLISHED BY THE HISTORIANS' PRESS
9 DAISY ROAD, LONDON E18 1EA

Printed in England by Antony Rowe Ltd

Contents

Preface

In the years 1964–69 I held the newly created post of Head of the Government Economic Service and – more important for an understanding of my duties – I was Director of the Economic Section of the Treasury (as indeed I had been since June 1961). I kept a private diary, as my two predecessors, Professor James Meade and Sir Robert Hall, had done.[1] This was contrary to civil service regulations but implanted events more firmly in my mind and now conveys a vivid and yet realistic picture of life in the Treasury in the 1960s. The diary entries grew longer in successive years but came to an abrupt stop when I left the Treasury at the end of 1968 to assume fresh duties as Master of St Peter's College, Oxford.

I was not unfamiliar with Whitehall, having served there almost throughout the 1940s, first in the Cabinet Offices in 1940–41, then briefly in the Board of Trade, followed by four years planning aircraft production from 1941–45 and a further spell in the Board of Trade in 1946–49 as Economic Adviser. I had even spent a week in the Treasury in 1941 deputising for Dennis Robertson. In the 1950s I had combined academic duties in Glasgow with membership of a succession of government committees, ending with the Radcliffe Committee in 1957–59.

Mixed in with these duties had been six months in Berlin in 1945–46 taking part on behalf of the Treasury in the quadripartite negotiations on a reparations plan, a second six months in 1946 on the staff of the *Economist*, a year in Paris in 1950 as Economic Adviser to the OEEC, and eighteen months in Washington helping to establish the Economic Development Institute for the World Bank.

When this part of my diary opens, l had already been in the Treasury for over three years as Economic Adviser to HMG, a title which the Labour Government abolished (without informing me) in 1964. I continued as Director of the Economic Section, of which I had been a founding member in 1940-41 when it was established in the War Cabinet Offices. In 1964 this was a group of a dozen or so economists, many of them of outstanding ability, although when I entered the Treasury in 1961 only one, Bryan Hopkin, was graded at Under-Secretary level.

In earlier years they had played an important part in educating their col-

---

[1] *Collected Papers of James Meade, Vol. IV The Cabinet Office Diary* (ed. Howson), (London: Unwin Hyman, 1989); *The Robert Hall Diaries* (ed. Cairncross), (London: Unwin Hyman, Vol. I, 1989, Vol. II, 1991.)

leagues in the Treasury in elementary economics and had advised on a wide spectrum of policy issues. By 1964 their main duty was to advise on demand management although I was also trying to brigade as many as I could spare with the expenditure divisions of the Treasury or second them to other key government departments. Advice on demand management was based on short-term economic forecasts, prepared in great detail three times a year and covering the next 18–24 months. In the 1950s there had been no other similar forecasts in Britain until Sir Robert Hall encouraged the National Institute to prepare regular forecasts, initially with Treasury help.

In the early 1960s Christopher Dow had urged that the preparation of all economic forecasts should be entrusted to a separate forecasting unit within the Treasury. Although this was not done, since other government departments continued to take an active part, the Treasury side of the work was undertaken in 1964 by a separate division, National Economy 1, staffed largely by members of the Economic Section. A major part was played by Wynne Godley, with Bryan Hopkin and/or Fred Atkinson taking administrative responsibility; all three of them being members of the Economic Section.

When the diary opens in October 1964 with the election of the Wilson government, the economy was on the brink of a major balance of payments crisis. The expansionary measures taken by Maudling in the 1963 Budget did not exercise their full effect until 1964 when domestic demand outstripped domestic production, and sucked in a rising flow of imports. At the same time, there was a large outflow of capital, much of it to finance investment abroad by the oil companies. The external deficit on current and capital account, as became clear shortly before the election, was likely to soar to £800 million in 1964.

When the Treasury urged corrective measures in June, the Chancellor, Reginald Maudling, had agreed to act in July by making a call for special deposits, but changed his mind, claiming that the economy was 'stuck', when he found that the index of industrial production remained flat month after month. As summer moved into autumn and the economic outlook steadily darkened, the government, paralysed by fears of public reactions to yet another 'stop' and to the implied abandonment of a 4 per cent growth target, took no action to prevent the impending crisis. Since the balance of payments had been a constant threat since 1960, voices were raised increasingly in favour of devaluing the pound and the issue of devaluation dogged the Labour government from the beginning.

I assumed that I should have no difficulty in finding a publisher for this record, but when I submitted sample extracts to six well-known publishers, one after another sent them back unhesitatingly without even asking to see the manuscript. Professor Kathleen Burk of University College, London then suggested that I should submit it to The Historians' Press which specialises in the publication of diaries and I was happy to accept her suggestion. It was necessary, however, to make extensive cuts, amounting to about a quarter of the original length, in order to reduce it to a convenient size. Readers interested in consulting the full manuscript can however, consult the copy deposited in the Library of the

University of Glasgow.[2]

My thanks go to Professor John Turner for rendering the manuscript into typeset form. I am grateful also to Mrs Anne Robinson who rescued the diary from illegibility, to Robert Pinder and to my daughter Elizabeth who transferred it on to disk, and made necessary adjustments.

I should also like to thank the Leverhulme Foundation for help in meeting the cost of editing the text and preparing it for publication.

Alec Cairncross
Oxford, 1996

---

[2] The diary for 1961–64 will appear under other auspices.

Abbreviations

ABA	American Bankers' Association; American Bar Association
ACAS	Advisory, Conciliation and Arbitration Service
AEC	Atomic Energy Commission
AFTA	Atlantic Free Trade Area
AP	Assistant Principal
ASLEF	Associated Society of Locomotive Engineers and Firemen
ATS	Auxiliary Territorial Service
BIS	Bank for International Settlements
BOAC	British Overseas Airways Corporation
BoT	Board of Trade
BP	British Petroleum
BR	Bank Rate
CAS	Centre for Administrative Studies
CBI	Confederation of British Industry
CEA	Council of Economic Affairs
CEGB	Central Electricity Generating Board
CM	Common Market
CO	Commonwealth Office (1966–68); Colonial Office (to 1966)
CPC	Commercial Policy Committee
CRO	Commonwealth Relations Office (to 1966)
CSC	Civil Service Commission
CSO	Central Statistical Office
DAVA	Douglas Allen
DCF	Discounted Cash Flow
DEA	Department of Economic Affairs
DES	Department of Education and Science
DHFR	Sir Denis Rickett
DTI	Department of Trade and Industry
EAC	Economic Assessment Committee
ECSC	European Coal and Steel Community
ED(O)	Steering Committee on Economic Policy (Official)
ED(PI)	Steering Committee on Prices and Incomes

EEC	European Economic Community
EFTA	European Free Trade Association
EPC	Economic Policy Committee
EPU	European Payments Union
FCO	Foreign and Commonwealth Office (from 1968)
Fed	Federal Reserve System
FHA	Finance Houses Association
FO	Foreign Office (to 1968)
FST	Financial Secretary, Treasury
FT	Financial Times
FU	'Forever Unmentionable' Committee on Devaluation
GDP	Gross Domestic Product
GES	Government Economic Service
HFIG	Home Finance Intelligence Group
IBRD	International Bank for Reconstruction and Development
ICC	International Chamber of Commerce
ICFC	Industrial and Commercial Finance Corporation
ICS	Indian Civil Service
IMF	International Monetary Fund
IMTA	Institute of Municipal Treasurers and Accountants
IPP	International Purchasing Power
IRC	Industrial Reorganisation Corporation
IRI	Istituto per la Ricostruzione Industriale
LBJ	President Johnson
LCES	London and Cambridge Economic Service
MIT	Massachusetts Institute of Technology
MPBW	Ministry of Public Building and Works
MTAC	Medium Term Assessment Committee
MTS	Medium Term Strategy
NABM	National Association of British Manufacturers
(N)AFTA	North Atlantic Free Trade Area
NBPI	National Board for Prices and Incomes
NEDC	National Economic Development Council
NEDO	National Economic Development Office
NIESR	National Institute for Economic and Social Research
NIF	National Income Forecasting
NMW	National Minimum Wage
NUGMW	National Union of General and Municipal Workers
NUR	National Union of Railwaymen
NUS	National Union of Students
ODI	Overseas Development Institute
ODM	Ministry of Overseas Development

OECD	Organisation for Economic Co-operation and Development
OEEC	Organisation for European Economic Co-operation
OSA	Outer Sterling Area
PCO	Plan Co-ordinating Office
PCSC	Plan Co-ordinating Survey Committee
PCWP	Plan Co-ordinating Working Party
PE Club	Political Economy Club
PESC	Public Expenditure Survey Committee
PI Comm.	Prices and Incomes Committee
PPS	Principal Private Secretary; Parliamentary Private Secretary
PSI	Public Sector Investment
PWLB	Public Works Loan Board
qr's	quantitative restrictions (quotas)
RES	Royal Economic Society
RFC	Reconstruction Finance Corporation
RIIA	Royal Institute for International Affairs
SCOW	Steel Company of Wales
SDR	Special Drawing Right
SEP	Strategic Economic Policy
SET	Selective Employment Tax
SIC	Standard Industrial Classification
SLA	School Leaving Age
SPC	St Peter's College, Oxford
SSRC	Social Science Research Council
SVIMEZ	Southern Italy Industrial Investment Association
TFM	Treasury Fortnightly Meeting
TGWU	Transport and General Workers Union
TIC	Temporary Import Charge
TOC	Treasury Organisation Committee
TUC	Trades Union Congress
TVA	Tennessee Valley Authority; Value Added Tax
UCL	University College, London
UDI	Unilateral Declaration of Independence
WP	No.3 Working Party No.3 of OECD

Chapter 1

October–December 1964

Friday, 16 October 1964

The 1964 election brought Labour to power with a majority of 5. The incoming government was given extensive briefs and advised against devaluing or floating the pound. Maudling[1] had asked the Treasury to consider the use of import quotas, or alternatively an import surcharge, and Treasury advice favoured a surcharge (following the example of Canada). When this was introduced it encountered strong criticism in Geneva from other members of EFTA,[2] particularly as the Government denied that the economy was suffering from overheating.

In a meeting of key Ministers almost as soon as the election was over, it was decided not to devalue. This occasioned little surprise in the Treasury in view of Harold Wilson's strong opposition to devaluation in 1949 but it shocked the government's new economic advisers, Professor Kaldor,[3] Sir Donald MacDougall[4] and Robert Neild[5]. Thomas Balogh[6] alone supported the government's decision and he, too, soon came to accept the need to devalue. I was myself convinced from the time when I rejoined the civil service in 1961 that the pound would have to be devalued at some stage in the 1960s. But I saw no point in devaluing in an overheated economy without the support of stringent deflationary measures which there was no likelihood that the Labour government would adopt.

[1] Reginald Maudling. Cons. Chancellor of the Exchequer, July 1962–October 1964.

[2] EFTA European Free Trade Association, made up of Austria, Denmark, Norway, Portugal, Sweden, Switzerland and the United Kingdom

[3] Nicholas Kaldor, (later Lord). Fellow of King's College, Cambridge from 1949: Special Adviser to the Chancellor 1964–67; a highly ingenious, fertile and knowledgeable economist with great faith in the power of taxation to make the economy work better; entertaining but rarely stopped talking.

[4] Sir Donald MacDougall. Econ. Dir., Nat. Econ. Developt. Office, 1962–64; Dir. Gen. DEA, 1964–68. Succeeded Cairncross in 1969 as Head of the Govt. Econ. Service and also appointed Chief Econ. Adviser to the Treasury.

[5] Robert Neild. Econ. Adviser to the Treasury, 1964–67.

[6] Thomas Balogh (later Lord). Fellow of Balliol College, Oxford, 1945–73; officially 'Econ. Adviser to the Cabinet', 1964–67; summed up by Robert Hall as 'the Prime Minister's spy'. A man of intuitive judgements that were often sound but of a violent temper and full of bile. As Keynes remarked: 'the trouble with Tommy is that he never went to Winchester'.

In the first month I took little part in policy discussion. I was chiefly occupied in ensuring the continuance within the Treasury of the Economic Section under a professional, non-political head. The post of Economic Adviser to HMG which I had held since 1961 had been abolished and instead I was asked to move to Washington in succession to Sir Eric Roll[7] as the Treasury's representative at the IMF/IBRD, without any clear indication of who would take my place and what was to happen to the Economic Section.

It was at first intended that Tony Crosland[8] should come to the Treasury and Robert Neild should go to the new Department of Economic Affairs but at the last moment the appointments were reversed. Robert became Economic Adviser to the Treasury and this appeared to involve taking over the Economic Section as his staff. As he was a former member of the Economic Section, this would mean taking precedence over former colleagues and at the same time make it difficult to maintain a non-political stance in Section advice. In the end an arrangement that proved reasonably satisfactory was arrived at. I became Head of a phantom Government Economic Service, while Ministers continued to assemble their own private armies of economists, sometimes with advice from Thomas Balogh, rarely with any reference to myself. Within the Treasury I continued to direct the Economic Section and shared advisory duties harmoniously with Robert Neild, with some overlap on major issues.

There was much discussion of the division of responsibilities between the Treasury and the Department of Economic Affairs and some attempt to use a short term/long term split. It seemed more important to decide how the main instruments of policy should be allocated. The exchange rate, monetary policy and the Budget all remained within the Treasury ambit and the forecasting unit in NE1 also stayed there. Incomes policy, as William Armstrong,[9] the Permanent Secretary, had envisaged, was readily transferred to DEA.

Friday, 16 October 1964   Election results started coming out at 10.00 p.m. last night. Like most people I expected a Labour majority of 30 or 40. At first the indications were of a Conservative victory (after seven results Transport House was obviously disconcerted and the bookies were offering 6 to 4 on the Tories. Then things swung strongly the other way and Robert McKenzie[10] on TV was implying that it was all settled while Robin Day[11] heckled Keith Joseph[12] as if there wasn't the faintest chance of a Tory victory. This morning at 1.30 a.m. I

---

[7] Sir Eric Roll (later Lord). Econ. Minister and Head of UK Treasury Del., Washington; UK Exec. Dir. at the IMF, or World Bank, 1963–64. Perm. Under-Sec. of State, DEA, 1964–66; Exec. Dir., Bank of England, 1968–77.

[8] Tony Crosland. Lab. Min. of State for Econ. Affairs, DEA, October 1964; Sec. of State for Education and Science, October 1965; President of Board of Trade, August 1967.

[9] Sir William Armstrong (later Lord). Jt. Perm. Sec. to the Treasury 1962–68; Perm. Sec., Civil Service Dept., and Head of the Home Civil Service, 1968–74

[10] Robert McKenzie. Professor of Sociology, LSE, from 1964; frequent broadcaster.

[11] Robin Day. TV Journalist from 1955 onwards; introducer of 'Panorama' 1967–72.

[12] Sir Keith Joseph. Cons. Minister, Board of Trade, October 1961–October 1964.

gave up and from then on the tide turned again. I was surprised to hear Otto Clarke[13] imply at 10.30 a.m. that it was still quite an open issue.

We met in William Armstrong's room to take stock, largely because of a false alarm on bankrate. The Chancellor had meditated putting it up before the election and had been persuaded that this was unwise. We all agreed at that stage that it was better to hold over a rise in case of a real run on the pound. But this morning the Prime Minister, seeing the news from Moscow of Khruschev's deposition, rang up Reggie to propose an immediate rise. It would have been done with Harold Wilson's agreement, if at all, but this would have been impossible to get before 12.45 or so, when he was due to arrive from Liverpool. William [Armstrong] readily got agreement that this would have been interpreted as a panic measure involving rejection at a few minutes notice of the bill tender. The market was, anyhow, pretty calm and in the end the trade figures didn't greatly excite it – no doubt because other events such as the Chinese explosion of an atomic bomb took precedence (even in Zurich).

Reggie [Maudling] had meant to go off to the country and lie low but he was at No.11 most of the morning and came in during the afternoon to say Goodbye. Later he was on television with Sir Edward Boyle[14] (and very good too). He was sad to go with things in their existing state and recognised that he was bequeathing a hard problem to his successor. He had been over the same ground with William earlier and my own comments followed William's. William felt that failure to control public expenditure and housing had been the major weakness with which he could be charged, and that we ought probably to have acted in June to call for special deposits. He did not say (but felt) that the 4 percent illusion was the other major weakness. I said that the truth was that expansion had involved grave risks, bigger than we had realized, and that in the circumstances it had been hard not to take the risks. Reggie agreed that he couldn't have followed a non-expansionary course and that the trouble lay not so much in economic gimmicks as in deep-set public attitudes. The businessmen were determined *not* to allow a policy of deflation time to take effect and agitated for expansion whenever there was a margin of spare capacity. Reggie is particularly anxious to be able to claim that action has not been postponed or withheld on political grounds and that he has done everything that officials wanted him to do by way of restraining action.

William asked me in the morning to consider taking over in Washington from Eric Roll who is to be Permanent Secretary to George Brown[15]. Gordon Richardson[16] wants the job but couldn't be free for several months at least. Eric

---

[13] Otto Clarke. Sir Richard Clarke, Second Perm. Sec. to the Treasury in charge of public expenditure, 1962–66; Perm. Sec., Min. of Aviation, 1966; Perm. Sec., Min. of Technology, 1966–70.

[14] Sir Edward Boyle. Cons. Min. of State for Education, July 1962 and for Education and Science, April–October 1964.

[15] George Brown. Deputy Leader of the Labour Party, November 1960–70; First Sec. of State and Minister for Econ. Affairs, October 1964; Sec. of State for Foreign Affairs, August 1966–March 1968.

[16] Gordon Richardson. Chm. of merchant bank J. Henry Schroeder Wagg & Co. Ltd,

himself is not very happy to be coming back a week after moving to his new house in Washington. Nor is Douglas Allen[17] very glad to be going to the new ministry as Deputy Under-Secretary. What the fate of the Economic Section is to be, nobody seems anxious to consider. Eric tells me that George Woods[18] still has some hopes of inducing me to come to the [World] Bank [as V.P.] and I pointed out to William that if I had to go to Washington I might prefer the Bank job.

Meanwhile the deficit has climbed to £800 m. this year plus £450 m. next and this is enough to make it impossible to delay action for very long. It is quite astonishing how calmly the foreign exchange market has taken each fresh revelation – no doubt a tribute to Reggie, but also a bit of a mystery.

This year has been incredibly like 1960 and even the course of exports and the output of engineering have run parallel. There was the same long spell of stationary output, drooping exports, and rising imports. I drew Reggie's attention to this today and he drew the inference that in 1961 things were getting better faster than we had realized and the same might happen again. But we're already taking credit for a big improvement, starting from a basic deficit about £300 m. bigger than in 1960.

Sam Goldman,[19] David Hubback[20] and I lunched at the Reform Club and debated whether Harold might decline to form a government. There was further discussion at 4.30 p.m. in William's room on this kind of issue. It seemed to me clear that the majority would oblige the government to take a pretty short view and avoid any action likely to cause unpopularity, knowing that an early election might be inescapable. It is also obvious that detailed legislation will be practically impossible. So far as Sam Goldman's proposition went, I said that politicians who had been out of power for so long would neither wish to refuse office, nor enhance their chance with the electorate if by declining it they made a second election necessary. Sam agreed that they must be very anxious to see the briefs and find out the 'facts' (of which there are very few that have not been made public). This would probably dispose them to take office, but Harold Wilson might seek a pretext for an early dissolution. William in the afternoon said that he thought the Conservatives might be quite willing to help the Labour Party to stay in power for a bit and might not act purely destructively. This tallies with the late Prime Minister's statement.

About 5 p.m. Eric Roll came along. Robert Neild had been asked by T. Balogh who had been asked by George Brown, to get Eric to ring! Eric was just too late to catch George Brown at No.10 but he went along to see him later with instructions from William to make sure that he knew the formal position

1962–72. Became Governor of the Bank of England in 1973.

[17] Douglas Allen. Third Perm. Sec., Treasury, 1962–64; Dep. Under-Sec. of State, DEA, October 1964–May 1966; Second Perm. Under-Sec. of State, May–October 1966; Perm. Under-Sec., October 1966–68; Perm. Sec. to the Treasury 1968–74.

[18] George Woods. President, IBRD [World Bank] 1963–68.

[19] Sam Goldman. Third Sec., Treasury 1962–68; Second Perm. Sec., 1968–72.

[20] David Hubback Principal Private Sec. to the Cons. Chancellor (Selwyn Lloyd), 1960–62, Under-Sec., Treasury, 1962–68.

and whether he was now Minister of Economic Affairs. George Brown waded right in and discussed his terms of reference which he thought (and Harold too!) weren't quite right. These terms represent presumably the paper William has sent along to him based on the Treasury Organization Committee Paper.

I lunched on Tuesday at the Reform Club with Donald MacDougall. He did *not* say outright that we ought to devalue but I expect that Douglas Allen is right in saying that this is what he really thinks. Donald seemed more anxious to get *me* to expound the situation.

Sunday, 18 October   I was told by Ian Bancroft[21] yesterday not to come in after all, but today I decided that I must. The Sunday papers were in pretty lurid terms; there was talk of devaluation and import controls splashed freely, and a rise in bank rate all but promised.

I saw Peter Jay[22] first and arranged that he should tell William that I was in (by now it was nearly 1 p.m.) as he hadn't come back from No.10. Then I saw Tom Caulcott[23] who is to be Secretary to George Brown and (in the corridor) Eric and a stranger, joined by Donald a moment later. We agreed to talk after lunch. William summoned me and it was clear that it had been a hectic day with outside advisors descending in swarms and almost bulldozing the Prime Minister into devaluation. Robert Neild is to come to the Treasury, but even he jibbed at coming if a decision on devaluation had already been taken. Nicky Kaldor is to be Tax Adviser. T.B. [Thomas Balogh] is to be taken on the strength at No.10 (how do they get released from their academic duties so easily?).

There is a battle over Evan Maude[24] to give William some leverage in case he is pressed to let the Forecasting Unit go.

I told William that I would be willing to go to Washington on a temporary basis if: (a) I could rest assured that the Economic Section remained in being, and (b) I had a job to come back to. But I would not decide finally until the middle of the week when all this was clearer. He thought that Gordon Richardson might be able to take over by Christmas.

When I finally saw Eric (very briefly) I told him that I thought it a very unfortunate day for the Economic Section if the post of Economic Adviser became a political appointment. I had served under both parties and the Conservatives left Robert Hall[25] undisturbed. I was in effect being sacked, and I was tempted to resign in protest. But if I did go to Washington I should do my best to explain and defend the Government's policies even if I was not personally persuaded.

---

[21] Ian Bancroft. Principal Private Sec. to the Lab. Chancellor, (James Callaghan) 1964–66; Under-Sec., Treasury 1966–68.

[22] Peter Jay. Private Sec. to Sir William Armstrong 1964; Principal, Treasury, 1964–67; Economics Ed. *The Times*, 1967–77.

[23] Tom Caulcott. Private Sec. to successive Chancellors, 1961–64; Principal Private Sec. to First Sec. of State, DEA, 1964–65; Assist. Sec., Treasury, 1965–66.

[24] Evan Maude. Treasury 1946–64; Assis. Under-Sec. of State, DEA, 1964–66; Dep. Under-Sec., 1966–67; Econ. Minister in Washington, 1967–69.

[25] Sir Robert Hall. Director, Econ. Section of the Treasury, 1947–61; Econ. Adviser to HMG, 1953–61.

Eric said that he too was very sad to have to switch in this way against so small a parliamentary majority and that although people might not believe him, his 'promotion' was not something that gave him pleasure. He suggested that I should wait until the end of the week since the Government intended to make a declaration of policy by that time, and this might help me to make up my mind. But I shall decide on the basis of the situation at the Treasury and in Whitehall, not on a Government statement of policy. *Somebody* will have to manage the economists in Government service.

Reggie in August when told the latest rather shattering figures of production and trade said over the telephone 'I see; inflation without expansion, eh?' I don't think I exchanged more than a couple of sentences with him between the Bank/Fund meeting in Tokyo and the election. He didn't like electioneering and was pretty tense (for him!) over some of his press conferences. 'X made a boob yesterday, it must be my turn to make a boob today'. Yet in fact he conducted the press conferences very successfully and without any real slip. He was first rate on T.V. against Crossman[26] and Jenkins[27] the night after the election.

Harold seems determined to be the elder statesman, unsmiling and suppressing any shafts of wit.

Monday, 19 October   We had one and a half hours with William in the morning and it soon appeared that utter chaos reigned. Nicky is making difficulties with the Chancellor about his title and location. He wants to sit in the Treasury, not in Somerset House (he is not interested in indirect taxation) and wants to be Adviser (*simpliciter*). T. Balogh seemed yesterday to take it for granted that he could go to meetings of the inner group (P.M., George Brown, Chancellor, plus W.A., Eric Roll, Donald M., and on Saturday – L.Helsby[28]). William reminded him he had to sign the Official Secrets Act and this couldn't be done except by arrangement with the Permanent Secretary but he had no Permanent Secretary. Harold Wilson gave instructions that T.B. was to have all the papers he wanted and access to him *but* the door from the Cabinet Office to No.10 was to be kept locked, and T.B. was *not* to have the key.

Some important changes even since this morning. Bruce Fraser[29] *not* to go to Technology but Education, while Maurice Dean[30] goes to Technology and Arnold France[31] to Health. Ministry of Housing to be split in two but to keep

[26] Richard Crossman. Lab. Minister of Housing and Local Govt., October 1964; Lord President of the Council and Leader of the House of Commons, August 1966–April 1968; Lord President only, April 1968; Sec. of State for Social Security, November 1968.

[27] Roy Jenkins. Lab. Minister of Aviation, December 1965; Chancellor of the Exchequer, November 1967–June 1970.

[28] Sir Laurence Helsby. Jt. Perm. Sec. to the Treasury, 1963–68 and Head of the Civil Service.

[29] Sir Bruce Fraser. Perm. Sec., Min. of Health, 1960–64; Jt. Perm. Under-Sec. of State, Dept. of Education and Science, 1964–65; Comptroller and Auditor-General, 1966–71.

[30] Sir Maurice Dean. Perm. Sec., Min. of Technology, 1964–66.

[31] Sir Arnold France. Dep. Sec., Min. of Health, 1963–64; Perm. Sec., 1964–68; Chm. Board of Inland Revenue, 1968–73.

Planning (after a weekend battle). Not clear what staff Donald MacDougall will have or how his functions differ from those of Eric Roll and Douglas Allen. Fred Atkinson[32] not to be promoted to Under Secretary. Difficult to recruit for an indefinite period but Donald is seeing a long list of possibles including W.Beckerman[33].

The question for me is whether the Economic Section is already dead. Donald and Robert Neild between them effectively end the post-war experiment. Robert told me that he would feel bound to submit his resignation on a change of Government. But he obviously wants to run the Economic Section as if nothing had happened. Bryan Hopkin[34] may well resign and Wynne Godley[35] is mutinous and may also decide to stay out. This would leave Andrew Roy[36] the only Senior Economic Adviser and a mass of Economic Assistants with no clear career prospects. L. Helsby tried to tell me at two successive interviews that Robert Neild was not a political appointee and I asked him what the House of Commons would make of that. He had no real understanding of the stink that must result if, say, Bryan and I both resigned. I told him that this would not be of my making but that, whether I went to Washington or not, I would ask to see the Prime Minister and speak my mind to him about the Section. If R.N. had been a private adviser on the political level no-one could object; but to bring him in as the head of the Section over Bryan, who had held the most senior post in the National Institute (and built it up almost from scratch), without any submission of the post to the judgement of other professional economists, was turning it into a political post of the same type as Walter Heller's[37]. This would have consequences all down the line for it would be difficult to hold out to entrants the prospect of apolitical advancement. In fact L.H. was prepared to agree that we might have to assimilate the Treasury economists to ordinary administrative functions or departments.

It is also far from clear where NE1 [the forecasting staff] will end up. Donald MacDougall has made it clear to Douglas Allen that he doesn't think that it is possible to leave the forecasting staff in the Treasury and even Douglas Allen has, I think, some hankering after uniting it with DEA.

The difficulty is to know what being a member of the Economic Section now means. If those outside the Treasury are put under a committee with Philip Allen[38] in the Chair, will they be content to stay indefinitely where they are? (e.g. Foreign Office). If within the Treasury there is no-one outside the

[32] Fred Atkinson. Econ. Section of the Treasury, 1949–69; Dep. Director, 1965–69; Head of Govt. Econ. Service, 1977-79.

[33] W. Beckerman. Fellow of Balliol College, 1964–69; Econ. Adviser to Board of Trade, 1967–69.

[34] Bryan Hopkin Dep. Dir., Econ. Section of the Treasury, 1958–65; Head of Govt. Econ. Service, 1974–76.

[35] Wynne Godley. Econ. Section of the Treasury, 1956-70; Dep. Dir., 1967–70.

[36] Andrew Roy. Econ. Consultant, Econ. Section, Treasury, 1962–64; Senior Econ. Adviser, 1964–69.

[37] Walter Heller. Chm., Council of Econ. Advisers, USA, 1961–64.

[38] Sir Philip Allen. Second Sec., Treasury, 1963–66; Perm. Under-Sec. of State, Home Office, 1966–72.

Research Unit above the level of Adviser and they are scattered and not under single control, do they any longer represent a common staff? If NE1 is moved, the position will be settled once and for all. William said that it won't be, but we'll see.

Thursday, 22 October   On Tuesday after lunch I cabled George Woods, telling him that my post had been abolished and asking if he was still interested. He rang me up in the evening to say he was very much interested, and would I fly out and see him? I made provisional arrangements with IBRD's London Office to fly on Tuesday next, returning on Friday night. I also told William what I was doing and that I couldn't bring myself to accept the Washington post if it meant leaving the Economic Section to Robert Neild. No-one, then or now, has told me what Robert Neild's title and functions are but Elsie Abbot [Treasury Establishment Officer] said last night that he was to be Economic Adviser to the Treasury. Wynne Godley called on Tuesday and assured me that he would not want to come back if the Section was to be directed by Robert Neild.

When I called to see William in the evening I had with me a Minute, addressed to the Prime Minister and Chancellor, that I drafted on Monday after talking a second time to Laurence Helsby. William thought that it should be in letter form and it went in letter form on Wednesday morning. But he warned me that Laurence Helsby thought it wrong for me to send minutes to the Prime Minister except through him.

I wasn't able to see Helsby on Tuesday evening but saw him on Wednesday first thing, having in the meantime seen the front page of *The Guardian* ('Economic Adviser to go'): we had rather a cross interview. He held to his view that no issue of principle was involved and this made me pretty mad until I told him angrily that it was his battle I was fighting. He also argued that Robert Neild was a better economist than Bryan which made me even angrier, although this time I kept my temper. He hadn't seen *The Guardian* and insisted that the announcement was not official (in which he proved to be right). He told me that he had talked to the Prime Minister who made it clear that there was no political animus against me and said he could think me politically less right wing than, say, Donald MacDougall. He didn't try to stop me from sending off my Minute although he made it clear that it ought to go through him and that it could not be treated as 'Top Secret and Personal'.

I asked what my duties were. He said to go to Washington. But he had nothing to suggest as an alternative and although he denied that after Washington I'd have to resign he had no concrete suggestions about that either. The general line was that I was an established civil servant like anyone else and must not expect to be retained indefinitely as an Economic Adviser. This is strange doctrine from the Head of the Civil Service.

When I had seen William the previous evening he said that there was no doubt that poison had been dripping for some time on my reputation and that it had not been appreciated that I was a non-political civil servant. Some of the Party obviously thought that I had been brought in to do the July measures and the pay pause in 1961 and the later National Incomes Commission evidence had seemed to confirm this.

So when I emerged from William's room and saw the Chancellor in the corridor I was not feeling particularly gracious. He shook hands and said he hoped to have a talk with me soon. I said 'I should doubt it' and walked away. He was obviously dumbfounded and sent Ian Bancroft (his private secretary) to talk to me, volunteering to come and see me. But I thought it best to talk on the basis of my Minute which was not yet ready and said so.[39] When I did see the Chancellor on Wednesday at 3.30 I began by apologizing for my boorish behaviour on Tuesday. He was as contrite as could be and spoke of 'throwing himself on my mercy'. He said he had been looking forward to having my help and there could be no question of lack of confidence. Robert Neild was one of the economists to whom he had taken a liking and he wanted him too, but had not foreseen the complications in my letter. Had I any proposals that would make it possible to meet my difficulties? I said that I had, and listed two of which the first obviously appealed to him. He then asked me to leave things with him.

Anything less like my successive interviews with Helsby is hard to imagine. It was obvious that the Chancellor had no conception of what the Economic Section did and when I described the links with other departments he was surprised. I doubt whether it was ever clearly put to him that the Director of the Economic Section should not be a temporary appointment and that Robert Neild could come in as Economic Adviser without being Head of the Section.

---

[39] I have no copy of the letter sent to the Chancellor and Prime Minister, but my original draft dated 20th October 1964 read as follows: 'I understand from Sir Laurence Helsby that the post of Economic Adviser to HMG to which I was appointed in 1961 has been discontinued and that other arrangements are being made for the direction of the Economic Section of the Treasury. The alternatives between which I have to choose are that I should take over Sir E. Roll's duties in Washington for a few months and resigning at once. The announcement in this morning's *Guardian* does not make it very easy to entertain the first of these alternatives.

I doubt whether the full consequences of the changes now being made have been foreseen. Whatever I decide or do, the Economic Section is now in serious danger of dissolution, and it may prove impossible to revive the idea of economists pursuing a professional career in the civil service without regard to the political complexion of the Government.

Up till now, economists in Government service, whatever their department, have been linked by common membership of the Section. This has now ceased to be true. The members of the Section have been recruited on a non-political footing, and efforts were being made to create an economic unit in each of the major departments. It will now be impossible to convince an academic economist of any standing that he may hope to be left undisturbed in a senior position on a change of Government. Younger members of the Section, who already see the wider prospects of promotion in the Administrative grade, will draw their own conclusions. Older members (who are rare but highly experienced) may well quit.

I am always prepared, if necessary, to change my job and have often done so. But I would think it wrong if the system of recruitment of economists to Government service were to be changed radically without a protest. It is not possible to combine the system that we have been trying to develop (with some success) and a series of semi-political appointments to top official posts, terminable on a change of Government.'

He was also surprised when I said that I rarely saw the late Chancellor and that when the Economic Adviser did a 12-hour day, it wasn't because he meditated on matters of high policy all the time. Much of my work was recruitment and establishment.

The Prime Minister at 5 p.m. had tea with me and was affable but didn't take things much further. He pointed out that the Washington offer was made before there was a government and that he would have been glad to think of it himself; nonetheless some of my predecessors wouldn't have been so well qualified to do the job. He said that Robert Neild was not as well 'house-trained' as he had expected and Thomas Balogh (Adviser on Overseas Development) was anything but 'house-trained'. The Washington offer carried ambassadorial rank and I could carry on, not just for a few months but for years. Nothing he said bore on the points in my letter on the matter of principle, and both he and the Chancellor were inclined to talk as if the matter arose out of some personal difficulty which he ought to have foreseen.

Since my main object was to get a basis for agreement and this had already been conceded by the Chancellor, I saw no point in raising anything in more detail or with more urgency.

I spoke to Elsie Abbot before leaving and she urged me to commit my interview to paper, which I did. I also spoke to Bryan Hopkin and he agreed that if we could make terms on the lines that I had proposed he would stay and he thought that Wynne Godley would too. He has talked to Robert Neild who is very much taken aback at the stir he has caused.

Today (Thursday) I stayed away but let the office know that I was available by phone. Both William and Laurence rang up. William was very helpful and agreed with the line I was taking. He particularly agreed about the 'new kind of animal' that was arriving in Whitehall, neither fully political, nor fully official.

Laurence was not clear whether Robert Neild would 'buy' but felt that, given 24 hours, he might be able to work out a satisfactory arrangement. I told him as I told William that we might have to act quickly because the Sunday press would obviously be full of speculation.

Bryan also rang up. He has spoken to Robert Neild who feels so involved in the preparation of the Government's statement that he can't find time to come to grips with the problem. Bryan raised the question of staff for Robert Neild and I said that we could give him Geoffrey Bell[40] to begin with. We agreed that the present situation was not an enduring one and that we had to see it through for six months and then take stock. Robert Hall on Wednesday morning said there were obviously now too many economists in top jobs.

Yesterday I was rung up after the *Guardian* headline by Duncan Burn,[41]

---

[40] Geoffrey Bell. Econ. Section, Treasury, 1961–69; Econ. Adviser, Washington Embassy, 1966–69.

[41] Duncan Burn. Industrial economist; leader writer and industrial correspondent, *The Times*, 1946–62.

Philip Chantler[42] (offering me Ronnie Edwards' [43]job again!), Bill Phillips[44] and Sydney Caine[45] (offering LSE Chair), and Wilfred King[46]. Otto Clarke came to offer sympathy and Denis [Rickett][47] took me to lunch. It was all very touching.

Sunday, 25 October   On Friday night at 6.15 p.m. William rang up to ask me to come in and I agreed. I told Peter Jay that I should call at the doctor's first and get some medicine.

[*Although the diary does not say so, I was suffering from pneumonia and had had to spend some days in bed.*]

We didn't get there (by Treasury car) till 7.30 p.m. and I had time to work out my proposals. I told William I wanted it to be clear that I would remain Head of the Economic Section of the Treasury and that I didn't think it right to call Robert Neild Economic Adviser to the *Treasury*, as if the Treasury had previously lacked for economic advice. He ought to be Economic Adviser to the Chancellor, as it was he, not the Treasury, who wanted Robert's help. William accepted both points but returned from the Chancellor to say that (a) the Chancellor held that there was no Economic Section now and that if I was Head of the entire Service, I was obviously Head of all the component parts (!) (b) that it would make Robert Neild's appointment look a political one if he were called Economic Adviser to the Chancellor. He didn't want him to seem his stooge. I found these pretty jesuitical answers after my letter since they denied two self-evident facts: there *is* a Treasury Economic Section and nobody has yet settled who is to take charge of it; and Robert Neild is without question a political nominee (equated by the Chancellor's own confession with Tony Crosland.)

William meantime had given me the Statement to read and this occupied me for a little. He told me that he had had over an hour with Robert Neild and felt sure that a working arrangement was possible. He had agreed that he should have one man only, preferably an Economic Assistant and access to the Economic Section papers, but there was no question of his taking over the staff now and my relations with the machine and with William personally would not really change. His conversation with Robert had ended with Robert saying that it looked as if William was asking him to trust him and William agreeing that this was so.

[42] Philip Chantler. Econ. Adviser to Min. of Fuel and Power, 1947–60; Under-Sec., 1960–65; Chm. NW Planning Board, 1965–69.

[43] Ronnie Edwards. Sir R.S. Edwards, Professor of Economics, LSE from 1949; Dep. Chm., 1957–61, Chm., 1962–68, Electricity Council; member NEDC, 1964–68.

[44] Bill (A.W.) Phillips. Professor of Economics, LSE.

[45] Sir Sydney Caine. Director, LSE, 1957–67; Governor, Reserve Bank of Rhodesia, 1965–67.

[46] Wilfred King. Financial journalist; editor of *The Banker*.

[47] Sir Denis Rickett. Treasury from 1947; Second Sec. and Head of Overseas Finance Division, 1960–68; Vice-President, IBRD, 1968–74.

While William was away Philip Allen and Rab [Chaim Raphael][48] looked in and we agreed a form of announcement that seemed to me satisfactory because it said outright that I would be directing the staff in the Treasury. When they next appeared with this, part had been cut out, presumably by William and it was read to me by the Chancellor himself. He had come into William's room when I was alone and had begun chatting with me (I had even gone as far as saying that I missed some increase in general taxation in the Statement and he had said that anything as small as £50 m. could hardly matter). Before very long William, Philip Allen and Rab were all in the room too. I held out against the new version which seemed to me the very one that I had decided in the car could not be accepted as it swallowed the point of principle without any perceptible guarantee for the future. In fact the Chancellor was being allowed to offer me *part* of my previous job as if this was a great concession and was left with the thin end of his wedge firmly in place, and was giving me (quite deliberately) no assurance on staff such as was implicit in my proposition No.1 of Wednesday. William made no direct appeal to me but obviously felt that we couldn't get better terms and that it was wiser to settle now than have a row. I wasn't so sure but what with a temperature at 102 degrees and the knowledge that Laurence would give me no support, I decided to settle.

The final press announcement had one or two touches that helped. I was 'continuing' (we had agreed on the use of this word); Robert's post was 'new'. The Chancellor professed not to know of my functions in relation to economists outside the Treasury but of course no one who had studied 'the new Treasury' had any excuse for not knowing. It was more disturbing to me to hear Philip Allen suggest (not in front of the Chancellor) that I had not been Economic Adviser to the *Treasury* since this was obviously just another bit of semantics. But if it makes Robert Neild's job a *new* one, okay.

I rang Bryan that night and told him of my mixed feelings; on the whole, he seemed to think that things had ended not too badly, given all the other changes in our relative positions. Fred Atkinson on Saturday was frankly jubilant; Wynne felt that the main point had been gained. Douglas Allen also rang to say how relieved and glad he was.

William said on Saturday morning that he was with the Prime Minister when the news came over the tape and he had said then how delighted he was. He had thought that perhaps he should concentrate his senior advisers in the Cabinet office (e.g. Zuckerman[49]) but on reflection he thought it right that the Head of the Economic Service should be in the Treasury, especially as he (Harold Wilson) was First Lord of the Treasury (he had made a similar point to me). I said that my earlier talk with Harold had been pretty superficial and that I was afraid that all except para 1 of my letter had made no impression. He said that he had gone over things later with Harold and there was no doubt that he had taken the other matters on board. Harold Wilson would therefore want to talk with me later at more length [*Note: he never did*].

[48] Chaim Raphael. Head of Information Division, Treasury, 1959–68.
[49] Sir Solly Zuckerman. Chief Scientific Adviser to HMG, 1964–71.

Saturday, 7 November   I have been off now from the Treasury for over a fortnight; on the evening of Wednesday 21 October I took to my bed and have been to the Treasury only on the evening of the 23rd (for an hour) and yesterday (on approval). I have kept in touch with and seen Robert Hall, Bryan Hopkin and Fred Atkinson here (i.e. at 31 Carlton Drive) as well as coping with as much paper as I could.

In all this time I have been bombarded with offers of jobs (LSE Chair, University College Chair, IBRD Vice-Presidency, Electricity Council, Gordon Richardson, Ray Vernon,[50] etc.) and have felt a lot of my old enthusiasm for the Treasury oozing away.

Early in the week I had a note from Philip Allen covering a letter to Donald MacDougall announcing the setting up of a Management Committee which is to include Robert Neild, Donald MacDougall and (by direction of the P.M.) T.Balogh. In addition the appointment of Dudley Seers[51] was announced as Director General, Ministry of Overseas Development, again without reference to me in any way, not even as to salary. As Robert Hall warned me, Roger Opie[52] is being taken on by DEA (at £4,500 as I learned from Ron Dearing[53] of EC yesterday).[54] On top of all this, William sent me a personal letter with terms of reference for myself and Robert Neild – terms already shown to R.N. These included a clause giving him the duty of joint supervision with me of the work of the Economic Section.

All this made me draft on Wednesday a long manuscript letter to William setting out my unwillingness to compromise the principle on which I had stood before: no direction of the Economic Section by anyone but a professionally trained economist recruited without regard to political affiliation. I had hoped that William would have seen it by Friday but on Thursday he flew to Paris for the OECD meeting and although he returned late that night he had not seen the letter when he rang me up on Friday.

The Budget is all prepared and the Speech is in draft but I've had no hand in it except for advice to William before I became ill and a few odd minutes fired in at random.

Looking back over the past few weeks it is strange how much the Treasury

---

[50] Ray Vernon. Professor at Harvard Business School, 1959–78; Director, Harvard Development Advisory Service, 1962–65.

[51] Dudley Seers. Oxford economist; Dir. Gen., Econ. Planning Staff, Min. of Overseas Developt., 1964–67; Dir., Institute of Developt. Studies, Univ. of Sussex, 1967–72.

[52] Roger Opie. Oxford economist; Dir., Planning Division, DEA, 1964–66; Econ. Adviser to Chm., NBPI, 1967–70.

[53] Ron Dearing. Establishment Division, Treasury, 1962–64; Min. of Power, then Technology, then Dept. of Trade and Industry, 1965–71.

[54] The salaries of 'irregular' economists were settled without reference to me and were not even communicated to me although the issue of fairness to my own staff was very much involved. In October 1964, my salary as Head of the Government Economic Service was £6,750, Donald MacDougall's £7,600, Thomas Balogh's £6,500, Nicholas Kaldor's £4,000, Dudley Seers' £6,500, Bryan Hopkin's £4,700 and Fred Atkinson's under £3,900. Half of my staff were being paid £1950–£2725 and the other half £815–£1345.

view has been given expression. This will become more apparent in the Budget but the emphasis on cutting public expenditure and particularly the singling out of the Concorde and of prestige projects is a decided triumph for Otto. Who would have thought, by the way, that we'd get to mid-November with bank rate at 5% and no drawing yet on the IMF?

The big squabble is on the import surcharge. It looks to me as if the Government had no real idea of the consequences of this and regarded it as a heaven-sent way out of an awkward dilemma. In fact as we've always said, it is an alternative to borrowing and the Party are so much set *against* borrowing that they don't stop even to argue the matter. But they ought to have known what a *furore* it would cause abroad and that they would be told that it didn't take us any nearer true balance if we are in fact, as we think, out of equilibrium. My expectation is that the Government will pull down the 15% to 10% in a few months and to 5% within a year so that the net gain in *non*-borrowing won't be more than perhaps £300 m. Was it worth £300 m.? I should have wanted £500 m. to make a move of this kind worth the candle.

But I fully expected it and I don't doubt that Reggie would have done much the same, if a little later, and with more preparation of key foreigners.

I am not clear why a Statement had to be issued in the first 10 days. But I suppose that they felt the need to show themselves Men of Action and there may have been a rebound from the pressure to devalue at once towards other action that puts devaluation (temporarily) out of court. I was disturbed to find that Ralph Vickers[55] knew that devaluation had been seriously considered before the Statement and that N.K. and R.N. both supported it.

Ian Bancroft last Sunday on the telephone said that the spirit of the new regime reminded him at times of the invading Scots at the Court of George III on the days of Lord Bute.

So far I haven't seen T.B. or N.K. and had only one talk with R.N. when I thought I was going. *The Economist* and the *Statist* both take a remarkably favourable line in discussing the influx. Apart from Cooper[56] of Ilford no one raised the matter in the House of Commons.

Monday, 16 November   Exactly a month since Labour took office. Harold Wilson delivered Mansion House speech but rather like a schoolboy reading a Lesson in Church. His evening coat didn't fit at the neck and shoulders and gave him rather a bogus appearance next to the ladies with tiaras and with the smoke drifting up to him from cigars.

I had drafted a long passage intended to show real determination to protect the pound but Harold did his own much more high-sounding version which, however, sounded very unconvincing. Meanwhile the losses today exceeded even Friday's.

Since last Wednesday's Budget, opinion has been hardening that the Govern-

[55] Ralph Vickers. Chm. of Vickers da Costa, Stockbrokers.
[56] Squadron Leader A.E. Cooper. Cons. MP for Ilford South; PPS to President, Board of Trade, 1951–54.

ment hasn't done enough if import restrictions really are temporary. The choice is seen as one between eventual devaluation and deflation with little suggestion of any *via media* such as we had in mind.

I got back last Monday and found the Budget speech in draft. I re-drafted the Economic Assessment but the Chancellor took very little of the redraft and in the end there was more of his own in the speech than has been usual with Chancellors. The final text wasn't ready until Wednesday morning.

Callaghan delivered it well except perhaps that he seemed at times almost too anxious to illustrate his point and get it over. I sat between the Governor and Robert Neild with Schweitzer [57] only a little further away. Later I went to help Tony Crosland with the foreign press. He spoke very clearly and I had to interrupt only twice: once when he implied that output was not rising and once when he was quizzed about the balancing item and whether it was included in the £700 m./£800 m. deficit.

The Tories didn't quite know how to attack the Budget but Home made a fair opening speech and Reggie was splendid on T.V. apart from a tendency to smirk that made it difficult to take him seriously (and indeed with some justice).

On Monday lunched with Eric Roll and others of DEA at Cabinet Office canteen. He has been sacked once, Tom Caulcott thrice and so on. George Brown never to be taken seriously after 6.30 p.m. says his wife. His speech was largely Tom's and Fred Atkinson's, not Donald's as *The Economist* supposed. I suggested he had to be wild in the office in order to be statesmanlike in the Commons. He never says 'Thanks' to his staff, offers a job to anybody seen in the corridor, drinks far too much. Sam Brittan[58] is speech-writing for him! George Cyriax[59] also offered a job. 'Instant government', says Tom Caulcott.

Schweitzer asked me on Wednesday night at the Bank what had gone wrong. Nearly everybody started talking about attitudes and taxation and long term factors. I said output had risen less than we had expected and money incomes more, the difference falling on the balance of payments. He has heard all kinds of different stories and the Board of Trade say that (a) we are competitive; (b) there is no real inflationary pressure, but don't add (c) that therefore we can't be in deficit.

Governor wrote on Friday formally asking for agreement of Chancellor to rise of 1%. We discussed in detail on Friday afternoon and again today and will see Chancellor tomorrow to reach a decision. We think it would be panic to act just after Budget with US assured to the contrary and discussions on income policy still going on. But we agree that some squeeze on bank credit will certainly be necessary.

Tuesday, 24 November   Tuesday night just back from Paris where Denis

---

[57] Pierre Paul Schweitzer. Dep. Governor, Bank of France, 1960–63; Man. Dir. IMF, 1963–73.

[58] Sam Brittan. Economics Editor *The Observer*, 1961–64; Adviser, DEA, 1965; Economics Editor *Financial Times* since 1966.

[59] George Cyriax. Journalist on the *Financial Times*.

Rickett and I attended Anglo-French Ec. Comm.[60] with Wormser in Chair. At lunch he told me that he had said nothing about our measures but was personally a strong supporter. He had no use for a modern Ambassadorship except in, say, Peking because it meant endless waste of time drinking, travelling to and from airports, and conveying messages to governments.

Bank rate increase to 7% yesterday at 10 followed discussions among Ministers. When I saw P.M. on Thursday night it was after he and George Brown had overruled Chancellor on bank rate – he wanted to go to 6% on Thursday. P.M. told me that they had been under heavy pressure to go up to 6% – they had everybody including God (meaning the Governor[61]) at No.10. Loss on Friday was over £60 m. and this made Chancellor decide eventually to go for a rise of 7% on Monday. But when we met on Friday morning in the Treasury with William to discuss President's cable nobody thought this likely. Sam Goldman was alone in suggesting it. It seemed to me then that Ministers might well take the American reaction as justifying doing nothing. I had to leave for Sheffield on Friday and wasn't in touch until Ian Bancroft rang on Saturday evening, by which time decision had been taken.

Denis said he and Governor discussed things on Saturday when William asked him to come in and that at first Governor had no firm view in favour of 7%. Denis put it to him that there would certainly be pressure to do more early in the week and that if so 6% didn't make much sense (Sam's argument). In fact Ministers did veer towards early action and were persuaded that 7% then became desirable. Roosa[62] had said this was preferable but didn't want to be quoted. We must have caused considerable strain in US administration since at first LBJ said no move to raise rate independently of US.

Chancellor took it all in remarkably good humour. He had said at Chequers that he could lose in a day or two as much as Beeching[63] and his 600,000 railwaymen could lose if they worked hard all year!

Harold apparently has contemplated possibility of devaluing *after* next election and this subject came up not only last Tuesday but also at Chequers. Ministers want papers both on possible tightening of exchange control and on floating rates (including wider spread). R.N. and I to prepare with T.B. on No.1 and possibly also No.2.

Maudling is now saying apparently that floating rates are the right solution. As Denis says, this is natural given his expansionist policy. Conservatives are

[60] Anglo-French Economic Committee. Failure to secure entry to the European Community led to meetings at intervals with representatives of France, Germany and Italy on economic affairs in proof of Britain's continuing interest. The leader of the French group was Olivier Wormser who had taken part in the negotiatons over entry into the EEC and whom I knew well from 1950.

[61] The Governor of the Bank of England was Lord Cromer (Senior Partner in Baring Brothers & Co Ltd from 1967), appointed in 1961 for the usual five year term after Sir Oliver Franks had declined appointment.

[62] R.V. Roosa. American economist and banker; Under-Sec. for Monetary Affairs, US Treasury, 1961–644; Partner in Brown Brothers, Harriman and Co from 1965.

[63] Lord Beeching. Dir., ICI, 1957–61; Deputy Chm., 1966-68; NEDC, 1962-64; Chm., British Railways Board, 1963–65.

going to be in embarrassing position if he really believes this.

Somebody must have spilt the beans about possible ending of switch market for the premium fell sharply last week on rumour of government action. [64]

Wednesday, 25 November

Pressure on the pound was surprisingly moderate until after the Budget on 11 November. The markets clearly expected a tough budget and when their expectations were not fulfilled reacted strongly. There was then hesitation in putting up bank rate that made matters worse. In spite of a two point rise in bank rate on 23 November, the drain on the reserves continued and with it the prospect of a forced devaluation. On 25 November papers were prepared by the government's new advisers and the Economic Section, spelling out the alternatives of devaluation and drastic deflation. The Bank of England had in the meantime raised three months credits amounting to £3 b. from other central banks. Ministers were jubilant and saw no need for either line of action recommended in the papers by the two groups of economists, which were rounded up for destruction unread while devaluation was pronounced 'unmentionable'.

Wednesday, 25 November   We lost over £90 m. today more even than yesterday. Bulletins appeared hourly on my desk. William called me about 10.30 and assigned papers to R.N. and me for 5.30 meeting at No.10. At that stage only W.A. and R.N. invited but I was subsequently included, not however Denis. My job was to prepare paper on deflationary measures, R.N.'s on floating rate, devaluation etc. Apparently there was a meeting last night that went on to 1 a.m. with P.M. and others. It seemed obvious to me that we ought to be mustering support from Central Banks, IMF etc. but William said this was being looked after as Task No.3.

With Bryan's help I got my paper ready but hadn't seen Robert's till 5.25. It was by him, Donald *and* T.B. They all said devaluation sooner or later was inevitable, and proceeded to discuss *only* floating v. fixed rates ending up with pros and cons and a request for more time!

I saw T.B. in No.10 and he asked for my paper. His only comment was that I was too optimistic. This appeared to mean that the measures I described ran completely counter to Labour programme and philosophy but I think he also meant that I put degree of deflation required to do the job without devaluation at too low a figure. I said four men could save us from devaluation – the leading

---

[64] The dollar 'switch market' was originally a market for the purchase and sale of foreign securities by British residents through the use of 'investment currency', which sold at a premium above the official rate for foreign exchange. Later, firms wishing to undertake direct investment abroad were obliged to buy 'investment currency' for the purpose. At the suggestion of a Treasury official (Anthony Rawlinson), it was decided to require sellers of foreign assets to surrender 25 per cent of the 'investment currency' received at the official rate of exchange, thus in effect imposing a tax on foreign investment.

Central Bank Governors – if there was enough resolution but T.B. obviously thought the battle lost.

When meeting started – and it was a big one including A.Bottomley,[65] Foreign Secretary,[66] E.Roll, Donald, T.B., D.Jay,[67] etc., etc. Harold told us of $3 b. loan 'without strings and they're all in it'. He then insisted that this meant we should go forward and use the opportunity and G.B. said a lot to the same effect: this would allow him to press G.Woodcock[68] to be more sensible, etc. etc. H.W. then went on to need for an inquest à la 1947 on the guilty men in UK selling sterling short. So T.B. and the other 'economists' are to do a *post mortem* although T.B. protested there were no statistics. G.B. made a passionate speech against even thinking of devaluation and said there must be no further talk of it. They had decided and reaffirmed their decision and now people should put it out of their minds or it would creep back into Swiss and other minds. R.N. spoke up at this point but when asked what longer term action he had in mind forbore to say devaluation although it was obvious that this was exactly what he thought.

It all had a curiously unreal, club-like air: sitting at the long Cabinet table without papers and with drinks afterwards. The talk was informal and not argumentative – only the advisers really seemed to want to argue.

But the whole machinery of government is now terribly amateurish. Nobody knows what is going on in other parts of Whitehall (or even his own department). I don't know what the Governor is doing, nor he what I'm doing. I don't know what the other economists are saying to Ministers. I don't even know what W.A. thinks about it all nor whether I ought to barge in and say my piece to J.Callaghan. I'm asked by H.W. to go and talk to F.Cousins[69] and by G.B. to come and talk to him – not to their Permanent Secretaries. The machine doesn't count. It's the economists who are expected to do the job and advise and of course they have direct contact with Ministers, *not* through officials like William and Eric.

Yet it was the old firm that did its stuff today: the Governor delivered the goods, and but for him the Government would have been in a sad way with devaluation inevitable.

Sunday, 29 November   Thursday: Whitehall Dining Club at W.A.'s. A

[65] Arthur Bottomley. Lab. Minister for Commonwealth Relations, October 1964, Minister for Overseas Developt., August 1966–August 1967.

[66] Patrick Gordon Walker. Lab. Sec. of State for Foreign Affairs, October 1964–January 1965, Minister Without Portfolio, January 1967, Minister for Education and Science, August 1967–April 1968. For a contemporaneous account of the 1964–70 Labour Government, see his diary: R. Pearce, ed., *Patrick Gordon Walker: Political Diaries 1932–71* (London: The Historians' Press, 1991).

[67] Douglas Jay. Lab. President of the Board of Trade, October 1964–August 1967.

[68] George Woodcock. Asst. Gen. Sec., 1947–60; Gen. Sec., 1960–69, TUC; Member of NEDC, 1962–69.

[69] Frank Cousins. Gen. Sec. TGWU, 1956–69; Lab. Minister of Technology, October 1964–July 1966.

depressing evening but highly illuminating.[70] As Leslie Rowan[71] drove me
back he said that the rumour in Zurich after the EFTA meeting was that we
were going to get rid of the surcharge and devalue by 5%. This because British
seemed to think everything fine after meeting.

William gave an introduction that was a lot more sympathetic to Government
than I should have expected and spoke of Cabinet as superior in ideas to last.
Impressed by mixture of those who had shed their pre-1951 shells and those
who hadn't. Also implied that people didn't take nearly enough account of
other changes since Oct.16 – the passing of Khruschev, the Chinese bomb, etc.
Labour expected adequate majority and resented being deprived of power they
felt entitled to by Tory delay over election. He also defended Foreign Secretary's
gaffe over bank rate. Leslie Rowan was foremost in attack on government
but others obviously shared his views. William had given the impression that
'the war of Jenkins Rear' had left us afraid that Johnson might be defeated
and that it was this that led to Cabinet conclusion that we mustn't embarrass
US government by putting up bank rate. It seems that Foreign Secretary was
pressed at press conference to say whether he had told President that we would
be changing bank rate and had felt obliged to say we weren't instead of telling
his questioner to ask the Chancellor. In fact Gordon Walker wrote subsequently
to Callaghan apologising: but the damage was done.

The most interesting contribution came from Maurice Parsons[72] who made it
clear that he and others at the Bank had had to make up their minds whether they
could invite support from other Central Banks with a clear conscience. They
were in effect pledging the good behaviour of the Government. It recalled to
me Callaghan's remark at No.10 when I tried to put the creditor's point of view
to him. 'If they had seen me fighting against the pensions proposal at Cabinet
they would know that we aren't an irresponsible government'.

But the fact is that they have so far taken the easy course of opting for
temporary solutions: first the surcharge, then bank rate; not for final solutions
which are bound to be unpalatable.

The papers which where circulated for the No.10 meeting were all recalled
for destruction. I succeeded in retrieving a copy of mine for a few minutes
from William but no doubt the manifesto of the other three has been completely
destroyed and no one can prove that they accepted devaluation as inevitable.

On Friday another paper from T.B. (unsigned) appeared mysteriously on my
desk. It was entitled 'A Medium Term Perspective' and was a curious mixture
of NIF working paper and policy document. Today one by the P.M. follows. It
is as bad as I feared – full of that preference for administrative gimmicks that
Harold used to show at the Board of Trade.[73] Where a straight economic analysis

---

[70] The Whitehall Dining Club in 1964 was a small group bringing together business
men and senior civil servants over dinner several times a year

[71] Sir Leslie Rowan. Second Sec. and Head of Overseas Finance Division, Treasury,
1951–58; Chm., Vickers Ltd, 1969–71.

[72] Sir Maurice Parsons. Bank of England, 1928–70; Dep. Governor, 1966–70.

[73] I was Economic Adviser to the Board of Trade in 1947-49 when Harold Wilson
was President.

is needed he goes for computer control of stocks, a Post Office unit trust, and a pig's breakfast of other irrelevancies to deal with a balance of payments deficit of £800 m.

We are to discuss both papers tomorrow night at No.10 and nobody else has apparently been told to prepare anything. An informal buffet supper that has caused William and me to cancel long-standing dinner engagements. The Chancellor won't be there as he goes to Paris.

The great difficulty is to get them to face up to further deflation and to cutting investment. The chances are that they will have to keep surcharges and 7% bank rate a lot longer than they imagine. But Harold does have a point when he says that we don't know yet how much damage we've done to investment in 1966 through undermining confidence.

Tuesday, 1 December   8 p.m. The buffet supper at No. 10 took place upstairs, with everyone sitting at table and rising to help themselves. No conversation of any interest except that George Brown kept insisting on the virtues of Bass Red Label. Eric Roll told us a little of his speech to IMF which at Schweitzer's insistence lasted 50 minutes and was followed by every member of the 10, India and Australia.

H.W. plunged right away by asking where we thought we'd be in the middle of next year. R.Neild answered first, followed by Richard Powell,[74] Donald MacD. and G.B. and of these the two economists spoke *against* further deflation. I put the other view insisting on the need to lighten the load on engineering and building and on the risks we ran if pressure increased. T.B. naturally was against any cut in investment (although I put the case (a) in terms of a cut in *orders* not output, and (b) insisted that if public investment was protected, private investment would eventually suffer). I don't expect to make much progress on this front but the prospect looks pretty awful.

In the end we were faced with committees on (a) an export incentive of the milk-cheque variety,[75] (b) an Ex.-Im. Bank, and (c) economic information.

G.B. enlivened the early part of the discussion by demanding if Tommy B. had flushed his second covert while Tommy, lost in the metaphor, kept insisting that he wanted a 10% export incentive. Curiously enough, we were sitting in front of a Morland painting entitled 'Rabbiting'.

Harold moved steadily from one item to the next, especially if it looked as if anything really controversial was about to break. When T.B. and I disagreed over the facts about the trend in US/stock-output ratios, he changed at once to a different aspect of the matter. T.B.'s main contribution was to insist on business irrationality – an argument used against investment-allowances, and in favour of a TVA. He also maintained that our balance of payments statistics were now inferior even to Switzerland's; and produced the story about 'the

[74] Sir Richard Powell. Admiralty/Min. of Defence, 1931–59; Perm. Sec., Board of Trade, 1960–68.
[75] 'The milk cheque variety' – i.e. a regular cash payment proportionate to the scale of exports.

Ministry of Health's' difficulties over the 1961 Census and access to the War
Office computer that were true some time ago but can hardly be typical now.

I found it all rather dispiriting: like a committee to appoint a committee to
search for the Holy Grail. 1965 is going to be a difficult year, far more so than
1964.

I did a policy paper for William and sent R.N. a copy but he is obviously
going to be very difficult to convert. His view is that there is more deflation
already than we think, that Labour Party won't buy deflation anyhow, and that
devaluation always was the right thing to do. So we'll get nowhere arguing
with him.

S.Brittan's book [*The Treasury under the Tories*] arrived. Bridges[76] told me
he thought passages about himself not too bad.

Thursday, 3 December   Chancellor, D.Rickett, R.N. still away in Paris returned
late this evening. William goes off on Saturday to USA with P.M.

First signs of renewed pressure – lost £24 m. This followed bad press reception of reserves announcement which didn't say (Governor's advice) how much
we'd repaid out of IMF drawing or whether there was anything left. Denis felt
this to be a mistake and Bank was divided, but D. also thought that Governor's
advice should be taken. Row in Paris also bad for sterling. *The Guardian* had
curious story that $3 b. long term loan was cooking. 4% growth also promised
in newspapers most of which got story quite wrong (especially *The Times*) and
thought government still wedded to *average* growth rate to 1970 of 4%.

William called Donald and me to see if anything worth doing. Agreed no
action possible. Couldn't rush incomes policy declaration or big defence cut.
Governor has written again to Chancellor suggesting public expenditure should
be less in 65/66 than this year but Estimates today show 9% rise and cut of this
order is impossible.

Donald agreed that pressure might well continue but didn't like the alarmist
view that I put forward that at £24 m. a day we'd be out of dollars by the end
of the month. Tomorrow bound to show fairly heavy loss and by weekend P.M.
and W.A. will be out of country and G.B in charge.

I spoke later to Donald and said that we *must* plan for devaluation or deflation
and not just treat them as dirty words. Indeed since devaluation must *require*
deflation we couldn't help examining a deflationary package.

What he did accept was that the talk of export incentives was all self-deception
and cloud cuckoo land. The most he could see in any scheme was something
of order of £50 m. He doubted if 5% devaluation would be thought enough and
cited reaction to German 5% change – people would speculate on next move.
I said that this depended on size of kitty and that if we waited till we ran out,
then of course 5% made no sense. He thought that we should have to let rate
go but that we'd get some of the outflow back but I argued that 1931 showed
how far down one might go first. Perhaps I'm too jumpy but I don't yet see

[76] Lord Edward Bridges (son of the poet). Sec. of Cabinet, 1938–45; Perm. Sec. to
the Treasury, 1945–56.

how we're to get through to April without a fresh crisis and don't see how in April if we get there we can hope for the right sort of package.

Donald told me he hadn't yet seen the paper I did for 'the day when manna fell'. He also said he had told the P.M. that we must do contingency planning.

Tuesday, 8 December   Dinner at Leslie Rowan's with Richardsons and Faulkners (Glyn Mills)[77]. F. said that on the famous day of the $3 b., it was impossible to deal in sterling at 4 p.m. and at one stage rather later it was even impossible to deal for dollars. The big business was on behalf of industrial clients with heavy forward commitments, e.g. tobacco companies, and there was very little speculation here or abroad except in the latter stages. Most of the dealing was spot, with more difficulty in covering forward. By the afternoon nearly all London dealers were acting for EEA and the handling of the market was brilliant. After London closed it was rumoured that the Swiss National Bank was about to make a statement helpful to sterling and Glyn's spread this rumour which stopped the run for an hour.

The City has no confidence that Ministers understand the gravity of the situation. George Brown apparently took some of the younger bankers to task for not defending sterling against speculation and letting their counterparts abroad, the foreign bankers, destroy confidence in the pound. It didn't seem to occur to him that it was for solid business reasons that people were cutting their sterling commitments. A Finnish timber exporter with a large business with England flew recently to London because he was so disturbed by the rumours about sterling, in order to decide whether to go on dealing for sterling or invoice in Swiss francs or some other foreign currency.

F. said that some of the people coming to his bank when the run was on were asking advice on commitments as low as £2-3,000.

Gordon Richardson said that it was very uncomfortable in N.Y. to be faced with US bankers ventilating prejudices against sterling and backing their prejudices with arguments.

Over dinner Leslie returned to his argument that we needed a fundamental change in attitudes of men and management. F. quoted a case where brothers worked in Richard Thomas at Margam on the same type of mills but wouldn't consult one another so that it was necessary to send them to US for advice there. Also quoted Amory[78] on his man who made machine break down 5 times when the Americans came to look at it.

Diamond[79] said this morning that we had to handle opinion rather like people using the kind of writing that looks blue in one light and red in another.

Thursday, 10 December   I.P.P. yesterday. T.B. present but said not a word. Yet

---

[77] Sir Eric Faulkner. Chm. Glyn Mills & Co, 1963–68; Chm. Lloyds Bank from 1969.

[78] Viscount (Heathcoat) Amory. Chancellor of the Exchequer, 1958–60; British High Commissioner in Canada, 1961–63.

[79] John Diamond. Chief Secretary to the Treasury, 1964–70.

he sends cables and minutes pressing on the Chancellor the ideas that Triffin[80] put forward about 1957 for ending use of sterling as a reserve currency by getting IMF to take over. Of course this means ultimately creation of liquidity by the Six in favour of IMF and indirectly of sterling area members, and therefore has no chance whatever. You can't just advertise for somebody to take over your liabilities. Rest of T.B.'s minutes are similar. Nearly all are addressed to a Minister, and most of them either ill-informed or about matters studied years ago (cf. his reference to 1961 Budget at No.10 evening). He doesn't know how to fit into machine. As for N.K., I've seen no sign whatever of his doings. Both seem to have very little influence on Ministers, while public is allowed to regard them as sinister and powerful influence.

The French seem about to ask for gold for their dollar holdings. General de Gaulle said to have decided and first $350 m. to be changed almost at once.[81] Sounds like 1929. Bound to be a major break.

Lunch with J.Brunner[82]. He claimed to be the only man in Treasury who opposed formation of EFTA. Said that we were now bound to the Americans and that chances of entering Europe had been set back indefinitely.

The DEA were (perhaps are) trying to get control of public investment and take view that Treasury is too parsimonious and un-Galbraithian. Otto put this down to Crosland which seems odd to me.

Ray Goldsmith said tonight that at time of WP No.3 meeting in late October he asked Swiss delegate whether he would rather have seen us devalue and was taken aback when Swiss said Yes. R.G. also says that this is usual Swiss view. He himself obviously shared it and so did J.B. who, after talking to T.B. last June or July, found himself cited in *New Statesman*, by T.B., who spoke of right wing economists already beginning to whisper devaluation. I didn't say that T.B. had changed his position on devaluation since.

I *did* tell C.Dow[83] on Tuesday that the government's economic advisers were in favour and that it was Ministers who were against.

Dinner at Ralph Vickers' last night. He said that Chancellor didn't seem to know that companies with the year ending after April '65 were already incurring liability to corporation tax. The statement made on Tuesday was published before I saw it and I doubt whether any Treasury official except Radice[84] had seen it in time to comment (*perhaps* R.N.). I didn't know until today that gains on gilt-edged were subject to tax. R.N. compared gilt-edged under par to growth stocks!

Still losing heavily on Thursdays – £17 m. today. $400 m. of support already

---

[80] Robert Triffin. Professor of Economics, Yale University; argued for the need to control the creation of international liquidity instead of depending on dollar deficits.

[81] General de Gaulle held strong views on reserve currencies which he thought enabled the United States to make foreign investments with the dollars held by the central banks of other countries.

[82] Sir John Brunner. Econ. Section of the Treasury, 1958–61.

[83] Christopher Dow Dep. Dir., NIESR, 1954–62; Treasury (Economic Section), 1962–63; Asst. Sec. Gen. OECD, Paris, 1963–73.

[84] I.L. Radice. Under-Sec., Home Finance Division, Treasury, 1961–68.

gone.

William back from US. I'll discuss our paper on Plan with him insisting on importance of balance of payments as an objective (e.g. balance by 1967). Meanwhile Donald, Robert and I have all done papers on contingency planning, without my even being allowed to dictate to Miss Davies. *Nobody* to know except David Walker[85] and *his* typist. No paper asked for on deflation.

Monday, 14 December   Trade figures not helpful – imports up and exports little changed. Much as I expected except that both figures a little higher. Next month is real test.

Reserve losses at end of last week heavy. I should judge that rate of loss is about as high as at peak in 1961 *before* 7% bank rate. Very nasty situation therefore shaping up before April. May not get credits easily renewed in February; figures for January not available till mid-February and it won't be until then that we can point to improvement in visible balance. In fact we're really going to have devaluation forced on us by incredulous opinion because nothing we can do before [the Budget in] April will reassure opinion very much.

Saw William for an hour on Friday and he shared my gloom. Didn't think that effort to get Plan on basis of 1967 balance externally would be successful but agreed we might try. Today R.N. took a more vigorous line and argued (a) plan ought to concentrate on structural adjustments, etc. (a good Treasury doctrine though he seemed to think it rather new), (b) policy was full of inconsistencies now and we couldn't get them settled before Budget so why draw up Plan for March publication that exposed them.

Lunch today with Otto and meeting of his new PSI committee. *All* the economists there. Astonishing orthodoxy and unanimity. Not a voice raised against Richardson except R. Powell's (and not very strongly). No disposition to argue for big tax changes – not even TVA. Little support for Merrett[86] line. Instead, general emphasis on undesirability of raising employer's contribution even for severance pay and certainly for income guarantee (Donald on first, Tommy on second). We could have reached the same conclusions unaided!

Ian B. told me that Chancellor performs very well at *big* meetings when he takes time to prepare e.g. when he saw P.M. and G.B. before they agreed Budget proposals he insisted on writing away by himself at No.11, refusing even to see William and then produced at the meeting two packages, one our own menu and one cooked at No.11 while he was waiting. Once G.B. had exhausted himself in attacking the second, Chancellor said 'Then we have no alternative but to accept the first'. P.M. is euphoric and won't do anything, Chancellor is gloomy and won't do anything for different reasons (keep your nerve and sit tight) and G.B. is gloomy and wants to *do* something.

---

[85] David Walker. Private Sec. to Perm. Sec., Treasury, 1964–66; Principal in Finance Division, 1966-73.

[86] A.J. Merrett. Author of works in mid-1960s on capital budgeting, stressing the importance of DCF (discounted cash flow) calculations.

Wyn Plumptre[87] called this morning. Told me that if we contemplated devaluation we ought to do it as an act of policy and not in a rout.

Van Lennep[88] has been talking at dinner parties and saying too loudly that we should devalue.

Thursday, 17 December   Frank Figgures[89] to dinner last night. Said EFTA thinking of putting us on m.f.n. and that this would lead to retaliation by EEC as well. Six mad at US interventions at GATT especially as we and US had forced through condemnation of France in 1958 and now sought escape for more flagrant offence. We would 'get nothing out of the surcharge'. He argued we *must* reduce by 5% in February and should abolish in the Budget. The high rate was interpreted as a sign of weakness and probable devaluation. If we meant to move at all we should do so of our own accord, not in order to avoid retaliation or breakdown of EFTA.

Ministers didn't seem to know what they were about: kept *lecturing*, talking of situation they inherited, self-satisfied, dismissing objections of smaller countries as legalistic (when they have only the law to cling to). Officials gave better impression because more courteous, starting from present, not the past.

B.Castle[90] went to Paris hoping to announce great increase in aid programme. When this was denied her she had to give talk on new Ministry and this provoked giggles. The previous day she had whispered (too loudly) to Chancellor as they exchanged earphones 'It's only the bloody Belgian'. Frank said Brasseur's[91] intervention was pure cant. He even handed his speech to press before Callaghan could possibly reply. Press puzzled what his game was, since speech was itself silly, and suspected row with Spaak[92] over NATO.

Governor called on Chancellor today and asked him to think of hire purchase restrictions. Exchange loss on the day £56 m. This makes over £200 m. so far this month.

Max Stamp[93] says he wants to know what we'll do *after* devaluation. Everybody seems now to take it for granted though F.F. saw no sense in it. M.S. said he thought about 30% right!

Nat. Inst. Party. Spoke to Crosland, Eric Roll and Douglas Allen, chiefly on misuse of economists. D.A. indignant that the October White Paper had

[87] A.W. Plumptre. Canadian economist who represented Canadian Ministry of Finance at meetings of Working Party No.3 of OECD in Paris.

[88] Emil Van Lennep. Chm., Working Party No.3, OECD, 1961–69; Treasurer General of the Dutch Ministry of Finance, 1951–69; Chm. of Monetary Committee of the EEC.

[89] Sir Frank Figgures. Sec. Gen. EFTA, 1960–65; Under-Sec. Treasury, 1955–60; Third Sec., 1965–68; Second Sec., 1968–71; Dir. Gen. NEDO, 1971–73.

[90] Barbara Castle. Minister of Overseas Developt., 1964–65; Transport, 1965–68; First Sec. of State and Sec. of State for Employment and Productivity, 1968–70.

[91] M.D. Brasseur. Belgian Minister of Foreign Trade and Technical Assistance to Underdeveloped Countries, 1961–65.

[92] P.H. Spaak. Prime Minister of Belgium intermittently, 1946–50; President OEEC, 1948–50; Sec. Gen. of NATO, 1957–61; Minister in Belgian Government, 1961–66.

[93] Max Stamp. Director, Hill Samuel & Co from 1958; Chm. Max Stamp Associates Ltd.

mentioned £800 m. as he had got G.B. and J.C. to agree to leave it out but P.M. insisted. Crosland attacked Treasury for handing tired Ministers enormous briefs on taking office without saying what should be done. This seems crazy criticism to me since nobody asked us and anyhow they would never have deflated at that stage as much as was necessary. But I don't know what William said or was asked. I just didn't know until the Friday night that they contemplated issuing a paper at once and knew nothing of its contents.

Crosland says the economists in Ministry of Overseas Development are T.B.'s private army and all good CND men. They will be used (he argues) to make trouble for us later on. (He saw me last night to say Alan Day[94] and Ian Little[95] disgusted not to be given jobs and also that D.Seers had got such a high paid one).

Lunch with D.L.Burn. The 'new' ICT computer is a two year old Canadian one developed by Packard for Ferranti, he claims. Americans expect to have breeder reactors producing electricity at $2\frac{1}{2}$ mills in 10 years' time (but he thinks this exaggerates because assumes low interest rate, etc). They specialise – one firm, one type where our firms try every type and tender for all possibilities.

Sunday, 27 December   Another buffet supper at No.10 on Wednesday 23rd just before we all left to go on holiday. Otto's paper on public expenditure was circulated but not mine on the outlook for 1965. As a result we spent most of our time on the outlook for 1965 and the position of sterling with neither Denis nor Otto invited and no effort made to give a forecast for 1965. Instead G.Brown who arrived late (and drunk) with Eric and Donald (to find a place short) tried to argue with everybody, very incoherently, and even more extravagantly. He thought there would be a million unemployed by the autumn but that we should cut defence expenditure (so as to make possible increases in other public expenditure?).

The meeting started in quite a relaxed way and rather more orderly than usual. The Ministers this time included the Foreign Secretary and the President of the Board of Trade (and Trevor Hughes,[96] the Public Relations man, was also there taking extensive notes for the first half hour or so). Callaghan was asked to open and did so rather well – arguing (a) that we got no credit abroad for what we did and that we ought to set out more openly what it all added up to, (b) that the increase in public expenditure would come as a shock when the Estimates were published in February, and (c) that if we were to make a cut it would have to be in weapons. He talked very Otto about the need to fix a ceiling now to defence expenditure and how his proposals would mean that the growth in public expenditure for the first time would be brought under control.

The P.M. seemed anxious to stick to the agenda in which public expenditure appeared as Item 3 but George could see no sense in dividing the subject up

[94] Alan Day. Professor of Economics, LSE from 1964; Economics Correspondent of *The Observer* intermittently from 1957.

[95] Ian Little. Oxford economist; Vice Pres., OECD Developt. Centre, Paris, 1965–67.

[96] Trevor Hughes. Press Secretary to Prime Minister, 1964–69; Chief Information Adviser to Government, 1969–70.

and the P.M. did not persevere very much. It was interesting to see how they all addressed H.W. as 'P.M.' - even G.B. at his angriest called out repeatedly to Donald 'Tell the *Prime Minister* what you tell me in my office and told me only this morning when you had breakfast with me'. This was à propos of the source of pressure on the pound.

After J.C., William was allowed to say a few words in his quiet way – and he hardly spoke again except when appealed to. He said the forecasters were more than usually baffled, in fact they were numb, and he made no attempt to indicate what the Forecasting Unit was predicting for 1965/66. I was puzzled by these tactics since we are in real danger of reflating and was therefore delighted to find T.B. speak up strongly of 'Surrender' as a summary of the line the more gloomy were taking.

After William came D.Jay who discussed the effects of the surcharge as well as what he proposed to say in January about export promotion. He rather implied that on the basis of Canadian experience there would be very little to show in January or February and that Canadian imports were as high in Q4 1962 as in Q1 so I intervened to say our calculations showed a more satisfactory outcome.

The Foreign Secretary, as far as I remember, was not asked to speak or if he was, was interrupted very early and got in very little all evening, although what he said was usually temperate and sensible. He was anxious to be able to announce some reduction in the surcharge in February but battle was not joined on this point. He did say, almost *sotto voce*, (à propos of H.W.'s suggestion that we should be ready to switch to q.r.'s) that we shouldn't threaten to use them if we didn't mean to carry out our threat - and on this D.J. had argued strongly against a switch. Nevertheless the Board of Trade will undoubtedly have to *get ready* to change over if H.W. has his way for he took this to be agreed.

Harold now asked whether the dealings in forward sterling arose out of speculation or out of efforts to cover commercial transactions. He adopted the curious device of asking the four economists in turn. Robert N. began by saying he didn't know and Donald said the same. Tommy launched into a great indictment of 'uncontrolled capital movements', the Hong Kong gap, the liquidity shortage, etc. etc., citing (without naming) John Dunning[97] on the poor return to Continental investment and claiming that £150–£200 m. of capital had poured through Hong Kong this year. I took the opportunity later, when T.B. returned to this theme, supported by R.N. and Donald, of pointing out that security sterling was above par but T. said this was *because* of the Hong Kong gap. The Ministers, especially G.B., were not much impressed by this tirade, the Chancellor saying he distrusted T. when he was so dogmatic and G.B. reacting against technicalities.

My own remarks, which, for once, I was allowed to go through with, were simply that all the bankers I had spoken to and the journalists who had been round the dealers, seemed to be in agreement that the trouble arose mainly from efforts to cover commercial risks: but that no one could be sure that this was the whole story, since no one knew the proportion of all transactions that this

[97] John Dunning. Professor of Economics, University of Reading.

represented. This was not allowed to go unchallenged even by the economists, who said that Heymann[98] had seen only 5 dealers and that they had had evidence of liquidation of foreign holdings of sterling securities – as if I had suggested the contrary! The P.M. and others took up the lack of statistics as their favourite theme but the talk turned next on what could be done assuming that it was commercial factors that were at work.

H.W. had two proposals: one to force bank customers to put up sterling when they wanted to deal forward (this didn't seem a very likely way of stopping forward sales) and another which I can't now recall. Neither of them prevented G.B. from discussing them both as not coming to grips with *his* problem. He had tried out on the Governor and Deputy Governor[99] the suggestion of half a per cent call for special deposits but said that the new Deputy had asked whether this was for show or to give rise to real deflation and that 'his bluff had been called'.

I thought the whole of the discussion amateurish and even childish in the way in which no one except the P.M. had anything constructive to say and the P.M.'s contributions were almost uniformly half-baked. It showed up very clearly the difficulty of conducting a technical argument without prepared papers by experts and in a meeting at which the Ministers were largely out of their depth and the officials included bogus experts like T.B. who didn't hesitate to deride the Bank of England for its conduct of market intervention (it was now intervening only in the forward market where before it intervened only in the spot and one couldn't see what the real forces were unless it allowed some of the pressure to come on to the spot rate). Yet T.B. is accepted as 'the greatest living expert on exchange control' by the P.M.

The Chancellor emerged rather well. He stood his ground against G.B. and got the decisions he wanted (though he could probably have gone further on defence and got support).

H.W. rode all his familiar hobby-horses – he still wants an Export-Import Bank, an import substitution panel ('to show that we're efficiency-minded, not protection-minded'), and subsidies for automation à la Bagrit. He thinks it easy to identify the industries that we should be expanding and looks to The Plan to spot them if the Board of Trade doesn't do it first.

They were all disappointed that nothing had yet emerged on export finance and T.B. (who remains silent at every meeting of officials he attends on economic policy) attacked the Treasury for conducting the discussions in a lackadaisical way (although he was present and so were the other 3 economists and he had no positive contribution to offer except that an export subsidy worth at least 10% *must* be found).

There was much talk of a great slump and of 1931, especially from G.B. who asked dramatically 'Does any one in this room think business is expanding?' to which I said 'I do'. 'Everybody who comes to see me says he is cutting

[98] H. Heymann. Journalist on the staff of *Neue Zürcher Zeitung*.
[99] L.K. O'Brien. Dep. Governor of the Bank of England, 1964–66; Governor, 1966–73.

out new factory building' (modified later to 'postponing'). He asked Eric if he
agreed and E. did. Then he asked me and I said 'Not for one moment'. Richard
Powell pointed out that he had been seeing the international companies like BP,
Unilever, etc. and that they were hit by the corporation tax. He also said that in
the development areas and elsewhere new investment was going up. This drew
some support from D.J. but the general tone, as interpreted by the P.M., was
that reflation might be necessary in the Budget.

(I showed Donald the latest NIF forecasts [100] and he merely whispered 'I
don't believe them').

There was some talk at times of Frank Cousins' efforts to modernise industry
and these clearly left G.B. pretty furious. *Not* kindred spirits.

At the end, Harold made a little speech about devaluation emphasising again
how passionately he felt against it and asking us all to put it out of our minds.
We were quite an influential group and could by our joint efforts make it clear far
and wide that devaluation was unthinkable. He recognised that the views of the
government's advisers were known (N.K. presumably, but I think he felt others
present might find what he said embarrassing for he alluded to things that had
come to his ears about what was being said). He had earlier repeated the rumour
from Zurich after the EFTA meetings that we intended to devalue by 5%. Now
and again the meeting of October 17 was referred to as the great climacteric.
It was all said very solemnly and with great finality – more deliberately even
than after the day of the $3 b. credits. G.B. gave an enthusiastic encore and the
proceedings ended (with some of the advisers looking a little sheepish).

Earlier, at dinner G.B. sat next to me and I took the opportunity of expressing
some misgivings about what might be publishable in March. He seemed to
misunderstand me and at one point turned and said loudly 'You presided over
the régime (this phrase was repeated thrice at different points) that committed
us to 4%' to which I replied that everybody regarded me as the man who had
said 2 to 2½ per cent in public as the basis of productivity growth, and that
I had presided over nothing that could be called a régime. But he lost interest
and said no more and as I thought he was drunk I saw no point in pursuing the
argument.

Tuesday, 29 December   Back to Treasury to find a stack of papers on foreign
investment: obviously a joint attack by T.B. and the other advisers on the
Treasury and Bank of England. But T.B. is remarkably restrained and his
proposals come very close to my own. A letter from G.B. to J.C. covers a
memo in similar terms. There is also a long paper on statistics and a memo on
statistics of the forward market, the latter signed by Michael Stewart[101] and the
former obviously largely his work. Neither a very fruitful contribution.

---

[100] Forecasts of Gross Domestic Product and unemployment were prepared by the
National Income Forecasts (NIF) Committee three times a year under the direction of
the Economic Section.

[101] Michael Stewart. Econ. Asst./Econ. Adviser, Econ. Section, Treasury, 1957–62;
assisting Dr Balogh in Cabinet Office, 1964–67.

Chapter 2

1965

Wednesday, 6 January 1965   Today meetings with MacD. over The Plan,[1] with Otto over means of promoting exports and with B.Trend[2] on Statistics. Also British Academy. T.B. was at first and third and Nicky at second. R.Neild at all 3.

T.B. at his most perverse. Twitted me with errors in government forecasting - didn't believe in forecasts, only strategy. All this à propos of our view that it was enough to say $22\frac{1}{2}$ to 25% for increase in GNP 1964–70 rather than 25%. T.B. told us Japan, Italy and France all showed that you didn't even need The Plan to be in operation. If you held out expectation of large increase in output that would do the trick. But if you made careful forecasts and extrapolations people would make preparations for still lower output. Vanoni Plan[3] had never been in operation – yet see how Italy had flourished. Didn't give us any alternative figure and shut up once I shut up so I guess he merely wanted to have a dig. But what rot!

Afternoon meeting on ports was interesting but not very relevant. Nicky seized on classic case for subsidy when he heard of port congestion and advantages of rail transport. But R.N. and I thought penalties for demurrage might be more useful.

On Monday night at Reform Club I had long evening with Roy Reierson,[4] H.Wincott,[5] R.Bird[6] and Co. They all agreed no devaluation but election likely by June or at latest this autumn. Their guess as to how much had been drawn

---

[1] The National Plan for which DEA was responsible, had already begun to take shape in the National Economic Development Council, many of whose staff (including Sir Donald MacDougall) moved to DEA. From the beginning, the Plan had been based on a 4 per cent rate of growth although it was recognized that that rate had not yet been reached. Without abandoning the 4 per cent target, the planners decided to frame an alternative target for the period 1964-70, consistent with an *eventual* rate of 4 per cent, and plumped for 25 per cent. This we thought too high because we were not convinced that productivity had accelerated very much or would continue to accelerate.

[2] Sir Burke Trend Second Sec., Treasury, 1960–62; Cabinet Sec. 1963–73.

[3] An Italian Plan for economic development in the 1950s.

[4] Roy Reierson. American financial journalist.

[5] Harold Wincott. Financial Commentator, *Financial Times*.

[6] Roland Bird. Financial Journalist, *The Economist*.

from \$3 b. was \$500 m. though Wadsworth[7] thought \$250 m. only. They all seemed quite impressed by argument that production this year might hold up pretty well and obviously started from gloomier presumption. They also took $2\frac{1}{2}$ per cent reduction in the Budget from surcharge as probable. On the whole willing to give government credit for eating crow and therefore willingness to go further if necessary. Wadsworth said loans already being restricted and horrified at idea of going back to 30% liquidity ratio.

Reierson sceptical whether confidence would return and thought losses might continue. But in fact situation has improved.

Sunday, 10 January   Lunch with Campion[8] on Friday. Told me of George Brown and other Ministers at High Commissioner's dinner party before the visit of P.M. to Ottawa. Chevrier[9] thought well of Bottomley and Healey[10] but not of Jay or Brown. G.B. arrived late and went to sit down without even greeting his host. Then Mme Chevrier came asking to sit beside him. Brown told her 'I sat here so as not to be forced to join in inane conversation' and when she offered to go said she 'might as well stay'. No doubt said half in jest, but showed himself plainly bored most of the evening and got up to go before the P.M. Simply went to the ladies and called out to his wife 'My dear, it's time for us to go'.

Jay argued that country's natural markets lay in the countries supplying it and appeared to be very anti-French even to the point of not drinking claret (and taking white wine under the mistaken impression it was *not* French).

T.B. at an early stage in the new government had a request to call and speak to G.B. He was kept waiting three quarters of an hour and then George got ready to go. His secretary reminded him that T.B. was waiting to see him. 'F— Balogh', said George. The secretary conveyed this diplomatically to T. (who had heard every word, sitting next door) telling him George had been called away to another engagement. 'F— Brown' said Balogh. Yet it was T.B. who called George 'the finest untrained mind in the country'.

Spent Saturday at Magdalene on NIESR Conference. Blackaby[11] told me that *no* firm had yet told him that it would cut its investment programme. Ford were going to spend twice as much as last year and ICI the equivalent of a quarter of their present net assets. Travelled back with D.L.Burn who spoke rather wistfully of the chair in Economic History at Colchester. There was remarkable agreement on the factors governing slow growth in UK.

CEGB have called for formation of two groups instead of four in electrical engineering but D.L.B. thinks there is a danger that this will leave constituent units going on as before (cf. aircraft and motor cars – he thought Austin

---

[7] John Wadsworth. Economist with the Midland Bank Ltd.

[8] Sir Harry Campion. Dir., Central Statistical Office, 1942–67.

[9] Lionel Chevrier. Canadian High Commissioner in London.

[10] Denis Healey. Lab. Sec. of State for Defence, 1964–70; Chancellor of the Exchequer, 1974–79.

[11] Frank Blackaby. Economist with NIESR.

and Morris still sold separately in Australia!). On the other hand he thought cancellation of TSR2 etc. a mistake because there *was* technological fallout.

Sunday, 17 January   Chequers yesterday for the afternoon meeting – drove back with E.Roll and D.Allen just after 6. We hadn't expected a very orderly discussion on the economic outlook but it was well conducted and quite different from previous evenings at No.10. There were no papers and I had let the Chancellor have only the shortest of summaries of our forecasts. He spoke to me before we went in and said he presumed there would be no discussion of Budgetary implications. This made it difficult for me when Crosland opened with a five point policy and I decided to stick to diagnosis although I thought that his programme leaned too far towards inflation and put too much on *directives* to officials to produce export incentives, cut foreign investment by £100 m. etc. In later exchanges Donald again took line that 1960/61 pointed to check to growth (he didn't quote employment experience). George kept quiet until his turn came and then spoke of big difference of view according to which businessmen you talked to last. Chancellor said difference was marginal and he wouldn't stand for 3% unemployment (the revised George estimate). Jay and Richard Powell helpful because they agree that home demand kept down exports last year – George furious that anyone should contest the doctrine that home demand should not be restricted in interests of exports.

We all had our chance to speak including F.Cousins and the Foreign Secretary but P.M. himself said nothing even by way of summing up. The reflationary school is obviously strong and G.B. is the pillar of it. But his visit to Sweden *has* changed his mind about the surcharge and he wants to announce a cut of 5% to take effect later in the year. Also impressed by Swedish investment allowances and their effect on exports (disguised as regional assistance). This was about the only thing that drew the P.M. to favourable comment.

Reasons for more rational discussion were that we sat round table, that Minister of State put a carefully prepared programme in front of us at the start, that economists had all seen the official forecasts, and that the meeting was over before 6.30 so that George was coherent.

But nobody would have judged we had a deficit of £800 m. and limited credits. In fact Crosland assumed we could fund the $3 b.– an astonishing misconception. Only the Chancellor referred to losses from reserves and need to take account of views of our creditors. No discussion of surcharge in 1966 at all.

I noticed at Chequers that Ministers all had the statistics bug and seemed to feel that with better statistics the future would cease to be in doubt. Every economic subject they take up leads them to this conclusion – as if more statistics would make them adopt different policies.

End of 100 days. Death of Churchill, after over a week in stupor, exactly 70 years after his father's death in similar circumstances. All kinds of government business held up, including P.M.'s speech on exports, statement by Jay, and press conference by Chancellor, Brown and others. At Chequers, over a week ago they had TV crew waiting for P.M.'s eulogy – a little gruesome especially in the light of after events.

Went to say goodbye to C.T.Saunders[12] and spoke to R.Fry[13] who felt that Treasury didn't know how the City worked and cited our reaction (especially D.H.F.R.'s) to paper on swaps by Ikle,[14] Coombs[15] and others as example. Told me that T.B.'s hostility to Bank of England went back to time he came from Fed. Reserve Bank of New York to work for Strakosch[16] who as Director of Bank of England had free access. Montagu Norman[17] saw T.B. going from desk to desk in discount offices copying down figures from papers, and took him by the ear to the door telling him never to come back. No doubt his great aspiration is to be a Director himself. When I saw him in his room at the Cabinet Office on Friday he told me that nowhere else would a Marxist be elected freely to be head of an educational institution like Balliol (Hill).[18] Expressed horror at salaries of economists in government service especially Fred Atkinson whom he thought a little sour (!) after nearly 20 years in Whitehall.

Leyton election result[19] on Friday morning at Cambridge where I had gone to speak to Marshall Society on Growth and was staying with James Meade[20].This makes it highly unlikely that the government will be firm and strengthens chances of devaluation. Costs will rise faster than for 10 years and so will government expenditure.

Had visit tonight from Richard Powell who is worried that we may be trapped into scheme for subsidising exports of capital equipment that is really intended to lead us into devaluation. I told him that I thought we had a diminishing chance of avoiding devaluation, whatever government said, unless they really would deflate and say so. He didn't seem so anxious to see demand for cars maintained and said they were at capacity so that bigger demand would push up imports.

Thursday, 28 January   Saw William for an hour last night about his minute to Chancellor who is increasingly isolated. George Brown ratting on TSR2 and supporting Minister of Housing on his claim for 15,000 more housing starts.[21] Similarly on interest rates. William has warned Chancellor that there is now literally nothing to point at to show evidence of 'stern review' of defence expenditure. Even rise in price of stamps in doubt. Since Leyton only interested

[12] C.T. Saunders. CSO, 1947–57; Director, NIESR, 1957–64; ECE Geneva, 1965–72.

[13] Richard Fry. City editor of *The Guardian*.

[14] Ikle. Director General of Swiss National Bank from 1964.

[15] Charles Coombs. Federal Reserve Bank of New York.

[16] Henry Strakosch (1871–1943). Banker, closely connected with gold mining in South Africa.

[17] Montagu Norman (later Lord) Governor of the Bank of England, 1920–44.

[18] Christopher Hill, the historian, was Master of Balliol College, Oxford.

[19] At the Leyton by-election in January 1965 the Labour candidate, Patrick Gordon Walker, was defeated although in October Labour had had a comfortable majority of 8000. At Nuneaton Frank Cousins was elected by a majority down from 11700 to 5200.

[20] James Meade. Professor of Political Economy, University of Cambridge, 1957–68; awarded Nobel Prize in Economics, 1977

[21] The TSR2 aircraft was ultimately cancelled in the April 1965 Budget.

in politics – G.B. for election in June or earlier. Crosland told R.N. that he thought if last government was so inactive this one had no cause to do more in advance of election.

Meanwhile at dinner last night Plowden[22] asked me point blank when we were going to devalue. He sees the muddle and the absence of clear line of policy.

I told William that I thought it was increasingly likely that we should have no option but devaluation and that I expected recrudescence of pressure in second half of February even in advance of Budget because it would then become evident that the Budget would not in fact be adequate and that chances of early election were very high. The only arguments we could use effectively were need to reduce bank rate and the surcharge. William agreed and told me that the only thing that clearly went home when he saw the P.M. at Chequers on the Friday night (to prevent too much talk) was the danger of having to retain high interest rates.

David Walker mentioned tonight that although they were trying to keep Budget discussions within the Treasury the Chancellor had referred to papers in a minute to P.M., and T.B. had at once been demanding to see them.

We had a very interesting meeting at Centre for Administrative Studies yesterday morning on the conjuncture and there was surprising unanimity that the outlook for private manufacturing investment was still little changed. Roy Harrod[23] kept pretty quiet but obviously didn't understand parts of the analysis (in terms of lags of employment behind output) and was puzzled at Godley's suggestion that output rose 4% last year (Q4/Q4). Everybody had something to contribute and seemed to welcome timing of the meeting.

Talk with Chancellor on Treasury publications – he accepted idea of remodelling *Economic Trends* and was even prepared to think of signed articles although at first preferring a high standard of anonymity.

Tax meetings proceeding. Chancellor had only 7 minutes for the last, chaired by Diamond, capital gains tax on gilt-edged, and double taxation of unit trusts. Chancellor complains he has too much to decide can't we settle more for him?

Monday, 1 February

As the Budget drew nearer, there were some signs of improvement in the trade balance and of a slight slowing down in domestic expansion; but the drain from the reserves continued, even if at a lower pace. The November credits of £3,000 m. were renewed in February for a further three months but would have to be repaid by the end of May and replaced by an IMF loan on IMF terms. At meetings

[22] Lord Plowden. Chm., Committee on Control of Public Expenditure, 1959–61; on organisation of representational services overseas, 1963–64; on aircraft industry, 1964–65.

[23] Roy Harrod. Student of Christ Church, University of Oxford, 1924–67; jt. ed., *Economic Journal* 1945–61; President, Royal Economic Society, 1962–64.

of OECD it was clear that continental countries saw British economic prospects very differently from the British government and that they looked for resolute action by the Chancellor in his April budget. The Chancellor, however, found his colleagues insensitive to foreign opinion and firmly against deflation in any form. Nevertheless the pressure on the pound, reinforced by the pressure of opinion in creditor countries, began to tell on the attitude of the Labour government.

The government's advisers concentrated on ways to improve the balance of payments without deflation. They suggested tightening exchange control and making use of the tax system as ways of reducing the outflow of capital; and switching to import quotas as the surcharge was abandoned, or introducing import deposits (as was ultimately done in 1968) as ways of acting on the current account. The Treasury, although bidden to close its mind to the possibility of devaluation, continued to give it constant thought.

Monday, 1 February   Winston's funeral on Saturday, 32 years after Hitler's accession to power. Had he retired like Rab[24] at 62, he would have been thought an unsuccessful politician, rather unstable and reactionary.

C.Dow today (with van Lennep) told us at lunch that Continental countries were not at present convinced that we justified extension of credits and that nothing less than £200 m. in the Budget would make them change their view. Real danger of misunderstanding between Europe and UK about the line each was favouring. Van Lennep gave similar figure to Denis and R.Neild. I told C. that (a) we had more Ministers, (b) more advisers, (c) more committees and consequently it was more difficult to predict what policies would be followed.

Later at meeting with Chancellor it became only too apparent that he was not looking for big additional taxes and if *he* isn't, then who will? Indirect taxes not very attractive to him although he still left alcohol and motor vehicle duties as possible sources. I should guess he might go for an extra £100 m. but not more.

Meanwhile Frank Cousins apparently insisted we couldn't plan for less than 4% growth from 1.1.65 and even George Brown had to take his paper back. This still seems to leave 25% 1964–70 accepted.

We had a long meeting on foreign investment with Nicky at which he took rather theoretical line and got indignant about Inland Revenue view of 'neutrality' between home and foreign investment. But we didn't really get to grips with the practical problems of non-mitigation.

Nicky maintained that ratio of retentions of profit was highly correlated with rate of growth. I challenged this because growth rarely takes undiluted form of new asset formation; and in UK most growing firms could still borrow and don't use their full credit (at least ones of a certain size).

Partial success on defence policy but TSR2 reprieved until April. Pound strong – but for how long?

Tuesday, 2 February   Governor has written again to the Chancellor – a better

[24] R.A. Butler, Cons. Chancellor of the Exchequer, 1951–55.

letter than usual but I doubt whether he'll get far with it. What *are* we to say in OECD when asked if we agree that the Budget should be a tough one? We have experience of last October behind us when William said in WP No.3 that the Autumn Budget would be 'brutal'. This year Chancellor doesn't seem to be thinking in very deflationary terms although our external debts pile up and the reluctance of the lenders is bound to get greater.

Another meeting today on foreign investment – all on oil. Nicky really showed mastery of the subject but somehow argued that foreign investment wouldn't suffer when this seemed the object of the exercise (Corporation Tax).

Friday, 5 February   In the morning today William discussed with R.N. and me the papers on the Plan for ED(O). The outline of submission to Ministers has shrunk to the kind of synopsis that consists of headlines with little trace of the argument. ('Balance of Payments problem outline of a solution – but *what* solution?). Donald seems to have a sketch of the balance of payments over the next few years with credits for 'Catherwoodery',[25] 'Incomes Policy' and so on when nobody could possibly predict any of these. Strong suspicion that the idea is to keep in circulation a counter-manifesto to the one expected from the Treasury.

We all agreed that the current ideas on export incentives were petering out one by one – subsidy to engineering products, taxes on direct investment abroad, tighter exchange control, etc. R. still thinks something may come from deposits against forward contracts or import orders but seems very doubtful.

Pitblado[26] told us that atmosphere in EFTA was better and they realized more clearly dangers to sterling, especially after Leyton. But he didn't think we could keep surcharge after Budget of 1966. I said that in that event we might be wise to plan for some limited q.r.'s from April 1966 on, so as to save £100 m. or so a year. General agreement at official level that we should cut surcharge by 5% about Budget time this year. Crosland, however, sent letter arguing strongly for 2½% now and promise of 2½% later. I think that if we come down now to 10% this will give us quite a long breathing space – long enough to make probability of election a good enough reason for staying put.

William sketched to us his ideas of Budget which were very close to mine: £100 m. if possible from motor vehicles, about as much again from National Insurance rebates (a regressive tax – the rich actually gain if standard rate is put up!), and perhaps a little more – but in the end maximum likely to be £150 m. R.N. said he thought we should do the arithmetic straightforwardly even if (as he guessed) it led to £350–£400 m. But this year there is no straightforward objective – we haven't got a strategy for the balance of payments into which the Budget should fit. Bryan warned us but nothing has been done.

Chancellor has been asking all and sundry what they want him to do in the Budget. The Governor, a little startled, came out with £300 m. – this has gone

[25] Fred Catherwood was Chief Industrial Adviser to the Department of Economic Affairs. He succeeded Robert Shone in 1966 as Director General of NEDC.

[26] David Pitblado – Third Sec., Treasury, 1960–61; Head of Treasury Del., Washington, 1961–63; Perm. Sec., Min. of Power, 1966–69.

to P.M. But it won't do to say this is what foreign opinion wants – although both van L. and C. Dow told us £300 m. was the minimum acceptable. We must try to lay the emphasis on individual items, not the aggregate. (Marcus Fleming[27] asked me today if I thought that there was anything in the idea that deflation in specific sectors would yield large gains in exports).

P.M. apparently spoke to de Gaulle rather warmly about his views on international liquidity and said they were in keeping with *Anglo-Saxon* ideas – a very odd misconception both as to French *and* US attitudes, all the more so in view of de Gaulle's press conference of yesterday.[28]

R.N. said this morning that he had had long session at Inland Revenue with Nicky from which it appeared that corporation tax would involve non-payment of income tax by US and other foreign firms and would cost us up to £60 m. or (allowing more reinvestment of profit) perhaps £40 m. in foreign exchange. We can't put withholding tax above 5% (OECD Code). Quite a bombshell!

Spoke to Robert Shone[29] about Sweden and this is now in hand at last.[30]

Yesterday had meeting on statistics at which we fed a list of 20 items into the machine – enough to clog it for some years! (DEA wanted Annual Census of Production, more regional statistics, etc., etc. – all requiring very big increase in staff) and had very vague objectives. T.B. was keen on savings survey, export and retail price indices that took stock of quality changes, etc.

Three more by-elections – this time without any marked change. Not clear how government will decide about early election but it will govern Budget decisions.

Sterling is still strong and public has little sense of crisis. Some holders of sterling getting nervous – Scandinavians and Middle East Central Banks. Germans don't want to renew credits for so long as 3 months; French not for so much as before. Meeting of BIS Governors this weekend will be very important. We can't draw on IMF for 6/7 weeks after the Budget and need cover to that point. If the Budget is unsatisfactory to foreign opinion, we'll no doubt still get IMF overdraft but only after long wrangle either involving activation of GAB or perhaps at cost of putting IMF itself virtually out of action. This could in addition be fatal to confidence in sterling because deficit won't end in May.

Friday, 12 February   Vast output of paper, interminable committees, low morale. Godley came to see me and asked if Ministers had been told how staff feel. George Brown apparently has heard of low morale in DEA from Patrick

---

[27] Marcus Fleming. Member of the Econ. Section, 1942–51; Dep. Dir., Research Dept., IMF, 1964–76.

[28] While the British Government thought that there was a shortage of international liquidity and wanted to create new international assets through the IMF, the French were more disposed to think in terms of the gold standard, and call for a higher price for gold.

[29] Robert Shone. Dir. Gen., National Economic Developt. Council, 1962–66.

[30] This is a reference to a proposed examination of the Swedish system of investment control. Taxes paid by Swedish businesses in good times could be released to them at times determined by the government for investment in new assets.

Sargeant[31] and called a meeting to discuss it but didn't get up in time to come to it.

Two extraordinary meetings on a paper by Donald for submission to Ministers on the Plan: the first in William's room on Wednesday, the second tonight in Eric's room. It dealt extensively with the balance of payments problem but had only a single disparaging paragraph on deflation. At the meeting on Wednesday, Donald made it clear that he would be willing to flog all available assets by running a deficit unchecked by restraint on demand until 1970. At lunch with Jukes on Thursday it was at once apparent that he shared Donald's views and that these were closely in line with Sam Brittan's.

Both today and on Wednesday it was not at all clear what Ministers were expected to do with the paper – no decisions, just education. Yet on balance of payments there was the underlying attitude that it could be dealt with in a way that needn't seriously affect the Plan (indeed it mustn't be allowed to) and the considerations bearing on the Budget were all set out for the benefit of ED(M) i.e., a group that won't make the Budget decisions. William pressed Eric step by step into a position of downgrading this section, compressing it, and presenting the final paper to a small group of Ministers, not ED(M). Nevertheless the draft has already gone to G.B. though nobody knows what attitude to it he will take. As a display of dialectics William's handling of the discussion was masterly and R.N. gave him full support. It was hard to see the point of the analysis of 1965–66 if the real issue (which we all knew to be deflation) was either to be pushed aside or left out altogether.

Unable to attend long meetings on taxes on foreign investment, franking, etc., yesterday. Briefing meeting for WP No.3 made it clear that we will be in difficulty over balance of payments objective – as indeed I pointed out to Denis after the last meeting was bound to happen.

Ministers buttressing the old vested interests coal-mining, housing, etc. We are to have at least as many starts as last year although there are now 440,000 houses under construction. Stevenson[32] today blamed P.M. for not laying down priorities and this is undoubtedly producing indecision and overload all round. Bryan commented on parallels with 1945-51 and there are many. But at that time we were far stronger *in relation to Europe*.

Trade figures not very good and some renewal today of week-end losses from the reserves. Governor had a rough time in Basle but is said to have handled things very well and it is thanks to his efforts that credits have been renewed. What seems clear is that we can't hope for renewal yet again nor, if we repay from IMF, a further rescue operation of the same sort.

Douglas Allen is trying to induce Donald to come to Paris for EPC. Denis was previously a little suspicious of enlarging the UK team to include DEA but I have no doubt that it would help if Donald could hear the Continental view at first hand.

---

[31] Patrick Sargeant. Financial journalist.

[32] Sir Matthew Stevenson (Steve). Dep. Sec., Treasury, 1961-65; Perm. Sec., Min. of Power, 1965-66; of Min. of Housing and Local Government, 1966-70.

Saturday, 20 February   WP No.3 rather tame in relation to expectations. We gave our forecasts fairly fully but WP seemed to shrink from offering advice outright, and in the draft letter to the UK only the most general guidance will be included. Christopher Dow had a figure of £100–£200 m. for the de-stocking effect that would now have to be continued by higher taxation and on this basis hoped to see a final 'twice as much' line erected (or rather, we told him this might be done). But it was not a very good way of arriving at a figure and none will now be included. The discussion was rather scrappy with Emminger[33] either below form or too disturbed to speak his mind (except that he obviously felt public expenditure *could* be cut and that we were taking a rise in wages far too lightly.)

The most substantial contributions were from Kessler and Wickman[34]. The atmosphere was sympathetic but also in a way apathetic as if they felt it was now *our* business to find a way out and all that they could say to us was how little time and money we had. At EPC Getzwold pointed out that if we were to redress an adverse balance of $2 b. other people in Europe and elsewhere would suffer and it looked as if it wouldn't be the 6. To this E. said the Germans wouldn't mind quite a large adverse balance, but they *might* have to tighten up to stop inflation, i.e. the Bundesbank is still guarding the Ministry of Finance's rear after the Budget cuts.

I had a tummy upset and was rather exhausted when I got back. Donald spoke at EPC (very well) on long term economic policy and this made some impression without diverting the discussion from our immediate problems. I was a little taken aback, therefore, when on Thursday at EAC on my paper he attacked our internal diplomacy and on being asked to elaborate by William said we might get more help if we changed our tactics and warned other countries in OECD how much they would suffer if we were forced to deflate. There may be a little in this but I can't see any of the key countries offering us more since they think we have made poor use of the time they've allowed us with past credits and some of them may even refuse either to vote for IMF help or short-term credits. The Belgians (de Stryker) thought we should get into equilibrium in 1965 (not at the end of the year). But the more serious of them simply harped on the way we looked like exhausting our 3rd and 4th credit tranches in the Fund.

At the EAC meeting T.B. only asked what I meant by a moderate deflation of demand and when I began at £100 m. and went up to £200 m. he asked if I was not thinking of as much as £350–£400 m. He seemed relieved when I said 'No' quite emphatically. The meeting opened one slight ray of hope for Donald didn't challenge the forecast that unemployment would change little this year and also didn't seem to reject the view that some tax increase was necessary although he rested this on the need to conciliate foreign opinion.

I had lunch at the Bank and spoke briefly to the Governor who has had a

[33] Otmar Emminger. German representative at meetings of Working Party No.3 OECD; later, Governor of the Bundesbank.

[34] Kessler, Wickman, Getzwold and de Stryker were the representatives at meetings of Working Party No.3 of the Netherlands, Sweden, Norway and Belgium respectively.

bad press for no good reason (except that he has focussed attention on public expenditure in a way that will aggravate the reaction abroad to the Vote on the Account). He said that £100 m. was not enough to prevent increasing pressure on the pound but that he saw little chance of getting more. What was done on the public expenditure side would be more helpful than extra taxation.

The press last week-end was full of rumours of Treasury/DEA dissension over the Budget. I expect they come from Sam B. – they certainly do a lot of harm and bring out very strikingly how many madmen there are around who take the balance of payments as something one can forget about. Roy Harrod has written to me twice and wants the Government to plan for an extra £1,000 m. of demand and renounce the extra 6d on income tax.

Wednesday, 24 February   Monday night dinner at No.10. David Hubback introduced T.B. to the Governor who sat on my right. I introduced him to Deming[35] who was told that W.Heller was one of T.B.'s oldest friends. P.M. joined us and we had quite a lively evening; with much chaffing of the Governor (none of the 'Cromer must go' stuff) all in front of Deming, George Willis, Sam Cross[36] and Co. T.B. insisted that the syndicate went back to 1934 and that he had some hand in it, while the Governor maintained it was set up in the war to ensure that the Government got its money. T.B. also argued that it was expensive and archaic.

Today William, Robert and I saw Chancellor for an hour at No.11 on my paper for Chequers. He wanted the references to devaluation taken out but didn't quarrel with the argument. Asked why he should believe the figures and whether any of us thought he should devalue rather than deflate. Only R. said Yes to this, agreeing that it would be judged the wrong time to do it but that it never was the right time since if the balance of payments improved we always inflated instead of devaluing. Chancellor didn't seem to blench at £200 m. although he knew it would take a lot of selling to his colleagues and the country. He wasn't quite clear at first whether our figures included the rise in income tax.

Devaluation came up because Robert put it strongly that those who would resist deflation, e.g. in DEA, really took devaluation for granted without saying so. We had to be quantitative (although the paper was not) and we had to show that policies of any other kind wouldn't let us get by.

Chancellor seemed to feel that we put the argument better orally but the paper will go round more or less as it stood.

Meeting of pseudo-Budget Committee in the afternoon (with Nicky present). Went on the whole very well and N.K. supported line that Robert and I took. William at one point said £200 m. but later £200–£300 m. (and this is what R. and I agreed on) and Denis picked him up.

In the morning Chancellor had said that if he had known the capital balance

[35] Fred Deming. Pres. Fed. Reserve Bank of Minnesota, 1957–65; Under-Sec. for Monetary Affairs, US Treasury and US representative at WP No.3, 1965–69.
[36] George Willis and Sam Cross – US Treasury colleagues of Deming.

forecast he would have supported Sam Goldman more strongly on portfolio investment at meeting yesterday with the Governor.

At lunch with NABM to hear P.M. Spoke to Donald who says that at Cabinet P.M. told Ministers they mustn't talk to press alone (and officials, too, as an afterthought. Should have a witness.). We've had a questionnaire over the Ian Aitken[37] article in *The Guardian* which made George Brown ring up from Geneva in fury because he thought it came from the Treasury!

Sunday, 28 February   Saturday at Chequers arriving at 9.15 leaving at 6. Two sessions, one on economic outlook, one on corporation tax and exchange control. P.M. and George Brown (who motored from Derby in two hours and drove himself back for a speaking engagement) and the Chancellor were the only Ministers. The P.M. and Chancellor had both had night train journeys, one from Liverpool, one from Cardiff.

George said hardly a word and P.M. did most of the talking. But it was soon obvious that he was strongly against deflation and would only contemplate tax changes that could be shown to be offset by balance of payments gains. On this basis, strictly nothing would be done but in fact no doubt £100 m. would be possible compromise. The P.M. saw some force in doing £600 m. if we really meant to deflate our way out but no point in doing half that. This is exactly what Douglas Allen told me on Friday was George's view.

The discussion was not reassuring at any stage except that Chancellor stuck to his guns throughout and though he didn't name a figure was obviously sceptical of the line that was pursued – that we could get out of deflating by cutting capital exports. A lot of rude and silly things were said about OECD that don't augur well for the day when we have to tackle European cooperation seriously. The P.M. dismissed WP No.3 as a bunch of officials and argued that it was political pressure that would have to be used on Erhard and de Gaulle. Why he thought de Gaulle particularly 'chummy' wasn't clear but he may be right in saying that in the end none of them will vote against a loan to the UK by IMF. As the Chancellor pointed out there are also the international officials and the traders and bankers to be thought of, and they may not be impressed by political pressures if the programme itself isn't very credible.

The proceedings started with a detailed exposition of the forecasts (which I gave) and this was accepted, though with rather bad grace by Tommy who (when challenged) wasn't prepared to offer a different forecast but pointed out that we had already changed our minds since December. He came back to the argument that nobody knows where the people who left the labour market in 1958 have gone – as if somehow, they might now re-emerge. George thought that labour could be used more efficiently and Donald took the line that productivity was already up to Neddy's forecast and still rising. There was the usual talk about the index of production and the failings of the Bank of England to get figures of transactions in foreign exchange. A post mortem on Nov/Dec was again ordered.

[37] Ian Aitken political staff *The Guardian*.

But apart from these lamentations we didn't get down to policy discussion at all. The P.M. was content to turn to the capital balance without pursuing the financing problem and took credit for £50 m. off the switch market very readily.

In the afternoon Nicky and Denis and D.Allen joined us and there was quite a good discussion on the corporation tax and capital exports. T.B. wanted us to go easy on *direct* investment but to be severe on portfolio. Unfortunately it wasn't easy to see how we were to operate in the switch market so as to get liquidation of foreign securities and then dispose of them in a way that allowed us to meet our deficit. All this was deliberately fuzzed. While the Chancellor was asked to prepare a scheme, it was taken for granted that this relieved us of the need to get a surplus on current account.

G.B. left early and must have been well content. His contact with the Swiss has made him feel that they aren't really so tough and will help us if we stand our ground.

It was all very like the discussion with the Governor before bank rate went up to 7% and the P.M. kept making his rather foolish metaphors about slitting the throats of sacred cows (à propos of threats of vengeance on the City if a fresh sterling crisis threatened).

Nevertheless when it came to T.B. arguing for cash deposits against forward purchases of foreign exchange it was the P.M. who seemed most sceptical and he argued quite strongly with him.

William as usual kept quiet though when he did intervene he did so very effectively.

Tuesday, 2 March   The P.M. apparently indicated to the Chancellor at the end of Saturday's meeting that he would expect to see 'the figures' before deciding on the shape of the budget.

Robert Neild doesn't think that we can count on agreement to + £150 m. – the most we're likely to get, he thinks is £125 m. It is pretty clear that the P.M. and George have joined forces and that both are being advised to go for a lowish figure.

From what Joe Fromm[38] and Percy Selwyn[39] told me at lunch it's an illusion to think that the French will scruple to vote against an IMF drawing. They expect us to devalue by 10% and are really much more interested in the dollar than the pound. There was no doubt in their minds that the UK would draw on the portfolio and try to realise US assets so that we improved our capital balance at the expense of the US.

We had a long meeting on exchange control today at which Nicky was present but not T.B. It became very evident that our chances of getting big accretions to the reserves from operations in the switch market are pretty limited. We may introduce a 15% tax that keeps down the switch premium but we're already taking some £50 m. of accruals out of the market and even the direct investment

[38] Joe Fromm. Foreign Correspondent, *US News and World Report*, 1946–72.
[39] Percy Selwyn. Senior Econ. Adviser, Commonwealth Office.

purchases are only about £20 m. a year so that it won't be easy to keep down the premium and take out still more. The P.M. seemed to envisage purchases of switch dollars on a scale equal to net private investment overseas (including reinvestment of profits, oil, etc.) but this would be a very formidable objective for 1965.

Monday, 8 March   Harold W. at Chequers indulged two of his gimmicks: a tax on business entertainment rebated for exports and a tax on coupons put through the letter box. The first is now supported by Nicky although everybody at Chequers thought it must be a joke. So it may yet feature in the Budget on Nicky's principle that people must be given something they can approve and understand.

On Friday we had a meeting of ED(O) on *Economic Report* which had been drafted at top speed. T.B. had told Eric it was a Tory Party Manifesto and accused the authors of a theory when like M. Jourdain they weren't conscious of one – Crypto-Paishery[40] no doubt.

Monday, 15 March   Last Wednesday at our dinner party both Geoffrey Crowther[41] and Charles Gifford[42] said that they would vote Labour at an election tomorrow and had not done so last October. This is in line with a lot of current thinking which is appalled at the poor showing of the Tories in opposition and correspondingly more willing to make allowances for the inexperience of the Labour Party in office. Yet the inside opinion of officials is not very favourable to the present government, especially because of the cumbersome way the machine works, and the indecisiveness of the P.M.

Still haven't seen the Chancellor since Chequers – he was off colour towards end of week. No indication yet of fate of *Economic Report* but T.B. was squared by Robert rather easily as he predicted and P.M. having first been bamboozled may now be debamboozled. George Brown seemed to be against publication, leaving the field (as William put it) to the Bank of England's *Quarterly Bulletin* but he may have been reacting to Ch. 1 only.

Now T.B. is off with a heart attack and had already been warned by his doctor not to go to Chile as planned. This is said to be not his first.

The doings of the Plan get odder and odder. Last week it emerged that Shone was redrafting the document for publication as a White Paper (on April 1!). G.B. also seems to have promised to submit each part of the Plan as it took shape for discussion by NEDC. The questionnaire to industry causes ribald comment from everybody – not least at Ashridge from John Brunner who wanted to know whether each industry (or firm?) was to be asked to adjust its plans to match

[40] An allusion to the views of Professor F.W. Paish, who argued for a minimum level of unemployment of 2 per cent.
[41] Sir Geoffrey Crowther (later Lord). Editor of *The Economist*, 1938–56; Chm. Trust Houses Forte Ltd, 1960–71.
[42] Charles Gifford. An old friend from Cambridge, interested in economics and finance (and football).

those of other industries once DEA had added them all up and made appropriate cuts.

John Jewkes was also there and told me that those economists still in Oxford were busy on little Neddies. Their post-graduate students were now writing proudly to the *Gazette* to say that they were making their contribution to the rebuilding of Britain by getting along unsupervised so releasing brainpower for the Plan.

Last week William minuted the Chancellor telling him that the planned increases in taxation were in his view insufficient. But it does look as if we might yet get to £200 m. The newspapers have recanted (even *The Sunday Times*) and nobody now features the great 'struggle' between Mr C. and Mr B. William thinks it likely that there may be more uproar over the corporation tax and its effects on overseas investment than over the Budget judgement whatever it is. We certainly have a difficult job of presentation to do and the first draft of the speech is far away from what is needed.

In the last fortnight the whole tempo has slowed down – not that there isn't still plenty to do but things are decidedly less hectic. Far fewer meetings which is a great blessing.

Tuesday, 16 March   Two long meetings with Chancellor this afternoon, one on savings media and one on the switch market. Chancellor took cautious line at both, opting for new P.O. savings scheme rather hesitantly and keeping open idea of unit trust which Diamond favoured strongly to give poor men opportunities of the rich. Chancellor was in good humour remarking on excessive merriment at the start as a sign of frustration and after the second meeting in which Sam and Nicky took strong positions on opposite sides he asked us jocularly what odds we would give on a run on the pound by the end of June. I said he wouldn't get any Swiss bankers to take a bet on the exchange rate on Dec. 31 (Lutz[43] said as much at Ashridge). There were other phrases that he used equally suggesting that he hadn't really any deep conviction that we could rally sterling although he is no doubt worried about it. Ian Bancroft tells me that we don't look now like getting more than £140–£180 in spite of William's minute and that is pretty certainly too little, as the Chancellor must know. The latest vacancy figures show a further sharp increase.[44]

I took action over a week ago to set on foot consideration of what a change in the rate might involve. There has obviously been no return of confidence on the foreign exchanges and the Budget will confirm fears if it seems to fall below £200 m. The unemployment figures are the last major recent indicator before the Budget.

Monday, 22 March   Lunch with Henry P.B. He thinks we should do some research on zones of wage relationships to establish what differentials need to be

---

[43] F. Lutz. Swiss economist.

[44] Unemployment in March, seasonally adjusted, was just over 300,000 nearly 50,000 lower than six months previously.

preserved – and watched. NEDC didn't explode at February meeting when 25% target increase in capacity was announced by G.B. the day before the meeting: but it boiled up in March when people implied that they didn't want any more by-passing of NEDC if it was to carry out its job. G.B. apparently leads the discussion, not Shone, who used to be called upon by Maudling to start things off.

Second draft of Budget speech. We agreed to turn argument round to demonstrate need for higher taxes to leave possibility of extra exports and need to balance one risk against another. Even so, as Roy Workman[45] shows, the argument that we will be aiming at balance by the second half of 1966 will not be easy to put across to the IMF and WP No.3.

Meanwhile last Friday the P.M., Chancellor and G.B. agreed on 6d. on tobacco, but want to take 1d. off petrol to the fury of Customs. This all started from Harold's feeling that Motor Duty was too high and some offset desirable especially as total went over £300 m. (But *no* TSR saving!). Chancellor also thinking that he might stop increase in bus fares, by slightly higher concession. Chancellor said that all this may yet be reviewed and withdrawn. Meanwhile Speech gets longer and longer but probably now nothing on monetary policy or public expenditure.

Also long meeting on housing. Crossman still anxious to cut mortgage rates *and* reduce private house-building. So he suggests using financial control to limit building by restricting loans of building societies on new houses; and goes on to ask that 30% of new mortgages be subsidised and guaranteed on a 4% interest rate basis. The saving is equivalent to 10% of interest charge or the equivalent of about half a per cent on mortgage and confined to those taking out new mortgage. It implements 'pledge' at perhaps fairly low cost but has otherwise little to be said for it.

Further agitation on coal prices. Robens[46] has now sent in data showing coal sales falling, stocking costs likely to be high and deficit of N.C.B. higher than ever. Yet price reductions for the summer already announced after his intervention with First Secretary and P.M.

Sterling remains weak and forwards largely rolled on. This is the second big week.

5 April   Last Monday we had a meeting with Chancellor at which he asked us round the table two questions in what he called a Buchmanite session. Was he doing enough in the Budget? And could he find some further way of giving the economy more thrust and dynamism? This came after quite a long discussion of the possibility of cutting 10% off overseas government expenditure. Otto said this came down to Germany and he and Raymond Bell[47] thought nothing really possible this side of the German election.

[45] Robert (Roy) Workman. Asst. Sec., Treasury, 1959–66; Under-Sec., 1967–74.

[46] Lord (Alf) Robens. Chm., National Coal Board, 1969–71; Director, Bank of England, 1966–81; Member NEDC, 1962–71.

[47] Raymond Bell. Under-Sec., Treasury, 1960–66; Dep. Sec. 1966–72.

My view was that if he wanted certainty – and he had said quite a lot about the people who were determined to see the government's policy in a bad light and would accordingly represent the Budget as irrelevant he could get it by limiting the extra taxes to £50 m. This would resolve matters by making devaluation inevitable. The most he could really hope for was doubt – the chance that he might *not* have to devalue. The Budget would be judged against the National Institute recommendations and if it did more he would score accordingly. (He had said earlier that if he had realised how near he was to coming to the National Institute £200/£100 m. he would have made a change in the Budget). Secondly, the last thing needed was any fresh stimulus through the Budget. His job was to use the pruning knife and cut out losses so as to let the profitable parts of the economy expand. I said coal was obsolete (no new apparatus was designed round coal) and we ought to choose this time to get men into other jobs. He said he couldn't challenge my economics but he did know about gardening and roses often bloomed best without pruning - but they didn't, as Otto interjected, bear losses!

Of the others (Raymond Bell, Ian Bancroft and Peter Vinter[48] had their say) William ended the round by suggesting holding over legislation on the corporation tax for one year: but Diamond gave three reasons against this. Otto also thought that there had been too much time spent on the new taxes but the Chancellor felt that the Revenue hadn't really wasted time since they couldn't have worked out details of Plans D and E and anyhow as Diamond said these plans might not prove politically acceptable. Diamond insisted that we must at all costs show £200 m. extra in taxation *this* year not just in a full year.

The Chancellor was in good form, and free from any sense of anxiety now that major decisions lay behind him. He prophesied that next April we would all be sitting there agreeing that we had done the right thing. We wouldn't devalue, there would be no recession, and things would come out to our satisfaction.

He said earlier that if the Tories wanted to be helpful they should take a leaf out of his book and say publicly that the pound need not and would not be devalued instead of saying like Cyril Osborne that it would be.

We had another meeting with him later on the New Taxes. This time Nicky and Alec Johnston[49] were there. At one point when N. was expounding the way public opinion would react the Chancellor said 'Well, we haven't had a revolution yet! And if we do, I'll see to it that you get pushed in front of the crowd'. Alec J. at the end tried to induce the Chancellor to give way on the reductions in personal allowances but had no success - 'throwing money away', Alec said.

The upshot of this meeting was that we reversed an earlier decision on capital gains taxation of insurance companies which we had thought justified, taxing capital gains on gilt edged because it ensured an adequate market. Chancellor seemed quite prepared to exempt insurance companies from capital gains taxa-

---

[48] Peter Vinter. HM Treasury, 1945–69; Third Sec., 1965–69; Deputy Sec., Min. of Technology and then DTI, 1969–73.

[49] Sir Alec Johnston. Chm., Board of Inland Revenue, 1958–68.

tion but none of us (to the Revenue's surprise) contested the point and supported the Chancellor. At this meeting the rate of tax was fixed. Other matters were still left open (e.g. treatment of unit trusts) and only settled on Friday.

William set us all going on Tuesday on a devaluation exercise because he felt we should be ready for trouble after the Budget, however irrational. He thinks a 3 figure loss three days running would be the signal for a submission to Ministers but in my view it would settle the whole affair and leave no time for a submission.

On Monday night we went to Italian Ambassador's for dinner. G.Brown was there and about 40 others. He ragged Cromer unmercifully at the table and passed messages to Lady C. comparing her with Mata Hari until Pieraccini, who sat between them and spoke no English, offered to change places with G.B., imagining he wanted to make eyes at Lady C. – although Mrs B. sat opposite, stern as a disapproving landlady.

When the ladies left he divided his fire between C. and me saying he couldn't make up his mind which of us to nominate for the Consulate Generalship of the Yemen (a favourite threat of his I gather). Somebody suggested the Leeward Isles and George at once corrected his pronunciation (twice, in fact) to Looard. He offered to drink to two Tories meaning me and Boyd Carpenter and then switched to attack B.C. for the Tory Bishops. 'You appointed atheists to be Bishops of my Church' – the fact that they were Labour sympathisers didn't deter him from pursuing the attack. B.C. couldn't make appointments now – that was reserved to the party in office. (But he didn't say much about past Labour appointments).

B.C. tried to stem it all by saying that I had given good advice but it was no use. However, Douglas Allen came out with high marks from George and this I was very glad to see.

Mary sat next to Cromer who was very annoyed (as who would not) and turned to her to engage in conversation saying he could see that George was trying to catch his eye.

I saw a lot of the Italians later and the 3 Ministers who made speeches to them all did it very well: the Chancellor, Diamond and George Thomson. I had lunch at No.11 then at 1 Carlton Gardens (with Mary) and also had a morning with their officials who seemed very intelligent.

It was a bad month, almost as bad in the end as January. But once the Budget is past we should get *some* money back (not perhaps a great deal), all the more if the TSR2 is cancelled as now seems certain. The final meeting of Ministers was on Thursday at 10 p.m. before Harold went off to Paris.

The press is now remarkably unanimous about the Budget – the range of £100–£150 m. is what one would like to see to get the right reactions.

Tuesday, 6 April

In the Budget on 6 April the Chancellor announced that he was acting to reduce home demand by £250 m. per annum. The TSR2 aircraft would be cancelled, and taxation would be increased by £164 m. in 1965-66 and £217 m. in 1966-67, mainly through higher taxes on drink and tobacco and higher licence duty on motor vehicles. The balance of payments was expected to benefit by at least £100 m. Two new taxes corporation tax and capital gains tax – were also introduced. There was no reflux of funds but neither was there an enlarged outflow.

A call for special deposits was made on 29 April and bank rate was reduced to 6 per cent on 3 June. Discussion in the Treasury dwelt on the danger of a shortage of international liquidity and on a long list of plans from A to F on various aspects of industrial policy. Plan E, which became the favourite, provided for the replacement of investment allowances by government grants, aiming at the same time to encourage investment in the development areas and in the equipment needed for automation.

Tuesday, 6 April   We spent nearly all yesterday in meetings on devaluation in William's room. A whole set of papers prepared in case we were forced to consider a change before May 25. Robert put in a separate paper arguing for floating rates but was more inclined after discussion to agree that this would be very risky especially if it meant forgoing IMF loan. None of us took view that Budget *would* precipitate a change but we felt it necessary to be ready in case of perverse reactions.

Budget day. Chancellor spoke very fast for two and a half hours, stumbling a little at beginning but showing more self-confidence than in November. Speech not ready as usual till last minute and I had not read final version. He told me yesterday that he thought I'd like Budget judgement section. It still sounded rather patched together but perhaps the sequence was about as good as could be hoped for given need to combine exposition of two new taxes, balance of payments problem, and the usual bits on Exchequer Accounts, etc. Heard uninterrupted throughout except for question on TSR2 (only it came out as TFX2) and supplementary from Home who was easily satisfied. Little or no noise till he got to talking about business expenses and savings which MP's obviously felt they understood! On motor cars he astonished them by saying no rise in purchase tax and still more by adding only £2$\frac{1}{2}$ to the cost of motor vehicle licence. No doubt at all he could safely have added at least £5. Similarly nobody seemed interested in removal of remission of tax on national insurance contribution.

I sat next to Nicky and R.N. (3 Soothsayers in Ordinary). Governor was in front and Shonfield[50] behind.

Wednesday, 14 April   Over Mont Blanc on the way back from Rome. I dined last night with Carli,[51] Baffi[52] and others from the Banca d'Italia after

[50] Andrew Shonfield. Econ. ed., *The Observer*, 1958–61; Dir. of Studies, 1961–68 and Research Fellow, 1969–71, Royal Institute of International Affairs; Chm. SSRC, 1969–71.

[51] Guido Carli. Governor, Bank of Italy from 1961; member of EEC Monetary Committee from 1959.

[52] P Baffi. Italian banker and economist; Bank of Italy from 1936; Italian deputy

addressing about 40 of the staff on the Budget (at 7 p.m.!). They were emphatic that if we are to get the Ministers and Governors of the Six to give us their backing in drawing on IMF we shall have to give a better justification of the Budget deficit. Carli said that a Director of Nestlé had told him that in the last few months they had observed a general falling off in sales in all the countries they dealt with. The Italians are obviously rather concerned about the prospects for world trade.

Looking back to last summer it seems to me that our undoing was that confidence was *not* shaken. It would perhaps have been better if there had been a mild tremor at least before the autumn so that the Chancellor would have had grounds for acting. It was also bad luck that the production index behaved so misleadingly: he would have been exposed to attack for hitting the economy when it was already down. But none of this justifies the supineness of the government in dealing with public investment and current expenditure. The Chancellor showed no interest in pruning the electricity programme and Otto was resolute in opposing cuts. Much the same is true of housing. To increase each of these programmes by 50% above 1961 in the middle of an investment boom was downright crazy. Even so, it is still obscure why our forecasts of the swing in the current account balance were so modest when we had the experience of the previous cycle behind us. Domestic activity expanded more or less in line with our own forecast.

The Italians are tremendously interested in our experiments in incomes policy and envious of our political stability. They feel the difficulty of coping with politically motivated unions and are conscious that their competitive position may weaken progressively.

There is an interesting cleavage of opinion on mixed enterprises. Marsan[53] recounted the advantages on the side of risk-taking, regional policy, managerial recruitment and efficiency in public enterprise. He said that it was counted no slur or disadvantage to enter state industry (under IRI) rather than private industry. The Banca d'Italia felt that the sharp break in UK between public and private enterprise was preferable since then private industry knew where it was in its dealings with the public sector. It is obviously true that a large undertaking like the steel plant at Taranto would have been difficult to finance privately. Marsan was interested in our own experience here e.g. in allowing freedom to a nationalized industry to manufacture for itself.

Thursday, 29 April   No great issue except special deposits and I wasn't even told of what was decided much less consulted. After all, I'd had my say earlier when the Chancellor decided against making a call in the Budget in spite of recommendation from officials and from Bank of England. The Governor suggested a call even *after* the Budget on the Wed./Thurs. partly because of what Al Hayes[54] and others had said on the telephone but the Chancellor decided

governor of IBRD, 1965.

[53] Marsan. Italian economist on staff of IRI.

[54] Al Hayes. American banker; President, Federal Reserve Bank of New York from

again – rightly as we thought – that he couldn't act then since it would reflect on the Budget. He agreed to wait for the April Bank Returns and when they showed a big rise in advances this settled the matter. He seems to have had no difficulty with G.B. but the P.M. cabling from Rome was worried about the effect on today's debate on housing and wanted announcement put off till late evening while Chancellor wanted to stick to Thursday à la bank rate (as on all three previous occasions of a call). P.M. in fact had tried earlier in the week to get agreement on fall in bank rate and call for special deposits – an idea floated by the Chancellor for use *if* the Budget produced a reflux of funds. Chancellor successfully contested this idea.

Today van Lennep was over just after meeting of Monetary Committee of the Six. William A. joined meeting at 12.05 just as we were about to start a discussion on monetary policy and he was able to startle Emil by announcing that Bank of England had made a call a few minutes earlier. He left us at 12.15 so it was quite a dramatic 10 minutes and a nice contrast to Emil's visit of last July when he was told that we were considering but in the end nothing was done. E. obviously didn't quite know what a call for special deposits involved but was impressed that action was being taken.

The effect of the Budget has been exactly as we thought. I told the Chancellor the day before that I expected no dramatic effect on sterling either way and we were all prepared for the storm to be concentrated on foreign investment and the corporation tax.

We did not expect quite so much argument about the budget deficit and monetary policy both with IMF staff and with the Six. But Baffi and Carli warned me that we had not made our case clearly at Basle and should do so in a paper circulated in advance. Unfortunately my minute on the subject lay around without anybody following it up in spite of the Chancellor's note on it as most of us went on leave for a week and neither R.N. nor S.G. had taken in the importance of the meeting in Cannes. I succeeded in getting a short note off on Wednesday night to Carli and copies were given to Emil today. But the key sections were drafted so badly by Radice that they had to be left out altogether. Even when he completed his draft a copy didn't reach me because it went to Fred Atkinson's P.A. who didn't know what to do with it. It was a classic study in bad organisation.

Yesterday we had a long session on international liquidity with the Chancellor.[55] Nicky was there and made an interesting point – that the amount of new liquidity was less important than the process by which it came into existence. There are to be further meetings and they should be illuminating although I don't think that much can come of it all this year.

1956.

[55] British politicians in the 1960s from Macmillan onwards were firm believers in the existence of a shortage of international liquidity (i.e. in the stock of internationally acceptable money) and feared that an international slump would result. The danger arose because America could not go on indefinitely supplying the world with dollars that ended up in central bank reserves but also added to America's liquid debts. Whatever the shortage of international liquidity, it did not prevent continuing inflation.

On devaluation, papers have been re-written but discussion deferred. R.N. now agrees that floating rate is not possible in position of weakness.

We must have been roughly in current account balance in Q1 but this is largely due to exceptionally low level of imports and unusually fast growth in exports. Rather expect figures for May to cause reaction and renew anxiety about sterling. Certainly not out of the wood.

Last week interesting because press swung over to very critical view of G.B.'s incomes policy and almost wrote it off; reported first whiff of deflation in form of mortgage famine (*Telegraph* even spoke of 'private house-building grinding to a halt'); but thought turn of the tide might have come in exchange market – at least till the autumn. The building hold-up is grossly exaggerated – only a little less overtime. Sterling may be in trouble again *before* August especially if any suggestion of an autumn election or pressure to get rid of surcharge. As to incomes policy, Douglas Allen said that G.B. had given a brilliant speech at Blackpool and swung the Conference, knew exactly how to put things to both workers and employers (a different style for each). Maurice P. thought that nobody else could hope to get policy across. But Ned Dunnett[56] on Wednesday was doubtful if we'd get anywhere for a long time because Union members had to be elected and were elected to mobilise bargaining power. G.B. is said to be still tired and depressed. He told D. Allen 'There's enough Treasury advice being offered in the Treasury'.

Spending a lot of time on staff. Shortage as acute as ever but I look like finding two Economic Advisers for this autumn. Aubrey Jones[57] wants somebody and has suggested Bruce Williams[58]. I asked Douglas Allen if Aubrey had threatened to resign (when he came into van Lennep's meeting to get him out). D. said No, not today but he has done so earlier. (*Express* headline implies a current threat over George Wigg's[59] silly speech.)

Sunday, 16 May   About a fortnight ago G.B. wrote to J.C. expressing concern about our commitments to IMF. Had we undertaken to *prevent* demand from rising more than $2\frac{1}{2}\%$ from 1964 (Q3,4) to 1966 (Q3,4)? Was he free to construct his plan on some more expansionary hypothesis? So I drafted a reply softly to say that things might not turn out as we feared and then, of course, more might be attempted. But it looks as if we were expanding at about 6% p.a., not $2\frac{1}{2}\%$, and the only sign of a check to the growth in demand is in private housing which the P.M. is determined to help by interest rate concessions. I keep being asked why expanding output should be a source of gloom but of course the investment boom produces expansion *and a deficit* simultaneously.

---

[56] Sir James (Ned) Dunnett. Perm. Sec., Min. of Transport, 1959–62; Min. of Labour, 1962–66.

[57] Aubrey Jones. Chm. National Board for Prices and Incomes, 1965–70.

[58] Professor of Economics, University of Manchester, 1959–67; Econ. Adviser to Min. of Technology, 1966–67

[59] George Wigg (later Lord). Lab. Paymaster General, 1964–70; Chm. Horse Racing Betting Levy Board, 1967–72.

Press has had a wonderful time at expense of G.B. over his last minute 'offer' in the steel debate. But this will only aggravate his desire to make the Plan a resounding success and win back ground that he feels he has lost to Jim C. My colleagues seem to think Plan can do little harm but I fear that it still prevents us from taking action and will go on doing so.

Chancellor anxious to reduce bank rate before it stays at 7% longer than under any other administration i.e. this week? It may be reasonable provided we intend to come up again in the autumn but even now the forward rate isn't back to last October level and we still seem to be getting currency coming in.

Chancellor very good at lunch speech after Trial of the Pyx. He is now beginning to make some concessions on Finance Bill.

Saturday, 22 May   En route to Washington for a week there and in Ottawa. Most of past week spent in interviews for positions in Government Economic Service.

On Thursday we had another meeting at No.10 – this time confined to Treasury and nominally about international liquidity and the economic outlook. Neither subject, as is usual on those occasions, was discussed. There was a formal agenda and we *did* take item 3 at some length (Plans D and E) because Diamond had to go off to the House of Commons. But for the rest, the discussion, though logical enough, was not directed to reaching an agreed conclusion, much less a sequence of conclusions. T.B. was present and was less disruptive than he usually is. Apart from an outburst against Loynes (Bank of England), and his habit of setting up Currency Boards, he seemed subdued and left early: in fact in the middle of a discussion of deposits against forward exchange purchases - his own pet scheme.

The P.M. did most of the talking and it trod the familiar path from gimmicks to autobiography and then hotfoot to the failings of statistics, this government's favourite alibi. He went over many of the suggestions that have been advanced under the head of D and E and in so doing brought out the reason why Otto has made such slow progress – a slowness on which the Chancellor commented a little sourly at the House of Commons in our preliminary discussion with Chief Secretary and others. But he and Chancellor then wandered off into a dream of docks and dock charges as a means of encouraging exports. The Chancellor in particular seemed to have in mind a subsidy to transport to the ports that would operate exclusively in favour of exports and yet be GATTworthy. Nobody else took this very seriously and N.K. pointed out that Tom Padmore[60] had already been over all this months ago and had made short shrift of the proposal.

At a later stage, after over an hour on D and E, we got on to the likely situation in the autumn and there was general agreement that if the current account didn't show continuous improvement (and the prospect of it) we should be in serious difficulties. Chancellor took the view that we had enough reserves to get by unless there was a run on the pound on the scale of last November and he

---

[60] Sir Tom Padmore. Second Sec., Treasury, 1952–62; Perm. Sec., Min. of Transport, 1962–68.

couldn't see why this should happen. I said we'd be bound to have trouble and the only question was how much – we'd certainly need luck. R.N. spoke quite openly of devaluation and N.K. said the budget hadn't been deflationary enough – we ought to have been more severe on cars. But N.K. is very inconsistent at times – he didn't say this at Chequers. He had just done a paper on liquidity with me in which he spoke of waiting for a fair moment before calling up UK foreign assets. This didn't stop him from arguing for it this autumn in the event of a run.

The statistical part of the evening was largely a monologue by the P.M. directed towards showing that we didn't know even now what caused the November crisis. No other country would allow itself to lack information about forward dealings as completely as UK Was there a Chief Statistician in the Bank whose job it was to assemble this sort of information? William and Denis raised the question several times what the information would go to show or be used to do, but the P.M. brushed this aside with the remark that one often didn't know the questions to put until the statistics were collected. (This went with a reference to John Jewkes[61] on finding the questions to the answers rather than vice versa.)

Earlier at dinner, he asked me what were the only two places in Britain where the water permitted the brewing of good lager and said Alloa and Wrexham, on the authority of *The Economist* for 1961 or 1962.

The Chancellor had to leave for a division half way through the evening and said as he went that when he had hurried to the House of Commons earlier in the week for a division on capital punishment he had asked himself why he should suffer premature death to save a murderer from hanging.

The Ministers were in high spirits over the Finance Bill. H.W. expounded the importance of boredom as a secret weapon and predicted the Tories would not be able to sustain their attack for long – he knew from experience how difficult it was to keep it up on issues that seemed highly technical to the back-benchers.

The Chancellor saw Heath[62] in the course of the evening and concluded a secret deal as to the amount of time to be devoted to the Committee Stage. He said that the Tories were in confusion, the bank-benchers hollering to divide on issues on which their leaders recognised it to be impossible.

At the House of Commons he made it clear that he no longer expected to take any major initiative on liquidity but we will be hearing more at Chequers on May 30. On hire purchase he takes William's view that to impose terms now would look like fidgeting, coming on top of the Budget and the intensification of the credit squeeze.

We talked this over on Wednesday night (R.N. not present) with William and DHFR. I came to the conclusion that it might not be worth pursuing the idea of a fall in bank rate and the imposition of hire purchase terms control, but that both remained starters, independent of one another: the latter perhaps at the request

[61] John Jewkes. Industrial economist; first Director of Econ. Section 1941; Fellow of Merton College, Oxford, 1948–69.
[62] Edward Heath. Cons. Lord Privy Seal, 1960–63; Sec. of State for Industry, Trade and Regional Developt., October 1963–October 1964; Leader of the Opposition 1965–70; Prime Minister 1970–74.

of the FHA to ensure fair treatment of all suppliers of hire purchase finance, the former partly to maintain the Chancellor's position in the Cabinet and strengthen his hand for other issues. William obviously felt that bank rate should come down unless we had a very strong case the other way. I was doubtful but willing to concede that we could probably afford to cut if the evidence of capital flows supported the view that interest rates were high enough. After all, the Budget was intended to leave room for some reduction. But the press comments today begin to throw doubt on the technical position and there is less pressure than appeared earlier in favour of reduction.

Later, en route to Washington   This has been a week of re-evaluation not unlike the week in April when I was on holiday after Easter and the press suddenly sailed into George B. on incomes policy and got worried about the prospect of wage inflation, while also becoming alive to the possibility of a set-back in private housing.

First came a 2 point rise in the cost of living. Of this, two-thirds was due to the Budget (though we had earlier put it at 1.2 not 1.4) but it was nevertheless a jar for the public. Then came a 2 point fall in the index of production (3 points in manufacturing alone) on top of a fall in February. Unemployment rose by 7000 on additive and 5000 on multiplicative method of seasonal adjustment and stands only 5000 below Jan. This took W.Godley by surprise especially as I had asked him a couple of days previously what he would say to exactly that change in unemployment.

Let me go back to the No.10 meetings. The drill is as follows. We usually hear of them 10 days in advance. Nobody is asked whether they have some other urgent engagement and usually I have to cancel something or other. The Bank of England are rigorously excluded so that rude comments about the Governor can be freely made. The economic advisers are present ex officio (except that Donald didn't get invited last night because DEA were not there – curiously, because Plans D and E are very much their affair). The Ministers don't monopolise the talk by any means and T.B. in particular calls them by their first name and doesn't hesitate to be pretty short, if provoked. At some point there is a round the room poll of opinion on some issue. The P.M. usually steers as far as anyone does.

When we arrive and have shed coats we go upstairs and find the home team (H.W., T.B. and some of the staff e.g. Burke Trend, Derek Mitchell, Robert Armstrong and the PRO, whom T.B. called 'the William Clark of this Administration') standing in the big dining room, usually with some walking up and down and lots of chaff. We then adjourn to have a buffet supper, without service of any kind. There is cold fish, meat, chicken and salad, cheese, and English beer – nothing else. Next we move to another of the upstairs rooms and sit in easy chairs taking coffee and brandy with us. (On Thursday we were in a rear room, quite elegantly furnished and adequate for a dozen or so guests, hung with English landscape paintings of the 18th century like most of No.10. In the dining room there are portraits of Wellington and Fox – the latter in some ways like N.K. with a wig – and outside is a big Romney of a lady). The only time any servants are in sight is on entry when they offer to show you upstairs and as you leave: or when one of them brings in a full brandy bottle and takes away the empty one. There are cigars (Jamaica only) and *sometimes* cigarettes. H.W. may smoke his pipe but more usually a cigar. The meeting was called for 7.30 on Thursday (rather early) and finished at midnight (relatively late). Only one paper was circulated in advance – one by T.B. on The Economic Outlook – and it was never mentioned; the Chancellor had not even seen it!

I made no note earlier of my talk with Brian Rose[63] or of a similar talk with Baffi. B.R. told me in mid-April that nobody in Washington could understand our Budget or the way we ran our economy. The Report submitted by the Mission would be largely unintelligible to his colleagues who took the simple-minded view that countries with big Budget deficits ended up with balance of payments deficits and that the cure for the second was usually a cut in the first. Why should Britain be a unique exception? Then there was the fact of last year's deficit which we could hardly be said to have predicted successfully – why should this year's predictions be taken any more seriously? It wasn't very convincing to say that the Budget accountancy (which was available to everybody) was misleading or irrelevant while the national income forecasts (which nobody ever saw) were the right basis and a reliable one. Baffi reported the same kind of scepticism in Basle and R.N. coming back from WP No.3 records a similar disposition to say that we are running our affairs on far too narrow a margin of risk.

Meanwhile in DEA the idea is strongly held that growth is proportionate to industrial investment and this in turn is proportionate to confidence in expansion so that nothing must be done to interrupt expansion for fear of killing the better prospect of genuine growth. Donald seems to believe this and it is an article of faith with Jukes, Grieve Smith,[64] Michael Shanks[65] and no doubt many others. I, on the other hand, say quite simply that all we are getting is an investment boom, chiefly in housing and electricity, that this inevitably produces a deficit and rising costs, and that we are heading either for a stop more sudden than any so far (with devaluation thrown in) or for a long slow adjustment to a sustainable level of investment and pressure of demand.

The government meanwhile is taking an increasingly firm position on housing and simply won't give up implementation of its pledges. They feel that electorally housing is too important and will contemplate any economic nonsense to keep down rents and keep up housebuilding. Similarly they are jeopardising the future of the nationalised industries by preventing price rises for coal (now put back to December) and bus fares. This will (Otto says) mean more government expenditure of just the kind our creditors can rightly criticise. Meanwhile Dick C. is agitating for 500,000 houses a year by 1970, 4% money for local authority housing, and some money for private mortgages at the same rate from

[63] Brian Rose. Member of IMF Mission to UK in April 1966.

[64] John Grieve Smith. Asst. Dir., Economic Planning, DEA.

[65] Michael Shanks*Financial Times*, 1954–64; *Sunday Times*, 1964–65; Industrial Adviser, 1965–66, Industrial Policy Co-ordinator, 1966-67, DEA; Dir.-Gen. for Social Affairs, EEC from 1973.

the building societies.

On top of everything, the fact that the government is in trouble on steel and doubtful of the trend in electoral opinion is going to make things very difficult. It was obvious on Thursday that H.W. was no longer so sure he wouldn't want to go to the country in the near future. There was none of the brave talk about seeing the whole programme through and more about the government's small majority.

Chancellor, on the Governor: 'You are speaking of the man I love'. P.M. did say M.Allen[66] taught him all he knew about economics and Chancellor made a sympathetic reference to L.K.O'Brien. Otherwise every reference to Bank was highly unflattering.

On Plan D, it was pointed out to Chancellor that DEA had not one but two departmental voices. This is something highly unusual in Whitehall but I can recall that Treasury used to be in much the same state in 1940's.

Burke Trend on Treasury in 1913 told me that when Waley[67] joined OF the duty of a young AP was to enter up *once a week* the exchange rates with each of the leading centres.

Sunday, 30 May   Three days in Washington and two in Ottawa landing me back yesterday morning.

The Chequers meeting today changed character from day to day last week and was finally confined to the morning, only because P.M. had to go up to London to look at the Queen. We therefore discussed The Plan and a mighty barren discussion it was although G.B., the P.M. and other Ministers seemed to think it splendid.

The P.M. opened with an attack on the press for giving a distorted picture of the purpose of the meeting at the behest of the Tory Central Office. Then came George B. followed by Donald, John Jukes and Catherwood in turn. Frank Cousins was next, 'roaming' as he put it and George and the Chancellor followed. The P.M. then turned to me but I declined and Tommy launched into a good old tirade about the Board of Trade and the Bank of England largely on the strength of a remark by Catherwood that it was proving difficult to get round the Restrictive Trade Practices Act in seeking self-imposed export allocations by a group of firms. The balance of payments problem was pushed into the background (though Tommy did say Plan wasn't really credible) and so was the 1967 'hump'. The Chancellor stressed the debt repayment obligations which the P.M. tended to assume could be 'rolled on' (or 'off'). But he thought q.r.'s might help and this drew criticism from R.N. and G.B. The P.M. thought that 100% q.r.'s *might* look different from 80% q.r.'s which would have been impossible last October.

Whitsunday, 6 June   When I got back from Ottawa I naturally asked where

[66] Maurice Allen. Fellow of Balliol College, Oxford, 1938–48; Chief Economist on staff of Bank of England from 1950.

[67] S.D. Waley. Entered Treasury 1910; Third Sec. 1946–47 dealing with external finance.

we stood on bank rate and hire purchase. After all, we had mooted a change in bank rate in Washington with FRB and Treasury and we had all been a little in favour of bringing it down (not, perhaps, Denis) until the set-back in the exchange markets seemed to put an end to the possibility. In fact, I had asked William why wait a fortnight more until June 3, since if we did mean to reduce bank rate it would be best to move at once.

Fred told me that it had been agreed not to proceed and that a meeting on hire purchase had ended in agreement to wait and see how things turned out. But on Monday evening William called me along partly 'to weep on my shoulder' – he was as depressed as I by Chequers and the evident satisfaction of Ministers although he thought H.W. too intelligent to be genuinely satisfied – and partly to tell me of the P.M.'s reaction to the idea of a 1% fall in bank rate with hire purchase restrictions. The Chancellor had abandoned the idea but *not* the P.M. who thought it a good bargain. I agreed to alert Denis to the idea but in the end had to wait until Tuesday before discussing it with him. On Tuesday evening I talked it over (after a day's Civil Service Boarding) and began to see a case for action because a reduced home demand for cars could conceivably be of help to exports or (more immediately) to relieving the shortage of labour in the Midlands (12 vacancies per unemployed skilled engineer). By next morning I was clear that we ought *not* to reduce bank rate and impose hire purchase (for how long, anyhow?) and said so. I found that R.N. was much more vehemently opposed than I was and in due course he minuted the Chancellor strongly advising against. R.N. felt the political case *against* was strong and that the risks were far too great in relation to the gains (economic *or* political). Personally I was mainly influenced by the fact that over £50 m. had been switched out of sterling in May and that a reduction in bank rate was not likely to improve the intrinsic discount against sterling.

William told us that P.M. had gone over the ground with T.B. and talked himself into a view of the future in which a fall in bank rate would complete the restoration of the Government's image. Later the Board of Trade arrived and showed us proofs of a H.P. order on the alternatives of A – a contraction in maximum period of instalment payments to 30 months, B – this *plus* an increase in minimum downpayments to 25% or 15% for furniture etc. with comparable change in hiring agreements. The second was the item to which the Governor said foreigners would attach most attention. The Board of Trade put the demand effects of A and B at £100 m. or so – mainly A.

I drafted a long minute just before lunch and it presumably was read by the Chancellor although when we all met at 6.30 at the House of Commons there was no sign of it. The P.M. and Chief Cashier were there as well as R.N., W.A., Denis and Ian B. The Governor had written to the Chancellor in terms more hesitant than before and stressing the risks but still arguing for a fall plus hire purchase restrictions (including deposits).

The Chancellor put a number of questions to the Governor without at first showing his hand. He *did* ask if this was not rather an odd time to reduce bank rate and if there was not a risk of a capital outflow. The Governor rather pooh-poohed this without denying that the confidence effect was a bit of a gamble. He didn't seem to know about the weekly figures of sterling and dollar liabilities. The Chancellor then made it clear that he proposed to move in spite of the views of his officials. He was a cautious man and so of course was the Governor. Why shouldn't he take the advice of the Governor when the very officials who now opposed a move had shown no anxiety or opposition a couple of weeks previously? If bank rate didn't come down now it wouldn't come down before Christmas.

Denis made his point that the Bank seemed to believe that it was only a rise in bank rate that took effect and that the *level* was of little consequence. How could a fall strengthen confidence if a rise was intended to do the same? The Governor thought that it *could* strengthen confidence if it showed that the authorities had the situation under control but I thought it more accurate to say 'if the situation *had been handled*' and it obviously hadn't been yet.

As we left, R.N. felt decidedly cynical and I concluded that we might end up with the fall in bank rate and nothing more. But the sequel was even more bizarre. Ministers met at 10- Jay, Brown (who had heard in the meantime about hire purchase but not, I think, bank rate), Chancellor and P.M. It was the evening of the dead heat vote (about 10.30) when the P.M.G. was in the Crypt and someone bet a bottle of bourbon if anyone could name the missing Minister. They were soon in a clinch. George Brown wouldn't agree to any hire purchase restrictions. They didn't know the facts – wasn't Nigel Lawson[68] saying in *The Financial Times* that motor car firms were spreading out deliveries of components? The Chancellor on the other hand insisted on the whole package. The P.M. who introduced the discussion didn't give the Chancellor any chance to intervene and went over the whole story without so much as indicating that the Chancellor wanted Draft B. Things began to get heated. There was talk by the P.M. of D-day and Eisenhower. 'So you're Eisenhower' said G.B. and launched into a tirade. Then the P.M. explained it was the Cabinet that was Eisenhower. Was the P.M. to decide between the different courses or was it be taken to the Cabinet? G.B. thought the P.M. should decide but when he came down on the side of Draft A he was faced with two threats of resignation for opposite reasons. The state of play at 2.30 a.m. was that officials were being asked to get out (i.e. W.A., Trend and E.Roll – Jay had gone long before), the Chancellor was ringing the Governor, and G.B. was getting thoroughly bad-tempered.

On Thursday morning [3 June, when the reduction in bank rate was to be announced] the Governor had breakfast with P.M. and they apparently agreed on the deposits side of hire purchase *only* and with furniture omitted. This was put to the Cabinet but it wasn't until 11.20 that agreement was reached. It was even then difficult to get hold of D.J. to sign the H.P. Order in time to lay it and impossible to have it printed for distribution. Nevertheless everything went out on the tape exactly as planned and the reception given to the news seems so far to have been in accordance with the Governor's expectations.

That evening I dined at the Governor's flat with P.P.Schweitzer, William,

[68] Nigel Lawson. City ed. *Sunday Telegraph*, 1961–63; Special Asst. to Prime Minister, 1963–64; Ed. *The Spectator*, 1966–70; Chancellor of the Exchequer, 1983–90.

Maurice Allen, Jasper Rootham,[69] John Fforde,[70] Jeremy Morse[71]. Most of the talk turned on the pledges of the IMF as to advances and credit (the £230/400 m.) and M.A. seemed to feel that he must justify his scepticism of these symbols. He also thought Schweitzer very angry because three times he had mentioned to the Governor that he was kept waiting 45 minutes at London Airport for his bags. William decided that in Paris that morning someone had chided him with not knowing of the fall in bank rate although in fact P.P.S. kept saying that he didn't mind the reduction and had told Stevens[72] that it should be combined with hire purchase restrictions as had been done: P.P.S. was strongly in favour of quantitative controls rather than higher rates on the basis of his experience at the Banque de France to which he referred several times. P.P.S. was also apparently incredulous of the idea that the Governor couldn't have known till 11.20 of the decision. My own impression is that P.P.S. was tired, tipsy and nettled by the constant attack on our monetary pledges without any constructive alternative being suggested. At any rate it was agreed that William should speak to Chancellor (with a view to get him to take P.P.S. to the P.M.) especially as the Governor had failed to take action to get him VIP treatment at the airport in the middle of his other preoccupations.

So next morning (Friday) when I called at No.11 for the interview between P.P.S. and Chancellor I found that the Chancellor and P.M. the previous night had brooded on what they might do and had decided on a motor cycle escort to the Airport: not, perhaps, so absurd as it might seem because the strike at the Airport was creating a traffic jam (but nobody knew that at the time). P.P.S. was amused.

It was interesting to see the Chancellor in bouncing form when he arrived; he had been completely pooped the previous evening according to Ian. In fact he retained the initiative throughout the interview and was very articulate and to the point. He told P.P.S. that the P.M. had decided (and told no-one else but him) that there would be no election this year. (P.P.S. was naturally perturbed at the prospect of an autumn election). He also said quite frankly that the bank rate decision had not been taken until 11.20 a.m. and that there had been threats of resignation. P.P.S. told us that de Gaulle had not been warned before his press conference that his proposals implied a revaluation of gold and that his speech had not been seen by Brunet[73] or by Giscard[74].

Going back to bank rate, the alliance between P.M. and Governor was not altogether unexpected since for their separate reasons both wanted to get bank

---

[69] Jasper Rootham – Bank of England.

[70] John Fforde - Bank of England, 1957–92; Chief Cashier, 1966–70.

[71] Jeremy Morse - Dir. Glyn Mills, 1964; Exec. Dir., Bank of England, 1965–72.

[72] John Stevens - Exec. Dir., Bank of England, 1957–64; Econ. Minister in Washington, 1965–67; Chm. Morgan Grenfell & Co, 1972–73.

[73] Jacques Brunet .President and General Manager, Crédit National, 1949–60; Governor, Bank of France, 1960–69.

[74] Valéry Giscard d'Estaing – Minister for Economic Affairs, 1962–66; President Comm. des Finances, de l'Economie Génerale et du Plan, 1967–68; President of France, 1976–81.

rate down now. The P.M. had read his briefs (unlike others?) and knew that what the Governor really wanted was an increase in hire purchase downpayments that might be very largely presentational. Presumably this also weighed in the end with G.B., since cars will be completely unaffected. So I was very nearly right in thinking that we would end up with a fall in bank rate *simpliciter*; and so far as there were other consequences (e.g. on opinion) we might as well have done A and B for all the difference it would have made politically. We have ended up by taking the political plunge and getting very little of the economic effect – indeed making it more difficult to use hire purchase in the autumn when we might want to use it. And if things *do* go wrong externally, will the Governor still call for 8% as he said he would on Wednesday night?

The amendments to Finance Bill are being pushed on Chancellor by P.M. as another step in restoring image of government.

Sunday, 13 June　　A relatively quiet week after Whitsun. William took off but still looked pretty tired on return. P.M. has sent a memo on housing to G.B. asking in effect for 500,000 houses whatever else goes into the Plan. Chancellor away all week and didn't see him till Saturday at No.11.

At Permanent Secretaries' meeting on Wednesday; R.N. recalled discussion on Plan at PCSG with Donald and underlined unreality of the big increases in public expenditure over next few years followed by small increases thereafter while personal consumption began to increase very fast in late sixties and had to be severely compressed in immediate future. The fact is that getting plausible *rates* of growth isn't compatible with fixed assumptions as to total *amount* of growth either of GNP or of public expenditure over 5 year period. It is also curious how willing DEA are to believe business replies to questionnaire on exports but how they take replies on labour requirements (and by implication, productivity) as basis for further *action*. There is also a continued mix-up between what to aim at and how to put the best face on things for public presentation; and this isn't helped by Donald's habit of presenting draft submissions that don't invite Ministers to decide anything.

Ned Dunnett thought we are nearing industrial anarchy. At Rover's, men are earning 700% on bonus and this sets a pace that men over 40 can't maintain.

Remainder of week involved several meetings with T.B.: one on statistics (Thursday); one on economists (Friday); one at lunch for W.Heller at No.10; one at No.10 on the trade figures. The first was largely waste of time but let us get across the point that it was on interpretation and analysis not collection of fresh data that there was too little effort. The second was equally futile, though Wolfenden[75] gave us some interesting figures about current output. After our advertisements we got 180 applications to join the Government Economic Service but none from an academic economist on the staff of a University.

The lunch for Walter Heller was interesting because the P.M. was remarkably uninhibited in what he said. For example, he said that Reggie had timed his

[75] Sir John Wolfenden. Vice Chancellor University of Reading, 1950–63; Chm. UGC, 1963–68.

move to Foreign Affairs badly and let Ted Heath steal the limelight, especially as it was the Leader of the Opposition who made the key speeches on Foreign Affairs. He himself had dropped finance when he got bored with it and that was the right time. Diamond disagreed over some of the comments on Ted and felt that he had been very effective in Finance Bill debates. There was an undercurrent of sympathy for Reggie but some suggestion that perhaps it was not a bad thing to keep out of the limelight at present.

When the conversation turned to the Corporation Tax, T.B. made the usual extravagant attack on the City as Tory to a man and argued that every concession would be taken as a sign of weakness. The P.M. didn't endorse this sort of talk and said that the Merchant Banks were becoming more professional than 20/30 years ago. Tommy retorted that this might go for 2 or 3 of them but that Lazard's for example were less professional than when he was in the City. Walter quoted John Thomson[76] and others to the effect that the City was reconciled to a Capital Gains Tax but worried about the Corporation Tax (his own views about this he kept to himself). This brought out the P.M.'s comment that the press seemed to think that the two Hungarians had made a special trip to Soviet Russia to be briefed on the most effective way of introducing Communism whereas in fact the only mission had been one of the Inland Revenue to USA.

This was interlarded with bitter references to *The Economist* ('nobody in the Government reads it now except in the lavatory') and to the editor whom H.W. referred to as a television interviewer and T.B. as 'an amateur'. Tommy tried to make out that *The Economist* was always hostile to a government of the left but the P.M. pointed out that it had had some pretty severe things to say about the previous administration. Tommy seemed to think that it was more reprehensible of it to attack a Labour Government and spoke feelingly of the way it had hounded the last Labour Government in 1950–51.

Earlier the P.M. had referred to Rees-Mogg's[77] article in *The Sunday Times* and singled out the suggestion that he should have gone to the country in March 'six weeks after Leyton'. He explained to Walter that the really controversial legislation was all going through this year, citing the Finance Bill, and implying that next year there would be fewer occasions for dividing the House.

He was asked by W.H. what could be done by LBJ[78] to help the UK over any withdrawal of funds by US corporations and banks. Harold cited some evidence that the corporations were trying to reborrow in UK and suggested that perhaps a quid pro quo might be found in the terms of a new Double Taxation Agreement since we were worried about the rate of withholding tax. It was clear that he had been reading the cables on this.

On Saturday morning Ian Bancroft told me to come to No.11 at 5.30 p.m. for a 6 p.m. meeting with the P.M. The trade figures were bad and the P.M. had thought up a new version of Plan E to take the heat off any reaction on

---

[76] Sir John Thomson . Chm. Barclays Bank, 1962–73; Union Discount Co., 1960–74.

[77] W Rees-Mogg. Deputy Ed., *Sunday Times*, 1964–67; Editor, *The Times, 1967–* .

[78] L B Johnson. President of the USA, 1963–8.

sterling. I came in through the Cabinet Office with Jack Stafford[79] who told me that exports were down by £8 m. only and imports up over £20 m. chiefly because of a big rise in imports of manufactures from W.Europe.

The Chancellor in white tie (for the Waterloo Banquet) and sports jacket joined William, R.N. and myself and we told him what we could. A memo had been prepared in the train on the P.M.'s way back from Bradford and was full of the most extravagant ideas about recalling troops from Germany, export incentives, etc. – all on the basis that there would be a run on sterling. We told the Chancellor that the main idea – subsidising the production of capital equipment – was really Plan F and that it had been examined and rejected as contrary to our international obligations. If we meant to go in for export subsidies we had better do so wholeheartedly and be prepared for a great row. But it would be taken as a sign that we were now bound to devalue. Q.r.'s didn't make sense as a substitute for the surcharge.

At No.10 the P.M. opened by a lengthy monologue on the trade position without quoting the figures or asking the Board of Trade to tell us what they thought about them. He was interrupted by a 'phone call from G.B. who was in Lancashire and obviously concerned to prevent any decisions in his absence. On this the P.M. gave an emphatic assurance. The meeting then quickly left the trade figures and went on to discuss Plan F. In fact, the P.M. really gave a directive as to how they were to be presented and invited the absent President to appear on TV and put the best face he could on things without being too dramatic.

This was the adjective the Chancellor started from since he thought the P.M.'s note was highly dramatic. But he soon wandered into the quicksands of port subsidies while the Board of Trade made short work of Plan F. Nobody said till the end that the Report on Plans D and G is now ready and nobody said even then that it begins by denying that any real export incentive is possible within the limits of our international obligations.

The Chancellor shook everybody by saying that he was coming to the conclusion that he would have to increase investment allowances by the amount by which the Corporation Tax 'devalued' them and it was left to Jack Diamond to point out how foolish this would be. R.N. passed me a note saying first that Nero would be at home in this company and then that he felt like Cassandra listening to Nero. Most people, however, breathed sighs of relief that the P.M.'s suggestions seemed to be dead.

As I came out the P.M., who was in white tie and tails, and smoking his pipe (somebody asked me if he had a pipe for every costume!) asked me how I viewed the figures. He had worked out that they weren't as bad as the average for Q2, or Q3 last year. I told him what Jack Stafford had said to me about imports of manufactures and this clearly came as news to him.

So he succeeded in wrecking the week-end for quite a lot of tired officials, some of whom are due at Chequers today, for the sake of a meeting that never discussed the subject that gave rise to it.

[79] Jack Stafford. Director of Statistics, Board of Trade, 1948–72.

I came out with Jack Diamond and was joined later by Eric Roll. He told us he had a long list of instructions from G.B. on what he was to say at Chequers on his behalf – most of it on non-economic matters such as what he thought of the Chiefs of Staff, the military value of Singapore, etc.

The obvious comment is that if there is such a panic in June when the figures are no worse than we might expect, what will happen in September when the heat is on? H.W. may still tell the Chancellor ('and no one else') that there will be no election this year. But what if there is? As Joe Fromm pointed out to me at lunch, the disclosure in New York that devaluation had been seriously discussed last October will be in everybody's mind and whoever wins will be expected to go through the same agonies and probably emerge with a different conclusion. The P.M. told W.H. at lunch that he knew of no body of opinion in industry or finance that favoured devaluation or thought we should gain from it. But he said nothing of what economists thought or said – including his own advisers. And when W.H. asked for an exposition of the present economic situation, he didn't get one.

Meanwhile sterling has been weakening again and we shall obviously end the month well down even if there is no run (and William told the P.M. he thought there was bound to be one. The Chancellor more guardedly said he had given up trying to forecast that sort of thing).

Lunch on Friday at Fielding, Newsome and Smith's. They wanted some forum for discussion between the City and the Government, spoke of the fund of goodwill when Labour came in and how it had oozed away, and suggested that some younger members of the Labour Party ought to be on the Boards of banks (including the merchant banks). They quoted Pakenham[80] on the absence even of a Jew from the Board of any of the Clearing Banks until a few years ago (David Montagu[81]). It was as important to get a link between the City and Labour as between the Trade Unions and the Tories.

One last recollection. Harold W. told Walter Heller that if Labour lost the election Roy Jenkins would have been editor of *The Economist* and added that he would have been a good editor, better perhaps than he was a Minister. He implied that Roy was just a little too admonitory and not a good enough politician.

Joe Fromm told me that we should never forget how much the Labour Government *hated* the Tories. For them it was war, not just a simple turn of the wheel. But they had manoeuvred themselves into a position where there seemed no hope that they could survive as a government.

Friday, 25 June   A quiet week before the Chancellor's departure for Ottawa and Washington. I had to lecture at Henley on Tuesday night, take the chair at Robert Triffin's meeting on Wednesday night, address the French Staff College on Thursday and prepare for another lecture next Tuesday at the Bank of

[80] Frank Pakenham, Lord Longford. Labour Leader of the House of Lords, 1964–68; Lord Privy Seal, 1966–68.

[81] Hon. David Montagu. Chm. of Orion Bank.

England.

Last week-end I drafted a paper on the economic outlook and revised it on Tuesday after talking to Wynne Godley. It appeared that the new national income forecast was flatter in 1965 than I had supposed and that the dilemma facing us was correspondingly sharper. It seemed to me that Ministers were not taking the danger of devaluation seriously enough and certainly not facing the price it involved. Foreign opinion is increasingly pessimistic and the loss this month looks like being very heavy. I spoke in this sense at Permanent Secretary's meeting on Wednesday and we discussed more fully on Thursday. Robert N. argued that key fact was that Ministers couldn't be brought to *say* that they were deflating and that neither party would opt for long period of unemployment over 2%. He has put in a personal note and William will be putting up mine, with a covering note of his own.

The tone of a later meeting on Thursday on fixed/floating rates was also highly pessimistic although Denis still holds that we might proceed by instalments and escape devaluation since *whatever* we do some deflation is inescapable. What is rather inconclusive is the *long term* forecast of a big continuing deficit. But Ministers haven't really had this put to them. I think now that if Ministers won't take further action and say the things that need to be said we won't in fact escape and that the great danger is putting off too long.

William told me on Tuesday night of a talk with the Chancellor at Chequers when they had gone for a walk together and the Chancellor asked William what he thought about the prospect of avoiding devaluation. William said he thought we'd be lucky to do so but that it wouldn't be the end of the road. The Chancellor interjected at once – 'It would be the end of the road for me'. He said nobody could tell what the P.M. really thought. As for G.B. he is still writing minutes complaining when we talk of too rapid expansion or imply that a rise in unemployment might be helpful. Of course devaluation might torpedo his plan as it stands but it would make it easier to re-write it in a credible way and there is also the danger that the publication of the Plan might torpedo the pound by making the present rate of exchange no longer credible. Sept. 16 as I pointed out on Monday is very close to the normal date for devaluation and Sept. 16 is publication day – P day we should call it.

On Tuesday night we went over to the House of Commons to see the Chancellor and he asked what we could put to the Americans as something they could do to be helpful – a high wide and handsome proposal was what he wanted. None of us could think of anything except more credit e.g. a bigger swap. But Nicky wanted us to suggest the Brookings type link with the dollar, both floating together. He took it for granted that the creditor countries would *allow* the dollar to depreciate, which I think far from self-evident.

The Chancellor before we began told us that Reggie had said that he had put the idea of floating to the Treasury when Chancellor and that this was what he favoured. We replied that he had had many ideas as Chancellor but it was not always clear what he really favoured.

Sunday, 4 July

*By the end of June the government had run up debts to the IMF of £850 m.
and had drawn £153 m. from other monetary authorities (mainly the Federal
Reserve System). The pound remained under continuous pressure and the Bank
of England, in addition to feeding in over £150 m. to the exchange market in each
of the first two quarters of 1965, had been supporting the forward market to an
undisclosed extent. The May trade figures had been particularly bad following
a cut in the surcharge from 15 to 10 per cent at the end of April. Fresh fears of
devaluation were aroused.*

*There was little evidence of any easing in the labour market. Unemployment,
although no longer falling, remained at about 300,000 or 1.3 per cent and was
down to 0.7 per cent or less in the London and South East and West Midlands
areas. Wages continued to rise at much the same rate as in 1964 or a little faster.*

*At a meeting of Working Party 3 early in July I found that everybody took
it for granted that fresh measures were necessary and on my return from Paris
reported this to the Chancellor. There was then a prolonged Ministerial battle
without much prospect initially of any action. After heavy losses of foreign exchange in the week ending 24 July, the government's economic advisers again
recommended devaluation (without informing me) but were ignored. George
Brown, however, had been converted and a long wrangle took place between
him, the Prime Minister and the Chancellor. At 1 a.m. on 27 July they finally
agreed on a package of measures that had quite the opposite effect to the one
intended since it followed assurances that no action would be taken and smacked
of panic. There was a run on the pound in August on a scale comparable to that
in November 1964.*

Sunday, 4 July   Leave for Paris WP No.3 tomorrow. Last week Chancellor
was in Canada/US with William, Denis Rickett, Robert Neild, so comparatively
quiet.

My paper for Chancellor went to P.M. and was commented on by T.Balogh
without any hint that it might be construed as an incitement to devalue. Chancellor has returned from US very gloomy. The US Treasury was so afraid that
he might have come to beg that they put him in a position by publicity for this
fear where he *had* to deny it emphatically. Fowler[82] tried to get him to think
of multi-lateral long term loan from Europe but there isn't much hope of this.
P.M. meanwhile has announced his intention of not holding election this year
but this hasn't really resolved doubts.

Value of Chancellor's visit was that he saw and spoke to lots of US bankers
including Bill Martin[83]. He was told by Bill that of the group with whom he
was about to dine all 36 had regarded devaluation of the pound as inevitable and
Bill had been the only one to take a contrary view. According to William, he
had taken all this very well and was persuaded that further action was required.

[82] Henry (Joe) Fowler. Under-Sec., US Treasury, 1961–64; Sec. of Treasury, 1965–
68.
[83] William M'Chesney Martin. Chm. Board of Governors, Fed. Reserve System,
1951–70.

There was a meeting at No.10 on Friday at which George said that a million unemployed was a bloody silly way to run a country and Jim retorted that 1.2 per cent unemployed was a still sillier way. They are all united against devaluation as firmly as ever. Out of the meeting came a whole series of measures for examination but, as Douglas Allen complained to me, with no judgement as to which were and which were not significant so that officials will again be overwhelmed. Evan Maude in Paris for EPC, half the top Treasury officials away, others immersed in PESC, the W.P. on agriculture, E.F. meetings and so on, put Douglas in a position where he can't really brief his Ministers adequately.

Douglas told me that George originally thought that his incomes policy would operate at once and that for this reason he pooh-poohed the people who were worried about rising pressure and claims. He was correspondingly downcast when things turned out differently but is now becoming more realistic. He has been off the bottle for a month.

But what does he (and the others) really know of the T.U. movement and above all of the TUC? Ministers feel let down because employers don't resist wage claims (and for that matter TUC officials don't either). The Chancellor on Saturday appealed to employers not to pay higher wages! (He also had a passage about not being able to carry out election promises that may not have been delivered; and another about the productivity breakthrough that Shone and Catherwood keep talking about – Wynne Godley puts it at 0.1% p.a.!)

Ned Dunnett is worried about all this because he feels that there is really nobody in the TUC that matters now except Woodcock who speaks for himself and can't lead the Unions. The Minister of Labour is put in a false position because he is expected to act solely as a peacemaker and if he tries to do more is liable to be attacked by the so-called Labour Correspondents who are largely the mouthpiece of the unions. For this reason Ned want a reorganisation in which Labour and Board of Trade are rolled up together and Overseas Trade taken away leaving a Ministry of Industry. This has some attractions, especially if DEA is reorganised.

I spoke to Burke Trend on Friday and he asked me what I thought of the position. He then asked if Ministers should go off on holiday without some indication of what might be in the wind. How could Harold dress up devaluation to his political advantage? And what was the latest date by which a decision was needed? To this, I said not later than the end of September because everybody would now have their eye on the Bank/Fund meeting, and preferably a good deal earlier.

A lot of talk this week about incomes policy and a crash programme. But it is probably too late now for anything like a 'freeze' although it probably could have been done and was half-expected last October (or so Fred Jones[84] told Ned).

Forecasts circulated at the end of the week. They look pretty bad.

---

[84] Fred Jones. Economist with NEDO, 1962–64; Senior Economic Advisor DEA, 1964–66; Asst. Sec. 1966-68; Asst. Under-Sec. of State, 1968–69.

Tuesday, 13 July   Last week began in Paris with WP No.3 at which everybody took for granted the need for fresh measures. It ended in the P.M.'s room at the H. of C. on Friday afternoon with no decisions at all (except to cancel a further meeting on Sunday) and no agreement that measures were urgently needed – at least not if they were deflationary.

The meeting began with a statement by the P.M. to the effect that the June trade figures weren't too bad and that therefore we could take breath – until next month's figures. The Chancellor then started by distinguishing fire brigade and longer term action but startled the P.M. by proposing a ban on all outward investment and startled the First Sec. by proposing a holiday on tenders in the public sector. The latter naturally asked why this should be raised now when the programmes for the Departments had just been gone over by the Ministerial Group last Sunday without any suggestion of this kind.

But the really disquieting feature of the meeting was to hear the P.M. equate deflation and 2 million unemployed and brush aside any more reasonable and limited proposal.We always had hit the economy when it was going down and it was going down now, so don't let's do it again. Exports weren't suffering through pressure of demand: could Douglas Jay name six industries in this position? This drove Douglas to cite toys and led to persiflage about dolls. But he need only have said: *any* six. He had cut the ground from under his feet by arguing against hire purchase restrictions because the motor industry's costs would go up and this would get in the way of their exports. So the P.M. naturally asked why the same argument couldn't be applied generally. Towards the end he ruled out further deflation as contrary to the policy of the government. Of course George supported him and D.J. wasn't the most effective ally. William obviously felt that the Chancellor didn't put his case nearly strongly enough but on the whole he talked better sense than most even if he had only the vaguest notion of what could be done to limit public expenditure.

As the Chancellor ruled out the regulator, D.J. ruled out hire purchase, and George thought that not much could be done about public expenditure, the whole discussion petered out. The one thing, as I had predicted, on which they all agreed (except the Chancellor who hadn't read his briefs) was that the arguments against import deposits were phoney and that indeed they confirmed the case *in favour*. This perversity won't last but they're all looking for gimmicks, and the P.M. was at his worst.

When I got back on Wednesday I found that William was assembling material for a package and that the P.M. had dictated a long memo with 28 points for examination (including, for example, foreign language training courses). It was a memo obviously influenced by T.B. but quite unrealistic in its appreciation of the true seriousness of the position. He suggested a moratorium on building and then, on Friday, said that he had only meant civil engineering (not housing) and attacked the Treasury memo which developed his own thought.

I prepared a memo for EAC on Sunday. This was duly discussed today – or at least the first half only. William kept most of the discussion to the details of the forecasts so that nobody could subsequently shoot them down. T.B. spoke only on public expenditure and chose the lack of a uniform set of *prices* as the starting point for a diatribe ('It is *absolu*tely ridiculous!') without any appreciation of what mattered for forecasting purposes. Maurice Allen and others insisted that output was currently limited by supply factors almost as much as by any change in demand.

The Fowler initiative was launched on Saturday but F. himself obviously hadn't thought of it until the last minute when L.B.J. pushed him into it. Not very well considered. T.B. rang up David Hubback to say that President ought to have consulted first!

T.B. has also been causing a lot of work to us by querying the use of the $4\frac{1}{2}$ per cent ratio [of public expenditure to GDP] on the grounds that one can use tax concessions *or* increase public expenditure. This is the kind of thing one could do without when the pressure is as intense as it is.

There is literally no central economic machinery of co-ordination now on budgetary policy as today's meeting showed only too clearly. It was a vast meeting and there could have been no real meeting of minds especially as George is cooking a package of his own and the P.M. has already spawned 28 titbits.

William's comment on the meeting on Friday was that it was quite a big step along the road to devaluation. But I believe that he still hopes it can be avoided. The Chancellor at least is determined to make a fight of it – but I fear on too limited a front.

Saturday, 17 July   There were two meetings today at No.10 to the first of which I was invited but did not go. It discussed Plans D, E and F while the second at (9 p.m.) was intended to deal with the short-term situation and consisted of half a dozen Ministers and only 3 or 4 officials. I gather that it was Callaghan who insisted on it but the Agenda appears to be a re-hash of the previous one with everything from training in foreign languages to nationalising the docks. As for D, E and F, Otto has narrowed it all down to the 'Northern Regulator', an idea of R.N.'s for giving a kind of payroll subsidy to the areas of high unemployment when the national average is over a certain percentage. Nicky has attacked it in a long memo to the Chancellor and T.B. has joined him in a note to the P.M. covering a memo by Michael Stewart.

Meanwhile the P.M. refuses to admit that there is a problem and has given assurances in non-attributable interviews that there will be no further measures. J.C. on the other hand put his foot in it in the Third Reading debate on Thursday by speaking off the cuff about the 'temptation' to deflate that had to be resisted until what had already been done had had time to take effect. On Saturday he seems to have tried to correct the impression at Durham (in the presence of the P.M. and George B.) but it seems likely to go for nothing. The Governor is increasingly upset (almost hysterical) in his letters and the IMF has now sent the letter that Whittome[85] suggested in Paris and London.

I did a memo on hire purchase which William has sent to the Chancellor and

[85] Alan Whittome. Bank of England, 1951–64; Director, European Dept., IMF, 1964–81.

he will probably back proposals for new restrictions along the lines discussed. But I don't think it is enough nor do I feel that the public expenditure moves will contribute enough in the time, desirable though they are. We are just beginning to contemplate the kind of action that was necessary last October but only the Chancellor has the measure of what is needed and there seems no way of getting it over to the Cabinet what is required or how serious the situation is. They are still fascinated by import deposits; and the effect of the dinner at the Bank of England last Tuesday when the P.M. sat next to Robarts,[86] was to confirm him in the view that bankers can keep down imports if told to do so. Seebohm[87] and Thornton[88] have meanwhile been to see the Chancellor with similar proposals for import deposits but agreed that it was more difficult the more they went into it. In the end, I fear that this is what they will go for.

On Friday we had a meeting on statistics to which Tommy came late as usual. He launched into an attack on Campion's report and on his failure to bid for more statisticians: said a lot about dissenting and the little that had been done: and spoke as if his proposals had been ignored completely. William said not a word except when asked by Burke Trend if he was broadly content with the Report. Considering what a full day he was having, he must have felt pretty mad.

The Plan is at last in draft but most Chapters in a form very different from anything circulated to the sub-committees. So that we have a week-end to digest and no time at all to brief. We did have a go at the Balance of Payments Chapter earlier in the week and it is certainly much improved from earlier versions. But there are long empty Chapters on, for example, regional problems that seem quite out of place.

Donald came to discuss staff on Friday after the Statistics meeting and at one point to my surprise used the phrase of the Plan 'if it ever gets published'. So the doubts are not confined to the Treasury!

Anglo-German Ec. Committee last Tuesday. It is clear that they half expect devaluation while the Regional Controllers of the Board of Trade half expect deflation. But the P.M. goes on ruling out both publicly.

I suppose that nothing much will happen now till September, given the increase in reserves at the end of this month and assuming that the August trade figures are not greatly different from July. But what will happen in September/October is another matter altogether.

Wednesday, 21 July   Lunch at No.11 for Coombs [Governor of Commonwealth Bank of Australia] who has asked for cover for £400 m. i.e. writing-up in the event of devaluation. Dinner last night with S.J.Pears,[89] Henry Benson,[90] John

[86] D J Robarts. Chm. National Provincial Bank, 1954–68; Chm. National Westminster Bank, 1969–71.

[87] F. Seebohm. Dir., Barclays Bank from 1947; Dep. Chm., 1968–74.

[88] Sir Ronald Thornton Vice-Chm. Barclays Bank, 1962–66; Dir., Bank of England, 1966–70.

[89] S. J. Pears. Partner, Cooper's and Lybrand.

[90] Henry Benson. Senior Partner, Cooper's and Lybrand, 1974–75.

Davies[91] and Ian Stewart,[92] given by Geddes[93] at Connaught [the first of several].

The week began promisingly, for William gave us an account of Sunday night's discussion that implied a greater willingness on the P.M.'s part to agree to hire purchase restrictions and an early announcement of a package of some kind. The afternoon discussion was pretty rambling but led to a decision to suspend further work on D and F and acceptance in principle of E. Don't know yet what happened to the Northern Regulator which both Nicky and Tommy have attacked, the latter as a palliative for deflation.

On Tuesday my paper on hire purchase was discussed with Eric Roll and Richard Powell, but they naturally couldn't speak for ministers. William said firmly that Chancellor was dead against the regulator. R.P. said the President took a similar stand against hire purchase. But he was very reasonable in his own comments.

We also had a morning on The Plan on Monday and William made the comment on the Conclusion to Ch.1 (with its appeal for co-operation between management, workers and government and the suggestion that a little more saving would help) that it gave 'a rather sketchy account of the next 12–18 months'. This with a solemn face and tongue firmly in cheek. I pointed out that it seemed to give priority to everything and Robert asked in what respect it differed from an NEDC Plan (answering himself that it committed the government, to which Douglas Allen replied that it had better not commit the government to 25% more by 1970 come hell or high water).

This morning the Ministers had a go at No.10 – P.M., Chancellor, First Secretary, Minister of Technology and Minister of Labour plus President of Board of Trade. They took a 'second reading debate' and on the whole maintained a high standard. George was realistic and relaxed and the Chancellor asked some pretty hot questions: for example, what is the latest date when we can turn this juggernaut back? and can't we give the idea of recovery from the balance of payments crisis top billing and priority over growth? George didn't mind changing the first sentence to give the balance of payments and growth equality of treatment. But he and the P.M. thought that on the substance if we aimed merely at restoring the balance of payments, growth would elude us and we'd stumble from one crisis to the next. The P.M. thought it 'inconceivable' that the Plan wouldn't be published and even George, while claiming that he would if necessary be willing to change, thought that if things were so bad publication wouldn't make them worse.

The Chancellor made the point that since the balance of payments section was not very credible the conclusion would be drawn that we wouldn't be able to pay off debt by 1970.

Before the meeting began the Chancellor asked us if we had been as gloomy

[91] John Davies. Vice-Chm. and Man. Dir. Shell Mex and BP, 1961–65; Dir.-Gen. CBI, 1965–69; Member of NEDC, 1964–72.

[92] Chm. Hall Thermotank Ltd, 1950–65; Chm. Fairfields, 1966–68; Dep. Chm. Upper Clyde Shipbuilders Ltd, 1967–68.

[93] Reay Geddes. Chm. Dunlop Holdings from 1968; Part-time member of UK Atomic Energy Authority, 1960–65; member NEDC, 1962–65.

in 1960 and pointed out that the Plan's statement that half last year's deficit
was temporary implied that his Budget hadn't contributed at all to reducing the
deficit.

R.N. also a little agitated over Coombs as he felt that we should say we'd make
an exgratia compensation in the event of devaluation. This was straightened out
later and the Chancellor decided against offering cover. But we all recognize
that it may be necessary to think further about compensation if we devalue.

All this arose also over Emminger-type proposals and at a FU (devaluation)
meeting on Monday. We are a little uncertain what to say to offers directed
towards providing guarantees to official holders of sterling.

It was the P.M. who was most unrealistic. But he did raise the issue of
control of investment in relation mainly to housebuilding but also to other social
investment. (Oddly enough he seemed to think a $4\frac{1}{2}$ per cent *limit* to the growth
of public expenditure made control of private investment *more* important and
he didn't seem to contemplate control for purposes of ensuring *fulfilment* of the
private sector element of the plan.) He insisted that the Cabinet had agreed to
control over private building but the others thought that this was not what had
been agreed or was likely to be agreed. (Otto said last week that he could think
of five previous occasions on which Conservative Cabinets had been recorded
as agreeing to control over private building and that this didn't seem to be quite
the major step towards it that we might otherwise assume.)

Sunday, 25 July   A week to go – thank God! – till we leave for Scotland.
Pretty exhausted. R.N. has gone and a lot more of us are due to go so it's just
as well that the statement will be made *this* week.

On Friday I had lunch with D.L.B. The AGR tender was likely to prove a
put-up job. The only working prototype was one of 30,000 kw. so why pretend
that one of 660,000 was proved?[94] Yet the rival syndicate had been warned
off a blown up version of 800,000 because so far 500,000 only was proved. (I
hope I've got my figures right.) The men running the big electrical companies
weren't very clever and under them the really bright fellows were going off to
the US or being moved off nuclear energy. And so on. The French wouldn't
touch the AGR and thought they could do better – were doing better – with
Magnox. We mustn't however run down the firms when the CEGB was just as
bad. This was the danger in the situation.

As I left I called in on Ian Bancroft and he showed me (a) a paper by the
four economists advocating devaluation. (This has gone to the P.M. who has
rejected it unhesitatingly.) (b) a letter from the Governor agitating yet again.
Given the heavy losses on Thursday (£48 m.) it is hardly surprising that the
temperature is rising. It goes without saying that neither Donald (with whom

---

[94] The Advanced Gas Cooled Reactor in question was Dungeness B and Burn's fore-
bodings were fully justified. It was many years before Dungeness B was constructed and
in working order and even then it remained well below its rated capacity. The episode
was a striking demonstration of the defects of arrangements for technical development
in Britain.

I lunched on Thursday) nor R.N. (who was at the same meeting on HP etc. on Friday morning) breathed a word of their paper to me. Nor did R.N. say anything of Nicky's note to William on floating rates in fact Nicky may not have told R.N. (but R.'s comment was that the government wouldn't bring itself to engage in the kind of rate war that Nicky *recommended*).

William came in and asked if I had thought of committing myself to paper. I said No; but if I did I should use different arguments in favour (e.g. the need to bring UK/US into quicker balance with a deflationary Western Europe) and that in the end it turned on what Ministers would be prepared to face. The Tories had a philosophy that let them take pleasure in squeezing. But how could Ministers openly pursue the sort of deflationary policies that were anathema to Socialist thinking.

On Saturday afternoon Ian Bancroft rang me to suggest that if I were moved to write he would collect a piece today at lunch–time. So I wrote a personal minute to the Chancellor, and one to William on top of the piece I had already drafted.

John Stevens called on Friday after lunch with Neustadt[95] and Bator[96]. He summarized things thus:

The P.M. had no mileage with the President on Vietnam.

The President thought we should learn to run our own affairs and that we had a lot to learn.

We ought to be thinking of a wage freeze.

There was a dispute about whether if we devalued they should follow us and on the whole the school favouring it were on the up.

The P.M. had got a completely false idea of how he stood with LBJ who had no particular regard for him or sense of obligation. It might be different if we sent a detachment to Vietnam.

Some of all this will go to the P.M. who has seen John and will see Neustadt on Monday.

Monday, 26 July   George was in the country over the week-end with Tony Crosland, Roy Jenkins and perhaps Donald. So it wasn't altogether surprising that he came in on Sunday converted to devaluation. After all, strength through deflation was hardly in keeping with the philosophy of the Plan and his staff under Donald have made no secret of their assumption that devaluation would intervene long before 1970. The P.M. however was firm as a rock and pressed George on hire purchase until a compromise was hammered out that waters down the full treatment to 30% strength. Nobody knows what has gone on in the Chancellor's mind but he apparently read the passage in my memo about Ministerial thinking very carefully.

[95] Richard Neustadt. Political scientist; Professor of Govt., Colombia University, 1954–64; Harvard, 1965–78.

[96] Francis Bator. Economist, MIT, 1951–63; Econ. Adviser AID, Dept. of State, 1963–64; Senior staff NBC, 1964–66, Dep. Asst. to President for National Security Affairs, 1965–67; Professor Political Economy, Harvard University, 1967–87.

The Ministerial group on public expenditure met today and William and Eric and others seemed to be at No.10 or 11 all day. The idea is that the finished draft will go to Cabinet tomorrow with a view to a statement in the afternoon by the Chancellor.

The battle was no doubt suspended in favour of the Irish who arrived today at No.10 to make overtures for free trade.

The P.M. sticks grimly to the idea of building controls. As Douglas Haddow[97] pointed out, whereas they were proposed six months ago in order to keep down private housing (in favour of public) now the aim is to make sure that private housing is *not* kept down by other (private) building.

But today I saw none of all this and had a quiet day reading Nicky on floating rates – a wonderful example of powerful logic driving a fairy coach. Nicky knows that we meet tomorrow and wants to come. But of course we couldn't have him without Tommy and all. The Chancellor has however been given the papers of the FU (Treasury) Committee discussing devaluation.[98]

Nicky wants us to raise our share of world trade from 13 to 16.5 per cent and to let the pound float down as each stage in export expansion is completed. The fact that this would leave us in surplus to the tune of about £3000 m. a year doesn't seem to have occurred to him. If £300 m. would do, why float?

D. Haddow told me at lunch of his troubles with Willie Ross[99] who thinks himself still in Opposition putting awkward questions. He finds everything wrong and hasn't put forward a single constructive idea. He persisted in going to a Fire Brigade Exhibition although it meant leaving today's meeting of Ministers after the first hour and blamed his staff for letting the two engagements clash (the meeting of Ministers was arranged on Thursday or Friday last week).

I suspect that the P.M. will now take the idea of an early election more seriously. He can't want to be caught in the Tory trap and find himself forced to devalue just when an election is inevitable. So he may go to the country after all in October – or even September? How will the Plan look in the light of all this?

It is only too obvious that the Tories won't speak up and promise to refrain from devaluing. They will give the government no real help on this. It may suit their book; but they may yet find themselves at the same disadvantage as Labour – taking over a mess that threatens to get steadily worse.

It was amusing yesterday to hear Anne Kirk Wilson tell us of the problems of No.10. Tommy B. churning out vast quantities of paper that defies filing just as much as comprehension. Derek Mitchell[100] deserting the sinking ship under

[97] Sir Douglas Haddow. Sec. Dept. of Health for Scotland 1959–62; Scottish Devel." opt. Dept., 1962–64; Perm. Under-Sec. of State, Scottish Office, 1965–72.
[98] Although officials were instructed to treat devaluation as 'unmentionable' senior Treasury officials met at intervals in the FU Committee under William Armstrong to review developments and prepare a 'War Book', so as to be in a state of readiness should Ministers change their minds. Ministers were not informed of the existence of this committee and neither Kaldor nor Balogh was a member.
[99] William Ross. Sec. of State for Scotland, 1964–70.
[100] Derek Mitchell. Principal Private Sec. to Chancellor (R Maudling), 1962–63; to

the last government and in close touch with Transport House for two months before, so that, had the Tories got in, he would probably have been out. The P.M. keeping at it into the small hours intellectually as alive as ever. The vast quantity of liquor consumed – the P.M. starting in on the brandy after lunch and alternating cigars and pipe. And George Wigg hating the staff as bound to belong at heart to the Tories and certain to be public school, upper class in outlook even when obviously not so in origin.

Thursday, 29 July   On Tuesday Ministers had a long wrangle and it was not known at 1 p.m. whether they had reached agreement and the statement would be made. I saw William in the corridor and he said he thought that it would be surprising if they didn't devalue by Christmas. In fact it looked as if there wouldn't be a government by the end of the week. But in the end they all accepted the statement as it stood. Yesterday I got down to quantifying it for transmission to John Stevens and this was continued today by Patricia Brown[101].

I joined the Chancellor to see the TUC and he told me he was grateful for my piece on devaluation on which he had drawn in his discussions with his colleagues. He felt pretty weary and said that he didn't think he could go on long under the same strain, not of events but of battling with his colleagues. He obviously put up as hard a fight as he could. But George made it clear that he wouldn't go an inch further on hire purchase and would resign if necessary.

The talk with the TUC was nearly all chaff and affability. But G.W. wanted to know what effect the Chancellor thought the measures would have on the balance of payments and the Chancellor wasn't prepared to say because he thought the effect on confidence the really important one. The Chancellor got in a bit of a muddle over the unemployment figures – using the uncorrected figures to show that full employment in January meant a lot more than now. Unfortunately this got into the press (though it was based on what was said in the morning at a different meeting). G.W. obviously thought that q.r.'s were the right answer to our problems and Len Murray[102] started asking one or two precise questions which the Chancellor dealt with rather brusquely by saying that he could think up the questions just as well as Len. To which Len replied that *they* had to find the answers.

Today, back from Cambridge, we had a long meeting on F.U. William said the P.M. was very firm on floating and that the Chancellor was of the same opinion. Three of the four advisers favour deflationary action at the same time (Donald is the exception!). They all favour floating, R.N. with qualifications 'floating between fixed and floating' to quote Maurice Parsons. All this made Denis pretty mad because he couldn't see why we had meetings at all if Ministers could make up their minds without giving officials or the Governor a chance to

the Prime Minister, 1964–66; Dep. Under-Sec. of State DEA, 1966–67; Dep. Sec. Min. of Agriculture, Fisheries and Food, 1967–69.

[101] Patricia Brown Senior Econ. Adviser, Econ. Section. Treasury.

[102] Len Murray. Head of Econ. Dept. of TUC, 1954–69; Asst. Gen. Sec. TUC, 1969–73 (thereafter Gen. Sec.).

explain what *they* think about it. William agreed to put to the Chancellor the need to let the P.M. (and perhaps T.B.) see some of the papers on devaluation. The theme of getting Ministers to see what was involved recurred during the rest of the meeting.

Saturday, 11 September

The Americans fearful for the dollar, were alarmed by the run on the pound in August and set about organising international support. The French refused to participate in this American initiative but the other central banks in the Group of Ten, together with those in Austria and Switzerland and the BIS, provided the necessary credit. This was announced on 10 September shortly before the annual meeting of the IMF and IBRD. (For the part played by Rupert Raw[103] of the Bank of England see entry for 15 March 1966.)

The selling pressure died away, the spot rate for sterling rose above par on 30 September for the first time since July 1963 and the forward premium for dollars fell progressively until May 1966. In the final quarter of the year, for the first time since Labour took office, the Bank of England was able to take in large amounts of foreign exchange from the market.

The National Plan was duly published, with little observable effect except to enlarge investment in electricity generation when it was probably already excessive. Unemployment, after a slight rise in the summer months, resumed its gradual decline in the autumn and remained at 1.2 per cent throughout the first half of 1966.

Saturday, 11 September   A long break since my last entry here. Not that August was uneventful. On the contrary it gave the lie to the civil service tradition that nothing happens in August. Only, this year it was the Ministers who did things, not the officials. It was the Month of the Hook-Up after the Hiccup. No sooner were the measures announced on July 27 (two days later than in 1961) than they seemed to backfire. Everybody wondered what was behind them and when the reserves were announced the following week there was quite a run, on the November scale. So questions were asked why the statement couldn't have been made to coincide with the reserve figures or the figures announced that much earlier. I spent the first week on the Solway reading the bad news which suddenly blew out at the week-end with statements that the Governor really *had* gone on holiday and the P.M. *had* gone to the Scillies. No wonder people called it the Scilly Season. I gather that a special effort to brief the Sunday press did the trick.

When I came back after three weeks, mainly to get peace to revise my text-book, I found the Treasury busy reading transcripts of telephone conversations between the Ministers. It was not clear how this could have arisen or what official advice was being got across. All the top Treasury men were away and

[103] Rupert Raw. Bank of England.

yet Ministers were busy simultaneously with a sterling support operation and new incomes policy, and the press obviously had better information about both (or certainly the second) than the officials, and presumably also most of the Cabinet. There were almost nightly talks between the P.M., Chancellor and various others, including Fowler. Much of this was en clair – in particular the last stretch to the Scillies was by radiotelephone and so beyond scrambling. Some of it must have been pretty revealing for according to Ian there was at least one conversation when G.B. was tight and insisting to the P.M. that he would have to choose between him and Jim. This conversation was terminated, no doubt as too unseemly with officials listening. It was then resumed half an hour later with George left out and all others in.

The main proposal originated at the early August meeting of the Group of Ten when it seemed clear that some fresh support for sterling would be needed and Deming had a talk with Denis, followed by a visit to London when he was given our latest forecast. Simultaneously there were talks between Cromer and the Fed. and Charlie Coombs drew up a paper setting out the strategy for a Great Bear Squeeze. This got approval from L.B.J. and was the Charter on which Fowler operated thereafter. The Americans at first wanted further deflation (there was talk of the regulator) and action to freeze prices and incomes based on their own policies in 1950–51. They also talked of a recall of Parliament, a 90-day 'freeze' until legislation could be enacted, and various other dramatic measures. This got caught up with earlier ideas about an early warning system for prices and wages and hints by the P.M. that it might be necessary to put the NBPI onto a statutory footing.

At the stage when I first came back to Whitehall on August 23 – Denis and R.N. also came back then – nobody quite knew what the timetable of action was nor how to link the two sides of the operation (sterling and incomes policy) without making it too obvious that this was what was involved. Eric was on the point of leaving for the US and G.B. was making his first approach to George Woodcock that very afternoon. It was pretty obvious that if we meant to move on incomes policy we'd have to do it unconditionally and not try to keep a kind of reciprocal conditionality with the sterling operation. Similarly it seemed clear that we had to line up the US firmly and then rally support on the Continent using the US card rather than incomes policy. But when Eric left it was not clear who was going to tackle the Europeans – us or the Americans – whether anything would be formulated before Fowler left on his European tour, what public statements were going to be made and by whom, whether the Central Banks or governments would be party to the operation, what scale it would reach, etc., etc. All we had was a page and a paragraph by Coombs sketching very generally the operation he favoured.

Meanwhile Schweitzer was seen at the airport by O'Brien and Sam Goldman and made it clear that he knew all about the proposals (when the Chancellor was insisting that he should not be told!). He maintained that the French would be offended if *not* approached and that they were busy with plans for bringing Britain into a new Europe. (This news set the P.M. off but seemed odd on the face of it.)

The press had carried (chiefly *The Financial Times* but *The Guardian* too) quite circumstantial stories the previous Thursday and Friday about what was on foot.

Douglas Allen had spent much of his time earlier in the month flying to and fro (he made 7 flights he told me) including a flight to Washington to sound out the Americans and one to Nice with Eric to square George. He kept trying to get some leave but was pulled back after 5 days to draft a statement on the new policy (it was never made but used by G.B. at his press conference at the beginning of September).

When I went off to the Solway it was clear that the Americans were solid and Fowler was in a position to raise the question with each country he visited. But he was in constant touch with the Chancellor by telephone at each stage. Of course there were misunderstandings, some created by Rupert Raw who had been to Paris before Fowler got there. Although Martin knew about his movements, Fowler hadn't been told. But this had nothing to do with the ultimate decision of the French not to participate. Of this there was no inkling.

The Chancellor sent a vague telegram to the various Finance Ministers but didn't mention the support operation (he probably drafted it himself) and when he spoke on the phone to Giscard he again made no mention of it.

It was altogether a very strange way to set about borrowing money and should have its place in the annals of financial diplomacy as the supreme example of the amateur approach.

The final announcement was made on Friday afternoon (10 September) but late on Thursday the Chancellor was still debating whether to call the operation off (after he had talked to Fowler and knew that the French were staying out while some of the others were insisting on swaps). Neither Robert nor I was brought into the discussion by the Chancellor. He is said to have been displeased with Robert over his memo on devaluation and hardly to have seen him once. But he agreed that Robert should go to Jamaica and Washington for the Bank/Fund Meeting while I stay behind.

Robert and I did a short brief for the Chancellor (our first joint paper) on Tuesday/Wednesday setting out why we thought any measures of reflation foolish for some months. But of course Ministers have begun to talk reflation – D.J. on hire purchase, the Minister of Works and Building [Charles Pannell[104]] about building licensing, the P.M. about housing and selected public works.

At Thursday's meeting of Ministers at No.10 (in preparation for the special Chequers Cabinet on Sunday) the discussion was almost entirely on the balance of payments, import restrictions, Plan E etc. Reflation was not mentioned. Harold still harping on his old gimmicks – 100% q.r.'s, Plan E to serve as stimulus to investment, regional regulator, export subsidy, etc. (all in one). D.J. was sceptical about any investment subsidy and particularly about one that did three things at once. He spoke for q.r.'s but G.B. overbore him, the P.M. *and* the Chancellor on the grounds of EFTA restrictions. D.J. was also *for* the reorganisation finance commissions (R.F.C.'s) that the P.M. favours.

---

[104] Charles Pannell - Lab. Minister of Public Building and Works, 1964–66.

As we came out, Richard Powell was fuming. We were coming round for the 10th time and getting no further. He and his Minister must find very little to agree on, as he is dead against FCI's, etc.

We had a meeting with him, Eric, and Robert on Friday morning about R.N.'s paper on export subsidies. Eric was strongly against, more so even than R.P. In the afternoon we had a meeting on Prices and Incomes Policy that made it clear that the TUC will be ineffective and that the only real outcome is likely to be a freeze of public sector prices for three or more months.

Sunday, 12 September   Yesterday I had tea at the Tugendhats with the Haberlers and Robbins[105]. Lionel very amusing on Attlee. If one went in the war to brief him he either listened enigmatically without saying a word or could break in with great eloquence and insight. Frank Lee[106] used to say that if someone explained circumstantially that hemlock had been added to Lady A.'s tea he would no doubt have given an abstracted 'Quite, quite' as he did to most expositions. When he was at the LSE he was rather an obscure figure among the great men of those days. But Lionel recalled him coming back one day and staying shyly apart. When L. went to talk to him John Coatman advanced and announced immediately after greeting them both: 'Do you know I'm the only man here who has kicked Laski's arse?'. 'Good', said A. (for it was just when L. was making a great nuisance of himself to the Labour Party). 'I hope others will follow your example'.

We had a long talk on the finances of Covent Garden and the Tate. Lionel says he thinks that there may be 300 first rate pictures still in private hands that might be acquired by the National Gallery now that it has more than £25,000 a year to spend on acquisitions. He also referred to Viner's 200 pp. when asked to contribute a page or two of preface to John Rae. 'By far the greatest scholar in the history of economic thought'.

Talked on Friday to George Ball[107] about his talk with de Gaulle. What alarmed him was the way de Gaulle almost snarled when discussing Germany. George said de Gaulle was ruled by his memory of past injuries. 'We will never forget what they did to us'. Similarly he can't forget Mers-el-Kabir. Rueff[108] still sees the General and leaves the Rue de Rivoli in a state of panic and uncertainty. I asked if his eyesight was any better. George said he obviously read very little so that the palace atmosphere was all the more pronounced. De Gaulle had done him the compliment of saying several times 'You may be right,

[105] Lionel Robbins. Professor of Economics LSE, 1929–61; Chm. *Financial Times*, 1961–70; Chm. Committee on Higher Education, 1961–64.

[106] Sir Frank Lee. Perm. Sec., Board of Trade, 1951–59; Food, 1959–60; Treasury, 1960–62; Master of Corpus Christi College Cambridge, 1962–71.

[107] George Ball. American lawyer and government official; Under-Sec. of State, 1961–66.

[108] Jacques Rueff. Counsellor, French Embassy in London , 1930–36; Dep. Governor, Bank of France, 1938–40; Chm. Committee of Econ. and Fin. Reform, 1958; Member, French Academy, 1964.

Mr Ball, but I think you're wrong'. He had seen Couve[109] and asked if it was true that he was going to give up at the end of the year. Couve said 'not at all' and added that this was put about only to annoy Giscard. But C. was in good spirits. There have also been rumours that Giscard might withdraw.

Tuesday, 14 September   Yesterday Chancellor called me in on long tap stock. Couldn't see why we should try to stop or slow down a rise in gilt-edged by making an issue 'saddling the next generation' with costly debt. I tried to explain the importance of market management at all maturities and relation between our interest rate policy and external deficit. He had deliberately not asked Finance to explain it all to him (but they were all away except Denis so it hardly mattered). Bank of England (Morse) think we're missing a golden opportunity to sell securities. How different from 1962!

This evening a real shindy at No.10 in the presence of a crowd of officials, including Nicky, Tommy, R.Powell, and quite a number of ministers, e.g. Michael Stewart[110] who spoke never a word. It was all on Plan E and there was no obvious reason for the row except frustration that the Plan is taking so long to get Cabinet approval and so be launched publicly.

George came in late explaining as he sat down that he had been getting Woodcock to agree a scheme for lining up TUC and DEA on the mechanism to be operated for the early warning system. The P.M. simply said 'Good. Plan E' and this gave G. the floor. He took a line that implied irritation with Treasury and insisted that abandonment of the investment allowance meant £300 m. had to be found to keep industry where it was (instead of £200 m. as we maintain). P.M. said it depended how you put the question. But Chancellor and G.B. got embroiled. Then G. started to argue that all three elements in Plan E as he saw it hung together. Yet he kept saying that item 2 (regional) *might* involve giving up free depreciation and he had argued a month ago on the other side when trying to extend the eligible area; and on item 3 (Bagritry) he began by assuming grants for particular machines when his own paper spoke of a new *agency* and this was a proposal that had not previously been considered. He wanted agreement *in principle* and Chancellor said he didn't *like* agreement in principle.

Meanwhile the P.M. was steadily grinding his own axe for the exclusion of building in the South so as to get a higher rate of grant for machinery. He can't see a scheme without passionately wanting to add frills. Most un-Puritan!

At this stage William mentioned in a whisper to the Chancellor (in reply to the latter's question) that Eric Roll was in Washington. The Chancellor began by making this point to the meeting and G.B. flew into a tantrum saying that this was what made him so stupid – no, he meant angry – to have Sir William A.

---

[109] Couve de Murville. French Ambassador to USA, 1955; to Germany, 1956–58; Min. of Foreign Affairs, 1958–66; Prime Minister, July 1968–June 1969.

[110] Michael Stewart. Lab. Under-Sec. of State for War, 1943–51; Sec. of State for Education and Science, 1964-65; Sec. of State for Foreign Affairs, 1965–66, 1968–70; First Sec. of State, 1966–68.

whispering to the Chancellor that Sir E.R. was in Washington. He had Douglas Allen who could perfectly well conduct any necessary discussion. The Chancellor then said he would ask William to call together officials including D.A. This made G.B. still more furious. There would be no change of Departmental responsibility. William could go to a meeting under D.A. The Chancellor said William was not going to be put in this position. G.B. said he didn't protest when he found himself at a meeting called by the Chancellor and chaired in his absence by the Chief Secretary or FST. Earlier the Chancellor had called on G. to withdraw his remarks about William but unsuccessfully (George had tried to get round William in the car on the way back from the US Embassy on Friday). In the end the P.M. had to stop the meeting as George and Jim were clearly getting into a pointless argument on protocol. So we all walked out sheepishly and silently.

Later G. got in touch with J. and it looked as if some arrangements would be fixed satisfactorily but again the conversation as it went on began to run high and it was pretty clear that G. if not tight before was getting that way.

G. also used a long intervention by T.B. to remind us that he had not been consulted over the 7 year mitigation on overseas investment (the famous typing error that converted 'several' to 'seven' hardly allowed of consultation).

Officials were silent throughout except for T.B. and N.K. The latter afterwards very gloomy and inclined to blame P.M. for failing to handle the discussion properly. True enough – he never singled out the matters for discussion – but then as Ian B. says it's meat and drink to him to see the boys quarrel and confirm his indispensability as leader of the Party.

Wednesday, 15 September   TFM on French non-participation in support for sterling. When Rupert Raw was in Paris the Banque de France said it couldn't pledge itself to come to Basle as this would imply participation. (Clappier?[111]) Nevertheless they did come and sat on the fence. Later Holtrop[112] rang up to say that it seemed likely France would join and they were put down for 90 but within 24 hours he rang again to say they would not be in. So it looks as if it must have been de Gaulle; and the French papers say it was intervention by 'the highest authority'. Vernay took the line with Chancellor that it was Anglo-Saxon clumsiness to mount the operation *before* the Bank/Fund meetings and so give the French a slap in the face by a demonstration of the importance of holding sterling. Quite clear that Schweitzer was all wrong – no eagerness to join with UK.

William also assured me that van Lennep had felt it would be a mistake to call WP No.3 – he came to this conclusion independently on aeroplane on way back from London as he told William after Basle week-end. William himself far from certain whether (a) Chancellor, and (b) Americans would welcome a meeting and had ascertained subsequently that they would have been strongly

[111] Bernard Clappier. Dep.-Governor, Bank of France, 1964–73; Governor, 1974–76; Vice Pres. of EEC Monetary Committee.

[112] M W Holtrop - Governor of Netherlands Bank, 1946–67.

against. Denis said it was a Central Bank, not governmental, operation so not for WP No.3. Also that over the Italian case it had been more failure to consult *anybody* (especially in Brussels) than to call WP No.3.

Chancellor had meeting on long tap and agreed in the end, rather on lines I had suggested. Asked Hollom[113] why we shouldn't simply use special deposits and let rate go up. He had consulted Kleinwort Benson's who had urged him to let industrial issues get out of the way first before making an issue and had assumed a $6\frac{1}{2}$ per cent coupon would be necessary. Interest in monetary and financial policy obviously growing. Gilt-edged back today to pre-trade figures level (which is quite remarkable). Even more remarkable that Bank took in exchange yesterday in the face of the trade figures and a *lot* more today.

Chancellor has been thinking of bank rate since he intervened last Friday with Building Societies. Apparently he indicated his hopes to Fowler (US Secretary of Treasury) who didn't demur but later got Sam Cross to tell Ian B. that it mustn't be thought US would be happy about, well, not a cut before Washington since he assumed this wouldn't happen, but *thinking* of a cut so soon. On Friday before the press conference Denis and I tried to indicate to Chancellor that he should think twice about cutting bank rate while deficit lasts. But he isn't altogether convinced. William told me he agreed strongly that we made a mistake in May to bring the rate down. I told the Chancellor that we ought at least to wait until forward rate had recovered.

Lunch with Otto who elaborated importance of quantitative thinking and 'identifying the jugular' in Treasury control.

William said it was clear that G.B. felt that now that Plan was appearing the time had come for him to take offensive and so he was feeling all the frustration of the past year and giving vent to it on the Chancellor.

No discussion whatsoever in Treasury so far of India/Pakistan fighting. But bound to react on us if it goes on. Algy Rumbold[114] agrees they may run out of materiel. He also said Radcliffe[115] had given way to pressure from Mountbatten over the boundary award in the area adjoining Kashmir. It was not true that 'the K— thing' was not in people's minds at the time. He thought it would have been better to do the job in two stages partitioning Punjab and Bengal and leaving British governors in office and going on later to set up two governments. He also had a pamphlet in which Pakistan was first mentioned, submitted to CRO by Moslem students at Cambridge in 1931. At that stage I stood for Iran and S for Scinde, A not for Assam but for Afghanistan. No thought then of Bengal or East Pakistan. Whole area and concept bigger. Idea of partition came very late. Indeed in 1946 when asked to prepare paper on viability of Pakistan he had asked his principal to do it because he hadn't taken it seriously.

Monday, 27 September   A very idle week once the boys had gone off to

[113] Jasper Hollom. Chief Cashier, Bank of England, 1962–66; Director, 1966–70.

[114] Algernon Rumbold. Commonwealth Relations Office from 1947; Dep. Under-Sec. of State, 1958-66.

[115] Lord Radcliffe. Chm. of numerous govt. committees including *Taxation of Profits and Income* 1952 and *Working of the Monetary System* 1957–59.

Jamaica and this week to all appearances equally idle. David Walker said William was on phone today from Washington a little suspicious and almost worried by lack of news as if there *must* be a crisis brewing of which he hadn't been told. In fact there is just nothing to report except that the figures as usual give a queer picture of rising bank advances, falling unemployment and even increasing industrial production! *The Financial Times* has at last got round to asking why the government says nothing in more detail about the ban on non-industrial private investment pending legislation. Meanwhile Crossman is seizing the opportunity to press for more housing.

Dinner on Friday 17 with Coombs, Donald, William and R.N. Not much discussion of the Plan. D. arrived very late from a party for his staff (70 according to Douglas Allen).

I had a word, as first arrival, with Coombs as to press reception of the Plan. This was before Alan Day and Heller dealt so trenchantly with it in *The Observer*, while *The Sunday Times* – once again inverting usual roles – was almost fulsome.

Lunch with Duncan Burn, mainly on nuclear power. He makes it all sound like a conspiracy to hush up the superiority of US design but at least we have the simple fact that capital cost is over 50% above US capital cost.

Tuesday, 5 October   Everything remains remarkably calm. Partly it's the fact of a second Indian summer but largely the continued absence of the Chancellor (I haven't seen him for weeks) and top officials. I had a talk with William today but I don't think that he has had a single Departmental or inter-Departmental meeting in his room since he got back from Washington. and I'm enjoying the free time that the falling-off in meetings (and the flow of paper) brings with it. Denis not yet back, nor Robert Neild. G.Brown in Switzerland. The press has also had other things to occupy it and keeps pretty quiet about the prospects. Ministers repeat their forecast of balance by mid-year or earlier but I wish we could say this with any certainty even if policies are not relaxed.

Lunch yesterday with Eric Roll. He hasn't had a holiday since he snatched a week in May and has had to make two flights to US, two to Nice, one to Copenhagen etc., etc. He sighs a little for the time when he was in Washington or at the Sugar Council (£10,000 a year and £1,000 for expenses was offered) and asks himself how long he can stick it. He has mixed feelings about George who can be attractive and difficult. He also finds it harder going within his Department than with the Treasury – Donald is not an organiser and creates quite a lot of problems. But Eric is nevertheless quite insouciant and can survive. He was Professor at Hull at 27, 30 years ago.

Later Otto had a meeting of the Public Sector Survey Group. Awful. He kept asking Donald if he 'had a man' to do this or that when the one thing D. is itching to do is to recruit more men to do research on items of public expenditure. John Marshall[116] tells me that these meetings tend to be a dialogue which Otto carries on with D. even when he has Douglas Allen sitting opposite

---

[116] John Marshall. Asst. Sec. Treasury, (Public Income and Outlay Division).

and far more the man to help him in DEA.

Meanwhile I intend to pursue the idea of trying to join forces with Donald in using staff for VLT [Very Long Term] and VST [Very Short Term] work leaving quasi-plan issues aside. We're still likely to be in trouble in discussing policy covering 1967-70 with D. and his men. Apart from John Jukes there doesn't look like being anybody full-time over 30 on that side pretty soon.

The P.M. is insisting on an inquiry into speculation against sterling. I can't see that this makes sense unless new facts can be uncovered. But the idea is that Richard Kahn,[117] Fry, Grierson[118] and another should be a secret committee to review the facts as we have them. The P.M. is thinking back once again to 1947.

On rates it looks as if Bruce Fraser made a major boob by mixing up the growth of real GNP and money GNP and has pushed the Cabinet into accepting a proposition for transferring financial burdens of unknown dimensions to the Exchequer under an unintelligible formula.

Wednesday, 6 October   Political Economy Club. Maurice Green[119] on The Plan with Kearton speaking up for George Brown. Plan *not* for his glorification. Donald not well but gave a good defence and Shone put the main points – the only member to speak of the public sector. George Schwartz[120] said we hadn't enough corruption in UK. Sat next Hawtrey[121] who began in Treasury under Heath and then was under Bradbury[122] before moving to Finance in time for Old Age Pensions. B. taught him his economics for, apart from lectures from Clapham[123] in preparation for Admin. Exam., he didn't take the subject at Cambridge. Heath was an expert on Greek Mathematics. Among his early responsibilities was the Treasury Chest i.e. remitting money to other countries for payments there e.g. to army stations, colonies, etc.

Miss Waller[124] on her saga of the Plan. She called at F.O. and they asked if she had a second ticket. Why on earth? For her baggage. Couldn't F.O. book one. No, this was Treasury's job. They promised to try but at the airport BOAC firmly said no second seat and no secret baggage in hold. Rang F.O. No good. So she worked out route via later plane. At N.Y. circled for an hour and

[117] Professor R F Kahn. Professor of Economics, University of Cambridge, 1951–72 and Fellow of King's College.

[118] R H Grierson. Exec. Dir. S G Warburg, 1958–68; Dep. Chm. and Man. Dir. IRC, 1966–67.

[119] Maurice Green. Asst. Ed. *The Times*, 1953–61; Dep. Ed. *The Daily Telegraph*, 1961–64; Ed. 1964–74.

[120] George Schwartz. Economist; Dep. City Ed. *Sunday Times*, 1944–61; Columnist, 1961–71.

[121] R G Hawtrey. Entered Treasury 1904; self-taught economist who crossed swords with Keynes and was an early monetarist; Director of Financial Enquiries, 1919–45.

[122] Lord Bradbury. Jt. Perm. Sec. of UK Treasury, 1913–19; Principal British Delegate to Reparations Commission, Paris, 1919–25.

[123] Professor J H Clapham. Professor of Economic History, University of Cambridge, 1928–38; Pres., British Academy, 1940–45.

[124] Miss Waller - Secretary to Sir Denis Rickett, Treasury.

then diverted – to Washington. She had to stay on plane guarding bags while Embassy sent out a guard. Captain gave her drinks but time went by – an hour or more. Guard not allowed out to plane. So Captain and others escorted her each with a bag to lounge. Passengers furious because they couldn't get their bags to go on by train while here she was with hers. Clamour even when it was explained she was Queen's Messenger and had two tickets. Couldn't go on to N.Y. because of fog. Couldn't go by train unescorted and guard said *he* couldn't accompany her. Could he give her money for fare. No – nobody had any. Harry Nissen providentially had rung around and contacted BOAC agent and he was bullied into letting her have appropriate tickets to take her to N.Y. and on to Jamaica. She finally got on plane from N.Y. on which Chancellor was travelling. But at Jamaica when bags were opened two of the three had 30 copies of Plan, 60 copies of Summary and 60 press releases for delegates – all unclassified, so that she could easily have travelled by first plane and put two bags in hold. On Thursday when she flew out the copies were still at the Embassy.

Sunday, 10 October   Wynne pointed out to me that hourly wage rates were likely to be 8% higher next spring than 12 months earlier and in fact they are over 4% up over last 6 m. This makes it hard to be optimistic about export outlook.

Evelyn Sharp[125] said on Wednesday that her Ministry was quietly approving more housing and that Crossman wasn't telling the Chancellor the truth. Approvals in 9 months as large as they should be in 12.

Plowden Committee expected to suggest nationalisation of aircraft industry. They certainly like radical solutions since only a short time ago Kit was proposing to wind it up.

I asked William if thought had been given to the cost of UDI in Rhodesia and he said 'Yes, £200 million'. There have been big withdrawals but when Minister of Finance was taxed with them he denied all knowledge and was taken aback to be told by Chancellor that one-fifth had gone in a week. Smith came over with suggestions that were clearly quite insufficient to meet problem. His Ministers have given rather poor impression. Minister of Finance asked to call on Chancellor made several excuses and Ian B. was finally told that he had just left hotel because his sister had called and he wanted to spend evening with her.

Indian summer continues, in more senses than one. But trade figures due tomorrow and capital expenditure forecast also.

Denis said on Thursday morning that Guindey[126] gave two explanations of French non-participation in sterling operation one political, one technical. The latter was that they didn't want to put up money for indefinite period without some indication how they'd get it back – they wanted a swap. The other was

---

[125] Dame Evevlyn Sharp. Entered Civil Service 1926; Perm. Sec. Min. of Housing and Local Govt. 1955–66.

[126] G Guindey. Dir.-Gen. BIS, 1958–63; French official dealing with minerals and oil refining.

that they resented Fowler taking the initiative, as they saw it, and felt that it was all being done as a piece of US policy. But of course we can't get P.M. to go to Paris every time there's an operation of this sort and Chancellor *had* spoken to Giscard (but without saying anything about the proposed operation!).

The Economist and other papers still treat Colombo's[127] speech at IMF as an offer to fund sterling balances and asks why British government is so hostile. But there was no more than a hint and we've never rejected the possibility – only said that officially-held balances aren't a major problem.

Monday, 11 October   Lunch with R.Sayers[128]. Did 9,000 miles in Australia and loved it. Wants to edit Treasury Historical Documents.

Called on Ely Devons[129] who pointed out (to Bill Phillips) that the attraction of mathematical methods was that they gave results. Never mind whether result was good or not or whether there should be any result at all. Other economists were bound to feel ill at ease in the presence of *results*. Bill said that use of mathematics was really to handle experimental observations and that in economics the dynamic factors were far more involved so that what worked at Rothamsted was useless to analyse economic change.

Capital expenditure forecast shows some slight *rise* in '66 and trade returns unexpectedly good. Crossman has sent a disingenuous letter to Chancellor on housing approvals pretending he is trying hard to keep within his ceiling. R.N. says Tony Crossland is annoyed that housing should get away with it while he plays fair on education. So there may yet be some shindy especially if G.B. and J.C. can pull together.

Wednesday, 13 October   Ely operated on today: Estelle says surgeon gives him at most a year. I mentioned that I was introducing Roy Harrod at the LSE Lecture next week and he exclaimed on the strange combination in him of naiveté about the way the world works and the range of clever ideas he produces.

Saw Chancellor (in corridor) for one minute for first time since early September. Indignant at suggestion he'd had a holiday – except in the Isle of Wight! Talked yesterday to Douglas Allen and today to William about forecasting procedures. ED(O) no substitute as a sounding board for the old Steering Committee. We have all sorts of makeshift arrangements but no real way of getting Permanent Secretaries involved in economic policy as they used to be. Economic Assessment Committee under William has met rarely and was intended merely to allow us to have some claim to discuss budgetary matters (in absence of

[127] Emilio Colombo. Italian Minister of Foreign Trade, 1958–59; Minister for Industry and Trade, 1960–63; Minister of the Treasury, 1963–70; Prime Minister of Italy, May 1970–August 1972.
[128] R S Sayers. Professor of Economics, LSE, 1947–68; member of Radcliffe Committee, 1957–59; Monopolies Commission, 1968.
[129] E Devons. Professor of Applied Economics, Manchester University, 1948–59; Professor of Commerce, LSE, 1959–65; Professor of Economics, LSE, 1965–67.

Budget Committee) without leaving DEA to take everything over. The weekly alternate meetings in E.R. and W.A.'s rooms involved only the two Departments. The Economic Forecasting Committee under Douglas Allen is really for us under the concordat. And the Plan Co-ordinating W.P. is too big and the wrong place under John Jukes.

DAVA told me today that G.B. has been asking why the *Treasury* issues the Monthly Econ. Report. William A. commented that it was getting so that anything with the word 'Economic' was not for us. He thought that Chancellor would not lightly agree to abandon idea of our taking on *Economic Trends* even if we felt ourselves that it didn't much matter who did what so long as the job was done. He (Chancellor) obviously feels that George is going to resume his empire-building and that this should be resisted.

Meeting with Harry Campion, DAVA and Osmond[130] on idea of merging economists and statisticians. The statisticians would be very suspicious and feel prospects of promotion might suffer. Much of this unreal (since not much would change) but we agreed to go slow.

Battle of the building industry proceeds. P.M. insists on more houses now that we have or will shortly have building controls and before we know what is suffering as a result of July measures. The architects have put out some extraordinary figures not easily related to government action.

Saturday, 16 October   Long talk on incomes policy with Elsie Abbot yesterday. She says officials completely cut off from ministerial thinking. On *M* rate officials agreed but in due course Ministers reached opposite decisions on grounds that don't make sense. George Brown won't hold ED(PI) meetings (none for months) because nobody senior enough comes. No real discussion of policy in Treasury because Chancellor feels he is lectured by Helsby who has no influence on him comparable to William's. In any event H. never calls us in when he is discussing policy so that two sides of Treasury are operating separately. Eric in DEA isn't strong enough to handle George. Paper on arbitration was amended and went up to George but hasn't uttered on it yet. Ministers in same frame of mind as Selwyn Lloyd[131] – this or that mustn't be allowed. George very effective when he sees people but of course it doesn't last because they think up the objections after. For instance, on the M rate he saw four of the Unions leaders and got them to agree to his propositions but as soon as they were out of the room they changed their tune. A letter in quite reasonable terms came in accepting that the *system* should go to NBPI but insisting that government should honour its obligation under the October review. The Chancellor and George think this 'insulting' but in the end they will settle for this and the retraction of one sentence in the letter.

[130] S P Osmond. Under-Sec. Treasury, 1962–65; Third Sec., 1965–68; Dep. Sec., Civil Service Dept., 1968–70.

[131] Selwyn Lloyd. Conservative Foreign Secretary, 1955–60; Chancellor of the Exchequer, 1960–62; Lord Privy Seal and Leader of the House, 1963–64; Speaker of the House of Commons from 1971.

Elsie thought the saddest feature was that Douglas Allen had given up advising George - felt he got nowhere with him.

I gather that 24 cases (or at most 30) is the utmost NBPI could do in a year. I don't see how they could handle 24 cases of the M rate type because it alone needs months. But they seem set on imposing a common pattern of fixed prices and limited income increases plus a productivity wrinkle. So far they've done nothing to upset the Trade Unions. But they can't go on very long with the same sort of recommendations in face of an 8% p.a. rise in hourly wage rates.

Gallup Poll very heavily pro-Labour. H.W. is firm on no election but he is taking a big chance, for something is pretty certain to go wrong in next six months and he can't go to the Polls now until March. But there is no doubt that so far he has been very much in the right about the wisdom of hanging on. The reputation of his government is far higher now than at any time in the past year and the Tories look correspondingly weak.

Tuesday, 19 October　　　I.C.C. dinner with G.Brown and Prebisch[132] as main speakers. Both very dull. G.B. defending Plan as effort to get away from 'year to year' running the economy ('like looking at the front wheel of bicycle and trying to keep balance') and hinting at new scheme of investment allowances. P. expounding differential tariff cuts. Sat next to Sir J. Carmichael[133] and Shawcross[134].

Lunch at Bank. M. Allen says continentals want us to produce some scheme for a loan that can be presented to their public opinion as a means of getting their money back. Had to rush off for 2.30 meeting with Chancellor, William and Robert. Chancellor asked whether we had really done enough to get balance of payments right. How was it we'd been able to get round the corner (or had we?) without the stop we had said was inevitable? If we expected growth at 1 to 1½ per cent next year was that really so disastrous? William pointed out that if he were still in Opposition he wouldn't be asking that question. Robert talked at some length about the car industry – his King Charles' Head – but Chancellor who is addressing SMMT tonight didn't feel expansion of car industry was necessarily the wrong course even if we got dragged into increasing sales at home. A lot of talk about need to control investment cycle. William argued for a sector by sector approach and this rather alarmed R. I said 'For God's sake sit tight. At least wait till we can take stock in early November.' He seemed prepared to take fresh deflationary action if urged to do so but of course he knows this is not really 'on'. On the other hand, nobody is pressing reflation strongly because unemployment isn't rising fast. In fact he's a little mystified why it isn't – almost worried! He also suspects that if he does nothing, economy

[132] R.Prebisch. Argentine economist; Exec. Sec., UN ECLA, 1948–62; Sec. Gen., UN Conf. on Trade amd Developt., Geneva, 1964–69.

[133] Sir J.Carmichael. Deputy Chm., Fison's Ltd, 1963–71; Dep. Chm., ITV Authority, 1960–64.

[134] Lord Shawcross. Attorney General, 1945–51; President Board of Trade, 1951; Member, Permanent Court of Justice at the Hague, 1950–67; Dir., Shell T and T Co, 1961–72.

may resume expansion in 1967. Asked if we thought that with 4¼ per cent increase in expenditure he would have to increase taxation next year. Clearly, presentation of budget may raise problems.

Tuesday, 26 October   The main interest last week was in my three dinners, one to hear George Brown at I.C.C. when he hinted at investment grants, one to Cost & Works Accountants when I saw Reggie M. for first time in a year, and the last at Leeds. Reggie told Donald MacD. and me of his encounter the previous evening with Lord Shawcross, George Thomson[135] and a third Labour member whom he greeted with the words: 'Ah! The three stages of socialism', which none of them liked. I sat next Shawcross on Tuesday at dinner but he said little of interest except a word of sympathy for John Belcher[136] and another of regret that he now had little active part to play at University of Sussex since he was made Chancellor – a 'dignitary' (to quote Sir Hector Hetherington).

Chancellor yesterday agreed to new short tap. He asked a lot of questions of Chief Cashier e.g. what would happen if he made no issue at all and went on buying in next maturity. But in the end he raised no objections to proposed terms. Bank don't want a medium tap for reasons that don't seem very strong to me – essentially they feel that yet another issue would discourage the market by making it clear that government would hold current rates. They are obsessed with idea that market can't be kept stable if sales are to be made and also hold that if Issue Dept ceased to deal the market as a whole would dry up.

Lunch with Henry P.B. [137] He wants to resign from NEDC at end of year. Still thinks incomes policy 'a little acorn' and will grow. But I minuted Chancellor in rather discouraging terms especially about NPBI and role of TUC. Henry looks on it all as 'wrestling with them in prayer'.

Meanwhile DAVA says G.B. won't be deterred by talk of heavy load on NBPI since he thinks he can expand the Board if need be. Nobody has told him of difficulty of getting good staff or of difficulty of by-passing Aubrey Jones.

Last week we got unemployment figures showing a fall of 12,000. The newspapers have made very little of this but it is obviously of first class importance. We think it may mean that unemployment has been level since early this year and didn't rise at all. But however it is interpreted it shows that pressure isn't subsiding very quickly and that next year may not show as much of a slackening as we expected. At same time balance of payments deficit looks like being bigger than expected this year and continuing next. We're already warning Ministers not to claim that it will fall to £300 m. in 1965.

[135] George (later Lord) Thomson. Ed. of *Forward*, 1948–55; Minister of State, Foreign Office, 1964–66; Chancellor of the Duchy of Lancaster, 1966–67 and 1969–70; Sec. of State for Commonwealth Affairs, 1967–68; Minister without Portfolio, 1968–69.

[136] John Belcher. Parliamentary Sec. to Board of Trade, 1945–49. In November 1948 irregularities in the operation of controls involving Belcher were alleged. A Tribunal presided over by Hartley Shawcross was appointed and on its report in February 1949, Belcher, a railwayman, resigned.

[137] Henry Phelps Brown. Professor of Economics of Labour, LSE, 1947–68; Member, Council on Prices, Productivity and Incomes, 1959–61; NEDC, 1962–65.

Everything now turns on our forecast of Nov. 5 and a great many decisions have been held over till we're ready. William will call a meeting of Economic Advisers (at which I can, if I wish, keep quiet) to consider the forecasts. But R.N. will be in Paris on Nov. 8/9 and I'll be away Nov. 9/10 at OECD.

The Times articles and the CBI Survey bear out the impression of a continuing boom. No wonder Chancellor and others are puzzled by contrast with 1961. But they forget 1960.

Wednesday, 3 November   Meeting with Chancellor on Group of Ten etc. T.B. was there but had just seen papers. We met in Chancellor's room in H. of C. The only thing Chancellor expressed himself on strongly was suggestion of a long-term loan. T.B. got him to say that this was because it might jeopardise other schemes for launching new reserve units in a way that would prop up reserve currencies. But in fact he obviously disliked idea of accepting surveillance that would go with the loan. R.N. obviously shares this opposition but I have little doubt that we won't get *other* help at less cost, and that long term loan might be *sine qua non* if we wanted multilateral swaps, etc.

Later meeting of CM(O) at which Nicky appeared for first time. Borrowing requirement for next year looks enormous. No obvious candidates for higher taxation. But more interest will gravitate now to prices because the efforts of government to keep down prices in public sector are *very* costly.

On Tuesday there was meeting with Chancellor and Heads of Divisions and main point emerging was that Chancellor was not clear whether to give prece-dence to Exchequer considerations or to incomes policy. Otto pointed out that 1% on assets of nationalised industries was £100 m. so he couldn't be too generous with subsidies.

Abs at lunch on Tuesday. Nothing new but a condemnation of new reserve assets plus an attack on efforts to correct deficits by stopping capital outflows.

Forecasts reached me last Friday and on Tuesday. The main feature is deficit next year of £150m. Once again we've underestimated import prices. We also expect as big an expansion as we did before July measures. The price policy has undone the cuts.

Saw G.B. in H. of C. today and he called me back and asked me not to put in such melancholy forecasts.

Tommy still agitating against Bank of England's market operations in letting spot rate rise so high. R.N. backs him up. I see something in this but doubt whether we should try to direct Bank of England in matters of this kind and Chancellor yesterday took same view.

Sunday, 7 November   We've had a lot of trouble over the Chancellor's 8%. If I alarm him about wage inflation by quoting a figure, out it pops as if I had pressed a button. It happened in April and here it is again. Yet *he* ought to know how dangerous it is to quote this sort of figure because it was he who ribbed Maudling in 1962 about the rapid increase in production. (One of my biggest howlers.) Unfortunately he got his 8% out in terms of the first 8 months of the year and this alarmed the CBI who saw that workers would feel cheated if they hadn't had *12* per cent and asked for a withdrawal. Miss Mueller[138] has worked something into a P.Q. for G.B. so perhaps we'll hear no more.

G.B. has now been raising the issue of the Monthly Report more openly and has got E.R. to speak to William. He wants it stated that it is the work of an interdepartmental committee and we have agreed to say it is prepared by 'officials' after interdepartmental consultation. We have also agreed that my assessment should be put on a different footing as *not* agreed interdepartmentally (as of course it isn't). But William refuses to go further. I foresee that if we start issuing reports in *Economic Trends* we may stir up trouble with George and that he will challenge our right to issue the *Economic Report* next.

Looking back to meeting of Chancellor with Heads of Division I see no record of my discussion with Chancellor of the building licensing situation. He spoke rather strongly against idea of advance licensing by MPBW but I reminded him that Ministers hadn't visualised a complete stop in new orders last July. To this he rejoined that he so rarely enjoyed uncovenanted gains that he didn't see why he should forego this one.

As somebody said the other day it's curious how in his squabbles with George it's so often the Chancellor who at first gets very excited while George acts the elder statesman and in the end the Chancellor usually calms down completely. Then George gets his way.

Tuesday, 9 November   Two very interesting days. Yesterday we had a meeting with Tommy and D. MacD. on the forecasts specially devised as a meeting of Economic Forecasters to let them express any disagreements. (We can't run Budget Committees because of Tommy and have to find some other way of squaring him and Donald.) The only points of substance were on exports, were raised by Donald, and led to a statement by Tommy of general agreement with D.'s objections, coupled with an attack on the B. of T. for not analysing their export forecast in terms of the competitive position and another on the Bank of England for not restricting capital exports more successfully. On the latter T. spoke without taking in that figures include reinvested profits and that direct investment in the £area is not restricted. However he went before the meeting was over to exult to Derek M. that he had 'wiped the floor with us'.

In the afternoon we saw the Chancellor who had already taken the measure of the forecast and wanted to discuss action not diagnosis although he had the analysts, not the policy-makers, at the meeting. He is already thinking of hire purchase and is a little shaken on price policy without yet fully accepting the need to let prices do some of the work of deflation. He is meditating a second bisque so as to get deficit within reach of £300m and believes that other measures might give him enough to get down to £300m.[139] He realises that P.M. won't

---

[138] Anne Mueller. Assist. Sec., DEA.

[139] The American Loan Agreement of 1946 allowed the United Kingdom to opt in specified circumstances and on a limited number of occasions for suspending the annual interest and repayment of debt due in December. This had been done in 1964 and was repeated in 1965.

be sympathetic to further deflation: 'When I talk to him about the Governor now, he thinks I mean the Governor of Rhodesia' and can't think of anything else.

Chancellor took it for granted that all signs pointed to renewed pressure though he disputed Fred's view that further deflation would put the balance of payments straight because it would simply aggravate labour hoarding unless we destroyed business confidence. He said we ought to act ahead of events because otherwise we should find ourselves having to do more once people awoke to the need to do *something*. He would therefore rather act at once than wait and didn't want to be held by fresh calculations. Also told us to stand our ground on best forecast we could make e.g. on exports and not just give way to other views if we thought them unreasonable.

Lunch with Brunet, Leith Ross, Denis, P. Reilly and a Mr M. of the Banque de l'Indo-Chine, at British Embassy. After lunch Leith-Ross[140] told us that in 1931 he was called down to see Chancellor when Keynes[141] and Stamp[142] were both advocating exchange control but that he and Governor (or Deputy Governor) had successfully countered the arguments. Brunet agreed with him that exchange control was a dangerous Socialist expedient but that Leon Blum[143] in 1936 had had the wit to see its dangers. He went to see L.B. 7 days after his nomination but before he had taken office as Premier and found him (on a Sunday morning?) in a rather gaudy dressing gown ('he was a man of Bohemian tastes') and expounded case for devaluing the franc. L.B. at once suggested that UK and US would be bound to retaliate and developed the dangers. Brunet asked him why he thought this and suggested that there was only one way to find out – to send him to Washington to discuss with the US authorities. L.B. was a big enough man, said B., to see the importance of maintaining agreement with UK and US and the mission on which B. was sent was the origin of the Tripartite Agreement.

Also spoke very highly of Marjolin[144] who is bound he says to be a P.M. of France and once worked with Michel Débré in his Cabinet before the war. Told us of M.'s mother who knew that she had hatched an eagle and when he left to go abroad felt she would never see him again. But in fact M. came back in 1944 and saw her two days before she died.

EPC – France and Italy – very dull. But a gay evening with E. Cohen and others at 69 Ave. Victor Hugo. Denis told story of Churchill as Chairman of the Cabinet Committee on A.R.P. and Shelters of which D. was Secretary. Churchill would come in in his siren suit and start at once on John Anderson. 'Lord President, I have been told on numerous occasions that the use of the

---

[140] Sir Frederick Leith-Ross - Entered Treasury, 1909; Chief Economic Adviser to HMG, 1932–46; Governor, National Bank of Egypt, 1946–51.

[141] Lord Keynes. Treasury, 1915–19; 1940–46; Ed., *Economic Journal*, 1911–44.

[142] Lord Stamp. Economist and businessman; Chm., LMS Railway; Dir., Bank of England; Chm., Survey of Economic and Financial Plans, 1939–40.

[143] Leon Blum. Prime Minister of France, 1936–37; March–April, 1938.

[144] Robert Marjolin. Sec. Gen., OEEC, 1948–55; Vice Pres., EEC Commission, 1958–67; Professor of Economics, University of Paris, 1967–69.

Tubes as shelters is open to the most serious objections and they have been explained to me in great circumstance. Now I see from the papers that they are being used by large numbers of the population without hindrance. How is it, Lord President, that all these weighty objections have been overcome?' To which the L.P. would make what reply he could for although they respected one another they had little in common. 'There was such a popular clamour that it seemed best to reach a compromise and draw a line three feet from the edge of the platform within which people could sleep'. 'But I am told that things are not all that they should be'. 'Yes indeed Prime Minister there are some important deficiencies in present arrangements'. 'Deficiencies! It is not a questions of deficiencies, I am told, but excesses!'.

Monday, 15 November   Meeting with Chancellor on forecasts. This time he did want to test them out. But again showed good judgement. He told George this morning on London fares: 'I'm the fellow who's done most to raise the cost of living this year. And what are you asking me now? You want me to do it again' which was a pretty forceful statement of the case for *not* holding down prices of nationalised industries. Later when Otto quoted next year's borrowing requirement as a figure 'mirroring the situation' he said: 'Mirrored – it's not mirrored, it's engraved'.[145] But where a week ago he was apparently ready to take action, now he wants to take time before deciding. He sees that G.B. will be strongly opposed and P.M. too, although he did plant his warning in a minute to the latter. They may be thinking of a Spring election, which would not go well with immediate action. R.N. agrees with me that (a) public expenditure is the root trouble; (b) if we cut demand (consumption) it would be better to use the regulator (petrol and purchase tax) rather than hire purchase.

On fares the meeting today was a draw but Chancellor thought more agreed with him than with George.

The week-end went on defence review, not too badly but nothing very concrete yet. Chancellor speaks of a slash at defence programme and other spending but he may not make much *net* progress. Even offered to look at school meals but Otto had already bargained it with Education so that if done they could claim compensation.

T.B. and R.N. spent over an hour on Government Economic Service. P.M. has apparently done a minute on this but not sent me a copy. I suppose the trouble is that I don't report to any Minister so I'm fair game.

Thursday, 18 November   Yesterday to reception at Bridgewater House and later to Phelps Brown. Talked to Selwyn Lloyd who was very gay and explained his intention of writing his memoirs in two volumes to be entitled 'Mistakes I have made'. I gather that both Otto and I were to feature among the mistakes. Frank Cousins greeted us as we left and told us how few of the Opposition had

---

[145] The borrowing requirement in 1966–67 was estimated in the 1966 Budget at £287m. but turned out to be £740m. As a proportion of GDP public expenditure rose from 33.9 per cent in 1964–65 to 39.9 per cent in 1967–68.

been in the House for yesterday's modernisation debate – only four according to him, and they had apologised to him later for the thin attendance. (In view of *The Times*'s rather savage summary of the impression his own speech left, he must be feeling a little edgy.) Heath was also there and I had a very brief word with him.

Later Henry Phelps Brown told us that before WWI the LSE had to choose between Cambridge Dalton and Oxford Attlee and chose the latter 'because he had the greater potential for development' (so the minutes record).

Today a very relaxed Chancellor discussed what to do. (We had already had one and a half hours with William in the morning.) He likes to chaff Denis and just as earlier this week he said that D. *looked* like a member of the Oxford Movement, today he said he'd like to know what it would take to make D. vote Labour. D. naturally made no reply.

Chancellor said the one thing he ruled out was a higher tax on petrol – which astonished us. He had earlier told Ian that it was not funk but a hunch that things might not be as bad as we were forecasting that made him hesitate to act. He was pretty realistic about *some* things e.g. he knew that he had to carry George *or* the P.M. He had obviously picked on George. This made him want to put the pressure at home in the forefront rather than paint the usual Treasury picture of a frightful deficit.

He still hasn't made up his mind to urge the others to let him act but will talk to them. I told him that we were running serious risks both at home and externally and that if we had to act to get the pressure down we ought to do so promptly and not drag it out into 1967. He asked me if in a few months' time I'd be coming to him to get another £150m off demand in the Budget and I said he was wonderful at reading my mind. We might very well have to ask for yet another dose in April. He laughed and said that made five Budgets. But the fact is that he doesn't worry as he did. When we began I had commented on the supply of candles (à propos of the cuts yesterday) and Otto said the Treasury ought to use up other people's candle ends. That took us on to Gladstone and the Chancellor said he was glad that after 70 years Otto had got the Treasury back to the traditions of the great man. I pointed out that it was 100 years since Gladstone was Chancellor and after some debate this was agreed. Otto said that it was in his 1860 Budget speech that Gladstone had looked forward to PESC. 'Is that what they will say of me in 100 years' time?' said the Chancellor and laughed.

Later he said there was only one thing for him to do and that was to give up being Chancellor and look for another job. But it was all banter and probably reflected his success in last night's debate (without using any of the material supplied to him).

Meanwhile they're putting everything to the NBPI – army, civil servants, etc., etc.

Lunch with T.B. of all people. His hero was Henderson[146] especially for his

---

[146] Sir Hubert Henderson. Econ. Adviser, Treasury, 1939–44; Prof. of Political Economy, University of Oxford, 1945–51; appointed Warden of All Souls, 1951.

attack on devaluation in 1949, and his demonstration that you need unemployed resources to profit from devaluation. He said that in 1924 the attack in *The Nation* on the idea of a return to gold was Henderson's, not Keynes; and that Keynes' later analysis was too clever since it suggested that what Churchill had done wouldn't be too bad because it involved widening the gold points. We agreed that in 1950 there was probably only one retired Professor of Economics in the UK (J.H. Jones[147]).

Unemployment figures fell again by 8,000. We must also expect very bad Q3 balance of payments figures next month. By end of year we'll also have published figures of public investment that may come as a shock to some people. But it probably won't be possible to act till January. As Wilfred King pointed out yesterday our July measures misfired at first because public didn't expect them and thought that things must be very bad if we couldn't wait till end of month or at least quote the exchange losses. P.M. also made matters worse by announcing a week in advance that we would take action but obviously before we knew what we should do. On top of that came Callaghan's gaffe. All in all, we made people suspect there must be reason for panic because *we* seemed panic-stricken.

Sunday, 21 November   On Friday we had a meeting with the Chancellor on liquidity. Chiefly interesting because T.B. made his first appearance at a meeting in the Treasury under the chairmanship of the Chancellor. N.K. also present. Curiously enough they didn't quarrel and T.B.'s first intervention was both sensible and intelligible (he pointed out that agreement on automatic distribution of assets – as against *ad hoc* – might prove to be trivial and might prevent the negotiation of larger increases when most required). On the whole, nobody had anything new to say and the only feature of the discussion was that the Chancellor did most of the talking without appearing less of an expert than his advisers. He began by saying 'I never thought I'd hear myself saying I'd *enjoyed* a paper on international liquidity'.

On Wednesday I talked to Steve about electricity. He says there is no doubt that the CEGB are trying to screen their suppliers in the interests of preserving their export potential; but they feel that development work is being done on the shop floor not at the design stage while the firms argue that they have been pushed into untried types of equipment faster than would have suited them. Nobody seems to know how much equipment is lying around waiting to be cleared. But the idea that power cuts are due to failures in forecasting demand is now being queried publicly.

Thursday, 25 November   Two dinner evenings, one on Tuesday with Reay Geddes, Ian Stewart, John Pears & Co. mainly on shipbuilding and labour attitudes and one tonight with Richard Powell introducing the theme of competition and monopoly to the Whitehall Dining Club. Denis R. slept and Leslie R. did

---

[147] Prof J.H.Jones. Professor of Economics, University of Leeds, 1919–46.

most of the talking. Bill Harcourt[148] had some interesting things to say about young men in the civil service and in industry pointing out that they had the satisfaction of writing minutes without the responsibility of deciding in the civil service whereas in banking their ideas might be derided but there was nothing on paper so they weren't inhibited from putting up new ideas without making sure they got them right. He couldn't use a 27 year old to be his man on the Vickers account because they *expected* somebody older and more responsible.

On Monday we had a long meeting with Chancellor on debt management. The Bank had submitted very late a revised draft of our paper and there was a lot in it which needed further discussion with us. Chancellor felt at a loss to know what questions to ask. William sat glum and silent and looked exhausted and bored. But next morning to my surprise he took the paper to bits exactly as I should have done, pointing out that the aims of debt management were discussed at three different points in quite different ways, that things in the original draft had been removed, and that important issues were not discussed at all.

Today meeting of T.O.C. at which Otto spoke at very great length, but not as clearly as usual, on manpower budgeting. I can see why Bryan H. said he wouldn't be willing to work under Otto. He pours out his ideas and talks everybody down whether they are elucidating his points or crossing swords with him.

Lunch with Donald Robertson[149] who told me of meeting of the arbitrators with George Brown which made them all furious. He interrupted Donald when he was about to explain his difficulties as Chairman of a Wages Council and harangued him on the duties of a Chairman and how Wages Councils worked ending up by saying *'Now* do you see'. To which D. replied quite calmly, 'Yes I see that you're trying to teach me my job'. He both tried to appeal to their better nature and denounced their attachment to a 'sinecure' (as if they were all paid or paid well). They tried to get over to him that he should insist that the *terms of reference* of arbitrators should be modified to require them to take the national interest into account and that they should give reasons for their decision, etc., but he kept insisting that they must do this without any change in their terms of reference. With one of the arbitrators he had quite a passage at arms by appealing to him to do his duty to the country in the next case. 'You mean the police'. 'Yes'. 'I'll show my terms of reference to the parties and see if they agree'. 'And if they don't.' 'Then I shall have to re-frame them till they do'.

Monday, 29 November   I told William last week it was like 1964 and so it is. Everything pours quietly on – towards the cataract. It's pretty obvious nothing will happen now before the Budget unless the P.M. feels so safe and

---

[148] Lord Harcourt. Chm., Legal and General Ass. Soc. Ltd, 1958–73; Man. Dir., Morgan Grenfell, 1931–68; Member of Radcliffe Committee, 1957–59.

[149] Donald Robertson. Professor of Economics, 1961–69; Professor of Industrial Relations, 1969–70; Member and Chm., Wages Councils, 1955–69; Member NEDC.

so disinclined to an election that he is prepared to be tough. Bread will be a good case since the employers have done all they were asked and the Unions may pay no attention to the NBPI.

Lunch with Freddie Fisher[150] of *F.T.* who says that production *can't* increase in '66 by more than 1% so if exports go up $6\frac{1}{2}$% and investment also increases what is the poor consumer to expect? And if wages rise another 8% everybody will get into investment dollars as fast as they can (at 15% premium? I wonder). He would go for a 25% devaluation if it came to that and he is opposed to devaluation precisely because he thinks nobody would pick as much as 25%. He wants something to shock the worker and give us the edge on de G. But what if de G. does 20% and what did the worker do in 1949–50?

I liked F.'s story of the managing director of a big firm in Birmingham who was blazing when F. called because he had just lost a toolmaker to a firm down the road. What made him mad was that this firm offered 40% more. Then there was the man who came into the board room and announced that he had just sacked a man. Consternation. Well, he'd been running a betting shop in firm's time and sent his brother instead. And anyhow other branches of the firm were still free to take him on!

P.M. wanted Simey[151] to chair Committee on civil service and got pushed off. Now he wants Teddy Jackson[152] on (this of course is Tommy). Teddy is also Tommy's candidate for CSO though he would agree to C.T. Saunders for the two years he still has to go (as a kind of hatchet man to do the unpopular reorganisation T. wants) and would also accept Bryan. I think that I'd advise Bryan strongly against taking it in those circumstances. He is due back tomorrow.

NIESR Review appears on Dec. 1 and will have forecasts virtually the same as ours. With IMF arriving this could be embarrassing.

Wednesday, 1 December   Dinner with Bryan, Fred, Wynne and Patricia at UU Club. Bryan was a little tired but we had a pleasant relaxed evening. After dinner Bryan and I had a furious argument about price control with him on the side of comprehensive – and I mean really comprehensive – price control as a means of getting leverage on wages. I pointed out that he was assuming: (a) that labour market was in balance (e.g. 1.8% unemployment!); (b) that *government* would stand up to threat of strike if employers would; (c) that price control was easier than wage control.

The first two assumptions were unwarranted and the last very doubtful. The case of the bakers showed that government would run first even after it had imposed price control to keep employers standing fast. The government's existing powers were considerable but were used to keep down prices in the public sector (without keeping down wages) and so aggravating excess demand that it really undermined the employers' bargaining position. Even the Dutch didn't

---

[150] Freddie Fisher. journalist on the *Financial Times*, later Editor.

[151] Professor T.S.Simey (later Lord) - Professor of Social Science at University of Liverpool, 1939–69.

[152] Teddy Jackson. Oxford economist.

use price control as a means of stiffening employers' resistance to wage demands. Price control was inapplicable to building and engineering – two key industries in the wage round. It meant an enormous staff and would ultimately require raw material and other controls – the specification of quality or style – and all for the sake of limiting wages when half the population had their wages fixed already by outside bodies. I can't say that I found Bryan for once, very realistic. But I was able to say how right he had been a year ago on the need for the government to look at what was going on and not just acquiesce in it.

Earlier we had a meeting with Douglas Allen on the bakers. He says legislation will get pushed back to next year, perhaps even to April. Meanwhile George and Chancellor were isolated in Cabinet on the bakers and P.M. was clearly not prepared to have a strike. The offer of an interim $3\frac{1}{2}$ per cent and reference to Board means an extra 8/- or perhaps 10/- against the men's demand for 20/- down. But the 10/- may mean 15/- in take-home pay and the men may accept (though not before the meeting of Cabinet on the subject). If they don't – and come out on strike - they may win and that will be that. Of course the Board might go on but it will be difficult to refer increases of, say, 5%.

I asked Douglas Allen where all this was leading. The NBPI now has practically all public sector prices and wages in its purview (which by itself is significant) and it is also taken for granted that its recommendations will be respected. Does this mean that government would welcome a situation in which the Board in effect issued awards on all wage cases in dispute?

D.A. said CBI wouldn't wear compulsion on prices nor TUC on wages while government seemed unable to take and hold a firm line on either. I said we must look to the *next* attempt to get a wage policy across. What should it aim at? Start off with a London busman's type of case?

This morning William, R., D., Otto and I talked over possible restrictive action. We were not optimistic and agreed that this month was out. P.M. seems to have taken line he was damned if he'd deflate any more and in DEA only Eric seems sympathetic to immediate action. We agreed it was best to think in terms of early January. But Otto won't be ready till about Jan. 18 and it might undermine his position if we got agreement to act via taxation or hire purchase earlier. In any event we had only the regulator and hire purchase to choose between and each was open to serious objections. Chancellor much influenced by Hodge's letter against hire purchase. I said we ought not to leave him without any view, that *something* was needed, and that I should myself go for 5% across the board with 10% on purchase tax. After all, what else would we have to suggest for April if we waited four more months? – only the standard rate and the top rate of purchase tax. Public expenditure cuts might not do more than tally with forecast assumptions and couldn't limit demand before April.

We saw Chancellor at about 6.30 at No.11. He was sitting with his feet on the desk talking to William about Rhodesia and entirely relaxed. Every now and again he'd say he hoped somebody had a speech ready for him (he had to be in black tie by 7.20). He began by offering us a drink and asking what we'd all done today, and reciting his own output, starting with the appointment of a Governor, and his Court, then saving a shipyard, and next a drawn battle on housing. Then he analysed the Rhodesia situation where he has been at odds with the P.M. but has now concluded that the sanctions taken *will* split the whites. He thought that the Javelins would make them most conscious of their dependence on the UK and that they would take the risks more seriously. They would be *relieved* by arrival of British forces in Gambia. The replacement of the Governor of the Central Bank by Sir Sydney Caine would be very effective. (I hadn't seen the measures but couldn't follow all this.) The P.M. had been careful to leave the door open for negotiations, even, if necessary, with Smith[153].

As to the economy he wanted to know whether he was to go and pound the table to get a specific degree of deflation but we advised him to wait till January without concealing his view that something would be necessary. Could we arm him with answers to all the things T.B. and M.S. had put the P.M. up to saying? Where were the measures biting? and why did we think more needed to be done? He thought the Treasury hadn't shown any great enthusiasm for cuts in public expenditure. (No 'glint in the eye' but he hadn't seen Otto's.) William said this might be so of aid but only because we were doubtful whether it would be carried through. R. said he felt for once a great ally of the Governor. The Chancellor also wanted to know if he should take on all spending Ministers or conciliate some and concentrate his attack on selected departments.

I thought it right to say my piece about the regulator, saying that we ought not to dismiss the old-fashioned style of using it because of arguments about tobacco etc. I qualified this, however, by saying that I could see how action in January might detract from the effect of the Budget if he were thinking of stronger action then. At no time was monetary policy discussed.

We all said that in the last resort action to limit demand was defensible only in terms of the balance of payments and the movement in costs and prices; and that in the present state of the labour market, productivity was being adversely affected and the thrust on wages was difficult or perhaps impossible to contain by incomes policy.

It is clear from the press that the argument about deflation is now going to get plenty of publicity and the Chancellor can hardly complain since his own speech started it. P. Davies tells me that he drafted the passage at the Chancellor's express request (he wanted 'a warning') and that it was obvious from *The Times'* account that he was determined to get it out even at the risk of being out of order. Strangely enough, a far more careful draft the previous week was not used in the debate on the address when the Chancellor scored heavily without using his official brief.

Sunday, 5 December   T.B. has been in Rome this week so one source of confusion is absent. The Chancellor duly saw the P.M. and apparently he poured little or no cold water on the forecasts as we had been led to expect but broadly accepted our diagnosis, perhaps because the NIESR had already produced identical forecasts. There were some curious points of agreement:

---

[153] Ian Smith - Prime Minister of Rhodesia, April 1964–November 1965; leader of régime after November 1965.

that hire purchase was comparatively painless; that public expenditure must be cut severely; and that it would be wrong to be faced with the need to put up taxation in the Budget and earn the reputation of a high-tax party.

There has been a lot of gossip about a successor to Cromer – no doubt because he is in the US – and the names run from Ian MacDonald[154] to William, Eric, and John Stevens. I think it unlikely that Cromer will be keen to leave while the future of the pound is in the balance. It seems years since the two of us arrived together but by now it would make little difference if I packed up and perhaps C. feels something of this as well.

We had a meeting on Friday on exchange control under Denis but as T.B. wasn't there, there was no real disagreement, even over the Hong Kong gap. N.K. claimed that he thought our estimate of the gain to the reserves from the 25% surrender of switch dollars was too conservative because nothing would stop the investment trusts from switching. But in fact the estimate was pretty close. On the other hand, the rise in the premium is now becoming a little alarming. It was over 17 on Friday.

Everybody is tied up with Rhodesia or Plan E or similar irrelevancies. When the Chancellor named his deeds the other day, he kicked off with the appointment of a Governor (Sydney Caine) and a new Court. Richard Powell was complaining of how much of a burden it puts on the Board of Trade, and in the Treasury Sam, Tony Rawlinson,[155] and even William are for ever pursuing it.

To get back to Friday's meeting. Nicky gave us a long discourse on double taxation from which it emerged that the investment trusts have at present a strong incentive to *add* to their investments in US up to quite a high proportion of investments because they can set foreign tax against management expenses and interest. But in fact the Americans are agitating in the belief (widely shared) that it works the other way and the Inland Revenue are resisting change on the quite different grounds that they can't start giving transitional relief or offer higher relief for underlying tax without bringing other complaints from allied institutions. So the Americans want a change because of an illusion and might easily end up by getting the reality. N.K. has a new clause all ready for the Finance Bill to reverse the incentives. (he was at the Cabinet Office canteen almost for the first time).

I am very puzzled by the transfer of engineering to the Ministry of Technology. This must have been a very sudden decision and one taken personally by the P.M. – perhaps after complaints from F.C. that he had too little to do and no doubt egged on by T.B. who has no love for the Board of Trade.

The bakers saved G.B.'s bacon by accepting to go before the NBPI once the terms of reference were suitably doctored to imply a minimum increase of £1. No wonder the *M.G.* burst out that the government had little reason to be satisfied. The Board remains but very badly compromised and it is clear from now on that the P.M. is ready to be frightened by threat of a strike. In any

---

[154] Ian MacDonald. Scottish accountant and banker; Chm., Lloyds and Scottish Ltd, 1959–78; Royal Bank of Scotland, 1969–72; Dir., Lloyds Bank Ltd, 1961–78.

[155] Anthony Rawlinson. Private Sec., to Chm., AEA, 1958–60; Asst. Sec., Treasury, 1963; Under-Sec., 1968.

event it was Gunter[156] who pulled it off and George himself had been 'pretty depressed'.

Robens is at it again and wants an extra £80 m. from higher coal prices, presumably to cover losses in '65 as well as '66. It needs only a rise in coal prices of this order to pull down the whole house of cards for steel *couldn't* stand an increase of that order, and Colville's is too obviously the weak spot.

What is pretty plain is that the Chancellor now thinks that if he can make cuts of £200 m. (including cuts in the Estimates) he'll be able to claim he's done enough and escape higher taxes in the Budget. He is also toying with TVA or something like it by 1967 Budget – or before! I very much doubt if the tax system could take this on top of all the rest, even if surcharge removed.

Tuesday, 7 December   Not very eventful days. Yesterday I was asked to get the five economic advisers to agree on a single paper of diagnosis for Jan. 4. Today we discussed 1967 but only to conclude that unless something unexpected happened we were unlikely to grow at a satisfactory rate and remain in external balance. Denis put the reasonable point that if we had more slack and then grew there must be some point at which we were in balance but Robert brushed this aside on the grounds that Ministers wouldn't stand the stagnation involved. DEA are arguing that if only we keep holding down prices for a few months longer the incomes gamble may come off because the rise this year is aggravated by a finite reduction in hours that is now almost over. Even DAVA seems to accept this line of argument. But when we're already standing in for about £100 m. in the nationalised industries alone and steel is obviously held down, we run the risk of springing a mine some months from now when prices *have* to be allowed to follow costs.

Lunch with IMF/Whittome very interesting on Spain. They believe they have a balance of payments problem because Franco was told this by a banker friend when on a shoot and repeated it to one of his ministers. But of course although the word goes round nobody organises a policy since nobody is charged with this duty. The head of the Plan unit is very competent but the Minister of Finance is quite otherwise. As I imagined there is simply no co-ordination, no regular exchange of views, etc.

On France, Whittome spoke highly of the ability of the French officials and their open-mindedness i.e. their willingness to expound and then controvert the official line (he mentioned Huet[157]). Of the Bank of France he said that the top three were very able but that the absence of promotion prospects made the rest of poor quality and the Banque counted for very little as against the Treasury. He thought that Pérouse[158] was in a strong position. But he had had

---

[156] Ray Gunter. Lab. Minister of Labour, 1964–68.

[157] Phillippe Huet. Financial attaché at the French Embassy in London, 1958–62; Dir. Gen. of Prices and Economic Enquiries in the Ministry of Economics and Finance, 1962; Dir. Gen. of Domestic Commerce and Prices, 1965–68.

[158] M.Pérouse. Treasury Director in the French Ministry of Finance, 1960–67; Chairman of the EEC Committee on Conjuncture, 1963–67.

an annoying time with St Geour's[159] balance of payments man who had *not* been open-minded.

I had on my left Gerstein who is Vice-President of the Per Jacobsson Foundation. There were *74* volumes and 56 cases of articles etc. He thought that much of the diary would be of little interest and provided clues only to what was said. But on Japan it is fascinating and this part is to be published. The papers will go to the University of Basle once their new library is built.

Had a long talk with Brian Tew[160] on steel. He agrees that reorganisation is necessary but the Board have no powers to call for necessary information. A part is being studied in conjunction with the Federation but the study is being protracted because the interested parties are in no hurry to supply data. Unless prices go up, there just won't be enough money to finance the investment programme, most of which is of a cost-saving type. Firms like Colville's will have to content themselves with patching for lack of profit out of which to meet capital expenditure. Nonetheless it was one of their schemes that the Board cut (or persuaded Colville's to cut) today. They again have no statutory powers to control *capital* investment.

I asked him what competition was supposed to do if it didn't drive out some plant and *why* it didn't drive out plant. He said this was a mystery and they (the members) didn't have figures of operating costs. He saw no advantage in nationalisation because of the need for flexibility in management but I couldn't see how investment could be successfully controlled (especially if price control was also present and was arbitrary) without some of the obligations of ownership. He reminded me that the Board wanted to give up fixing maximum prices but the Minister wouldn't permit it.

On the US discount rate, we as officials had no forewarning of a rise but presumably neither had the President. We *were* told of the US measures to cut direct foreign investment but that isn't the same thing. I wonder if the Bank of England had any hint. Joe Fromm told me that the rise must have been timed before Balderston's[161] departure in the expectation that it wouldn't be reversed if left in force for a month before the next governor (Chandler?[162]) arrived.

Sunday, 12 December   On Thursday Mary and I went to Fr. Embassy to say Goodbye to Louis Franck[163]. Place full of financial journalists including Nigel Lawson to whom I made some flattering remarks and Sam B. to whom I did not. Fisher said of Otto's lecture that it had shown DEA to be superfluous (in

---

[159] Jean St Geour. Head of Econ. and Fin. Research, French Treasury, 1963; Dir. of Forecasting, Min. of Finance, 1965–67.

[160] Brian Tew. Professor of Economics, Univ. of Nottingham, 1956–67; Part-time member, Iron and Steel Board, 1964–67; East Midlands Electricity Board from 1965.

[161] C.C.Balderston. American banker; Vice-Chm., Board of Governors, Federal Reserve System, 1955–65.

[162] Alfred Chandler. American business historian; instructor/professor Johns Hopkins University, 1963–71; Director, Centre for Study of Recent American History, 1964–71.

[163] Louis Franck. Chm. of insurance companies; Adviser to Bank of France, 1955–62; Financial adviser to French Embassy in London, 1962–65.

spite of Otto's anxiety to be fair). Both Lionel Robbins and Louis Franck made remarks to Sam about his book that did not conceal their feelings.

Chancellor had meeting on liquidity to discuss paper by R.N. and Lucius Thompson-McCausland[164] but it became apparent that proposition was a non-starter. As usual, T.B. and N.K. got across one another but, fortunately, were kept under control.

On Friday I had a meeting of the five advisers with Jukes in place of Donald (who has pleurisy) to prepare a paper for Jan. 4. They all talked very hard and almost exclusively about what should be done although we were asked for a 'diagnostic' paper. But by the end we seemed agreed on the short and simple points that had to be made. Nicky praised Paish's[165] lecture at York (but for the reason that I felt in disagreement with the argument viz. that we have not *allowed* investment to increase). Jukes said a lot of silly things to the effect that we mustn't in any circumstances deflate but none of the others gave this much of a hearing. T.B.'s line is that if we get three good months' exports we can stand two months' bad news and so can escape acting before the Budget (i.e. before the election). R.N. and N.K. weren't so sure and both stressed the precariousness of it all. Of course, they want higher investment and think that the balance of payments will remain a constraint indefinitely but on the main issue I think we are all agreed.

R.N. told me afterwards that the Chancellor had had doubts about Plan E and was getting calculations made by the Revenue on 'free' depreciation. Tommy somehow found out (how does he do it?) and saw George B. Chancellor was looking for allies and had been in touch with D. Jay and others. Nicky and Robert are busy trying to argue him out of it but there may be a rumpus yet. Presumably what worries him is not just the extra cost but the fact that the CBI will hate grants.

Today to see Ely who was remarkably vigorous. We talked at considerable length about Ministry of Defence, statistics, Local Government Commission, etc., etc. On the first, Ely said he had tried to get Henry Hardman[166] to appoint an economist who would report to him directly but he was unwilling. He started off things and then lost track of them because his staff either had no sympathy or no understanding of his ideas.

On statistics E. wanted a statistics and economics unit in all government departments with the head of it acting as Economic Adviser. Hence he was strongly against centralisation in C.S.O. Need for the head of the department to be interested in policy so as to prevent statistics being treated too technically. GRO issuing population projections that everybody had to accept but economists could say were wrong. Need also for access to data held by Departments but untapped e.g. Census of Production where recent analysis of, say, shipbuilding

[164] Lucius Thompson-McCausland - Bank of England, 1931–65; consultant to Treasury on international monetary problems, 1965–68.

[165] F.W.Paish - Professor of Economics with special reference to business finance, LSE, 1949–65.

[166] Sir Henry Hardman. Perm. Sec., Min. of Aviation, 1961–63; Min. of Defence, 1963–64; Perm. Under-Sec. of State, Min. of Defence, 1964–66.

lay buried.

On Local Government Commission he said staff was still about 100 but it was obvious that Minister would take no notice of any recommendations. Extraordinary to see a Minister rise in H. of C. to say he wanted to change local government completely (without reference to existing Commission) and to sweep rates away (with not the least suggestion that he knew what to put in their place).

Sunday, 19 December   On Thursday evening we saw Chancellor at No.11 on *Economic Trends*. Chancellor left us in no doubt that he thought our idea pretty feeble. 'I suggested you should take over Ec. T. last April and nothing has been done yet. Of course I'm not saying this in any critical spirit but it's your battle, not mine. You've let DEA steal a march on you and they'll be in a still stronger position if you wait'. William took him up and said he couldn't see why *we* should worry if DEA published things rather than Treasury. Chancellor might, but weren't we servants of the government? Chancellor repeated his theme of Chancellors come and go and I may not be here when this thing has taken root. Read some passages at random from latest DEA broadsheet and said I bet you won't have anything like this in your articles. Scored a point for they were fulsome stuff about DEA pioneering this and that. Denied he had ever agreed with DEA we should refrain from publishing. But relented when William said my prospectus was too modest and that perhaps like all shells we might yet put something into it.

Chancellor spoke sourly of Bank of England's *Quarterly Bulletin*. Who thought up the idea? William said Radcliffe and I kept quiet. Wrong to have two voices. If anyone spoke for government on economic policy it should be Treasury, not Bank of England. We must in time get over this two-centred arrangement for organising policy (this à propos of DEA not Bank of England).[167]

Fairfield's no go. George saw Isaac Wolfson[168] and wanted £4 m. '£4 million!' said Isaac. 'I could buy these assets for £1 or at a generous estimate 30/-. Good day'. Then Thomson[169]. Somebody with T. said to George he wanted T.'s money. 'Not just his money' said George, 'I want his name too'. But he got neither.

Monday, 20 December   Last Thursday at Nat. Inst. Party, Mrs Weeks reminded me of my remark on incomes policy – Do you believe in fairies?

[167] The Chancellor put it to us that the Bank of England's Quarterly Bulletin and the broadsheets issued by DEA were expositions of a view of the economic situation that the Treasury might wish to counter without the power to do so. When we then made arrangements with the CSO to include in *Economic Trends* a monthly economic assessment, prepared by the Treasury, it had to be called off at the last minute on two occasions because of ministerial reluctance to allow publication. It was not until January 1967 that regular publication began.

[168] Sir Isaac Wolfson. Chm. Great Universal Stores from 1963; Founder/Trustee Wolfson Foundation, 1956.

[169] Lord Thomson. Chm. The Thomson Organisation Ltd including *The Times*, and *The Sunday Times*.

But this remark applies far more to the confidence view of investment and planning (if everybody believes the plan and invests, the plan is fulfilled because investment raises productivity as postulated).

Saturday, 25 December   We had a final meeting on Wednesday of the Economic Advisers. T.B. again fired in a comment on the draft in advance and typically complained that I seemed to be lamenting that unemployment wasn't higher although in fact there was no foundation for this at all. Nicky was much more forthright and at the meeting said his reflections over the week disposed him to favour higher unemployment even if he did sound like Paish. He thought 1.8 quite a reasonable target – i.e. he is where the Treasury was some years ago. But he also came out strongly for a long passage on ways of reducing the capital outflow and I had no option but to put this in the draft. When we discussed it at Higher Directorate on Thursday (N.K. making his first appearance) he didn't say this passage represented his views but said that the principle was right. When William asked if de facto he thought anything could be done he agreed not.

I got each to say what he wanted done. J.J. said no deflation, tiptoe along to the Budget, and export subsidies in the Budget. T.B. as usual havered (and was careful to wait for J.J. in case he could shelter behind him) but seemed willing to accept hire purchase restrictions in January. He obviously wanted to keep the final recommendation dependent on the date of the election. I didn't point out – what is obvious – that an election in May would make it even more important to do something in advance of the Budget since otherwise everybody would fear a weak Budget followed by devaluation after the election.

T.B. and J.J. have not exactly seen eye to eye so that T. hasn't been able to take his usual line that what he is suggesting is exactly what somebody else thinks too (as he would with Donald). J.J. has rather crazy idea of what is 'on' politically and no real economic insight to offset it. Fred is worth two of him any day.

We agreed that the next draft should be prepared by R.N. and myself and be the subject of telephoned amendments only. Nicky had none and T.B. confined his to cutting a paragraph in two! But J.J. came twice to see me, all for the sake of a minor change in the final paragraph which anyhow said that we weren't agreed on the main issue (the only clear dissentient being J.J.) of action in January or not.

R.N. was away on Thursday but sent a brief supporting minute to the Chancellor. Nicky did a piece of his own which I signed with him.

On Thursday Chancellor had a party and arrived late from Cabinet so we were already drinking. Ian B. told me that George had stayed away from Cabinet because he first heard of Cabinet changes on the radio and thought that as Deputy Premier this wasn't good enough (but the press makes no mention of his absence). He already told us that the Chancellor was pleased at Roy Jenkins' promotion but qualified this by remarking 'We'll have to watch him. He's too kind to these buggers'.[170]

What is really interesting is the NIESR contention last May that the sum total of government measures up to May '65 had no net effect on GNP. This seems to me to go too far but is an interesting point for those who keep asking why the economy doesn't lie down.

[170] In a Cabinet reshuffle Roy Jenkins became Home Secretary and Barbara Castle Minister of Transport.

Chapter 3

1966

Sunday, 16 January 1966   Left for US on Jan. 1 and returned on Friday morning (14th). P.M. in Africa (Lagos and Nairobi), G.B. in Delhi (Shastri's[1] funeral), and Chancellor in Wales(?). I saw R.N. briefly and talked to Fred before going home with a full bag of papers.

Contrary to what I gathered from David Hubback in Washington, Ministers do mean to use hire purchase. But on Jan. 7 there was no agreement at all. I'm told that the three met in the afternoon without officials and that George was so impossible that the P.M. finally walked out. R.N. was asked to put in an agreed paper with the other advisers on the 'relevance' of further hire purchase restrictions in present circumstances and was taken off the plane to Geneva in order to prepare it. He got Tommy to accept and J.J. was pushed into a reservation in the final paragraph, the paper being submitted on Saturday evening so that R. could get off for his skiing before the EFTA meeting. The Chancellor then spoke to P.M. on telephone and P.M. to G.B. and we were then authorized to go ahead without even a quibble about the total effect (although the Chancellor himself had been prepared to accept a lower figure than £135m. and may yet cut it unilaterally). Douglas A. was brought in to see the Chancellor to let him have the advice he had given to G.B. mainly to make sure that action was part of a visible strategy extending beyond hire purchase.

It was also agreed to study guide-lines for sterling area capital exports and to tighten monetary policy. In fact it looked as if the Bank of England had been prepared to issue directions to the banks in advance of the hire purchase restrictions which won't come until early February (after the Hull by-election) and may never come at all because Ministers may not hold fast to their decision.

The continued strength of sterling and rise in exports made one doubtful if they would take action in advance of the Budget although I had told Schweitzer and Deming that it was not ruled out.

Excitement also about the leak over the Indust. Reconst. Corporation (said to be by DEA) and about the goings on over Tom Padmore, Foster[2] and Co. at the Ministry of Transport.[3] I can't be very content to hear of appointments

---

[1] Shri Lal Bahadur Shastri. President of the Republic of India.

[2] C Foster. Dir. Gen. of Economic Planning, Min. of Transport, 1966–70.

[3] Barbara Castle, the new Minister of Transport, was said to ignore her Permanent Sec-

like Foster's from the newspapers since they make nonsense of the Govt. Econ. Service, however sensible in themselves.

Geoffrey Wilson[4] is returning to be Deputy Head of ODM. He said that George Woods, though a man of outstanding ability as an investment banker, ran the Bank too much as if it were his and regarded the staff as subordinates, not colleagues. Hence he didn't hesitate to dress them down in front of others until it was difficult to feel any enthusiasm for coming into the office. Where Black had selected specific areas of responsibility and left the rest to his colleagues, Woods kept a finger on everything so that there was, in effect, a lowering of status all along the line with the No.2 becoming a No.3 in each Division because Woods became the No.1. G.W. agreed that in the first year Woods had helped to restore morale, which up till then had been low because of the uncertainty over Black's successor. But things were different now and there were signs that Woods would want to continue in office. This would make the Bank an all-American institution especially if G.W. were not replaced from Europe since most of the non-Americans had been in the US now for 20 years and were no longer genuinely representative of their country.

On Monday 10th we went by train to Boston and called on Rosenstein Rodan[5]. R. was fascinating. He began by telling us how expert the undergraduates are nowadays in all the technicalities of economics. They are thorough, elegant, learned, and will never commit the mistakes of our generation. But, said R., they also won't construct and innovate with the boldness of older economists. No inspired guesses for them, no clutching at dimly perceived truths – only more polished versions of things already said. On the other hand, they are also more limited in range. We are the last examples of the humanist tradition that allows physical chemists and classical scholars and philosophers to emerge as economists. Although it is not how he put it, the poetry is dying and the symbolism is becoming almost wholly mathematical.

Then he talked of Italy imagining that I had some special interest in it. He agreed that there were no major figures to compare with Pareto[6] and said a word in praise of Marco Fanno[7] for whom he had a great admiration and who died only a couple of years ago. The Fascists were unable to touch him, so great was his reputation. Then he spoke of his first encounter with Pareto. Paul's father believed that the right way to learn a language was to go to school in the country and he was in fact ready to be packed off to Paris when the First World War prevented this so that instead he was sent to Lausanne. When they called his name he found he couldn't recognise it although French was spoken in his

retary, Sir Thomas Padmore, and consult only her recently appointed Economic Adviser, Christopher Foster.

[4] Sir G Wilson. Vice-Pres. IBRD, 1961–64; Dep. Sec. Min. of Overseas Devlopt., 1966–68; Perm. Sec., 1968–69.

[5] Paul Rosenstein Rodan. Dept. of Political Economy, University College, London University, 1931–47; IBRD, Washington, 1947–53; Professor of Economics, MIT from 1953.

[6] V Pareto. Italian sociologist and economist.

[7] Marco Fanno. Italian economist.

home in Vienna. He was then 18 and it was at a party that he met Pareto without any inkling of his identity. He found himself talking to a bearded man with cigarette ash on his lapels who listened patiently to his exposition of modern physics and the modifications that it involved in the laws of thermodynamics, quantum theory, etc. etc. Pareto suggested that difficulties similar to those in physics existed in economics. But the mention of political economy only moved Rodan to say 'Mais ce sont des bavardages pour le bourgeoisie!' Nevertheless he was invited to dinner. When he knocked at the door he was faced with Problem No.1. 'Is this Mme P. or the maid? If Mme P. I must kiss her hand. But if not I must on no account kiss her hand'. He was just forming the conclusion that it was the maid when he saw behind her Prof. P. who said briskly: 'Let me introduce you to my wife. There are some women you have to marry in order to get rid of them'. Problem No.2. Should he laugh? Was this intended in jest. But it was at once apparent that it was no jest. In fact it was quite an evening.

We talked – or rather he talked – for an hour in the most entertaining way, and when we eventually went upstairs to see Bob Solow[8] and others he continued to talk because they were at lunch. He commented on John Adler[9] that he had the American failing of verbosity. 'Americans', he said, ' go on talking under the illusion that if they circumnavigate the point their meaning will be clear in proportion to the number of words they use'. Then on Tommy Balogh he cited Keynes' remark that the fatal defect in his education was that he didn't go to Winchester. Later he said that Tommy's exposition of any economic argument was so childish that he would expect first year undergraduates to do better but that Tommy's conclusions were often on the mark. He had a kind of feminine intuition that was at the opposite pole from Nicky's overwhelming professional skill in economic analysis but Nicky's judgements were often very dubious and Paul said he distrusted them profoundly. He spoke rather sadly about his attitude to the Labour Party – indeed with more hesitation than when he identified himself with a Left of Centre position in Italian politics as something he had believed in all his life. What he said was that he thought that the Labour Party had more chance of making things acceptable in England that were necessary for her eventual prosperity. But he obviously had his reservations about the P.M., deriving to some extent from his friendship with Hugh Gaitskell, dating from the time when both were at U.C.L.

Sunday, 23 January   What a week! News came thick and fast and nearly all of it made nonsense of what went before. First the index of production for November showed a fall (at least if the effects of intense cold on gas and electricity production are left out). Then unemployment fell 19000 in the Jan. figure. We also heard that retail sales in December were up two points and that the latest investment intentions survey showed little or no fall. All this suggested that production *was* rising – both exports and retail sales pointed this

[8] Robert Solow Professor of Economics, MIT.
[9] J H Adler. Staff of IBRD; a joint founder of the Econ. Developt. Inst., Washington, 1955-56.

way – and that stockbuilding might be lower. But what could we make of the unemployment figure? Even if the labour supply *was* steady, employment was plainly increasing. Then on Thursday as I left C(M)(O) after expounding the situation, Ned Dunnett told me that the latest figures for June 1965 showed a big rise. In fact we hardly know how to interpret the situation except that unemployment is undeniably lower than a year ago and apparently falling instead of, as we have hitherto maintained, flat. (Vacancies fell slightly, to make things even more confusing.)

G.B. in obviously worried and trying to hedge his agreement to hire purchase restrictions. D.J. wrote to the P.M. arguing for a cut of half in what we proposed. Now G.B. wants to know just what the effects of our proposals would be. Also hesitant about credit restrictions. T.B. also minutes the P.M. without consultation to say we should withhold action till mid-February (after the trade figures). Note that he is free to tell the P.M. what he thinks and interpret the unemployment figures to suit his thesis. But at least a copy comes to the Chancellor *and so* to officials.

Since the hire purchase restrictions and extra purchase tax may be alternatives it looks as if we may yet have to wait for the Budget – with possibly an election in between. Can they really want to have an election with no action since July and unemployment *falling*? It would look uncommonly like 1964 except that imports are not rising.

Tuesday, 26 January   Far too much paper – can't even read what comes to me and tray piled higher than ever.

Spent nearly an hour with the Chancellor on recent indicators. Last night at Tuesday Club Denis Barnes[10] told me that earnings were up 10.1% (I guessed 9.6) in the October enquiry but when I told the Chancellor this, he merely asked 'What's the usual increase?' He agreed that the employment indicators were more reliable than the production ones. But he has made up his mind not to increase taxes and obviously regards the hire purchase restrictions plus the cuts in public expenditure as meeting the need. At first I thought he was joking till he said 'Don't give me that cynical laugh' and went on to explain that he didn't trust the figures. This referred to a change of £200 m. in the revenue estimate which completely offset cumulative cuts of £150 m. in expenditure. He argued that the budget deficit couldn't be taken seriously in the face of this and that he could easily reduce it by £500 m. if he pushed the local authorities on to the market for funds, although we agreed that this had no real economic advantage. He didn't want to argue that the *real* changes that we forecast would be affected by the revision in the revenue estimate or that he should take no stock of the probable change in demand. But it seemed pretty clear that he would take a lot of persuading and was rather glad not to have to set about persuading his colleagues. I said we needed figures for early 1967 to judge how much action was needed and that we'd have them in a fortnight or so.

[10] Denis Barnes. Dep. Sec., Min. of Labour, 1963–66; Perm. Sec., 1966–68; Perm. Sec., Dept. of Employment, 1968–73.

Nicky spoke to me at Zecchi's[11] party for Ossola[12] tonight in some consternation at the same reaction from the Chancellor whom he saw to day. He thought that we were faced with a pre-election Budget and that the Chancellor would go for hire purchase in the very circumstances where we said they were inappropriate.

For this was the outcome of yesterday's discussion between us and William. We felt that the mix of hire purchase and tax needed to be considered in the light of election timing and that it was only right to go now for hire purchase if sufficient time elapsed to let the restrictions be modified in the Budget.

I spent Monday night at *The Economist* arguing with MacRae that 1.2% unemployment made nonsense of any attempt to get the balance of payments straight or to accelerate industrial growth. I drank too much brandy but enjoyed the debate. Last night I heard Aubrey Jones on Incomes Policy and on the whole thought his defence more astute than his critics rather half-hearted attack. Eric Roll said a few things at the end to throw doubt on the functional relationship between unemployment and wages. But he pretended to keep his tongue in his cheek.

Today we had two meetings on Government Economic Service. Tommy B. said both *The Observer* and *The Sunday Times* had offered him £6,000 for his memoirs. He said he could easily have accepted without infringing the Official Secrets Act since Mallaby,[13] for example, had written his by carefully refraining from quoting secrets or reflecting on policy but had given plenty of gossip about the great in the manner of somebody observing whether each had his fly undone.

Yesterday gave evidence to the Select Committee on Estimates about economic forecasting. Jeremy Bray,[14] having insisted that Campion and I appear in spite of great inconvenience (C. should have been in Bangkok) was himself half an hour late because he wanted to attend statement on Rhodesia. But at least his questioning was good-humoured and to the point.

So tonight (after Ossola) is the first chance that I've had of reading papers and getting them back into order.

Thursday, 27 January   N. Hull result a resounding victory for Labour. This puts paid to any thought of a pre-election Budget.

A day of scurry trying to get agreement to a paper on the economic situation for Friday's meeting. R.N. leaving for WP No.3 at lunch, J. Jukes at 4 p.m. and T.B. and myself tied up with meetings. When I rang T.B. on Federal he started reading a note of his own with all sorts of details about government intentions (e.g. hire purchase restrictions) and I persuaded him to send it over. Of course it wasn't purely the factual piece asked for and went on to argue

[11] Zecchi. Italian financial representative in London.

[12] Rinaldo Ossola. Economist with Banca d'Italia, 1938–79; Dir. Gen., 1976–79.

[13] Sir G Mallaby. First Civil Service Commissioner, 1959–64.

[14] Jeremy Bray. Chm. Labour Science and Technology Group, 1964–66; Parliamentary Sec. Min. of Power, 1966–67; Jt. Parliamentary Sec. Min. of Technology, 1967–69.

strongly against hire purchase or any other restrictive action until after Feb. 14 and perhaps none at all even in Budget. When Nicky asked him why he had changed his mind he fell back on (a) the strength of sterling, (b) the contingent need for stronger action in event of a strike. But what had he in mind? All we could get out of him was a rise in bank rate – this was the really stern device that a strike might call for. So I insisted we give up arguing about what we were not asked to decide and concentrate on a purely factual paper. This went in signed by all but seen in final form only by myself.

R.N. said this morning that Chancellor was sounding us out individually to find an ally for a soft budget. It looks as if he will argue for hire purchase on the assumption that this will absolve him from raising taxes while his colleagues will oppose him because they fear it will prove just one more instalment.

I spoke to William and told him of Chancellor's line with me including the suggestion that we ought to bring down bank rate to 5 per cent. This last was new to him and I explained that I had argued strongly that with an international boom under way a fall in interest rates would be very dangerous for us. William said that for past 5 days Chancellor had been trying to wriggle on higher taxation, arguing as he did with me that people would say we were the highest taxed country in the world and that he was forever raising taxes. William told him that it all sounded very like 1955 and that he had then heard similar doctrine in the same room. Chancellor then tackled Governor without indicating size of prospective deficit and rang up William to say that Governor was offering agreement. But of course when Rowley saw figure he changed his tune as William warned Chancellor he would do. In fact this was another parallel with 1955. Chancellor asked William if he was suggesting that he would lose his reputation and William said "And a great deal more". He thought things pretty black but didn't despair and said he judged from later remarks last night that I must have made some impression on the Chancellor. The odd thing is how relaxed the Chancellor is about it all.

Sunday, 30 January Thursday was frantic but Friday calm. The four Ministers met at noon and agreed on the new lending restriction but disagreed on hire purchase. The line-up was (according to Chancellor via Ian B.) Chancellor and P.M. v. G.B. and D. Jay. But (again according to Chancellor) there was agreement in principle to let him go ahead. Only, nothing must be done until the NUR had decided whether to strike or not. This last is plumb crazy and William has spoken to Chancellor pointing out that if nothing is announced by next week-end when the Party leaders meet at Chequers nothing will be possible thereafter whatever the NUR do.

G.B. saw Sydney Greene,[15] and according to Hunt,[16] told him that a nod was as good as a wink. When S.G. asked if this meant that his Union would get

---

[15] Sydney Greene (later Lord)– Gen. Sec. National Union of Railwaymen, 1957–74; member of NEDC 1962–75.

[16] John Hunt – Asst. Sec., Treasury, 1962–67; Under-Sec. 1965–68; Dep. Sec., Civil Service Department, 1968–71.

all they were asking for, G.B. gave him a pretty free hand along predictable lines. But never a word was said about productivity. We look like having one more sell-out with nothing to show for it. Meanwhile G.B. is anxious that the earnings figures should not appear yet awhile and Chancellor is trying to make Governor's letter coincide with their publication on Tuesday. Ministry of Labour will insist on publication.

Contretemps on electricity prices. The Chancellor looks like being manoeuvred into the position of having to accept no change in bulk supply tariff before April 1967. This means sacrificing about £50m in receipts from electricity.

Saw Ely on Saturday. He thinks that whatever Crossman now does local government reform may go back, not 5 but 15 years.

Newspapers almost completely empty of economic comment over the weekend. Entirely engrossed in politics and speculation about election. What a contrast to 2/3 years ago! But Tories beginning to get round to prediction of calamity ahead.

Sunday, 6 February   A rather uneventful week although it may have been decisive from the election point of view. We started off with the annual meeting of forecasters at C.A.S. and found little new. Everybody seemed to follow F.Paish in expecting unemployment to rise rather belatedly in a few months' time. Obvious that people were optimistic about exports and so about balance of payments. Wadsworth said demand for credit was easing and Paish that fall in profits was sure sign of a change in climate.

On Tuesday Fred brought me provisional forecasts showing increase of £100m in deficit in 1966 and no increase in unemployment (very little even in 1967). I did a note which was discussed on Thursday at Directorate. Nicky and Robert were sceptical about the supposed new *trend* in productivity and hence about the unemployment forecast but probably not seriously at odds. The main discussion was on what could be said in advance of an election. But this will settle itself since we'll probably have a Budget first.

To go back to Tuesday. I spoke to Governor and Deputy Governor who were now thinking not just of what we needed for debt repayment but also of what would cover transition while we joined EEC. They wanted to know whether a cut in Government expenditure could be made in continuation of the good work of last July.

Douglas Allen told us how things stood on the Prices and Incomes Bill and the fix the government would be in if it was once introduced and no election intervened to kill it. (*The Times* had the whole story next day.)

At the Pol. Econ. Club on Wednesday, Victor Feather[17] gave a rather flippant talk. Enoch Powell[18] argued: (a) that productivity and the movement of money incomes had no logical connection; (b) that this was also true of individual industries; (c) that "restraint" was ineffective and wrong in principle.

[17] Vic Feather (later Lord) – Asst. Gen. Sec. TUC, 1960–69; Gen. Sec. 1969–73.

[18] Enoch Powell – Professor of Greek, University of Sydney, 1937–39; Parliamentary Sec. Min. of Housing and Local Govt., 1955–57; Financial Sec. to Treasury, 1957–58; Minister of Health, 1960–63.

Of course, this brought in Robert Shone and others till Aubrey Jones gave us his views: (a) that restraint had to be within the power situation; (b) that there was also a wider question of reform.

He argued on (a) that lower pressure was not a substitute for an incomes policy but complementary to it. I thought it right to point out that in the first year of the Incomes Board hourly earnings had increased at a record rate; and that so far as wage structure, restrictive practices and all that went, there might be a place for a pillory but nobody could take the responsibility away from industry itself with the government still responsible for general policy. The Board could only play a subordinate role and it would be a mistake to pin everything on its success.

Earlier, Hawtrey had intervened and predictably (as I murmured to Max Stamp when he began) led up to a demonstration that the pound was undervalued and it was the bankers in whose hands incomes policy really lay.

Tommy's antics about statistics have led to a proposal for a new Committee of Enquiry (Jackson, Reddaway,[19] Worswick) with terms of reference very like Douglas Allen's. I discussed this with William on Friday just before a separate meeting on the C.S.O. where G.B. again is trying to take over. On top of this, Bray is busy and will tie up a lot of the time of senior statisticians.

We had a meeting on *Economic Trends* with Eric Roll and may yet get our proposal for a Monthly Comment back on the rails. At any rate we're agreed we can't amalgamate the DEA *Broadsheet* and the CSO *Trends* as Ministers suggest.

Agreement reached with D. Jay on H.P. Luckily new car registrations were high in December and hire purchase sales very high in January. So at least there is *some* justification even if we take a gloomier view than others of the prospect for cars this year. The Chancellor will be pretty satisfied if he can score £90 m. towards the Budget. But he will no doubt be correspondingly mild in his proposals for taxation. I must confess I am surprised to see him get his way (to be announced tomorrow) and can only conclude that he must have made some reassuring noises about tax changes.

Tuesday, 15 February   The hire purchase measures were duly announced and calmly received.[20] The Chancellor then made a statement on the 8th about public investment and the July deferments which was interpreted as severe although it did no more than ensure that the deferments weren't caught up in 1966-67. All this, combined with the Governor's letter prolonging the credit squeeze, made some journalists suspicious and Anthony Vice[21] called on me, no doubt for this reason. I thought that each item could be explained by a separate logic and said

---

[19] W B Reddaway – Director, Dept. of Applied Economics, University of Cambridge, 1955–69.

[20] Downpayments on domestic appliances (other than cookers but including radio and TV sets) were raised from 15 to 25 per cent and the maximum repayment period reduced to two from two and half years. Motor vehicles were unaffected.

[21] A. Vice Journalist with *Sunday Times*.

so. But of course Mary hit it at once when she first heard of the hire purchase restrictions and said: "Is that to make the budget easier?"

Anyhow by last Monday the P.M. and others, after their Chequers week-end, had got well along the line towards a firm decision on a March election. William gave us a tentative timetable with May 5 as the latest date for the Budget and he and Robert spent a good part of the week drafting a minute for the Chancellor to send to the P.M. on the character and timing of a statement. By Friday it was in draft but I didn't see it till Monday (yesterday) and the Chancellor had by then amended it (in significant respects e.g. he said he was coming round to the view that a more direct attack on the balance of payments was necessary). We had a talk last night on the outline of the statement, assuming that P.M. and G.B. agreed it should not be a full Budget but a bid to keep the Budget judgement open. Ian B. drafted an outline which we discussed today.

It's clear that R.N. must have been working on the Chancellor over the pound. I'm not sure where William stands on this and the P.M. may have a fixed position. But if the Chancellor changes sides, he and George together are bound to prevail. So it looks as if the strategy is going to be the one Nicky has always favoured – a tough Budget and then – let go!

My own activities last week were largely on the preparation of a Budget submission which now goes into cold storage. I did a draft on Tuesday for William and R.N. and redrafted it on Sunday on the basis of revised N.I.F. and BP forecasts. Wynne gets little if any increase in unemployment over the next two years but he is likely to revise this a little.

Lunch at Bank last Tuesday. Governor dwelt rather surprisingly on additional reserves needed if we went into EEC. He has since written, on guide-lines for sterling area investment, a pretty forcible letter which I hope will scotch the project. It seems to be most strongly backed by Catherwood and Co. although R.N. and N.K. obviously find it congenial. I can't say it makes much sense to me.

Sunday, 20 February   Not a very eventful week. Wednesday and Thursday in Hanover including a whole day to get there! By Monday it had become quite clear that election date was practically settled and Chancellor's statement for March 1 was a firm part of the programme. Chancellor sent a minute to P.M. drafted by Robert but with some significant amendments (e.g. he is "coming round to view" that a more direct attack on balance of payments will be necessary). This set out to show that it would be best if he did not make Budget commitments but kept the position open. Chancellor was to discuss this with P.M. and First Secretary on Monday evening but I never heard the outcome. By Tuesday we were sketching the statement on basis of Ian B.'s draft outline and by Friday R.N. had circulated a fairly complete version. William was uneasy that with so much paper there would be a leak and wanted to use camouflage (e.g. calling it Option X) but of course the press had guessed almost exactly what is in the wind. On Monday Chancellor was still telling Ian that we mustn't assume that Budget would no longer be at beginning of April final decision would be put off till P.M.'s return from Moscow.

I had a long talk with F. Figgures in Hanover about 1964. He had earlier attacked the "nonsense" of the sterling area guide-lines and said the submission was at fault for not denouncing the whole idea. I thought this a little simpliste. F.'s point was that it might mean a small saving in foreign exchange or an actual loss and that if we were prepared to do that much we ought to think of extending Exchange Control and getting something worthwhile. He made the same point on the Armstrong Report in 1964,[22] that Ministers did not think it said there was any need to deflate. On this I felt a little to blame for I only pressed William *after* it was in draft – but felt that as he had taken it out of my hands I wasn't going to push the point since it was such an obvious one. Frank thought that we should have insisted on deflationary action in July or August 1964 and this also gave me a twinge of conscience since I recalled the minute I wanted to send in June to say that special deposits ought not to depend on the flatness of the index of production but on the *level* of activity (which was already too high). F. pointed out that D. Jay was able to say in Geneva later that the suggestion that the British economy was overheated was not in accord with official advice. This showed that we did not put up our minutes forcibly enough and pandered too much to Ministerial brain-waves. He obviously had the surcharge at the back of his mind. But I can hardly imagine that Richard Powell ever told D. Jay that there was no overheating. When I tried to argue that it was hard to know who was being advised in the first six months of the new government, he showed little sympathy with this. Even if Ministers disregarded what they were told they ought to be told. But how does one tell *other* Ministers.

I wonder, looking back, if I should not have forced myself more on the Chancellor or even insisted on seeing the P.M. But at that time we didn't think that the deficit would be nearly so big, and by the time we were into July and the foreign exchanges held firm we thought we had a promise. The critical period was between late July and the time I left for Italy and I can't recall what went on although I certainly wanted increased taxation – at least the rise in petrol which was later put into the November Budget.

F. also said that in January 1965 Ted Heath had told him that there was no official advice to act. This surely is not true. William told me at the time that the Chancellor argued strongly that the regulator for 4/6 weeks (i.e. about £10m) wasn't worth it – i.e. he could wait till after the election.

On Friday when I got back there was a terrific cascade of paper: the final forecasts for 66/67, the *Economic Report* in draft, an enormous paper on costs here and abroad, and a sheaf of others on everything from housing to coal and liquidity.

Donald MacD. away for another month, i.e. pretty well till end March making four months in all.

Wednesday, 23 February   Revising the Statement. The Chancellor's version is full of political scores and not the statesmanlike survey of the economic outlook

[22] Armstrong Report – presumably the brief prepared for the incoming government in 1964.

that we had postulated, or he himself seemed to favour. William troubled about our original advice and seemingly doubtful whether statement will serve. It has both to be cast in a form that explains why there is no Budget before the election and yet holds things open till after the election and will be seen to do so.

This morning Robert and I discussed strategy with William who reported a conversation with T.B. (he hasn't gone to Moscow for health reasons but lunched today with R.F. Kahn). T. said his experience in government left him more humble and that if he were outside he would be lambasting the civil service, not knowing the true situation. He thought now there was no way out except devaluation and that perhaps the thing to do was to combine it with entry into EEC. This would mean that he had to eat a lot of words since he had no love for EEC (he made no mention of the Commonwealth) and he was at a loss to see how we could get through to 1967, when the negotiations might be far enough advanced, except by breaking the rules, e.g. export subsidies. Robert said he found this pretty sane but felt that in order to join Europe we might have to pander to a lot of unspoken anti-Americanism and he was doubtful whether the P.M. could head a campaign of this kind however he might be drawn to the idea of a link with Europe. For T.B. the fact that it was now a Europe des Patries made things easier. R. thought that the idea of overcoming the evident state of fundamental disequilibrium by deflation over 5 years was out and not worth pursuing but was willing to see the Economic Advisers do a submission in which devaluation was only part of the story and not pressed as *the* solution. Nobody said we could do more on the capital balance and indeed it was T.B.'s thesis that we had to get the current account into surplus.

Many promotions well in advance of July 1, all starting from Philip Allen's shift to Home Office. Bill Nield[23] lamented his continuing responsibility for Rhodesia which he felt to be "a mess" and wanted treated à la Palestine by our "clearing out". He was fed up with instant government from Harold, drunken government from George and seemed incredulous that the public could possibly return this government with a bigger majority. Paul Bareau[24] put the majority at 40 but I thought this was likely to be a considerable understatement because the Tories wouldn't pull out the marginal voters and still less the marginal non-voters.

Sunday, 27 February　　　Cobham to see Ely. He commented on H.'s success with journalists of whom 17 went to Moscow. They were always willing to swallow his story although the best of them must be aware of his tactics (government by intent; constant bustle, frequent starts, no need to follow through). I said we were approaching U.S. situation where one didn't look for differences of principle between leaders of opposing parties. E. pointed out that on foreign policy there *had* been genuine differences but that H. had already begun to

[23] W Nield – Min. of Agriculture, Fisheries and Food, 1949–64; Under-Sec., 1964–65; Dep. Under-Sec. of State, DEA, 1965–66; Dep. Sec., Cabinet Office, 1966–68; Perm. Under-Sec. of State, DEA, 1968–69.

[24] Paul Bareau – Journalist on *The Economist*; later, Editor of *The Statist*.

change his ground when he became leader of the Party. The one thing neither party would put to public was relations with U.S. He thought that Conservatives missed a chance on Local Government Comm. which they saw abolished without a murmur. Crossman might think that the R.C. would report and that new legislation would be possible by 1970 but 1980 was a better guess. We talked about Evelyn Sharp on T.V. and Ely commented that she seemed very sorry for herself until at the end she was asked if she'd rather have been a man.

On Thursday we had a meeting on Economic Strategy with Eric and it was agreed that we should prepare papers for March 31. Robert and William both talked of a rogue elephant line of policy but I said that one had to change character to get that sort of change of policy.

William also spoke of Harold's anti-economist (in the sense of anti-hero) approach. But this merely means he likes gimmicks – administrative rather than market methods of control. The administrators will think of what is open to us politically while the economists examine the various ways of softening the deflation/devaluation dilemma.

Wednesday, 2 March　　　Meeting on forecasts – rather tame although Fred got in one or two digs at DEA by pointing out how fortunate it was unemployment was so low when we were in balance of payments trouble.

Told William after TFM that I might want a year off. He made no comment except that he was glad Bryan could take over and had I spoken to Laurence H.

Chancellor's statement yesterday a great success but the *F.T.* got the point in its headline "The Budget still to come" and *The Times* and other papers were also a little acid on the contrast between the first and second halves. The BBC on TV starred the decision in favour of a decimal currency (and this was what went over big in the House, as Ian B. had prophesied) and it was only when their second commentator came on that there was any reference to the economic situation.

Meeting yesterday on economic strategy with T.B. and Co. in T.'s room. Mainly on controls.

Sunday, 6 March　　　Election campaign in full swing. Henry Brandon[25] on sterling in 1964 in *The Sunday Times* – William spent most of Friday trying to get it held over. It makes juicy reading and it is obvious that Maudling has talked freely (and not just Maudling).[26] Nicky came to see me on Friday on Robert's draft for our Economic Report (R.N. being and WP 3) and we had a brief discussion on export-led growth and floating rates. It is clear that Nicky attaches importance to opening of wider markets by devaluation and entering Europe and I have some sympathy with this. But I regard the clog on faster growth in UK as the shortage of resources to the most affluent firms (unless they push up

[25] Henry Brandon Washington Correspondent, *Sunday Times*, from 1950.

[26] Two articles by Henry Brandon on the sterling crisis of October 1964 appeared in *The Sunday Times* on 6 and 13 March 1966 and a fuller account was subsequently published in book form in *In the Red*.

wage rates) plus imperfection of the market. I doubt whether new markets in Europe (or abroad) can change this very much, or the restrictive practices etc. by which we are plagued. Once bitten (by expansionist doctrinaires) twice shy (of export-led growth – which I called by a slip "export-led inflation").

There wasn't much 'humility' in T.B. at our meeting with E. Roll, R. Powell and Co. when he told R.P. that there was no one, but no one, in the Board of Trade *capable* of judging whether French growth had been faster or French production was higher than in UK. He still thinks we need a powerful economist in every key department including Health (and has been writing to the Minister to say so).

T.B. has done a paper on the Hong Kong gap – a critique of the Treasury paper. It is quite a piece! – and certainly justifies my denial of F.F.'s suggestion in Hanover that he is a charlatan, even if I disagree with the whole philosophy.

Neil Caplan[27] told me on Thursday that at the NEDC meeting the CBI pressed for more deflation and Robens wanted 500,000 unemployed. I said the paper by Robert Shone was incredible because it never once mentioned the balance of payments and offered quite unreal choices – more unemployment and less output or less unemployment and more output. The TUC had told the Chancellor that they wouldn't object to 1.8% unemployment – the figure he said he expected by end of 1966. So who was standing out? The whole Neddy business was a shady deception the outcome of which could only be devaluation and those who egged Ministers on to expand were well aware that this was their unspoken assumption, although they took no trouble to tell Ministers.

Henry P.B., according to Neil, was too nervous before speaking and too academic to cut any ice. In fact he doubted whether there were any really good independent members to be had.

R.N. told me not long ago of his talk with G.B. who made it plain that he didn't mind higher taxes if the resources released *did* go to exports (i.e. if we devalued). But he obviously still wanted the same pressure on the economy.

John Jukes told me on Friday of his week-end at Nuffield with G.B. at the time of the railway settlement. George got pretty fu' by 10 p.m. and in the common rom when silence descended attacked them all for contributing not a single new idea. Here he was, left school at 15, and they the leading academic institution in the social sciences and what had they to say by way of comment or criticism? One man ventured to ask about Vietnam and this set George off again. Of all the things they might hope to enlighten him on, etc., etc. They got him to bed and the telephone kept ringing but George was sound asleep and when awakened muttered "Where's Sophie?" and couldn't take it in.

ED(O) on Economic Report – a small group and a poor discussion. I gather the Committee has never really got off the ground. Haven't been there since the much bigger meeting on The National Plan.

Sunday, 13 March   On Thursday morning William told R. and me (Denis was

---

[27] Neil Caplan – Under-Sec., Scottish Devlopt. Dept., 1963–65; Under-Sec., NEDO, 1966; Asst. Under-Sec. of State, DEA, 1966–60.

still in Paris) of the Governor's call the previous evening (I had seen him go into William's room). He had been increasingly uneasy over the fall in sterling and asking whether a rise in bank rate was not advisable. By Wednesday morning he was firmly of this opinion and had told the Chancellor after consulting a number of other members of the Court and finding them of the same opinion.[28] He feared that the loss would be very heavy if bank rate was not increased and that the market had come to expect it (the press said the very reverse). Continental opinion in particular was alarmed by the P.M.'s reiteration of the Labour Party's steel nationalisation plan.

The Chancellor at some stage was persuaded to agree but when they both saw the P.M. late on Wednesday he dissented. He said that in ordinary circumstances he would have been prepared to put up bank rate but these were not ordinary circumstances. The Tories accepted that they would lose and were now in a mood to be vicious. He had just seen Heath on TV saying that sterling couldn't be kept out of the election and that a Labour victory would damage it. If bank rate went up they would at once point out with glee how right they were and that things must be a great deal more serious than the government had admitted for such a rise to take place now. The argument went on for some time and it was agreed that it would come up at Cabinet on Thursday as the first item. It must have been the subject of a long squabble because at 10.45 it still hadn't led to the promised telephone call to William.

Robert took the view that a rise might well alarm not calm the market and was interested chiefly in how to counter Heath's efforts to make sterling an election issue. Both he and William seemed to think this dirty tactics but Harold hadn't been altogether silent in October 1964. I contented myself with the comment that there was nothing much we could do if the Cabinet was already sitting and that a rise in bank rate made more sense either at the *beginning* of the election campaign (cf *The Economist* on 8%) or *later* once the financing problem came home and interest rates had to be levered up at the longer end. Both R. and I found the housing situation disquieting.

Later that day it emerged that the French had bought sterling and that we took in £2m. from the market. This news was greeted with much merriment when brought to the Chancellor's room although he didn't think it quite so funny after having been persuaded by Rowley C. The fact is that the big drop on Wednesday and earlier seems to have been due to Hamburg bankers who went bear of sterling, rightly judging the Bank of England's tactics which were to let the rate take the strain. The Chancellor himself had earlier (on Wednesday, I think) expressed some indignation that the Bank might use its reserves to steady the pound, pointing to the low rate to which the pound was allowed to fall in

---

[28] In the final quarter of 1965 sterling had remained consistently above par and the Bank of England had taken in £175m. in foreign exchange from the market. In February and March 1966, however, the sterling–dollar rate fell steeply but was held above $2.79 and recovered slightly in April. Over the first quarter as a whole, the Bank of England took in a net amount of £47 m. in foreign exchange. These results were partly due to an improvement in the current account, which was in surplus in the last quarter of 1965 but chiefly to an inflow of funds from abroad in both quarters.

October 1964. So he doesn't emerge much more satisfactorily than R.C. from the affair.

On Friday morning the economic advisers and others met in Eric Roll's room for a run over the paper we are to prepare. There then took place, for the first time in my recollection, a seminar on the factors governing growth in the UK that may not have been on a high standard but did at least show the different angles. Nicky gave us his dissertation on wider market opportunities and I said my piece on overloading and sluggish responses and John Jukes explained why there must never be any spare capacity and T.B. said that market forces were not enough and indeed very feeble. *Who* would reorganize British industry – was Beeching the best suggestion that we could put forward? So we moved on to Catherwood[29] (in his absence) and variety reduction, standardisation, and direct stimulation of productivity increases. Then William, who had got T.B. to be a *little* more specific, pointed out what a considerable administrative effort it added up to and the way in which, say, building controls were already exercised in three different departments (MPBW, Ministry of Housing – through talks with the building societies if they do take place – and Board of Trade).

In the meantime I had drafted a couple of pieces on Deflation and The Outlook and left Nicky to redraft them. He told me he thought we were really in agreement on most of the issues but I still find his and Robert's objective too ambitious for my liking, and they take too readily for granted that they can get agreement to devaluation. (In fact if their target of +£500m is accepted it *implies* devaluation so I've told Nicky he must put all he knows into this bit.)

Henry Brandon in *The Sunday Times* – where on earth did he get it all unless the main actors spilled the beans? It makes the secrecy of government a little silly.

Paris, Tuesday, 15 March   Dinner with Rupert Raw at the cafe in Rue Beaujolais. We discussed on the way back to the Bristol his part in the August/September operation. Originally he was went off to visit three countries and the idea was that he would visit Carli first because he was to mount the operation. But he argued – and his views were accepted – that the French were the key to the operation and that he should begin in Paris. It wasn't till he got to Germany that he became quite clear that it would not be possible to do the job bilaterally and that it would be necessary to get everybody round the table. Nor did anybody think till he suggested it of using the monthly meeting in Basle for this purpose. In fact he put it to Leslie O'B. that he'd have to go on to the Netherlands (his 4th country) and get Holtrop to agree. If the meeting were in Rome it would be obvious why the Central Bankers were meeting in force there whereas in Basle no one would suspect anything.

So off he went to Paris to see Clappier (and in fact get him back from holiday). Clappier [Deputy Governor of the Banque de France] at once said that the fact it was to be on a governmental footing made it more difficult, little as was

---

[29] Fred Catherwood Man. Dir. British Aluminium Co Ltd, 1962–64; Chief Industrial Adviser, DEA, 1964–66; Dir.-Gen., NEDC, 1966–71.

the room for manoeuvre by the Banque de France. The views of his Minister were known and didn't make for confidence in French participation. But he would try. Rupert at least felt justified in getting in first before the Americans because he rightly believed that it would be argued that it was all an American contrivance (and it was so argued in spite of his visit). The French at one time seemed to be in but an hour later phoned to say they were not. Similarly nobody knows now whether they will come in on the facilities discussed at the Basle meeting this month.

From Paris R. went to Rome and saw Carli, the Chancellor having spoken to Colombo. Then to Frankfurt where he saw Blessing[30] from 11 p.m. to 1 a.m. and B., after some dinner, offered to go at once to see Erhard. B. felt that the rate should go and said so. Erhard when B. spoke to him in the middle of his election campaign didn't mince his words and was not willing to help. He too thought the rate should go and didn't approve of the Labour Government's controls. Nevertheless B. was still prepared to listen. Rupert used both the pistol – the danger that sterling couldn't be held – and at the same time the carrot (that it might need only a little to rally sterling and get us round the corner). We couldn't stand another month like August but perhaps September could be quite different with a little help.

Meanwhile R. went off to see Holtrop whose wife had died very recently and who was pretty angry over the whole business. How could anybody suggest that he should simply buy guaranteed sterling? R. shouldn't be such a bloody fool to propose such a thing. B. had said much the same. It would be crazy to think of the Bundesbank buying sterling whatever Charlie Coombs might say. The market for sterling was in London not Frankfurt. There the market was in dollars and if he bought sterling people would think him crazy. It should be left to Bridge to use whatever facilities the Bundesbank offered. And in the end that is exactly what was agreed. The Nederlandsche Bank made a dollar deposit and the Bundesbank in effect did the same, so that it was left to the Bank of England to activate the facility except vis-à-vis New York where the Fed. could and did buy sterling. Total facilities were under $1 b. and we've only recently used the Italian facilities.

R. returned from Amsterdam to see B., again at 11 p.m. and B. on his own responsibility agreed to help. R. had previously engaged in argument with the Board of the Ned. Bank. He had to avoid any reference to freezing wages although this had been part of the original idea and had in fact comparatively little to go on. But he was enormously impressed by the courtesy and attention shown by the Central Bankers (especially when B. got him a room as a pseudo-President of a Landes-centralbank!).

I said that on the recent bank rate move Cromer had overplayed his hand and riled the Chancellor by suggesting adverse market reactions where none had shown themselves. Even on Thursday morning the market had been quiet

---

[30] Karl Blessing – Asst. to Dr Schacht,1929; Deputy Head of BIS,1930–34; Dir., German Unilever Group, 1939–41, 1948–57, Chm., 1952–57; President of the Bundesbank, 1958–69.

and it seemed a little unlikely that it was the hint of better trade figures that accounted for the inflow of foreign exchange from France in the afternoon. (R. said the Banque de France didn't know what had caused sterling to strengthen.) To bring in steel nationalisation was a mistake. (I made no reference to his threat of resignation which was an even bigger mistake on this particular issue.) But on top of this his speech on foreign investment was a direct attack on settled government policy. R. said that at Basle our capital exports were themselves the subject of criticism and he had pointed this out to the Governor. On the other hand, he was a man of great sincerity who spoke up for his beliefs and had undoubtedly great influence on his colleagues in Basle.

R. also told me a little about the last Basle meeting. Ansiaux said bluntly that he had no use for a new monetary unit. Emminger spoke for an hour summarizing the position on the Group of Ten "very lucidly". Blessing said that he thought the dollar was in a very different position now in the sixties from ten years ago, that we were in danger of entering an era of floating currencies and that if this happened he didn't see the French supporting the gold pool. (They were unwilling to feed in gold up to the previously agreed limit.)

R. also quoted Vocke[31] as saying some time ago that he didn't want the Dm. to be a reserve currency because the obligations involved weren't worth a minor German export industry.

Tuesday, 22 March   Last week in Paris for two days (recorded above) at E.P.C. on Tuesday and Wednesday. R.N. told me he had breakfast at 8 a.m. with Chancellor regularly before his press conferences.

Yesterday I told William I had decided against taking a year off. Suggested rise in bank rate on April 1st but William said it would be Maundy Thursday before we could act and that by April 15th the point of it all would have gone. Also drew attention to awkward position of D. Rickett and S. Goldman in relation to MTS since they knew that something was on foot.[32] I *didn't* say that Fred had already begun a paper on strategy in ignorance of what was afoot and that others might be doing the same.

Unemployment down again.

Monday morning: another long MTS meeting on R.N.'s draft which I hadn't read. T.B. said that Ministers would plump for deflation solution unless we made it absolutely obvious that this was too risky to be worth while. We wouldn't get them to pay any attention unless we made them see that there was no other way out than devaluation. (That afternoon he attacked Nicky again on this because Nicky insisted on keeping W. Godley's calculations). Douglas Allen said that coming fresh to the paper his question was what we did if Ministers refused to devalue and this was left very obscure. William said in reply to T.B. (who appealed to him as somebody standing closer to Ministers than the rest of us)

[31] Wilhelm Vocke – President, Deutsche Bundesbank, 1948–57.

[32] This is the first reference in the diary to the Medium Term Strategy Group but there had been previous meetings some of which may have been less formal (see entries for 23 and 27 February 1966).

that he thought they would not devalue in their present mood– there was so much to be unsaid, matter of honour, etc. Then the talk switched to the need to get strategy fixed since keeping options open was to have *no* strategy. We should fail to get enough deflation if Ministers didn't have an understanding that they would devalue later. William said he thought in matters of this kind it was almost impossible to keep secret and that it would only be if P.M. kept strategy hidden even from his colleagues that it would be successful. (This seemed to me far too pessimistic, given 1949 precedent.)

My own line was (a) to query the £500 m. target for balance of payments as excessive and insist that we needed to see where £300m would take us, (b) to doubt the passages about floating rates.

R.N. spent today on Fulton [33] so he couldn't do any redrafting. He goes on leave tomorrow night.

Lunch at Bank yesterday. Discussed interest rates with Governor. He is thinking of putting in a paper re-opening the question of capital gains tax on gilt-edged. I found him sympathetic to idea of a rise in bank rate in early April but I doubt whether he thought in terms of getting gilt-edged prices down in advance of the Budget.

Economic Trends is now firmly billed for the 31st in spite of T.B.'s intervention to get the Q4 balance of payments figures published earlier and support from George Brown no later than yesterday.

Wednesday, 23 March   Houblon Norman. Lunch at Bank of England next Bill Carron.

We spoke of wage structure in engineering, of Birmingham and of Scotland. He agreed on the virtues of time rate for the motor car industry and felt the BMC would have to go over to it sooner or later. The present arrangement meant built-in inflation through a succession of minor improvements that left piece rates unaffected and generated wage anomalies. The skilled man only too often got very little out of his training. But it was not only here that the industry was overloaded. It was true also of the US. And they had their weaknesses e.g. a more severe limitation on apprenticeship (1 in 7 only compared with 1 in 3). I didn't think it fair to ask about their union structure in comparison with ours. He cited the example of Cummins who finally came round to accepting that workers should vote for or against being represented by a union and choose their union (but 1 only) if they wanted one. They duly voted for the AEU. Cummins then produced a Bible-size agreement to be signed from which it appeared that Sunday work was to command no premium – this in Scotland! The founder, it appeared, was a Seventh Day Adventist.

Carron also spoke of the pace of work in Birmingham which he attributed entirely to historical circumstances. Then he praised the transformation of Lanarkshire. But he added "there is no news in peace". So nothing of this gets publicity.

[33] The Fulton Committee on the Civil Service, of which Robert Neild was a member, reported in June 1968.

Robert Hall said that he knew of at least two Permanent Secretaries who were thinking of getting out. I said that William complained of the shortage of good Deputy Secretaries. When I said that Douglas Allen was highly regarded by G.B., Robert said "Yes, but is G.B. highly regarded by Douglas Allen...". He also said how much at one time he would have been delighted to hear the news that Otto had left the Treasury. As for Tommy B. he was the P.M.'s only spy and not somebody the P.M. felt any need to turn to for advice. But of course it meant that people were more cautious with him around and he (R) didn't say things to Ministers because they would get to T.B.'s ears and through him to the P.M. Tony Crosland was an exception, as an old friend.

In the afternoon, the advisers held a final meeting on the paper for Ministers. We discussed the Summary of Conclusions and Nicky argued strongly for a recommendation on floating rates even if it were said explicitly that it was backed by four not five of us. R.N. persuaded him to leave the threefold choice in all its nakedness and I suggested that the third course might be headed "Letting the pound float or changing the parity" which seemed to please them. Tommy regards it as a useful pretext (like joining the Common Market) and Nicky is full of explanations of its strategic importance. I don't yet know what R.N. will do to the main part of the text.

T.B. said that we should certainly be cross-examined on our paper at Chequers or No.10. We shall see – I'm not so sure. I pointed out to Robert that it nowhere brought out the danger that we would go on thinking that *the Plan* was feasible when 25% was quite dead and even 20% increasingly hard to plan on. We've drafted exclusively in balance of payments terms.

T.B. had a similar objection. (Mine was just privately to R. alone.) Where did we say that industrial policy needed re-examination and the Whitehall arrangements for it needed overhauling? Were the Permanent Secretaries not going to sign a Report? Was this the last meeting? He was appalled and went off to see William after much backchat in which one after another of the Permanent Secretaries was sneered at: R. Powell for his hunted look, Eric for taking care not to associate himself with any advice we offered, etc.

They were all, for once, remarkably amiable even over my line on fixed rates which they accepted as a kind of natural outgrowth of a Treasury man, like a moustache.

R.N. has done a heroic job in getting a single document out of five such different economists and I'll be interested to see what the final text looks like. Nicky is still busy with appendices and T.B. will also have one on controls. He is torn between his past attitudes and his recognition of present needs so that he wants simultaneously to show how much *could* be done by controls and to acknowledge that they would not add up to the full amount needed. His preoccupation is with the political problem of assisting the digestion of Ministers if they have to make a heavy meal of their own words.

Heavy losses today and total for month now up in the fifties. Sent off my minute to William on bank rate yesterday.

(From mid-March the tide turned and losses on the month were exactly as declared in the form of reduced reserves – £27 m.)

Sunday, 3 April   The week was dominated by the election and by MTS meetings. I expected a majority of at least 100 and probably 140. In fact the swing was only 3% and pretty uniform between different parts of the country. Labour won fewer votes and a lower proportion of the total vote than in 1951 and its majority may be no better guarantee of a long spell in power than much larger majorities have been.[34]

Ely D. today commented that it should be seen in the light of the majority of 5 in 1964 which showed how difficult it was to dislodge the Tories in spite of an extraordinary series of bloomers and a hostile press with hardly anybody saying a good word for them.

We had a talk about the 2-party system and the resulting absence of sharp divisions on principle. E. pointed out that Ted didn't go very far with his attack on Trade Unions because he didn't dare to – he had to seek the middle ground. Elkin said this seemed to justify Marx's view of the two parties as part of a dialectic process with each defending the system and asked what the point of an election was if there was no genuine option. But Ely and I said that competition took this form under duopoly and remained competition in the sense that it was the pressure of one party that forced the other to adapt its policies. (E. quoted the way each party attacked the US while in opposition but rallied to the US when in power.)

MTS met thrice: on Monday and Tuesday I was at C.G. Boards and could do little. On Wednesday morning we had a frightful meeting with Nicky and Catherwood arguing about investment at enormous length. C. believes that we ought to have higher wages and would (apparently) up-value the pound at the same time if one took him literally. But what really emerged was that Eric and William meant to put in a paper of their own and that Tommy and Eric were making common cause. The P.M. had been told of what the Economic Advisers were doing and had exploded so T. was now trying to backtrack. William also made a number of simple points that expressed dissatisfaction with the idea that "going on as we are" wasn't viable. (He had seen me on Monday night and I let him have my paper.) T.B. had circulated a paper of dissent in which he said that he couldn't regard 2% unemployment as intolerable. But when I said that we should get calculations on this basis he went into his usual act about the horrors of deflation.

The next day R.N. was back and we had the paper by Permanent Secretaries handed to us. This was attacked in very moderate and sensible terms by R.N. and we had a good discussion in more realistic terms than any so far. R. had squared us all beforehand and I had pointed out that we couldn't devalue before about December and that Ministers couldn't be expected to make up their minds finally this month. Equally most of the devices for direct action or new taxes needed two or more years and were therefore not very relevant to the immediate situation. Tommy gave us a repeat of earlier arguments about the danger that Ministers or Perm. Secs. would have heart attacks and his desire to improve their life expectancy. He stressed the vulnerability of the pound with £400 m.

---

[34] Labour's overall majority was 97.

to be drawn on if the trade figures were bad for a quarter. But he was equally seized of the disadvantages of devaluation. The 10% surcharge hadn't done much good, so why should a 10% devaluation?

Nicky provided the counterpoint with long expositions of his latest theory of growth, Verdoorn's Law[35] and the need to make the manufacturing sector expand (if necessary by taxing services).

T. had distributed a new introductory section to the Perm. Sec.'s paper (which fortunately it was agreed to redraft). R. suggested (as previously agreed) that only our conclusions should go to Ministers and that they should be embodied in the Perm. Sec.'s paper.

What we all dislike were what N.K. called the "tranquillizers" in the paper – the long list of things to be looked at when we knew that they wouldn't stand examination. He said it was a well-known dodge to provide plenty of bulk so as to convey the impression that there must be *some* substance in it.

On Thursday night we went to the club party at Henry Hardman's and came away before 1 a.m. E.R. was there and so was Tom Padmore, Otto C., Plowden, etc., etc.

On Friday the final meeting also went pretty well. In the morning R.N. got us to accept his redraft of the conclusions. In the afternoon we had a long session on a revised draft which seemed to offer the prospect of meeting us all. There was some chaff about Ministerial reactions. N.K. told Tommy: "Don't let us ask what Ministers will say" to which T. replied "We *know* what Ministers will say". "You're unduly sensitive", said N.

William asked us at the end about the Plan and public expenditure and got over the point that the Plan would have to be revised drastically and that it was urgent to get public expenditure reviewed if GDP was going to increase by less then 20% instead of 25%.

We had had a CM(O) meeting on Wednesday and this passed off uneventfully on the basis of my draft submission. I talked after it with Denis who felt that we were making a tactical blunder in talking of £200-250 m. so I stiffened my Conclusion and made it "preferably at the upper end of the range". D. was also unhappy about control of capital exports on a basis that had proved highly unpopular in 1962 but recognized that the decision had to take account of the wider discussions from which he was excluded. He agreed that if deflation didn't improve the balance of trade he would be ready to contemplate devaluation in a year's time. (Which is exactly what I had put as my view to William.)

Tuesday, 5 April   George Brown asked to see me at 3 today. I chatted in the private office to de Burgh who told me that at Christmas nothing was done except Fairfield's and oil for Rhodesia. George was single-minded when worked up. In due course the Paymaster General [George Wigg] emerged, giving me a hard look as if I were a horse he had not yet decided to back. G.B. was cheerful and informal and spared me the persiflage I had half expected. Of course I

[35] Professor Verdoorn, a Dutch economist, laid it down that economies of scale made output rise faster than employment, so raising labour productivity as market expanded.

knew what he was going to say. He started by explaining the difficulties he had had in finding someone to take Shone's place. The names acceptable to one side were blackballed by the others. So he had in the end decided that he'd just have to make an appointment. It appeared that there *was* some possibility of finding someone acceptable to everybody and he thought that I would be. I expressed surprise. George said he wanted to know whether I was interested. I said that the job seemed to call for gifts that I didn't have: a political sense, a capacity to administer, etc. George replied that he regarded me as an economist interested in applying theory to industry. I told him that I knew my limitations and my instincts were against accepting but that I'd like a little more time for reflection. Did he want to know by tomorrow? He apparently had had some hope of trying it out on NEDC at tomorrow's meeting but didn't press this. At rather a late stage, he mentioned that Catherwood was also acceptable to both sides but whether he had talked to C., he didn't say. I asked if he had spoken to the Chancellor. No. he said, but he *had* spoken to the P.M. who entirely approved.

I remained non-committal and George made no effort to persuade me beyond saying as I left that there would be a lot to be done. He had earlier stressed the work of the little Neddies and spoken critically of Robert Shone – he was not very articulate, and he dragged in the things he was personally interested in instead of getting on with what G.B. obviously thought was the job (i.e. he put in papers on savings and taxation instead of industrial efficiency).

I had already made up my mind quite firmly against accepting. Five years in NEDC would drive me mad: I should be associated with the Plan, like it or not; no decent staff; turned into a diplomatist with no real experience of industrial relations. And what about the Economic Section? The only attractive side to it was the idea of a change of job.

Naturally I made no mention of Selwyn Lloyd's offer of the job to me in 1962.

Yesterday we had a further MTS meeting, most of it very unexciting. But at the end T.B. spoke up strongly against *contemplating* going into Europe until we were strongly competitive. He now accepts that we might hope to be in this condition in a few years' time – presumably through devaluation although he keeps twitting Nicky about the exaggerated hopes that Nicky places on devaluation. "I'm not so sure of my theories as some people are". They both enjoy explaining how we must dynamise British industry. N. said he thought the danger (à propos of Europe) was that our financiers would be far quicker off the mark than our industrialists. They were full of ideas for mergers, cartels, etc. that would mean pouring more British capital into Europe when our balance of payments wouldn't support it. He also really wants to blow up the payments system and so isn't at all worried by the stock rejoinders to the idea of a floating rate. T.B. on the other hand does see the drawbacks of putting up import prices in a sluggish economy and antagonising everybody (including those who hold pounds) at the same time.

At Friday's meeting last week T.B. in recounting the P.M.'s attitude told us that he had argued that the Americans would bale us out if necessary. None of us thought this at all likely.

Victor Chapin drew my attention at lunch to the *Guardian* report that Michael Foot[36] had been offered the Home Secretaryship last year when it went to Jenkins.

When I talked to Ely on Sunday he made the point that Trade Unionists rarely want to go into the House of Commons since they have a wider scope in their own Union or in the TUC. He quoted Lewis Wright[37] when half drunk to the effect that, after all, you might end up Chairman of a Nationalised Industry if you were on the TUC General Council but if you went to Parliament and bored it with speeches about cotton you got nowhere. (He had Ernest Thornton[38] in mind.)

Wednesday, 13 April

In preparing his 1966 Budget for introduction on 2 May, the Chancellor was anxious to avoid an increase in any existing tax but agreed that additional tax revenue was needed. He was therefore attracted by a proposal by Professor Kaldor for the introduction of a new tax later described as Selective Employment Tax. With a Budget due in under three weeks it seemed inconceivable that such a new tax could be devised in time, especially if it did not take the form of a simple tax on services. A scheme was, however, introduced, to come into operation in September, and was expected to raise £315 million in the current financial year. It involved levying £1.25 per week on employers for all adult men in employment, half that amount for women and boys, and 40p for girls. Manufacturing industries would receive a 130 per cent refund and there was to be a 100 per cent refund for the public sector and for transport undertakings.

All this meant the collection and subsequent refunding of vast sums of cash with an unknown length of time between collection and reimbursement. The delay was bound to intensify the credit squeeze. There would be a large and immediate demand for additional credit, and the consequences for industry if no additional credit could be provided were hard to foresee. A further difficulty was how to draw the line between manufacturing and services when work done in manufacturing was fundamentally a form of service. So far as the public was concerned, they could see the point of a tax on services and of a subsidy to manufactures in the interest of encouraging exports, but they were mystified by Professor Kaldor's rationale which seemed to imply that the tax was designed to force labour out of services into manufacturing and yet raise productivity in both.

Wednesday, 13 April   I've made no entry on the events of last Wednesday and Thursday which included further MTS meetings and a meeting with the

[36] Michael Foot – Managing Dir., *Tribune*, 1945–74.

[37] Lewis Wright Secretary of one of the Unions in the textile trades.

[38] Ernest Thornton – Sec., United Textile Factory Workers' Assoc., 1943–53; President, Amalgamated Weavers Assoc., 1960–65; Lab. Jr. Parliamentary Sec., Min. of Labour, 1964–66.

Chancellor on Wednesday on the Budget. This began with a declaration that he didn't like the idea of raising purchase tax one bit and some questions about domestic pressure e.g. the slower rise in hire purchase debt. I gave my usual account of the forces at work (but all on the domestic side since this was what was asked for) and agreed that demand had been checked although unemployment had gone on falling. He then raised the question of a possible surcharge on the employers N.I. contribution and I tried to ride it off by saying that higher wages would do the job just as effectively (he wanted to cut labour hoarding by a species of pay-roll tax). But Nicky now intervened and it became apparent that he was serious about trying to get into the Budget a surcharge that would be rebated on manufacturing as defined for the purposes of the investment grants, and would therefore fall exclusively on "services". Robert was not present but he was said to favour this. It seemed to me inconceivable that such a scheme could be worked out in time but the Chancellor was obviously set on something other than raising purchase tax. So further meetings were fixed up, one for 5.30 that evening and the idea is still in play in spite of heavy blows on Thursday. The Chancellor raised it with the P.M. on Thursday and went off on holiday without giving any idea to Customs what options he wanted kept open (and they need to know at once) for purchase tax changes. Naturally the P.M. is sympathetic and according to the Chancellor on Wednesday was absolutely thunderstruck at the idea of raising a further £200 m. in purchase tax. As well he might be ! It was Jack Diamond who said how such a budget would look to the Labour Party fresh from its victory at the polls. He wanted something on the surcharge allowance to make it look a little less regressive. But the Chancellor did not query our assessment of £200-250 m. even if he first said £200 m. and then had to correct it, almost absent-mindedly, to £200-250 m.

When I saw William this evening about all this he was a little desperate. We still have to get the Chancellor to decide on an increase that is feasible as against one that is not and then to persuade his colleagues while the options narrow steadily as time goes on. G.B. knows what is our assessment but is naturally as strongly against higher purchase tax as the Chancellor and more strongly against disinflation.

As to MTS we had a brief meeting with R.P. present but not Robert N. on Wednesday morning before we saw the Chancellor. The draft by this time was one incorporating as Pt II the conclusions of the Economic Advisers but with a general introductory part on how we got to our present situation and a concluding part on the changes in policy that could be made, consistent with present parity and no severe deflation. Discussion focussed on Part III and the quantification of measures on invisibles and the capital flow: then moved on to the conclusion. As William pointed out a great deal of Part III made sense *without* any consideration of the alternatives and did not really represent an alternative in itself. But he didn't draw from this the conclusion that we must therefore devalue or deflate.

When we met again in the afternoon the time was wasted with Catherwood at his most tiresome until at last William decided to intervene with his own views. It then became clear that the three Permanent Secretaries were not prepared to recommend devaluation and William gave six reasons why he was unwilling to do so. It was a very able performance, heard sympathetically by everybody, especially T.B., (I couldn't quite fathom that) while I tried to get across the point that if Ministers waited too long they might let the reserves go before making up their minds.

When I asked today what had happened on strategy William said that the P.M. had heard what was going on from Burke T. and had said flatly that he was not prepared to receive advice based on a change in parity. (Now abideth these three, faith, hope and parity and the greatest of these is parity.) It would be for each Minister to let his advisers know that this was the position and that they should frame their advice accordingly. Of course if, as William emphasised several times, the way to a successful devaluation of the pound lies through a single-minded strategy not communicated to everybody but kept close by the P.M. himself, we may yet see a great stroke later on. But, remembering 1949, I doubt whether this the right way to go about it.

Meanwhile the Chancellor has charged ahead on control of investment in the sterling area and the Australians are already arriving to discuss the scheme. D.Jay asked why we couldn't wait until *after* the Budget and the answer is obscure. It also seems odd to consult, without taking the major decision first. William said today that we might easily see the end of the sterling area any day now. The P.M. was sent a minute last Tuesday, agreed on Wednesday almost by return, and a cable went off that day. T.B. had the minute at MTS and (if I heard aright) thought it crazy.

He also got very worked up over the absence of any discussion of the H.K. gap in the memo on strategy and exploded about the months that had passed since he had drawn the Treasury's attention to the losses involved. William soothed him down, pointing out that other gaps might take its place.

But what of the memo? William proposed to cut out Pt II (so that the Economists' Report disappears for good) and develop Pt III and present the document as the best we can offer on the middle course recommmended.

I've left out any mention of the meeting of the Pol. Econ. Club last Wednesday at which Nigel Lawson gave a disquisition to a large group on the necessity of devaluation. I took Fred Atkinson with me and made extensive notes for William (which I didn't use). Went by tube with V. Feather who seemed anything but enthusiastic about Catherwood as a successor to Robert Shone. He said he had understood that I was to succeed him. From earlier remarks by N. Lawson I should judge that he too had heard this but was more up-to-date.

Monday, 18 April   I came back to work last Wednesday, R. on Thursday (I think), Nicky on Friday, T.B. (I believe) today. Meanwhile the great pay-roll levy gathers momentum.

Yesterday Ian B. rang me up to say that Chancellor wanted to talk to me today with a view to a paper from me, as a bystander, on the scheme. I went in to meeting at 4.30 and found William and Eric in the private office. They gave me the gist of it before we adjourned to go over Peter Vinter's draft with Nicky, Robert and Wynne. It then became clear that it was pretty well accepted although Chancellor had nearly been argued out of it on Friday. He had seen P.M. and G.B. and had apparently claimed that the Inland Revenue could collect a tax on services, only to find that when he saw A.J. this idea was knocked to bits in five minutes.

On Friday morning when I saw R.N. (we went off to lunch at the canteen) the scheme seemed far from accepted and Chancellor had been spouting ideas about bringing in Min. of Labour. R.N. made it clear that idea might have originated with him but it was Nicky who seized on idea of using surcharge and that he (R) didn't see how the scheme could be framed adequately by May 3. When I saw him tonight he still had deep reservations about it e.g. because it might do very little for the balance of payments and quite a lot by way of disinflation.

So today I had to prepare two memoranda for the Chancellor for submission before I left the office and also spend the morning (after 10) interviewing cadets. All largely without benefit of consultation although I saw Fred in the afternoon and Wynne for a few minutes before he went to one more meeting. I left the office after 8 leaving William still at it. He told me he hated the scheme with its vast surges of money to and fro all for the sake of £100 m. of disinflation. In his view the P.M. wants a tax on services, not this great machine of collection and refunding with well over £1,000 m. flowing into the Exchequer. But he thinks that there is now too little time to adapt the scheme so that it is a pure tax on services.

I told him that the real difficulty was to avoid doing too much in the Budget if the scheme were introduced, because its effects would be largely unpredictable and it would therefore be necessary to have *on top of it* some predictable disinflation. This seemed to me to point to an increase in income tax which would be necessary sooner or later anyhow and would have an effect on opinion about the pound quite different from the levy. But if income tax *were* increased, might we not overdo things?

My other memo (on the scheme itself) was too general and lacked bite. But there was no time to redo it. P.M., Chancellor, and First Secretary meet tomorrow to make key decisions.

Fred suggested use of regulator to cover "summer gap". But we *couldn't* do that in a Budget.

Chancellor said after his talk with me and once Ian withdrew that he was glad I hadn't taken Neddy job and that he had other things in mind for me which he couldn't specify. He hoped I would warn him before I went off to do anything else. I said I didn't propose to quit but that he didn't lack for economic advice. I also said that my first question to G.B. had been whether Chancellor was aware of approach to me. Chancellor said G.B. had told P.M. he would speak to him (Chancellor) before approaching me.

Tuesday, 19 April   Had another brief word with Chancellor who was worried about the summer gap and about the discrepancy between the effect of his scheme on the Budget and on the economy. He seemed to have a lot of revenue for very little deflation. I reassured him on the gap, especially if he were prepared to put up income tax but he himself raised the possibility of petrol tax.

I wasn't clear whether he had in mind a full year or some shorter period.

By the time I got back from C.S.C. William had called a meeting to give us details of agreement between Ministers (the 3). They want to exempt *all* transport and practically all Group B (public services and nationalised industries) and repay manufacturing no more than it pays. This drove N.K. and R. to despair, R. saying that the baby had been given away and the bath water kept. Wynne went home to do the calculations in peace (from N.K.) and I had to get Fred and Jim Shepherd[39] to brief me for my own paper. Ministers don't want to use any other taxes and it looks as if they won't need to if they want effects *next* year. Their plan is excellent for *1967* but is being rushed through as if it were vital to *1966*. There is now no balance of payments twist which R. thought the key to it all.

Earlier N.K. had rung me up to congratulate me on my submission of yesterday but when he saw my supplementary paper he was very depressed and said I was not on the side of the angels. When I suggested that he would only lower export costs by 1% he rejoined that we were likely to break up the sterling area for £40 m. and his scheme would add £120 m. to exports.

Once again it was 8.30 p.m. before I got away and William was still at it. The Treasury is obviously being kept busy.

Chancellor mentioned that G.B. had pointed out to him that scheme would mean big increase in *net* revenue this financial year since repayments would be delayed. He wasn't clear how this affected the economy and suggested we might use special deposits but left this very obscure (he may have meant *reduce* them but I think he still had the summer gap at the back of his mind).

Sunday, 24 April   Saturday morning at Academic Advisory Committee for new Institute at Sussex. T.B. came late saying he couldn't possibly get up for a 10 a.m. meeting (it was 9.45) and offering to interest the P.M. in opening the Institute.

On Wednesday William told us that Ministers had now taken decisions involving no rebate in excess of the levy, private and public transport left out altogether, and agriculture and local government practically exempt. This left N.K. "very low" and he and Robert stayed to see what could be saved. By Thursday there were working out projects involving a subsidy again (I don't know how this got back in) at higher rates of contribution. We thought an increase in petrol duty would be needed but were told that this was out. Nevertheless Chancellor seems to have kept the option open.

We had a long meeting with Chancellor on Thursday on exchange control proposals – not on policy but on administration – with Governor and others. We agreed *not* to raise 25% retention from switch surrenders to 50% – N.K. spoke up against because he wanted to see sales and too high a figure would cause switches to be very expensive. But he was against *exempting* switches as the Bank of England proposed, again because he wanted net realisations.

---

[39] James Shepherd – NIESR, 1960–64; Treasury, 1965–80 (initially with Economic Section).

Sam G, seemed keen on the whole range of proposals, including those for controlling cap. inv. in sterling area. The Australians have asked why we should risk breaking up the sterling area for so little.

Sunday, 1 May   On Monday we had a meeting which I took to be MTS but proved to be on the surcharge. It was mainly of interest because T.B. while unwilling to argue positively in favour of retention wanted to rub in the risks that its removal involved. We were all pretty clear by the end that whatever followed (and T.B. obviously wanted to keep import quotas in reserve) the surcharge could not be retained beyond Nov. 26. Eric tried to argue for an announcement at Berne but William was irrefutable in his claim that it would have to be the Budget. The alternative would make the government look like dithering or yielding to pressure and create general consternation *before* Berne.

On Friday morning we had a meeting on monetary policy to which M. Allen came for the Bank. I said that we might get pressure in gilt-edged market and shouldn't resist it because long rates should go up if we meant to enforce a squeeze. But Sam is obviously happy at renewed strength of market and takes no account of fact that in Q1 we took in £350 m. in stock, a fact that will emerge in a few months.

Meanwhile the Chancellor has abandoned his compulsory scheme for limiting investment in sterling area and the voluntary scheme is being substituted with Ireland in. In fact the scheme won't look very voluntary, given the procedures to be followed.

I've had less of a hand in the Budget this year than ever before except in Nov. 1964. But Wynne has been kept very busy and was at work today with R.N. when I called at the Treasury. R.N. was also in yesterday.

On Thursday as I left I looked in on Ian B. and he told me of the day's high comedy. First they had to cope with Crossman who was due to deputise for G. Brown in the debate on Address and had a speech ready extolling what the government had done for construction industry. This obviously needed to be rewritten and Ian had to intercept him at No.11, charging upstairs at 2 p.m. and hollering for food. His first remark on hearing of the levy scheme was: "And what will it do to us poor farmers?". No thought of housing! But on Wednesday Tony Part[40] had launched an irate note in defence of construction and on Thursday the Chancellor had to face a threat of resignation from Reg Prentice[41]. But he did it in his best Big Jim style lying back and telling Reg, "Well, of course, you can always take it to Cabinet but that won't take you anywhere. Or, put it another way, I'd have to go!".

Lots of fun about Governorship of Bank, announced on Tuesday. It is true, as *Sunday Times* says, that Leslie O'Brien was told when appointed Deputy

[40] Anthony Part – Dep. Sec., Min. of Education, 1960–63; Min. of Public Building & Works, 1963–65; Perm. Sec., Min. of PBW, 1965–68; Board of Trade, 1968–70.

[41] Reg Prentice – Lab. Minister of State, Dept. of Education and Science, 1964–66; Minister of Public Building and Works, 1966–67; Minister of Overseas Development, 1967–69.

Governor that he mustn't regard this as stepping stone to Governorship and in fact that this was excluded. But I don't know why they think the big row was with Maudling. Obviously Leslie won't take a public stand with the same backing as Cromer could and can hardly be a public figure in the same way. But doubtful how long Bank of England can remain spokesman of the City on essentially political matters. *Guardian* had a silly leader and Fred Hirsch[42] is also well off beam today. When I commiserated with Leslie on Wednesday about press publicity he told me, "Well, I rather like it".

Tuesday, 3 May   Budget Day and *The Times* carrying front page news. The Budget was better received than I feared – at least by the House of Commons. The Chancellor had gathered an enormous number of minor proposals which occupied the first $3/4$ hr and had the House somnolescent if wary. He raised a laugh on Siamese Twins and later on the bookies. But it was only when he seemed to be playing cat and mouse over purchase tax and income tax that he had their undivided attention. This was partly due to a passage by William about his budget judgment which *seemed* to imply that he *would* impose higher taxes of the usual type: for the succeeding passage knocked this down as if by design. The exposition of SET was very good and well done, thanks, I imagine to R.N. but with an unmistakeable Kaldoresque flavour of ingenuity and complexity that didn't escape Sam Cross. I got in one passage on the effect in terms of prices that obviously stuck.

Ted Heath made an effective comment when his turn came – after a seemingly endless series of resolutions. He asked the question we expected: why we thought a tax on services should save labour if a subsidy to manufacturing didn't waste it. (Richard Marsh[43] had taken a somewhat similar line in Cabinet.)

As I left the House with Sam Cross I met Bruce-Jardyne[44] who felt that the Chancellor couldn't know what the tax would do and was therefore in the dark about the risk to the balance of payments. Ted H. had taken the line that the Budget was insufficiently deflationary and that the Chancellor had scrupled to tax the consumer because of the nearness of the election and had devised a way of taxing industry that hid from the consumer what was being done.

At P.E. Club the discussion was disappointing. William spoke at length, nominally on matters of fact, but in the end in defence of the tax (which he doesn't really believe in). Nicky foolishly came next and gave a defence of Mercantilism that prayed in aid the sacred name of Adam Smith– he also made it clear that it was the structural and balance of payments effects that he was after, not just the redressing of the balance between services and commodities. E. Boyle said that you had to get exports up first and draw in more labour into

[42] Fred Hirsch – Leader writer on *The Economist*.

[43] Richard Marsh – Chm., Inter-Departmental Committee to Coordinate Govt. Policy on Industrial Training, 1964; Parliamentary Sec., Min. of Labour, 1964–65; Jt. Parliamentary Sec., Min. of Technology, 1965–66; Minister of Power, 1966–68; Minister of Transport, 1968–69; Chm., British Railways Board, 1971– .

[44] Jock Bruce-Jardyne – Foreign Editor, *The Statist*, 1961–64; MP for South Angus, 1964–74.

manufacturing, not vice versa. He also thought that more deflation especially via cuts in collective consumption was necessary. E. Compton[45] pointed to clumsiness of the financial arrangements and the temptation to industry to adapt its structure and escape tax. M. Parsons also wanted cuts in expenditure. Morton thought GATT would object. F. Paish pointed out that it was not as deflationary as it seemed (which I reinforced) – contrary to Cockfield's[46] introduction which suggested that it involved deflation of the order of £500 m. David Eccles[47] and V. Feather seemed to think that Trade Unions would ask for the 37.5p refund offered to manufacturers. On the whole, not a very good discussion – I thought Ted Heath made a better job of it at less notice.

Sunday, 8 May   Plenty of discussion on the new tax. Spoke on Friday to A. Vice who used my remarks in *Sunday Times*. Very naughty of him as he had seen Chancellor previous day and had no need to call on me. Opposition to tax is greater than I had expected but on the whole more sensible line is emerging (e.g. M. Naylor today). I suppose my own attitude derives largely from suspicion that poll taxes, pay-roll taxes etc. don't have the effect on productivity that is commonly believed and that I therefore measure taxes in terms of the harm they avoid not the good they do. A great deal of the feeling regarding this tax is due to the double or treble discrimination – not just that somebody pays but that others actually get paid. The fact that the tax is popularly associated with idea of labour hoarding makes it worse since even in the Cabinet some Ministers (e.g. R. Marsh) think that it is manufacturing that is the hoarder. (I took a lot of trouble to pour cold water on this idea. Nearly every manufacturer wants *more* labour not less and it is only in long run terms that employment is excessive in relation to output – except perhaps for 30–50,000.)

Economist line that philosophy runs counter to investment grants already urged by R.N. But this is only if it is thought of as a tax on employment not on services. Distinction between tax on commodities and tax on employment is more apparent, and so no similar objection urged against indirect taxation.

Business men think we could easily find better export incentives that don't infringe GATT and so can't see why manufacturers should get this payment on their employment.

Tuesday, 10 May   Tuesday Club on the Budget, Robert Hall speaking for first time on this since leaving Whitehall. He approved *The Economist* line and said at one point that he regarded a pay-roll tax as ideal type of indirect taxation (though not for Shone's reasons). He also attacked the timing of the Budget and thought that if we meant to depress demand we should do so now, not in

[45] Sir Edmund Compton – Third Sec., Treasury, 1949–58; Comptroller and Auditor General, 1958–66; Ombudsman, 1967–71.

[46] Arthur Cockfield (later Lord) – Man. Dir., Boots Pure Drug Co Ltd, 1961–67; NEDC, 1962–64.

[47] David Eccles (later Lord) – President, Board of Trade, 1957–59; Minister of Education, Oct. 1959–July 1962; Director, Courtaulds, 1962–70.

September. There were some signs of the cycle turning and by September the Chancellor might want to go back on the tax or use the regulator if he was really serious about full employment as one of his Triple Objectives.

E. Boyle asked if we really thought that faster growth could be triggered off by a transfer from services to manufacturing and in private told me later that he recognised that this was Nicky's idea but that it couldn't in his view offer us enough leverage, as export-led growth would. He cited Japan as the outstanding example of a country where exports had not been leading element in early stages.

Wednesday, 11 May   Trial of the Pyx. On the way back with the Chancellor he asked me (a) to speak to the Prime Warden about the manufacture of sovereigns (which he thinks we should stop), and (b) to do a study of housing statistics with T.B. There was apparently a disagreement with Crossman on the figures this morning and the P.M. suggested that I should do a report in the next fortnight (with Tommy, though this was something of an afterthought). Spoke to Bill Nield who didn't have the minutes but read out chunks (the P.M. said that I had been "a progress chaser of aero engines in the war and used very modern techniques"! – what a travesty by somebody who ought to know better). Spoke also to Steve who said he knew better than to accept his Minister's version without checking against the minutes.

Evening in honour of Otto who spoke of the impact on him of his new Ministry (Technology). He had found how remote they were from Treasury, how they still thought of Treasury view as it was 5 years ago so that he had to suggest gently that they had the wrong end of the stick, how they thought the Treasury actually well disposed to the Concorde, and how little they understood the more general aspects of economic policy down the line. (He mentioned 450 people earning over £3,000 a year and total employment of 40,000). I thought most of what he said not at all surprising and a reflection on the Treasury if it came as news to them.

Sam Goldman said he thought that eventually Treasury would be fragmented and we would lose the Management function and control of public expenditure to DEA.

Monday, 16 May   On Friday before TUC meeting Chancellor suggested that I talk to Gordon Dennis of Eastman and Dennis who, he said, thought that the housing market was saturated partly because of the security offered by the new Rent Act. I saw him today in a little office in Westminster Palace Gardens and he talked ten to the dozen, mainly about the financial difficulties of buyers and builders. What is clear is that people who see the market in operation know far more than comes out in the figures.

The TUC meeting was a bit of a pantomime with the Chancellor acting the ex-Trade Union leader and Harry Douglass[48] being very solicitous about

---

[48] Harry Douglass (later Lord) Gen. Sec., Iron and Steel Trades Confederation, 1953–

productivity and thrift. He felt that deflation would injure the one and high rates of interest on mortgages damage the other by preventing the spread of house ownership. Harry Nicholas[49] said that SET would cost his union £60,000 a year, and that his men wouldn't understand why their Union paid while their opposite numbers involved no similar liability e.g. to employees in the docks or on London Transport. The Chancellor congratulated him on his efforts to raise productivity but felt that some cooperation from him on incomes would help, which provoked the usual stuff about members on rates below £10, followed a couple of sentences later by the remark that rates hardly mattered compared with earnings. Chancellor told them that we expected growth by 2 – 3% this year which is in fact too high.

After the meeting we chaffed Harry D. about his interest in unit trusts, and he told us that he had put his Union's money into equities 12 or more years ago. He had cut down on benefits, pushed hard on subscriptions and now had £4 m. invested and growing steadily. He told us that this was the way to make men hesitate before striking. If they had something to lose they would be more willing to make terms.

There was some talk about the seamen and we were told that the men were in a mood to strike even if there were given all they asked for. In fact last year's agreement was a bad one and affected the men unequally (e.g. it hit the coastal shipping workers compared with the others).[50]

Today lunched at Bank. Governor didn't seem worried by exchange losses which had already reached £15 m. (but were over £50 m. by the end of the day). We concentrated on interest rates and I argued that over the year we could hardly hope to hold up gilt-edged so that we ought to beat a retreat while the going was good. Governor not in disagreement but wanted to consult his staff.

Dined at LSE with Henry P-B., Douglas Allen, Barnes, Roberts,[51] Albert Rees, Aubrey Jones. Very illuminating on US labour practice. At one point Henry said, "Yes. We quite understand. We had the same situation here in 1891–3 when the Royal Commission on Trade Unions was told that employers liked strong unions, etc.". But, he added, with full employment the Union may be helpless and the Union official too busy (e.g. Denis B. said they couldn't arrange a meeting with the Railwaymen before July 1 at the earliest). I suggested that Conferences would have to be programmed but perhaps they should be taken before the Nat. Boards. Aubrey Jones said that he'd like a clutch of productivity agreements brought before the Board.

First meeting of ES(G) under Eric. We did little except list the jobs to be

---

67; Member, NEDC, 1962–67; Chm., TUC Economic Committee, 1962–67; Monopolies Commission, 1967–70.

[49] Harry Nicholas – Treasurer, Labour Party, 1960–64; Asst. Gen. Sec., Metal and Engineering Group, 1956–68; Gen. Sec. of Labour Party, 1968–72.

[50] A seamen's strike began on 16 May after the breakdown of talks with the Prime Minister and was settled after 46 days on 1 July, on terms rejected earlier by the National Union of Seamen.

[51] Ben Roberts – Professor of Industrial Relations, LSE, 1962–84; Editor, British Journal of Industrial Relations, 1963–89.

done. Donald was back (and Tommy) but took very calmly the statement that we needed to know rate of growth by May 24 for purposes of planning public expenditure. G.B. is committed to issuing a review of the Plan by the end of the year but *may* be able to wriggle out. T.B. and N.K. both want review of sectoral problems only (e.g. fuel). T.B. very excited about price of North Sea gas. But I recall M. Stevenson on Friday saying that if there hadn't been a long struggle by himself and others who had shown the necessary foresight there would *be* no North Sea gas. The Sunday press even suggests that T.B. is in charge of the negotiations over gas!

Friday, 20 May   Friday night and a report on housing to prepare over the week-end. D. Butt[52] for lunch, Saraceno[53] for dinner and Vlady Pertot[54] to stay the night.

Saw T.B. in many curious places: on Monday at ES(G) the new steering group under Eric; on Tuesday at Judith Hart's meeting to find an economist for the C.R.O.; on Wednesday first at No.10 (where he is now installed) and then at the Committee of Management for the Economist Class under Philip Allen; today at my housing meeting. P. Allen tells me that in evidence to Fulton he was excellent on his first appearance when he made a statement but left no time for questions: then destroyed this good impression on his second appearance.

When I called on him on Wednesday it was after I had gathered from Bill Nield that he had made a fuss about the decision on housing to get me to make a report when he had just submitted one. This had moved the P.M. to set up a further group, clearly for the purpose of keeping T.B. happy.

Lunch at Bank on Monday. Tried to get the Governor to think of letting gilt-edged fall in price while the going was good. On Thursday lunched with Mr Wellby (the Prime Warden) who travelled to Tokyo last year with his sister by Trans-Sib. He wanted us to mint gold coins of £10 face value and £5 gold content like the beautiful ones minted for Tonga.

Took A. Williams[55] to see Sir C. Cunningham[56] this morning. Sir C. thought he might be able to tell us in a few days that there really was no point in having an economist in the Home Office. But D. Butt said this was nonsense. For example, an economist would soon point out that Borstals cost several times as much per head as Oxford Colleges!

Little Frogs, Whitmonday, 30 May   Last week was pretty uneventful if very busy. I worked through Saturday and Sunday on my housing report and got it

---

[52] David Butt – Econ. Section, Treasury, 1946–52; Asst. Sec., 1952–62; Australian National University, 1962–76.

[53] Pasquale Saraceno – Italian economist; joined IRI 1933; Prof. of Indus. Economics, Univ. of Venice from 1959; Vice-Pres. SVIMEZ.

[54] V. Pertot – Croat economist; fellow student at Cambridge in early 1930's.

[55] A H Williams – Economic Consultant, Treasury, 1968.

[56] Sir Charles Cunningham – Permanent Under-Sec. of State, Home Office, 1957–66; Dep. Chm., UK Atomic Energy Authority, 1966–71.

round for discussion on Tuesday. Tommy came half on hour late and by that time everybody had agreed on the document so that all he could raise were points of detail. The Ministry of Housing were very pleased. On Thursday evening we all went to No.10 to see T.B. about *his* draft (which hadn't reached me). He had spoken earlier as if it were to be full of recommendations and of course it did end with a whole series of them when he was asked for a *forecast*. But he cut them all out when Douglas Henley[57] said he couldn't accept them on behalf of his Department. This still left no forecast, but none of us wanted to press this on Tommy. His thesis is that we need to go for contingency planning (i.e. be ready to give more approvals for public sector houses) because there is an inherent instability in the present situation – either starts will go up or they will come down but they won't go on at their present level (which is *exactly* what they *have* been doing for quite a time).

There is still tremendous activity over SET and many officials went in on Friday. Anxiety about the effects of the seamen's strike also beginning but on the whole our losses have been modest.

I gather that the Chancellor has been rather prickly recently e.g. on Erhard's[58] visit and that there were times when both of them went on talking at the same time for nearly a full minute.

Lunch with Bruce Williams on Thursday. He was very impressed with the Soviet Institutes he saw in Russia and argues that even if they represent what British Universities fear, it may be better to go for Institutes. I said that it seemed to me relatively easy to build up big research units on heavy industry and defence but far harder to get science geared to needs of consumer and that Institutes were not as satisfactory as adequate staff in the individual enterprise. I doubt whether the Russians are more successful than we are in *organising* application of science (except in the directions where we are relatively successful) but their manpower is far more highly trained on the technological side. B.W. admitted that where commercial considerations entered, the Russians were just beginning to confront the problem (hence their use of British management consultants).

Sunday, 5 June   Lunch on Friday with B. Hopkin. We discussed the importance of uncertainty: in data, in interpretation of data, in the outcome of decisions; the consequent need to make planning an exploration of contingencies not a set of fixed instructions; and the failure of economists to get all this over, indeed the deliberate playing down of uncertainty in mathematical expositions of economic problems. To me this corresponds to the under-rating of management in the broad sense, and the attitude of so many economists that the administrators needed to carry out a policy can be treated as a free good. The theory of profit in the private sector is well understood but there seems to be a lack of appreciation that the same theory could be extended to the public sector.

[57] Dougals Henley – Asst. Under-Sec. of State, DEA, 1964–69; Dep. Under Sec. of State, 1969.

[58] Ludwig Erhard – Fed. Min. of Econ. Affairs, 1949–63; Fed. Chancellor, 1963–66; Chm., Christian Democrats, 1966–67.

Earlier in the week I lunched with Henry P.B. and he told me of the attitude of economists in Chicago ("What did you say was the rate of increase of wages in Britain last year?") to the idea of incomes policy. Yet the Americans are groping after the same things as we are. Henry said the constitutional lawyers were worried at the inroads into freedom of the subject involved in guide-lines. They felt that Congress should first be asked to agree to the procedure before individuals were exposed to moral pressure with unspecified sanctions that might be taken all the more seriously because uncertain.

Chancellor away all week and comes back on Tuesday. William remarked on Thursday on sense of drift and lack of direction. This doesn't prevent great accumulation of paper. But little of it deals with major issues. Press is beginning to go for the Plan and get windy about balance of payments. Curious scare by *Telegraph* on Wednesday or Thursday about a wage freeze said to be urged by Chancellor; and the Sunday press sticks to it that this *must* come from Treasury although there is nothing whatever in it.

Meeting on Europe under Derek Mitchell on Friday at which Donald gave a very good exposition of the argument that we might lose industrial markets on joining. Derek very quiet in Chair and meeting went on far too long.

Sunday, 12 June   Last week was one of increasingly low morale. Seamen's strike in its fourth week. Heavy losses on Monday and Tuesday following Indian devaluation and even Wednesday not very good. Thursday even, and Friday back to Wednesday level so that for a week as a whole losses on spot and forward were in excess of £130 m. Yet throughout the week I was never called for consultation (except once by Denis), never saw the Chancellor, and know of very few occasions on which officials took stock (except when Chancellor happened to be holding a meeting on something else) – certainly William lay very low and said nothing at all. Of course I saw the papers, including minutes of meeting on Wednesday at which possible change in bank rate was discussed.

Wednesday, 15 June   Three very quiet days since I got back from Ditchley. Chancellor at meetings all day on Monday (including housing and wage policy) so I still didn't see him as indeed I haven't since meeting with TUC weeks ago. R.N. said that on Friday after meeting on liquidity he had a long discussion with Chancellor and succeeded in getting him to see that a wage freeze made little sense except in context of a shift of policy involving other measures. I had submitted a minute on Friday in same sense, and yesterday Chancellor apparently didn't come out against G.B. on this issue. None the less Sam B., William Rees Mogg, and all the other Sunday asses have heehawed for a freeze– as if they had taken that line all along.

R.N. also argued over housing policy saying that they shouldn't try to outdo the Tories but pick something on which they failed like hospitals that also cost less. But in committee Chancellor appears to have been pushed into agreeing additional approvals by P.M. and Dick C.

The trade returns came out yesterday and as expected showed no apparent dip in exports (which strengthened the pound, coming on top of Basle, exactly as we had thought likely though Maurice Allen was surprised as he took the change in the deficit to be the really significant fact). We shall no doubt have some respite particularly if the strike gets settled within the week. But from early July we'll be back in real trouble.

Lunch with Bob Bryce[59]. He said he was having difficulty in keeping down Canadian reserves and couldn't even buy back enough Canadian bonds from US ("their bond market isn't as good as ours"). In trouble over reform of Bank Act (6% ceiling) and having to look at taxation, provincial relations, etc. Would be glad to have more Indian cotton textiles but had to invoke anti-dumping legislation because they were so high cost. Japanese goods increasingly easy to compete with in Canada. Need to let in more Chinese because of wheat purchases. The limiting factor to wheat exports was purely physical and the dockers' strike, followed by Seaway strike, made things very difficult. Russians mad and tried to move out one of their liners. Had a lot of goods for Expo 67 that they couldn't unload.

Yesterday meeting of PCSG that seemed to go on for ever under Donald. He said we could take 18% as limit of growth with present balance of payments difficulties and 21% limit assuming they didn't exercise a constraint.[60] This at least is an advance. But George is still set against any change in Plan.

Meetings on Value Added Tax – I avoided going to them. Invitation to visit Delhi to talk to Medical Conference in November. Marion B.[61] reminded me that George Allen's[62] chair would fall vacant in a year and was I interested in taking it. I said I'd love to, looking at Tommy, "anything for a quiet life". And indeed I would.

Franks[63] came to see me yesterday about his keynote speech to N.I.C.B. in San Francisco and we had an interesting talk, mainly about how to run a mixed economy and the constraint of guide-lines.

Sunday, 19 June   Various meetings on public expenditure in 1967–68 and 1970–71 under William or chez Donald, all of them essentially about the Plan and all of them pretty inconclusive because the 18 and 25% models that have been constructed are both implausible, one because it leaves an impossible external deficit anyhow and the other because it assumes that business savings will be very high in conditions of slow growth. I cut meetings to make sure that I got through my papers.

[59] Robert Bryce – Canadian economist, a Cambridge contemporary; Sec. to Treasury Board, 1947–53; Sec. to Cabinet, 1954–63; Dep. Minister of Finance, 1963–70.

[60] The models of the economy referred to yielded an increase in GDP between 1964 and 1970 of 18 per cent on one hypothesis as to economic growth and 25 per cent (as in the National Plan) on another.

[61] Marion Bowley – Economist, University College, London; daughter of the statistician.

[62] George Allen – Professor of Political Economy at University College, London, 1947–67.

[63] Lord Franks – Chm., Lloyds Bank, 1954–62; Provost of Worcester College, Oxford, 1962–76; member of NEDC, 1964–66.

Disenchantment with the government and with Harold very much on the up. Some of the journalists beginning to come clean and agree that Harold's tactics may be first rate but they don't lead to the kind of breakthrough that he promised in 1964. It would seem from what T.B. let fall yesterday at Sussex Academic Advisory Council meeting which Blackett attended that the two of them took credit for Harold's Science and Socialism speech at Swansea and at the Party Conference; Tommy coupled Carter[64] and Williams with the thinking but I doubt whether they were *politically* engaged. In any event, I can't share their admiration for Harold's endorsement of science as if it had somehow been appropriated by the Labour Party as their contribution to Britain's future and certified safe for us all to use. From the start I suspected that he didn't really understand what had gone wrong with our use of scientific discovery and over the past two years I've become convinced of this. Blackett,[65] I was glad to see, insisted on the importance of the commercial aspect of technical progress and I think that he had a fair understanding of what it takes. But Tommy is too mixed up between the common sense that he sometimes produces so devastatingly and the malevolent tosh with which it is sandwiched.

At any rate it looks as if things would now come to a head in a matter of months – certainly by next year's Budget. The Chancellor is out of favour because of SET; G.B. is baffled by the Plan which is fastened round him like a millstone and no longer campaigning for incomes policy; the P.M. hardly ever makes a speech in public (his last one was supposed to be private but he asked permissions to leak it). Rhodesia, the seamen's strike, Vietnam, the deficit – all go on as before while the rest of the world begins to think that we just don't care for anything but frivolity. The whole country is going to be badly infected with a deeper sense of frustration than ever and without any sense that a different government would change things for the better.

William spoke to me on Thursday evening and proposed a division of duties with Robert. This involved R. taking "the conjuncture" and I said that I should have to talk to my colleagues who might not be willing to operate on this basis. William admitted that it seemed to imply having two Economic Sections. I told him that the absence of clear terms of reference 18 months ago had been an advantage not the reverse and that I could understand nonetheless the awkwardness of having to consult both of us on everything. (Not that William *has* consulted me on anything formally for ages.) The fact is that although I'm very busy I'm also largely superfluous. Tommy goes ahead with finding people and writes to Ministers without bothering to tell me (or anyone else). The Chancellor speaks to R. about economic affairs, rarely if ever to me. I am in practice just one more senior adviser. So if there has to be a division of the Economic Section I might as well clear out and leave the whole, not just half, to R. I'd like to stay until after the next Budget but not longer.

[64] Sir Charles Carter – Economist; Vice Chancellor, University of Lancaster, 1963–67; Editor, *Economic Journal*, 1961–70.

[65] P M S Blackett (later Lord) – Prof. of Physics, Imperial College, London, 1953–65; Board of NRDC, 1949–65; Dep. Chm. Advisory Council, Min. of Technology, 1965–70; Pres., Royal Society, 1965–67.

One other thing that William mentioned was that the Chancellor had had it in mind to put me on the Court. (I rather guessed this was what he was hinting at.) Leslie would have been quite prepared to accept this but felt that he already had in Maurice Allen all the economic advice needed and preferred an operator (Hollom). However, the idea is now that I might take on the Chairmanship of a Committee on Finance with the Bank of England and the Treasury represented on it (rather like HFIG).

While we were discussing Nicky's ideas at Section Meeting on Friday Ian B. came in to say that the Chancellor had decided firmly against letting us publish the draft assessment of the economic situation in *Economic Trends*. We just had time to stop it without holding up publication although it will involve printing new covers and a great deal of rearrangement and redrawing of graphs.

Sunday, 3 July   Leave tomorrow for Paris for EPC. About 300 pages of text plus 100 pp of briefs!

The news of the end of the seamen's strike came to me from Paul Bareau who also reported the bombing of Hanoi oil installations and the P.M.'s "declaration of independence". The previous evening Nora Beloff[66] told me that P.M.'s House of Commons speech had fallen pretty flat and disappointed the journalists who looked for something more concrete than where trade unionists slept when in London. I thought that the strike might be prolonged by this intervention but once again P.M. brought it off and this will be put to his credit even if what he said hardly affected the upshot. (It would surely have been enough for him to make clear that the NUS was fighting the government.) Nora B. is being urged to write a full-scale biography of the P.M. I said she couldn't tell the truth and remain on speaking terms. The journalists are fascinated by his gifts and don't see what he lacks.

The Cabinet is very restive about economic policy. At the meeting on prices and incomes several ministers (including Healey) said that it wasn't possible to judge prices and incomes policy without taking in the economic situation as a whole and the Cabinet was promised an opportunity of discussing this (July 12). As William said last Monday the voices raised on this issue were really attacking the way in which the P.M. has elected to conduct economic policy (by confining it to himself, G.B. and J.C.). Then last Thursday came a discussion on housing policy at which the methods of setting public expenditure were attacked. This still let Crossman get his 7,500 extra approvals (or at least *nearly*, for the Chancellor left early and his position was reserved). They were to rank outside the PESC total and no other programmes were to be cut in consequence – the usual absurd compromise since all expenditure is in competition with other expenditure and can't be "outside". Some ministers e.g. Kenneth Robinson[67] have been indignant because they play ball and others don't. Why, he asked,

[66] Nora Beloff – Correspondent of *The Observer* in various countries, 1948–78; polit. correspondent, 1964–76.

[67] Kenneth Robinson – Labour Minister of Health, 1964–68; Minister of Housing and Local Govt., 1968–69.

does B. Castle get agreement to keep 11,000 miles of railway and where does the money come from for the extra 3,000? Crosland feels much the same on educational expenditure.

Meanwhile Nicky is in Persia for a fortnight and Tommy was in Rome last week. This *partly* accounts for the peace. But in the main it is due to the pressure of the Finance Bill and indecision. On the morning of Dahlgrun's[68] visit the Chancellor was up till 8 a.m. at the House of Commons and the following day it rose at 10.40 a.m. So it's hardly surprising that we have seen little of what the Chancellor thinks. It's over a month since I set eyes on him. But within the next month something will *have* to be done. We are back to where we were last July, but with far heavier debts.

Wynne finished his first draft of NIF and points out how little we can foretell how public expenditure will move. If the shortfall were to disappear there would certainly be no increase in unemployment this year. In fact the situation is very different now from 1962/63 with persistent pressure in the public sector and every likelihood that an easing in the private sector will merely accelerate the progress of work in the public sector. In the special case of housing this has not happened but this is because labour has left building altogether for other jobs.

The press makes remarkable reading – most of all those commentators who were so scathing about Selwyn Lloyd. They now clamour increasingly for a wage freeze as if we hadn't tried it before; and talk of heavy unemployment as if we hadn't tried hard to produce it with no effect. The fact is that disinflation in the UK is a lot harder than it seems.

But G.B. still talks as if it could be had for the asking. He has done a long paper for consideration by the P.M. and Chancellor last Friday in preparation for the Cabinet meeting on July 12. It poses rather silly alternatives, hints at devaluation, still seeks the growth target and proposes an extraordinary solution "outflanking de Gaulle", getting the US to pay for our East of Suez costs, joining Europe and generally getting the best of all impossible worlds by siding with the US against France and yet getting France to bless our union with the Six. Most of the specifically economic proposals were nonsenses or slogans like discrimination.

Public expenditure next year is due to rise by 7% (even leaving out SET and Investment Grants) so there can hardly fail to be a first class row.

Wednesday, 6 July   Just back from EPC, my second visit to Paris this year. Eric and I defended UK policy on Tuesday and WP3 begins it all over again tomorrow, with R.N. and Denis Rickett performing.

The general atmosphere was that sterling has had it. Stopper[69] said the bankers weren't interested any more and didn't believe it could recover. In EPC the language was guarded but unmistakeable. We had wasted a year (Kessler). The one thing we didn't have was time and the thing we proposed to use most freely

[68] Rolf Dahlgrun – Federal Minister of Finance, Bonn from 1962.
[69] Edwin Stopper – Swiss banker and official; Dir., Swiss Fed. Commercial Dept., 1961–66; Chief of Dept., Swiss National Bank from 1966.

was time (Ockrent[70]). There was no room for error any more, and the risks were not in the least symmetrical (Emminger). They felt that with unemployment lower than a year ago they could not rely on forecasts unless backed by action. The SET fascinated them but did not leave them convinced: it might or might not work but things were past the stage at which there should be room for doubt.

The French and the Americans were silent and the talking was left to the Dutch, Belgians, Germans and Swiss. I had a talk with van Lennep on Monday night after dinner at Edgar Cohen's[71] and he indicated that he saw little now to hope for. If we meant to devalue why didn't we at least reduce the load on the economy in a way that would allow us to profit from devaluation and might conceivably make it unnecessary?

Getzwold in an intervention today said that in 1899 Norway had had the choice of six countries from which to borrow at 3% for 60 years (75 years was a little more expensive – $3\frac{1}{4}\%$) and she was actually repaying some French loans contracted (in francs) about 1880. How many under-developed countries could do so today? I pointed out that if US long rates were at their highest for 40 years our long rate was now effectively on a 7% basis something unknown since 1815 and indeed probably since Charles II.

Eric's discourse yesterday was largely on the need for structural change. It was well delivered and several countries afterwards expressed interest because they saw symptoms beginning to show in their own economies. But the questions were all on the urgent problems of the balance of payments apart from a single comment by Langer.

Before I left on Monday I had a note from William asking me to prepare a paper for the Chancellor to circulate to Cabinet on July 12 giving (a) a conspectus of developments since October 1964 and (b) a forecast for the next 12 months. Fred put it in hand at once and both William and the Chancellor demanded to see it. So by tomorrow we may know what he proposes to say – it has to be delivered by mid-Friday.

I told Eric in the car on Tuesday morning that I didn't feel inclined to stay more than one more year and he confessed to something of the same feeling. But at 58 he had only 2 years to go anyhow. He felt he could handle T.B. but that it was just that extra element of strain when there was already more than enough. E. recognises the absurdity of the split of the two main departments – creative tension is really destructive tension or just tension – but appreciates that the P.M. prefers things that way and that, given the three personalities involved there is now probably no other basis for letting them play their parts. It is a curious classical drama of almost Greek simplicity.

Stopper last night was amusing about the stereotypes that blocked the thinking of university economists. They talked of "markt-conform" policies and condemned credit ceilings as opposed to raising minimum reserve ratios without thinking that inflation itself was not "markt-conform". In his view there

[70] Roger Ockrent – Belgian diplomatist; Chm., Exec. Cttee., OEEC, 1957–61 and OECD from 1961.

[71] Sir Edgar Cohen – Second Sec. Board of Trade, 1952–60; Econ. repres. of UK to EFTA and GATT, 1960–65; to OECD, 1965–68.

was an extraordinary difference between economists who had been inside government and those who had not. But when I asked about Lutz and Niehans[72] he said they had made little use of either: Lutz I think because of his views on floating rates and Niehans because he knows a lot about US monetary policy but isn't so familiar with Swiss institutions. I think that this must conceal other reasons and some dislike of Niehans' criticisms.

Monday, 11 July   Thursday and Friday busy tidying and catching up. Paper for Chancellor to circulate was ready, thanks to Fred, but in the end Chancellor took cold feet about including forecasts and while I was at the Garden Party, P. Davies[73] had to rewrite Pt II. P.M. subsequently still more doubtful about including even an indication of this year's deficit so that Ministers will only hear orally what we have in effect already told OECD. Apparently the paper, watered down, still strikes Tony Crosland as pretty gloomy. (R.N. saw him over the week-end and also saw Chancellor with William on Sunday night).

Late on Friday afternoon I managed to dictate a hasty piece on the dangers the government was running. William said he agreed and thought things worse even than I represented them. (I was anxious to point out that if we did devalue we'd have a very bad time at 1.2% unemployment.)

Today I found five papers to brief on and had little time to let William know what I proposed. But R.N. told me that Chancellor was thinking of hire purchase so I got Wynne to prepare for 4 p.m. meeting with William and R. Powell on that and put in a hasty note. William had told me on Friday that Chancellor was trying to resist the July itch. I said then that the obvious package was almost a caricature of Selwyn's – the regulator, 7%, wage pause, etc., etc.

At ESG William told us that P.M. intended to try to deflect Cabinet discussion onto increasing productivity which as D. Allen remarked, was like trying to fight a forest fire by subsidising water-divining. There was general agreement that Europe was now out, since Pompidou's visit.[74] But D. Mitchell will go ahead with his interminable elegy.

G. Brown is preparing to introduce his Bill on Thursday and has spent week-end writing speech. It will presumably coincide with rise in bank rate. G. said to be gloomy because the French have really denied us the pretext for devaluing.

Spoke to John Stevens who says US will help us until after November but no longer. They are all briefing President that the pound and dollar don't hang together but in last resort John thinks that they would bale us out. Visit of P.M. won't be a love feast. President told Walt Rostow[75] that we were treating US

[72] Jurgen Niehans – Swiss economist.

[73] Peter Davies – Entered Treasury 1955; Economic Section from 196 ; Press Sec. to Chancellor and Head of Information, 1978–80.

[74] Pompidou, the French Prime Minister, had visited London on 6-8 July with Couve de Murville and had discussed a number of subjects with Harold Wilson and other Ministers, including the Common Market, technical co-operation, and the Channel Tunnel. There had also been talks at the Foreign Office between Couve and Michael Stewart. The main discussion (entry for 2 February 1967) had been on sterling balances.

[75] Walt Rostow – Prof. of Economic History, MIT, 1951–60; Chm., Policy Planning

like a lot of f****** Pakistanis in denying them military equipment without guarantee against use in Vietnam. He said that expansion would go on at rate between 1st and 2nd quarter rate.

As for Vietnam, Ho is said to want to wait for the election too because he thinks US government won't carry enough popular support. Once election is past, truce is on the cards.

US will resent rise in UK bank rate especially if we don't consult them first. J. himself felt it would do little good, but failure to act on Thursday could have serious effects.

Tuesday, 12 July

In June it was clear that a fresh exchange crisis was approaching but Ministers seemed unprepared. The support arrangements for sterling made in September 1965, which were due to expire on 15 June, were replaced by fresh arrangements on 13 June at the annual meeting of the BIS and involved about £2,000 million in new credit. On this occasion a separate bilateral agreement was reached between the Banque de France and the Bank of England. Substantial support was used before the end of June.

On 8 July the Governor of the Bank called on the P.M. to warn him that exchange losses were on a scale endangering the parity. At the same time the Treasury was pressing on the Chancellor the need for drastic action. The key ministers seem to have debated devaluation over the week-end and there was a point at which the Chancellor, in despair of support from his colleagues wavered on the rate.

The first Ministerial action was to announce on 12 July the prolongation of the credit ceiling to 1967. There would be 'no general arrangement for the clearing banks to provide special assistance' to offset the effects on credit of SET. Two days later the Prime Minister announced an increase in bank rate to 7 per cent and a call for special deposits. Although it had been put about by No.10 at the week-end that there would be no mini-Budget and the Lobby was advised to the same effect on 11 July, the Prime Minister went on to announce that 'further measures will be necessary which will have the effect of providing the restraint necessary in internal demand, public or private'. The measures would include 'a substantial reduction in overseas Government expenditure'.

Unfortunately the Prime Minister was unable to say what measures he had in mind, making it clear that he had been caught unprepared. It was not until 20 July that a further statement by the P.M. provided the details. The measures were intended to reduce home demand by £500 million and overseas spending by £150 million. They included the 10 per cent indirect tax regulator; tighter hire purchase restrictions; tighter building controls on private and office building; cuts in public investment in 1967-68; cuts in government spending overseas; a 10 per cent surcharge on 1965-66 surtax liabilities; a limitation of the travel

Council, Dept. of State, 1961–66; Spec. Asst. to the President, 1966–69.

allowance (on travel outside the sterling area) to £50; and a voluntary wage and price freeze. The measures failed at first to steady the market and the losses in the following week were particularly heavy, but by mid-August the crisis had passed.

Tuesday, 12 July   Not quite so hectic. Ministers settled nothing but their common opposition to cuts in public expenditure. Cabinet was "all over the place". William told me that Chancellor, P.M. and G.B. had had long talk last night but he didn't know the outcome. Chancellor was settling character of his statement on credit and SET for House of Commons today and took a pretty tough line with an "out" in the use of the word "general" i.e. no *general* relaxation of the ceiling would be allowed. P.M.'s attitude to bank rate not known for certain. I thought Chancellor right to make his announcement today since it would make rise in bank rate obvious next step and might be some reassurance to market in consequence. Similarly William had agreed with R.P. not to go ahead with preparations for Hire Purchase for Thursday. S.G. commented favourably on new flexibility of the Bank. They accepted formula for credit ceiling and were also writing on next steps to William (letter arrived about 5 p.m. but had little new except preference for hire purchase over regulator and unspecific suggestions for cuts in public expenditure including expenditure overseas).

After lunch William told me that the earlier expectation of a meeting of P.M., G.B. and J.C. at 5 had now changed and G.B. would not be there. At 6 Burke T. would hold meeting of officials (William, Eric, R.P.). William also said that Burke had told him what P.M. was contemplating. This included hire purchase, part or all of regulator, ban on *all* office building and lowering of £100,000 limit on miscellaneous private building. There had been some talk last night of a fresh deferment operation but this was not mentioned. William suspected that P.M. wanted to get Jim on his own for special confrontation on holding the rate. ("One of the faint-hearts").

It seems that within past 48 hours Chancellor has begun to have doubts about the rate because he can't get any support from his colleagues on cutting public expenditure. Meanwhile P.M. has drafted speech for Australia Club reaffirming his belief in rate in very strong terms which will commit them all. He wants package before he goes off to see LBJ and seemed to have in mind action on all fronts on Thursday. This we agreed was a mistake. The P.M.'s speech gives figures for cumulative deflation since 1964 which he insisted we should provide; but no one will understand them or be in the least convinced.

(When William and R.N. saw Chancellor on Sunday night William put it to him that the only way to hold the rate was by massive deflation. Chancellor reacted strongly.)

I had already got Fred to work this morning on the scale of action. We agreed to take 1.8% next July as a starting point, with 2% by end of 1967: this made sense whether we devalued or not and was bound to yield as big a package as anybody could imagine. (In fact some £400–£500 m.) At 5 William discussed this with P.V., F.J.A., R.N. (fresh from Fulton) and myself, Ian having left to go in search of the Chancellor in the House of Commons and show him P.M.'s draft speech with its 3-fold references to selling Britain short. There was no dissent from general proposition and agreement that we couldn't put whole load on consumption.

There will certainly be trouble if anything of this sort is done and the public expenditure part will require agreement of all the Ministers concerned so it can't be put into practice by the 3. In any event it will all be whittled down by P.M. and will probably end up with £200 m. at most. The big target *ought* to be housing where total in '67 shows climb of £100 m. in public sector alone. Fact that credit squeeze may hit private sector might lead to efforts to compensate in public sector.

Ian says it's the last 100 days. For him, certainly. He did his best to prevent another Guildhall speech on sterling and underlined problems of giving figures on deflation while Chancellor remarked as he put down telephone "You were pretty rough on him, weren't you?". "All in your interests", said Ian.

Reception at Marlboro House for Commonwealth Finance Officials. Saw Raphael who told me that it was No.10 that put out all the confident stuff about no mini-Budget at the week-end and followed it up with the Lobby on Monday. Sam B. is apparently wild with us for now tightening credit after such a release (but more because Chancellor won't see him!) and we may get unfavourable headlines when we badly need favourable ones.

Wednesday, 13 July   Spent morning at Marlboro House expounding economic situation to Commonwealth Finance officials and a good part of afternoon doing the same to a group of foreign economic correspondents so that I was effectively out of action during a critical day. P.M. was at Brighton but he, G.B. and J.C. met in the evening.

Upshot was to postpone package till Aug. 2 and shift heat to overseas government expenditure which they want to cut by £100 m. a year by next April. P.M. also insists on special deposits in spite of William's efforts to explain this adds nothing. In fact we just *must* repeat Selwyn. J.C. even proposed that he should include in tomorrow's statement something to indicate that more measures were in store to deflate demand; and G.B. duly proposed a wage freeze for 12 months which he thought he could sell to TUC but was willing if necessary to "impose". Up till 7.30 it was not clear what would be done tomorrow if anything.

All are agreed on a "jumbo" package of the dimensions we proposed (£400 m.+) for Aug. 2 provided we can wait that long. P.M. doesn't insist he should have it done before he sees LBJ. But it will presumably all have to go to Cabinet this time and it isn't certain that everybody will be helpful over proposals. I don't know who argued them out of action tomorrow but presumably they recognised how difficult this would be.

It's a strange conception of planning. To do now what would have made all the difference a year ago and still more in Oct. 1964. But even now the P.M. might retract, I suppose. At any rate Ian was sitting down to draft a letter from J.C. to him setting out what was agreed. Astonishing that G.B. will take it.

Trade figures out and their effect was small – to judge from negligible loss today. P.M.'s speech plus Chancellor's PQ steadied the market.

Yet here is P.M. propounding a package (without any agreement as to contents up to this evening) when a few days ago he was telling the press "No mini-Budget".

It will be difficult to get Ministers to hold their hand until Aug. 2 and in due course there are pretty certain to be leaks.

The £100 m. off overseas expenditure was to be £50 m. from Germany and £50 m. off Far East. J.C. proposed that the bombers should be flown back just before or just after his visit to Dahlgrun. Ian had to tell him that there were certain logistical difficulties about that sort of thing. Neither he nor J.C. were in the RAF but he was in the army and J.C. in the navy and no doubt the RAF had regard to similar problems.

Sunday, 17 July   The Cabinet met twice on the economic situation, once on Tuesday and once on Thursday. On Wednesday the Chancellor had a meeting of his Committee on Public Expenditure and another is due tomorrow. The fact is that total P.E. is due to increase by 11% in 1967-68 if the additional proposals are accepted and by 7% even if they are not. These figures are at constant prices and cover public sector housing, etc. but not investment by nationalised industries (i.e. they are on the $4\frac{1}{4}$% basis but exclude SET and Investment Grants). They are inflated a little by uprating of benefits in 1967-68 but this isn't the decisive factor.

A good part of Thursday and Friday went by on routine stuff. I had to scrap the Section Meeting on Friday to hear the package. But in the end it came only to organising a meeting with Board of Trade and DEA (Donald) on hire purchase at 11.30 and putting in an assessment at 6.30 to William. I also fired off an attack on the housing programme because it seems to me very dangerous to cut consumption exclusively and this is what programme looks like doing in 1966-67.

Thursday's statement by P.M. was based on preceding Cabinet at which Chancellor said his piece. Details of the package were given (including stopping all office building and cutting £100,000 limit on miscellaneous building to £50,000) but no reference to regulator or hire purchase. This must have been prudence (even in Confid. Annex) because Burke told William that it was all raised. A lot of the discussion fell on overseas expenditure with the same old propositions in the forefront (£50 m. off Germany: cut of £100 m. p.a. by April 1 1967, etc.), but Healey wasn't present. The University of the Air featured twice in the Confid. Annex either on Tuesday or Thursday (I'm not sure which) and was obviously a contribution from the P.M. Barbara C. gallantly offered to get liner trains moving.

Now that the moment of truth has come so swiftly it is instructive to ask why it should have come so soon. The journalists lay stress on Cousins' resignation and this obviously put paid to an agreed incomes policy. But there were also the first quarter figures, the bad trade returns on Thursday, and the cumulative effect of rising interest rates abroad (Euro-dollars at $6\frac{1}{2}$%). Even on Monday it didn't look altogether certain that bank rate would be put up but in a couple of days all that had become a thing of the past. The major factor must have been the statement that there would be no mini-Budget (inspired from No.10) from which the only possible conclusion was that we were heading for devaluation. The Chancellor's deliberate resort to a PQ to announce an apparent further credit restriction also had a bad effect and it might have been better to wait for Thursday and get it all in together. But on top of all this came the P.M.'s statement on Thursday promising further measures. This repeated the tactics of July 1961 without the excuse (the regulator was still not passed into law) but although people quoted Lear they had forgotten Vicky's cartoon of Selwyn. It all smacked of panic because it was obvious that the government was caught unprepared and would have to work out new measures. Then there were the rumours of Cabinet disagreement (in fact very subdued so far as I know).

The measures were at first to be included in a short statement: then left out till more fully considered: then for Wed. 27 July (afternoon); and now for next Wednesday (20 July). The press, smarting from Harold's phrases of Tuesday, seems to have ferreted out nearly all that is in prospect or that went on. They editorials already have an elegiac note. Yet here is H.W. in Moscow and J.C. going off to Bonn on Wednesday after the statement.

When we were discussing on Thursday morning at Higher Directorate what might be asked of the Chancellor or said by him after the P.M.'s statement, William summed it up nicely: "he can't gild the P.M.'s lily".

The Treasury is an odd place in comparison with 1962. Otto hasn't been replaced so that the top echelon of civil servants looks pretty thin. Denis is away for long stretches; Louis Petch[76] has moved over to Management; even Bryan Hopkin's absence in noticeable. But we get meetings with N.K., R.N. and myself. Far more is left to William individually and no one is completely posted on what is afoot in spite of the vast quantity of paper. I've seen no Treasury Minister for well over a month and there have in fact been very few meetings of officials with the Chancellor.

Wednesday, 20 July   Wednesday night and the statement has been made. I leave for Edinburgh tomorrow for Anglo-German Economic Committee just after Chancellor has left for Bonn on the offset agreement.

First, some facts. On Monday we met at 12 at ES(G) in Eric's room and there was T.B. very solemn. He button-holed me as I came in and asked how things were going. He was thinking of the market and in due course William told him that loss had already gone over £50 m. (it reached £100 m. and for once was mainly on spot although BBC comment that night said little Bank of England intervention and that mainly in the forwards and no sign of speculative, as distinct from commercial, pressure).

The meeting was rather desultory until Nicky asked what happened if we were forced off on August 2 when the reserve figures were published. He thought government might be choosing greater evil by first seeking to defend the rate and

[76] Louis Petch – Third Sec., Treasury, 1962–66; Second Sec., 1966–68; Second Perm. Sec., Civil Service Dept., 1968–69.

then suffering humiliation of having to give up, losing all remaining reserves in the process. Did Ministers know the reserve figures? It became doubtful to me whether even the P.M. or George really appreciated what the position was and William promised that a factual paper would be prepared. Nicky said, on being challenged by William, that he would instruct the Bank of England to give up supporting the rate. William said that the Chancellor would then be faced with the resignation of the Court. It would be in breach of an international obligation (and an obligation to our chief creditor). William was asked how much more we could borrow from IMF and gave an immediate off-the-cuff account of our residuary drawing rights and their relation to the Basle agreement. At one point he said to Nicky that his advocacy of a floating rate "raised all the issues that were discussed elsewhere on Saturday night".

Talking to N.K. after, he said it all hung on the P.M. Jim and George would both devalue if the P.M. would allow it but Jim had been talked round by appeals to loyalty while George was torn. Later, on Tuesday, I had another talk in the corridor and was joined by Sam. N.K. said that he personally felt like resigning but thought that his resignation would be misinterpreted and that he did not want to do it on his own. (His view was that the press would think the government was throwing him out.) Of three possibilities the strongest was that the package wouldn't be big enough; next that it would not stop the drain; and only after these two that it would both be big enough and effective. On the day after the statement we might take in £5 m. (S.G. said £50 m. and I guessed £20 m.) but by August 2 we'd be in trouble when the reserve figures were released. It was these that caused the panic (he was called in by the Central Bank of Iran because they were worried when they saw the reserves fall by nearly £50 m. in June and he had reassured them that we would not devalue). He believed in getting free from "serfdom to the international bankers" and that if we broke out of the box in which we had shut ourselves we would grow more rapidly.

Monday was relatively quiet. I did a brief on the package which rubbed in some of the uncertainties and the importance of what was *said* about the package. I thought we had a 50/50 chance of escaping devaluation even with the package (which, unlike N.K., I fully expected to get). But most of the work fell on Wynne who kept calculating the effects and getting different answers.

The first thing I learned on Monday was that the car deposit was now being talked up to 50%. This left me pretty scared even when Wynne explained the need to overinsure and the possibility of quick reversal (this I didn't believe – these things are *not* quickly reversed). But in the end it was all academic. We advised the Chancellor strongly not to go above £160 m. on hire purchase *unless* he failed on public spending.

On Tuesday we were still completely in the dark on what would eventually be agreed but William explained the line he was taking in brief. He started from the need to get £250 m. on the balance of payments, scored £150 m. on direct savings and then worked on a conversion factor of 4 to convert the balance of £100 m. into domestic deflation. This gave him a total of £550 m. and a *method* of organising the discussion.

I had to go to Savoy for Unit Trust Dinner but came back at 10 p.m. and stayed till 1 a.m. Cabinet broke up a little before 10 and resumed this morning at 9. Yesterday they hardly touched on the difficult items: public expenditure, overseas expenditure, the freeze. Some had to go off to the Palace and this by itself prevented discussion of defence and foreign policy.

About 10 p.m. Sam, F.F. and I relaxed in S.'s room swopping reminiscences of previous crises (e.g. the 1947 one when Sam and Frank couldn't get their figures to agree because F. used a dollar rate of 4 and S., a statistician, one of 4.03).

F. said that when Douglas Jay and Patrick Gordon Walker came to Geneva in 1964 they acted like a couple of economic illiterates. Patrick G.W. was lectured by Stopper on the importance of confidence in sterling, that so many people held sterling and it was important to reassure them. "If people tried to take their money out of London we should stop them" said Walker. "You mean you would make it impossible for them to withdraw it". "Certainly". "Thank you very much" said Stopper and that was that. The story came from Olivier Long[77]. The Swiss banks were duly told and acted accordingly and who could blame them? Jay maintained strongly that there were no signs of excess demand, a view he equally strongly contests in a recent minute to the P.M. where he thinks our deficit in 1964 largely attributable to excess home demand.

This brings me to today. The P.M.'s statement naturally couldn't be circulated until it was written and only a first draft existed at 9 a.m. I spent the morning on notes for supplementaries and had an early lunch. But there was really nothing to do and I left William, Robert and Wynne to handle things until Robert called me over and asked if I would brief Lord Longford.

I went over to the Lords for 2.45 and found three of the Ministry of Defence already there to explain: (a) that they wouldn't save at the rate proposed until the *end* of 1967-68 (b) that defence commitments would be unaltered.

Longford didn't really want a brief on the statement but asked me why things had changed so suddenly. He said quite a number of things about the Cabinet meeting. For example, he had wanted tobacco to be included but the smokers voted him down. Harold had not taken too rigid a position on devaluation no doubt out of consideration for George Brown. He (L.) had been rather surprised by this. The Cabinet had agreed to introduce import restrictions next year and he couldn't quite understand the argument for not doing so at once or when the surcharge came off. But D. Jay had persuaded them on this point and indeed the President had played quite a commanding part in the discussions. He had been one of the leaders of those who were firmly against devaluation. So was Longford who asked, however, if all economists were in favour. He had put this question (I think) while waiting to see the Chancellor and Ian had pursed his lips and said that it would be true of "the later arrivals" among the government's economic advisers. L. had also talked to Donald who was familiar with his arguments. He thought the press had behaved rather well over devaluation and had refrained from playing up rumours about George's intention to resign and his conviction that we ought to devalue (this is now apparently common

---

[77] Olivier Long – Head of Swiss Deleg. to EFTA, 1960–66.

knowledge).

Tonight on T.V. Harold gave the usual sermon quite impressively. But Jo Grimond[78] later was quite devastating on "this government that believes in planning" and changes its mind every week. Crossman thought that it was good selective deflation, protecting essentials (he didn't mention £95 of investment by nationalised industries) meaning housing – and implied that in a fairly short time expansion could be resumed.

Harold was *not* impressive in the House of Commons and is said to have rattled off the statement very fast.

Sunday, 24 July   On Thursday I had to go to Edinburgh for Anglo-German Econ. Comm. We took off about 2 p.m. instead of 9.20 and I came back by the 8 p.m. plane. Talked to Murison of Schroeders and travelled with John Owen[79]. Kaiser[80] asked me why we didn't devalue and cited his three examples: Turkey, Spain and France. In each case it had been a brilliant success. Other Germans were sceptical of our chances of avoiding devaluation because of rise on costs and prices, and failure of exports to respond.

Brown after all withdrew resignation. I had judged this on Wednesday night impossible and I still think it very embarrassing to government. If both Cousins and G.B. had been in opposition, the question "How long will H. last?" would have real point. Would Selwyn have been sacked if H. had been P.M.?

On Friday Wynne asked how it could be so easy to add £40 m. to gas programme (since last forecast) and so difficult to cut £40 m. off again.

William asked for brief for P.M.'s trip to Washington. Ambassador reports talk with Bator and Rostow which implies willingness to give us support if we can show long term prospects of recovery. I have spent week-end drafting it. Chancellor went ahead with his schoolday speech in Norfolk and P.M. went to Liverpool to Beatles' launch. Press on the whole not unfair but obviously sceptical about the forecast of unemployment. General tendency to assume that devaluation was preferable course. No one argues that we needed to move to lower pressure of demand (but this was put by Maurice Laing[81] to P.M. on Wednesday). Public attention will be focussed on prices and incomes and the policy looks very obscure. At the last meeting of the official committee just over a week ago, most of the Permanent Secretaries were strongly in favour of an absolute freeze – including Denis Barnes[82] and of course Steve, and (less

---

[78] Jo Grimond – Leader of Parliamentary Liberal Party, 1956–67; Ambassador to UN, 1967–68; Dir. Gen., GATT, 1968– .

[79] John Owen – in 1968, Under-Sec., Overseas Finance Division, Treasury, dealing with Western Europe.

[80] Kaiser – German representative on the Anglo-German Economic Committee.

[81] Maurice Laing – Building contractor, on the Court of the Bank of England.

[82] Denis Barnes – Deputy-Sec., Ministry of Labour 1963–66; Permanent Sec. 1966–68; Permanent Sec. Dept. of Employment, 1968–73.

surprisingly) Herbert Andrew[83] and John Winnifrith[84] (who thought he could control food prices in the light of what happened in the seamen's strike). It all looks cockeyed to me unless they mean to take statutory powers or frighten everybody with references to NBPI. But what Trade Union is going to be frightened that way?

Sunday press seems agreed that origin of the present measures was visit by Leslie O'Brien to P.M., before he left for Basle, on July 8 to warn him of threat to the pound in current exchange losses. This was, as it happens, the day when I fired in my own minute to the Chancellor. I think in retrospect that if we *had* had a package ready (as the press was willing to assume) we could have had it introduced on the 14th without the fatal delay that followed. In the end what was announced differed very little from what we should have proposed (and did propose so far as checks to consumption are concerned). But we had nothing ready on the freeze and we needed to get Departments to accept the various cuts in public expenditure.

Interesting references to William Davis'[85] article in Friday's *Guardian*. Chancellor seems to be visualising a change round and some way of ending the silly split between Treasury and DEA.

Wednesday, 27 July   Monday chiefly of interest for ES(G) meeting at which once again T.B. sought to explain that P.M. needn't go to Washington as a beggar because we had so many cards in our hands e.g. we could threaten to liquidate the portfolio! This showed utter disregard of the element of time since no one else will pay *this* month's cheque but US. Nicky made the point but William deliberately put best gloss on it as he always does when T.B. speaks.

Today we had an interesting Permanent Secretaries' meeting at which William rightly put his finger on reason why Ministers couldn't get rational explanation of public expenditure control. So long as policy is settled by three men of such different views it can't be coherent, and if it isn't coherent it can't be expounded in public. Indeed there can be no rational discussion of it, and officials are at a loss to know what to say about it. It is this that drives argument underground until it suddenly emerges in a crisis with explosive force. Bill Nield commented on attitude of Ministers in recent Cabinet discussions as based on failure to understand whole economic background. Deeply suspicious of PESC as a Treasury device for allowing outlet to its masochistic urge. No real picture of antithesis of public and private spending or spending for consumption versus spending for investment. But the situation is really more complex than Bill's Four Square notion. They want to salvage *some* priorities (housing, schools and hospitals) partly so as to *say* that they still have these priorities and therefore

---

[83] Sir Herbert Andrew – Permanent Under-Sec. of State, Dept. of Education and Science, 1964–70.

[84] Sir John Winnifrith – joined Treasury, 1934; Third Secretary, 1951–59; Perm. Sec., Min. of Agric., Fisheries and Food, 1959–67.

[85] William Davis – City Editor, *Evening Standard*, 1960–65; Financial Editor, *The Guardian*, 1965–68; Dir. Gen., Nat. Trust, 1968–70.

aren't cutting indiscriminately like the Tories. But immunity from cuts isn't priority; and *all* cuts express priorities if made with any deliberation.

Some of the discussion seemed to imply that PESC had failed – William will have later discussions. But I suspect that we are really caught between Ministerial emotions, bad figures, and inadequate contact with the real points of control (e.g. between Treasury and CEGB).

Lunch with Bryan who felt that the Labour Party had now been forced to abandon its old shibboleths. I'm not so sure, looking at the banker's ramp type of reaction. If you shut your eyes, you can see queer things. Besides, the press still has religion about investment, expansion etc. Sam B. still draws all the wrong conclusions in today's *FT* about Treasury and DEA because he doesn't accept the overriding need for limited pressure of demand and has a false picture of what Treasury does and did before 1964.

Saturday, 30 July   Lunch today with the Rolls and to our great surprise the Roosas. Mrs Roosa was bitten by a snake on the main road to Moscow about 150 miles the other side of Kalinin and they had to stay in Kalinin nearly three weeks, with their plans to tour Europe all ajee. They were full of praise for the Russians and their medical services.

It's been an odd week, punctuated by visits from foreigners – Sam Katz[86] on Monday, Giersch[87] on Thursday and Bill Smith[88] on Friday. Sam asked why Ministers couldn't keep their mouths shut after the Chancellor's unfortunate remark at the Hague about the wage freeze being "a bonus" and not indispensable to the government's plans. (He was no doubt being needled by sceptical journalists and anxious to show that *everything* didn't turn on complete success).

By Friday night Ian B., at the end of his P.S. job and heartily glad of it, said the sooner Ministers got off on holiday the better. He felt that some resignations (e.g. by Nicky and Tommy) would be just what was needed to restore the government. I thought it a wonderful idea that Nicky should save the pound from "floating" by coming forward and offering his resignation. What had moved him to this was the mess that had been made of the Prices and Incomes Bill where the Government, having thought they would get their bill because they had squared the Opposition, suddenly tumbled to it that they hadn't squared F. Cousins and made a quick procedural change to make sure that he wouldn't be there to oppose it. But they hadn't revealed all this to the Opposition who went wild on Friday thinking that *they* were being diddled. Ian says that if a dozen of the most brilliant men in the country had been charged with planning the worst possible mess they couldn't have done better. 'I can't remember a government discrediting itself so completely and so quickly.'

The poor TUC are being forced to accept one humiliation after another. The conditions they attached to acceptance of the White Paper in one of the oddest

[86] Sam Katz – US economist at the UK desk in the Federal Reserve Board.

[87] Herbert Giersch – Professor of Economics, Institut für Weltwirtschaft, Kiel.

[88] William Smith – Professor of Economics, University of Fredericton, New Brunswick, Canada.

documents I've read have now had to be withdrawn because the government has simply disregarded them. It is fascinating to see the TUC persuade itself on the say-so of the P.M. that devaluation would increase unemployment to 1 1/2m. (in fact in the interview with the TUC the P.M. started off at 3/4 m. and as the TUC leaders laid more and more stress on the impossibility of the proposals he stepped up his estimate, Sir William Carron[89] concurring). (Carron was subsequently invited to dine at No.11 on Fowler's visit, R.N. dropping out to make room.)

I read the White Paper in its successive drafts with increasing incredulity. The early drafts were in the spirit of Nelson: England expects every man to observe the wage and price freeze. As Nicky said on another occasion: why don't they pass a law requiring that productivity must rise by 4 per cent per annum? (He drew me aside the Monday before last to ask if the previous government had been as bad in a similar type of situation.) I don't believe that the policy of overriding commitments to make increases can succeed. It makes for an immediate rather than a delayed challenge to the policy. There may be no such challenge. But it doesn't rest with the TUC to decide. Their signature, like their signature of the Declaration of Intent, goes only part of the way to assure success. There are also the individual Unions and behind them the men themselves who may well be very angry, e.g. the railwaymen, and reject the leadership. Once unemployment is rising this reaction could be mastered. But why provoke it *now*? Of course, *The Economist* and other papers still write as if it were all within the power of the government to control wages.

R.N. came to have a word on Friday about further work on devaluation. I'm afraid it will all fall on Wynne, who is also doing a paper on public expenditure. We agreed that it would be sensible to visualise a withdrawal of the SET premium and possibly of investment grants (since export profits would rise and provide finance for the investment most required).

We lost over £80 m. on Friday, mainly forward. But the Bank has had to strain itself to get even the necessary spot finance to keep down the published loss on reserves. We're still relying on overnight borrowing from the Fed., and hush-hush borrowing from B.I.S. Market forwards are back up near previous peak. In a single week we lost nearly £350 m. on spot and forward. The public can have little notion quite how bad it is – though I recall that the Kahn Report said that last year's position was not quite as bad as the press implied. What is odd is that even on days like Friday the papers say the pressure was small (e.g. *The Times*).

There was a curious meeting on Friday in L.H.'s room on the proposal for two Treasuries. It was obvious that a tussle was in progress between William and Laurence but I couldn't then make out why or to what purpose. Elsie Abbot tells me that the proposal comes from a Fabian pamphlet of which R.N. was part author and he is pushing the idea on Fulton. It sticks out a mile that we couldn't set up yet another new Department in present circumstances but for

[89] Sir William Carron (later Lord) – President of Amalgamated Engineering Union, 1956–67; Dir., Bank of England, 1963–69; Dir., Fairfields, 1966–68; NEDC, 1968–69.

some reason William seems to back the idea without specifically saying so. He was, as always, very impressive in his handling of the points, completely sure-footed: while Laurence also was at his best and said a lot that was very important – the need for a short line of communication from the head of the Civil Service to the P.M., the impossibility of asking a Senior Minister to devote himself to purely C.S. matters and no more, and the futility of leaving a *junior* minister to be titular head of a C.S. Dept. LH suggested that the Paymaster General might be put in charge and William said that while there was something to be said for this it narrowed the P.M.'s room for manoeuvre in sharing out other Cabinet appointments. L.H. couldn't see this since the P.M. could always create another Minister without Portfolio.

When I suggested that every Cabinet Minister would be briefed on civil service of all matters, L.H. said No, there was usually a special effort to keep down the circulation of papers to the Cabinet on the C.S. (e.g. Franks). But the *P.M.* would be briefed. The subject broadened out to the organisation of the P.M.'s office and L.H. said that even if H.W. treated the Cabinet Office as his own secretariat he took the *formal* position that it was the *Cabinet* secretariat. If the P.M. acted as indirect head of a C.S. Department this would raise at once the issue of a policy department under the P.M. To this William agreed at once.

But why the Treasury should discuss this only to prepare a paper for the Fulton Committee, God knows. There are lots of other problems in the machinery of government we *ought* to be thinking about.

R.N. looks like being a victim of the freeze. His salary is unchanged since 1964 and so is D. Seers'. But Nicky is to get more and T.B. has had both a Franks increase *and* "something more" by edict of the P.M.

I told Elsie that the Treasury organisation on price and incomes policy was chaotic because L.H. didn't supervise it and William couldn't. She agreed that L.H. either refused to interest himself or expressed pique that he hadn't had the papers. But the organisation is bad, with one set of people dealing with the public services under L.H., another with the nationalised industries under Peter Vinter and nobody with the private sector except me. The draft White Paper didn't reach me till Thursday and I couldn't comment until Friday i.e. till too late.

In fact one thing that stands out over the past month is that we are paying for having been so over-extended by SET and other problems. We ought to have been ready with a policy statement on the credit squeeze well before July 12 (even if it wasn't made until them) but S.G. and the Bank didn't hold their meeting on this till the beginning of July. Had we raised bank rate on the 7th and added the statement about the credit squeeze most of the subsequent collapse might have been avoided. On this my own conscience is clear because I had suggested a rise in bank rate much earlier and was not even asked to the meeting in June where it was discussed with the Chancellor. I wonder what Denis thought of all this – he had the Group of Ten and WP3 very much on his plate in early July. The liquidity will o'the wisp has been almost as bad as SET. I remember that he called me in at the beginning of the month to ask me what I honestly thought we should be saying to the Chancellor and it was this that moved me to write on the 8th, about a week later.

The open discussion of devaluation in the press and Parliament makes it seem very doubtful whether we'll avoid it even this year. I think that I'd now give odds against devaluation but on July 20 I thought the odds no better than evens, and by July 21 as slightly less than evens.

Tuesday, 2 August   Two rather unexciting days. At ESG we discussed mainly export prices, the favourite subject of T.B. At one point, speaking of the scope for import substitution he said "Let's take something I happen to know about – sulphuric acid". Eric said "You mean vitriol. Yes, of course, you know all about that, Tommy". When the laughter subsided Tommy said "Touché", with a wry smile.

I had a word tonight with William à propos of a meeting of ED(O) on the revised forecast. Douglas Allen thought that he didn't intend to have such a meeting because of the awkwardness of chairmanship etc. but William said at once there was a misunderstanding. We talked briefly about a number of things and he then said that he had thought over my minute on distribution of duties and saw some substance in my argument. He told me that there had been a meeting at which the Chancellor had openly meditated resignation and both Nicky and R.N. had said that if he did resign they would go too. This had rubbed in the possibility that they might not be in the Treasury for the remaining period of this administration and given force to my line of argument. William had not spoken to R.N. and agreed to leave things as they were until after the holidays.

On incomes policy he agreed that line taken by government meant courting trouble and running very considerable risks. He had got Bank to write saying that it was not necessary to go back on past commitments to reassure foreign opinion and had urged moderation on Chancellor without avail. He rather feared that it might have been something of what he said that influenced the Chancellor in his retort at the Hague on "a bonus".

As in 1961, plenty of talk of reflation. In fact P.M. talked of "when we come to reflate" when he saw TUC in week of the 20th. T.B. yesterday thought that if we deflated "just like the Tories" we couldn't reflate like them too – that would be too much. So he wants to go for higher investment not higher consumption, without quite knowing *when*.

William said yesterday that P.M. undertook no new commitments to LBJ. He had almost got agreement to talks on liquidity with US on bilateral footing when Fowler insisted we must wait until after Bank/Fund meeting.

Chancellor is cutting down delegation and has cancelled his Canadian tour. He has tried to leave out R.N. but of course he must go anyhow for WP3.

Sunday, 7 August   On Thursday afternoon Chancellor had a meeting on interest rates and later held a party at NO.11 to celebrate the passing of the Finance Act. So I saw him twice, for the first time since May (I think) and with the feeling that when I next saw him he might no longer be Chancellor. He greeted us by asking "Why do you all look like strangers?" and seemed his normal self, cheerful, interested, avuncular. We spent all our time on PWLB rates without getting to Building Society rates at all although this was obviously the hot item. In the end George B. let loose the storm in the House by *appearing* to express agreement in a freeze when he was only indicating that Part IV of the Bill didn't apply. Then he had to make it clear that the government was not washing its hands of mortgage rates at all. Of course since rates to new borrowers are already up it would be more than usually nonsensical to keep down rates on existing loans especially as no increase in current payments would be involved on practically all mortgages: the Building Societies would merely stretch out the period of repayment. In effect, as Steve pointed out, there is a freeze already in the normal practice of the Societies.

Bank lunch on Thursday. Cecil King and Robens were there and, for once, Niemeyer[90] looking a lot older. I talked afterwards to Leslie who asked about the new arrangement to form a Finance Group of the Economic Advisers. I told him that William had linked it with other plans and that he had probably put it aside for the present. But I would make a point of keeping in touch with Maurice Allen and Kit MacM. (and if he wished, John Fforde). Cecil King said the country needed leadership and never seemed to get it from either party.

Wednesday, 10 August   On Monday we had a discussion on incomes policy at ECSG with Nicky at his Nickiest. He wanted us to decide how much there was available for higher wages and then allocate it exactly like Selwyn Lloyd in 1962. And he got the two customary replies – one from me that *we* don't settle these things nor do we plan the TUC membership; and one from Douglas Allen that the money has already been given away.

In the afternoon we had brief meeting on export prices followed by Chancellor on Capenhurst.[91] He asked good questions from a state of professed innocence and I told him that such innocence was an enormous advantage in matters of fuel policy. I got across my doubts about the wisdom of spending so much on yet another protected industry.

Yesterday we had a very long meeting of PCSG to deal with assumptions about 1970. On the whole everybody was pretty reasonable. In the afternoon William gave a masterly exposition of the relation between NIF and PESC and of the state of play on public expenditure and the decisions to be taken. But of course T.B. asked how he reconciled what he said with PE11 and William replied that we were under instructions to show how public expenditure could

[90] Otto Niemeyer – UK Treasury, 1906–27; BIS, 1931–65 (Chm., 1937–40; Vice Chm., 1941–64); Director, Bank of England, 1938–52.

[91] The meeting on Capenhurst related to a project to use cheap electric power for the production of aluminium and save imports. Although it was argued that it was legitimate to offer electricity in bulk at a price below the usual charge there was no real doubt that the scheme – later code-named 'Uncle' – involved a subsidy. Once one scheme submitted by RTZ was adopted, another was submitted by British Aluminium and loans of £33 million and £29 million respectively were made to the two companies for the building of smelters. A year later, when devaluation threw further doubt on the scheme, it was too late to turn back (see entry for 24 July 1968).

be kept within limit of 3 1/2–4 1/4% [increase per annum]. Also the paper was the Chancellor's expressing a *political* preference against higher expenditure, not a Treasury paper outlining the political decision called for between higher taxation and various changes in public expenditure.

Later at dinner with Clearing Bankers, William was again in very good form and held the floor almost continuously. We discussed disclosure of profits and the submission to NBPI. Archie Forbes[92] was the most categorical, John Thomson the most incisive but, like Stirling,[93] understanding. The Governor kept fairly quiet but pressed the bankers nevertheless to consider disclosure. Thomson said he was rung all through the week-end by people who were in danger of being bankrupted by the squeeze.

Today we had official meeting on Capenhurst with Nicky and T.B. squabbling violently and Posner[94] and Bruce Williams appearing for the first time. Alan Neale[95] supported the RTZ project.

William said that at Cabinet when P.M. announced the new Economic Strategy Committee [SEP] only Barbara asked who the members were. She was told at once that this was not the kind of thing discussed in Cabinet and that was that. But the members do not included a single critic of Harold's machinery of deciding policy (and no representative of the spending departments).

Monday, 15 August   On Friday I had lunch with Fred and went over with him the present state of play. He had been off for a month (i.e. from before the week of the 20th) touring Europe. I went over the points William made earlier in the morning about the first meeting of the new Strategic Economic Policy Committee. When first announced in Cabinet, the rebels were silent but Crossman no doubt knew what was only known to the public later – that he was to be Lord President and as the offices, not the names, were given, he took over membership.

It was first made clear that there was to be no record of the new Committee except one copy to be kept at the Cabinet office under lock and key and shown only to authorised persons for stated reasons. The conclusions would however be circulated. The Committee will meet monthly (Sept. 6 next) and there will be an official committee which will parcel out the work but engage in no substantive discussion. Wonderful make-believe!

The ministers ran over the usual business: better statistics to be available for each meeting, perhaps a chart room (H.W.!), a report similar to the one I had submitted (it was explained that NIF does only 3 per annum); for the Oct. meeting there should be the new short term and five year look commissioned for end of September, and perhaps (or probably) a look at public expenditure.

---

[92] Sir Archibald Forbes Chm., Midland Bank, 1964–75.

[93] D A Stirling- Chm., Westminster Bank, 1962–69; Chm., National Westminster Bank, 1968–69.

[94] Michael Posner – Director of Economics, Ministry of Power, 1966–67; Economic Adviser to Treasury, 1967–69; Economic Consultant to Treasury, 1969–71.

[95] Alan Neale – Board of Trade, 1946–68; Second Sec., 1967; Dep. Sec., Treasury, 1968–71.

Then a bit of philosophy: were we pointing towards US or towards Europe (I said due North)? Then some talk of reflation: had we done enough? Was it working? But not a word of the Plan or even of growth. (The dog that did not bark.)

They did talk of import controls and import deposits and I pointed out that if it was seriously intended to introduce import controls we should need further restraint on demand and it could hardly come from the taxation side so that it would be wrong to fix expenditure and *then* go on to look at import controls.

I also raised the issue of a liquidity crisis (which N.K. refuses to take seriously). I thought that Ministers kept getting agitated about contingency planning when the main contingency was a series of bankruptcies in the wrong places or industries (Harland and Wolff) combined with a request for bank or government money. In the light of Thursday's discussion at HFIG we might have a *real* liquidity crisis since people were scared they wouldn't be liquid enough and the government was intensifying their fears. They might react by making desperate attempts to improve their liquidity, hoard cash, cut commercial credit, and bring on the very state of affairs they feared. Maurice Allen said that his views were not those of the Bank but he agreed that this pessimistic hypothesis was not to be ruled out. The government has left no loophole and the state of the reserves makes a public change of front very difficult.

On all this N.K.'s comment was that the government had been attacked in the past for not barking when it bit. Was it to stop biting and be attacked for barking too loudly?

The change of Ministers took everybody by surprise.[96] On Monday Burnet[97] was saying simply: "Brown must go" and I found myself in the position of emphasising his merits as a go-getter (in the right job) and his bad luck in being handed The Plan (when planning for anything except the balance of payments was bound to be impossible) and Incomes Policy (when this too was incompatible with the rest of the government's economic policy). But it was perhaps going too far to excuse him for not seeing that the policies did not add up when this is what planning is all about, and he had had nearly two years to say so. Later in the week Douglas Allen was also expounding the impossibilities of George and particularly the problem of dealing with somebody so essentially irrational and liable to fly off the handle.

Saturday, 17 September   My first impression on coming back from holiday was of how little had happened either in Whitehall or in the country. The papers had just begun to feature redundancy and the motor industry hit the headlines on Wednesday. Fred told me that Chancellor was insisting that Treasury took a more operational line by which he seemed to mean that other Departments

---

[96] As part of the Cabinet changes made on 10 August, George Brown moved to the Foreign Office to knock at the door of the EEC, Michael Stewart succeeded him in charge of DEA and Dick Crossman became Lord President.

[97] Alastair Burnet – Leader writer *The Economist*, 1958–62; Political Editor, ITV News, 1963–64; Editor, *The Economist*, 1965–74.

were not to enjoy our confidence. He was said to be rather browned off and not reconciled either to being No.4 below Michael Stewart or to trying to run the Treasury in tandem with DEA.

Later I talked to William (on Wednesday) and he said that this mood was getting under control and the Chancellor recognised that coordination involved exchange of information. T.B. was his bete noire and it was T.B. that he wanted to keep at arm's length. Ian B. said that it was the usual post-holiday mood of the Chancellor to suspect the worst – to feel that his Department was keeping him in the dark and not coming clean, to ask that there should be a work programme, to complain about his own burden of duties and ask for some of it to be pushed onto other Treasury Ministers, etc., etc. But of course there is no holding the Chancellor to a regular programme as Ian quickly discovered. He has just started seeing City Editors but this will probably not last more than a month or two.

William said that the real trouble was that he had nothing solid to occupy him and was therefore inclined to reach after lots of rather gaseous topics- he had kept him from 12 till after 2 discussing this and that, mainly large and shapeless subjects like the future of world trade and liquidity.

On Thursday we had a meeting on tax reform at which he seemed his usual buoyant self, but a little puzzled as to what *could* go into the next Budget if, as we agreed, major reforms must be ruled out. He gave us his usual harangue on savings, confessing willingly to heterodoxy but pleading that he must be able to *appear* to be on the side of the saver.

Chancellor spent a lot of the week fighting the Minister of Agriculture on credit and won his battle at Cabinet on Thursday. Sam G. said it kept him very busy and had taken up practically an entire day. Now he's off to Montreal and won't be back in the Treasury for about 3 weeks Commonwealth Finance Ministers, Bank/Fund, then Party Conference follow one another.

On Friday afternoon I had a late call from T.B. After some polite exchanges, he went right off the deep end about Harry Johnson[98]. Why hadn't I told him that he was working for the Board of Trade? What had happened to our agreement? He became more and more livid with rage at this "rabid defender of laissez faire". Then he switched to Wright[99] who was going to the C.R.O. and knew nothing about the very intricate problems of Commonwealth countries (to which I pointed out that he had only recently returned from Singapore). Peston[100] and Ely D. came next. I asked if I was to let him know of economists appointed to government committees as well. He ended by insisting on an early meeting so that he could find out what fresh surprises were in store.

[98] Harry Johnson – Professor of Economic Theory, University of Manchester, 1956–59; Professor of Economics, LSE, 1966–74.

[99] John Wright – Economist, Chief Scientific Adviser's Staff, Min. of Defence, 1961–66; Senior Econ. Adviser, Colonial Office, 1966–68; Head of Economists' Dept., FCO, 1968–71.

[100] Maurice Peston (later Lord) – Economic Section, Treasury, 1962–64; Min. of Defence, 1964–66; Professor of Economics, Queen Mary College, University of London, 1965–88.

The P.M. hearing of the motor car redundancies, was apparently pleased that they had chosen that option but whether he will say so in public is quite another matter. It seems to me that there is a certain euphoria about the price and income freeze after two months and that people are forgetting that it had to escape challenge for a much longer period if it is to be successful. It's only now, when the deflation is beginning to bite and the atmosphere of industrial relations is changing, that one can judge the chances of maintaining the freeze. We could easily have a repetition of the electricity supply case in 1961.

Sunday, 9 October　　Didn't see Chancellor till Walter Heller's party on Saturday at Carlton Tower and then had a brief word with him on Euro-dollars and high interest rates, Dewey Daane[101] and Alan Holmes[102] standing by. Chancellor said it seemed dotty to do things that did no good to US balance and actually hurt ours. He also presumed that there would be more emphasis on tax weapon and less on monetary after November. The Americans hoped so. Dewey said that he found it hard work at the Fed. – they meet every morning at 10 and go on till 12 or later (stopping for tennis). He gets papers at 6 p.m. and so had more home work than at the Treasury. Most of the work is on merger cases and all Governors join in.

Main event of the week was meeting on public expenditure on Friday in William's room. William handed out table (which he gave to Robert and me the previous evening) showing cuts proposed for 1967-68 to get back to level assumed on July 20. This added up to £300 m. and included some increased charges (e.g. school meals 12 1/2p from 5p). T.B. at once said figures alleged to have been prepared to meet specification from Ministers had now acquired a life of their own and were now to be basis of decisions. He didn't think for a moment Ministers would agree to suggestions and they would certainly raise whole issue of Budget. He also attacked Treasury for presenting figures in same old way instead of in economic categories and said that some Ministers would feel free to ask for higher taxes. William seemed a little nettled and said that it was decisions to increase expenditure since July that had given life to figures. We *had* used economic categories, even if they were full of anomalies. As for the Budget his withers were unwrung. Let them raise it.

Douglas Allen then said that the rise in charges would be awkward from incomes policy angle since 12 1/2p from 5p for family of three could be a lot of money. Ministers might prefer to go back on earlier decisions than take this politically difficult step.

On Wednesday I went to Pol. Economy Club to hear Dewdney[103] on productivity agreements but the best contribution came from Ben Roberts, who spoke of the absence of all such agreements on the continent where they are unnecessary because of the labour legislation that we used to deride.

[101] James Dewey Daane – Dep. Under-Sec. of Treasury for Monetary Affairs, Washington, 1961–63; member of Board of US Federal Reserve System from 1963.

[102] Alan Holmes – member of Federal Reserve Bank of New York.

[103] D A C Dewdney – Managing Dir., Esso Petroleum Co., 1963–67; Vice-Chm. 1968; Jt. Dep. Chm. NBPI, 1965–66; pert-time Member Bd., 1967–69.

On Thursday a very interesting session of the Whitehall Dining Club at the R.A.C. on foreign policy. At the end Paul Gore Booth[104] said: "There have been two occasions in my life when Ministers have deliberately cut themselves off from their officials. One was Munich and the other Suez. Officials may not always keep them on the rails but you see what happens when they're not used". Leslie Rowan said that according to Horowitz[105] the Israelis had a 10 to 1 superiority in the air and never had to fight an air battle and a 5 to 1 superiority in tanks but fought only one tank battle when some of their units failed to identify another Israeli unit. It was simply one great muddle with the air force thinking of a 7 day strafe before they had complete air control. He also recalled how in the war there appeared on Churchill's desk on the same day the intelligence report on a German invasion indicating that the Germans could get a foothold in a week and a staff appreciation of the time required for us to land in Ireland six weeks.

Maurice Parsons said that George Humphries[106] had ruled that we were not to get a penny from the IMF until all our troops were out of the occupied zone. Paul Gore Booth also told us how Denis Rickett had rung him up on the day hostilities broke out and when he got over to the Treasury asked him as he sat down: "Well, is this war and if so whose side are we on?". Makins[107] didn't know until the Sunday that a decision had been taken and Leslie R. learned only on the Monday when the fighting had already started.

Monday, 10 October   Chancellor and Chief Secretary had a field day with us. Why did we let public expenditure keep on growing? What had happened to the injunction to limit the increase to $4\frac{1}{4}\%$? "If you get the increase down to 8% when asked to keep to $4\frac{1}{4}\%$ perhaps you would get down to $4\frac{1}{4}\%$ with a nil permitted increase!" (In saying this the Chancellor wasn't aware that if the incomes policy is a success we may see wages rise by 5% over the next year.) And why was there no attempt to carry out the remit to show how we might limit expenditure increase to $3\frac{1}{4}\%$? (The Chief Secretary explained that if $4\frac{1}{4}\%$ was right for a 25% growth in GDP then it seemed sensible to take $3\frac{1}{4}\%$ now that growth was going to be a lot less.) "There isn't a word here about defence except to say that no cuts will take effect till 1970". Of course he was told that you couldn't cut public expenditure so quickly. To which he replied that you could cut civil servants' salaries and (for that matter) numbers.

He had his tongue in his cheek: but obviously meant to ferret out other possibilities without accepting increases in charges which he dismissed as not really limiting expenditure. He recognized that he and Chief Secretary would be alone in fighting for the private sector while other ministers would fight for their

---

[104] Sir Paul Gore Booth (later Lord) – British High Commissioner in India, 1960–65; Perm. Under-Sec. of State, Foreign Office, 1965–69; Head of HM Diplomatic Service, 1968–69.

[105] David Horowitz – Israeli economist; Governor, Bank of Israel from 1954.

[106] George Humphries – Secretary of the US Treasury in the 1950's.

[107] Roger Makins (later Lord Sherfield) – Jt. Permanent Sec., Treasury, 1956–59; Chm., UFAEA, 1960–64; Hill Samuel Group, 1964–70.

bit of the public sector; and that it was difficult to cut while the big spending departments were sheltered (as in July) or could point to exceptions like housing. When I asked how he could seriously ask his colleagues to agree to cuts of £500 m. *on top of* the July cuts of £500 m. in demand, he admitted that he didn't know in July just how big the increase in public expenditure would turn out to be. It was plain that he was really anxious to find some guide to the just balance between public and private sector. Would it help or hinder growth if he cut new hospitals from, say, 10 to 7? In all this he was remarkably unconcerned about the level of demand. He just wanted to cut expenditure: in fact he rebelled against calling it a cut to limit the increase to 4¼%. He said perhaps he was old fashioned (and the Chief Secretary said he was too) in his attitude to public expenditure. Chancellor wanted a neutral budget – certainly wouldn't think of increasing taxation in circumstances of 1967 and couldn't see why expenditure should increase either. Spoke of "all that nonsense about constant prices" and really hankered after constant money outlay. I doubt if such doctrine had been heard in the Treasury since Thorneycroft[108]. One naturally reflects on the fate of Thorneycroft.

Earlier Wynne had analysed the cuts in NIF terms and was excited because this is the first time it had ever been done on the Budget Committee Public Expenditure side. R.N. said it was an historic day for the Treasury. I told him to wait an hour till we saw the Chancellor. On reflection I think we were both right!

Monday, 17 October   On Friday we got preliminary unemployment figure – up by 98,000, of which 60,000 wholly unemployed or 34,000 seasonally corrected. This will come out on Thursday and have a devastating effect on week-end press, reinforced by CBI Investment results. Panic clearly beginning although Chancellor was very restrained at today's discussion. P.M. has minuted Chancellor who rather resents (so he says) having his own ideas flung back at him with no indication of their origin. (This à propos of a temporary increase in investment grant). Nicky said flatly he welcomed increase in unemployment – sooner the better, etc. – economy had suffered too long from constipation brought on by scarcity of labour. He didn't like my suggestion that we ought to relax bank advances and preferred cut of ½% – not 1% – in bank rate. Chancellor disposed to agree. Sam G. was against both but felt credit ceiling the easier to change. William favoured liquidity move rather than increase in investment grant. Wynne pointed to fact that SET payments lay ahead with no *assurance* that they would be repaid before March. It was all very inconclusive but at least no sign that Chancellor was anxious to take lead in reflation. On contrary, he wanted to know where he could most safely make a concession to his colleagues.

Donald, à propos of unemployment, quoted Wynne's dream of the oboe con-

---

[108] Peter Thorneycroft- Conservative President, Board of Trade, 1951–57; Chancellor of the Excheuqer, 1957–58; Minister of Aviation, 1960–62; Minister of Defence, 1962–64.

certs when as he was about to start someone jumped up to ask if he was sure his notes were seasonally adjusted.

R.N. has now decided to take the job in Stockholm but won't issue statement till he goes there with Fulton and gets it all sown up. He will go in May.

Sunday, 23 October   On Friday we had a fascinating discussion on Europe in which T.B. (who has submitted a paper prophesying *two* devaluations if we enter EEC and arguing for a tie-up with US) attacked the F.O. for not setting out the *political* conditions of entry. In his view France would never allow us to enter if we persisted in a pro-American policy, or unless we became "fully European" in our attitude. He claimed to have talked to Brunet when he was over and confirmed that the French had not budged and would not budge on the central proposition that, as Bill Nield put it, quoting de Gaulle, we would come in "tout nu" or not at all – i.e. stripped of our reserve currency function, of our special relationship with the Commonwealth, and the US, of our agricultural policy, etc.

Meanwhile Frank Figgures has done a very good brief explaining that we couldn't get in before Jan. 1970 at best and would certainly be allowed a 3 year transition period so that the balance of payments in 1967-68 is not very relevant.

The argument on Friday was that if we joined we should certainly have to devalue. On the other hand we could probable shed our East of Suez commitments. It is consistent to think that antagonising the US and devaluation would go together and of course if antagonism is the price of entry the rest follows. But it is not altogether clear that this is so especially as a few years ago it was the US that actively pushed us to negotiate. It was also argued that we should devalue *before* negotiating and this too makes sense, given the assumptions.

It was rather comic to hear T.B. and N.K. telling us where our true interests lay and what the Anglo-Saxons ought to do, especially as the moral of it all was to turn our backs on the Continent and face our destiny across the Atlantic. After all, even Lionel Robbins in 1950 didn't go quite *that* far in thinking up the Atlantic Community.

Earlier in the week Douglas Allen said at lunch that there *had* been a plot and the leader of it was G.B. The *New Statesman* had probably got the story right. George had almost certainly put out some feelers to see what support he would get if he challenged H.W. for the leadership and George Wigg must have known this.

I spent a good part of the week trying to get the investment outlook into focus. The press, as I expected, simply brushed aside the Board of Trade survey and took the CBI results at face value, working themselves into a panic. I saw Hugh Weeks[109] before his press conference and he was pretty reasonable. But Peter Jenkins in *The Guardian* didn't even get his figures right and spoke of a 15-*35*% drop next year instead of a 15-25% drop to the second half of 1967

[109] Hugh Weeks Director, ICFC, 1960–74; Chm., NIESR, 1960–74; Dep. Chm., Richard Thomas and Baldwin, 1965–68.

(which I judge is what Hugh Weeks must have said).[110]

The Chancellor took it all pretty calmly. When we met on Monday we soon got on to investment grants and monetary policy and I found myself arguing with Nicky (who wanted to cut bank rate by $1/2$%) and S.G. (who was averse to changing the ceiling on bank credit). My line was that now that the July measures were working we ought to let up on credit restriction especially as this plainly had aggravated the slump in business confidence and investment plans (so far as there has been a slump!).

We had later meetings on all this and there has clearly been a change quite recently. Both in bank credit and in debenture issues the demand has fallen away in the past month or so, the fall in issues under planning being the more recent and the queue still a long one. Banks could lend plenty if they said they could. H. Weeks said ICFC still had big demand on their funds at 9–10% on debentures and were lending strictly within the criteria.

Chancellor on all this seemed to favour a one year investment grant and a cut in bank rate rather than an increase in supply of credit. But things may change. Unfortunately I missed the later meeting on tap stock where I think the maturity date a good deal too long. Leslie O'Brien was there but itching to get away to Zecchi's Memorial.

Tuesday, 25 October   Ministers yesterday seemed in no hurry to decide on an increase in investment grants – they thought £100 m. a lot to spend on psychology and unlikely to make much difference to level of investment.

Sunday, 30 October   A fairly quiet week. Dinner party on Friday night. Chapin[111] told us story of the Scots in Argentine who tried to import haggis and found themselves up against the usual health regulations. After chemical tests it was allowed an import licence – as a fertilizer!

On Thursday we had meeting with Governor and Chancellor on public expenditure. Governor's second letter since he took office and very well argued (Nicky said it was "a pleasure to read"). Chancellor at a loss to see how he could devise a formula for control of public expenditure and recognised that $4^1/4$% had had its day. He suggested a task force of Bank and Treasury economists.

On Wednesday Chancellor took a press conference at which he reiterated his figure of 400,000 as his aim for unemployment but declined to tell Sam Brittan whether it was seasonally adjusted wholly unemployed. After the conference he and Sam had a word together and Chancellor said that he could recall three separate occasions on which he had very much resented what Sam had said. But of course he couldn't recall any of them for Sam's benefit.

---

[110] The *Board of Trade Journal* reviewed 'The Investment Outlook' in an article on 28 October 1966. This showed that investment in manufacturing increased by 12 per cent in 1964 and 9 per cent in 1965 but was expected to fall by 4 per cent in 1966 and 8 per cent in 1967. If oil refining was omitted, however, the falls in 1966 and 1967 became 11 and 16 per cent. In due course the official statistics showed a *rise* in manufacturing investment in 1966 by $2^1/2$% and fall of 2–$2^1/2$% in 1967.

[111] Victor Chapin – Canadian commercial attaché in London.

Denis Barnes on Tuesday said he was quite clear that we had to stick at 2% unemployment and he thought his Minister was of same opinion. He had never believed we'd stay below 2%. But why did Treasury accept risks of unemployment forecasting when they could get Ministry of Labour to take it on? I didn't argue the point but he was right in saying Chancellor is in exposed position. So is M. Stewart. It's almost as if P.M. wanted to keep Jim ready for the chopping block.

With George B., the same fatal urge to act is again at work. He wants to move now to get into Europe when there is really nothing to be done. So we'll have these probes – lunar or not – with no possibility of telling the foreigner what we want. For we'd either have to give away our negotiating position or appear to want terms that the French could cite as proof of our unwillingness to be good Europeans. In any event as F.F. pointed out, they all know that we haven't really made up our minds. The German Ambassador told him: "I'm not interested in what the Cabinet thinks unless they've decided. I'm very interested in what your P.M. thinks and he hasn't decided".

Unemployment figures are now being collected weekly but the fact is being kept very secret. The rise goes on at about the same rate as in the past month.

Tuesday, 1 November   John Stevens very interesting on US monetary policy where the Fed. is now split down the middle on possible tax increase after election. Idea would be to get ready for the cut later before 1968 election. Governor told me yesterday that Bill Martin had thought at Bank/Fund meeting that economy had peaked out but that taxes would still be increased. The Fed. made bloomer over discount rate. Anxious to keep it down even if below market rate and use discount window to enforce selective credit policy in interests of debt management. But it had been a flop because people didn't like to go to discount window too frequently and didn't want to be in state of uncertainty about access to credit. US borrowing will continue heavy and this will make them anxious to keep other borrowers out of market.

We agreed that real issue now was 1968 since by then any détente in Vietnam might have serious effects on US, with government spending *and* private investment both high and vulnerable. Similarly in UK real issue is how business investment will move in 1968, not 1967, and current uncertainties more likely to affect 1968. Possibility of devaluation next year can be ruled out, given P.M.'s line, and he can't use Europe as alibi because he can't guarantee that we'd get in or tell his Cabinet what it's all in aid of. J.S. also thought that he couldn't stimulate consumption in next Budget and since we can't stimulate government spending either, we're bound to be at mercy of export developments, whether we like it or not.

Monday, 7 November   Evening at No.10 – first time this year I think – for IRC dinner. Enormous– 11 members of Bank and 5 Ministers and their Permanent Secretaries or Economic Adviser plus 2 officials. Formal dinner upstairs – none of the old beer + do-it-yourself stuff – with wines, liqueurs, cigars and all, then discussion in Cabinet room led by P.M. but with chance for all Board members to join in. G.B. not there and this helped towards more consecutive discussion. M. Stewart spoke in middle and good sense but somehow lacked force. Chancellor silent. Minister of Technology (Benn[112]) quite amusing. Best of the industrialists, I thought, was Lockwood[113] with Stokes[114] a bit wild on consortia and Mike Wheeler[115] backing him. Kearton[116] good on mergers which he pointed out were rare and usually concealed as take-over bids for sake of amour propre. He wanted aggressiveness and nobody of course opposed this although nobody seemed very clear *what* IRC was to be aggressive about. General attitude – not content with gradual reconstruction via mergers, must do something more forceful to help exports. Government procurement should be used to assist regrouping. But of course persuasion important and government backing of IRC as instrument of policy essential. Leslie O'B. spoke up in praise of it and even R. Powell pointed out that only IRC could take initiative, a point that P.M. took up at once. P.M. seemed relaxed as usual, made his quota of cracks, but concentrated on cross-examining and eliciting opinions.

Lunch with Sir D. MacD. and walked with him in the park discussing the Plan etc. He pointed out that there was nothing to cause unemployment to *fall* after 1967 unless one took a very optimistic view of exports. He also spoke of early days with G.B. when he had tried to persuade George that one couldn't in 1970 have bigger public spending and had to *choose* between programmes. G.B. very indignant and unbelieving – like Varga[117] in 1952 on need to increase supply not ration demand by price. I said it looked as if Treasury were now the only surviving believers in planning because we needed to plan public sector within appropriate framework. I also suggested that full employment was the secret weapon by which we controlled public expenditure, a topic discussed on Friday with William and P. Vinter (I've since asked R.S. Edwards, John Wall,[118] Tony Part, etc. whether their programmes are accelerating now that labour market has eased).

Chancellor tonight said he had shown my paper proposing extension of incomes freeze to M. Stewart. On Saturday Kahn and Berrill[119] phoned me again about draft White Paper and I had a further word with B. today after K. had

---

[112] A W Benn – Lab. Paymaster General, 1964–66 ; Minister of Technology, 1966–70.

[113] Sir J Lockwood – Chm., EMI Ltd and subsidiaries, 1954–74; Director NRDC, 1951–67; Chm., IRC, 1969–71.

[114] Lord Stokes – President, SMMT, 1961–62; Man. Dir. and Dep. Chm., Leyland Motor Corp. 1963–66; Chm., 1967; Chm. and Man. Dir., British Leyland, 1968–75.

[115] Sir Charles Wheeler – Jt. Man. Dir., Guest Keen Iron and Steel Co Ltd, 1946–54; Chm., 1959–60; Chm., AEI Ltd, 1964–67.

[116] Frank Kearton (later Lord) - Dep. Chm., Courtaulds, 1961–64; Chm., 1964–75; Chm., IRC, 1966–68.

[117] Varga – Hungarian economist living in Moscow and advising government of USSR.

[118] Sir John Wall – Unilever Ltd, 1952–58; EMI, 1958–64; Dep. Chm., Post Office Board, 1966–68; Chm., International Computer Holdings, 1968–72.

[119] Kenneth Berrill – Lecturer in Economics, University of Cambridge, 1949–69; Special Adviser Treasury, 1967–69; Head of Govt. Econ. Service and Chief Econ. Adviser to Treasury, 1973–74.

rung me up about paragraphs on productivity agreements and low paid workers.

Chancellor also said he understood forecasts were pretty gloomy and that he didn't want to circulate them. This seemed to apply to NIF as well as to BP. I don't think he realises that Departments already have them.

Wynne's forecasts in fact show total investment falling or flat from 1964 and now beginning to increase. Same with housing. All very odd. He had a 3% rise in production next year but has whittled it down to 2%. This in fact yields much same level as in August forecast. The public investment element in forecast is major uncertainty because we simply don't know whether it will go along flat as before or rise with programme, i.e. very steeply. We are in fact forecasting a 10% rise next year.

Thursday, 10 November   Harold made his statement on EEC. So we were wrong in thinking that nothing would come of it all and unsuccessful in dissuading them. But they did put in something about the pound having to be "firm and high" like some decayed bird.

Chancellor saw financial journalists on Wednesday night (?) and William Davis reflects this (as does the *Telegraph*). He seems to have said that investment was encouraged "last time" by announcement we were going to join Common Market. Where *did* he get that impression?

P.M. has asked that *all* appointments of senior economists be referred to him and if necessary should go to an informal committee of myself, T.B. and R.N. This all comes from Ely's appointment to Monopolies Commission of which I was quite unaware till Frances told me. While existing arrangements are bad (e.g. I'm not told myself) the P.M. can't possibly keep track of all the negotiations for "senior" economists including part-time consultants.

Saturday, 12 November   On Monday night Chancellor said he didn't want forecasts to go round to other Ministers. He thought they would be misused and leaked. On Friday he returned to the same subject with P. Baldwin,[120] obviously under the illusion that he had had the conversation with him. But of course other Departments already have the forecasts since they collaborated in their preparation. Reggie used to have the same desire to play his cards close to his chest.

When I asked P.B. what SEP was for if it couldn't discuss the forecasts, he said the trouble was that the Chancellor didn't think it *had* any point. He certainly won't be willing to show his hand and yet he is bound to be under pressure to relax or at least not cut public expenditure. He is now taking a less extreme position and willing to see an increase of 6% in 1967-68 instead of 4 1/4%. But as William has emphasised the delay in reaching decisions means that the forecasts will be prayed in aid by those who don't want to make cuts.

The P.M. has been asking what our present estimate of the fall in hire purchase debt is and we have repeated £160 m. He has also asked for a note after being

[120] Peter Baldwin – Cabinet Office, 1962–64; Principal Private Sec to Chancellor of Exchequer, July 1966–Jan. 1968; Under-Sec., Treasury, 1968–72.

told by Chancellor that we deflated by £800 m. not £500 m. in July. (P.B. thinks however that he treats £800 m. as 18 months' deflation instead of 12: but I can't believe this.) It happens that we now get nearer to £500 m. but this is because (in part) we have reduced exports, are taking a higher figure for public expenditure, etc.

On Friday I had a succession of meetings. First ESG discussing a paper by Donald on the long term outlook. Tommy raised an odd question about some plan for advance factories that might run to hundreds of millions. Donald is now arguing that increase in potential to 1970 is 19½% but that on GEG calculations output will rise only 13/14% with unemployment steady at 2½%. (I don't think this can be right but my query was shouted down.) The paper went over q.r.'s, mobilisation of foreign assets, cuts in defence expenditure, etc. and showed that none of them will make a great deal of difference. As Nicky put it, it was precise, clear and gloomy. We agreed that entry into Europe finally ruled out q.r.'s.

Then followed F.U. on guarantees, etc. I asked why the central banks of the sterling area should be excluded from forward market (they are alone in this) and offered no option that would give them similar cover (e.g. a kind of Roosa bond[121] at lower rates of interest and with less liquidity).

After lunch a meeting on shadow rates with Posner, one with Maurice Allen and then William on draft for SEP, followed by A.H. Cameron[122] from Toronto.

Lunch with James Murray[123] on leave from Indonesia. He said he was the only expert on genocide in Indonesia (he watched it among the Watutsi) and could tell just how to reckon how many bodies could be disposed of in a given time without trace, how many could be reckoned to give rise to X at a particular bend in the river, etc., etc. He thought 30/300 thousand the best estimate he could offer and Malik[124] has since said 100/200 thousand or, say, 150,000. The Americans had to change their tune abruptly since they didn't want the new regime to seem too blood-thirsty. In Bali the estimate is 20,000 or so. I asked how so permissive a society could be so savage. He thought the bad boys of the village had been willing to act for the Communists and had turned themselves into nasty little fuhrers so that once the protection of Soekarno[125] was withdrawn and they were clearly not in favour with the central authorities the villagers took the law into their own hands.

Murray said one of his first instructions was to send no cables on Soekarno's health. He had seen in a state paper a printed report by a Harley St. specialist and thought it one of the most awful documents ever. Gilchrist[126] used to send

---

[121] Roosa bonds – Dollar-denominated bonds sold abroad.

[122] A H Cameron – Dealer in bond market, Canada.

[123] James Murray – HM Consul Ruanda-Urundi, 1961–62; Ambassador, 1962–63; Dep. Head of UK Delegation to EEC, 1963–65; Counsellor, Djakarta, 1965–67; Head of the Eastern Dept., FCO, 1967–70.

[124] Omar Malik – probably Pakistan Ambassador to Indonesia in 1950.

[125] A. Soekarno – President, Republic of Indonesia, 1945–49; of United States of Indonesia from 1949; Head of State for life, 1963.

[126] Sir Andrew Gilchrist – Diplomat, 1933–70; Ambassador at Reykjavik, Djakarta

a cable one week saying that S. was in very poor health and follow it the next with a casual description of an encounter with an obviously ebullient S. He is said to have only half a liver. But his Japanese wife is about to give birth. Everything is still done in his name – even the ordinances requiring him to stay put. The army are firmly in power and see eye to eye with the government.

Murray said the economists were the best of the people around. There had been an improvement in the degree of pilfering etc. of imports. But prices rose 1,000 times last year. Expenditure by the state came to 29b, revenue budgeted for was 9b and actually received in six months $1^1/_2$b (the seasonal factors operate to make the second six months rather better). Presumably the balance of payments is similar and the prospects of debt repayment very remote.

Cameron told me that Canadian banking system was getting highly illiquid because the squeeze was making it part with its best assets. C. warned Mike Pearson[127] that rising wages were going to force devaluation within the next couple of years. He was full of gossip about Morgan's (who had gone long on US gilts and taken a heavy loss), about the City Bank and US/Canadian legislation on banking, the danger of hire purchase finance houses being in trouble in UK. I had little chance to talk about UK. He did tell me of a conversation in 1962 with P.P. Schweitzer in Paris when he was given the official French line on perfidious Albion. We had tried to prevent the EEC from coming into existence, organised the EFTA as a counter attraction, and now wanted to join EEC to smash it up from inside, dishing the Commonwealth which wouldn't trust us in the least.

Sunday, 20 November　　　Three days in Paris for OECD meetings and two in London with the usual enormous pile of arrears.

Stopper and others who had told me that it looked as if it was all over in July were naturally delighted by the measures we took. Ossola even feared we might have gone too far (like Italy in 1964) and that we ought to be thinking of relaxations were it not for the international misgivings this might arouse. Only Ockrent seemed determined to get us to be more explicit about the path on which we had set out.

Tuesday, 29 November　　　Back from Geneva/EFTA with Derek Mitchell. He told me yesterday that for the first time Burke Trend had confessed to him that he really didn't know where the P.M. stood on Europe. There was "layer upon layer upon layer". T.B. told us that he had no doubt at all after his visit to Paris where the French stood. They would repeat Wormser's tactics and "screw and screw and screw and screw" until we found ourselves having to choose whom to disappoint – the Commonwealth, the US, the Germans, etc.... ending up by disappointing everybody. Then the French would be ready to put their cards on the table. R.N. thought we had to make some gesture and it could only take the form of a proposal on sterling balances or on defence.

and Dublin.

[127] Lester (Mike) Pearson – Canadian diplomat and politician.

Derek Mitchell told me of the first day at No.10 in October 1964 (when T. didn't get his key to the gate from the Cabinet Office – he got it the day D.J.M. left No.10) T.B. came in late in the evening to say, "Dear boy, there's just one thing that hasn't yet been arranged for me: do you think you could see to it? – I haven't got a title". To which Derek at once said: "You can't expect that on the first day – you'll have to wait till you go!".

When in Geneva I had some talks about the CM. I gather that Olivier Long was able to give a precise summary of the line-up in the Cabinet and the views of the leading exponents on both sides. At the Lisbon meeting of EFTA the members had judged from our "relaxed" attitude, the jolliness of George Thomson, the open hostility of Douglas Jay, the detachment of Michael Stewart, that we had no immediate initiative in mind. At first they felt that we might be in danger of repeating the folly of the Danes but they have since been somewhat reassured, no doubt once they saw the French reactions. Douglas Jay said "over my dead body" and this is in strange contrast to the views of Richard Powell who in other respects is very much in sympathy with him.

T.B. said on Friday that the P.M. had been obliged to go as far as he did or he would have had a Cabinet crisis on his hands and he didn't want a Cabinet crisis. Derek Mitchell said much the same when he said that if we were intending to go in, a Cabinet re-shuffle would be a preliminary and a signal.

I had a long argument with Sparks Davis[128] on Saturday night when he was discussing the future of electronics. He seemed to be saying that the size of the U.S. market gave them an overwhelming advantage since they could engage in a development effort related to their market opportunities and this would reinforce their grip on the market. But while he attached importance to scale he was also insisting on the need for mergers in the U.K. between the small family businesses engaged in scientific instrument manufacture. In Germany, Siemens had always played a major role and another large private firm (Hartmann's?) was also in a position to undertake the necessary development. AEI could have done the same and had a strong Cambridge connection before the war (with Cockcroft and Walton and others). One of their people invented the foot pump but AEI now paid royalties to GEC of USA for their designs. The simmerstat was still almost a monopoly of AEI (70% of the world market and made at lower cost than in 1937) in spite of attempts by GEC to improve on the British model. Nobody in 1931 appreciated that the electron microscope would generate £10 m. a year business by 1966 (1000 are made annually – half in Japan) – but it was an AEI invention and they had gone on assuming that they had a grip on it until too late. I put it to him that while Siemens had come back from next to nothing AEI had succeeded in losing £100 m. and neglecting the lines in which profits were there to be made. He didn't disagree, recollecting his own experience in Sunvic and the failure of AEI to attempt takeovers in this line of business, much less putting up the capital for expansion. The business Sparks built up in Germany had been pretty well on a basis of handing over £10 a time to cover expenses! Yet the turnover is now well over £1 m. a year.

[128] Ryland 'Sparks' Davis – Engineer with Met. Vick., later AEI; Man. Dir. of Sunvic.

I said that I recognized that there were lots of factors behind our poor performance but management was a major one. Economists tended to single out
investment, education, size of market, development effort, etc. without recog-
nising how all these interacted and how much the sheer will to make money
and improve efficiency counted. Our society was too relaxed, too willing to let
well alone and not face a row or a major upheaval. One could put all this in
terms of competitiveness. It was certainly associated in some ways with the
forms of central control. Yet I could not dispute that if mergers were needed
some central initiative by the government or IRC would probably be required.

Sparks described the opposition within AEI to the setting up of a technological
forecasting committee, drawn from the scientists, to review the technical changes
against which they should be on their guard or from which they should be ready
to profit. The Finance Division insisted that programmes and forecasting were
their affair. They were uneasy about scientists meeting on topics of this kind.
In the end S. said he had to change the title and to some extent the function.
Yet there *is* no real link between the scientists and the financial experts and
little appreciation of how each functions (e.g. the scientists regard DCF as
involving absurd questions and giving magnitudes where the risks of error are
subsequently ignored or misunderstood).

It is also true that the problems of government and society are much the
same as in a large firm where the Chairman may in the end do no more than
change the climate of thinking or the framework of decision-taking without
making a lot of difference to individual decisions. He can't sack or disregard X
because that would react on the morale of X's Department. After a merger the
constituent units will retain their original loyalties and welding them together
is a long drawn out process. (BTH/Met. Vickers is a splendid example of
in-fighting). Even on local councils, as Barbara Davis said, if you get a left
wing staff a right wing council will still be faced with left wing specifications
at the technical level. Truman was hitting the nail on the head when he said
that his only real power and privilege was to sign the documents handed to him
for signature.

Thursday, 1 December   Yesterday we had a long meeting on regional policy
in which I did my best to rebut Nicky who is now on the war-path to extend
SET in a kind of colonising mission in the Development Regions. I'm afraid it
will all lead to a repeat of last year's budget with SET pre-empting the limelight
and side-tracking the main drift of reflationary policy.

Fred said today that he was now doubtful if civil servants really could keep
Ministers on the right lines and instanced the Budget as a prize example. He
wondered if William had put the objections forcefully enough and on this, of
course, I could say nothing because I don't know. Indeed, given William's
relationship to the Chancellor I hardly ever know what he is saying on current
issues. On regional policy I can't judge whether he will support my line or
Nicky's. On Capenhurst I suppose that I could have minuted again but he never
asked where I stood in the light of later discussions.

Yet as Donald MacD. said last night when I discussed regional policy with him, it is a relief to have someone so entirely rational to advise. D. feels far more content now that he has Michael Stewart and Douglas Allen to deal with in place of G.B. and Eric Roll. But even he, after 5 years, wonders if he will stay much longer.

DEA, I gather, take a lot of pains to brief M. Stewart before SEP meetings but don't know whether he says anything at the meetings. He has obviously had several sessions with Donald and no doubt with Douglas Allen and so is conscious of the significance of the paper on 1970 when the Chancellor is still apathetic.

Barbara Castle has written a very good letter to the Chancellor on roads, pointing out that the programme now extends only 3 years ahead. A very different letter from Richard Marsh admits tacitly that the electricity estimates are 5,000 MW too high in 1970, as we claimed, while the Ministry of Power refused to back us and the CEGB said that we had no right to make such calculations and were unwilling to modify theirs till the National Plan was revised.

Saturday, 17 December   We had some comings and goings with *The Economist* over Norman Macrae's[129] article 'Crystal Ball' a week ago.[130] The Chancellor was naturally indignant that his speech should be described as "deplorable" and still more when he had it quoted against him by Débré[131] on his visit to Paris. Raphael thought that I should write a "devastating reply" but in the end the Chancellor spoke to A. Burnet and got Macrae to come and see him on Friday. The Chancellor asked me to join hum after he had been talking to Macrae for nearly an hour. "Sit over there Alec", he said as I came in, "we have the enemy on this side". When we got round to forecasts Norman agreed that there might be special difficulties over balance of payments forecasts but argued that we were now falling badly behind in not giving official forecasts of GNP as other European countries did. This was coupled with some tilts at the Budget accounts for not showing the effects of the Budget on GNP and the difficulty of explaining to continentals that we were really more sophisticated than we seemed. On all this I pointed out that the Chancellor was in a unique position since he had the power to *act* on a forecast in a way none of the Europeans could so that a forecast was a statement of policy in the UK far more than anywhere else. There was also far more neuroticism about GNP forecasts here than abroad so that they were the basis of a great deal of comment in the press and Parliament. Some elements in the forecast could not be disclosed without revealing government policy (e.g. in relation to public expenditure) that it might

[129] Norman Macrae – Leader writer on *The Economist*.

[130] In its issue of 10 December 1966, *The Economist* pointed out in an article headed 'Crystal Ball' that the forecasts and comments of the National Institute in its latest *Economic Review* hinted at devaluation as the obvious policy. Asking whether the Government had an alternative, the article went on to suggest that its alternative was only too likely to be to deflate further.

[131] Michel Débré – French Prime Minister, 1959–62; Minister of Economic Affairs and Finance, 1964–65; Foreign Affairs, 1968–69; Defence, 1969–73.

be premature to announce. And so on.

The Chancellor after listening to all this suggested a Conference at Nuffield on what should or should not be published. He would be glad to promote this so long as he wasn't required to come.

Macrae said at one point that his judgement of the success of Chancellors was in proportion to their lack of vagueness. Butler got top marks for the Budget of 1952 even if the forecast in it had proved wrong. The Chancellor was unimpressed. Macrae went on to list Amory and Maudling among the less vague and this brought the Chancellor to the defence of Selwyn, who he said inherited a position that made specific forecasts difficult. M. rejoined that Selwyn *started* vague. His nostalgia for the old *Economic Survey* was rather amusing in view of Marjory Deane's[132] disenchantment with the National Plan since the problem is very much the same in the two cases.

I saw William earlier in the day and he told me a little of what went on in Paris. At the interview with Débré, he was taxed with bearing sterling in word if not in deed and D. denied this (our information implies he was lying) and pointed to 'Crystal Ball' to show that we needn't look outside Britain for bears. Rueff he dismissed as not responsible for government policy. After all the French government didn't think there was a shortage of international liquidity so why should they support an immediate increase in the price of gold? But when an increase was called for, this seemed an obvious device. D. talked of "doubling" the price and this upset his officials who passed a slip to him and led him to substitute "increase". But when William and the Chancellor asked whether a rise would not set off fresh gold hoarding in the expectation of a later rise, D. seemed uncomfortable and it was not clear whether he had really thought it all out or was reacting to pressure – from Rueff on one hand and from his officials who saw the fallacies on the other.

The Chancellor was also determined to make a bid to get interest rates down and had apparently talked Joe Fowler into a meeting on this in mid-February although it is still quite likely that once Fowler is back in US he will think better of getting involved in this. At any rate the Chancellor won't want anyone else (e.g. officials) to handle it as he wants if possible to have it on record for the benefit of his standing in the Party that he did his best to get international action. The Germans, represented by Brandt,[133] couldn't say very much but they did claim that they wanted lower rates and that Blessing was being told that he must get rates down (no doubt he will make the obvious rejoinders).

All this meant that William would no longer be going to Washington in January and that I ought to make my own arrangements. I dare say that I might also be able to find something out about alternatives to the Common Market and all that. William said that Débré had volunteered his own opinion that the major question to be resolved was not agriculture or the Commonwealth but what sort of community there would be after we joined. What would its political and

---

[132] Marjory Deane – Commentator for *The Economist*.

[133] Willie Brandt – Mayor of Berlin 1957–66; Fed. Minister of Foreign Affairs 1966–69; Federal Chancellor 1969–74.

defence orientation be? It was quite apparent that the French attitude rested explicitly on anti-Americanism and that this was the feature that would govern their willingness to admit us.

Joe Fowler also saw Débré and spoke to the Chancellor afterwards. They agreed that it would be desirable to explore what should be done if admission to the C.M. was not "on". Of course, in Whitehall this work is going ahead on a U and non-U basis (i.e. we join Europe or we don't) but I haven't heard that much that is new has emerged from the non-U analysis.

We had a great meeting in my room on export credit at which Nicky, having written most of the Treasury paper, took every opportunity of damning the Treasury line, sometimes with faint praise and more often without.

On Wednesday Denis Rickett and I lunched with Pete Collado,[134] Norman Biggs[135] and their European manager. P.C. told us that he had negotiated the two earliest agreements in war-time for aid to UK and elsewhere that introduced a 5% repayment in local currency. This condition he thought might have originated as a suggestion of Maynard Keynes. At any rate he had discussed with Keynes how something could be introduced that would give the agreements some appeal for Congress, something that the US could claim to its own immediate advantage. It was this 5% that had provided the funds for the Fulbrights.

He was proud of having been at Harvard in the days when Taussig's[136] pupils were all producing their fat red volumes on international trade and payments and he had himself written his thesis on the Japanese balance of payments so that he knew what it was to work with very limited and unreliable data (I assured him that this was ideal training for economic forecasting). There was then no series for the US (or British) balance of payments and the only study was Bullock, Williams and Tucker until some charlatan about 1935 minuted the President announcing that he had found that there was no American balance of payments and he had given instructions that one should be drawn up. In England, according to Biggs, the Bank of England had started in the thirties trying to prepare a balance of payments and had been obliged to ring up Logie (of Lazard's?) every so often because they couldn't follow what was happening to the various clearing agreements. All this arose à propos of the abundance of statistics nowadays compared with before the war.

Denis Rickett quoted the story of Chalmers[137] and Heath[138] when both were joint permanent secretaries. Chalmers arranged to see H. at a certain time and went along to find the Chancellor there. "Chancellor" he said at once, "what you told the House of Commons yesterday was a lie and you knew it was a lie. That's all, Tom" he said to Heath and shut the door. His appointment as

---

[134] Emilio (Pete) Collado – US economist and oil executive; US Exec. Dir., IBRD, 1946–47; Standard Oil Co of N.J., 1947–75.

[135] Norman Biggs – Director, Esso Petroleum Co., 1952–66; Chm., 1968–72.

[136] F W Taussig – Professor of Economics, Harvard University to 1935.

[137] Lord Robert Chalmers – Perm. Sec., Treasury, 1911–13; Governor of Ceylon, 1913–16; Perm. Sec., Treasury, 1916–19; Master of Peterhouse, Cambridge, 1924–31.

[138] Sir Thomas Heath – Jt. Perm. Sec., Treasury, 1913–19; Comptroller General, Nat. Debt Office, 1919–26; authority on Greek mathematics.

Governor of Ceylon followed soon after.

Denis had a chat with me after we got back. He said that someone had quoted a high official of the Bank of England as taking the view that we might not be in surplus after all next year. On this D. is reasonably optimistic and does not think that the government, having done so much for the sake of the parity, will want to throw it away because of pressure to reflate. He would qualify this if an election were likely but it seems years away. I said that if we encountered a further spell of concentrated speculation we should be in difficulties because I found it hard to believe that the government would go further down the deflationary road. On the other hand, by next spring they would be on the horns of a dilemma, particularly if unemployment continued to increase right up to the Budget. But the latest unemployment figures suggest a more hopeful conclusion.

Sunday, 18 December Two other things I omitted. First the pantomime over the increase in Building Society lending rates ten days ago (which brought rates on all loans to $7\frac{1}{8}\%$ instead of on new loans as previously). This took up the better part of two days in discussion of presentation until finally the Chancellor decided to issue no statement at all and leave it to the Press Office. On the whole, a sensible decision but the preliminaries showed how determined he is to make increases in rates difficult. He wanted to imply that those societies with sufficient reserves should not raise rates at once but wait till their funds become inadequate, i.e. he wanted more competition but not too much!

The other incident was the reference to North Sea Gas at Collado's lunch. They pointed out that they were under pressure to show a return by the US Treasury on all their sterling outlays and that it was becoming difficult to justify further heavy investment especially if negotiations took such an odd form that the most secret parts erupted periodically in the press. There are few things about which more leaks have occurred (no doubt gas is liable to leak) and Dr B.'s name has been freely included as if to sow prejudice. The natural suspicion is that the Gas Council has a hand in it although some Ministers may also be playing the game. Relations between Marsh and Sir H. Jones[139] are very strained as often happens with Chairman and Ministers.

I must record Denis' paraphrase of a Belgian view of aid: "Aid is what the poor in the rich countries give to the rich in the poor countries".

Tuesday, 20 December

Towards the end of December the Chancellor advanced a new economic strategy which he proposed to submit to SEP. He elaborated it into a six point programme (entry for 23 December) of which a key element was willingness to accept a 2 per cent level of unemployment. This was, however, an ambiguous target since it might be interpreted either as a working average, or a maximum – with very different outcomes. There was also some doubt whether the Chancellor really

[139] Sir H Jones – Dep. Chm., Gas Council, 1952–60; Chm., 1960–71.

meant 2 per cent or 1.8 per cent (entry for 23 December) – again, it made quite a difference. The rate of economic growth that 2 per cent unemployment permitted was open to argument; and calculations of tax revenue requirements and permissible public expenditure were highly uncertain. But the key uncertainty, as events were to prove, was the balance of payments. Any strategy was at the mercy of changes in the rate of growth of foreign markets and the course of international prices; and in 1967 the changes were large, unfortunate and unforeseen.

Tuesday, 20 December   We had a long meeting this morning of ESG mainly on the guidance to be given to nationalised industries. DEA now want to use upper and lower limits not only for investment planning but apparently for the next edition of the National Plan. This seems to me daft and I didn't hide my views. Nicky had a lot to say but was obviously quite ignorant of the electricity programme and the whole background to investment programmes.

This evening William called me to join Peter Vinter, Raymond Bell and himself at 6. Chancellor wants his paper on long-term growth of public expenditure to be based on 2% unemployment, £100m. surplus balance of payments and implied growth in GDP. We'll have to work this out by Thursday night but it does involve some wishful thinking and my economist colleagues will say so far more emphatically. Chancellor would settle for cuts of £200m. in defence (of which £70 m. might be overseas) but William thinks £100 m. might be added for civil expenditure and leaves housing on one side. M. Stewart on the other hand is probably persuaded that only solution is to push up output via devaluation but will hesitate to argue this.

Not much of interest at Natwest lunch except that there are rumours of Cobbold's[140] returning to the City and Cromer rejoining Baring's. Sir E. Reid[141] was the other guest and he is going off to retire to Edinburgh. Eddie Playfair[142] seemed to me a generation younger than his fellow directors who included Salisbury, Sylvester Gates, and about 25 others. Chesterfield[143] expressed himself strongly on Boards that were ignorant of their own bank and its affairs and believed that the Bank of England did a lot of harm in preventing contact between Treasury and clearing banks. They had told Ronald Thornton that they thought it wrong of him to go and talk to the Treasury (when he was still in commercial banking). But the outcome of this absence of contact was misunderstanding of what the other party was doing or trying to do.

Friday, 23 December   Three busy days mainly on the Chancellor's paper on long-term expenditure and the calculations needed for it. By Wednesday

[140] Lord Cobbold – Governor, Bank of England, 1949–61; Lord Chamberlain, 1963–71.

[141] Sir E Reid – Godson of King Edward VII; Director, Baring Bros and Co, 1926–68; Chm., Accepting Houses Cttee, 1946–66.

[142] Sir E Playfair – Perm. Sec., Ministry of Defence, 1960–61; Chm., International Computers and Tabulators Ltd, 1961–65.

[143] A D Chesterfield – Chief General Manager Westminster Bank, 1950–65; Director, 1963–69.

morning the marching orders were that the Chancellor needed a draft by lunchtime on Thursday, and so the calculations had effectively to be complete by Wednesday night – i.e. in one day. In due course Wynne reported and I talked to Fred who suggested that it would be a serious error to push all this into the SEP paper. For example, Ministers would see a set of figures for the first time which they would not be able to reconcile with the earlier SEP figures. The Treasury might have to defend its calculation without having enough time to be sure they were right. Other departments would be critical when, if we sheltered behind the First Secretary's paper and Donald's figures in it, we could establish all that was necessary without sticking our necks out.

When Peter Vinter and I saw William in the evening, he resisted this and told us that the Chancellor was now full of his strategy which had blossomed into a six point programme. He had been to see the PM who said snap to it all and did not mind being accused of doing Michael Stewart's work for him. It was obvious that William took some wry pleasure in contemplating the First Secretary's reactions when faced with the dilemma of supporting or opposing the Chancellor's paper. Donald's draft, which merely set out the calculations asked for by SEP, seemed to him (William) rather feeble precisely because it laid down no strategy whatever. I drew attention to the difficulties of the calculations, to the margins of error involved, and to the dependence of the Chancellor on a bit of luck. William for a moment thought I was attacking the Chancellor's judgement but I agreed that it was quite reasonable to take a chance particularly if he really did mean 2% unemployment. With unemployment steady at 2% we should probably be able to pay our way to and after 1970 unless things changed suddenly in foreign markets. To this William said Chancellor had told him that he would now accept the advice given to him when he entered the Treasury that 1.8% was the right operating ratio for unemployment. But of course 2 and 1.8 are not quite the same, especially if there are oscillations around the figure and if the repercussions on costs are not symmetrical.

William had also raised Europe (as I did on Tuesday) and the Chancellor had taken the line that he did not propose to run at $2\frac{1}{2}$% for the sake of joining the EEC. This carried the implication that he would be willing to look again at the rate if we did decide to join. William repeated to me on Thursday that this should not go any further (although P.V. was present on Wednesday and it surprised me that William was prepared to say this in his presence).

I did some redrafting on Wednesday and then talked to W.G. and J.S. on Thursday morning. In the meantime the ministerial meetings were put back and the idea of giving the Chancellor a draft for the train to Cardiff was dropped. From what W.G. said it became clear that we took 2% unemployment to imply an increase of only $14\frac{1}{2}$% in GDP from 1964–70 and the balance of payments seemed to work out at £150 m. a year. So in the end we seem to emerge with everything as before except that the unemployment figure has come down to 2 from $2\frac{1}{2}$%. The balance of payments of £300 m. that used to go with 2% 6 months ago has now been cut in half. The fact that Ministers have had 13–15% quoted to them as consistent with $2\frac{1}{2}$% unemployment will be decidedly awkward.

Late on Thursday William held an ESG meeting which I had to leave at 6.15 for the Section Party. He gave the gist of the Chancellor's line to Douglas Allen, Donald and John Jukes who took it all fairly calmly. They still concentrated on the Chancellor's paper although William pointed out that the real problem was what the First Secretary would say in his paper to SEP (Donald's draft). Douglas felt that the First Secretary would certainly have a lot of reservations and want to add "conditions". Even the Tories had never accepted 2% as a basis for planning. In fact it was the problem of the plan that D. raised first. The Chancellor's strategy would rule out any plan in 1967 – or perhaps later. This led to a discussion of debt rephasing and to the impossibility of saying anything publicly about a strategy so dependent on the rephasing of debt. Then came – at last – some questions about the figures and it became clear what a wide gulf there was between Donald's figures and ours (he takes $1/2$% fall in unemployment as yielding about $2 1/2$% extra output).

We had a long debate this morning with Donald and John Jukes and it became clear that they were basing themselves on our 1968 forecast of unemployment when Wynne was disposed to argue that it was too high in relation to the output forecast and that there would be a fall back to 2% even if production increased only at the rate of productive potential. Donald said (in effect) that it would be a bold man who advised the Chancellor to count on a fall from $2 1/2$% to 2% without any faster rise in GDP than 3%.

Meanwhile William had done a more extensive redraft deliberately inserting into the paper on Public Expenditure a reasoned statement of the Chancellor's strategy. This we agreed to leave with some amendments (after a 3.30 p.m. meeting) although I still had doubts whether this was desirable. The only really important figure is the increase in taxation that is necessary and this is very sensitive to price and other data. At one moment A. Roy[144] seemed uncertain whether *any* increase would be needed, then he had figures £150 m. below and subsequently £750 m above. So the really material figure is virtually a guess and the Chancellor is shouldering one more uncertainty the increase in taxation he will have to budget for *whatever* the cut he secures now in expenditure in 1970.

The whole episode is a good illustration of the fatuity of having two separate sets of planners: those dealing in short-term calculations and those dealing in long-term. We used to be brought in when the Plan was taking shape and we also came in on GEG (although neither of us liked the assumption about productive potential). But now ESG papers are fed in at the last moment without underpinning by the forecasting staff and even in DEA Donald does the sums on what seems a plausible basis without adequate cross-checking.

Nicky meantime carries on a denunciation of the whole idea of productive potential since he says (rightly) that it is a function of policy, that there is no model or hypothesis underlying it, and that it takes no account of changes by sector or region. He and Donald both want to go in for sub-aggregation while

[144] Andrew Roy – Fellow, Sidney Sussex College, Cambridge, 1951–64; Economic Consultant, Treasury, 1962; Senior Economic Adviser, 1964; Under-Sec., 1969.

Wynne opposes this idea as not useful for short-term analysis.

We also had a lot of discussion of the Chancellor's initiative on interest rates and it looks as if this will lead to a meeting at Chequers on Jan. 7-8 of Fowler, Schiller[145] and possibly Débré. This all started in Paris through a conversation with Fowler who was keen on the idea of combined action to get rates down. But it will be a little odd to have the Finance Ministers (or Economic Ministers) sitting at Chequers (while the P.M. and his family keep to their quarters) and the Central Bank Governors meet in Basle: each group meditating on what it would like the other to do. It would be easy for the Finance Ministers to reach conclusions that they had then to sell to their Central Banks and after a discussion in which none of them really appreciated how the others' monetary systems worked. Anyhow Schiller may already have got the Bundesbank to move (or been rebuffed) so he will be promising to carry on. Joe Fowler may jib at reducing the discount rate (or telling Bill Martin to reduce it) without seeing what the others have done first. The French may simply offer to stay put.

At the meeting of Permanent Secretaries on Wednesday R.P. said they were having great difficulty with the President who was insisting that his reservations should be entered on any brief implying that we might be willing to accept the common agricultural policy or deny free entry to Commonwealth food, etc. The reservations will be the President's, not the Board's. Tom Padmore commented that it was just as well they did not have to enter their Ministers' views on Rhodesia as reservations whenever the subject came up.

The Chancellor's six point programme as spelled out at Thursday's Directorate consists of: (i) Around 2% unemployment (perhaps $1\frac{3}{4}$–2%). (ii) £100–150m surplus. (iii) Debt rephasing after repayment of this year's maturing debt in the autumn. (iv) No reflation this year (or perhaps before September – or even July). (v) £200m off defence expenditure. (vi) Not more than £300m on taxation to 1970 (or perhaps £100m off civil expenditure).

As to (iv) the P.M. is in agreement. The word has gone round that even hire purchase must not be changed till July or later. This is supported by Nicky who suspects that I am not with him. And indeed I am not sure yet that I am because there may well be a need to offer some minor reflation in the Budget. I rather think, however, that it would be useful to hang on and use hire purchase relaxations, especially if there is to be any regional concession.

For the moment there is a kind of sub-optimal euphoria because a lot of the news is either good or not as bad as it was. Unemployment has been falling for 2 weeks, exports are well up, the balance of trade is in substantial surplus, etc. But it won't last.

Friday, 30 December   Not much news till Thursday of the meeting of Finance Ministers. Débré couldn't manage 7 or 14 January and the Chancellor, instead

[145] Dr Karl Schiller – Prof. of Economics, University of Hamburg, 1947–72; (Rector, 1956–58); Member of Bundestag, 1965–72; Federal Minister of Economics, 1966–71; of Economics and Finance, 1971–72.

of proceeding without him, asked the views of the other two and finally settled for the 21st. I talked to Sam on Wednesday and he agreed that we were dealing with a case of financial transvestitism in which the Finance Ministers were going to dress up for a discussion of monetary policy while the Central Bankers dress up for a discussion in Basle of fiscal policy. While we might want concrete decisions to be taken it seemed increasingly unlikely that the Conference could do anything more than set the stage for decisions by the monetary authorities, some of whom would not be represented at Chequers. The Governor is obviously rather contemptuous of the whole affair and a little concerned at Ministers meeting to discuss things they don't understand. But nobody wants to have the Central Bankers present and only Débré wants a preliminary meeting of experts. The big danger is that it all leaks out too far in advance – a pity that it was not possible to hold the meeting this week-end as the Chancellor originally proposed.

We had a briefing meeting on Thursday afternoon and Jeremy Morse took the line that it would be bound to be rather indefinite and inconclusive. We all thought that it might be a Canute quadrille chasing the receding tide since rates are already falling.

Today Sam called with a letter from the Governor to the Chancellor suggesting a cut in bank rate by $1/2$% on technical grounds. The tenor of the letter made one react the other way but the conclusions ran counter to the argument. The Conference was touched on only at the end and it was made clear that by Jan. 12 it would probably be *impossible* to cut bank rate because the trade figures would be bad.

I pointed out to Sam that we had had all this in 1961 when a cut was resisted for a long time on incomes policy grounds. (Curiously enough, Robens urged the same objections on the Court and Carron didn't dissent.) In the end the fall had to be extended to 6% after my own preference for a clean cut of 1% had been overruled. The Bank would find themselves pushed into a second cut now, even in advance of the Conference, if they started with $1/2$% on Jan. 5.[146] How would Blessing like the British taking the initiative in this way? Why excite foreign opinion by being in the van when we could probably get support by waiting 3-4 weeks?

The Governor assumes that the PWLB rate will be increased simultaneously but of course the Chancellor won't stand for that and will probably represent the proposal to the P.M. as one commanding the Governor's approval *without* this (or any other) condition. It is clear that the Chancellor is tempted though it seems dotty to us. (I haven't spoken to William or Denis.)

When we discussed publication of forecasts at Section Meeting today Patricia Brown reminded me that in July the P.M. wouldn't allow the balance of payments forecast to be passed on to other Departments but he himself within a fortnight was issuing precise forecasts even down to the quarter in which we

---

[146] In 1961 bank rate was cut from 7 per cent to $6 1/2$% on 5 October and 6 per cent on 2 November. Presumably the reference is to the October cut. In 1967 the cut from 7 to $6 1/2$ per cent was delayed until 26 January *after* the Conference.

would move into surplus.

I was also reminded recently by William that the Chancellor's views on interest rates involved Sam in going to Brighton to get his agreement to the terms of the last issue of Government stock.

John Hunt told me this morning that Marsh has now written to tell the Chancellor that giving up Drax (power station) will involve him in so much difficulty with Robens that he would prefer to settle Drax and Hinckley Point together implying that he could dispense with both if forced to do so. At least he agrees that he can't programme on a basis that specifically assumes slippage from the start.

Wynne pointed out to me that both in medium term planning and in short term forecasting we may want, not one plan or projection, but several. For example, if we think that balance of payments constraint is likely to prove intolerable we should not plan public expenditure on the basis of that constraint. If we are forecasting we should not make it seem that the figures *are* the forecast: what matters is the policy advice we offer on the basis of the figures. This applies equally in the longer run: the plan is not the collection of figures included but the series of decisions of policy to which it leads. From the point of view of publication therefore Wynne is on the side of the poets: dealing in epithets indicating in very broad terms what the predominant trends in the economy are likely to be. Hence he didn't really like having to produce charts for a post mortem.

We all agree that it is much easier to give post-Budget forecasts since by that time all the key decisions have been taken and the forecasts do not then disclose either policy decisions that are not public knowledge or failure to take decisions of a kind that the figures suggest as necessary. At that point in time, forecasts are not made for the purpose of policy decisions but to register those decisions.

Chapter 4

1967

Sunday, 8 January 1967   A good deal of week taken up with incomes policy. Richard Kahn's report arrived on my desk on Friday and he rang me up on Saturday afternoon. Meeting earlier with Evan Maude – mainly on statutory powers and largely occupied with moans from T.B. that if incomes policy was going to be so ineffective we ought to warn Ministers since apart from unemployment we had no other weapon left if we went into EEC.

John Stevens on Tuesday told me that attitude towards our joining EEC was changing in US administration. Treasury and Fed. naturally far from keen for obvious reasons and departure of George Ball left State Department more open with John Leddy[1] still in favour but E. Rostow[2] doubtful. Agreed to go to US in late April and told William.

Bank rate proposal died but I gather that it has been revived since Bundesbank reduction. Ministers foregather in a fortnight at Chequers and no leak yet but may well be one before next Monday. Italians may still be included if they express anxiety.

Ministerial changes make government look bigger than ever without getting rid of more than a couple of chaps. Impression bound to grow that Harold isn't a good butcher but that may do him very little harm.[3]

Monday, 16 January   Today the conference of Finance Ministers announced at 4 p.m. – no leak apparently although Sam says that George Bolton[6] heard of it from his man in Paris by last Wednesday. The Governor at Basle found other Central Bankers unaware of the project.

Italians now invited after Colombo took a sour view in advance of visit to Rome by P.M. and Foreign Secretary. Timing could be better since we are

---

[1] John Leddy – American official dealing with commercial policy.

[2] Eugene Rostow – Professor of Law, York University, 1944–84; Under-Sec. of State for Political Affairs, 1966–69.

[3] 28 new appointments were made, including three to DEA (Fred Lee,[4] Harold Lever and Peter Shore[5]).

[6] George Bolton – Director, Bank of England, 1948–68; Chm., Bank of London and South America, 1957–70.

to have WP3, Group of Ten and Joint Meeting with IMF immediately after Conference and this made journalists suspicious.

Fowler has issued a long addition to press release in terms that may offend Germans and French.

Chancellor this morning contemplated a special conference, or perhaps a special session at Chequers, on the arguments about price of gold. We insisted that this was highly delicate since for Americans it was equivalent to devaluation and while it was true that people did argue about gold price it was quite another matter for Chancellor to recognise that it admitted of discussion.

He is undecided about bank rate this week and said he hoped for 1% fall within next month or two. The journalists warned us that markets would interpret conference in a very bullish sense whatever we said.

Meanwhile John Stevens has written to say that Bill Martin doesn't mean to accommodate the President and resents the State of the Union Message and the arm twisting tactics of getting Walter Heller's bank to lower its rate. Blessing will also resist further move at once. So if we move it will be without further immediate support. Fortunately, *Economist*, *Financial Times*, and other papers support caution. Governor, however, inclined to argue that we are losing chance to get rates down and that by disappointing the market and *not* lowering bank rate we have been producing an outflow. Unfortunately for him the figures show the reverse. Recent large inflow which must be due to our rates *staying up*.

Tuesday, 17 January   Long meetings in William's room chiefly on rates, (in the morning) current price forecasts and the Budget deficit (in the afternoon). As William reported to me last week Chancellor has tried to get Worswick[7] to replace R.N. but W. says no. Chancellor will pursue Worswick via R. Hall but also hankers a little after Kit MacMahon.

We debated bank rate today by ourselves and agreed that we should move this week or next since to refrain from doing so would involve marked shift of policy that would be hard to square with Conference at week-end. We also agreed after some hesitation on my part that next week would be preferable. My fear was that if we waited we might be pushed into doing *more* whereas by acting before the Conference we could make it plain that no *immediate* results should be expected. The Chancellor has accepted our advice and Governor seems quite satisfied although he wrote only yesterday renewing his suggestion.

Nicky still arguing that Ministers ought to be warned that they may have to raise taxes in Budget. He is thinking of a recovery in stock-building that makes for renewal of pressure especially if public expenditure still rising strongly, unlike 1962-63.

Saturday, 21 January   Mainly occupied over Chequers conference. Chancellor held briefing meeting on Thursday at which he began as usual with an ambitious target pour épater les bureaucrats: a reduction in bank rate by 2%. Of course

---

[7] David Worswick – Fellow and Tutor in Economics, Magdalen College, Oxford, 1945–65; Director, NIESR from 1965.

it soon appeared that he was thinking of a reduction in stages over the cycle, asking why we shouldn't do as much as we did in previous cycles, and using the 2% to focus the discussion. William argued that even abstracting from international pressures we couldn't go down to 5% and seemed to be following a line I had developed a week or two ago.

There is still a dependence on monetary weapons (including hire purchase) that can't be dispensed with if public expenditure is going to go on rising. William didn't specifically point to the gilt-edged market as I did: but I said we just couldn't abstract from external pressure since we were consciously slowing down the economy *because* of the external situation, including our indebtedness. Chancellor couldn't follow the argument in terms of liquidity: he doesn't really see why creation of more money matters.

It was quite an amusing discussion since Chancellor wanted to know *what* to talk about on Saturday night when everybody had unbuttoned and was gossiping in the Long Gallery. Débré had said he wouldn't come if we were going to talk about Europe (Denis says there was a somewhat similar hitch about Giscard earlier). Fowler didn't want the subject of gold raised but according to John Stevens he was quite anxious to discuss conversions of currency into gold. The Italians can't be very interested in interest rates when they have changed their bank rate once only since 1950.

First meeting of panel on economists with T.B. there. He made quite a number of suggestions (including Nita Watts[8] for F.O. and Ken Berrill for, presumably, O.D.M.). Andrew Cohen[9] had seen me earlier about the latter and indicated four names: Sidney Dell,[10] Ian Little, Bryan Hopkin and K.B. He told me that when Barbara C. took office he was told of his appointment as Permanent Secretary and of proposal to appoint Dudley Seers as Director General. When he went to see Barbara she showed no interest in the fact that he was the Permanent Secretary – instead, her first words we "Well, how about Dudley?" and she was more concerned about his grading than any other subject.

Wednesday, 25 January   Burns Night – reception at Lancaster House. I arrived with Donald MacD. after a long argument on the economic effects of regional differentiation of SET. It was a curious gathering with T.B., John Stevens, Lieftinck,[11] Sam Brittan, Alan Dudley,[12] Anjaria,[13] Esteva,[14] etc., etc. On the

[8] Nita Watts – Economic Section, 1940–555; ECE, 1959–64; Vice Principal, St Hilda's College, Oxford, 1968–81.

[9] Sir Andrew Cohen – Dir. Gen., Dept. of Technical Co-operation, 1961–64; Perm. Sec., Min. of Overseas Develop., 1964–68.

[10] Sydney Dell – Economist on the staff of the UN in New York.

[11] Pieter Lieftinck – Dutch economist and politician; Minister of Finance, 1945–52; Exec. Dir., IBRD and IMF from 1956.

[12] Sir Alan Dudley Foreign Office, 1942–49; Dept. of Technical Co-operation, 1962–64; Dep. Sec., ODM, 1964–68.

[13] Anjaria – an Indian official.

[14] P Esteva – Under-Sec. of Finance, 1960; Jt. Dir. of External Finance, 1964; Technical Adviser to the Cabinet of the Prime Minister (Pompidou), 1967–68; Director of Cabinets of Couve de Murville and Ortoli, 1968–71.

very day when Harold is trying hard to convince the French of our sincerity about EEC, T.B. was warning J.S. to keep the options open in Washington and telling him that the Ambassador was too enthusiastic a "European" to see the difficulties of joining. John agreed with this view and wanted to know where the work on AFTA stood. I told him that T.B. didn't really take it seriously but thought it useful to keep it running. Lots of people in DEA and Treasury were being kept busy doing exercises for T.B. without much conviction.

John told me that the Ambassador had had a lunch party with the Rostows, Bator, and some others to discuss British entry into EEC and had mentioned that there might be some "financial difficulties". They all looked at John who said bluntly "For example, what about devaluation?". Stunned silence. Bator asked him to come to White House and expressed surprise that John should even mention devaluation to which J. replied that the official line was of course unchanged but any realistic assessment could hardly leave this out.

Bator himself is churning over a scheme for US demonetisation of gold following UK devaluation (but of course the President is unaware of this and nobody else is known to be of this view). The idea is that if we moved it would break the log-jam and *allow* the US the freedom of action she needs. Her aid and foreign policy is being hamstrung by the need to defend a weak balance of payments and so, B. argues, she ought to be ready to take initiative and make dollar the currency of the future. Yet when B. was at Chequers he spoke not a word of all this and told Chancellor they were still anxious to see us in EEC. Too many Hungarians double-crossing each other, says John.

WP No.3 on Monday. Débré has to go for three weeks to Réunion for the election! Very interesting discussion on Germany which has already a large surplus and rapidly rising unemployment. They mean to use a "full employment" budget. Emminger claimed that Bundesbank would move if situation was getting out of hand: but it may be July before much is done. At Chequers Schiller said the Italians were not being sent home but were now fully integrated.

Emminger gave excellent talk on liquidity at lunch today to large audience but is not reported in evening paper.

Chancellor has now reconciled himself to failure to get Worswick to come to Treasury. Suggested Berrill to William. Robert N. returns tomorrow.

Wynne has pointed out that Board of Trade survey of investment intentions implies upward not downward revision of investment plans (press seems to have got it all wrong again).

The volume of leaks about family endowment plans is now unbelievable. In fact very little now goes on that *doesn't* get into the press.

Sunday, 29 January   Ditchley week-end on CM and NAFTA. At the station there was a great crowd to see Bobby Kennedy and newspapermen hung around Ditchley later partly to photograph him and partly for Shinwell[15]. He looks

[15] E Shinwell (later Lord) – Labour Minister of Tech and Power, 1945–47; Sec. of State for War, 1947–50; Minister of Defence, 1950–51; Chm., Parliamentary Labour Party, 1964–67.

very young, handsome, almost undergraduate. Curious reddish complexion with chestnut hair over left brow and cast in one eye. Either seems to be staring you out of countenance or looking away. I found his expression rather sulky and his talk a little staccato, with something of a drawl like his brother's, a touch of Welsh in the rhythm and climb of words. There was a great burst of laughter when he interjected as he did twice or thrice.

The Americans were full of good will but lacking in sustained argument. The British showed plenty of reservations about the CM and only the business men came out hot and strong: Beeching, very brief, almost inaudible, dogmatic and anti-economist; Kearton, Gaullist in sentiment, confident, pro-European, realist in his assertion of British interests; and Shawcross,[16] smooth, articulate, and basing himself mainly on economies of scale. (But when Snelling[17] put Jay's question in private, what a market of 200 m. did that one of 100 m. didn't do, he veered away towards the older argument from competitive pressure and a new spirit).

Senator Brewster asked what would happen if US suspended gold dealings but I got no chance to find what this question represented in Senatorial thinking.

Con O'Neill[18] made an effective speech posing the choice as one between evils but he later felt he hadn't gone far enough and argued that if we were "in" we could change the policies of the Six. He was naturally asked if we had told the Italians this.

The gist of the matter was plainly that our entry would alter the whole character of the EEC since others would follow and the voting pattern would be altered. Hence it was fundamentally an issue between one kind of community and another and the rest of the issues were subsidiary and the arguments a pretext. Jo Grimmond talked at length about strength and defence and political participation – having an effective voice, etc., etc. – but only political content that I can find on close examination is anti-Americanism. If de Gaulle were asked what was the political character of the Six, he would be bound to see it in these terms and has advanced no other intelligible ideas except a vague Europeanism. However, Jo denied strongly that there were no political overtones and thought that if that were so we ought not to join.

The Americans were uniformly keen on our joining although their enthusiasm diminished as the day wore on and they began to canvass an Atlantic Association – as did some of the British e.g. Sir M. Wright[19]. It remained so much talk and when I asked Tydings what substance it had he said it might be possible to

[16] Lord Hartley Shawcross – Lab. Attorney General, 1945–51; Chief Prosecutor, Nuremburg Trials, 1945–46; President, Board of Trade, 1951; Member, Permanent Court of Arbitration at the Hague, 1950–67; Director, Shell T and T Co, 1961–72.

[17] Sir A W Snelling – Dep. Under-Sec. of State, CRO/FCO, 1961–64.

[18] Sir Con O'Neill British diplomat; Ambassador to Finland, 1961–63; to the EEC, 1963–65; Dep. Under-Sec. of State, Foreign Office, 1965–68; Leader of deleg. to negotiate entry to EEC, 1969–72.

[19] Sir M Wright – British Diplomatic Service from 1926; Chm., Atlantic Trade Study; Member, Board of International Movement for Atlantic Union; Founder Member, British N. American Cttee.

sell a political association to Congress but not an economic one. The Middle West would not welcome exposure to Australasian food imports. Some British speakers also felt that the UK would be dominated and ultimately absorbed by the US if it joined NAFTA. But they were uncomfortable at the prospect of being dependent on European joint defence.

Kennedy stressed the change since Cuba (as Jo G. had done previously) and the release this had given both E. and W. to new alignments. Nationalism was growing. Different generation was rising to influence, born since 1939, both in US and in Germany. He saw the possibility of a détente with Russia. But he wanted British leadership in Asia and Africa and said that in 1962 we had saved the US from large scale escalation of the struggle in Laos.

I had interesting talks with Senator Percy and his wife. P. gets up regularly at 5 and finishes after midnight but thrives on it. He went off to see Crossman who told him the Yanks ought to get out of Vietnam and repeated a story of what de Gaulle said to H.W. on the subject which likened the Americans to a second rooster coming into the yard.

Con O'Neill says that the French disclaimed any intention of pressing for an immediate increase in the price of gold and played down the sterling balances issue. He said that de la Martinière[20] had suggested repaying sterling balances out of our contribution to the Community Fund in import levies.

Thursday, 2 February   Lunch today with Velebit[21] and yesterday with Joe Fromm and Perry (?). They knew from US Treasury sources that our short term indebtedness to Central Banks had reached 1\frac{1}{2}$b. and didn't ask for confirmation. Nor did they inquire whether the January inflow was £100 m. or £200 m. since they already knew that it was large. They *did* put it to me that we were bound to have a difficult financing problem this year and hence had no margin for manoeuvre and that the US would have preferred the Chancellor not to commit himself so publicly to repaying the first $1b. to the IMF this year. (In fact, the surplus for the month on spot was £188 m. although against this must be set a large increase in market forwards that didn't escape Sydney Gampell's[22] attention. We've already had an inflow of the magnitude Sam G. wanted for the whole year to see him through.)

Kahn called to see me on Tuesday. He had been disturbed by the press account of last week's Cabinet discussion: all the more because, as he said, *The Guardian* obviously insisted on checking against the minutes before publication (!) while other papers on Tuesday appeared to have seen the text of Ministers' Cabinet papers before circulation. Michael Stewart wrote his over the week-end and it bore all the traces of the intellectual twists and turns through which he had gone to be convinced by the TUC and CBI of their ability to do the job voluntarily, coupled with an advance declaration that he would be very hard to

[20] G de la Martinière – French Commercial Attaché in London.

[21] Vladimir Velebit – Yugoslav politician; Under-Sec. for Foreign Affairs, 1956–58; Exec. Sec., UNECE, 1960–67.

[22] Sydney Gampell – Reuter's Correspondent in London.

convince. Nearly all of this one could read openly in the *Financial Times* and *The Times*.

Today we had meeting on The Plan. Chancellor had seen a paper on Monday by M. Stewart saying that he proposed to develop new plan for publication in 1968 and to tell NEDC on Wednesday. He at once telephoned to protest that this was all too leisurely since incomes policy hung on a deal with the TUC involving his six point strategy. But of course we don't know yet what we *can* promise in the way of sustained expansion and the strategy has not yet been accepted by the Chancellor's colleagues except as a hypothesis on which to base expenditure plans. So if he means to say anything to TUC before March 3 it will have to be pretty vague. First Secretary is right to insist on careful examination of alternatives as the root of good plannning.

Ryrie[23] said he thought that Chancellor was offering too much and in the wrong posture if he pressed for declarations about expansion instead of biding his time and not whittling down his balance of payments target. William doesn't like balance of payments targets of any kind and N.K. wants an export target because he thinks exports critical to the strategy and would accept that failure to achieve the target ought to be reflected in higher unemployment.

We also discussed sterling balances. William insisted that France attached importance to this. Pompidou had discussed little else. Couve had remained unconvinced that the position of sterling was essentially the same as that of other currencies. The fact was that we should be bound to remain conscious of our obligations to sterling creditors once inside the EEC and that these obligations would influence our policies and might have to be shared by others in the Community. Yet no one had suggested what we should do or shown interest in the P.M.'s offer (however vague) to let them share in the benefits. William pointed out that if Basle went into reverse we should be involved in extending credit to Europe.

He then mentioned conversation with Schweitzer who had recently seen Débré for the first time and come away very depressed. D. seemed convinced that there was a US imperialist plot which only the French had spotted and that they must protect others from falling victim to it. S. was satisfied that we should not be allowed to join the Community. William went on to suggest that we should do further work on sterling e.g. pursue the idea of a common European currency but it was hard to work up enthusiasm for this given the summary of French ideas that we had just heard.

Yesterday we had a meeting of Methodology Group for first time and T.B. appeared. What is more, he was pretty reasonable, insisting that we ought to know what the price tag was on any deal put up for Ministerial blessing. Most of the discussion was more appropriate to C.P.C. but there were some useful suggestions, Nicky arguing that we gained from a *flat* tariff rather than one that varied greatly from item to item.

Meanwhile battle has been joined on NAFTA between DEA and the Cabinet

---

[23] W S Ryrie – Treasury from 1963; Asst. Sec. for international monetary affairs, 1966–69; PPS to Chancellor of Exchequer, 1969–71.

Office. We don't take it very seriously and the Ambassador has reported that several Americans in high places have gone out of their way to warn him that it won't lead anywhere. It is true that the Fed. and Treasury have some doubts about seeing us pushed too violently into EEC but they are not the most influential voices in Washington.

When the subject came up at the Tuesday Club in conversation with R. Powell he said things were now beginning to move in Brussels and the political side of the EEC would progressively become more and more of a reality. I said: "We don't know what we're in for if we're out. And we don't know what we should be out for if we're in". Difficult to translate.

We're in for a difficult month. NIF should be in first draft by tomorrow week but we don't really know what is happening or will happen to public expenditure. If we want to do something in face of large prospective deficit it would make far more sense to cut expenditure than clap on new taxes in April. For it would be quite a time before the cuts became effective.

At lunch Derek Mitchell told me of George's lunch with the EFTA Ministers which went on far too long. D., sent to bring him back, was welcomed in with a roar, "Derek, get me a girl!". And when the P.M., looking like thunder advanced in person to collect George he exclaimed: "Christ! I ask for a girl and what do I get but the bloody Prime Minister!". Derek says that this (or something like it) was in *Private Eye* but in no other part of the press.

Joe Hyman[24] gave us a long disquisition on capital and its misuse in British business. In some ways very much to my liking but not what I want to hear. Joe claimed that British companies that starved their overseas subsidiaries of expenditure got a better return in consequence. We'd never get British industry really efficient so long as it could borrow so easily and cheaply from banks. The tax system needed overhauling to put a premium on output, not investment: to encourage double shifts even at the cost of more unemployment and to give bigger incentives to business men.

Thursday, 9 February   William tells me that Chancellor has had a refusal from Kit MacMahon and is now contemplating an approach to Posner. We agreed that this was not a very good idea since P. is doing a good job where he is and there is no one to take his place. Chancellor hasn't responded to idea of Berrill, who called me on Tuesday to say he was interested.

Reception for Kosygin[25] last night at Lancaster House. Everybody was there: David Frost, Mary Quant, Peter Sellers, Mary Rand, Percy Mills,[26] etc. (1100 I believe). K. entered via a door opening into the large reception room and there was soon a crowd like an indoor garden party as he progressed between the mob, with his daughter in white ermine cap and coat as a convenient landmark. He seemed relaxed and given to mini-smiles.

[24] Joe Hyman – Chm., Viyella International Ltd, 1962–69; Chm., John Crowther Group from 1971.

[25] A N Kosygin - Vice-Chm., 1960–64, Chm. from 1966, USSR Council of Ministers.

[26] Lord Mills – Minister of Power, 1957–59; Paymaster General, 1959–61; Dep. Leader of House of Lords, 1960-6?.

This afternoon Chancellor took on the Economic Section for $1\frac{1}{2}$ hours and we had a chance to get his views on employment policy, taxation, and other subjects. He gave everybody a chance to talk, and made a good impression. I first took care to let Wynne tell him about shortfalls in public expenditure, mainly to show that the published figures and the forecasts would look quite inconsistent. But he approached the subject from the angle of cuts, concluding that the cuts might have had no effect. It was control, not presentation, that struck him as the major issue. Then we went on to discuss how the economy should be run, starting with Jim Shepherd. The Section line was that it was better to let up a little at an early stage rather than overdo it under pressure later; and that there should be a bigger margin of unused capacity to stop us constantly hitting the ceiling. It was William who drew attention to the question: what governs the growth of potential? The Chancellor said he was to do a George Brown on TV on Monday and hoped we could put him wise to how to deal with Shonfield. He was content to see growth at 3% for a bit so long as it was steady and didn't mind if this fell below the rate in European countries. There was a dangerous tendency to belittle the need to aim at an increase in reserves.

Frank Figgures said at a reception for AP's that Michael Stewart isn't a horse, and that Cabinet Ministers had to be horses. He is liable to fall asleep in Committee or not to read papers because he is too tired. He will agree with his Department and then say nothing in Cabinet. For example, he had done nothing to stop Chancellor from demanding that full foreign exchange costs in Germany be met and threatening to withdraw troops in proportion, when this was an absurd threat. (But it was, after all, the Chancellor who made it.) He had gone off agreeing with F.O. in their view and then sat silent through the Cabinet at which the matter was discussed. Frank said it was one thing for Ministers not to read papers because they thought it unnecessary but another because they were too tired.

Bill Nield's view of the Chancellor in Cabinet was that he was weak and very much inclined to sit on the fence until he saw which way things were going. I was trying to elicit the Chancellor's view on incomes policy (D. Barnes says he is lining up with Gunter but this seems mistaken to me). Bill thought that last summer he could have had his way quite easily by threatening to resign because this would have endangered the pound more than even the P.M.'s resignation. This, however, is only a half truth: resignation by *either* would probably have done the job. Similarly Bill now thinks that he can get G.B. to toe the line by pointing out how indispensable a strong pound is to our entry into Europe.

There are, in fact, as was evident in Paris, only two good arguments against our joining: the "cosy nest" argument and the "can you run your economy properly" argument. The French fully appreciate how different things will be if we enter the EEC and don't want the tight knit group to be disturbed, least of all by the undisciplined British.

H.W. apparently took the wind out of the General's sails by indicating at the start that the UK didn't mind taking a line independent of US except in defence. But according to Denis Rickett he said many things that are simply not true: speaking of other countries that were in deficit and including Germany in the list; implying that we could liquidate our foreign securities without difficulty; and so on. The General used one phrase that suggested he thought out entry unlikely ("il parait difficile si non impossible") but this was not included in the official record.

Friday evening at Terence O'Neill's reception. Frank Cousins was there and Con O'Neill and I had a long talk with Mallabar[27] about the Harland Wolff shipyard which he thinks can be saved. Great mistake had been over marketing. He himself went to Monte Carlo for a week to see Greek shipowners one of whom was afraid nobody would take an order from him for a liner.

Sunday, 19 February   Quite a busy week, preparing Budget submission. In the end, not a very good paper as I was trying to keep pace with the forecasters and had completed my draft ahead of them.

William told me early in the week that Kit had changed his mind and was willing to come to save us from a worse appointment. Meanwhile the Chancellor had seen Richard Marsh who was not happy to lose Posner and had promised to write after reflection. He did write and continued to ask for mercy but the Chancellor is determined to get Posner.

Germans cut their discount rate on Thursday and William asked me on Friday as we walked into the Treasury if we should move. Governor had suggested Feb. 23 before leaving for Pakistan. Spoke to Denis and Sam in the afternoon and we agreed it would be best to copy January tactics. After all, Vote on Account had shaken the market and it would seem irresponsible within a week to cut bank rate. Sam felt that on domestic grounds alone we ought to go slow while I thought that we should at least wait and see if US moved any further. But I think that a cut to 6% won't be delayed more than a week or two – certainly not beyond the Budget.

Saw D. Jay on Friday about legislation on restrictive practices and advised him to swallow easing in direction of agreements on standardisation etc. if we got a tightening up on information agreements etc. as part of the deal. He obviously felt that there was very little case that would satisfy an economist for action to offer exemption by administrative decision but he would certainly lose if he took it to Cabinet and it seems better to win on the whole packet, as I think he would if Board of Trade retains power to administer. He didn't seem put out by all the fuss in the papers about his speech on Common Market.

We had our meeting with Chancellor on Thursday on regional proposal. I came in halfway through while he was asking about Cardiff and the possibility of bringing it into Development Area. Once he was told that the scheme would leave out one of the three big Welsh steelworks and include the other two he said it would be impossible. Then he asked N.K. to give the case for and afterwards I gave him some of the objections. I accepted the objective and the principle but said I wouldn't have the nerve. I listed some of the difficulties that discrimination would involve, but didn't make a dead set at the whole thing.

[27] Sir J. Mallabar – Chartered accountant; Chm., Ruston and Hornby, 1964–66; Harland and Wolff, 1966–70.

R.N. spoke in favour and the administrators gave some mixed but unenthusiastic reactions. Even Bretherton[28] ended by saying that the alternative might be some other scheme that would do less good and cost more. McDermot[29] was mildly pro and the Chief Secretary very much so.[30]

The Chancellor appeared to agree but not to inclusion in the Budget, and did not commit himself to more than consultation of outside opinion which, as Robin Butler[31] had said, might well make it impossible to proceed. NEDC would certainly be split. I had made a special point of the difficulty of reckoning the effects of the scheme if it was not supported by both sides since it calls for investment and that implies continuation of the cost advantages. Only one speaker pointed out that if you change the calculus of business action too often, you end by getting very little out of a further change.

Unemployment flat and exports in January far above level we can hope for this year. Average of last 3 months over 10% up on a year ago. No wonder government in a state of euphoria. When Chancellor saw the Section a week ago he wanted us to plan for a fall in unemployment to, say, 550,000 by September with no further increase over the winter. This would call for some pretty powerful reflation. He also hasn't quite taken in the difference between wholly unemployed and registered unemployed.[32]

He was on TV on Monday and although he routed Shonfield and R. Day he talked too much about pure reflation. He simply couldn't raise taxes after talking that way even if it were the right thing to do.

Monday, 20 February   Budget Committee. Nobody in favour of cutting taxes but divided about what to do. N.K. wanted to put up corporation tax 5 points to soak up cash not to cut demand. A.J. wanted a cut in public expenditure and of course M. Parsons took the same line. R.N. and I were for a neutral budget. The discussion centred on company liquidity although that was really meant for Friday next and N.K. quoted from figures that Lovell would incorporate in the paper for that meeting. Denis put up most reasonable line for higher taxes that we are at limit of risk on balance of payments with no real assurance of a surplus. N.K. argued that exports would go up faster still if we cut demand and that forecast didn't allow enough. If we ended up with more spare capacity and not enough exports there was an easy solution. So why hesitate to put taxes up?

[28] Russell Bretherton – Economist; Fellow of Wadham College, Oxford, 1928–45; Under-Sec., Treasury, 1961–68.

[29] Niall McDermott – Labour Financial Secretary to the Treasury, 1964–67; Minister of State, Minister of Housing and Local Govt., 1967–68.

[30] The attempt to find a way of discriminating in favour of regions with high unemployment issued in the introduction in September 1967 of the Regional Employment Premium (see also entry for 28 February). Additional SET refunds for at least seven years were to be made in Development Areas.

[31] F E (Robin) Butler – Principal in Central Economic Division of the Treasury.

[32] The number of *registered* unemployed in the United Kingdom reached a peak of 644,000 in February but for Great Britain the number of wholly unemployed, seasonally adjusted, was 461,000 or 2 per cent. By September this had *risen* to 540,000 or 2.3%.

He talks of a future torrent of liquidity.[33] But in fact it merely reflects depression in the private sector and the extra liquidity will furnish later means of expansion once they see better market prospects. There will be no real acceleration of demand in public sector.

A real change has come over DEA under the new dispensation and the papers on planning are very sensible. This is mainly Douglas Allen's work but I expect that the Planning Staff is also very much chastened. In retrospect our influence must be due quite largely to the superior *rationality* of W.A. + J. Callaghan as against E.R. + G. Brown. But it also reflects the virtue of the forecasting staff which has throughout given us a kind of moral ascendancy, since we were talking realities and knew the way to make our views effective.

Saturday, 25 February   Two long meetings yesterday (Friday) in preparation for the Budget submission and two others earlier in the week on the forecast: one on Monday (CM) and one on Wednesday (ESG) that made me miss a lunch. (It was just before David Devons' wedding). Yesterday we also had a meeting with Marjolin followed by a lunch at Lancaster House. I chiefly recall as a saying of the week T.B. at ESG. He had insisted again on the impossibility of prolonging the uncertainty about Europe (which of course is just what Harold intends to do) and pointed out that we can't be nasty to the French because we want to enter EEC nor to the Germans over offset costs for the same reason, nor to the US because we may need to fall back on them. "We can't be nasty to anybody any more and I don't know how long we can go on living that way". Nobody seemed to see the joke.

The first CM meeting was intended to deal with the forecast in real terms but Nicky soon dragged us into discussion of company liquidity and he was arguing on this basis for an increase in the corporation tax of 5%. Of course this shook Alec Johnston who wondered why we had introduced the tax at all if we meant to raise it at once by 5%. R.N. supported my line and William kept quiet although he didn't suggest that I should re-write anything and Andrew Edwards told me later that William saw no reason to revise the text since he accepted the conclusion. It was a good discussion even if it was essentially about matters we had agreed to leave until Friday. Nicky had got some figures from Lovell about company liquidity in 1966 that none of us had seen; and on Friday he again had a table that nobody had seen before. I found Denis far more convincing in arguing that we were at the limit of risk than Nicky that we were in for a profit inflation. Some of what Nicky was arguing sounded very P.J. – as if the budget deficit in itself would ruin the prospect of a surplus in the balance of payments in 1968. At times he seemed to argue from the crude deficit, at times from company liquidity and one didn't know (nor did he) whether he was challenging the NIF forecast.

---

[33] Company liquidity at the end of March 1967 was less than at the same date in any of the three preceding years but was expected to increase later in the year as public investment rose. In the next nine months the rise in company liquidity was nearly three times as fast as the average for 1964–66.

On Friday he made a passionate speech which Maurice P. wished he could have tape-recorded about the need not to *prevent* an increase in exports and investment and make sure that supply difficulties were minimal. He and T.B. (at ESG) both now talk as if exports were limited by pressure of demand (which is especially odd, coming from T.B.). When asked what he wanted to do, N.K. said he thought the sustainable Budget deficit was £700 m. so we must cut the prospective deficit of £1400 m. in half and this he took to mean increasing taxes by £300 m. at least this year and repeating it next year unless we could cut expenditure. He would raise this partly by putting up Corporation Tax and partly through SET in October. (Wynne subsequently estimated that this might in due course add 50,000 to unemployment but this took no account of multiplier effects). N.K. also said – in reply to Fred, who recalled a talk in which Nicky had seemed to defend no addition to taxation last year – that he had pleaded again and again with the Chancellor to use purchase tax *in addition* to SET.

My own line was clear. We were bound to have extra liquidity if we chose to expand in the face of a slump in private investment. But the way to deal with this was by keeping money as tight as possible, ensuring that interest rates were on the high side of expectations, and using Tax Reserve Certificates as far as possible to mop up some the liquidity generated by the oddities of the tax arrangements. (I wanted 3 year certificates at good rates but William has just had a minute seeking agreement to a reduction.) I also saw the possibility that Ministers might more willingly increase taxation this year than next since they had the prospect of a bare balance this year and the risk of a renewed sterling crisis (Fred said 1 in 40 and N.K. 1 in 2!). But the right analogy was 1962 not 1963 and we might push Ministers into switching too violently towards reflation if we forced them now to put up taxes.

Wynne, in the afternoon meeting, reduced N.K. to silence more effectively than I have ever seen it done by pointing out some of the differences now from 1963 (and indeed there are plenty). He also challenged the idea of a sustainable deficit, pointing to the decline in private housing and the increase in public housing as a factor bearing on the normal size of the Budget deficit.

N.K. seemed to follow a number of different strands of argument: (a) the increase in liquidity was itself dangerous and should be reduced; (b) there was a double risk externally because we might not achieve a surplus and foreign confidence might evaporate; (c) the deficit would lead to an inflation of prices and profits followed by an inflation of costs; (d) we ought to make sure that there was enough unemployment to exploit an increase in exports that occurred spontaneously or after devaluation.

Some of these points I argued more forcefully than Nicky himself (especially (b)); and I see that whether exports rise appreciably faster or less fast than we expect we should be in trouble. I was at pains to emphasise that we could *not* guarantee that there would be no sterling crisis this year. But there was also quite a risk of appreciably higher unemployment than we were predicting and it seemed difficult to create still more unemployment if we saw in front of us a prospect of an eventual steady surplus – a point William made when the discussion got round to devaluation.

Marjolin at the meeting we had with him had little new to say. But he did claim that his visit to Rome in 1964 had helped to get the Italians on to the rails and had strengthened Carli's hand. The Commission felt that there had been too much use of monetary policy and too little of fiscal policy. They believe that in 18 months devaluation will be virtually impossible for any member and that they are moving towards Monetary Union. But M. could not say for sure that capital movements within the 6 were increasing and agreed that most capital movements were now via Euro-dollar market. The Commission did not think that EEC had reached the point of no return: there was no such point. In the US they hadn't reached that point even in 1861 as the Civil War proved although he didn't want to suggest that Europe might have to go through Civil War.

I talked to Devons about the founding of the Economic Section. H.W. was *not* a member but came with Beveridge on his Man Power Survey and was found a room in our corridor. Lionel R. on his first day in the Section became so agitated on seeing a Report by the Chiefs of Staff that he had to be taken home in a taxi.

Sunday, 26 February   Henry P.B. talked about some of his Oxford Professors. He said that he had been told that MacGregor[34] was the most eloquent speaker at the Union before the war. As a Signals Officer he ran the greatest risks and returned from the war shattered. Then he left his magnum opus (on German cartels) on the table and had to go off for an operation. On his return it was gone and although he went out to the town dump and dug he never found any trace of it. MacGregor was a Cambridge graduate but I don't know of what year.

I have my second meeting tomorrow of a Methodology Committee, and we shall discuss Kennedy round and round.

Tuesday, 28 February   Investiture. Queen was in short skirt, blue dress with side strap, rather simple, and looked remarkably young. Cobbold introduced us and I came after Leslie O'Brien.

Yesterday, I spoke to William after the Methodology meeting and said that although I had not changed my view I saw force in the arguments for higher taxes especially if we meant to be taken seriously in Europe. I also didn't want to be told in July that we couldn't reduce hire purchase restrictions because taxes hadn't been increased. It wasn't as if unemployment was already perceptibly higher than we thought that it should be. (I had earlier talked to Fred and Jim Shepherd who said we should expect 20,000 or so of the temporary stopped to melt away at the present level of unemployment.) My view was that we should be hedging by considering a possible increase in SET in the autumn, possibly July or August, and if necessary bringing the uprating of benefits forward. William pointed out that it would have to wait till August or September (i.e. till Finance Bill was enacted) and that it would greatly complicate the new regional

[34] D H MacGregor - Professor of Ecoomics in Oxford before the Second World War.

proposal. In fact we should have very great discrimination locally between manufacturing and services; and it would not be enough, as I suggested, to exempt services from payment in the regions.

Today we had a 2 hour meeting with the Chancellor and other Treasury ministers, Douglas Allen, Fred, Wynne, and the usual CM attendance. It was all a little ragged but the Chancellor got the points. Unfortunately William gave too much emphasis to disagreements between Nicky and us on diagnosis and this started things off badly. The other 2 Ministers were obviously foxed by the figures and Diamond argued straight from Exchequer deficit or from figures of Government investment without regard to special elements we had emphasised. He backed idea of rise in corporation tax by $2\frac{1}{2}\%$ *and* an increase in SET *and* a cut in expenditure. MacDermot, while also impressed by the case for higher taxes, did see the difficulty of increasing SET and having the new regional scheme. Chancellor repeated his view on unemployment but promptly unsaid it all by agreeing we should consider what form higher taxation might take. Everybody except the Economic Section took it for granted that we'd need to raise taxes next year.

Tuesday Club in evening. Yamey[35] on Monopoly. Brandt suggested that discount market could finance inter-European trade with Euro-dollars if there were a lender of last resort. European banks reluctant to engage in third country finance. But this may change. German non-banks can borrow freely in Euro-dollar market but not others of the Six because they had put a stop to the practice when Treaty of Rome was signed.

Wednesday, 1 March   Dinner at the Pitblados with the Marshes and Willis Armstrongs[36]. M. has been Minister of F. & P. for one year and is already looking ahead to his next Department. Works very hard and is at it from early morning till after midnight. He has a calm off-hand manner that is deceptive. Spoke more frequently when in opposition than perhaps any other MP. Always prepared his *theme* but spoke without a text or even notes. Lives in Eltham and was on holiday last year at Porec for 3 weeks. He said he hoped for the early fall of the Labour Government to restore his leisure.

Marsh said he was not convinced that Posner was the right man for Chancellor who didn't need a theorist while he did. Later he said he was impressed by way P. held Tommy at bay. "We all have to bear Tommy" he said, "but some people don't find it easy".

Monday, 6 March   Lunch on Friday with Blackburn of Viyella who told me quite a lot about present state of cotton industry. He confirmed that the real economies of scale lie in marketing and lamented decline of the best Lancashire brand names like Horrocks and Tootal.

[35] Basil Yamey – Professor of Economics – LSE and a member of the Monopolies Commission.
[36] Willis Armstrong – American diplomat in London.

Lectured at Exeter University which has a fine site but buildings are disappointing. Mrs David Walker said that some of the students felt like conscripts, doing time for the welfare state and entitled therefore to complain of inadequate treatment because they were losing employment and pay in "civil" life. She was indignant that anyone should feel this when they could run a car and relax in the gardens and sunshine in the University precincts.

Friday, 10 March   Most of the week interviewing candidates for SEA and EA posts. Some fascinating contrasts. One young tiger with a 2.2. from L.S.E., aged 26 and already a Senior Lecturer at Enfield Technical College, had been President of the L.S.E. Students Union. Then there was an engineer (Michael Fores[37]) who took his BA in Mechanical Sciences in two years, and nearly got a first in economics the next, who was so laconic that none of us could recommend him. He was earning only £1600 at 32 and had worked as a design engineer for Ove Arup and many other firms in Australia, Greece, Persia, etc.

On Wednesday morning we had a long meeting of CM(O) notable for a strong attack by Alec Johnston on our fiscal laxity in which of course Nicky joined. This time, instead of Nicky producing a table that nobody else had seen, he led us into a discussion of the sustainable deficit on the basis of a paper he had not yet circulated. He brought out the rise in public expenditure as a % of GNP since the mid-fifties but it was not clear what one deduced in respect of 1967 or even 1968 from the trend nor even whether the trend would necessarily continue after 1968. Robert took a solid line with the rest of us against both Alec J. and Nicky. William had said from the start that he didn't want to repeat the previous debate and was obviously bored.

At the end Nicky played his best card by asking how we stood if hire purchase restrictions had to be relaxed in July. He prefers this course partly at least because it allows demand management to remain neutral and yet reduce the Budget deficit.

When he saw me this afternoon he said he had bet Wynne G. £1 for every 10,000 by which unemployment next January exceeded or fell short of unemployment this January. I asked if this meant he was now challenging the forecast for 1967 and he said that this was so although he wouldn't want to say it too loudly. Our forecast rested on unsafe foundations since the only falling elements were business investment (which was small in relation to GNP) and stocks which could turn round fast if public expenditure really did what he expected it to do. He thought that we couldn't have been non-competitive all through the past 16 years and that it was the lax approach to fiscal policy that had undermined our competitive position. He had never expected to find the Treasury such a hotbed of Keynesians. I told him that he was now at the point I was at in 1961 and that if he stayed longer in the Treasury he would be a pillar of orthodoxy and a "good Treasury man".

Friday, 10 March   Dinner last night at Cromer's. I sat between Mrs Anthony

[37] Michael Fores – Engineer-economist, latterly in the Board of Trade.

Barber[38] and Dame Ruth King. Mary was next to Cecil King of whom she knew nothing at all. The Plowdens were there too, Edwin as gloomy as ever. Barber said that if the Conservative Party was defeated at the next election he would think seriously of giving up politics. He marvelled at D. Jay sitting on the Opposition Front Bench for so long and said that the sensible man like Crosland and Jenkins found other things to do. Rowley was denouncing Hungarian goulash to Cecil King and Mrs B. asked me to explain what was wrong with the thesis of "The Affluent Society". She seemed worried by the waste of a dozen varieties of hair lotions and not at all troubled by any loss of freedom to choose between them. I said the waste could hardly be very large or somebody would produce a variety at lower cost in bulk and wipe out the others.

Edwin Plowden lamented the unwillingness of the young of any ability to choose a business career – "it's the result of 70 years of Fabian teaching". The others agreed that many firms in industry would be happy to be taken over by the government but that the *City* was stoutly capitalist.

Rowley Cromer was strong on tax incentives. He said that fortunately his wife had a little money but that his salary net of tax just about covered his season ticket. Edwin said that there was a noticeable let-up by executives once they got as far as £6,000/£7,000. Rowley thought that there were fewer people earning over £5,000 in this country than there should be (and were in other countries), and that this indicated the absence of incentive (rather an odd doctrine). Later I heard Lady Cromer say that they had the worst of both worlds, living and earning in England and having to maintain a house in France. She would have to go abroad some time: she couldn't afford to die in England. "It's unpleasant but I have to face it. I don't look forward to dying abroad but I know that I'll have to".

On Tuesday I gathered that Walt Rostow & Co. have come forward with an extraordinary proposition — McCloy[39] calls it "crap" – to lend us $4,000 m. to help us maintain our troops in Germany. This is coupled with a self-denying ordinance about holding gold to which Germany would have to subscribe. But it seems completely out of perspective in relation to the cost of keeping two brigades in Germany (an extra bisque or two would be enough to handle that) and to take for granted that Germany and the UK could flout the French when we are both (for different reasons) anxious to stand well with them.

Governor wants his extra $\frac{1}{2}$% off bank rate and although Sam Goldman is doubtful since it will be taken as a sign of the slant of the Budget, William is inclined to let the Bank decide for themselves this time. I think that it might be quite useful to have something in hand for later in the summer provided we believe that a 1% rise would by itself be a useful weapon. The fact that US policy is rather decidedly relaxing should be the main reason for our moving

[38] Anthony Barber – Conservative Economic Sec. to the Treasury, 1959–62; Fin. Sec., 1962–63; Minister of Health, 1963–64; Chancellor to the Exchequer, 1970–74.

[39] J J McCloy – American lawyer and administrator; Pres., IBRD, 1947–49; Chm., Chase Manhattan Bank, N.Y., 1953–60; Asst. to Pres. on Disarmament, 1961; Chm., Ford Foundation, 1953–65.

now – they shouldn't be exposed to too large and sustained a drain – and lower rates would be a more sensible form of reflation at this point in time than tax concessions. The situation will look different by, say, the end of the year. But nothing will be decided till next week when we get the new trade figures.

Monday, 13 March Colombo at the Treasury for over 2 hours – my first sight of him. He is short, handsome, with dark wavy hair, relaxed in manner, obviously intelligent, and pleasant to deal with. He seemed optimistic about the attitude of France on liquidity, saying that Débré had changed his usual line at Brussels and seemed willing to accept an increase in automatic drawing rights as well as an increase in quotas and hence in conditional credit. Chancellor was a little sceptical and felt that this might only be a tactical move designed to delay agreement. He suggested that Colombo should tell the Americans (to which Colombo replied that he would have to give up his job if he kept flying off for several days at a time). He didn't say that the Americans are trying to get the Germans to hold Roosa bonds and forswear additions to their gold reserve. (But they may not have put this yet to the Germans since their ideas are still taking shape.)

Chancellor encouraged the Italians to give us their forecast for the balance of payments in 1967 but seemed a little taken aback to be asked for his. Still, he got out of it quite well by saying that we expected as big an improvement this year as we had last year and making this out to have been about £240 m. (including payment of interest on US debt). He also fought off C.'s request for his view of the case for bigger quotas for EEC countries in IMF by saying we'd certainly agree if we were *in* EEC. There was a suggestion from Colombo at one point that the Washington joint meeting in April should be postponed. But he withdrew this very quickly, arguing that the Munich meeting of the Ministers of the Six would be based on the IMF paper on drawing rights.

First draft of Budget speech was ready by Friday (which seems very early). I have circulated a piece on hire purchase restrictions coming down firmly against a tax increase in this year's Budget, even as a prelude to relaxation.

Saturday, 18 March Lunch on Friday with Ronnie Edwards and Douglas Allen. We had a long debate on pricing (where RSE is playing for a *small* rise in the price of electricity because he doesn't see why we should recover more overheads on electricity than on for example chemicals in a slump). We also discussed gas and the unfairness of letting gas have all the new cheap fuel from the North Sea while electricity *had* to use coal. Then we got on to RTZ and the discrimination involved in a 20 year contract at the price of electricity proposed. There were some swipes at investment grants and the tendency for industry to look now at self-supply of electricity on the basis of a 25% (or 45%) grant.

The amount of paper over the week was formidable, with Ec. Report, Budget Speech, Monthly Report (for *Economic Trends*), White Papers on Incomes Policy and on Regional Policy, long minutes on credit control and dividend control (Reddaway still in the background). There was also quite a lot on forecasts and disclosure and I got the final arrangements for Nuffield Conference agreed.

At the end of last week, S.G. reported that the Governor was proposing a cut in bank rate. He and Denis Rickett were doubtful because of the colour it would give to the Budget. Meanwhile the Governor was just going off to Basle and not back till Tuesday. William came down in favour and I minuted on Monday in the same sense. But so far as I know, there was no meeting of officials at all. By Tuesday evening Leslie O'Brien was able to tell me that a reduction had been agreed [to 6 per cent on 16 March]. It seemed to have very little effect on the market.

Of course, we've had such a plethora of good news that it would have been hard to stick out. Even the trade returns were on the whole very good (although *The Economist* is waking up to the prospects for imports). The Q4 results, the renewal of the Basle arrangements, the re-establishment of the US swap facility, etc., all have been announced in the first half of March so that it is hard for the Chancellor to bring in a tough budget. On the other hand, unemployment is clearly still rising and the public has had no recent figure to bring this home. The March figure will show a fall in the number temporarily stopped so that the trend may not be clear to the man in the street.

Lady O'Brien told me that they had been burgled four times. So Rowley's preferences for staying ex-directory is understandable.

Thursday, 23 March   The row over the L.S.E. has gone on for most of the past fortnight. It was the main topic when I went to see Ely Devons last Sunday. He said that what mainly worried him was the behaviour of the staff. The lawyers and the sociologists were egging on the students just when they seemed about to pipe down. It wasn't true that the economists paid no regard to their teaching duties and were too deeply taken up with research and consultancy. The Director didn't command the unquestioned respect of the staff who were inclined to talk wildly about "power" and "rights" as if somebody exercised dictatorial influence over the affairs of the School. He quoted Nye Bevan[40] who was advised to join the Parish Council if he wanted to influence affairs but found that the Council had no real power: then the County Council, Parliament, and finally the Cabinet, where on each occasion he was disappointed and could find no sign that he was sitting where "the *real* decisions were taken".

The Director also was too indecisive, first siding with the hardliners and then making concessions at the wrong time. He was the last man to engage in argument with students because he got excited and raised the temperature of debate. Early on, the day after the incident when the porter died, Ely moved at a meeting of staff that a fact-finding committee be appointed and the lawyers argued that this shouldn't be the Disciplinary Board because they would have to pronounce sentence if anyone were found guilty of wrongdoing. Once they were reassured on this point the Committee *was* set up and Ely asked if anyone dissented from this. Nobody in an audience of 200 or so voted against. Yet once the report was prepared, the lawyers again argued that no action should be

---

[40] Aneurin Bevan – Minister of Health in Attlee Government, 1945–51; founder of the National Health Service.

taken because the students might be upset.

He wondered what Hahn,[41] Gorman & Co. would do and felt that after all his exertions to bring them to the School they might change their minds. At least two Professors would retire early instead of continuing after 62. And what would it be like when Adams[42] came?

Monday, 27 March   It has been agreed that Wynne will now go over to the public expenditure side of forecasting and leave Jim Shepherd to do NIF. This appeals greatly to Wynne and is a job that badly needs doing.

Just before Easter we had an IPP meeting to which T.B. came (late as usual – in fact at the end of Denis' exposition of the state of play). T. asked the question: did we *want* to agree with the Americans on a scheme for the creation of more liquidity. He was afraid that if we sided with them it would provide the French with a fresh Nassau. We had not thought out our attitude to the Kennedy Round, liquidity and the Common Market from a consistent stand-point. Of course he had his orders although they weren't to his liking and he could only observe that, given what his master was saying, we ought not be in a hurry to make friends with the Americans and side with them against the Six. Reticence was the word. "Surtout pas trop de zêle" in the immortal words of Talleyrand.

I thought that the Chancellor had chosen a more discreet line when he said, à propos of drawing rights, that he was not averse to a settlement on this basis provided it was clear that it was not put forward purely as a tactical move and did represent a genuine effort to arrive at a workable solution. After all, it was the French who proposed a new asset and we who thought drawing rights preferable; and now we have changed right round and can hardly claim that it is really indispensable to cling to our new view even if we do think that it is technically superior. Of course, too, a lot of the manoeuvring does centre on the dollar and the original proposal by the French was aimed *against* the dollar just as, no doubt, the most recent change of front, rests on the view that the units solution may be too favourable to the dollar.

Who would have thought, two years ago, that I should find myself having to argue against Nicky over a proposed £300 m. addition to this year's tax burden; or over the view that a reduction in home demand might well put the balance of payments straight. "It hasn't been tried", as he no doubt rightly contends. In fact, as I told Nicky, his current position is very close in many different respects, to mine when I entered the Treasury – though I would never claim to have been capable of expressing it with such force, elegance and articulateness. This is true, for example, of his emphasis on scale of manufacturing activities (but I wouldn't single out manufacturing), his attitude to deflation, his scepticism of fixed estimates of productive potential, etc. What I did not share was his conviction that changes in taxation would work wonders or even improve the

---

[41] F Hahn – Univ. Lecturer in Economics, University of Cambridge, 1962–67; LSE, 1967– ; Vice Pres., 1970–71, Pres., 1971, Econometric Society.

[42] Sir Walter Adams – Principal, University College of Rhodesia and Nyasaland, 1955–67; Director, LSE, 1967–74.

sense of equity. Maybe I shall come to that view yet; but I rather doubt whether all the changes that have taken place in the tax system have been accompanied by much of a change in our economic performance.

Sunday, 2 April　　　I had three days in the office and saw William briefly at Directorate on Thursday. But although he expressed anxiety about the Budget Speech, I have had no hand in it since and indeed am more completely outside the whole process of preparing it than I have ever been.

Tuesday, 4 April　　　Lunch at the Bank on Monday. We discussed public expenditure along traditional lines. I asked about market forwards and the Governor said that there were still £700–£800 m. outstanding, falling at £100 m. a month. In 1961 the total rose to the alarming figure of £150 m. starting off at £60 m. but they are calmer about these things now. I asked why so large a forward position should still persist in face of a surplus, spot and forward, of £329 m. in March alone and £205 m. spot. They thought that some of the positions involved transactions with maturities of six months or more. They (i.e. M. Parsons and the Governor) pointed out that there was little or no interest incentive to switch into sterling so that presumably the continentals are replenishing normal holdings of sterling.

Today Rivel of Chase Manhattan called on S.G. and me and asked if the discount market was right in thinking that there was a large hot money inflow. We gave him the answer suggested above and he confirmed that the inflow did not seem to be from dollar sources. He was notably concerned at P. Jay's piece in *The Times* (a scoop on his first day) and insisted that his bank could not have intended to embarrass the US administration by throwing doubt on the future convertibility of the dollar.

Later I had dinner at the Reform with George Schwarz, Sydney Gampell, P. Wilsher, G. Haberler, A. Tugendhat and Co. and we all discussed this at some length. Sydney was also excited about the Press Conference on the Regional Employment Premium and the precedent it set for democratic planning of new taxes. Haberler was on his way back from Bellagio and explained James Meade's latest ideas on unilateral free trade.

Meeting today with Chancellor on credit control. S.G. very long-winded and Nicky in good form. William as usual kept quiet until the end and then put a devastating question. He said he wanted some figures and elicited that if things went as we foresee we might have to increase special deposits by 7 or 8 % to mop up surplus liquidity.[43] So (after some interruptions that increased our interest in the punch-line) why didn't the Chancellor raise special deposits *now*? Could he remove ceiling on advances without tightening up in some other way? Of course, the figures are all wrong and would involve the government meeting

---

[43] Company liquidity at the end of March 1967 was less than at the same date in any of the three preceding years but was expected to increase later in the year as public investment rose. In the next nine months the rise in company liquidity was nearly three times as fast as the average for 1964–66.

nearly the whole of its borrowing requirements from special deposits whereas it is bound to sell *some* gilt edged if only to the banks. N.K. took the line that we needed to limit the powers of the banks to lend and that it wouldn't be enough for the Governor to talk to them and indicate how he wanted them to interpret an increase in special deposits. Sam wanted a fixed change in the ceiling in *addition* to all this but this was fortunately argued out.

Lunch with N.K. and Bill Nield. After SEP Crossman challenged the minutes in a note which spoke of the "P.M.'s brilliant idea" (the Regional Premium) and attacked the low balance of payments objective (really a plan for devaluation in disguise). This was obviously drafted by T.B. as William had hinted to me and, as Bill Nield said, the P.M. had spotted. Bill is still fed up with the indecisiveness of Ministers and also attacked Norman Hunt[44] for his lack of understanding of the way the Cabinet functions. There is no voting in any formal sense and most people say nothing at all so that sense of the meeting comes from the run of argument between the few who do. There isn't just a tussle between two views but when "voices" are asked for there is first one, then another, then some combination or compromise between the two, and so on until no one could faithfully indicate what was agreed because nothing is agreed. It is left to the P.M. in his summing-up and to the Secretaries in drafting the minutes. It is very rare for Burke Trend or Bill to ring William, usually to consider the implications of a particular conclusion before circulating it.

Saturday, 8 April   On Thursday I took the pre-Budget Press Conference – my first experience of taking one – and there was Frances representing *The Times*. Most of the discussion was on productive potential but there was also some interest in price movements and Wynne gave them his estimate that manufactured goods were selling about 2% lower than the behaviour of costs would suggest. The press is much more rational in its comments on what the Budget should do than it was in, say, 1962-63.

British Academy banquet at night – I had to cut L.S.E. meeting – and long speech by Kathleen Kenyon[45]. Jenny Lee[46] looked more like a Hollywood film star than a Minister, her hair carefully styled, with bow lips and a rather cautious look in her eyes – not surprisingly when everybody made an appeal to her in turn to spend more on their pet projects. She smiled across at her neighbours at the table when references were made to them and seemed relaxed in spite of the thoughtful cast of her eye. Not at all like an ex-schoolmistress and more like the subject of a Pop Song (as of course she was 35 years ago).

Tuesday, 11 April   Budget today after a morning meeting on the balance of payments cost of entering EEC.

[44] Norman Hunt – Fellow of Exeter College, Oxford.

[45] Dr Kathleen Kenyon – Archaeologist; Principal, St Hugh's College, Oxford, 1962–73.

[46] Jenny Lee, widow of Aneurin Bevan – Labour Parliamentary Sec., Ministry of Works and Buildings, 1964–65; Parliamentary Under-Sec. of State, Dept. of Education and Science, 1965–67; Minister of State, 1967–70.

I felt drowsy in the Distinguished Strangers Gallery but the Budget speech was not very thrilling or novel. Keith Joseph at the Political Economy Club in the evening said he thought the Chancellor had an excellent voice and delivery and that it was a good speech even if there were no major proposals. The one moment of high spirits was when the Chancellor announced a relaxation of hire purchase restrictions on motor bicycles and 3-wheel cars: this cause loud laughter. The House listened respectfully and there was not a single interruption in $1\frac{1}{2}$ hours nor even an interjection (I thought I heard *one*, but not very loud, "not enough" when he talked of falling interest rates).

The Political Economy Club discussion was not very enlightening. I sat next George Wansbrough[47] and Keith Joseph and we discussed the absence of academics, tycoons and T.U. leaders in the House of Commons – à propos of a move to Windsor of the House of Commons as suggested by the *Telegraph* supplement. K.J. thought it was already cut off from reality and this would complete the process, citing Canberra and the division of the House into 300 M.P.s who had rooms in Bloomsbury and 300 who lived in hotels when in London.

Edward Boyle said to me as I left that he had just re-read three textbooks, Samuelson, Lipsey and Cairncross, and that he thought mine undoubtedly the best. Samuelson was too American and Lipsey too uppish.

Thursday, 13 April   A bellyful of methodology. First an hour on Kennedy Round and then a couple of hours on the effects of entry into EEC.[48] The second meeting was opera bouffe with Nicky at his nickiest. First he said we needn't report till the 27th when he had promised not to say this in the morning. Then he danced on a Treasury paper on capital movements which he alleged he hadn't seen, repudiating the conclusions as absurd. Then he practically took over the meeting telling everybody what they were to do – most of it they needn't do or had done already. Finally he returned to his taxation hobby horse, and told us again that taxes would have to go up by over £2,000 m. At one point John Wright, whom nobody had invited and who had read none of the papers, let loose a succession of red herrings starting with the need to help New Zealand, the consequent rise in butter prices, expansion of butter production in Scandinavia after *it* entered EEC and ending with a bill for £200–£300 m. when, as Nicky said, we could buy all the New Zealand butter for £150 m. and throw it in the sea.

Yesterday we had dinner with de la Martinière and N.K. was there, but for-

---

[47] George Wansbrough – Dir., Mercantile Credit Co. Ltd, 1934–75; Investment Consultant, 1952–73; Member, PWLB.

[48] A formal application to join the European Community was made on 11 May. A White Paper giving an assessment of the costs and benefits of joining the Community was subsequently published in 1970 (Cmnd 4289). Such estimates were necessarily confined to predictable and measurable changes of which the most obvious was the higher price of food. The balance of payments cost reflected higher import prices and probably also higher capital exports. The resource cost measured the reduction in real income once the adjustments necessary to restore external balance had been made.

tunately rather less exuberant. It's curious that T.B. is relatively calm at these meetings and it's only N.K. who won't stop talking and delights in being perverse. They squabbled at the earlier meeting about the importance of investment but saw eye to eye today. Nicky could see no connection between fiscal policy and food prices and took it for granted that all tax changes would be upwards.

Nominally the meeting was for the preparation of a report *by officials* helped by economic advisers but of course the officials couldn't get a word in and most of them were from the Board of Trade and felt committed to support the President's paper. N.K. is happy so long as we can show a whacking balance of payments deficit but only a moderate resources cost of joining. T.B. said we needn't mention devaluation since he had 15 other ways of saying it.

Saturday, 13 May   A gap of exactly a month. I had quite a hectic week before leaving for Washington and the paper on the balance of payments cost of joining EEC was not in the end complete by 8 p.m. on the Tuesday night when I had to quit. However F.F. managed to get a version in agreed by everybody largely by dint of tackling the main protagonists one by one. The fact that T.B. was in Moscow no doubt helped. Although the figures looked a little on the low side by comparison with our earlier discussions, they must have been enough to give the Cabinet a jolt, and *The Times* on May 1 carried rather similar results but less coherently. The distinction between the resources cost and the balance of payments cost has escaped all the commentators so far as I can see.

When I tackled William, he explained that we had to pursue as firm a policy whether we entered or not up to 1970 and that if we had the surplus we needed out of which to repay debt we could presumably stand the shock of entry at that point in time. So there was nothing inconsistent between the Chancellor's strategy and joining EEC. This seemed a little too neat and William did go on later to say that we ought to dig up the F.U. papers and have a look at accompanying measures.

On the morning I got back from Washington I went straight to Directorate meeting and when the issue arose of what was to be said in the debate on EEC I drew attention to the fact that 10 speakers out of 43 backbenchers speaking in the Budget debate had either advocated or contemplated devaluation. William said that although advisers were asked to the week-end meeting this was confined to Saturday morning only at No.10 and there was no intention of allowing advisers to join in the discussion. They would answer factual questions only and would take part only when these questions were put to them by their Minister. As I was going to Belfast for the week-end William thought it best to "let me off" and took Nicky. He said later it was a complete waste of time and that the arrangement was devised simply to please Tommy. The questions, like most Ministerial questions, had all been loaded and the only ones that gave him anything to do were about value added taxation.

Conference on May 1 at Oxford on disclosure of forecasts, then on Tuesday I had to start off the IMF discussions, go on to a Methodology meeting and then to ESG, all in one morning.

At Oxford I sat next the Chancellor at dinner and he told me that he had been under pressure at the Cabinet on EEC. He had made it clear that he would not devalue whatever the pressure. "There comes a time", he said, "when you must play your historic role". Denis Healey told him that "You put us in a difficult position, Chancellor".

When I spoke to William about this he said that the Chancellor had squared his conscience by deciding that he must be free to go on saying publicly that he would not devalue even if he thought that this might be necessary. But unlike Stafford Cripps[49] he would make way for somebody else if it came to the crunch. "Of course", William added, "this means that if we consider what to do, we may be thought to be planning for a new Chancellor".

The Oxford discussion was really rather funny especially after T.B. and N.K. joined us after dinner, with the Chancellor. The Chancellor wanted to dissociate himself from the official forecasts while T.B. wanted to argue both that the forecasts were very bad ("My dear boy, you have no idea, but no idea", he told Teddy J.) and that of course they should be published. The journalists were unhappy at the suggestion (a) that the Chancellor had some other way of deciding what was going on, and (b) that there was simply a judgment what should be done that did not flow directly from the forecast. So there was quite a debate on the differences between a forecast and a judgment. Fortunately Wynne wasn't there.

I should record here that at a meeting on the long term prospect for taxation held by William before we went off to Washington, Wynne told N.K. quite amicably at one point to "shut up, Nicky" and Nicky dutifully did just that. This was the only time I've seen it done. It arose when W.G. was arguing that N.K. was foolish to ask us to decide what tax changes would be needed next year or the year after since one ought only to *decide* when decision was required – although one should of course have an eye on longer term trends and probabilities. Nicky still feels that somehow our long term assessments are inadequate. John Boreham, on the other hand, returning to the fray after some years in G.R.O., told me on Friday that he was appalled by the MTAC work and thought it far less sophisticated than he recalled from 1962-63.

The fall in bank rate [to 5½ per cent on 4 May] was not unexpected. William told me before I left that the Governor had written (I saw the letter later) in terms that implied that he was quite prepared to see an early cut, even before his return from New Zealand and Australia. It seemed inappropriate in mid-April but when William asked me again in the first few days of May (May 2, I think) I said that I saw nothing against it in the next week or two and a cut was duly made on May 4. What did surprise me was the anxiety to put the inc. in reserves over £50 m. in April. I protested (but the figure was put *up*, at N.K.'s suggestion, from £48 m.) that we couldn't possibly reach £50 m. in May because we were sure to have a reaction to a decision to join EEC and might have bad trade figures (as we eventually did). Did we mean to tell the truth from now on? If we had to come clean, we would find May awkward.

[49] Sir Stafford Cripps – Labour President of the Board of Trade, 1945–47; Chancellor of the Exchequer, 1947–50.

The impressive feature of the last week or so is how often T.B. turns up at a critical meeting and how forcefully he puts his points. He was at a joint meeting on "Uncle" and spoke for 20/25 minutes (according to John Hunt) just after H. Lever had hoped to get a straight answer to the question whether everybody was in favour. (T.B. was afraid it would mean too high a profit for RTZ – I wish he was right: the real trouble is that we should have to subsidise electricity!). For one occasion when he is sensible and indeed penetrating and witty there are half a dozen when he is intemperate, vitriolic and downright bullying. I think it is quite a reasonable judgment by the outside public that if this is the sort of man the P.M. relies on, how can we expect good administration.

I was amused on Thursday at Directorate when Raphael started to talk about the way the press was beginning to harp on devaluation, to hear N.K. say "Can't they issue a D notice about devaluation?" He told me afterwards – as William had done already – that he thought we should devalue this summer. Next spring wouldn't do, it must be this summer. I said the P.M. wouldn't look at it and N.K. said it depended on the advice he was given. I replied that the advisers had given him the advice before and it had had no effect. The Chancellor certainly wouldn't listen to advice.

On Tuesday the Chancellor gave a party for R. Nield whom I talked to briefly – my first sight of him since the Budget. I had time only to say "Good luck and thank you" and I meant it for he will be a great loss. The Chancellor was just saying "Those of us who arrived in 1964" when T.B. arrived, so he repeated it, saying that he would expect T.B. to agree with him, and went on "how many days ago?" when William interrupted with "932" to everybody's amusement. In fact, William said, the Chancellor has now all but equalled Amory's period of office but still falls short of Butler and Cripps. Peter Vinter pointed out that William had developed a paunch.

Wednesday, 17 May   Richard Powell, back from Geneva, told us that Alan Westerman [50] said once it was all over (Kennedy Round) "I've never worked so hard by night and done so little by day since my honeymoon". When it looked like breaking down, Richard told Wyndham White[51] that he would take on his shoulders a cut in the steel tariff if this would get the others going. This led to successful pressure on the US and the Japs (who alone had a Minister – with an elongated head as if it had been pressed in a vice – Douglas Allen said it probably had). This put the EEC on the spot and Rey[52] wanted to consult his Council of Ministers and give a decision on Wednesday. He was argued out of this – there would obviously have been stories of a major crisis in the press and great difficulty in getting an eventual settlement – and ultimately agreed by 10 o'clock to the remaining concessions. These were, of all things, on cottonseed

[50] Alan Westerman – Leader of Australian delegation in meetings on commercial policy.

[51] Sir Eric Wyndham White – Exec. Sec., GATT, 1948–65; Dir. Gen., 1965–68.

[52] Jean Rey – Belgian Min. of Econ. Affairs, 1954–58; Sectional Pres. for Ext. Econ. Relations, EEC, 1958–67; Pres. of Combined Exec. of EEC, ECSC and Euratom, 1967–70.

oil and the sugar content of canned fruit! Richard said the EEC played the game, respected the British team (which was the most expert of those represented) and didn't try to make use of our application to join the EEC except in relation to the special case of steel. Rey had to take it out on us as he couldn't pick on the Americans without a breakdown; and he apologised to R.P. for having done so, quite deliberately. The Americans made bad blunders in Geneva and Washington and had no top leadership to cope with Rey. The Japanese kept out of the way "in the underbush" and had some genuine difficulties, not unlike ours, over cereal aid, aggravated by the situation in the Assembly. But they will probably be the biggest gainers.

General de Gaulle spoke at more length yesterday on the UK application than I had expected but the gist of it all was exactly as in 1963 and it is hard to interpret his speech as anything but a veto. This leaves Harold to raise other possibilities in Washington. When I was there at the end of April John Stevens couldn't believe that H.W. would make an application to go in because he must be contemplating a different move on his visit to Washington. But as William pointed out on my return this served the purpose of a long stop if General de Gaulle proved obstinate. It looks as if George Brown would now bang his head a second time against a closed door.

Last week we had a meeting on hire purchase relaxation at which N.K. took a much firmer line against a general relaxation than I was proposing. I thought on reflection that Nicky was right but in the meantime Andrew Edwards put round a paper in which the two of us figured as protagonists of opposing policies. N.K. rang me up on Monday (when I had already told William to postpone action) to say that he hoped the paper would not go forward representing the two of us in this way and I heartily agreed.

Trouble in the gilt-edged market partly it is said because steel shares are so attractive to the institutions who are therefore shedding gilt-edged. I think it is more likely that people now fear a steady deterioration – this is the third year running that the market has weakened in late May (if my memory is right). The trade returns were ominous (like Jan. '64) and the fact that unemployment is still rising doesn't help. The Bank of England have put the government broker in and actually raised prices on a falling market – which was asking for trouble – and have naturally taken a beating.

Sunday, 21 May   Some gossip about the C.M. At Directorate William said we had the melancholy pleasure of being able to say "I told you so". F.F. said that, as on the last occasion when we negotiated, many people had assumed that, as we had an apparently well-conducted government, we must presumably have taken all necessary precautions to assure ourselves that our application would meet with no foreseeable obstacles and could reasonably be expected to succeed. There was corresponding surprise that the P.M. should have gone ahead *after* talking to de Gaulle only to encounter the familiar reaction. Matters were not made any better by *The Times* comment that we had been supporting the franc – a comment obviously inspired from No. 10 which we had done our best to delete from the P.M.'s speeches. "A negotiation isn't a battle" said

Frank. "You've got to leave your opponent anxious to settle and with room to manoeuvre for a settlement".

At the previous Directorate meeting Nicky told us of a conversation with Uri[53] who emphasised that France might face a constitutional crisis in the autumn. The government had a majority of 2 and with the resignation of Pisani this would fall to 1. De Gaulle intended to make use of decrees but it wasn't clear how long this would continue. Uri also tended to make light of the agricultural policy as an obstacle.

When in Washington I talked to Larry Krause[54] who couldn't see how the French could possibly agree to our joining, given the advantages they enjoyed under the present arrangements. Yet Kermit Gordon[55] said that Walter Heller had argued when he came back from Europe that all the signs were that the French would accept us. This wasn't just his reading but what he heard on all hands. I told John Stevens that I thought H.W. could quite well say that in the light of what he had gathered, and given our present economic situation, he thought it right not to apply just yet, though this was his intention. But I judged that George wouldn't stand for this as he wanted everything to be decided so that we could join by 1970.

On Friday night we had a long talk with Bent Hansen[56] about UK fiscal policy and his view that the cycle since 1960 was almost entirely of the government's own creation. It is really impossible to discuss this in abstraction from the longer term aims of the government and the over-anxiety to maintain full employment.

In the last fortnight the general situation has changed dramatically, especially since the trade figures appeared, and the Chancellor's strategy is under attack notably by Sam B. (who won't pull his punches). The gilt-edged market changed round violently and so, to a lesser extent, did the exchange market. The car industry is largely demoralised and pressing for a cut in purchase tax to 15% and measures to raise sales *this year* to 1,150,000 – a quite impracticable change. (Otto got quite heated on Thursday about our attempts to pooh-pooh it all). Unemployment is up and there are a few signs of real recovery (except that housing is active and John Laing says his firm is flat out). In some ways it's like the summer of 1962 – especially in the motor industry which is touting for similar concessions. The Chancellor is jumpy and now reluctant to move. He went through a fairly harmless draft Monthly EC Report in detail to get the tone of it more optimistic.

Meanwhile the press openly discusses devaluation and some of the papers are strongly pressing for it. If we're *not* going into Europe there ought to be less case for devaluation but the pound weakened after de Gaulle's speech. The press is also sour about the government and everything runs against them. Even

---

[53] Pierre Uri – French economist; Econ. Dir., ECSC, 1952–59; Econ. Adviser, Common Market, 1958–59; Chm., Experts' Group on long-term development of EEC, 1960–64; on competitive capacity of EEC, 1968–70.

[54] Larry Krause – Economist of Brookings Institution, Washington D.C.

[55] Kermit Gordon – Director, Brookings Institution, Washington D.C.

[56] Bent Hansen – Danish-born, Swedish economist; Prof. and Head of Institute of Economic Research, Stockholm, 1955–64; Special Consultant, OECD, 1965–67.

the Chancellor is thought to be "pompous".

Tuesday, 23 May   Lunch yesterday with Phelps Brown and Buchanan (Virginia). Henry told me of Trenchard's[57] claim to get along on two languages: English and loud English. We discussed the C.M. and Buchanan[58] took little part in the discussion except when we got on to minimum wages when he explained that it was only now that they were beginning to bite anywhere except the South. They had slowed down the development of the South but were now being extended to distribution and would effectively end the use of High School boys at week-ends. The University of Virginia had been forced to go over to automats and sack its canteen staff. Yet the minimum is only $1.40 an hour.

Later George Garvy[59] called. He spoke in praise of the humans who without contact with the West or recollection of an earlier system had worked out the virtue of a market economy and did not hesitate to urge that all that had gone on since 1920 was wrong – not just inappropriate to modern conditions as Fekete[60] might urge in Hungary in 1966 – but wrong even at the time. It was more important to get the Russians to move forward than any of the Eastern European countries since they would then move all the further.

He spoke also of a book by a daughter or niece of Menshikov (who was once Ambassador to the US). It was the best book on US agriculture, according to the experts in the Department of Agriculture although she had never set foot in the US. He also told me a story of Papic[61] in the mid-fifties explaining the difficulties that the Russians would have when they came to adapt their system to market forces. The Yugoslavs had quickly learned the need to bring back experienced managers even if they were not politically reliable but in the USSR the managers have become so used to plans that they wouldn't know how to behave if asked to make economic choices.

William Davis had a long article in yesterday's *Guardian* suggesting that the Chancellor needed to be replaced. Today the Chancellor referred to it rather unexpectedly adding suddenly that it must have been Crossman who put William Davis up to it – he recognised some of the material.

Originally he had called us together to hear our independent views of the state of the economy – Fred, myself, Nicky and William. Nicky veered towards talking devaluation, by saying that people would rightly ask us why we weren't in surplus at this stage in the cycle instead of worrying over higher imports. The Chancellor said laughingly that he'd take the rest as read. Nicky had had a good innings yesterday and should be restricted to a quota if he put the record on at every meeting.

The upshot of the meeting was nevertheless that the Chancellor who a few days ago refused to be "hustled by Otto" came round to the view that perhaps he

[57] Lord Trenchard – Air Marshall, 1919; Marshall of the RAF, 1927.

[58] James M Buchanan – Professor of Economics, Univ. of Virginia, 1956–68.

[59] George Garvy – US economist with Fed. Reserve Bank of N.Y.

[60] Fekete – Hungarian banker acting for Moscow Narodny Bank in its international operations.

[61] Papic – Yugoslav economist.

ought to do something for the car industry and not wait too long over it. William patiently went over the timetable – R.E.P., uprating, children's allowances etc. – and convinced the Chancellor that perhaps he should wrap the hire purchase relaxation up with the R.E.P. announcement some time between the two bits of bad news – the reserves and May trade figures.

Later when I saw William he was obviously chuckling over the meeting which had gone further than he had hoped but very much in the right direction. Nicky would have liked an offsetting increase in taxes but agreed (a) that this meant SET or petrol and (b) that it wasn't "on" politically. Fred rightly insisted that next year's Budget would still be in sufficient time.

Friday, 2 June   Paris for EPC and WP3. Denis was particularly interesting on the post-war years. It irks him that at the Group of 10 Emminger is liable to say that he is the only one present who was in EPU from start to finish when Lucius goes back to Bretton Woods and Denis had a hand in nearly all the post-war bilateral agreements. When E. suggests a parallel between 50% settlements in gold and units (or drawing rights) and fractional gold settlements in EPU he forgets that these were a way of handling inconvertibility (and hence imply inconvertibility between gold and units). As D. points out the Continentals won't treat units as a new form of reserve asset but insist on treating them as credit and hence subject to creditor limits and all the usual safeguards associated with the extension of private credit.

D. also laments that in the post-war agreements when Stafford C. was asked whether the French should be given a credit or a grant he insisted on a grant because of the huge franc debits already accumulated. He didn't think it possible that repayment would ever take place. Yet we were simultaneously refusing Rothschild £75,000 in francs to purchase Chateau Margaux – now worth perhaps £2m. Did economists ever make long term forecasts that turned out right?

Earlier D. recalled the disputes with the Belgians over conditional aid. They persuaded Harriman that when we submitted our balance of payments forecasts we were getting aid by a cheat because we forecast deficits with other European countries that didn't happen and yet drew aid to cover them. D. argued that there was no cheating because what mattered was our deficit in dollars and whether the forecast here was correct. There had been a visit to Brussels to argue with Spaak (Hall-Patch[62] flew from Paris but had his Rolls Royce driven to Brussels to meet the plane and "you can imagine what Cripps thought about that": H.P. wasn't going to let "that fellow Rendall"[63] handle things). The proposal was made that in the bilateral agreement we should buy freely if not asked to pay to cover the deficit and allowed a perpetual credit (or perhaps non-reimbursable credit). The translator got the phrase wrong: and Spaak broke out, like a French

[62] Sir Edmund Hall-Patch – Asst. Sec., Treasury, 1935–44 (shared a dug-out with Chou-en-Lai in Szechuan); Foreign Office, 1944–48; Chm., Exec. Cttee., OEEC, 1948; Treasury rep. in Washington, 1952–54; Chm., Standard Bank, 1957–62.

[63] P S Rendall – Chm., British Nylon Spinners, 1960–61; Man. Dir., Courtaulds, 1943–61; and Dep. Chm., 1949–61.

taxi driver offered only a fraction of his fare, "Mais ce n'est pas un credit, c'est un don").

When the EPU was being set up, the Bank of England thought it would be the end of sterling, *i.e.* sterling held by Europe, and their fears excited Jay and Gaitskell. One of the last things that Denis did before leaving the Treasury for No. 10 was to have lunch with them and meet the argument that the Belgians would be able to claim payment in gold by pointing out that we had the reciprocal advantage if we were in surplus with other countries. (Under the previous arrangement the Belgians would only have been able to use their sterling under administrative transferability i.e. would have required our agreement: now they could automatically ask for a fractional gold payment). As for the other danger, that the Europeans might run down their existing holdings of sterling, this was covered by the Katz-Gaitskell agreement[64]. Some years later George Bolton actually cited as one of the *advantages* of EPU that it had led to a running down of sterling holdings which he said had become very low and hence no threat to his scheme for a floating rate.

As for Germany D. had great difficulty in advising whether the mark was a hard or a soft currency because of the peculiarity of the support arrangements. The Americans insisted on dollar payments for all exports because they provided most of the imports, and did not recognise the division throughout Europe between hard and soft payments. Yet if we didn't buy from Germany we were liable to make larger payments.

I suggested to D. that in spite of all this, trade increased remarkably smoothly so that it was difficult to say from the figures where EPU started (or EEC). The most important feature of the post-war scene was rising employment levels and this dragged up trade in spite of the obstacles. However, there was a real danger of breakdown in 1947 and the injection of US payments made all the difference.

Ditchley, Sunday, 19 June   Rupert Raw told me that he had had a useful morning at the Banque de France and that they had agreed to renew the swap, provided we kept it secret and on no account let it reach the ears of the General!

The EPC meeting was chiefly interesting because of the emphasis laid by the Germans on the state of domestic opinion about balanced budgets. It seems that Emminger is regarded in Germany as a dangerous radical. But it was clear to us that they still don't really know how the German economy is likely to behave this year and are hoping for an expansion that may be late in coming.

People in Paris expressed some sympathy with the UK for being so foolish as to back Israel and get itself into a position where we should be obliged to offer some naval or military support. But in fact it was clear within 24 hours that Israel had won hands down.[65] Apparently for once we had the right intelligence.

---

[64] Katz-Gaitskell Agreement – an agreement between US and UK governments offering reassurance to the UK against possible calls on her exchange reserves as a result of the operation of the European Payments Union.

[65] War broke out on 5 June between Israel and Egypt, supported by four of the Arab States. Arab oil supplies to the US and UK were stopped and the Suez Canal was closed. A cease-fire followed on 8 June.

According to Kermit Gordon, the US Intelligence thought that 7 days would be enough and we thought 10: this emerged when the P.M. saw Johnston and underlay the subsequent actions of both governments. The British reaction is typified by Brogan[66] who wrote to *The Economist* to point out that in 1956 one could quote the boy whose homework was badly done: "Daddy *would* help me!" What nobody can foresee is how the Jews and the Arabs are ever to be reconciled before the H bombs start falling.

The fortnight since I got back from Paris has been busy but unexciting. Most of this week seems to have gone on the methodology of public expenditure. Donald felt that the distinction between transfer and other expenditure was drawn much too sharply and that it was premature to report agreement on the precise ranking of the two.

We also on Friday had our first FU meeting for months. Of course the newspapers and Hansard are full of devaluation talk and it is coming to be taken for granted that only somebody very stupid would fail to see how advantageous it would be. N.K. is not a member of the FU Committee but he now feels amply borne out by the trade figures and in spite of rising unemployment would stick to his view that we should have raised taxes more in the Budget. He points out that the MTAC assessment ignores the impossibility of maintaining a smoothly descending unemployment rate from 2 to 1.75 over 3 years (we just don't have the instruments) and the aggravation that loss of confidence may introduce. The new MTAC report was discussed on Thursday but N.K. did not go and T.B. was comparatively genial, pointing out that in primitive communities like Hungary *non*-working usually worsened the balance of payments whereas somehow in the UK, an affluent society, a withdrawal of workers (through raising the school-leaving age) or a loss of productivity actually improved it.

What is obvious is that we shall have difficulty this year again if things go on like this with a substantial visible deficit and rising unemployment since the Chancellor's strategy will be called in question and the impression will grow that the only possible alternative if devaluation. There isn't now much hope that exports this year will go on growing since recovery in the US and still more Germany has been delayed.

It is odd what a capacity T.B. has to get hold of gossip. He knew exactly how much every Economic Adviser was earning. He had also found out about two statistical appointments of which none of us had any knowledge.

Wynne was much annoyed to have his memo. on Public Expenditure entirely revised by Miss Cooper[67] without any consultation with us or indication by T.B. that this was how it was amended: all the more because it was full of mistakes and badly argued.

This week-end in glorious sunshine I'm at Ditchley for a discussion of incomes policy, the outcome being that there is room for something, but not very much, to bring pressure on price and wage settlements. Nobody seems to like dwelling on machinery.

[66] Dennis Brogan – Professor of Political Science, Cambridge, 1929–68.

[67] Miss Cooper – Fellow of St Hugh's College, Oxford.

Monday, 26 June   Geneva. EFTA. Derek Mitchell told me that when P.M. had to give a broadcast in Russian he had typed it phonetically and then attempted to read the teletype only to find that the phrases extended off the page so that he had ultimately had to give up at 2 a.m. Derek also said that Giles Wilson was seen off every morning by his mother from Charing Cross Station, even at 16, that he was now at Ealing topping up A levels, and that there would be a lot of topping up to do. He thought that Mary Wilson, having lost "Robin", was not reconciled to parting with Giles and was secretly relieved that he found his A level exams so forbidding.

Eugene Melville[68] gave us dinner and his guests included Olivier Long's wife, Mr and Mrs Curzon[69] (he is a Professor at the Hautes Etudes and will alternate with Chicago) and another lady. Curzon told me about the duty free zone, part of French territory, which dates back to the 1850's. The trade of the zone is now very large especially in butter. Before the war the area was quite a centre of smuggling and apparently the main items imported were Japanese bicycles (not subject to quota) and petrol.

We had a talk about the C.M. and its political role. I expressed some doubt on the proposition that if we entered the Community we could hope for a great extension of our political influence (modifying existing economic decisions would after all be no more than a mitigation). Eugene supported this view pointing out that General de Gaulle hadn't consulted anybody about the Middle East. Did anybody suppose that the existence of the EEC had made the slightest difference to the reactions of its members to the dispute or to the handling of it?

The previous evening Getzwold had asked us what was wrong with the division of Europe. Weren't we getting along splendidly? Wasn't the main thing to keep expansion going? Derek said association was an obvious attempt to side-track us and wasn't seriously intended to lead to eventual membership. If it were, there might be something worth studying but how could we decide, say, on agricultural policy unless we had a firm undertaking that went beyond association? We then got on to the subject of inward investment and I argued that whatever the French said, their actions showed an interest in getting US participation in French industry. They merely wanted the satisfaction of some strong anti-American sentiments stuffed with lots of nationalism and laced with a little logic, that was pretty feeble when tasted. As for the technological community with which we were so anxious to endow the Common Market, were any of the 6 likely to build up a really successful opposition to the US in aircraft, nuclear designs, or computers? We alone tried all these and tried to meet the US head on, but did it pay? Was it not better, like the rest of Europe, to concentrate effort where the disadvantages were less apparent? The market didn't really hold up when it came to aircraft development and sales. Even

[68] Eugene Melville – Minister (Economic) Bonn, 1962–65; Perm. UK Delegate to EFTA and GATT, 1965; Ambassador and Permanent UK rep. to UN and other international organisations in Geneva, 1966–71.

[69] Mr and Mrs Curzon – Economists at the School for Advanced International Studies, Geneva.

collaboration was not a satisfactory substitute, as we had found. Then there was the problem of the big international companies which, as Getzwold pointed out, had obliged the Norwegians to join the aluminium racket because Alcan & Co. already controlled such a large proportion of the fabricating outlets *in Norway* that there was no obvious alternative.

Curzon mentioned to me tonight that the Swiss commercial banks are said to have foreign exchange holdings twice as large as the Central Bank's holding of Fr 10b. Hay[70] said that when the Sudanese transfer took place it was the commercial banks concerned that approached the Swiss National Bank for advice. The news was probably leaked by the Bank of England to show the futility of such proceedings by the Arabs.

On Friday morning William and I had a long talk with the Chancellor about the paper on methodology. Chancellor found it difficult to follow – quite rightly as it turned out because I had put a rather different interpretation on one of the main points from Wynne. William and I had a long discussion in the afternoon and this cleared up a lot of it for me but made the proposition a rather different one, centred on the kind of relationship we use in short term forecasting between employment and output: to release 100,000 men you have to reduce demand by the equivalent of the *average* output of about 300,000 men. As Wynne said this hinges on a very high profit/output gearing which is not so likely to hold in the longer run although it remains true that some reduction in profit is likely if output is reduced.

Wednesday, 28 June   Last night I went to the 50th Anniversary of the Tuesday Club and heard Leslie Rowan read out a letter from O.T. Falk,[71] now 88, celebrating ballet and ballet music. He took Keynes to see Lopokova and he said afterwards: "She's a rotten dancer: she has too tight a bottom". Only once did a woman gain admission to the Tuesday Club – when P.J.[72] entered with Erin in his powerful wake and nobody was able to turn her out. Geoffrey Crowther drove me back and told me that Falk was a dictator when it came to guests ("Foxie Falk" he called him), that he built the club up with all his staff as guests till it was a public meeting, and there was a rebellion. He used to bring Maurice Hutton[73] and Tommy Balogh regularly and G.C. remembers T.B. shaking his fist at some unsuspecting American guest and shouting "Blood will run in Wall St within six months".

The argument developed by G.C. and others seemed to be that there was now nothing in economics to be discussed or if there was, the officials present would be unable to speak and the others would get it wrong, or if this didn't happen, it would all be shown to be nonsense by some young econometrician who would

[70] Alexandre Hay – Swiss banker; representative at WP No.3.

[71] O T Falk – associate of Keynes and delegate with him to Paris Peace Conference, 1919; Founder of the Tuesday Club.

[72] Per Jacobsson – Swedish economist; Economic Adviser, BIS, 1931–56; Managing Dir., IMF, 1956–63.

[73] Sir Maurice Hutton – Dep. Sec., Ministry of Food in war-time; Man. Dir., O T Falk and Co.

demonstrate in a series of unintelligible equations what "really" happened. Otto said financial journalism had raised the level of discussion so that there was little to add. G.C, pointed out that there *was* no government economic policy 30 years ago whereas now there was practically nothing that *escaped* government economic policy; and that anything said could be refuted by those who knew the facts who were few and not given to discussion. But somebody drew attention to the phenomenon of leading articles which still developed on argument on a thin basis of fact and no statistics. Geoffrey's main points were the rise of statistics and of TV, the two things contracting the area of fruitful debate. I entered a demurrer, and Robert Hall supported me: the Club did provide a useful clue to the impact of policy.

G.C. also said (when I remarked that *The Times* Business Section needed an editor) that it had been an extraordinary decision that denied Denis Hamilton the post of editor of *The Times* in order to put him in the spurious post of editor-in-chief and installed Rees Mogg as editor when he was quite unsuited to the job.

Jeremy Raisman[74] told me that when he suggested running a deficit in India in 1937/38 P.J. Grigg[75] had replied: "I heard enough of that Keynesian stuff when I was in the Treasury". So that Keynes was certainly not in the ascendent at that time.

Saturday, 15 July   I have seen nothing of the Chancellor for weeks. The forecasts were ready a week ago and on Monday I had a note ready on them which, in William's absence, I sent to Peter Baldwin. It brought out the gloomy side quite deliberately and avowedly. But the trade figures and the (unpublished) unemployment figure all told in the same direction. William spent some time with the Chancellor on Tuesday and told me that he was in a state of acute depression, as if his strategy had crumbled. On Thursday William again discussed the outlook, this time with T.B. specially sent for and asked for his views. Of course T.B. started at once to revile the forecasters and explain how uniformly wrong they were (as I've now heard him do 3 or 4 times). William asked if he thought things might be worse but T.B. wasn't prepared to say and when asked for advice had nothing effective to suggest since q.r.'s (his first idea) were obviously inconsistent with the approach to EEC. The Chancellor was apparently in a better state of mind at the outset and William thought that he had stated the position quite fairly. William said that if it was finally clear that the rate should be changed he would prefer to do it in the spring ("when unemployment will be 700,000") not now and that he would be more disposed to favour a change in the rate if he saw any sign of willingness to take the necessary accompanying measures. The Chancellor had been thinking of a relaxation of h.p. on cars

[74] Sir Jeremy Raisman – Finance Member, Govt. of India, 1939–45; Dep. Chm., Lloyds Bank, 1953–63; Chm., PWLB, 1948–70.

[75] Sir P J Grigg – Chm., Board of Inland Revenue, 1930–34; Finance Member, Govt. of India, 1934–39; Under-Sec. of State for War, 1939–42; Sec. of State for War, 1942–45.

(to be tightened again in the spring) and seemed surprised that this idea had already been put to him and rejected. He also thought of using the regulator. I undertook to set out the possibilities by Friday night and duly did so, adding post-war credits, etc. for good measure. William had advised the Chancellor that h.p. would only reduce unemployment by 10,000 or so next February and this is probably about right. The fact is that the Chancellor regards 700,000 with horror and thinks that it will cost him his seat: but even in February we were saying 680,00 and all that has happened *on this front* is that we may see unemployment rise by 50-100,000 more than we expected while on the balance of payments we face the more serious possibility of a deficit as large as last year's. The big problem is imports which are running well above the level forecast at this stage of recovery. The delayed recovery of exports is something we had already provided for in the forecasts.

In addition to the paper on lines of action, I sent forward another on the world economic outlook in response to a suggestion by Peter Baldwin. But again I had no direct contact with the Chancellor at any stage.

Another interesting episode was Butler's speech on Wednesday to the Stock Exchange. The more I hear him the more his political record baffles me. He gave us the usual half-jocular stuff at the start with that detachment that lends piquancy but makes one ask how much he really cares. Then he went on to talk about his post in the Treasury and painted a picture of a never-never land in which Lord Bridges came in from time to time to congratulate him on an improvement in the balance of payments and on the wizardry with which he was running the economy. He told us that we were growing at 5% per annum, etc., etc. Now it was important that we got into Europe and we must pay regard to what the French had to say. Of course there were two difficulties, one that they felt that we were in the pocket of the Americans and on this he felt no comment was required. But the other was sterling balances and here we ought to do something to get rid of them. He himself would have liked to do this when in office but didn't get round to it. He knew Couve well and was sure that he would want this to be a precondition of entry. (Couve had in fact spoken earlier in the week to that effect.)

I tackled him afterwards and told him that the French were only using sterling as a stalking horse for an attack on the dollar and that we could only "get rid" of sterling balances through schemes that the French would dislike even more (or else by obliging the holders of sterling to try to acquire gold). He said that when one was out of office it was very hard to discover the arguments behind policy and that it would be useful if something could be published by H.M.G. setting out the problem.

Wednesday, 19 July   Group of Ten on Monday and Tuesday,[76] WP No.3 today and tomorrow. Last night we had Whitehall Dining Club at Vickers with Schweitzer, van Lennep, Emminger & Co. all present. The discussion, in which

[76] The Group of Ten were engaged in negotiations leading up to the creation of SDRs (supplementary drawing rights) to ease the pressure on central bank reserves.

those three all took part, was on the prospects for a recovery of international trade. I sat next to Emminger who told me how he had worked out a compromise plan for Ministers. On Monday night the Chancellor had been rather despairing and had asked the Deputies to have something ready for the following morning. But everybody had to go to Hampton Court and it was the hottest day of the year. While the Ministers joked and walked in the gardens, E. and the others had a discussion indoors. Dewey Daane said he would do a draft since he was used to working all night. But next morning he had not only not shown up at 8.30 but when he did arrive at 9.30 had his draft in mss so that it wasn't ready till 5 minutes to 10 when Ministers were due to meet.

Fortunately Emminger had been unable to sleep because of the thunder and had stayed up to do a draft which he was able to give the Chancellor and which formed the basis of eventual agreement or half-agreement. At lunch he had used his opportunities of sounding out the Deputies and knew what concessions were necessary to the various points of view. He got a draft communiqu, ready with brackets round disputed passages (largely in deference to Larre[77]) but it was agreed in 10 minutes by Ministers without brackets (e.g. he put in "expected", not "hoped" to reach agreement at Rio). Débré was easier to deal with than Larre (it was Pérouse's swan-song and Larre made heavy weather of quite minor matters because he wasn't sure of his ground). But Débré got very excited when he heard that E. had said he would have to invent a zebra (i.e. it had to involve a new reserve asset to please the Americans and yet involved only an extension of credit to please the French). The Belgian minister tried to soothe him by saying it was "un mouton à cinq pattes" and Débré exploded that (the scheme) was neither a zebra nor a sheep but *"un crédit"* (which he kept on repeating). E. says he has no humour at all and is highly excitable.

E. also said that Ministers rarely had any idea how to *negotiate*. He cited the events of '64 when the Deputies referred to Ministers the question what increase in quotas was politically acceptable (the Belgians said nil, the Americans 50% and everybody had widely different views with no apparent possibility of agreement). In Tokyo Ministers met twice, made long statements of their position, and were unable to do anything except refer the whole thing back to the Deputies. After some intensive negotiation, involving the intervention of the gold mitigation clause, etc., the officials reached agreement – but only when allowed to make the political judgment of what was acceptable.

Again, he agreed that the matters in dispute often proved to be quite unimportant afterwards, e.g. he had asked Deming on Monday whether he really thought that the scheme would come into force if France, Germany and Italy were all against it; and if so, why the veto conditions should be an effective stumbling block. Obviously if the scheme does ever come into force it will not take the precise shape now being settled, e.g. as to amount, etc.

Both Emminger and van Lennep said they had found the academics at Bellagio quite out of touch with the arguments about the investment aspects of the debate

[77] René Larre – French Financial Minister, Washington, 1961–67; Fr. Exec. Dir., IBRD, 1957–67; IMF, 1964–67; Dir. of Treasury, Fr. Min. of Finance, 1967– .

(too much Kindleberger[78]) and they had taken refuge in the afternoon discussing the problems of the Group of Ten.

Lunch with Wynne who says the statistics of the public sector are worse than he imagined and prepared by junior clerks who don't appreciate any of the nicer points.

Sunday, 23 July   At WP3 Denis told me it had been a mistake to split the management and policy sides of the Treasury and that promotions were now made without consulting him. The T.O.C. never met. Had I been asked to give evidence to Fulton about the civil service? (not just economics) – he hadn't.

What brought on all this was a discussion (of all things) on trends in multilateral surveillance and on the desirability (or otherwise) of a US drawing on the Fund. E. was discreetly in favour although at the last meeting he had spoken up for the right of Germany to add to her dollar holdings. Milton Gilbert[79] had a crushing retort to the French when he pointed out that there was no question of pumping out dollars – only of contrived credits to the US. But Larre had left by the time he got round to making his point. I lunched with Milton Gilbert afterwards and he insisted again that the system was not viable and would break down inevitably once the US gold gave out or earlier. If I had sat through the meetings of Ministers I would understand why nothing but an increase in the price of gold would do. It was useless to say that a US surplus would alter matters. It would merely make the Europeans devalue. They could not or would not recognise that the US deficit was an inescapable part of the process of generating liquidity. What was equilibrium for a reserve currency? There was no book that set it out or explained the rationale of a gold exchange standard. But he was himself writing a book – how he can get it published I can't imagine.

M.G. claimed that at Bellagio nobody had been on the side of Despres[80] & Co. V.L. and E. might be impatient with the academics but they had no reply to the question he put to them: how can the system be made viable without a rise in the price of gold?

I was told that the Chancellor might want to talk to me but in fact he never did, nor did he ask for a brief. If any request comes to me it is via William. It's a little ironic in these circumstances to receive a request from Lundberg[81] to give a "challenging chat" [in Sweden] on "How to succeed as an economic adviser"!

Wednesday, 26 July   Peter Davies tells me that the Chancellor didn't get down to dictating his speech for Monday's debate until 10 p.m. on Sunday night although Peter was kept busy most of Sunday doing little essays (e.g. on French devaluation – the Chancellor had been told that Schweitzer said it reduced real wages by 10 per cent but of course this is absurd and I had already

[78] C P Kindleberger – Professor of Economics, MIT.
[79] Milton Gilbert – American economist with OEEC in 1950's, BIS in 1960's.
[80] Emil Despres – American economist.
[81] Erik Lundberg – Swedish economist.

minuted him to say so). There was an earlier draft of the speech which the Chancellor tore up.

No copy of the speech was sent to N.K. But when I rang later in the morning to ask to see William about the passages on devaluation N.K. was with him and had obviously already made the comments I was about to make. (He was reading William's copy.) We both made various suggestions to get some things removed or watered down and sent in an amendment to a later paragraph. But the speech was delivered almost unchanged and brought cries of "Nonsense" just in the sentences I wanted removed.

Peter thinks, however, that William drafted some of the passages on devaluation. I rather doubt whether this can be true of the final text.

Lunch with S. Goldman on Tuesday at the Reform. He reminded me that the Chancellor had originally included in his Budget speech a passage of praise for his officials which later disappeared. Sam says this reflects the P.M.'s abiding suspicion of the Treasury.

I wondered myself if it wasn't a little sinister to let D. Jay wind up and Callaghan open the debate on Monday – in sharp contrast to 20.7.66.

Last night went to cocktails at John Partridge's[82] and found Plowden gloomier than ever. He has told his people to expect no improvement for a year. He says that wages are not being held at present levels of unemployment but it wasn't clear if he thought that at some reasonable rate they would be.

Arthur Bottomley said that he had known Gandhi before the war and found him no saint but a very astute politician. He said for example that he never read the newspapers and this was true because he had them read to him.

Wednesday, 2 August   On Monday we had a short meeting of EN (O) about the issue of a planning document this winter. Douglas Allen told us that a draft was needed by the end of the month without any certainty that Ministers would want to publish it. They won't want to use projections and they will hesitate to say what is proposed about public expenditure. Indeed, if they *can* say, they will prefer a White Paper to something that might be leaked after submission to NEDC.

The politicians were baffled by the Chancellor's antics on public expenditure in last Monday's debate and thought that there must be a big cut next year. But of course the increase is of the order of 6 per cent followed by two smallish increases in the ensuing years *if* Ministers hold to their decisions and don't come up with the usual additions. The Chancellor is simultaneously arguing that he isn't cutting at all and in fact all that will be taken from the civil programmes is a maximum of £100–£200 m. in 1970-71. *Nothing* has been agreed for 1968-69. The item Ministers will most want to conceal is that they don't propose to uprate in proportion to earnings next time round – but this is only a pseudo-decision and political pressure would change it.

Meanwhile Ministers are still brooding on reflationary measures and waiting

[82] Sir John Partridge – Chm., The Imperial Group Ltd, 1964–75; Chm., Council of Industry for Management Education, 1967–71; Pres., CBI, 1970–72.

for the trade figures before making up their minds. The Prime Minister is thinking of a purchase tax cut on cars and the President is arguing strongly for relaxation of h.p. on other durables. This the Chancellor thinks "bitty" but if it weren't, it would be too much! He is attracted by import deposits, stopping pit closures, and other will o' the wisps but Marsh is firm on pit closures and import deposits would be an absurdity when we expect company liquidity to go leaping up. At the same time as Ministers are scared by the unemployment figures, some officials are scared by the prospective Budget deficit of £1700 m. or so, and others by the prospects for the balance of payments. We had the usual debate at CM(O) today on current price forecasts and their interpretation.

Yesterday we had a meeting with William to prepare for the next SEP meeting, probably on the 15th. This concentrated on reflation but we didn't even debate *whether* any reflation was needed. Ministers want only "something factual".

Methodology Group tonight. Tommy inevitably came late and although pretty quiet laid down the law as usual about trade statistics in front of the statisticians. Then he explained how he had predicted to "his master" the "NIF forecast" (he meant the balance of payments forecast) in June at – £100 m. by study of the previous forecast.

I notice from the press that he is going to France and that Crossman will stay with him while Judith Hart[83] will call on him and so will Roy Jenkins. Wedgwood Benn copies minutes to him when minuting the First Sec. or the Prime Minister. T.B. writes to the Chief Secretary and sends the *same* letter to Douglas Allen (even including references to his "responsibility for public expenditure").

At the Chancellor's party, Gregor Mackenzie[84] said he didn't think for a moment that Peggy Herbison was moved by concern for family allowances. She had allowed herself to become the protagonist of her Department and been pushed into a position where she had to threaten resignation to get her way and in the end was the victim of over-enthusiasm for what was at bottom a pose.[85] His mother, asked what was the biggest mistake made by the Labour Party, had answered, "Putting up public assistance to £4 a week". The average Labour voter in Glasgow was not sold on bigger family allowances which would go to support the families of Catholics and "socially irresponsible" parents.

Saturday, 5 August   On Friday evening I had a word with William about the papers for Ministers. He had seen the Prime Minister with the Governor and they had discussed the US tax proposal. I said that its effects on interest rates depended on how the Fed rated the chances of Congressional approval and William said this was also Leslie's view. But he had gone on to imply

---

[83] Judith Hart – Jt. Labour Parliamentary Under-Sec. of State for Scotland, 1964–66; Minister of State, Commonwealth Office, 1966–67; Minister of Social Security, 1967–68; Paymaster General, 1968–69; Minister of Overseas Development, 1969–70.

[84] Gregor Mackenzie – Parliamentary Under-Sec. to Chancellor of Exchequer, 1966–67; to Home Secretary, 1967–70.

[85] Peggy Herbison, Minister of Social Security, resigned on 24 July over cuts in the social services.

that any damping down of the US economy was not altogether in our interest. The Prime Minister had assured him that he need have no fears that L.B.J. would go too far in that direction with an election only just over a year away. On purchase tax the Prime Minister was persuaded by William not to think of a reduction on cars, and he showed little interest in a reduction in textiles which the President is being pushed into proposing. (It seems that Lancashire regards it as "unfair" that there has been no government enquiry into the textile industry when so many other industries are having one!) The Prime Minister took the view, however, that any relaxation on h.p. should cover both cars and other durables because it would be impossible to do one without making the pressure for the other irresistible. William accepts that they will be obliged to do *something* and seems reconciled to both h.p. relaxations. Hence perhaps his revival of FU meetings on Friday.

The Chancellor meanwhile has begun to pursue import deposits enthusiastically and the Governor seems to be encouraging the idea too.

At the Group of Ten last month the French came with instructions not to agree to *any*thing. In fact it looked as if a compromise was in sight, the US yielding on the veto, when the Chef de Cabinet arrived, whispered in Larre's ear (I suppose it was Larre) and brought about an abrupt change of front. The French tactics were to wait for compromise suggestions and then suggest a fresh compromise near to their own position.

Sunday, 6 August   I went out to see Ely who told me that his efforts to raise money for L.S.E. had failed to move Sydney Caine to effective action. It was arranged that Joe Hyman should be invited to dinner and Sydney Caine agreed. But the dinner was a complete flop for the talk ran on anything but the School.

Monday, 7 August   At Friday's meeting of F.U. William said that he had it from van Lennep that the Monetary Committee of the Six discussed the whole French government programme in advance of the 1958 devaluation and also (this surprised us) the German revaluation in 1961. Holtrop was certainly unaware of the latter and abroad at the time (indeed, on the Atlantic I think) so van Lennep must have kept the secret closely.

I had lunch today at the Bank, and talked afterwards with the Governor, Deputy Governor and Maurice Allen. I was interested to hear Maurice Parsons address Leslie as Mr Governor and M.A. speak of Mr Deputy Governor in quoting Maurice Parsons. Yet at the dining table nearly everybody was on the *staff* of the Bank (except Sir Arthur Young – the Chief of Police) in the sense that they were not outside Directors or even recent arrivals.

They were very despondent about the prospects and strongly against *any* immediate reflation because of the effect on sterling. There was no doubt that they felt very vulnerable to a fresh run on the pound but saw no attraction even in a forced devaluation. They are also concerned at the prospect of a large budget deficit and don't believe that government expenditure will flatten out in 1969 and so leave room for private investment. What isn't clear to me is what they would propose since they can hardly want higher unemployment even if M.P. tries to belittle it by calling it dishoarding of labour.

They agreed that confidence was at a low ebb in the City and that only a sustained rise in exports would restore it - but probably not *this* year. Leslie said that the pound would be in danger till after Rio and even through October. But by November we'll be giving hints about next year's Budget deficit so that there can hardly be much improvement. I also pointed out that Ministers, however courageous, had to carry their Party with them and this might prove impossible if they stuck absolutely rigidly to existing policies. But I was sufficiently moved by their arguments to go back and do my draft for the Chancellor in the same sense as their arguments.

Wednesday, 9 August   We had another meeting of F.U. at which William had to expound Nicky on floating rates. We were left very uncertain what US would do if we devalued but the general impression was that the US would not move and would instead tighten up control over capital movements. If however US did move, European countries would probably seize the chance to get gold prices up and we should all go back to square one. Also in difficulties about sequence of informing various governments and doubtful whether we could tell *any*body till markets had closed. If we told Prime Minister of Australia and bound him to silence and inaction he would deny we had ever consulted him. But if not so bound, he might try to get rid of some of his sterling.

Trade figures were available last night and William gave us them this morning. I can go off for a month with an easy mind but September may be very different. Unfortunately Ministers may take it out in a little more reflation.

Thursday, 10 August   Another rather frantic day. I had got off last night both the Monthly Economic Report and my paper on reflationary measures. This morning there appeared on my desk first a covering note on the latter by William, then a paper by the President suggesting that the trade figures justified more reflation, this time a cut from 11 to 5 per cent in purchase tax on textiles and haberdashery (over £100 m. a year) from Sept 1 to April 1. Comments by 4 p.m. I went to see Jack Stafford who told me that of the fall in imports of £23 m. over £10 m. was diamonds! Called back to the Treasury I found a minute by the Prime Minister insisting on the need for reflation, saying our forecasts were poor and too gloomy, and predicting that imports would soon feel the benefit of the fall in commodity prices. The most remarkable statement was that the improvement between June and July in the trade figures was at the rate of £600 m. a year! I did a hasty comment, got Gower Isaac[86] busy supplementing it, and got my piece off by lunch-time and did my comments on the President's proposal by 4 p.m. This was interwoven with meetings with Goronwy Daniel[87] at noon and Maurice Allen at 3.30. I didn't see William all

[86] A J Gower Isaac – Private Sec. to Chief Secretary, Treasury, 1964–66.

[87] Goronwy Daniel – Min. of Fuel and Power, 1947–64 (Chief Statistician, 1947–55); Perm. Under-Sec. of State, Welsh Office, 1964–69.

day and tomorrow he goes to a funeral so that I'll be the most senior character in the place (for one day). Denis has left by car for Sardinia.

Lunch with John de Burgh[88] who told me that George B. would be staying on in Norway on holiday after official visit "to save his fare". "He's terribly mean", he told me. But George does run a Jag. after all.

I've had work home every night so far this week and dictated a full cassette tonight. But at least I have a holiday in prospect while Peter Baldwin and William's staff don't look like getting any.

Wednesday, 16 August   Left for Gothenburg with Mary. Today Peter Jay has his leader on government expenditure in *The Times* and finally establishes that public expenditure in 1970 will now be as high as total in Plan. Trade figures out yesterday – newspaper comment in *The Times* very negative and critical. *N.Y. Herald Tribune* doesn't even print the figures. This may, however, deter Ministers from taking reflationary initiative.

Wednesday, 23 August   At the Ulricehamn conference I had several long talks with Ohlin[89] who asked whether, with an election approaching, H.W. might not by 1969 be willing to listen to the French hints of a new form of association with free trade in industrial products for the 7. Iversen who was present thought that this would be acceptable to the Scandinavians. Ohlin made it clear that the French were considering some move but wondered how far Wilson would insist on the political objectives of his approach to Europe. He might have very little to offer the electorate if unable to enter EEC and his rear would be amply protected since the move could be represented as similar to Maudling's efforts of 1959. I must say that since I think very little of the purely political objectives it would seem to be a much better bargain than membership of EEC.

In an earlier discussion on Thursday evening, Ohlin spoke rather sadly of his life as a politician – leader of his party since 1945 but never in power and now resigned to a less active life, no longer leader but dreaming even now of joining a future Cabinet. The S.D.s have never had a clear majority all that time and are currently dependent on the Communists. They haven't dared to nationalise very much and even their tax and distribution policy has not been very radical. So Ohlin contents himself with the thought that if not head of the government he has yet shaped what the government did.

Walter Heller was about to tour Norway and I explained to him how matters stood on devaluation. He had got the impression that this might now be inevitable.

Thursday, 14 September   The Cabinet changes over Bank Holiday weekend are unmistakably to the advantage of the Treasury (as I had presumed).

---

[88] John de Burgh – Asst. Sec., DEA, 1964; Principal Private Sec. to successive First Secs. of State and Sec.s of State for Economic Affairs, 1965–68.

[89] Bertil Ohlin – Swedish economist and politician; Prof. of Economics, Stockholm School of Economics, 1930–65; Leader, Volksparte, 1944–67; Nobel Prize, 1977.

The Chancellor and the Prime Minister are working closely together and have arranged to see one another every Monday evening. They are also to be co-Chairmen of NEDC with P.Shore Deputy Chairman. SEP becomes a regular Cab. Comm. with the usual procedures in circulating papers and allowing attendance by Ministers involved in issues raised. We shall have to work closely with DEA over incomes policy (William says that Chancellor was offered full responsibility but declined – he will, however, be Chairman of the P.I. Committee under SEP). Meanwhile, as somebody at No. 10 remarked, the Prime Minister has left DEA under a "Lee Shore". (Fred Lee is nominally in charge of incomes policy but nobody quite knows where he comes in). Not a breath about the plan.

William said that reflationary measures were taken against Treasury advice.

Monday, 18 September   I decided that government will be forced either to devalue or to introduce q.r.'s within next few months and that of these two the first is obviously preferable. I discussed with Fred and with William who told me that Leslie O'Brien had expressed a view to him within past 3 weeks that we might have to devalue before Christmas and that we should be in a position of readiness now.

My reasoning is simple. The government cannot do *nothing* in face of estimate for 1967 of a £300 m. deficit and serious doubts of any surplus even in 1968: in that sense latest forecasts are comparable with those of October 1964. It would be impossible for government to justify its inaction *ex post* and in any event public will form its own view. We have lost share in our own market and in foreign markets in conditions calculated to help us to be *more* competitive. If exports were at level of early 1967 we would be in balance (i.e. + £25m a month) but it looks as if exports will not shoot back to that level and will be lower *throughout* 1968 than we previously forecast. Without some recovery in exports soon, we have no option but to act and q.r.'s wouldn't offer any prospect of ultimate equilibrium at present rate. We can't afford to let reserves run out and we may face this threat if next month's figures are bad for second successive month.

William said that the Prime Minister was in curious mood and quite inflexible about the rate. He believed that L.B.J. would be bound to have a boom next year with the election and would help sterling out even if the boom did not. He was intending to brazen it out at the Labour Party Conference by pointing to changed trend in unemployment (he told TUC of this a week ago, speaking of a hunch, but the figures will bear him out) and to the succession of acts "between consenting adults" (as William put it) to "re-structure" each industry in turn: the Cunarders, computers, etc., etc. It is as if H.W. single-handed meant to reorganise British industry. He put in G.B. and that didn't work, then Stewart and that failed, so now he proposes to do it directly.

William said Chancellor was more realistic but felt case for a change was not proven and that we should wait till the Spring (as Fred also argued). But he was realistic about the chances – only he recognised that he'd have to resign if devaluation proved necessary. By tomorrow he'll be off and won't be much in the Treasury till Oct 9 when the next but one SEP meeting takes place and the trade figures will be known.

William said that Prime Minister speaking to City Editors had given the most convincing arguments ever against q.r.'s. No mention of them at the SEP meeting and D. Jay's advocacy may make them less acceptable. But in the end government may well have no choice if they won't devalue.

Friday, 22 September   End of my second week back: on the whole a very quiet fortnight mainly occupied with staff and recruitment problems.

William put round a minute from Maurice Allen arguing rather obliquely for q.r.'s and this brought forth sharp reminders from Frank Figgures and N.K. It then appeared that the Governor had told William that these views were not the Bank's but W.M.A.'s own. I was asked to put down my own ideas and have now done so. The right thing to do now is to devalue because the chances of coming through to a persistent surplus (either at all or without having to overcome a succession of crises) now seem very remote. But if Ministers don't take this view the choice is between q.r.'s and doing nothing at all and I'm not sure that they should be encouraged (or would be allowed) to do nothing.

We had a meeting of F.U. yesterday – the second since I got back – and this was attended by the Governor and Deputy Governor as well as Kit M. and another man from the Bank. Posner, at the Chancellor's request, is to see the pp. and come (which implies acceptance by the Chancellor of the need for the work we are doing) but so far he hasn't been able to attend. Douglas Allen came for the first time and William spoke of letting the F.O. and C.O. know of the provisional conclusions as to timetable etc.

The main argument was over the size of the package and D.A. had obvious hesitations about doing so much at once. Kit pointed out that we couldn't tell what the reactions would be and it was this that justified over-insurance: we had to base our actions on the *success* of the move and do nothing that might reduce the chances of success. I pointed out that in 1949 the accompanying measures were virtually nil but that there was really no chronic deficit and only a need for redirection of ex. and imp. William said he knew but Ministers would not that our package was of the same size as we had proposed a year ago in an economy fully stretched. It was also the same whether the rate was 2.40 or 2.50 – a circumstance that might well make Ministers suspicious.

At the end D.A. summed it up by saying that the message of the paper seemed to be: rape may be inevitable but you're not going to enjoy it.

We also had an ESG earlier in the week which was remarkably relaxed. T.B. at one point explained what difficulties the B/T would put in the way of q.r.'s and this moved N.K. to say "Then hats off to the B of T!" which William suggested should go in the minutes.

"Uncle" is now settled and the capacity is to be 2 x 120,000 tons. The Fin. Sec. is enthusiastically in favour but the companies have still to tender. I think that we've bought 2 pups instead of 1.

Meanwhile the Government is busily looking for other large losers of public money: QEII, the Beagle, etc., etc. The colliery closures are being postponed

- always with the assurance that the programme for the next year has to stand, i.e. there has to be an acceleration later to make up for the postponements now. Of course, this is make believe but the Minister of Power [Dick Marsh] is not in a position to get the P.M. to see this. He has been hauled over the coals for his handling of the rise in electricity prices and slapped down in Cabinet in front of his colleagues. I am told that he has in the past taken little trouble to conciliate other Ministers and tended to go his way without bothering what they think. But I can't help thinking that he has been more frequently on the right side than any Minister I can recall in that post.

It is also ludicrous to hand over to Aubrey Jones such full powers over public sector prices and for Jones to tell the P.M. that he can handle 100 cases a year when he is obviously fully loaded already and has difficulty in coping with 30 cases a year. I confess also to some doubt how far his recommendations have taken effect case by case: and he simply could not combine more cases with any follow-up of previous cases. He is absorbing quite a high proportion of the experienced economists: *far* more than, say, the B. of T. or Neddy and more in some ways than the Treasury or DEA, if one counts members of the Board and consultants helping in individual cases.

Cambridge and Walthamstow results have been given sufficient space to make the unemployment figures take second place. I suppose this means that there will be no General Election till 1970 or even 1971.

Tuesday, 27 September   Peace, perfect peace with the Chancellor far away. No meetings for 2 days. Tomorrow we dine with V.K. Rao[90]. He made about 150 speeches in a month of campaigning and still seems to get through half a dozen a day. He addressed his audience in Mysore in Tamil as well as English and Kanaris and in Delhi volunteered to use Hindi to talk to the "rural women" he was invited to address. He says he has established a real rapport with a mass audience – something he didn't reckon on. His choice of seat in Mysore was not of a safe one but of a constituency that seemed in danger of being lost. He also explained that for a Brahmin to stand in Mysore was like and old Etonian standing for a mining constituency.

Lunch with Brian Reddaway who had 3 months in Ghana as Ec. Adv. and thinks that his main contribution was to act as honest broker between the big international companies and the Government. He asked me what was the rationale of the Government's policy on the pound and I explained that they were prepared to run high risks so long as there was a chance of maintaining the parity at reasonable levels of unemployment.

N.K. had a bad car accident on Tuesday last week, skidding and smashing his car but emerging safe, thanks to his seat belt. He came to ESG in spite of this and didn't seem at all perturbed though he had a fracture of the wrist as was later revealed by X-ray. He is hot against quotas and told me last night that my own more qualified attack was "a typical Alec minute" – in which I agree with

[90] V K R V Rao – Indian economist and politician, Cambridge contemporary; Minister of Transport and Shipping, 1966–69; Minister of Education, 1969–71.

him.

Sunday, 1 October   We discussed the Chinese and N.K. told us of his encounters with Mao and Chou – both mild men but with the ruthlessness of idealists. If we lose the first battle, they had implied or said, you may take 5,000 prisoners: if the second, 50,000; if the third, 500,000; and so on. But what will you do with them? We can lose 50 m. and still have plenty left to carry on. T.B. said Chou was like Litvinov[91] rather than, as I suggested, Mikoyan[92].

Monday, 2 October   Lunch with Jo Fromm at the Connaught. Jo started by saying that for the first time in his 11 years in London he thought it possible that we might now be driven to devalue – not an easy beginning since it seemed a fair judgment to me and I had to make plain that I had had little or no recent contact with the Chancellor.

Jo also recalled that at the beginning of September the *Washington Post* had come out in favour of devaluation. This made H.W. panic and send for Jo to collect the American pressmen and bring them to No. 10. The continentals were also invited for the first time and naturally asked what it could be about. Had Jo ever been called in this way? To which Jo innocently said "Not quite in this way ever". But how the correspondents refrained from cabling their papers to expect instant devaluation he couldn't imagine.

There was also some panic about a cable from Marjoribanks[93] from Brussels indicating the conclusions reached by the Commission in their Report. The Chancellor wanted Fred to go north at once but was talked out of it by F.F. – apparently it was George B. who was most concerned.

The winter is setting in. Another week and the exchanges will begin to rock gently.

Tuesday, 3 October   Lunch with Sam Goldman. Early in September after the h.p. relaxations and the electricity price increase, there was general gloom as the reserves drained away and it looked as if very little would soon be left. The Governor shared these anxieties and went off to Basle after a 2 hr talk with the Chancellor having warned him that we were unlikely to get much support in Europe and nearing the limits of US credit arrangements. However, in Basle the atmosphere was remarkably friendly, there was agreement that we had done all the right things and understanding of the moderate relaxation we had allowed, and suggestions of help came spontaneously from the Swiss and the BIS. Indeed it looked before Rio as if we might be able to mount yet another

[91] Maxim Litvinov – Russian Commissar for Foreign Affairs.

[92] A N Mikoyan – Soviet politician; Member of Politburo, 1935–52; Minister for Foreign Trade, 1938–46; First Dep. Chm., Council of Ministers, 1953–64; President of Supreme Soviet, 1964–65.

[93] Sir James Marjoribanks – Asst. Under-Sec. of State, Foreign Office, 1962–65; Head of the UK Deleg. to EEC, European AEC and ECSC, 1965–71.

international support operation but somehow it fizzled out. Zijlstra[94] had some technical objections but we don't yet know what went wrong. Still, the Swiss are going to make a quite substantial deposit in London, and this will probably be announced this week.

Sam felt danger of a renewed period of "Go" and consumer-led boom and agreed that it was touch and go for the pound. There was a decision to jack up rates first by putting the market into the Bank at BR. and then later at BR + ?% but the latter is still to come. Not possible unless threat to raise BR implied in it can be implemented and this couldn't be done this week with Labour Party Conference still in progress.

For some unexplained reason the pressure last month died away in spite of rather poor trade figures. This month the fall in unemployment we may yet reveal could operate either way: causing alarm that we should have swung round so quickly, or, as Fred thought, reassurance because no need for fresh reflationary measures. It will be odd if imports don't reflect *some* of the change of trend and strikes at Liverpool may react on exports.

Sam said that Chancellor in a TV interview had been rather unguarded about his prospects and had made it clear that he had no longer any reason to fear a Selwyn Lloyd operation. Not only much closer to P.M. but P.M. can't use him as a scapegoat for a policy to which he is so fully committed. Chancellor gave every evidence of enjoying the relief and of determination to stay where he was.

Monday, 9 October   We dined at 35 Cheapside with the Governor, just back from Rio. Norland was guest of honour (Gov. of Bank of Iceland). "Surviving?" I asked when Leslie shook hands. "I hope so" he said. "You can be sure" I said, knowing that the Chancellor has sent him a reassuring message. He then said that "they" were trying to get at H.W. through him, and that it was all due to his efficient public service in London which had made the text of the speech freely available: a point on which S.G. and I had agreed earlier today.

On Friday the export figures became available and clearly heralded trouble. I told William that we ought to put up B.R. this Thursday, not in another week and I repeated this to S.G. today but he argued that we must associate the rise with rates of interest abroad and that it would be better to wait a week. To move B.R. now would look panicky.

William said that we must await events and that he, Leslie and I should keep in close touch. We couldn't tell the Chancellor that he had now no option but to devalue but he agreed that we shouldn't wait till the reserves ran out.

Denis won't be back until Thursday or Friday and S.G. goes on leave at the end of this week so we remain less than fully prepared for an emergency. Fred also proposes to take some leave next week. Meanwhile Richard Powell talks gaily of a trade deficit of perhaps £50 m. this month – and he may well be right.

[94] Dr Jelle Zijlstra – Dutch Minister of Finance, 1959–63; Prime Minister, 1966–67; President, Netherlands Bank from 1967.

Wednesday, 11 October   And by George he was!

Lunch at Savoy for French journalists given by the Chancellor. I sat between M. Massip and M. le Cerf (both of the *Figaro*). They explained that the French intelligentsia was anti-Gaullist and indeed M. Massip drank the toast to Gen. de Gaulle with obvious reluctance and (as he pointed out) in silence. The Chancellor answered questions brilliantly, giving the *effective* but not always the technical answer to the questions e.g. about sterling. He pointed out that this difficulty had never been raised in his first two years as Chancellor. He also asserted strongly that the economy was on the road to recovery and that, with "restructuring", the economy would emerge from the current balance of payments difficulties stronger than ever. Jock Hunter[95] at the end said no Chancellor had stood higher in the City's estimation. When I congratulated him later he said (of his replies) "if only it were true". It was an impressive performance because it carried conviction even if he didn't feel it and was good-humoured even when the questions were awkward (e.g. when did you begin to see the advantages of joining EEC?).

Cocktails at US Embassy and dinner with H. Cheadle and Charles Walker of A.B.A. with Maudling, P. Jay, Gordon Newton,[96] H. Johnson, etc. Discussion mainly on NAFTA with P. Jay making most of the running. Reggy said that he thought the best solution would be one of association and that we might have to come back to that. The others asked the Americans why *they* wanted us in the EEC. But as F.F. pointed out to me on the way back from the Savoy it's no use asking for association at this stage since there is no basis on which to begin negotiations and France would soon begin to insist that we ought to come in as they have done before, varying their proposition whenever we switched and implying that the *alternative* was the right course whatever we proposed. Later we *may* begin to talk of association but let the others first propose it and give it some shape.

Bank rate talk with S.G. who wants to wait for rise in US rates as the appropriate indicator. My view is that if government wants to react at all to the deficit and not stick it out nonchalantly doing nothing, a rise of **?** – 1% would help to calm the market. In that event *this* Thursday is the right day. Maurice Allen at US Embassy took a similar line. I fear that if we don't use this weapon now we not only won't be able to do so later but won't have any others to use either.

Roy Bridge[97] also tried to enlist my support for Euro-bond borrowing and claimed that market was growing. Earlier I found Michael Posner on my side against N.K. and S.G. in this issue. If US corporations and French public corporations can use the market why shouldn't we?

Wednesday, 11 October   S.G. to lunch at Reform, after he had spent morning

[95] Jock Hunter

[96] Sir Gordon Newton – Editor, 1950–72; Dir., 1967–72 *The Financial Times*.

[97] Roy Bridge – Bank of England, 1929–69; Dep. Chief Cashier, 1957–63; Adv. to the Governors, 1963–65; Asst. to the Governors, 1965–69.

arguing on Euro-bonds. Full of admiration for H. Lever's pertinacity even if he keeps putting up propositions like an A.P. for officials to knock down. B. of E. via Roy Fenton[98] came down unenthusiastic about Euro-bonds but now Morse is arguing strongly on Lever's side and Posner and I rather agree while Revenue send along Willis[99] who has no hope of standing up to H. Lever.

On B.R., Governor has weighed in for a 1% rise now and I argued with S.G. in favour but unsuccessfully and no doubt Chancellor will decide against. So let's see how the market takes it. Chancellor, says S., hopes to see big rush of exports in Q4 making up for strike. I suspect that exports will remain pretty low even if no strikes. Even £5 – £15 m. doesn't explain present figures.

I found that F.F. yesterday thought that P.M. would seize joining EEC as pretext for devaluation. So he may but that isn't how he seems to be playing it. I told S.G. that we could go to Chancellor and say the time had come when we really must devalue and know that this meant telling Chancellor he'd have to resign: but we couldn't do that to P.M. And nobody quite knows how P.M. *does* form his views of economic policy since on this he does not see eye-to-eye with any of his advisers and doesn't necessarily agree even with Chancellor. Very dangerous to have a P.M. who doesn't have to argue these things out. Of course, William would say he *has* to keep it close to his chest but this is true also of Chancellor and we *do* know exactly how he feels and why.

Unemployment likely to be down 15,000 this month. But that won't be known for another week.

Maurice Allen told me last night of new French weekly (*Business Week* type) sponsored by *Express* and McGraw Hill which discussed UK situation and explains that devaluation wouldn't change structural problems and yet what is needed is a devaluation of 30–40%. This would be very embarrassing, it goes on, because everybody expects one of only 15–18%!

Reggy Maudling last night said that he reckoned economy had been expanding for past 2 months. This would go on but rise would be less steep this time and shorter because balance of payments would force a new stop.

Maurice Allen said however that Court was always sceptical of his investment forecasts and analyses and tended to say: "not true of us".

Sunday, 15 October   Trade returns had expected effect. I guessed £100 m. but this was a little too high – at least on Friday but not if Thursday is included. We took it mostly on the forwards. The week-end press was curiously silent but we'll certainly have a renewal of the loss.

Fred and Wynne came to see me on Friday evening to say they had come to conclusion the game was up and that we ought to devalue. Their arguments were very much like mine. I explained that whatever advice we gave would have little effect on Chancellor and P.M. Fred pointed out that if Governor

---

[98] Roy Fenton – Governor, Central Bank of Nigeria, 1958–63; Dep. Chief, Central Banking Info. Dept., Bank of England, 1963–65; Chief, Overseas Dept., 1965–75.

[99] J R McK Willis – Dep. Chm., Board of Inland Revenue, 1957–71; Vis. Prof., Bath Univ., 1972–79.

joined us he could hardly be disregarded. I said we had no access to P.M. so that argument with him was impossible, and even with the Chancellor difficult.

When I saw William he agreed that it rested with Leslie, whose tactics were to exhaust all possible lines of assistance before throwing in his hand. He himself had found Chancellor unwilling to listen although he had put to him my point about irresponsibility. The Chancellor on Friday asked to see me but later postponed it so he may yet want to sound me on this issue.

Meanwhile unemployment is likely to be down by 15,000-20,000 this month. This is biggest fall since early 1964 although we should say it was in part a fluke and unlikely to go on.

Wednesday, 18 October   Chancellor had two meetings yesterday – one with Nicky, Michael P. and myself on the domestic outlook and one on SET. At the first he refused to be rattled by our joint warnings of trouble ahead and told N.K.: "Why do you worry Nicky? I'm the one who's paid to worry". He is determined to wait till his next Budget before doing anything but is at least resisting acceleration of investment grants in the expectation that he can if necessary postpone this till Q1 1968 (but it now transpires, *after* the SEP decision, that he can't). He won't raise B.R. ahead of a rise in US rates, preferring if necessary to use swaps. He also lays stress on reduction in regional unemployment and feels that REP is a great success even if it also means that firms leave Cardiff for a black area like Caerphilly only a few miles away. (All this to N.K.'s annoyance, reflecting on the difficulty of selling the idea to the Chancellor earlier this year.)

After the meeting I talked with N.K. and M.P. who both felt that something should be put by officials to Ministers warning them that the strategy of last year was no longer viable. I underlined the difficulties when the P.M. wouldn't listen to the Economic Advisers as a body and did not ask for any new assessment. The natural occasion for a submission was the next set of forecasts and this William fully realised. I would think over how I might put something down but it would have to hinge on the balance of payments forecast. The only other possibility was intervention by the Governor – as in 1931 as N.K. pointed out.

At the meeting on SET and prices the Chancellor was persuaded not to refer surcharges and absorption of SET to NBPI and instead to agree to an enquiry by Reddaway. Chancellor felt that tax was not accepted yet and was anxious to bring pressure against politically motivated use of surcharges.

We had another hour of ESG at T.B.'s instance because he feared that Treasury was now veering round in favour of association with EEC, not joining. He was assured that this was without foundation. William then asked "What more spilt milk would you like us to cry over?" He had pointed out that if complaint was over our briefing for Kiesinger or our rejoinder to EEC this was in response to Ministerial directions and he ought to complain at the source (i.e. to the P.M.) against "ridiculous" suggestions that we were fully competitive. The EEC chapter on finance, said N.K., was not written by Barre or even accepted by the others as part of a bargain with the French but was unanimous view and fruit of much re-writing. T.B. said we had managed to unite Commission with

French against us by our attacks on their Report. William said he was awaiting quite calmly outcome of any discussions in Brussels since he didn't think that there would *be* any negotiation and why worry therefore if Chalfont exaggerated and didn't understand the dangers of high capital export. If we were serious about negotiations it would be natural to invite Comm. to come over and open the books to them: but we had no intention of doing anything of the kind.

N.K. said he couldn't fathom what lay behind our approach to the C.M. It must have been clear that we had first to be strong to benefit from joining and that the French would oppose our entry, almost certainly with success. So why had we started the whole affair?

T.B. harped on the figure of £50 – £100 m. for net addition to capital outflow, which he felt completely misrepresented the major risk. Douglas Allen said others had tried to explain risks to P.M. but he simply wasn't interested in macro-economic problems and wouldn't discuss them. William said his reading of G.B.'s mind was that he was hoping for a veto and T.B. agreed that this was likely though he had no recent personal contact.

L. Franck to dinner last night. He says Wormser not happy in Moscow. On the Common Market he said that it was originally a compact in which industry looked like losing but agriculture stood to gain. Now it was becoming clear – as it was not in 1960 – that within agriculture there was a sharp division of interest with the cereals group very much the gainers while the vegetable, dairy produce and other groups were greatly discontented. In fact the whole of France south of the Loire and West of Normandy was suffering from the international competition released. The concentration of industry in and around Paris was greater than ever. I told him that we would expect rather similar consequences, in part fortuitously because it so happens that the area near London is flat and lends itself to wheat production.

He told us that each ministry had a man of about Under Secretary status in the Elysee who was not the spokesman of the ministry but was likely to deal with its affairs. He denied that a superior corps of Insp. G. made appointments but agreed that the man in the Elysee might be consulted about them.

Louis F. also told us that amalgamations and mergers in France, although all the rage, were not very popular with the administrators since they involved a limitation of the top posts which they could eventually fill.

Friday, 20 October   After Ec. Directorate yesterday William told me of the $1/_2$% rise in B.R.[100] Denis was just as surprised as I was since the Chancellor had given no indication of his intention. He suggested that perhaps the rise in the exch. rate by 5 points in expectation of an increase in B.R. might have persuaded the Chancellor to move but I think it must have been the Governor

---

[100] Bank rate was raised to 6 per cent on 19 October. The reduction in the number of wholly unemployed in October, seasonally adjusted, is now put at only 8,600 but *any* reduction in the circumstances conveyed a warning of renewed pressure. The winter peak was 547,000 or 2.4 per cent, seasonally adjusted, but the peak in the number of *registered* unemployed, unadjusted, was 671,00.

plus the fall by 21,000 in unemployment. On the latter point, the papers are very wide of the mark, with headlines about rising unemployment. S. Brittan dismisses the fall as "a fluke" and nobody says that it is $3\frac{1}{2}$ years since we had so big a fall in the s.a. figure. We would now put the peak winter figure at about 675,000 where a month ago we should have predicted 750,000: and I think we are quite likely to revise downwards yet again, for the weekly increase in the crude figures is very small.

I had a letter from St Peter's suggesting that I might let my name go forward for the Mastership. It is tempting, just as the Canterbury[101] idea is tempting and I think I ought now to fix a date for winding up in Whitehall.

Monday, 23 October   William this morning said that crunch was coming and we ought to be warning Chancellor ahead of other Ministers. In spite of what he said last week to us Chancellor was very much exercised. William had even drafted message to L.B.J. because he foresaw that this would be P.M.'s first thought. V. doubtful if Cabinet would approve accompanying measures such as we proposed. (W.G. rang me yesterday on all this saying his proposals added up to more than he had reckoned but that more was needed given change in unemployment.) Surely we could wait till Budget? N.K. also felt smell of approaching battle and felt need for us to consider measures as well as case for floating rate. N.K. now anxious for rise in SET *not* income tax (partly because of effect on profit) and agreed in light of Swedish experience that a poll tax might be useful. He would withdraw premia from manuf. and also refrain from repaying 100% of tax. As for floating rate he would want this on tactical grounds because he was doubtful if French would stay put. (W.A. said our sources said Bundesbank was considering revaluation of DM.)

When I asked about B.R., William said Leslie had taken up firm position and Morse had argued strongly for $\frac{1}{2}$%. Chancellor now thought this was a mistake but he was not clear whether this meant Chancellor preferred 1% or 0%. The argument was (a) that nobody would think $\frac{1}{2}$% intended to offset strikes, etc; (b) market response already discounted a move and no move would therefore be worse than $\frac{1}{2}$%; (c) too big a change might make a devaluation increasingly more difficult. On (c) Leslie thought 8% was the right post-devaluation rate, whatever the rate before devaluation. So this argument wasn't very strong.

Spoke to Fred, Wynne and Michael Posner in succession. M.P. not committed on floating rate and according to William unconvinced that devaluation was right solution (he thinks like P.M. in structural terms). W.G. convinced me that strong measures would have to be announced at once or would never be taken later. Moreover need to plunge was strong because to get given balance of payments improvement meant big increase in GNP and in imports so that some offset was very necessary. (Big multiplier since no import or factor cost offset). I pointed out risk that engineering sector might not effect big enough adjustment very quickly. On our reckoning total engineering output would have to increase 8%

---

[101] Canterbury – I had been offered a post as Master of Keynes College, Canterbury which I had thought of accepting.

faster in $1\frac{1}{2}$ years and this might not be easy since it was necessary to ensure expansion in right *sectors* of engineering, not a uniform increase.

Not much left in the till. Enough for October settlements, but by end November situation will require fresh borrowing.

N.K. puzzled by balancing item which he connects with B. of E. forward transactions, i.e. he thinks this may cause foreign banks to hold more sterling.

W.G. very interesting on statistics of public expenditure. CSO use data for local authority investment quarterly which they discard completely once they get capital spending figures once a year but these don't really relate to actual investment so we don't get either quarterly or annually any reliable guide to what is happening; and tend every year to be thrown off previous interpretation by annual data.

Wednesday, 25 October   I had drafted a short paper for the Chancellor on the forecasts, going on to discuss the alternatives, and sent it to William on Tuesday. This morning he showed me an incoming telegram from Fowler which (a) said the US would be adding a further $100 m. to our credit line, (b) suggested an approach to IMF for postponement of repayment next month and (c) indicated that European Central Banks might be asked to go beyond the $300 m. so far promised. Most important, however, of all was a passage which implied that the US Treasury regarded our troubles as temporary and reflecting state of world trade. Clearly Ministers may treat this as showing we are not in underlying deficit at all and have a blank cheque from Uncle Jo. I agreed that my minute should not go forward but William said that I ought still, at some stage if I wished, to put forward my own professional opinion to the Chancellor even if he obviously wouldn't listen now to talk of devaluation.

Lunch with Gallop[102] who says that the figures sent by SCOW raise 100 queries while non-computerised, manual, 19th century figures sent by Colville's never raise any. Trade statistics "full of holes" (e.g. no sign of 80,000 tons of scrap exported via Immingham to Japan; exports of bright steel bars = 4 times total U.K. production because heading "bright bars" separated in the ledger by about 30 pages from heading "iron and steel"). Steel investment not much affected by nationalisation – much more by lack of profit since some firms down to 3–4% on assets. There will be a large number of mixed companies now because nationalised companies often have a 50% holding in a non-nationalised one. The Fed. is treating only wholly owned and one 90% owned company as constituting the nationalised industry for statistical purposes. Gallop also mentioned case of 16" tubes where system of fabrication has changed to resistance welding from hot welding so that orginal reason for treating under a different S.I.C. heading has disappeared. One group of buildings may count as 2 or more establishments if there are records of transfer and if new and separate process is involved (e.g. wiredrawing). But the old distinction of semis in terms of cooling after the ingot stage prior to re-rolling has ceased to have a technological foundation. The line between industries – and establishments – changes as

---

[102] L Gallop – Economist with the Iron and Steel Board.

technique changes.

Monday, 30 October   On Friday we had an ESG and FU meeting, the first as usual at T.B.'s request and to listen to his vendetta against SSRC, the second to give Michael Posner his first chance of expressing a view and consider the technical arrangements for announcing devaluation. The most memorable part of the proceedings at ESG was William's remark: "Other people have strikes: we have meetings". T.B. wanted Perm. Secs. to be free to pay the market rate to academic economists for government research, not see us limited by a fixed tariff. Of course, it wasn't William's business at all, but (if anybody's) mine and so it was referred to me.

Tuesday, 31 October   A quiet day on Monday. I passed through William my verdict on devaluation; composed yesterday, for submission to the Chancellor.

Thursday, 2 November   William spoke to me on Tuesday about the memo and suggested some minor amendments. He also recommended me to enclose it with a personal note in mss for the Chancellor alone, making it clear that no one but he (William) had been consulted. I had to think of it as an invitation to resign addressed just when the French were firming the government's resolution to persevere.

He then told me that last Wednesday, he, the Gov. and the Chancellor had called on the P.M., with Burke present, to discuss the situation. They had gone a long way, including some discussion of accompanying measures, but the Chancellor showed increasing disquiet at the trend of the discussion. He had finally argued strongly in favour of letting things work out further before taking any final decision. He wanted to wait till the spring when the trends might again be in our favour. The P.M. accepted the Chancellor's line and there the meeting ended. William felt that it would be impossible to leave things there – and indeed we haven't the resources to survive without further borrowing. (All this he has told no one else and I'm not supposed to know.)

Yesterday we went to SEPO for a discussion of a long draft of what might go to Neddy and eventually be published as "a planning document". It has been written and re-written like so many documents nowadays without Ministerial direction or agreement about what if anything should be published. It was agreed all round that we couldn't say anything at all about the balance of payments but of course this is tantamount to saying that nothing can be published. William also argued that we had to decide what the status and usefulness of the document was as a "plan" since it was obviously not like the last Plan but yet had some of the same overtones. *How* did the Government propose to influence the private sector's plans?

Douglas argued for something that could go to NEDC but this really meant deciding what Neddy was there for and what they could be enlisted to support or clarify. Here T.B. was far better than seemed conceivable: largely insisting on the importance of incomes policy as the last fling.

Saturday, 4 November   Friday was one of those days! I was trying desperately to dictate a note on the latest forecasts to the Chancellor when a series of phone calls were put through: Donald to say he'd be unable to stay beyond 11.30 at the Methodology meeting, Glyn Davies to tell me of fresh trouble over his secondment from Strathclyde, Nicky to tell me that Ian Little was the man for Power, William to ask me to call at 10.45, etc. On top of all this Miss Davies kept bringing me the wrong minutes. It transpired that yesterday she had sent to N.K. and M.P. my first draft Top Secret memo to the Chancellor thinking that this was the short half-page on the forecasts that N.K. had asked me to copy to him. So I had to get it back from N.K. and then from M.P.; the latter hadn't read it but N.K. had spoken about it to William to his great embarrassment and with real enthusiasm. N.K. promised to keep its existence secret and make no reference to it.

Then followed nearly two hours on Methodology with T.B. at his most vocal, inveighing against Heyworth[103] and SSRC. I had a brief word with M.P. on the dv. speech and went off to lunch with Bill Nield and Steve. At 3.30 I was to see the Chancellor but he was late and I was asked to come back at 5 i.e. just when Peter Hart[104] was due to call.

When I did see the Chancellor we were alone and this must be the first time I've had a chance to talk to him alone since 1964 (except a short exchange at Nuffield, or No. 11). I commented on the lights for they were all blazing and the walls were newly painted white. The Chancellor said that Jack Diamond had made the same comment. Then he turned to my memo which he said he still kept in his pocket and had shown to nobody. He thanked me for sending it and I said it was perhaps unkind to strike at his nerve when he needed all he had. He said he saw the force of the arguments although he might not be able to set them out so expertly. He had been conscious that I was gradually changing my attitude to dv: was it the forecasts that had completed the change? I said Yes. When I came back from leave and saw how things were I felt that we couldn't defend inaction in the face of such a poor outlook. He then asked if I thought it irresponsible of him not to devalue: my thrust about 1964 had gone home. Why shouldn't he borrow? What if there was an inflow of capital from abroad on a big scale? I said it depended on whether it was short term (and so unreliable) or long term (a la Canadienne) and calculated to develop our productive power. He thought it would be wrong, when the future was so obscure and everything at its worst, to devalue: we might later regret it. Why not wait till the Spring? I mustn't think that it would be possible to hold incomes and prices or that he would be there to do it. His mind was made up. If devaluation proved necessary, he would not remain Chancellor. I said that as time went on and the bad news accumulated it would be difficult to explain how we expected to emerge in balance. If we had to say that we saw no need for further action and that it would all turn out right in the end, the explanation

[103] Lord Heyworth – Chm., Unilever Ltd, 1942–60; member, Royal Comm. on Projects and Income, 1951; Chm., Council on Productivity, Prices and Incomes, 1960–62; Cttee. on Research on Social Sciences, 1963–65.

[104] Peter Hart – Prof. of Economics, Univ. of Reading.

would be pretty thin. "Then we'll just have to start getting used to being thin".

Earlier he said that he had noticed but been rather puzzled by my remark in May that we'd had all the good news. We had needed all the luck there was to get into surplus and instead had no luck at all. He didn't complain of the forecasts but after all they had shown a handsome surplus in 1968 last Feb. and now showed a deficit of up to £200 m. I said that other forecasts had been further out than ours. World indus. prodn. had probably fallen since the beginning of the year – something almost without precedent since the war – and world trade in mfrs. had certainly been flat or falling. All this was worse than we could safely have predicted. Could we *really* have said as a basis for planning that exports would fall? We *had* said that exports would be flat and this was implied in his Budget speech although few people had noticed this (he said he hadn't and I elaborated the point with a little graph).

We also had a few words on competitiveness while debating the rights and wrongs of borrowing abroad. I agreed that our competitive position seemed to have slipped a little over the years, and had not improved as we had hoped over the past year because of the deflationary policies elsewhere. It was wrong to speak of competitiveness in any absolute sense and one could measure changes only after taking the level of world activity into account.

I went on to remind him of the total amount already borrowed (over £1500 m.), the enormous total for market forwards (£1100 m.+) and the danger that our lines of credit would run out this month. We'd need a *lot* of money to wait till the spring.

After we got up I asked him if he slept at nights. He said Yes he had slept last night till 4 a.m. then woke and remembered my memo but was asleep again by 4.10. He felt that if it did come to devaluation in the end, he had at least the satisfaction of guiding the country for three years and would be able to look back on a great deal that had been accomplished over that time. He gave no sign at any stage of worry or perturbation. His demeanour was that of a man who has thought it through, come to a firm conclusion, and is incapable of being ruffled. He assured me that I must always speak my mind even if it meant disagreement. But I mustn't give comfort to Nicky and the rest of them by lining up with them. (He referred twice to Nicky as having been constantly at him on devaluation and obviously resented it.)

Curiously enough at 12.55 when I saw N.K. he told me that Jim wouldn't devalue, and went on to explain why. If he did, H.W. would get rid of him at once and it would be the end of his career because H. would saddle him with all the blame. He had to wait till H.W. himself would feel obliged to take the lead and identify himself with the change. This may be what N. took from what the Chancellor told him but it seems to me too simpliste.

Donald described a visit to the White House to talk to Sorensen and had just asked "Is the President going to Texas?" when L.B.J. entered carrying a telegram and said "Yes I've told him he must come to Texas: that's my State" and walking on, plugged in, asked to be connected to President Truman and two minutes later was talking to him in a barber's shop in Kansas City. D. remembers registering that the telephone service must be a lot more efficient in the US than in the UK.

Tuesday, 7 November   Lunch with John Stevens. He is enjoying Morgan's and says that his prep. school and Winchester prepared him for the working conditions with all the partners sharing one room and overhearing all the others' affairs. He finds it a welcome change that he doesn't have to bother what to do about bank rate etc. but merely react to what *is* being done.

Thursday, 9 November   Crisis moves nearer. B.R. up another $1/2\%$. We had heavy losses last Friday (£100 m. spot and forward) and this week the same story goes on. Next Tuesday we will be saying that the trade deficit was over £100 m. in October. I very much doubt whether the exchanges will stand that.

F.U. this morning. William told us of yesterday's discussion between Chancellor and van Lennep at which Ch. seized opportunity to ask about EEC reactions if we did devalue. (In fact van L. was asked to call on him while over here for Shell Lecture.) Ministers are inclined to take the line (put to me this morning by Nicky after Directorate) that markets are so jumpy nobody can say who will move and who will not. Only *they* deduce from this that if others will follow they shouldn't move, while N.K. argues for a floating rate (not just an unpegged one but a rate seen to fluctuate to keep people guessing).

It seems that at a cocktail party van L. heard Larre say that Fr. wouldn't let UK get away with devaluation; and he expressed great indignation to Chancellor about this, saying that EEC should act together. On Tuesday the six will meet over lunch in Paris with Larre as host and van L. will try to get an agreed line. Chancellor asked about reactions if there was a general disturbance and van L. gave all the right answers about the dangers of dislodging the dollar. This led on to question of support for the pound if it was in anybody's interest not to risk "chaos". Van L. was less emphatic about the chances of mobilising support. Curiously, he thought that this was conjuncturally not a favourable time for devaluation, citing the position in France and Germany.

Meanwhile Denis has gone to Bonn to see Schellhorn (and Emminger at an airport) about support. D. is due back tonight and may go off to Washington tomorrow on the same quest. William warned us that next week-end might be D-day and asked us to leave a note of our addresses.

Wrote last night to St Peter's refusing but didn't post and am still undecided.

Monday, 13 November   Wrote to St Peter's accepting. A very difficult decision.

This evening Wm. called us about 6 and told us the score. No previous news but the papers had carried headlines about international help after Basle and the Mansion House speech gave nothing away.

The big 3 are now together again but very worried about party support especially over Vietnam. George is said to be against devaluation and Wm. thinks it may derive from fear that he might get the blame from insistence on entering

Europe and doing what the French want. P.M. also still against but Chancellor has changed round and now sees futility of going on.

It is a long story starting with teleg. last week indicating that French might follow us. When Denis got to Bonn he learned little from Schellhorn; and Emminger took much the same line as van L. – that the French were inclined to follow us and mustn't be allowed to.

Meanwhile in Basle Governor found that Zijlstra thought that we should devalue: so did Ansiaux: Blessing after much havering, which revealed his true attitude, thought not – no doubt to stand by the Americans: Carli was stoutly against and tried to mobilise support but without being able to offer any himself: Brunet wouldn't give any opinion – not even his own (but he was driven to say that if we did devalue by no more than *10%* the French wouldn't move): but Hay and Coombs were firm that we mustn't.

In Washington Denis arrived armed with instructions to make their flesh creep with talk of pulling out of Singapore (to keep control of the party) and of Germany. Fowler and Deming were already worried about a possible devaluation and its effects on the dollar and had begun to think of a package of $3b. This would have involved a drawing of $1.4b. from IMF; a further $1 b. to be put up by US ($½ b.) Germany and Italy ($¼ b. each); and $600 m. from sources unspecified. At first Schweitzer thought that a standby of $3 b. might be done given UK acceptance of a long string of conditions in a "nice letter". But on reflection he concluded that IMF couldn't tie up its resources to this extent (GAB would be heavily involved) and it became clear that IMF felt we should devalue.

Americans were prepared to make a further effort and came up with smaller package of $2b. of which their contribution would be $600m. and the rest our IMF quota.

Meanwhile Chancellor had decided that he could not accept the larger package on the terms implied and had spoken to P.M. The smaller package was only introduced into Basle discussions rather late and was kept alive chiefly because some smoke-screen is obviously needed if pressure on the pound isn't to become insupportable.

(I'm not sure if I've got the authorship of the package right, but there is no doubt that Leslie went straight to Washington with suggestion of the $3b. standby without first sounding out London. Naturally we should feel pretty horrified at such large additional debts.)

The disarray in the Party means that they can't be sure of carrying Parliament on the accompanying measures. This is what horrifies G.B. but equally Wm. and Denis made it clear at the week-end that devaluation without these measures would be futile. Wm. spoke of possible vote of 50 M.P.s against Government as something the Chancellor had introduced into discussion of the measures. He reacts against 6d [2½p] on income tax on grounds of incentive and speaks lightly of bigger cut in public expenditure (bad conscience of this year's experience?). This is rather frivolous in the circumstances.

Of course, it's all rather late. We *need* a decision this week but Cabinet doesn't even have the forecasts or realise how far things have gone; and they have insisted that any *measures* should be discussed in full Cabinet at leisure not pushed through as in July 1966 at top speed. So we may yet find ourselves with an empty till and no real leadership.

Tuesday, 14 November   Wm. told us early on that probability of devaluation was now "in the high nineties" and that I had better not go to Paris. I eventually prevailed on Ken Berrill to go in my place with M. Posner taking on the main job at EPC tomorrow.

There was a meeting of ministers last night (presumably the 3) and they had a cable from US implying that it was now apparent that US was reconciled to devaluation. But Denis after talking to Deming in Paris phoned this morning that Deming strongly took the view that this was *not* US government policy. We will continue to try for support but more as camouflage than in earnest.

William and I saw Chancellor at about 12.15. William asked if N.K. should be brought in and the Chancellor left it to William who said "Not to this meeting". (N.K. is very disconsolate and just as William was preparing to bring him in, P.M. said the "two" economic advisers were *not* to be told. William did, however, hand over N.K.'s papers on a floating rate).

We agreed that main issues were size and composition of package, guarantees, and fixed or floating. Of these the first occupied us a good while and I stuck out for £600m. of which £400m. for devaluation itself and £200m. because economy would need checking next year anyhow. When we turned to taxation Chancellor said P.M. wanted a *cut* in income tax by 6d as an incentive and he himself asked us to look at 3d until we made it clear we thought this a bit of a joke. He made no great difficulty over h.p. or credit restriction or even 8% (these had been discussed last night) though not too keen on h.p. and thinking more of p.t. (upper range). Then came betting duties (he wanted to treble them $- 7^{1}/_{2}\%$), heavy oil (doubled – for the sake of coal), the rate support grant (flatten out), corporation tax or a tax on dividends. But no enthusiasm for a rise in income tax or SET. Instead he harped on expenditure and totted up nearly £200 m. but threw out the "refit of Ark Royal" cancellation. When I tried to argue that it was important to announce it all now because it wouldn't be possible later he checked me by pointing out that this was a political judgment and he preferred to take these himself. Then he said: "Professor Cairncross we have here a package of £450m. excluding income tax. Would you not consider that enough?"

He asked William to think of something to distinguish the package from the usual blend. Guaranteed sterling or something like that.

They are still worried that they may not carry the Party with such a big package.

In the afternoon William took the first meeting of the Steering Group and I later stayed on for a discussion of taxation with Alec Johnston and W. Morton. No great problems but Paul Gore Booth reverted to incentives and the need to provide some – as if devaluation didn't do that automatically. Ned Dunnett felt the extra £60m. cut in defence unfair when cut in civil exp. was less. Of course we are sceptical of both and prefer the certainties of higher taxation.

At 6 the Overseas Panel got going under Sam Goldman and was still sitting at 9.30. Quite a day. William was returning to a meeting at 10.30.

Wednesday, 15 November   Another full day. William told us of outcome of Ministerial meeting last night and then this morning. They went round the houses last night with Denis Healey rounding on the Chancellor as he has never been rounded on in his political career and asking why anyone should trust him now or believe his forecasts after all he has dragged the party through. George B. had breakfast with him to quieten him down. Crosland also sceptical last night but he rang N.K. at midnight and asked if he should believe the £500m. calculation. N. told him it was too little. More progress at 9 a.m. meeting but P.M. still saying we were old fashioned and should get motor industry to export more by talking to them not by h.p. restrictions. Doubtful at that stage if we'd get *any* measures.

We saw Chancellor at 11.30 with A.J. and W.M. This showed him willing to consider reasonable package but still aiming for betting tax, fuel oil duty, etc. and no mention of SET.

After lunch Steering Committee at 3 then Chancellor again at 3.30, this time with N.K. (brought in at last). He made case for SET and against H.P. (he also wanted regulator but no Inc. Tax) and got short shrift from Chancellor. William looked bored and said nothing. In the morning he had spoken up for H.P. because without it we wouldn't be able to stick to credit restraint but he thought it might be deferred till Jan. or so if we had some understanding with motor trade. In the end Chancellor had all the alternatives but hadn't decided what package he would ask for. But by 6.30 he was at the meeting and got most of what he wanted. Then he, William, and others went off in white tie and tails to Actuaries Dinner where he was principal speaker.

I had prepared for him with Wynne a 2 page summary of argument for £500m. and this was all that Chancellor handed to his colleagues at the meeting. The paper on Accompanying Measures hasn't gone to any of the Ministers.

M. Posner returned about 7.30 and I saw him in private office where he was rightly indignant that Chancellor should be considering doubling the fuel oil duty. N.K. however seemed happy with this and argued that it would not affect the price of fuel oil! M.P. inclined to agree it might be recovered via higher petrol prices.

Meanwhile Denis is still busy trying to assemble support for the Fowler package in Paris. Daane was at B. of E. today and implied that if we devalue the US might do nothing to help us over our difficulties. Fed. Open Market Comm. met without advisers for first time and the view was expressed that US should put dollar first if we did devalue.

Yesterday's meeting of 6 at lunch ended with French still being evasive on their probable reaction.

My earlier picture of negotiations in Basle and Washington is very inadequate and confused. Leslie tried to get agreement to holdings of guaranteed sterling and failed. Then came idea of $3b standby from Fund which Schweitzer at first seemed willing to accept and then rejected because it would commit whole of resources of the Fund, etc. Then Fowler came forward with his $3b proposal but could find no takers for the non-US part, while in Basle idea of a $2b package was canvassed. Whole problem has been to get European Central Bankers involved, especially Germany and Italy.

It is also clear that Deming before seeing Pres., was willing to regard the hunt as up but that Pres. took a very different line and insisted that he should "go at them" when he got to Paris and drum up support. Americans are clearly scared of consequences for the dollar.

Cabinet tomorrow at 10.30. Most of them can't know yet what will be put by Chancellor and none of the spending departments except Defence have been told anything.

Chancellor in favour of guarantees *after* devaluation. He said today that the £100m loan was really to the US as much as to us since it was to avoid consequences of our making a $ repayment.

On the whole he seemed in good humour and remarkably quick and alert. Only once really cross over a statistical disagreement between W.G. and N.K. in the afternoon.

The odd feature of it all is the series of engagements that nobody can escape in the middle of the discussions.

Friday, 17 November

The package when announced after devaluation on 18 November included a rise in bank rate from 6 1/2 to 8 per cent, limits on bank advances, further hire purchase restrictions on car sales, an increase in corporation tax (but not income tax) to be included in the 1968 Budget, and a number of cuts in public expenditure. These included £100 million off defence spending, a further £100 million off other public spending (including spending by the nationalised industries), another £100 million through withdrawal of SET premiums due to be paid to manufacturing firms outside the Development Areas, and the withdrawal (from 31 March 1968) of all export rebates. Although superficially substantial, these measures fell short of what the occasion required and look positively modest alongside the successive deflationary packages introduced at intervals in 1968 by Roy Jenkins.

Friday, 17 November   This last observation particularly true today with Chancellor off to S. Wales and P.M. to Liverpool to meet speaking engagements while exchange loss roared up to £500m or more. Chancellor came back in heavy fog and much delayed.

To go back to yesterday. I stood around a good part of the day and/or sat in on rather fruitless re-drafting of telegrams. But I got W.G. busy on an estimate of the value of the package as it emerged from Cabinet and he and Patricia gave me the results about 6.30. At William's Steering Committee there was general feeling that size was insufficient and Bank felt this particularly (M.P.). I went over to No. 11 at 9.30 p.m. to find William with Chancellor, and Gore Booth arriving, followed by Governor. We had a long session on telegrams, then Governor came in and argued strongly that we should tell Pres. earlier. Chancellor insisted that we should wait till US markets closed and that US would help us anyhow.

Then Gov. expressed disappointment with size of package. This too made Chancellor indignant and he flatly refused to think of going back to Cabinet and asked if we could perhaps choose a lower rate or float. I backed up Leslie as far as I could and explained that we should still be in real trouble in 1969 and lose the advantages we would gain by devaluation if no further restriction of home demand. Chancellor rounded on me for doing forecast on basis of cut of £60m in defence which he had not agreed with Healey. Then said he couldn't go to Cabinet with detailed cuts for agreement there and then or explain that cuts would be half frustrated by "slippage". Anyhow we could make further reductions in next Budget. Leslie was unimpressed by all this and stood his ground.

When this was over Chancellor suddenly gave way on the timetable and was about to agree to 12 and 2 for Schweitzer and Pres. when Gore Booth came in and asked for parity of treatment. Eventually they reached compromise of 1 p.m. for both. It all seemed a little unnecessary to me, and events have shown that advancing the time was a clear gain.

Earlier Chancellor was in difficulties over a personal cable from Fowler virtually insisting he should go for a standby to protect the pound but Chancellor decided to send no reply.

Today we spent ages on statement for TV on Saturday. This goes back to change of plan by P.M. last night when he decided not to announce all the changes in his broadcast but get a press announcement half an hour earlier. I got away and did a summary of how things would look in 1968.

Lunch with N.K. who told me that Chancellor wanted to speak on Tuesday as a back bencher but was persuaded by P.M. who appealed to his patriotism. Of course the P.M. would be left rather solitary and exposed without Jim. He will probably stay for a week and be succeeded by Tony Crosland or Jenkins.

Just as Tony rang N.K. to ask about £500m, G.B. rang Donald MacD. who in fact came up with the same figure and much the same package. As he left George, Jenkins came in so he wasn't totally ignorant of what was going on.

Great confusion tonight – foreseeable and only avoided earlier by great good luck. Very heavy losses. At 3.40 Posner called William out of meeting to suggest immediate action but Chancellor had gone off, and Governor had already turned idea down flat as likely to make return to a fixed rate of 2.40 impossible.

Later I found Sam wrestling with proposition to announce at 2 p.m. tomorrow before close of Middle Eastern markets (all this as I suspected was much exaggerated). Since they open at 5.30 our time no great adv. but William thought we could get better news presentation and was sure that France would leak whenever they got the IMF paper at 2. I argued that losses in US till 10 p.m. would dwarf any losses in Middle East and suggested to Sam that we might be wise to let Americans stop supporting the pound. But he quoted the Governor and both Fred and Kit Macmahon said we should stick out, so I didn't press it. N. had argued that the drain showed massive incompetence and that we should invoke the leak procedure. All this arguing went on in corridors and without connection while the Ministers concerned were out of London. If anything had to be done it lay with the Bank and they preferred to make no move. They took comfort from the view that it would all come back and made little of the 15% loss on the deal. But had things broken earlier in the week we couldn't possibly have held. (Dealings today were for Tuesday so no actual spot loss.)

My impression is that we "overplanned" and lost flexibility in doing so. The P.M. said to William our War Book was the best he'd ever seen and no doubt it was. But we tended to get too absorbed in telegrams, press conferences, and drafts of statements instead of holding ourselves free to devalue at once as we might theoretically have done last night (but without the blessing of IMF). In fact, with a reserve currency I suppose that it is not only very difficult to bring oneself to devalue but just as difficult to organise because there are so many people to conciliate and inform and so large a possibility of misunderstanding that the operation *has* to be planned and becomes pretty inflexible whatever we do.

Last night Roger Lavelle[105] read me some of the P.Q.'s for Tuesday which will sound very funny e.g. asking Chancellor why Gov. was allowed to put bank rate up to $6\frac{1}{2}\%$; what change in import prices he expects; and so on.

N.K. is drafting speech for Chancellor. But tonight I got a paper from Peter Baldwin outlining the argument *by the Chancellor* to N.K. in his car to Paddington and asking me to do a draft for Tuesday's debate.

IMF arrive tomorrow and we will have to tell them what we think the measures will do. Schweitzer refusing to be hurried over standby. He may now get exactly 1 hr to get the Board to approve our new parity since paper goes out at 2 and we are thinking now of announcement at 3.

Poor Denis still in Paris this morning and unaware of final decision. Chancellor said last night we should leave him without guidance on this so as to avoid embarrassment today. But I see Chalfont[106] has put his foot in it again by saying devaluation "not in our minds".

One thing M. Posner accomplished was a cut in fuel oil duty from 2p to 1p and he nearly got it left out. Marsh put up a fight and it went to P.M. but he upheld Cabinet decision and left Chancellor to fix a figure which he did: so 1p it is.

N.K. told me that the right time to have moved was in June or July. He still feels that Cabinet haven't got the right feel of tax requirements and thinks a new Chancellor may find this easier to do.

Saturday, 18 November   Der Tag. At 9.30 the statement became public and at 10.25 I saw the TV screen show a £1 note with DEVALUED printed across it.

[105] Roger Lavelle – Spec. Asst. to Lord Privy Seal in negotiations with EEC, 1961–63; Private Sec. to Chancellor, 1965–68; Asst. Sec., 1968–75.
[106] Lord Chalfont – Defence Correspondent, *The Times* , 1961–64; Minister of State, FCO, 1964–70.

First, however, an addendum to N.K. on J.C. He told me that in Cabinet there had been murmurs that people hoped he wouldn't feel obliged to resign. He had replied rather equivocally. N. himself thinks he should resign in the tradition of British public life and that he could rejoin Cabinet soon after. Would be treated sympathetically both by H. of C. and by public. When Tony C. went to B. of T. it had been understood that Peter Shore would go and Tony was last minute appointment, probably to block Roy J. At least this was N.'s interpretation. Roy has *not* been brought in to the devaluation discussions. N. saw some advantage in a Chancellor who could take a fresh view of taxation requirements.

As to today, I first saw William with Denis sitting there and Rab and others also standing around. They said first reactions very good especially in US. L.B.J. told Daane that earlier in the week he "had a feeling in his bones" that we might have to go but he would put the US "stack of resources" right behind us.

William said P.M. would now broadcast on Sunday at about 6.30 in place of a programme of "Songs of Praise".

It emerged that N.K. *was* to do Pt I of the speech so I gave him some comments and in the evening got on with Pt II. It will obviously be a major speech and needs a lot more work, since it should be of Budget proportions.

Afternoon with Fund Mission. They are very critical of scale of measures and got quickly to the nub of the matter. They also want credit ceilings on government expenditure i.e. a target for sales of bonds. I asked how you could set about forecasting sales and what instruments could be devised to promote them. The B. of E. said that sales of government securities to the market last week reached £75m and that even on Friday they were probably net sellers. That rather shook the IMF.

No news from Australia and New Zealand; Malaysia took it all rather badly. Governor organised necessary support very quickly, mainly out of the familiar Fowler items. Germany on Friday wouldn't go beyond $250m for 3 months which gives some idea of what we might have borrowed if no devaluation.

On the whole, my fears of yesterday were unjustified. We lost only $50m in US (presumably because loan rumours revived) and things have gone more or less according to plan today. Only the Danes, Irish and Israelis are known to have devalued and the Six and Japan have both held firm. The French made it clear at once that they wouldn't move. In fact everybody had the answer ready.

Chancellor has had letter from Gov. saying that he thinks measures not really adequate and asking for assurances about next Budget. We are asked to prepare a reasoned reply. William said Governor told him he didn't "tip the wink" to IMF about the measures but W. suspected that Morse or somebody else might have done so.

Sunday, 19 November   Of course as Mary said when I told her, it is rather comical that the P.M. should have ruled that the two Economic Advisers weren't to be brought in. Last Monday at ESG Tommy was fulminating against the forecast, obviously ignorant of the decision that had been all but taken (or afraid that a loan might be accepted). Nicky up to Wed. or Thursday was still not free to see the papers and more or less weeping on everybody's shoulder. Then by Friday he was deputed to draft a speech justifying the Chancellor's change of mind and failure to devalue earlier. He went off yesterday to Cambridge to entertain Lloyd Reynolds[107] having felt obliged to stick to this engagement for fear cancellation would arouse suspicion (but he did – at the last minute – cancel his lecture). Last night he rang up at 9.40 afraid that as he heard nothing on BBC the operation was cancelled.

Denis maintains that there was a leak in Paris. How otherwise account for the heavy losses on Friday while on Thursday we more or less balanced out (as Gov. told Chancellor losses in afternoon of the order of £10m only). At airport the Duty Free Counter (govt.-run) would not accept sterling and many hotels took same line. Graham Turner of BBC said his informant on Wed (on $1b loan) was non-British "member" of OECD – D. says this means French. His "source" told him on Friday that we were about to devalue by 17% but he didn't broadcast this at 6 p.m., not because of anything Denis said but because his source had cold feet and rang up withdrawing (cf. US market).

Of course, too, nobody ever mentioned 30% devaluation or laid down conditions for loan. Whole discussion was in terms of timetable in event of standby or short term assistance to see us through on assumption of no devaluation.

Ch. is saying (e.g. to R. Butt in *Observer*) that he made up his mind a fortnight ago and Denis finds this embarrassing in view of what he was instructed to say to Fowler and Emminger. But it isn't really true and perhaps Chancellor said something more qualified.

Trouble with IMF. Schweitzer thought we meant an absolute reduction in public expenditure by £400m and wants (a) a commitment on balance of payments in e.g. 1969 or late 1968. (b) a commitment on borrowing requirement. (c) credit ceilings on government borrowing from banks. They are thinking in terms of conditions laid down for France in 1957/58.

P.M.'s broadcast at 6 pretty awful in spite of efforts to change it. Full of "roots" and "speculation" and attempt to pretend we might have had loan on unacceptable terms. Badly delivered.

Press reactions bad. All taking v. gloomy line as if major disaster. *Observer* not too bad. Few stress importance of releasing resources and nature of adjustment required.

Chancellor told George Woodcock that prices would go up 6% and G. repeated this widely. Doesn't make DEA's job very easy. He no doubt added 2 1/2% to 3 1/2%.

We saw S.B., Peter Jay, etc. for seminar at 2.30 and it seemed to go well but Shonfield went off and said on BBC measures would be very deflationary after arguing the contrary with us. (He expected swift rise in exports).

William wants the contingency planning to go on, e.g. for dollar emergency. I asked if we couldn't also review all the things we do because we are in balance of payments difficulties so as to undo them later.

Yesterday I heard of final extinction of fuel oil duty proposal in middle of

[107] Lloyd Reynolds – Professor of Economics, Yale Univ.

meeting with IMF. Fortunately I had said nothing but William did mention it to Deming. Otherwise we killed it just in time and press today supports Marsh on final policy.

P.M. apparently told the Lobby that unemployment would fall to 1.7% by middle of year. (We say 1.8% by end of year because we don't expect any real change relative to forecast of $4\frac{1}{2} - 5\%$ inc. in GDP).

Some discussion on statement for tomorrow. William had drafted a narrative of events (God know when!) explaining the events of last week, and it may be included tomorrow to put an end to argument about whether decision was forced on government by Friday's run (Denis said it was the other way round since run reflected leak of decision: *Figaro* and *Le Monde* had headlines asserting we would devalue by 17% on Thursday or Friday). We have also to explain what we were negotiating *about* in Paris and Basle and in fact we can do so quite candidly now.

Monday, 20 November   Long meeting with IMF over credit ceilings and, still more, borrowing requirement. They are taken aback to find borrowing requirement up by £400m this year since May and no less next year than this. But it doesn't help to ask for fixed targets for money supply or government recourse to bank borrowing, quarter by quarter.

Governor wrote to Chancellor on Friday on public expenditure developing his views and asking for 6d ($2\frac{1}{2}$p) on income tax now. Chancellor is sympathetic up to a point and has a bad conscience over public expenditure. Last week he was suggesting cuts in it to William as if they were a new idea. Ministers have agreed *privately* to raise taxes in next Budget but won't want to make a definite pledge and if pushed by IMF would react the wrong way (e.g. if some item like Higher School Leaving Age were picked out).

Papers this morning remarkably full and well-informed. Most of what we know is there somewhere or other including behaviour of the French.

Tuesday, 21 November   A little peace at last. More meetings with the IMF which I kept out of. William had prepared a key section for the Letter of Intent and this may save us from specific commitments on credit ceilings provided Chancellor will accept undertaking to raise taxes in next Budget. William had an eye on publication (and no doubt on the Governor's letter). IMF wanted a firm figure for the borrowing requirement and for balance of payments in 1968 II. Meanwhile on TV Schweitzer practically conceded the standby, and Emminger made short work of attempt to denigrate the whole operation and to suggest that there were strings attached to loans.

In first half-hour when Stock Exchange opened B. of E. sold £250m and was nearly out of tap stock. So much for the doctrine which IMF seemed to be supporting yesterday that there is a clear ceiling to possible sales of government bonds to non-banks.

Crosland's speech took shape as a blend of N.K. and A.K.C. but seemed to leave out the key passages explaining how the total of £500m was reached – indeed seemed to leave out the £500m and talk only of terms of trade.

M.P. has already started up idea of shadow rates again but I can't say it thrills me. William was onto "Uncle" yesterday as a possible victim and M.P. said if Norway hadn't devalued then it ought to stand on its own feet. We may yet kill it.

Chancellor made a very good showing in the House yesterday and rises in popular esteem even when people are shocked by devaluation. As a nation the English love their Dunkirks and Sir John Moores in retreat more than the victorious generals. But then there are no victories at present and the public mood reflects this. People are cynical about devaluation even when they howled for it: S.B., for example, goes round saying presumably this will be bungled too. There is an intense lack of self-confidences which we can't afford for long without disastrous consequences. The sooner morale is restored the healthier it will be for any form of democratic government. But I can't believe that we'll always be out of luck and this may prove to have been a good time to devalue provided trade now begins to expand. The foreigners, curiously enough, are far more impressed than the British press.

In Scotland 37% of those sampled in Gallup Poll said they supported a Scot. Nat. Government – twice as many Scottish Nationalists as Conservatives. Given that the older generation is presumably not so much impressed this must represent a very high proportion of the younger generation. Yet net migration from Scotland is now nearly half the birth-rate and gross outward migration must therefore be even higher as a proportion. This in spite of a rise in the ratio of earnings in Scotland to earnings in UK.

On Thursday evening in the argument over the timetable the Chancellor said: "Did you ever read the 1949 devaluation debates? I've read them right through". Then he went on, I think, to say that there were a lot of references to telling people while their markets were still open – a thing he was determined to avoid this time (hence his insistence on not telling the Americans till 5 p.m.).

Total losses for the month up to last Friday (together with foreseeable losses to end of dev.), spot and forward, totalled £1,000m. Quite a total, however you look at it!

Wednesday, 22 November   N.K. said profits would be £1,200m higher even on a pre-devaluation basis and how could you hope to run an incomes policy on that basis.

I had a talk with Donald about the calculations. Douglas told me that Donald reached conclusions very close to ours and told G.B. that £500m was about right for cuts. He also agreed that by end '68 we should aim at releasing about £600m in resources and this was also Blackaby's figure on Sunday.

Douglas was at the Palace yesterday and sat next to the Queen who discussed devaluation with him. She first heard "some weeks ago" from the Governor of the possibility but while in Malta her attention was on other things. She had seen Cousins on TV and deplored his attitude. Philip, however, wanted less incomes policy and more incentive for more work which seems very close to Cousins' view.

Saturday, 25 November   A week since devaluation. Too early to judge how it has gone. Recognition by the press that measures are insufficient but (a) the government has said so already (speeches by Crosland and Chancellor in Debate) and (b) the press takes our forecast of $4\frac{1}{2}$ – 5% for granted *now* but was arguing differently only a week or so ago.

On Thursday P. Jay issued his piece in *The Times* on the destroyed memoranda [in November 1964], and the press took it up enthusiastically just as they took up Chancellor's final speech. But of course it's the policy not the advice that matters and there is nothing horrifying about Ministers deciding not to take advice. The P.M. and others no doubt went further by insisting on *not having advice* on the main issue. The Advisers equally went beyond what is usual by putting in a memo direct to the P.M. and by-passing officials. The really odd feature is that essentially the advice throughout was political, rather than economic: the advisers thought themselves better politicians than their masters.

This came out on Thursday at a meeting held by Donald when N.K. referred to Ministers as "babies". The meeting should have been on import substitution under my own chairmanship but Douglas at ESG (W.A. not present) explained that William and he had agreed that there should be a review of the problems post-devaluation under Donald and I at once intervened to say I had called a meeting on the key issue (shadow rates etc.). When I protested to Douglas at lunch that we were in danger of organising a parallel Forecasts Committee he said he wanted the work of NIF to go forward separately.

William also raised the matter at my suggestion at Directorate and emphasised that the NIF work was not affected. This didn't prevent N.K. as I had foreseen from trying desperately at the meeting to get on to the assessment and away from shadow rates and similar general issues. T.B. was relatively quiet.

I've made two correct guesses so far on devaluation. I said the dollar premium would fall about 10 pts and that the Stock Exchange was only buying equities at first as a kind of conditioned reflex to devaluation and in continuation of the devaluation hedge spirit of recent months. Sure enough, in two days the market turned round but without any very big fall. Things should settle down now. What *is* rather disconcerting is to find sterling coming down from the ceiling as early as Thursday morning.

With the IMF we have reached agreement and practically published it including the fact that we will aim to limit the borrowing requirement to £1,000m. This was agreed by P.M. as well as Chancellor. On Wednesday morning William came in with a draft which he had dictated straight off and which provided the basis. He saw that the main hope of quick agreement was to promise fresh consultation when we did our successive forecasts; and he knew that the borrowing requirement was more important to them than the credit ceilings etc. But I was surprised that this commitment was accepted so readily and suspect that in the end the local authorities will be asked to bail out the Central Government by taking less from PWLB. After all, money costs *will* increase.

Given this agreement, the Chancellor will have a ready answer for the Governor and will indeed have committed himself to a Budget judgment months in advance. N.K. will be delighted. When we argued at Donald's meeting I said to him that I should be surprised if he wanted less additional taxation than I did at the next Budget (this when he was arguing for what seemed a lower level of unemployment than I should favour). He took the point; and when he next mentioned an unemployment target he made it 2% next year. N. still wants very heavy taxation and regards the Economic Section as somehow in disagreement with him when all we jibbed at was £300m in *last* year's Budget. N. would say that we might not have needed to devalue if this addition to taxation had been made.

Sunday, 3 December

On 29 November James Callaghan resigned as Chancellor but remained in the Cabinet, exchanging Ministerial positions with Roy Jenkins, the Home Secretary. The IMF was approached for a standby of £1,400 million and additional support was sought from foreign central banks. In its Letter of Intent to the IMF, submitted on 23 November, the UK Government gave as its target an improvement in the balance of payments of £500 million and a surplus in the second half of 1968 at an annual rate of at least £200 million. It undertook to keep the borrowing requirement within a limit of £1,000 million and the increase in the money supply in 1968 to no more than the increase in 1967. These limits were in fact observed but the target for the balance of payments in 1968 proved much too ambitions. Although there was a rapid and almost continuous improvement in the balance of payments in 1968 and a surplus at an annual rate of £200 million was reached by the second quarter of 1969, confidence in sterling was slow in returning and in 1968 alone the exchange market had to be supported to the tune of over £1,400 million – nearly as much as in the three preceding years of tumult taken together.

An important issue that emerged early was whether enough had been done to damp down domestic demand. The IMF and OECD would both have liked to see a target of 3 per cent growth in production in 1968 when forecasts predicted (correctly) an expansion at 4 per cent or a little higher (and the TUC was pressing for 6 per cent). The high rate of expansion in demand contributed to a boom in imports which were 10 per cent higher in volume in the first quarter (compared with the average for 1967) in spite of a 12 per cent rise in price.

Immediately after devaluation there was a sharp rise in consumer spending which ran counter to the government's economic strategy. The nearness of Christmas, however, made it difficult to check demand at once and it was doubtful how far a check would release resources to boost exports. The Chancellor decided to concentrate instead on securing agreement from his colleagues to substantial reductions in public expenditure. Cuts of £700 million in 1968–69 were announced in a statement by the Prime Minister on 16 January while on the same day proposals were published for the expenditure of £165 million on aid to private industry for modernisation. The cuts were in defence, public housing, road construction, and education. The total also included increases in various charges (e.g. NHS contributions).

Sunday, 3 December   On Monday and Tuesday we had meetings under Donald of PCSG which were a pretty good illustration of the way in which the government of an underdeveloped country is conducted. I came late to the first from a briefing meeting and found the discussion centring on figures for the balance of payments showing a deficit of £600m early next year. Donald had elaborated all this in a series of tables in spite of a previous understanding that he would cut out forecasts. Then on Tuesday he took up most of the meeting briefing himself for the CBI on prospects for profits. We sympathised with his insistence on getting it right when the CBI is being so misguided and unhelpful but this was not the aim of our meeting. Nicky also talked a lot.

I talked briefly to William who has been busy on gold pretty continuously. He said he wished he knew what the Chancellor's intentions were (this was on Tuesday at 6.15 p.m.). The gold situation was now under control and some had come on offer during the day. But, as R. Raw told me later, we still haven't had a return of all the sterling withdrawn on the Friday (only about 2/3). William also asked about the state of morale in the Economic Section and I said it was high since they felt that they had done the work.

WP No. 3 was hard going. My initial presentation of the measures was a little halting but I worked up plenty of steam in the afternoon. There was no doubt that the reception was highly critical even if not unfriendly and even Larre made it clear that he did not propose to object to a standby. De Stryker was the most forcible of those who spoke and kept to an elegiac note, arguing that WP No. 3 had failed to protect the system and that we must re-examine our work de novo. Van L. was helpful and didn't accept this thesis but he said that the measures should "lead not follow".

We dined at Edgar's. Denis had announced to the W.P. the resignation of the Chancellor and the continuity of policy but I was surprised that, even so, he was staying behind and leaving Crosland to handle the meeting. C. arrived at Edgar's about 11.30. M.P., Denis & I stayed to brief him. He told me that the Chancellor must have changed his mind as he was generally expected to go to the back benches.

Talked before lunch on Thursday to C. Dow and after lunch to R. Bertrand[108]. Both conversations left me very depressed and I had started with some worry after an aggressive and wrong-headed intervention by M. Débré in the Ministerial Debate. I pointed out to C.D. that the US willingness to continue in deficit in the 50's was the basis for the unprecedented prosperity we now enjoyed. He thought that there was still a lot of sense in Débré's argument and I said I though it dangerous nonsense. Then C. said we had left everybody dissatisfied yesterday. There should have been more drama, less glibness. Calvet had wept in 1957. We however had failed even to answer questions. This riled me a little for we used up all our time and nobody had brought this reproof against us in the meeting. I said nobody would believe us whatever we said: they wanted performance, not words. C. said he thought words could still help. They thought our forecasts must be a lot better than what we quoted to them and distrusted

---

[108] R Bertrand – French economist with OECD.

Denis' smooth presentations. I pointed to the IMF commitment and what it meant. He said they didn't believe we would honour the commitment. Perhaps it would have helped if we had brought out what a concession it represented.

Bertrand took a rather similar line. He pointed to what the P.M. had said. This was no call to sacrifice and renewal but the usual shuffling away of responsibilities. If we had announced import quotas or a wage freeze of something as big, even if it couldn't be done, then the impact would have been quite different. France had cut real wages. We weren't even trying to do so. So of course they didn't think we were serious. I told him that the Labour Party couldn't afford to let this fail and he saw the force of the argument, but came back again to the P.M. and 1.7% unemployment. People thought we were going to expand at 6% in 1968 and this was a sure recipe for failure. I told him as I told C.D. that we had doubled unemployment since mid '66 but he pointed out that France had also 2% unemployment so we couldn't say it was an intolerable level whatever the political outcry. (in fact what alarmed me most in Débré's speech was his readiness to encourage everybody, including France, to maintain a higher level of unemployment *indefinitely*).

Bertrand urged me to consider sending a paper to delegates *before* the January meeting setting out our new forecasts as soon as we had them. (Of course there won't be new forecasts till February but we were thinking of something rougher and readier).

I had lunch with the Franck's, the Chapsals, and M. Fabbra[109] on Saturday. M. Fabbra is a young, keen type who struck me as intelligent and sensible. He understands the need to make sure of his facts and avoid doctrinaire journalism from which at times *The Economist* (he said) suffered. He reads the *F.T.* and *The Economist* regularly. He agreed that growth was faster in France before the devaluations of 1957-58 and faster in Britain in the Sixties.

Tuesday, 5 December   I told William of the St Peter's position and he in turn told me that he would be succeeding Laurence Helsby as Head of the Civil Service in April. The P.M. had made up his mind just as the Chancellor was resigning (I think he said on Tuesday). Of course he welcomes it – and the chance of being "his own adviser" because it won't be such a rush. Denis R. also goes about the same time and today Richard Powell's resignation is announced.

William said that Roy J. told them on arrival that he didn't take work home and proposed to come in at 10. He did finally take some papers away but didn't read them. He chaired a meeting with J. Rey on Monday afternoon quite successfully and today had another meeting on his speech. This was written out in his own hand on Treasury paper and a very skilful bit of work which needed little amendment. But it dodged the main issue: what does a borrowing requirement of £1,000m imply for next year's Budget?

Another meeting of the economists. T.B. arguing *against* a large target for balance of payments surplus, N.K. *for* a big one. Donald did his best to get

---

[109] Fabbra – French financial journalist.

progress but it was hard going. Berrill made it seem more than ever like a Mad Hatter's Party by changing places with Nicky to get on the lee side of his cigar. I got in a few words arguing for a surplus of £500 m. in 1969 if we could get it because we wouldn't get more later. T.B. is sceptical of the idea that 15% should let us improve balance of payments by £1,000m on the grounds that the French wouldn't allow it. But of course nobody wants £1,000m and we all agree that there are foreign political as well economic responses. T. still injects his usual jibes at all forecasts, long or short, because they are consistently too optimistic and lead to bad policy decisions. In which he had just enough justice to make this reiteration dangerous.

D. Rickett off again to Washington for discussion of gold certificates with van L., Emminger, Ossola and Co.

William was certainly right when he prophesied that the economists would be "kept busy" by the remit from P.M. I've hardly seen them except at Donald's meeting.

Thursday, 7 December   I asked R. Powell in the car about the rumour that Crosland had been offered the Chancellorship until Callaghan had changed his mind. He knew nothing of this but said that as they got off the Golden Arrow C. had a message from Roy J. asking if he could call and see him that evening. C.'s message in reply was given hesitantly and after some delay and was to the effect that he didn't want to see R.J. that night and indeed wasn't sure if he'd be staying in the government. Later, he asked for this to be left out of the message and next day told R.P. to forget it. But Raphael agreed with me that in Paris he was obviously under some emotional strain over the whole affair. He asked me as we entered the Bristol to repeat what I had said about William not knowing when I left for Paris on Tuesday night; and he volunteered that Jim must have changed his mind over the week-end as he had planned to go to the back benches.

I had 15 minutes with the Chancellor alone at 10.30. I said that it would be a difficult year and that there would have to be a nice judgment how consumption could be kept down without letting output go up too fast. There was a danger of consumers spending now to lay in stocks and of producers stocking up too. He made little comment except to show some scepticism about output expanding fast.

Sunday, 10 December   When I saw Roy J. on Thursday he asked me about N.K. who would one day have to go back to Cambridge. I said that he was very much liked and respected even when he wasn't able to convince and that he had been a thoroughly valuable influence on the Treasury. Perhaps he could carry on part-time? We didn't get on to policy very much but I did point out that spending might go on rather fast from fear of rising prices.

Forecasts reached me on Friday and are rather reassuring if they can be trusted.

Sunday, 17 December   The week began with the Report of the Economic

Adv. which we discussed on Thursday at SEPO to little purpose. William looked bored and asleep and most of the discussion was with R. Powell, M. Stevenson and D. Allen.

On Thursday I agitated for a paper to give a lead on exports and in due course dictated one. I was also kept busy on the TUC Economic Review which wants a 6% expansion mid '68 – mid '69 and is a curiously naive document full of half-digested wisdom and policy pronouncements. The forecasts arrived on Wednesday and were amended by Friday.   They call for £850m cut in *demand* (or, say, £1,000m in taxation) to keep expansion down to 4%. I did a quick note for the Chancellor suggesting £500m in extra taxation plus £300m in expenditure cuts taking effect in 1969. This would probably mean about $4\frac{1}{2}\%$ expansion and very little scope for increase in consumption.

The Churchill Incomes Policy Conference was interesting because there seemed to be pretty general agreement that real wages would not fall in 1968 if things were left to go on as they are. John Davies said so point blank. Aubrey J. seemed to agree. Unfortunately A. talked far too much; he opened, he closed, he made speeches in each session; and he was too mannered to carry a sympathetic response. He had a curiously French style: expressive shrugs, elegant phrasing (without genuine fluency), a preference for the oblique generality and an almost dainty avoidance of hard economic reality. He opposed "social forces" to supply and demand as if social forces didn't operate on wages and prices *through* supply and demand. He has also swallowed the doctrine that the *level* of unemployment has little influence on wage settlements. N.K took a somewhat similar line in terms of prosperity and profits citing pre-war experience and Italy.   But C. Saunders disputed his doctrine by pointing to the European phenomenon of faster increases as full employment approached. This led to a dispute over Fiat and the Italian example and it was later explained to me that Fiat's had set out to outdo the Communist unions and had paid high wages for (in a sense) non-economic reasons so that they were not a typical oligopolist and the Italian experience was not the same as Fiat's.

The Governor has written asking for immediate action and by a curious co-incidence I did a piece for William on Wednesday along very similar lines, pointing out that our reserves and our debts to central banks roughly balanced, with IMF debts and the forward position completely uncovered. I suggested a Budget in February but I really meant January and it now looks as if this might be a serious possibility. That is, the exp. cuts might be accompanied by a statement of the tax increases to be introduced in April. Denis weighed in on Friday in support of this idea. But I gather that the Chancellor is still thinking in quite moderate terms – certainly not £800m.

Nicky laments that we didn't devalue in July, '66 and so threw away the chance of a freeze. But I still think that we can't hope for a freeze, that we *could* have got acceptance of a 4% ceiling, and that the last 18 months have been well spent in getting some deflation and nearer to the end of the world recession. July '66 would *not* have been a very auspicious start to devaluation: though no one can say that November '67 is auspicious either! July 1967 would probably have been the best choice and one that could have been justified to outside opinion without the need of a forced devaluation.

Tuesday, 19 December   Yesterday morning I was asked to do speaking notes for the Chancellor and spent about 1½ hours on them but I doubt if he even read them. Then when I was at William's meeting on the forecasts I had to go off to No. 10 for a briefing meeting at 4.15 and stay on for the meeting with the TUC. So a fair proportion of my time lately has gone on their blasted Economic Review instead of on consideration of measures to match the forecasts.

At No. 10 the P.M. let in only two officials at first (Douglas and myself) and Michael Halls[110] kept T.B. out to his obvious indignation. But he came in later and told the Chancellor what to say: that we ought to work up to a progressively faster rate of expansion, not start off at 6%. T.B. had seen Len Murray earlier and made little impression on him just as D. and I made little on Lee.

The P.M. had just come from the House of Commons after his statement on public expenditure and South Africa and was anxious to give an account of how it had gone: more quietly he said than he had expected.

On the TUC side of the table there were 14 in all with Sydney Greene in the lead speaking the purest cockney with a glottal stop if not like an idiot boy at least like an argumentative bus conductor. Of course Cousins in the end did most of the talking and George W. also spoke (one couldn't say spoke up for as usual he was hardly audible). Carron took a line nearer to the Bank of England than the TUC and some others were also pretty candid and off the normal TUC beat. The Chancellor spoke well on the theme set for him by T.B. and committed himself (a) to a balance of payments target of £500m for 1969, and (b) to 4–5% increase in GDP in '68 with the emphasis on 4 rather than 5. But the whole atmosphere was wrong. The TUC want 6%, not because they are keen on over-expansion but because they think anything less forces them to reduce their 3%-4% norm proportionately. In fact as Peter Shore pointed out, current settlements are at 5% or more and it would be absurd to expect less in 1968 but it is the *government* that is insisting on a nil norm. So the unreality of the government forces a parallel unreality on the TUC.

Harold handled the TUC well, pointing out how nobody wanted a consumer boom but that we were having one currently. But of course he won't look at any suggestions of statutory powers and is relying on the vetting procedure when it obviously isn't proving sufficient.

His face was rounder, more expressionless than it used to be and he had a double chin.

Wynne told me tonight (a) that Bryan would be happy to take over from me; (b) that Jim Shepherd *could* be persuaded to stay in G.E.S. So things look a lot brighter.

Friday, 29 December   I went in to see Ely on Christmas Eve and Boxing Day and both times found Olivia standing by the bedside. She had had a miscarriage

[110] A N (Michael) Halls – Treasury Under-Sec.; Personal Private Sec. to Prime Minister.

only a week before. Ely looked gaunt, black and wasted like a man from Belsen, with his big brow puckered at the eyes on Christmas Eve but smooth on Boxing Day. He stirred in pain but didn't wake and his eyelids half-opened and sunk back again as if held by some adhesive. Above his bed was a drawing of a lifebelt with HMS Jolly Roger on it. In the rest of the ward everybody else was out of bed and sitting up and eating a hearty meal or drinking a bottle of beer. A coloured man sat on his bed next to Ely paying no attention to him and obviously enjoying his food. The nurses tried to feed him while still unconscious and got a few spoonfuls of soup down, then gave up. He was heavily doped as if to ensure that he would never wake.

Nearly all the economists are away and won't be back till 1 January. So the draft for Ministers that I did last Thursday (before Christmas) can't be discussed for some days yet ("The Economic Outlook"). William said yesterday that it hardly mattered, since Ministers seemed agreed on the biggest cuts they could make in public expenditure and had accepted broadly the need for a major re-casting of the Budget. Only T.B. is unhappy and he has now gone off for a few days.

I had S. Fay and Hugo Young of the *Sunday Times* to see me about wages policy and public expenditure yesterday. They are naturally puzzled by the nil norm and by the idea of switching to 2% (a figure the press have conjured up presumably from the TUC: by putting the increase in GNP at 4% and deducting drift, etc?) as the standard increase in wage rates in 1968. On public expen-diture, figures of £800m and £600m have appeared in the *Financial Times* and *Guardian* and it looked as if this was intended to discredit the economy drive. But William says the obvious suspects (the P.M. and Crossman) are putting their weight behind the cuts. However, these various leaks must leave the public in a state of complete confusion and may cause unnecessary disappointment when the figures are finally announced.

William told me that D. Allen is likely to replace him and that he had discussed the possibility of uniting the two forecasting teams. I agreed that this would be a welcome move – say, when D. joined the Treasury – and William said that the P.M. might bless it because he had so little interest in macro-economic problems.

When I saw Callaghan before Christmas on my way to lunch he asked me who would succeed me and I gave him a short list: B. Hopkin, D. MacD., and Brian Reddaway. We discussed economic help for him at the Home Office for he is on the main economic committees and could be very helpful to the Chancellor.

Chapter 5

1968

Thursday, 4 January 1968   Donald held a meeting today on the forecasts after miscellaneous efforts on my part to find an acceptable way of getting them to Ministers. We may succeed in drafting a sequel to our earlier report but debate today wasn't very promising. T.B. launched forth on methodology and K.B. on the impossibility of reducing consumption so that little time remained especially with N.K. in full spate.

Earlier at Directorate we discussed the cuts in public expenditure on which the public must be by now thoroughly confused, especially since the press has got hold of a figure of £1,000m. Last year's figure was £500m which was both the swing in the balance of payments, the switch in resources and the fiscal change. This year's is £1,000m which may or may not include measures already taken. People are ringing up from Brussels to ask if this is the intended cut in public expenditure.

William described a talk with Denning Pearson [Chairman of Rolls Royce] who was worried about the credibility of the UK economy and felt he might lose contracts for $2b for engines for US, not on grounds of price or technology but simply from fears that we were incapable of running our economy properly. He had gone to Min. Tech. to get an assurance that import quotas wouldn't get in his way. He felt that the government should make some cut in its expenditure to show that it didn't intend to let socialist ideas get in the way: prescription charges would mean nothing to the Americans and deferring the rise in School Leaving Age might be unfavourably regarded. But what about cuts in public housing? Or in the civil service? Of course we needn't cut at once – only establishment: and we shouldn't be moved by squeals from staff. Tell them to name the 10% that they would like to push off on somebody else and offer to take it over: it would never be named. Rolls had got rid of over 1,000 staff when no change seemed possible. John Wall had also argued that restrictive practices were worse in government service than out – no doubt the G.P.O. does suffer in this way. Then A.G. Norman[1] had argued for abandoning the Trade Expansion Bill and said that the C.B.I. would not mount the favourable campaign it was preparing if this did not happen.

---

[1] A G Norman – Man. Dir., De La Rue and Co, 1953–77; Chm., 1964–87; President of the CBI in 1961.

William also mentioned a firm in Glasgow that employed 200 workers all of whom drew unemployment benefit. He had been told that there was practically no *real* unemployment there.

Geoffrey Heyworth said he reckoned never to give more than 25% of his time to work outside Unilever and to take on only things he would put effort and time into. He regarded his 3 years on the Royal Commission on Taxation as the one really unfruitful use of his time because N.K. had spoken for 70% of the total time at each meeting and often contradicted himself. He had had understandings with N.K. on, for example, capital gains tax and lower rates of surcharge but in the end N.K. had lined up his Minority none the less. In future G.H. would not go out of his way to seek a unanimous Report. He had just been on point of resignation when Cohen[2] persuaded him to stay – and then resigned himself.

He spoke strongly on need for more study of psychology (no chair at L.S.E.). Also thought that Roblin, not Stanfield, should have been chosen to lead Canadian conservatives. Manitoba had gone furthest to resolve French-English problem: joint language in schools since 1971.

Friday, 5 January   Second meeting at No.10 at 11.30 with TUC. They felt entitled to urge that government plans should be based firmly on the assumption that productivity would rise twice as fast as in 1950's. Firms ought to be given export targets as a means of getting exports up more quickly. If the government wanted TUC support it would have to make a deal covering all kinds of selective intervention and innovations in policy.

The discussion at No.10 was pretty typical. The P.M., armed with a good brief from Donald, took firm charge while Sydney Greene tried to work through the series of questions that Murray had set for him to ask. The P.M. had the ability to out-talk anybody else, to speak sensibly on general issues, diminish potential disagreements, and yet in detail make the most foolish propositions in the knowledge that they were meat and drink to the TUC. The Chancellor spoke twice and to considerable effect, making the main points about the risks and objectives. Peter Shore and Ray Gunter intervened mainly on side issues. On the TUC side, it was Cousins who inevitably did most of the talking, with Len Murray on his left and Woodcock on his right. I have rarely heard such a passionate declaration of protectionism. He wanted everybody to Buy British and indulged in a long attack on imports of all kinds without reflecting that with full employment, cheap imports become more important that job security. He also failed to take the point that if the balance of payments is to improve, *total* consumption has to be checked in relation to *total* production.

The discussion brought out the essential étatisme of the TUC leaders. They wanted a fussy intervention in detail and like the P.M. distrusted all *general* policies. If the subject was training of skilled labour they wanted to know *which* Scottish firms claimed to have difficulty recruiting it so that action could

[2] Lord Cohen – Chm. of the Council on Prices, Productivity and Incomes, of which Lord Heyworth was a member.

be taken there. If there was a shortage of capacity they wanted to know *where* it would arise so that it could be expanded in time. If firms didn't expand their exports fast enough they wanted the firms identified so that their workers could "get after them". The economy was to be regulated and planned down to the last detail. The P.M. pandered to all this and "enthused" one of them by his description of how joint consultation might be brought to bear on exports. But he stuck to it that we shouldn't aim at too fast a rate of expansion or generate a consumer boom. He also spoke sensibly at the end on incomes policy and insisted that while they couldn't take on an unrealistic target we couldn't risk seeing them bless a uniform or minimum increase of 4% in wages.

The P.M.'s interventions were also satisfyingly circumstantial. He could say exactly what was happening to unemployment, region by region, what the plans of the motor industry amounted to, what the Express Dairy Co. had just done to Back Britain by keeping its prices down. If a problem needed some government pronouncement, he was just about to make it on his visit to Wales or Liverpool or .... He knew what the Green Book had said about the closing of reg. unemployment differentials. There wasn't the least suggestion that he had a difficult Cabinet meeting less than an hour away. He just puffed on his pipe and kept on talking. And whatever one might think of what he said the TUC were just appalling.

In fact Victor Feather said as much to me at the end. He was shocked that they should be pressing a 6% expansion on us when we thought 3% normal on past form. He agreed that George W. had somehow linked the 6% with his 3%/4% norm and that it made more sense to think in longer run terms of wage norms. But nobody else on their side said any of this: Carron contented himself with a brief question about the effect of the American measures. I wonder what Walpole would have made of it, looking down from behind the P.M.'s chair.

I gather from Peter B. that the Cabinet meeting went well and that the Chancellor lost nothing and is well on the way to his main objectives: prescription charges and the raising of S.L.A. are both settled in principle. My US visitor today (O'Leary) said that the restoration of prescription charges would have a great effect in US because they would feel that this was typical of socialised medicine and the over-spending to which it led.

Friday, 12 January   Most of this week and last were full of public expenditure cuts and final decisions don't look like getting taken till Monday or even Tuesday when the statement is to be made. I spent Tuesday and Wednesday in Geneva on EFTA business with F. Figgures.

Yesterday we had CM(O) with Nicky and me as the two Treasury economists at M.P.'s suggestion. We agreed to work on £600m as a basis for extra taxation and were told that Budget might be as early as March 19. N.K. asked why the anxiety to get it early. William said (a) to put an end to uncertainty, and (b) to get out of the embarrassment of being about to do something and not able to say what. (The IMF will be in London in mid-February and people will ask what was agreed.)

N.K. saw no virtue in advancing the date of payment of corporation tax (on which I've been pressing A.J.) so I feel free to make light of his anxieties about liquidity. He also took issue with me on direct taxation when I said that this would have to do half the job. He thinks that doubling SET plus some indirect taxation would be enough. But we *won't* double SET.

All this led to some pantomime on the Reddaway enquiry which we won't announce now till well after the Budget because N.K. thinks that it would tie the Chancellor's hands on SET to get this going and then suddenly double SET.

Lunch at Unilever's with Zinkin[3] who said that what matters for growth was receptivity to change and this was a function of education. The A level stage meant a diminution in emotional involvement and a degree the beginning of a rational approach to problem identification. Business men had to be taught to identify their problems, to give priority to the major ones, to think clearly about solving them. I said if Unilever was struggling with these shortcomings with so many graduates what hope could there be for the rest of industry? Z. said that in 1950 they had no economists – now they had over 50. They hadn't gone for graduates until 1950. I asked whether non-graduates weren't more money-oriented: where did drive begin? Robert Hall said that morale suffered most from muddle. With clear thinking, drive would be generated because there would be a clearer perception of role and identification with that role. I pointed out that taking on graduates might lead to disappointment: they might feel neglected by the management and yet be envied by their contemporaries working alongside them as enjoying the favour of the management.

Thursday, 18 January   Whitehall D.C. at Brown's Hotel with W.A. as host. Very depressing discussion opened by William with quotation from Jim Callaghan in the car: "Why do Labour Governments always handle finance the wrong way?" Of course we didn't stick to the question and Franks in particular took us on to much wider issues about prospects for democracy. He spoke of balkanisation in the absence of leadership – assertion by powerful groups of sheer self-interest. William said government had looked too exclusively to legislation, to existing political institutions, to continuing its Parliamentary majority when Parliament no longer had the same significance. In non-Parliamentary relations, foreign, financial, press, etc. the Government had been conspicuously unsuccessful but now it might have difficulty *in* Parliament as time wore on and Party Conference approached.

The business men spoke strongly and scornfully of the P.M. Bill Harcourt thought his removal alone would help to restore confidence. Foreigners had told him that nothing we could do would restore confidence without this. Rowley said he doubted whether we would get to another election under the same P.M. without a change of parity.

I doubted whether there was much in it between Labour Chancellors and Conservative and thought that it was much more in the handling of a crisis that the distinction lay – Tories could rally the country where Labour fell apart or aroused antagonisms.

[3] M Zinkin Economist with Unilever.

William also spoke of various forms of social malingering – of the way people had no need to think of work since they could live without it and draw a comfortable income.

Denis cited Uruguay as an example of the ultimate in the welfare state: with power to bequeath a pension.

The odd thing was how little was said about the economy or the policies required and what *was* said (e.g. by Oliver) was not very sensible (e.g. on incomes policy where he recited the dilemma but didn't point to clear solutions).

Yesterday I went in early for the Chancellor's speech. He left at 11 for the meeting of the Party without having written the chunk on defence but saying that he would have 2½ hours from 1 p.m. to put it together. He seemed more concerned about whether it should be single spaced or double spaced than about the language and was advised that he should use single spacing as there would be less pages to turn over and less appearance of reading from a prepared text.

He is against giving balance of payments forecasts (like Bob Roosa whose advice to Fred D. was never to give one to WP No. 3 since it would invariably be wrong) but agreed to put in an "undated target" of £500m.[4] He also felt that exposition in terms of increment in output and allocation of resources in 1969 was too much like counting chickens and would make it seem too easy.

Wynne raised fundamental doubts about big increase in taxation because balance of payments might not improve as fast as we assumed. We had a long argument and I minuted William. But all the pressure is now on government to do maximum in Budget (or earlier). People are *anxious* to have their consumption cut even if it won't benefit balance of payments much and might merely increase unemployment. Difficult to tell them not to be silly if we mean to levy big increase in taxation in two months' time. But their outlook derives from the form of calculation that W.G. favoured since they are told the eventual bill and assume they ought to be paying it now (even while they resent higher prices in the shops!).

Sunday, 21 January   Morale is very low and the papers full of assured proposals for putting things right. At first the business reaction was bad because spokesmen like John Davies said that there would be no real net advantage left for exporters. Then that wore off and I thought we had reached the watershed with the *F.T.* Monthly Report on Jan. 8 showing improved prospects, the rise in exports, the fall in unemployment and the cuts in public expenditure. But for the moment, the pundits have decided that the government should have done everything at one go to provide £1,000m for the balance of payments and feel appalled at the government's mishandling of affairs. They are turning their guns on the civil service. But of course we advised Jim C. to do more than enough and he asked me if I was talking politics. I don't know what advice

---

[4] The current account deficit in 1968 came to £273 million, much as we had expected *before* devaluation. The improvement at which we were aiming was in progress but was much slower than we had expected, largely because of the remarkable buoyancy of imports. By 1971 there was a current account surplus of over £1,000 million.

William gave the Chancellor but I made it clear that I thought there was a case for announcing the main tax changes along with the public expenditure cuts. Even so, it is arguable whether this would have been right and there is no real justification for the press hullabaloo except that the public have been lashed into a state of masochistic fury and want to know what price they must pay in higher taxes. It may be that by March they will be less willing to see taxes go up but it will certainly be more necessary.

ESG on Friday rather quiet – on Donald's paper. Had a long talk with Douglas Allen afterwards about the use of computers in forecasting.

Ministers debated use of hire purchase in Friday and we briefed Chancellor against. They agreed that a plan should be prepared for emergency use of hire purchase and regulator but apparently were not in favour of doing anything now.

Tuesday, 23 January   Extraordinary to think that P.M.'s speech on 16 January is only a week away. On Sunday the 14th there seemed to be dozens of us in the Treasury reading bits – Ian Bancroft, Louis Petch, Peter Vinter, etc., etc. – and then came the preparations for the Chancellor's TV talk and his speech. There had also been lots of confusion in Cabinet with the Chancellor talking wildly of a shift of £1,600m in resources and corresponding budgetary requirements (based on taking the deficit at £400m in Q3, and doubling it). I thought the P.M.'s statement lacking in a theme and rationale: too much a shopping list. The Chancellor got this right in his speech after some efforts by M.P. and myself to get him to do some forward-looking arithmetic. But he dislikes showing extra output and allocating it when it is still to come as if it meant counting chickens.

We had a quick run over his speech on Wednesday morning and the Chancellor proved a quick editor and quite confident about the way he would present things.

Yesterday we had another long session on the Budget with N.K. and K.B. present but not M.P. who is in Paris. N.K. of course got in first and was full of ideas. Chancellor began by asking if he had made a mistake in not using the regulator. William said it was "an expenditure occasion" and the others agreed that it would have been wrong to operate in advance of the Budget although N.K. had a hankering after hire purchase on cars some time soon. I said there was a case for announcing the main tax changes but it would have been difficult if not impossible. Chancellor said if it had been a full Budget, Chief Secretary would have had to prepare it.

Later N.K. pushed SET saying that there was no real outcry against it since no questions were ever put in Gallop polls. Chancellor said that one could imagine various forms of poll tax that would be economic nonsense and never excite mass opinion. N.K. at once protested SET wasn't economic nonsense and Chancellor had to explain that he was talking "purely in hypothetical terms".

Later N.K. referred to a Select Committee of 1909 (on the earned income allowance) when they had ignored salaries of over £2,000 as practically non-existent. Chancellor trumped this one by referring to minority report by Sir Charles Dilke and saying that it was not an occasion on which he showed to greatest advantage.

I don't think I ever noted down the occasion when at S.P.C. T.B. talked of "hometake pay" while all the native British kept quiet only to hear N.K. say impatiently: "the word is take-home, Tommy, not hometake. Why don't you talk English?".

Wednesday, 24 January   CM(O) took my paper on Budget measures and discussed the shape of the Budget. Very little real argument since we were merely looking at possible menus. We agreed to stick to £600 m. although this excludes Corporation Tax and might include things to take effect in 1969 like investment grants or FAM. The clear argument is that we can't count on supplementing whatever we do by later action (except perhaps HP) and must err and be seen to err on the safe side. In Paris we were told that 4% was too high a rate of expansion but it was assumed that 3% and £600m would be compatible so we may yet please everybody. William said to Chancellor on Monday that it would be best to do more than commentators thought likely.

Chancellor on Monday also spoke of opening a window on the incentive debate: by which he seemed to contemplate not raising the marginal rate on earned income whatever was done on unearned income. He enunciated the principle that when you had to do a lot it should be with the current of public opinion and this justified a higher betting tax and apparently little or no increase in income tax. But of course there is nothing to speak of in betting tax and a possible £250m or more in sixpence on income tax.

Bill Nield spoke to me at lunch about the "arrogance" of ministers and about their inability to understand macro-economic problems. Crossman was particularly bad and Bill felt deeply about his TV performance on "the worst informed government in Europe" – the reverse of the truth. He said that Roy was more successful in Cabinet than Jim who had been weak or mulish while Roy remained firm. When Roy had spoken of two separate £1,000m in Cabinet nobody had contested it except Crosland who was at pains to be helpful except on Departmental issues. I commented on the extraordinary absence of any document setting out the economic outlook for the Cabinet but this has been typical of the past three years and more. If they lack information it is because they don't ask for it.

Thatcher[5] says that many firms that found themselves eligible to pay SET because classified as non-manufacturers have insisted on re-classification and this means that the SIC itself is now being revised and that the figures of employment will be correspondingly delayed (to end of February). Naturally this implies that apparent fall in employment in distribution etc. is exaggerated. The Ministry of Labour and Board of Trade will use different systems of classification in 1968.

Thursday, 25 January   I had a long meeting with Treasury advisers and F.F. on export credit; an earlier one with Burke on the future of the C.S.O. in which B. came out for full centralisation. He also accepted that there would be an

[5] A R (Roger) Thatcher – Dep. Dir. of Statistics, Ministry of Labour, 1963–68; Director, Dept. of Employment, 1968–72.

increasingly political angle to work of the C.S.O. and yet somehow thought that C.S.O. (without a Minister) could be left to issue press releases on balance of payments, etc. His reason for wanting a single centralised service was the tendency among Ministers to dispute each other's statistics and regard the departmental statistics apparatus as suspect. But of course this is why the C.S.O. was set up in the first place. Most departmental statistics are not handled by professional statisticians (e.g. public expenditure) and may be used for operational purposes. Social statistics are another problem – or Inland Revenue.

M.P. and D. Rickett told us this morning that they had a difficult time at WP No. 3 but the French said little. On other hand, they were very obstructive on what seemed purely technical matters in Group of Ten. They want to see Ministerial meeting as do the Swedes (Wickman is in the Chair); they see advantage in making difficulties even if they finally give way. F.F. said this might well be their way of keeping the Six together: ensuring that meetings had to take place to get them to come into line, or at least to try to iron out differences. But the Dutch line is not to agree to *any* meetings of the Six and it isn't clear that Luns[6] even knows that the Monetary Committee has met. The other 5 can see no point in reaching a common line on things about which they differ even inside their own governments.

Sunday, 28 January   A quiet week-end with some sporadic work on export credit.

On Friday I was busy at meetings on Stat. Policy and Export Credit. The first was remarkably sensible with Edmund Dell[7] in the Chair and some of the younger ministers doing most of the talking Mrs Lerner, Roy Hattersley,[8] and Freeson[9]. T.B. was absent then and in afternoon.

Monday, 29 January   At lunch I talked to Brazier[10] and Wadsworth on economic advisers in business and to whom they should report. B. said he reported to the Head of the Marketing Department and did some work for the Chairman (when he went to NEDC). I asked if his work was on company internal affairs or on external relations and he said the latter. Dunlop's are a large international company and so have to keep track of world events and trends. B. also said that domestic affairs come under the Financial Director but that on long term planning the economists and accountants get together. In many businesses the economist reports to the Finance Director. John Wadsworth said that in the Midland the Economic Adviser was now head of an operating division and

[6] Joseph Luns – Dutch Minister of Foreign Affairs, 1956–71; Pres., NATO Council, 1958–59; Sec. Gen., NATO, 1971–83.

[7] Edmund Dell – Parliamentary Sec., Min of Technology, 1966–67; Jt. Parliamentary Sec., DEA, 1967–68; Minister of State, Board of Trade, 1968–69; DEA, 1969–70.

[8] Roy Hattersley – Labour PPS to Minister of Pensions and National Insurance, 1964–67; Jt. Parliamentary Sec., Dept. of Employment, 1967–69.

[9] Reginald Freeson – Parliamentary Sec. to the Min. of Power, 1968–69.

[10] Brazier – Business economist with Dunlop Rubber Co.

took part in the main Executive Committee under the Chief General Manager and alongside the eight Joint Managers. This was the new style managerial revolution. B. said economists should be used more as staff officers and that industry didn't yet use properly the military distinction between line and staff. He agreed that forecasting and planning was the natural operational sphere of the economist. I said that few economists were trained for business and that the Business Schools should teach them what was involved in the *planning* of a business with programmes, monitoring, etc. instead of *DCF*, model-building, etc. The Glasgow tradition of economist, accountant, and industrial relations expert was best.

Tuesday, 30 January   35 years since the burning of the Reichstag....

I saw William this morning and confirmed my willingness to take over from Denis at Gp of 10. He made it clear that he thought Donald should replace me as Head of GES, go to No. 10, and make life more difficult there for T.B. I agreed that we ought not to bring in yet another academic economist.[11]

Lunch at Bank of England. Talked first to M. Parsons then (at lunch) to Governor. Overby said he lunched first at Bank of England in 1947 when the IMF Annual Meeting took place at the Institute of Civil Engineers in Great George St. The lunch was in the Court Room and it was the first time the C.R. had been used for a Bank lunch. Hugh Dalton[12] was also there.

M.P. worried about February maturities which will be over £1,000m (William told me Chancellor had also been brooding on them over the week-end and was still unsure whether he might not have to act to check consumer spending). He thinks that everything hangs on the Budget because we may find that with loss of confidence other countries cash their sterling and even refuse to trade in sterling. I said that people had far too gloomy a view and seemed to think that an extra 1% or 2% on wages this year would offset the whole of a devaluation of 1/7. Once the export orders came in, and they would, the whole atmosphere would change. It was clear that M.P. shared the gloom and felt that the caution shown by business was thoroughly justified. I pointed out that every time a survey was taken it showed that what the City was alleged to think bore no relation to what business was planning. The clearest example was export prices where there was now abundant evidence that sterling prices were being quoted some 6–7% higher – not 14–16%. On export prospects and investment prospects the same story could be repeated.

With the Governor and M. Allen the talk was mainly on incomes policy and they both stressed (like M.P.) the importance of a tough line. But they don't really understand incomes policy and are thinking rather nostalgically of a freeze like that of July 1966. M.A. even contemplated one of three months only. They don't like to be reminded that wages are rising faster in almost every other European country or that if we *did* have an effective wage freeze it would mean

[11] As explained below (p. 284), it was subsequently arranged that Sam Goldman should be the Treasury representative on the Group of Ten.

[12] Hugh Dalton – Labour Chancellor of the Exchequer, 1945–47.

an *enormous* increase in profits and further deflation on a big scale.

The question now is going to be whether we stick to the proposed tax programme even if our forecasts show an increase in output of only 3%. But I doubt whether this is at all likely. We could easily show 4% on one basis for exports and 3% on another, *after* a big tax increase.

We discussed arrangements for IMF consultations starting Feb. 20 with OECD joining in at the start but IMF don't like the idea of OECD participation.

Chancellor going to Washington April 2, P.M. Feb. 8.

William said Douglas Allen would want to concentrate mainly on financial side and spend some time going with Chancellor to IMF/OECD/etc. He doesn't know Schweitzer.

Jasper Rootham told me tonight that 3 or 4 weeks before Cromer left the Bank, J. had said to Leslie O'B. that Cromer would be going and Leslie should and would succeed him. L.K. said "You're mad". But Jasper had stuck to it. Leslie, too, is going to US and had hoped to go on to Caribbean for a holiday but Chancellor has vetoed it because of his anxieties for month of February. He has promised Governor to do *more* than people expect. This he may yet do if everybody keeps quiet. But in the light of the public expenditure exercise this may be too much to hope.

The Treasury still thinks that the Letter of Intent was leaked by the French to Fabbra after it reached the French Governor of the IMF. But of course it was leaked in London and the British press only took note after it had *reappeared* in *Le Monde*.

Denis Barnes was very hot tonight about economists in general and *The Economist* in particular, because of the simple-minded approach to incomes policy. He waits for the day when the Government will announce that it hasn't got an incomes policy. R. Kahn was equally vehement on Postan because of his piece in *Encounter* (H. Wincott in today's *Financial Times*).

Sunday, 4 February   Bill Nield appointed Permanent Secretary of DEA. Not a very exciting week. We had a great set-to with N.K. on SET on Friday at which he was very much put out by the way we threw doubt on all his evidence.

We also had a meeting on dividend control at which N. waved away all the administrative difficulties and came up with a fresh proposal to meet each of them. It was quite a lesson in resourcefulness and in the first hand knowledge he has of finance.

Long debate on Thursday evening with Thornton and Hillage of Bank of England on the proposed article for *Economic Trends*. It was interesting to see what kind of mind the Bank breeds. By the time we were finished Thornton was quite willing to say "Exactly" when I suggested that perhaps "as a layman" I could form a better view of the reception the article would get. They feel such pride in their own achievements that they don't stop to think that other people may have worked it out for themselves.

The press is now completely quiet about the P.M. and the economic situation: the Stock Exchange is having a wonderful boom: and most people have forgotten all about the Budget but *are* alive to the way prices are rising.

First results of forecast to hand: $4\frac{1}{2}\%$ this year, 4% next and no increase in consumption even if no increase in taxation. This will need some reflection and doesn't point to quite so severe a Budget as we expected – one that would surprise by its severity.[13]

Wednesday, 7 February   William called me today to say that Barclays, Lloyds and Martins were about to merge and that this would be announced tomorrow together with a reference to the Monopolies Commission. Could I see whether R. Sayers would be willing to serve as reinforcement? I was lunching with John Wall and R.S. joined me at 2. Troubled but obviously trying to see how he could do it alongside all his other duties. He rang William later and will be seeing him.

Thursday, 8 February   W.A. seems more relaxed now. After hearing us all at Directorate on our various problems he remarked: "I'm very sorry for you all" which as the first sign that his mind is gravitating away from us produced a slight shock followed by a good laugh. Of the announcements about planning – at NEDC the Government was committed to submitting papers without any real forethought on the implications of the commitment – he said: "It looks as if we'd built another shell without waiting for the hen". And at ESG when Douglas Allen arrived he said that we were starting by preparing the agenda – "a practice I normally associate with disarmament conferences".

On Tuesday I gathered from William that the Chancellor had arrived at tentative proposals for £620m in taxation. He had talked to N.K. who said "Fine". The Chancellor asked if N.K. hadn't been arguing for £1,000m and N. then told him about the forecasts (which I lent him overnight) but added that he shouldn't believe them.

Nobody seems to know what view Chancellor takes of incomes policy (e.g. freeze or ceiling) or of planning. But he did receive miscellaneous and conflicting advice on the latter. He hasn't discussed dividend control with us but is putting in the paper by officials while they, too, are in disagreement.

N. now says budget deficit will be only £800m allowing for items like investment grants etc. which he treats as non-income generating. This is his "normal deficit" and ought to mean *no* increase in taxation but he won't, I expect, take this line (cf above on talk to Chancellor).

Chancellor and Co. will discuss on Monday after SEP possible use of regulator and hire purchase. But there would be little point in acting now with the Budget just over a month away.

P.M. in Washington but nobody can see what he can usefully do there.

---

[13] Our forecast was that there would be no increase in personal spending even in the absence of higher taxation and further hire purchase restriction. This seemed on general grounds very implausible, as DEA maintained, and in fact consumption was 3 per cent higher in 1968 than in 1967. The big increase took place in the first quarter, before the Budget.

Monday, 12 February   A quiet week-end in which I got quite a lot done – two sides of tape. The forecasts arrived punctually on Friday afternoon and I discussed them with Fred and Co. in advance of today's meeting of Treasury economists and others, tomorrow's of the Economic Advisers as a Group and (in the morning) CM(O).

N.K. was, for once, not ill-disposed towards the forecasts and quite moderate in his arguments (though no doubt £300m in taxation last year would seem moderate to him in comparison with £600m now). Nobody bid under £400m. Denis argues that we ought to go now for 3% instead of 4% because 3% is "politically possible" now where it wasn't before (£1,300m in taxation!). He says OECD will regard £400m as just adequate, £500m as good, and £600m as very good. My own line was that we could afford to come down a little from £600m especially if action was spread over the year.

N.K. also strong on SET, less hot on taxes on consumption. He claims that the latest Ministry of Labour figures *prove* that SET did increase productivity greatly.

Afternoon meeting with Chief Secretary on trade, aid, loans, at which he shared my scepticism but, like me, was persuaded by F.F. and Denis to take a less hostile view of the new export credit proposals.

Tuesday, 13 February   Two long meetings on Budget, one of CM (at which Douglas Allen and Richard Powell appeared, resuming the Board of Trade link that broke in 1964) and one of Ec. Adv. under Sir D.M. The first was comparatively uneventful. We all agreed on £500m at my suggestion and N.K., who spoke after me said only: "I do not dissent from what has been said". But he made up for this unwonted taciturnity later by embarking on a long exposition of the virtues of SET. He spoke of the irrationality of arguing about lack of evidence of a switch of labour into manufacturing when employment in manufacturing and distribution was contracting and this provoked Douglas to say: "You mustn't expect politicians to be convinced by rational arguments" and when N.K. protested that they should hear the arguments D. reiterated: "You can get them to listen but you don't necessarily convince them".

Later N.K. had a long argument with me on the statistical evidence and when I finally told him that I thought he had "a strong case" he embraced me and urged me to say so to the Chancellor. I said I would want to talk to Wynne G. first. I rang W.G. in the evening and he satisfied me that what I had said to N.K. was consistent with our view of the operation of SET while N.K.'s view went a lot further.

The meeting in the afternoon at DEA seemed to me nonsensical. The Economic Advisers were being asked to comment on the forecasts without any of the forecasters being present.

Aside from this the idea of preparing a paper by the Economic Advisers for submission to W.A. and D.A. of exactly the same character as my own submission to the Budget Committee also seemed preposterous, especially as the Chancellor will be reaching conclusions tomorrow and will have virtually settled what to do by next Tuesday (i.e. the day before the IMF discussions begin: the reason for this is that Custom Duties need to be settled that far in advance of the Budget).

In the car, going to the CAS, William said of Denis: "I know nobody who is more successful in making the straightforward answer look like the sensible one".

At the reception I talked to Alfred[14] of Courtaulds who was arguing that there could be no theory of the firm since everything rested on personality in management, that the one advantage of economists was their understanding of marginal theory (preferably in the first Chapter of Joan Robinson on *Imperfect Competition*) and that it was best to recruit scientists who did economics *after* graduation. But he spoke up for the Arts men who appreciated that there were several answers or different questions to be asked: a combination of arts and science was best.

Wednesday, 14 February   On Monday after SEP Ministers agreed not to use the Regulator or Hire Purchase although P. Shore was in favour of tightening Hire Purchase and this view reflected Donald's.

We had a long meeting today with the Chancellor on taxation. He began by saying that it had been quite chastening to see how volatile our forecasts were. He had made a speech earlier in the week in terms of 4 per cent and had he not been careful to express himself rather guardedly he would have felt some resentment because he hadn't been warned. He took us through the export forecast, enquiring why we had changed our view of world trade. How often had the forecasts been right? Was the last one right? etc.

Nicky gave the Chancellor a long account of his independent calculations which showed that with 3% we'd have a surplus of about £340m in 1969 but with 4% it would only be about £100m (all based on calculations of the Budget deficit and nothing else, except the assumed swing in exports, I believe). The Chancellor pulled his leg by asking how *he* allowed for a poorer outlook for world trade and how he could calculate down to the last £10m.

The interesting feature of it all was that the Chancellor would like to get away with a Budget raising indirect taxes only – no income tax, no SET. So we had, as N.K. foresaw, a tussle on SET but didn't seem to make much impression on him or shake him on grounds of regressive taxation. I said that he ran the risk of a rise of 4% in the cost of living in two months because 2 points on taxation might coincide with 2 points through devaluation effects and high seasonal prices for food.

At Jap. reception tonight at 1 Carlton House Gardens I spoke to Joel Barnet[15] who said that P. Jay was putting it about that J.C. had been in favour of devaluation in July 1966. Barnet didn't believe this and said that if true it reflected badly on C. because he and G.B. could have forced the P.M. to agree. He also

[14] A M Alfred – Head of Economics Dept., Courtauld, 1953–59; preached the need to use DCF calculations in capital budgeting.
[15] Joel Barnet – Chm., Labour Party Econ. and Finance Group, 1967–70 and 1972–74 (Vice Chm., 1966–67).

said he couldn't forgive Peter for his famous article on the P.M. after devaluation. I said he was tight when he wrote it but J.B. said that Peter still took the same line in conversation with him. As J.C.'s son-in-law he should have shown more circumspection.

At today's meeting with Chancellor William was remarkably quiet. The only surprise to me was that he showed obvious scepticism of our forecast of personal consumption and took the DEA line. I minuted the Chancellor on SET after talking to W.G. and N.K. and on the whole sided with N.K. on the statistical evidence.

Sunday, 18 February   Nicky told me that in William's view (but William said nothing to me) the danger was that Chancellor would go to P.M. with Budget proposing increase exclusively in terms of indirect taxation up to £450m and find that P.M. would insist on maximum of £250m. This doesn't seem to me a very likely story except as it applies to the Chancellor who is plainly determined to rely almost entirely on indirect taxation. He would listen to neither N. nor to me on SET nor even to the argument that if the cost of living went up by 2 points it might become 4 because of seasonal and other influences in March and April. Such a rise could hardly fail to provoke strong reactions. N. himself would now like £200m in SET, not o130 m. and would rest content with £200–£250m in indirect taxation (including motor vehicle licences).

We had a meeting with William and the other Treasury advisers partly to let them put their views, partly to prepare for IMF/OECD, on Friday morning. Some disposition again to contrast big increase in consumption in 1967 (4%) and small increase in GDP with opposite situation forecast for 1968. Donald rang me up to say $1/2$% off the savings ratio seemed very small and I told him that this was what DEA had asked us to try. But I agree that there are various links in the argument that are all rather weak so that consumption might well rise more this year than we are allowing. The budget changes we propose cover this possibility.

I have not been asked for a formal submission to Chancellor although I have written several papers for CM(O). But Fred's E.F. paper seems to deal adequately with assessment and no doubt William has conveyed orally the gist of our conclusions about £500m.

Chancellor will make up his mind this week-end about the shape of his Budget and we will see him on Monday and have a final CM(O) on Tuesday followed by EF on Wednesday (by which time IMF will be upon us).

Chancellor will also have to decide on publication of forecasts. Curiously enough, it is the political advisers who now have cold feet: on the whole the regulars are in favour though we recognise that an official forecast will be treated as a plan and should be issued, with that in mind, *after* the Budget.

Government out on a limb on submissions to NEDC on medium term plan: one after the Budget and then a fuller one in the autumn. This could quickly land us back with a full scale plan of the old type. P. Shore also arguing for more selective intervention to help the balance of payments *after* 1970. He thinks economists negative when they point out what a mess the aluminium smelter ['Uncle'] has got us into and how long it takes to settle an issue of that kind. There has been well over a year of argument and nothing is settled yet. In fact they seem to want the smelter to run on coal *stocks* and speak of stocks still mounting in *1974*![16]

Another ministerial committee thinks that the Economic Advisers are now a separate department and have a staff at their disposal. Of course, it may yet happen but the marvel is that they agree on anything. As I told Hester Boothroyd,[17] the economists *will* argue while at least administrators know the value of reaching agreement. Economists are passionate for truth but don't always appreciate that they don't know it and never will. It helps when there is an opposite camp to solidify them.

Wednesday, 21 February   We had a meeting on Monday with Chancellor and on Tuesday of CM(O) on Budget. This morning I gave a kind of address to IMF/OECD teams on the forecasts.

The Chancellor strongly resisted efforts by Nicky to get him to use SET. "The only people I have met who have a word to say in favour of SET" he said "are in this room". Nicky told him that it would be regarded as a Tory budget and that if Labour were in opposition it would "tear it to bits". The Chancellor didn't flinch. I took the line that so heavy a dependence on indirect taxation would not make for industrial peace and that he ought to consider again direct taxation or SET. Opinions about the latter would change once the figures were available. But the Chancellor said that SET was, after all, indirect taxation. We all agreed on rejecting corporation tax *this* year. Nicky also attacked strongly the proposal to get more revenue from marriage allowance – "perks of the poor" – and surtax on investment income ("millionaires don't pay surtax – only civil servants who can't escape it").

Later Chancellor saw P.M. who took no exception to shape of budget even though it does nothing really to help the poor (*no* give aways) or tax the rich (except the surtax). He did remind the Chancellor that the CBI had proposed that corporation tax be increased and income tax cut (before devaluation) but as A.J. pointed out there is really nothing in this because the cut in income tax would be negligible.

N. came to see me in the evening to suggest that we should combine our forces better. This was because I had queried the idea that employment changed by 2 times unemployment and so there could have been no evasion of SET (the Chancellor raised this hare). I told him that it was not just the Chancellor who would have to be convinced and that P.M. might be of same view. If we persuaded Chancellor *not* to impose indirect taxation he might later draw back from SET or income tax and therefore we mustn't push this too hard.

Yesterday we had a meeting with D. Allen and William on forecasts and planning. Forecasts are *not* to go to ministers since P.M. feels they may draw

[16] Alcan were building one of the aluminium smelters using cheap electricity under the scheme code-named 'Uncle'.

[17] Hester Boothroyd – in 1966 Asst. Under-Sec. of State in the General Planning Group of DEA.

wrong conclusions and instead Economic Advisers will do a paper on lines of Donald's note (the one that carried an addendum saying that although incomes policy was given little space we really thought it pretty important!).

On planning Douglas insisted that we had to give figures in form of a target for, say, 1972 – not just 3% potential or the assumptions we would make for our own purposes. He agreed that he would like to see the whole thing scrapped but politically Ministers were committed to putting in something high as guide to little Neddies. But I don't see how we stop short of another Nat. Plan once we start on this tack.

Meeting today uneventful since we gave them our forecasts very formally and trust them to keep quiet. They are still suspicious of monetary side of the forecast. N.K. gave them a long harangue on sectoral surpluses but they really want to know how we stop liquid funds from defeating the squeeze.

Alexander Gray[18] died earlier this week. A.J. reminded me that in 1905 John Anderson stood first, Gray second and Crerar (another Edinburgh man) third in the Home Civil Exam.

Friday, 23 February   At Directorate atmosphere as R. Armstrong[19] said later was a little like that of a Russian trial with Nicky confessing that P. Jay had spoken to him on Tuesday but denying that he gave anything away. Nevertheless P. Jay has a pretty accurate view of what it all adds up to though he has nothing on 1969 and gets some facts wrong.

John Fay[20] gave us his view after discussions of the prospects for 1968-69. He thought that we needed to cut demand in the Budget by £800m basing this, not on our forecast, but on our forecast plus maximum exports. We pointed out that this meant double insurance and would imply an enormous surplus in 1969. We also said (as we did to IMF) that 3% growth after the Budget (i.e. 1968 I –1969 I) didn't require action on anything like this scale. Fay had no draft and seemed quite prepared to circulate one after his return to Paris without showing it to us. Naturally we protested and I rang up C. Dow to reinforce this. A delay of one day is hardly material compared with the risks the Secretariat would run if they put in (unintentionally) a damaging phrase or figure.

I haven't heard how later discussions with IMF have gone. They leave on Tuesday and this means that Chancellor will be able to say on Tuesday in House of Commons that he hasn't seen them except for a few minutes over drinks.

Lunch with Ronnie Edwards alone and lots of gossip. I asked him about NEDC and he regards his morning a month at meetings of Neddy as the most fruitless and futile use of his time. He didn't think it could come to anything with Catherwood as Secretary. I said it was difficult for the government to find a role for it although Ministers seemed to be curiously enthusiastic. It could

[18] Alexander Gray – Prof. of Political Economy, University of Edinburgh.

[19] R Armstrong – Sec., Radcliffe Cttee, 1957–59; Asst. Sec., Cabinet Office, 1964–66; Asst. Sec., Home Finance Division, Treasury, 1967–68; PPS to Roy Jenkins, 1968; Under-Sec. (Home Finance) 1968–70.

[20] John Fay – long-serving member of staff of OECD.

either sponsor an able secretariat, issuing documents that educated opinion and focussed public attention on important issues, or it could try to get agreement on some common declarations especially on incomes policy. But it was doing neither. There had to be some useful continuous activity involving the Secretariat. But the Secretariat had no prestige and nobody of real ability.

Meeting this morning under D. MacD. at 9.45 to prepare a paper on forecasts for SEP. T.B. actually arrived first! This is all because P.M. doesn't want to circulate EF forecasts in case they are misunderstood – when most members of SEP have access to them anyhow. The P.M. also wants to see the report we prepare before circulation. It was a little comic to hear Ken Berrill speaking of not affronting the Chancellor and so making him less sympathetic to building up the Economic Advisers as a group.

Later had a somewhat heated argument with Hester Boothroyd and Nankivell[21] over the way DEA dissented *after* all the work on the forecasts was over.

It is really a fearful waste of time to thrash out drafts of this kind after the Budget has in all essentials been settled – indeed the Chancellor is bound to claim in time that he had settled it before he saw Goode[22] (which means long before he can possibly see the draft).

Sunday, 25 February   I should have recorded that at Tuesday's meeting R. Armstrong said it was "95% certain" that Chancellor would not use SET. There was obviously pressure on him at SEP to raise family allowances but the coding has gone too far to claw back most of the increase on the same basis as the 35p increase through the Inland Revenue. The paper by Ec. Adv. will no doubt concentrate on the shape of the budget but here again the battle is really over.

Press has long lost its hysterical tone and now has little on the economy except incomes policy. Not even very much on IMF or OECD (presence of OECD not even known to the press). Immigration issue has stolen the headlines. But there are indications of storms ahead within the Party (see Nora Beloff in today's *S.T.*).

Ronnie Edwards talked to me about Jewkes[23] and said how much better he could have written the attack on planning. But who had stood up among the critics to denounce indicative planning in its heyday? Who had said that the National Plan was nonsense at its birth? (Answer: Ely Devons?). It was no use getting worked up over government interference and bureaucracy – you had to live with them. Indignation settled nothing.

We also talked about Alcan[24] and I said what an excellent case study it was in selective intervention. It was over a year since it all started and nothing had been decided even now. The government got into deeper and deeper water, and the worst was probably still to come.

[21] O Nankivell – Statistician in DEA.

[22] Dick Goode – Economist with IMF who was usually leader in negotiations with UK.

[23] John Jewkes – First Director of the Economic Section, with which Harold Wilson was associated in 1941. Author of *Ordeal by Planning*.

[24] Alcan was one of the firms scheduled to build an aluminium smelter.

Tuesday, 27 February   S. Brittan today has a scoop on Treasury forecasts. William read the article to ESG but nobody could account for the leak any more than we could for P. Jay's. The OECD (for the first time) enter and are said to favour an extra £1,000m in taxation (they mentioned £800m). I suspect DEA as the source.

Lunch yesterday with Milton Gilbert who convinced me that a rise in the price of gold *would* help the US balance of payments. He had spent nearly 3 hours with Denis R. on this on Friday. He told me that after devaluation $1b of Euro-dollars were withdrawn in a week and that this helped to explain the Frankfurt meeting – not just gold.

Appeared today before Select Committee with Mikardo[25] in the Chair. It went not too badly.

Nicky still pleading for SET and arguing with Donald. N. thinks of it as a "paragon" of a tax which doesn't raise prices or reduce consumption but is paid out of higher productivity. Tommy half arguing for hire purchase in the Budget to keep prices down.

C. Dow will bring draft of OECD paper but we've seen none of it yet and they are being incredibly casual about the whole affair. We ought to have had a sight of it long ago. This morning, after all, Dick Goode told us *his* conclusions and read them from a paper. He wants £500–£600 m. in taxes (or h.p.) and 3% growth but at least he says 3% *from now on* and recognises that this means 3.7% from half year to half year. So he isn't far away from us. Very likely it will all be leaked before March 19. The French have just leaked the Canadian drawing on IMF.

Phil Tresize[26] called me on Monday to say the US pretty certain to restrict imports (or boost exports) in early March. Not clear if this would be before or after EPC.

Wednesday, 28 February   C. Dow arrived last night and at once rang up Dick Goode at the Hilton. He left the OECD paper for me this morning and it simply appeared on my desk in a pile of papers. I felt very annoyed since he first promised that John Fay would bring a draft last week (which he did not) then that we would have the policy conclusions yesterday via the Delegation (which we did not) and finally made no attempt to contact me in advance of today's meeting at 11.30 in William's room. In addition it was a highly controversial paper with a proposal to add "something more" than £500m in taxation written into it (in terms that suggested this was the *demand* effect not the revenue effect): i.e well beyond what IMF have suggested. In addition, the balance of payments forecast at 6 1/2% expansion over 2 years is put at the same level as our estimate of 8% expansion: yet we had not a whisper of this from Fay and Co. The whole conduct of business has been incredibly casual with no perception of

[25] Ian Mikardo – M.P.; Member, Nat. Exec. Cttee. of Labour Party, 1950–59 and from 1960; Chm., 1968–70.

[26] Phil Tresize – Dep. Asst. Sec. for Economic Affairs, Washington, 1961–65; Head of the Delegation to OECD, 1966–69; Asst. Sec. Gen. for Economic Affairs from 1969.

the consequences if any of this leaked and very little clear thinking even in the conclusions. Since John Fay's opening gambit was: "what can we do to help?" I find the paper quite extraordinary and the manner of getting it into circulation even more so. It is still being translated into French. Yet this is Wednesday and we finished with Fay last Friday morning.

Van L. took a very different view and seemed willing to leave figures out altogether from WP3 discussion. Lunched at Savoy with him, C.D., and M.P. Dinner at Connaught with Roy Reierson, Harold Wincott, Paul Bareau and Co.

Roy Reierson took view that US ought to stop selling gold but agreed he hadn't thought out the consequences for Euro-dollar market. Relying on Carli, Emminger and Co. to hold dollars and see the US through.

Monday, 4 March   I missed a meeting with the Chancellor on Thursday on the Budget because I had to appear before the Select Committee. Nicky was in despair because the total was working out too low in demand terms, but felt that all was not yet lost on SET. In fact he got me to agree to two paragraphs of press guidance on the new figures and Frances has quite a useful piece in today's *Times*, helped unofficially by our press officer and by instructions from P. Jay. (The others at *The Times* don't find any real evidence that SET is working.)

I went yesterday to a second meeting and there is to be another on Monday. Arranged badly so that I wasn't told and had no papers. Discussion first on dividend restraint. Chancellor wants a $3\frac{1}{2}\%$ norm (which won't matter much this year) not the more complex flexible Dividend Restraint Scheme that is now in its 21st or so edition. Also wants a special contribution à la Cripps (which he rejected earlier when I brought it up). Nicky said at Directorate that he thought the earlier scheme "a shocker" and that when he heard of it in Paris he was shocked. He argued with Chancellor that it would have no effect on demand (though he lays great stress on demand effect of capital gains!) but Chancellor insisted it had *some* effect. Main debate was on hire purchase and SET. We tried to dissuade him from using hire purchase but fact it doesn't raise cost of living is strong argument in his mind. He established that "the official Treasury" was unanimous in wanting SET increased while the other Ministers would use it only if no other way of reaching necessary total. He then said that the two biggest mistakes he had made in office had been on unanimous advice: one in each Ministry and one in accordance, one against, the advice offered. William said the moral was that decisions were difficult when advice was unanimous but in this case it wasn't! Chancellor promised to think it over during week-end and he will also have a look at family allowance clawback.

Main interest of the week has been the immigration bill which has done more even than devaluation to destroy L.J.C.'s reputation. It would seem almost unthinkable now that Labour Party would treat him as successor to H.W.

Paris, Tuesday, 5 March   EPC in Paris. Denis Rickett's final appearance. W.P. No.3 tomorrow afternoon. Lunch with Milton Gilbert and Denis Rickett at Talleven's. Discussion lasted till after 7 with some questions about the French franc area that super-saturated the audience.

Hay greeted me before the meeting with a strong dose of pessimism. He fears that the gold fever won't die now. If one Senator can cause a loss of 70 tons of gold in a few days, it means that people have persuaded themselves that a rise is inevitable and they won't be easily persuaded to the contrary. Milton Gilbert of course would like to say in public what he thinks, and in private he must already be generating a good deal of distrust of gold among central bankers. Rupert Raw argues that the Eastern European bankers are already influenced by the B.I.S. where they are all enthusiasts for a rise in the price of gold. Kessler has done a paper arguing for a sharing arrangement to maintain similar gold ratios in reserves and show conclusively that price will not be increased. At least this means second thoughts on Rio, which is something.

I spoke on UK and said we were unlikely to do more than 4% from now on even in absence of budgetary action and that year on year increase would be under 4% – again on a pre-budget basis. But I insisted that it would be a mistake to rest too much on forecasts. More important to make it possible for exports to grow freely. Public already taking Budget for granted and looking anxiously to movement of money incomes and costs. Business opinion much more buoyant and orders now beginning to respond to change in competitive position.

Emminger was apparently impressed by what I had to say about export prices. The typical reaction in Europe is that British exporters are not exerting themselves and are no great competitive obstacle. This is combined with gloomy views about the US and leads to apocalyptic visions of future disaster. We must brief the Governor for Basle.

Wednesday, 6 March   This morning Denis spoke in the car about devaluation and told me that Everson had tackled a high French official in December about their failure to tell us in advance whether they would move with us. The reply was that they didn't know officially that we intended to devalue until the last moment not till the Friday afternoon. But, said Denis, they weren't supposed to know officially even then. So wasn't there a leak? He still felt that something odd went on in Paris that day and that there was no run on Thursday after the Chancellor had spoken. I said it took time for people to react – but they did!

He also spoke of a conversation he had with the Chancellor at the House of Commons about 8 November when after the business was done he stayed on and the Chancellor locked the door saying he wanted to consult him. The Chancellor told him of my letter and wanted to know what he thought. Denis said he agreed that devaluation seemed inescapable but the Chancellor asked him if it wouldn't be possible to wait till the Spring. Denis naturally said that this must depend on how he would use the time and indicated some of the things he thought might be done.

In the plane from Paris Rupert Raw told me of his own part in the affair. He was with the 8/9 Governors at Basle the previous week-end when the debate went on for hours – no-one else present except himself, and the only minute of the meeting in William's possession. They were all more worried about the gold pool than about us and all agreed that we should devalue. There was no need for further consultation after that. In Rupert's view we made a mistake in devaluing at week-end – we should have picked middle of week. In the previous two week-ends there had been big movement of funds.

He then told me the extraordinary story of his telephone call to Brunet on the Saturday when O'B. agreed that he was the better French speaker and should take on the approach to France on the support operation. Rupert wrote out what he had to say in longhand in French, rang the Banque de France and spoke to Clappier. Clappier told him where he could find Brunet and gave him his private telephone number at the Banque (where he in fact was). Rupert nevertheless gave Clappier the message before ringing Brunet to whom he repeated it: "La Grande Bretagne souhaite vivement la concours de la Banque etc., etc.". Next day or on Monday Ansiaux and Carli rang up the Governor to say that they understood that Brunet was denying that he had been approached. Rupert immediately rang Brunet to protest warmly. Brunet said there must be some misunderstanding. Rupert insisted that Ansiaux had left no room for misunderstanding. Brunet took refuge in havering and shortly afterwards Débré, made his announcement that the French had not been asked to take part.

At the Basle week-end, asked about his government's attitude, Brunet had said that he could not commit the government and that there were political factors. Any credit for Britain would be decidedly better on a post-devaluation than on a pre-devaluation basis. But Rupert thought that we could have raised $2b had we decided not to devalue, chiefly because of fears for the dollar.

Today's proceedings at EPC were made extraordinary by Larre who at one point in the discussion of the Chairman's summary insisted that we must not say that a tightening of monetary policy was the necessary alternative to higher taxation. This meant endorsement of higher interest rates and the unleashing of a world deflation. For his part he thought the US might adopt a third policy – drift: and he preferred this to higher interest rates. Dewey Daane was plainly shocked at the inconsistency with earlier pressure for US deflationary measures and van Lennep at the lack of economic logic which called a big US deficit plus tighter money deflationary.

Larre took exception to a sentence imputing common interests *and responsibilities* to both creditor and debtor countries although the gist of it came straight from the Report on the Adjustment Process and implied that this was "merely a report of experts" and not approved by the OECD governments.

After the meeting of the EPC Deming held a press conference in the hall of the OECD where anyone who wanted could have taken part. It was not a good augury for W.P. No.3 which didn't start till 4.45 p.m. so that I heard only the first hour.

Saturday, 9 March   On Thursday night Eric Roll rang to press me to drop everything and do a job on Arab refugees for Carnegie at a fee of $30,000 for 6 months. Of course I said it was too absurd – if I could leave Whitehall earlier I'd go to St Peter's but I don't want to go while the outcome of devaluation is still in the balance. Last week it was Jack Beaver[27] asking me to succeed William Clarke[28] as Director of O.D.I. Then Austin Robinson[29] told me on Thursday that I had been elected President of the Royal Economic Society and I will also be President of Section F of the British Association next year. So I don't look like having too quiet a life.

Rupert Raw said that the Belgians have been earmarking for some time their contributions to the gold pool (which really means that they have withdrawn) on the grounds that they don't propose to supply their speculators with gold and would prefer to deal only with other central banks. The Italians look like following suit. If anything of this got out, there would be a headlong flight from the dollar since the US is more and more isolated in feeding the London market. This week-end Bill Martin is in Basle and the idea is that a general declaration should be made by all the Governors (except perhaps Brunet?). But even this won't stop the rot if US stock goes on falling. Kessler has done a paper on harmonisation of gold ratios but one can hardly see the US accepting this, with its implied holding of other currencies.

Michael Posner told me that WP3 went off quite well. The UK let the others discuss appropriate policies and even express their own reservations about what the more extreme advocates of deflations were saying. Larre was rude and practically called Denis a liar, shrugging his shoulders when assured that the Budget was not yet in final form. C. Dow first made a long speech which ended with a figure of about £500m, then went into the uncertainties and said perhaps the figure should be doubled: then towards the end he made another speech full of hire purchase and monetary policy and seemed to want *half* his original figure in extra taxation. So he had less influence on the discussion than seemed likely. But on the whole, people seemed to want about £600m in extra taxation (not too specifically defined) and some sighed for cuts in public expenditure like Hay and Ossola. No doubt they felt on safer ground discussing growth rates! Emminger was absent, which was a pity.

Wednesday, 13 March   Chancellor had a final meeting yesterday which was good fun because N.K. got quite excited about various minor provisions (e.g. aggregation of capital gains tax for minors with parents) and shouted a pained "No" at the Finance Secretary when the latter was explaining that it didn't really amount to very much. Then somebody appealed to the ghost of Gladstone, who initiated the fixed fraction of income on which tax relief could be offered for life insurance premiums: and Alec Johnston remarked "a great deal has happened since Gladstone's time". Chancellor has decided to play safe on total size of budget and selected two items out of three where he had invited us to choose one only. In all, the extra revenue from new taxation will be about £900m so

[27] Jack Beaver – Retired member of staff of IBRD.

[28] William Clarke – City Editor, *The Times* 1957–62; Financial and Industrial Editor, 1962–66; Dir., Cttee. on Invisible Exports from 1966.

[29] Austin Robinson – Cambridge economist; Jt. Editor, *Economic Journal* 1944–70; Sec., Royal Economic Society, 1945–70; President, International Economic Association, 1959–62; Director of Economics, Min. of Power, 1967–68.

he can't be accused of doing things by halves. He ruled nearly always against N.K. on the grounds e.g. that the surtax payer was already having quite a lot put on him and minor pin-pricks weren't worth while. But he ruled in favour on bonus shares and probably also on relief from SET for the elderly.

I saw Chancellor again this afternoon over the press conference which obviously has him worried. He is really anxious to get next Tuesday over without incident, knowing how bad the trade figures are and how precarious also the international financial situation.

Denis Rickett is *not* going to Stockholm so Sam Goldman will go. I didn't object since I regard my Group of Ten assignment as dating from 1 April. But it does seem pretty silly to divide up the responsibility in this way, especially as we may shortly be in the middle of a major dollar crisis. Many of the key papers don't come to me and I couldn't read them if they did.

Incidentally I don't now see even the state of play Budget papers showing the score of the successive decisions. Of course the process of decision-taking is over now; but it does seem odd. I think the organisation of the Treasury increasingly awkward and yet I don't see how it should be improved. But one thing is certain: we need two Second Secretaries. We also run the obvious risk of a division between economists and administrators with many of the economic issues being discussed simultaneously in the two groups without effective contact between them.

Friday, 15 March

Currency uncertainties increased the temptation to seek refuge by switching into gold. This put pressure on the price of gold in the London gold pool which the central banks sought to hold steady at about £35 an oz. by feeding in gold when required. The United States, however, the chief supplier of gold, was unwilling to part with its gold reserves indefinitely. It was necessary, therefore, to devise new arrangements to limit gold sales that might involve letting the price rise so as to check demand, or putting an embargo on US sales (which would have had much the same effect) or accepting a division of the market into dealings at the fixed price between central banks and dealings at a higher and variable price between all others. Agreement was reached in Washington between central banks to the latter arrangement and a closing down of the gold pool for the time being, but there were good reasons for regarding this as a temporary solution, paving the way to an eventual reunification of the market at a higher gold price.

One effect of the pressure in the gold market was withdrawals from sterling when there was only a diminishing stock of gold and foreign exchange to cope with them. In what was the first of repeated sterling crises in 1968, the government went over a series of proposals for radical measures to protect the new parity: floating, blocking, and borrowing. The suspense was the greater because within a couple of days of the week-end conference in Washington on the gold pool, the Chancellor would introduce a Budget to raise an additional £923 million in 1968-69. This seemed likely to reassure the markets but if blocking or

*floating had been introduced it would have come too late and we would be unable
for a long time to restore confidence in sterling.*

*One casualty of the crisis was George Brown who resigned on 15 March com-
plaining that a Bank Holiday was declared without his being informed and attacking the system by which governmental decisions were taken.*

*In the Budget which followed, indirect taxation was raised to bring in £314
million (in a full year) in higher taxes on drink and tobacco, £333 million in
purchase tax, £152 million in SET and £125 million in motor vehicle duties. It
was the largest increase in taxation in British history.*

Friday, 15 March   The Ides of March. Bank Holiday. George Brown resigns
three times and the third time is lucky.

The crisis blew up very quickly. We discussed with William on Wednesday a
passage on international liquidity for the Budget speech because the Chancellor
could hardly disregard what was happening in the gold market. But it was only
on Thursday that things got out of hand. At Directorate we debated the discount
on forward dealings and I asked why the Bank stayed out of the market at so
high a discount. This brought out that it was due to distrust of sterling and that
we might therefore have to face spot losses which up till Thursday were small.
But they were heavy on Thursday. William called a meeting in the afternoon
and this led to a further meeting with the Chancellor and Governor.

William told us that Bill Martin had rung the Governor in the morning (i.e.
at 4.30 a.m. Washington time) to say that the Americans were proposing to
adopt the Carli plan of dividing the market for gold into two channels. What
should we do? William himself looked dreadfully fagged and his eyes closed,
as sometimes happens, in the middle of the debate that followed.

I insisted on the dangers to sterling from any course other than a straight increase in the price of gold. We all agreed that the double channel plan wouldn't
work and that the rise in the free market price would cause withdrawals of
sterling. It was important that we should get US credits in almost any circs. but
the Bank was reported to be against further borrowing. We discussed blocking,
floating, and credits, and agreed that blocking would be preferable to floating.
The Bank was said to favour floating which amused N.K. "That was predictable",
he said and in fact he had come very near to predicting it earlier. He thought
that floating before the Budget would be disastrous for the Government but (as
he said today) after a decent interval of a fortnight or so (to give the US time
to float too!) it would be fine. So he wants blocking, *followed* by floating. We
also disagreed on the embargo solution which I thought would also be dangerous for us and would not necessarily have the effects on European countries
he supposed. I emphasised in particular the large dollar liabilities including
Euro-dollar liabilities that would have to be absorbed by central banks and the
likelihood that international trade would suffer through credit contraction.

When we saw the Chancellor we found that the Bank had gone through
much the same analysis but ended up rather differently. The Governor spoke to
Martin and reported that they were divided in Washington and that Martin did
not exclude an increase in the price of gold. The idea of a Bank Holiday was

mooted but we weren't sure how this would improve the position of sterling if it were still dealt in in other markets. We wondered if a Bank Holiday on Monday and Tuesday would be possible. The Chancellor said he understood that we had $1,500m to see us through, and the Governor put the figure at $1,200m – in view of the losses. But it was not clear how far this took credit for any of the IMF standby. He also expressed himself strongly against floating. Then he went off to see the P.M.

I had to leave the office early for my dinner party with E. Roll, B. Trend, D. Pitblado and R.C. Vickers. It was quite an evening with Ralph affronted by the state to which the government had reduced sterling and Burke worried about what to do. Eric gave us a sketch of opinion in Washington and favoured the embargo plan, followed by a conference. He thought the level of expertise in the Administration much reduced with so many people leaving and no one of stature in the Treasury. Okun[30] and Deming lacked the panache and width of Heller and Roosa.

Today we had a brief meeting with the Chancellor on the Budget Speech and at 6 p.m. I joined a 3 hour non-stop meeting with Sam and the Bank. Earlier I talked to Donald who said he had been in favour of putting up the price of gold since 1950. (He held a meeting of Ec. Adv. with none of the Treasury Advisers present). William and M.P. have gone to Washington and Denis is being called back from Ireland.

It quickly emerged (N.K. brought out the importance of the matter) that the Fed. had let the rate slip to 2.3740 although there had been an assurance from Martin that if we suspended gold dealings the rate would be looked after and held above the floor. Maurice Parsons was reluctant to move and it took some combined pressure from N.K., S.G. and myself to get him to ring Charlie Coombs and get him to support the rate. N.K. insisted that in a matter of this kind the Chancellor ought to be told; and it seemed pretty evident that if losses were light today they wouldn't be on Monday if it got around that we weren't holding the parity.

Then began a long debate on blocking and floating against the background of a possible failure of the Washington Conference and no US aid. I opted very reluctantly for blocking and as they left Maurice Allen and Maurice Parsons both insisted that this wouldn't do. Maurice Allen said reserves were –$200 m. so we had no option. I quoted yesterday's discussion. But the Deputy also said the till was empty. Yet neither said a word to this effect in the debate.

The three blocking schemes were called Brutus I, II and III in honour of the Ides of March and the Treasury line is that we should adopt B.I. I argued strongly (a) that we should not block on Sunday night, (b) that we should aim to get through Monday and Tuesday without blocking or floating, but that (c) we might find ourselves without the option. Kit Macmahon argued that once we blocked we would never revive the sterling system and so would pay for a generation for the decision. Eric Haslam argued that if we blocked nobody

[30] Arthur Okun – Economist, Yale Univ., 1962–64; Council of Economic Advisers, staff, 1960–62; member, 1964–68; Chm. 1968– .

would feel impelled to assist us while if we floated they would be bound to.

It was only on Monday night that Gordon Richardson told me how worried he was to find Dean Acheson[31] and Bundy[32] (in the West Indies) speaking of the folklore of gold and suggesting that if only they could get rid of these antiquated ideas all would be well. No wonder, said Gordon, that people are convinced that the US will increase the price or suspend sales.

Eric Roll put the point in terms of arithmetic when he said that of course dealers looked at the size of the gold stock, the rate of loss per quarter, grossed up for Vietnam, and decided that the stock wouldn't last many months.

It is all very like November in the psychology and we could lose just as much as we did then ($1,400m in one day) and end up with nothing at all in the kitty on Tuesday. But there would seem to me a reasonable prospect that the Americans will help us out and if we can get over the immediate panic the Budget will help to put things straight.

But Haslam told us that Malaysia and Singapore were already refusing to deal with one another in sterling. There have also been conversions of sterling on quite a large scale today in New York by Libya and Singapore. Over the past two years the OSA central banks have added some £600m to their reserves but practically none of it in sterling.

Saturday, 16 March   The Economic Advisers met at 11 and Donald rang me up to say they were meeting. I said I couldn't come in because I had a lunch party and undertook to ring him at 5. But the redraft wasn't ready so I went instead to a meeting in S.G.'s room on the paper for Ministers. Only Kit Macmahon was there from the Bank − not the golden horde of yesterday − and he made his points very effectively. In particular he pointed out that blocking still left us with all our forward commitments to honour. So it probably would not save the rate if we were already in trouble. It is agreed that the gold market may never re-open and certainly won't before the Budget. It also emerged that when Charlie Coombs entered the market yesterday the Fed. pushed the rate up to 2.3825 at a cost of only $3m. So much for the Bank of England view that by letting the rate go through the floor we were saving a large outlay in $.

Denis is back, thank God, and injected a welcome note of common sense. He got the cover note to say that "some of us" would want to refrain from blocking *or* floating if we got even minimal help from the Conference. It would be incredible if we blocked on Sunday night and an extraordinary comment on the negotiations in Washington. We just could not move before markets opened. N.K. thinks that if we got no help now we could still get it if US floated so that we could unblock at that stage. But he very much underestimates the permanent harm that blocking (even "suspension of convertibility") would do. Rawlinson thinks, however, that we might call off Brutus I after a short time and I suppose that we *might* just get away with it.

[31] Dean Acheson − American lawyer and politician; State Dept., 1941–53; US Sec. of State, 1949–53.

[32] McGeorge Bundy − Harvard Univ., 1949–61; Spec. Adviser to the President for Nat. Security Affairs, 1962–66; Pres., Ford Foundation, 1966–79.

Douglas explained that after the George Brown episode P.M. will have to summon five Ministers to discuss the situation tomorrow. Chancellor will meet his Advisers at 12 but it will be late in the evening before we really know how things have gone. He said our paper dealt exclusively with contingency that we got no help but didn't address itself to real issue: how bad did things have to be to make it right to block or float. Both Donald and Douglas are for a rise in the price of gold.

It seems pretty clear that the only likely argument is on the Carli Plan but it may be a partial agreement between a limited group (including Germany and Italy but *not* France?) and the demand for gold will certainly not cease. But if there are no gold dealings in London perhaps sterling will escape the worst pressure if only because there is no gold available for purchase on any scale.

Burke asked me on Thursday if I was scared and I said "Yes". In fact I'm far more scared by the situation now than I have been for nearly 20 years – certainly more than before devaluation. People here don't realise that this is a sterling crisis far more than a dollar crisis since the Americans are fundamentally in a very strong position while we are terribly vulnerable.

Sunday, 17 March   I was called at 10.45 to come in and at 11.15 M. Posner gave us an account of his day in Washington yesterday. We then adjourned to see the Chancellor who went off at 1 to talk to the P.M. Ministers met at 3.30 and again at 7.30 and I came home at 8 as I was not summoned to either Ministerial meeting and could foresee how things were likely to go.

M.P., K. Berrill and I had lunch at 2. T.B. said: "Who would have thought that the most progressive, advanced thing to do would be to treble the price of gold?" On this issue we agree. He also said he owed his career to H. Schacht and that Blessing and he had written articles together for him when B. was Schacht's Kit Macmahon. S. got him a German Rockefeller and that started him off.

My final session was with N.K. and M.P. at 7 and I rehearsed once again the drawbacks of deciding here and now to block, before markets opened on Monday, without having taken the measure of the effect of the Washington Conference, knowing that we might end for a very long time the willingness of foreigners to hold and accumulate sterling etc., etc. If we had to gamble why not wait two days till the Budget had registered? Would people sell unless they feared a second devaluation *in* the Budget (as some do) or wouldn't they wait a couple of days? And surely the communiqu, would not be an invitation to get out of sterling at any price? N. said he was converted and I think that M.P. agreed. But I'm pretty sure that T.B. doesn't. However, of the five Ministers, R.J. and A.C. will almost certainly oppose blocking and I doubt if the P.M., P.S. and M.S. will overpower them. The only worry is that it may be put to the Chancellor that he can't take the chance of having to block *after* the Budget and so destroy its effects on confidence. But I felt sufficiently sure of the outcome to leave the office.

M.P. said the meeting started at 9.30 two hours before the publicly announced time and that they had police protection and were shown in by the back entrance.

Most of the discussion centred on gold and the dollar, not sterling, and Deming made it clear that the US administration would not consider a rise in the price of gold. (Brimmer[33] privately made it clear to M.P. that an embargo might yet come especially if we floated.) The continentals were puzzled by our fears for sterling and thought that if the gold price rose this would damp down the scale of dealings and hence the run on currencies. The Governor also declared his unwillingness to ask for or receive further short term assistance and they couldn't see how to give us longer term aid and professed the need for consultations with their governments. They regarded $5b as quite out of the question but there seemed to be some prospect of $2b M.P. thought that this was not enough.

One point that was cleared up during the day was that the standby could be activated in 24 hours – according to Schweitzer. This together with $1.4b of unexhausted credits (my earlier $1b plus guaranteed sterling) and $2b extra aid on a Basle M type agreement would yield nearly $5b.

The Chancellor asked Denis to ring William to say that we couldn't have two Bank Holidays on Monday and Tuesday as everybody assumed in Washington (N.K. was right in insisting strongly that this would provoke panic if London were the only centre to remain closed). He was also to press for more aid if possible against the background of possible blocking. William, roused at 7.15 a.m., asked us to provide a draft of what we would like in the communiqué. This we did, in Sam's room.

One subject that caused some disagreement was the London Gold Market. I had Roy Bridge, Kit Macmahon and Jasper H. in my room most of the afternoon and Roy was adamant that we shouldn't close the market just to please the Swiss. But the Governor had promised this and I had understood the Bank to be quite ready to close it indefinitely. The P.M. also showed an interest in keeping it open and apparently none of the experts in Washington except the Swiss really insisted. So it will presumably open after all.

The whole business is fortunately being pushed out of the headlines by the appalling riot in Grosvenor Square, George Brown, Bobby Kennedy, etc., etc. So long as people still think of it as a *dollar* crisis we can breathe. If, after Tuesday, there is a run we can only react by blocking and will almost certainly float as well. What M.P., N.K. and I agreed (and Kit) was that all that is in question then is the sequence: since blocking and floating are almost certain to follow one another.

Denis spoke very effectively at meeting with Chancellor but I didn't see him at all afterwards.

The US will of course have to supply gold to *all* countries not just to the Club if this is needed in order to support the parity. But if the recipients feed the free market the US may be forced to put on an embargo and this may spread. So we may yet see an embargo without any formal announcement and a rise in the price of gold without any US change in the gold parity (because the other countries need an accounting price for transfers between them or because the French force the pace).

[33] Andy Brimmer – American banker with the Federal Reserve Board.

Tuesday, 19 March   Yesterday was uneventful and I saw nothing of William or the Chancellor. Sam implied that at No. 10 the Economic Advisers had dithered but the P.M. had stood firm against blocking. If so, we had a very lucky escape. Market reactions couldn't have been more helpful.

Budget Day. The Chancellor spoke for $2^1/_4$ hours and was cheered by his supporters more loudly at the end than I can recall in other recent budgets. He had just enough for the Left Wing but it was astonishing to hear them cheer a speech imposing over £900m in taxation, mostly indirect. Perhaps, as Bentinck said to me at P.E. Club they were cheering an alternative leader to H.W.

The Chancellor had obviously rewritten chunks of the early part of the speech but it referred too often to the Washington talks and seemed to me boring till he got to the Budget judgment where I was glad to see that he had preserved my final text. He didn't get a laugh till well on, with an announcement that beer would not go up (I exclude an early laugh at the Speaker's expense).

The Tories gasped in horror at a 30% rise in SET – much more than at the £923m of extra revenue in the peroration. There were few interruptions but one or two shouting matches e.g. over the investment income levy.

At the P.E. Club Eric Roll gave a rather perfunctory introduction, more on tax reform than on the Budget judgment. The only man to draw attention to the 3% judgment was Harold Rose and nobody took him up; Richard Fry emphasised the danger of strikes and Nigel Lawson drew the corollary that the government might exhaust its limited political strength in seeking to impose an unrealistic incomes policy. Geoffrey Rippon[34] made an attempt to reproduce Ted Heath's criticism but sounded bone-headed. Hawtrey interposed his customary drone on the undervalued pound. Frank Paish thought we might have to impose just as much additional taxation next year. Then there was a long and arid discussion on how far the balance of payments aims could hope to be achieved if the US had equally ambitious aims. In short, quite a typical inconsequential and unilluminating discussion. But the undercurrent of opinion was that this was the right medicine if a little late in coming and provided cuts in public expenditure were out.

Sunday, 24 March   Week-end at Sunningdale. Businessmen far more articulate than usual and William at his best in a long piece of fantasy.

Earlier in the week William told me that the Chancellor had "taken a fancy to Sam" and wanted him to come to Washington. This was preliminary to asking me to forego membership of the Group of 10 in favour of Sam which I did willingly because it is quite obvious that one can't detach the "international representation" from the policy direction; and this is not a problem in relation to W.P. No. 3 or EPC. I told William that without wanting to do a G.B. I thought the week-end arrangements had been bad and that we had had a narrow escape. To have T.B., N.K. and M.P. as the three economic advisers at No. 10 on the issues under discussion was taking a chance and I had neither been told what I was supposed to do nor supplied with the relevant cables. By accident, no

[34] Geoffrey Rippon – Conservative Minister of Public Building and Works, 1962–64.

doubt, I was not invited to hear William's account of the episode from the US end although Sam told me that it would make a Penguin.

William said à propos of the closing of the gold market that there was no truth in the Bank of England suggestion that the Swiss had pressed it on us. On the contrary, they had been entirely content that it should stay open. The Americans took a different view and were not alone in wanting the market closed for good. The ultimate decision to shut it for a fortnight was a compromise. Ansiaux who pressed to have it shut rang the Governor on Wednesday after the Budget to say he would be willing to see an earlier re-opening.

The feature that interested William most was to be the one Treasury man admitted to the hagglings of the bankers. I thought of EPU in December 1950 and he told me that in Washington as in Paris Carli used Ansiaux to get an agreed proposition.

It was clear that the low point came at the end of the second session (i.e. just when M.P. left to come back, full of gloom). But the show-down came later and, curiously, in defence of the pound not the dollar. When the Europeans were unwilling to provide the necessary further assistance there was a moment of silence and Martin said deliberately: "Well, Gentlemen, if we can make no further progress on this we shall have to impose an embargo on gold dealings and our plans for this are all ready".

Chancellor held a party on Thursday evening to celebrate the Budget. He took Friday off and William also went off to Glasgow for a wedding in Shotts. Jennifer made it clear that he was still pretty exhausted after his week-end. (Dowler[35] spoke on Monday of Chancellor lying down and asking if somebody couldn't say something cheerful).

William looking forward to dropping his Treasury responsibilities. He is an extraordinary man with tremendous resilience and an astonishing mixture of frankness and reserve. He will say so much and yet seem to keep back even more, giving the impression of layers below layers while remaining superficially candid and almost voluble. It is impossible to get cross or excited with him. I know nobody who can bring down the temperature more successfully and ensure rational discussion. He has such a well organized mind that he recalls without effort the rationale of any policy and the issues involved, even when it is not of immediate importance to his normal duties. When he does so, the logic is clear, the facts are stripped of inessentials and he brings out some facets that even the expert might not notice especially if they have a political slant.

He told me this morning of negotiations with Distillers at which McDonald had been very tough and the Treasury had forced conditions of sale on BP that had subsequently proved awkward for Distillers. William remarked that he "rather liked" this kind of hassle with somebody who showed equal relish.

When on Thursday we were discussing the week-end on the Social Services that Ministers have in mind, it was pointed out that the Ministers would like to base their policies on a 4% rather than a 3% rate of expansion. "Then they'll have to export like mad", he said and went on to indicate that the point of the

---

[35] Derek Dowler – Private Sec. to the Home Secretary, 1967; to Chancellor,1968.

exercise (which emerged once one got to discuss the period after 1970) was that it would provide a first draft of the Manifesto.

His final intervention this morning at Sunningdale ranged from an analysis of the decline of the UK and the repercussions on the 23 year old who had lived all his life in peace-time, to the release from the slavery of reading afforded by T.V., and the mutual hatred of parents and children. The attitude of parents to spending money on their children varied from "the mean to the downright cruel" and it would be best to give the children the money for family allowances, or, if not, vouchers. Watch the effect on a girl of letting her buy her own clothes at 13. All this verging on flippancy and yet "thinking in depth" so that one hardly knew how seriously to take it. As Reay Geddes said "Anybody prepared to follow William along the same line of thought would need his head examined".

B.R. cut by $\frac{1}{2}\%$. Sam Goldman spoke to me on Thursday morning and told me Governor now thought of $\frac{1}{2}\%$ rather than 1%. I agreed that it would add to the confident impression of the Budget and that we probably got very little out of 8% except a continued sense of crisis. The comic side of it all is that the Governor regarded it from the start as a vote of confidence *by the Bank* in the Budget as if – to quote Denis – the Bank was quite independent of H.M.G. and itself decided what to do with bank rate. The Governor also spoke in the evening in the same vein to the Finance Houses and I expected to see plenty of press criticism and derision (e.g. he said the Government had been too slow in acting, hadn't cut public expenditure enough, etc.). Harold Lever was there and the toast was to Her Majesty's Opposition!

Wednesday, 27 March   On Monday attended meeting with TUC at No. 10. Roy gave a first-rate statement of the strategy behind the Budget: appalling risks of expanding faster when we are borrowed up to the hilt, folly of repeating 1964, dangers of an international financial crisis which we might ourselves precipitate. George Woodcock and the others were clearly impressed although I doubt whether they took it all in, for Roy is so fluent: the argument pours out of him in all its complexity at a great rate. George began "Then we're in a pickle" when the Chancellor insisted that we couldn't go faster. He and F. Cousins were remarkably moderate and merely insisted that their difficulties in handling wage demands were as intransigent as the Chancellor's in coping with the bankers. Could the Chancellor show that what he asked was *necessary* and that nothing else was possible? Why couldn't we rephase our debts? The Chancellor had dealt effectively with the idea of selling the private portfolio because it served as a kind of collateral, couldn't be realised quickly, and if touched, might start a run. P. Shore spoke once only and at the end: supporting the TUC on selective intervention. The P.M. said comparatively little but pointed out that the hole that the Chancellor had spoken of in January had been filled in advance by the consumer spree.

Saturday, 30 March   17 to lunch including Ann Kirk Wilson who was back for six months at No. 10 to help the Archivist sort out the Attlee papers. She spoke of Tommy's habit of coming in and taking away papers of all kinds, many of them not copied to him, or even papers he was not supposed to see, making off with them without a word. Some papers were locked away by the staff but even this wouldn't stop him since he would insist: "Open that box" – and what could a poor secretary say when no firm instruction came down from the P.P.S. He would even paw the secretary's in-tray like a card-sharper, till papers collected in his hand and his attention fastened on key passages. I asked how they filed his papers and she said this defied all attempts. There was simply a large cabinet with Balogh Misc. since he ranged over every subject without pursuing them systematically. Every now and then he would bring in a stack of pieces of blue paper and her heart would sink. I asked if he would be able to take them all away and she said: "And a lot of other papers too".

The Cabinet papers are put on file at No. 10 along with Briefs and other material – unlike any other Department. But this means that No. 10 files probably provide the best source for general policy.

The Attlee papers were very complete and included all sorts of communications from the public – Lord Mayors, retired Colonels, etc. – which she weeded out. Attlee's private papers he took away and as he did much of his work in mss., this means that they afford very little clue to his methods of work and his thinking. The papers of the Conservative government were all in a fairly small room. Harold M. thought by talking and there are carbons of most of what he dictated.

We had final meetings with William of Ec. Directorate and E.G.S. on Wednesday and Thursday.[36] I didn't hear the end of the first as I had to go off to British Association. At the second, the idea of an inquiry into forecasting was discussed and the arrangements agreed. All was sweetness and light. William said how useful E.G.S. had been from his point of view and Douglas promised to carry it on and congratulated William on keeping such an awkward team in harmony. Ken B. pointed out that there had never been a minority report (since October, that is quite true, and indeed all our documents have perforce been agreed). William wound up by saying: "Let us put it that we have all learned quite a lot". But the truth is that E.G.S. has been from the start a way of handling T.B., that he has initiated nearly all the business (generally when it was already proceeding elsewhere or when it was no affair of those present), and that, however fascinating the discussions, they rarely gave rise to concrete action.

The bye-election results were not known on Thursday and on Friday the Chancellor was in Stockholm. I don't see how they can change matters very much except to weaken the authority of the government and make resistance to wage claims feebler. It is just possible that the Unions will be less willing to take industrial action but I should judge that their authority, too, has been weakened and that we shall see the impotence of both unions and government at an early stage. William took the line at Ec. Directorate that the best we

[36] Sir William Armstrong moved from the Treasury to the Cabinet Office as Head of the Civil Service at the end of March and was succeeded at the Treasury by Sir Douglas Allen.

could hope for was that 3 $^1/2\%$ might become the norm rather than a ceiling but I doubt whether norms count for anything now.

At any rate in a rather critical fortnight the Chancellor will be out of the country, first in Stockholm, then in US for a good part of the time.

Chancellor said on Monday in his winding up speech that he expected unemployment to fall. This was done *against* official advice and was not included in the speech as circulated for discussion on Monday afternoon.

Nicky recalled at Ec. Dir. how in the 1965(?) Budget a typist inserted "seven" for "several" (years) in a phrase about the relief on overspill and how the Chancellor became committed to seven years as the period for the taper. But as William pointed out it happened to fall in with the Chancellor's own predisposition. So often somebody names a critical figure and it gets accepted uncritically (like 4% growth) but only if it is within limits that the layman accepts as reasonable.

Monday, 1 April   L.B.J. "quits" as the headlines put it. This can hardly be good news when the US position in world affairs is so critical and the election is over six months away. From the point of view of getting peace in Vietnam it may well work the wrong way and make the North Vietnamese, if anything, more intransigent and less willing to negotiate. From the point of view of the world monetary system it might set off new strains because there will be no effective leadership in US policy. L.B.J. is still the nominal leader of the West, as Kennedy was before him.

Lunch with Sam Brittan. We discussed George Brown's article and the future organisation of the Treasury. Sam wanted to know when the "regulars", the inner core, came round to the view that we should devalue. I had to say that the question never arose since the Government never asked for our advice on this point and no memorandum was prepared after 1964 weighing up the pros and cons. The only issue was: at what point did we have to say that the government *must* devalue. But in fact I don't know *what* William thought in 1966 or 1967 or whether he felt compelled to take a view. All we could say was what the price of devaluing or not devaluing would be: and on this my own conscience is clear.

Sam also asked me, when I spoke of George Brown in a John Anderson role when he was really a Beaverbrook, who else had coordinated policy outside the Treasury and No. 10 and I could think of no one. But of course in peacetime that is where coordination takes place and it is only in war-time that you get a John Anderson outside the Treasury. I said that there was room for a coordination of policy on nationalised industries although this was more doubtful since the Treasury had a bigger stake in this. George had had strange notions of disputes between civil servants and probably hadn't noticed that these disputes made the ultimate job of coordination easier for a strong chairman. Yet this went on all the time in Cabinet where Harold was in fact the John Anderson of the Government. Sam felt that I was overlooking the unwillingness of some civil servants to think of the right thing to do rather than their own departmental interest.

He agreed that there was gross ignorance in the Labour Party in 1964 about the Treasury and that they had shown little interest in policy in comparison with machinery of government.

Tuesday, 16 April   The Ministerial Reconstruction was announced on TV on the 6th and was more extensive than I had expected.[37] The gradual erosion of DEA continues but P. Shore moves up to No. 10. The press, even the local press, takes the early demise of DEA for granted but Harold – although now stepping out of it – won't kill it.

David Serpell[38] asked me (Radice and Rawlinson) about bank rate as the Chancellor is obviously anxious to use a cut of $1/2\%$ to stop the Building Societies from raising their rates. Poor D. had no idea how to proceed or where to seek advice and asked Radice what the form was about bringing in the Bank of England. There was nobody else around because nearly everybody is still on holiday and the Chancellor himself is going off tomorrow morning although he only got back just before Easter. David went to the Bank with R. and duly sent up a minute which seemed to me rather unconvincing. But I expect that the Bank's opposition will prevent anything happening this week. Not that a further $1/2\%$ is unthinkable but to time it so as to head off a move by the Building Societies seems to me pretty odd, futile, and characteristic of Chancellors in the same fix.

My first remit from Douglas Allen is to prepare a brief for Dick Taverne[39] for the Bildesburg Conference.

Tuesday, 23 April   Paris for W.P. 3 with Jeremy Morse. All day on US with $1/2$ hr on Canada at the end. Alan Hockin[40] said he would be "mercifully brief" and I bet J.M. that he would take 20 minutes, which he did.

Before I left yesterday I talked to Douglas Allen about bank rate, Ditchley and staff. He agreed with the point made to me at lunch by John Jukes and later by Donald M. on the telephone that Barbara Castle would need a really good economist, given her new responsibilities. In fact, now she *does* need one she probably won't find one. (Denis Barnes agreed on Friday to sound Donald Robertson, not very hopefully. He also asked for Ted Whybrew[41]). Douglas – to

[37] The Cabinet was reconstructed on 6 April, the most important change being the appointment of Barbara Castle as Secretary of State for Employment and Productivity (i.e. Minister of Labour) with responsibility for wages policy. Meanwhile Michael Stewart, having moved from the Foreign Office to DEA in August to replace George Brown, moved back again to replace him in the Foreign Office. Harold Wilson took over the direction of DEA with Peter Shore as Minister in place of Michael Stewart.

[38] Sir David Serpell – Under-Sec., Treasury, 1954–60; Dep. Sec., Min. of Transport, 1960–63; Second Sec., Board of Trade, 1963–66; Second Perm. Sec., 1966–68; Second Sec., Treasury, 1968; Second Perm. Sec., Min. of Transport, 1968–70.

[39] Dick Taverne – Labour Parliamentary Sec. of State, Home Office, 1966–68, Minister of State, Treasury, 1968–69; Financial Sec. to the Treasury, 1969–70.

[40] Alan Hockin – Canadian representative at WP No.3.

[41] E G Whybrew – Economic Adviser, Economic Planning, DEA.

come back to him – pointed out that DEA was nominally still the coordinating economic department and provided chairmen accordingly; but the committee structure and the ranking of the ministers involved were all out of line. He would take over the ES Committee without trouble, but what about the others?

At lunch on Wednesday at B.P., Hancock said he recalled a meeting of Ambassadors from Asia and Africa at which there had been surprising unanimity that the most valuable man on the staff was the *Junior* Military Attaché because he knew the Colonels and the Majors, not the Generals, and whenever there was a coup d'état he was the best informed man in the Embassy about the new rulers.

Lunch with C. Dow, van Lennep and Schwarz of IMF. Van Lennep complained of Paul Samuelson's[42] two articles on gold, the first insisting that price must rise, the second retracting. He said academics *would* dwell on the two non-starters – a rise in gold price and a demonetisation of gold – instead of the real issues between these extremes. I asked what would happen if US did suspend dealing and suggested that we would suffer most since people would flog pounds more than dollars. Van Lennep dissented strongly and implied that sterling would get support if these conditions did arise but dollar would not. I asked him which Blessing would choose: to stockpile dollars or let rate for DM rise and he said at once the latter. The EEC would not accept a dollar standard: this was a *political* issue and should be looked on as such. I asked if they had considered what IMF would do and at first Schwarz took view that it would go on as before. I said the world would have changed and their assets and liabilities would be subject to new uncertainties. Would they accept a US request for a drawing?

All this started from a remark that if US had no obligation to maintain parity by gold sales somebody else would have to do it (unless US drew on IMF or used up its existing foreign currency). I asked what EEC would do about price of gold for dealings with one another but Emil had no reply to this. He was content to assert that higher gold price would not help the US balance of payments.

S. is flying out specially to go to a dinner for members of Group of 10 (to which I was originally invited). It is not the dinner à dix but a small clique under Dutch chairmanship that does not include the Belgians or a lot of other people but is designed to allow some discussion of gold without involving formal meeting of the Ten. (Deming insisted that if gold was to be discussed, it should be a matter for Treasuries, not Banks). So Milton Gilbert was probably wrong in saying that they had never discussed a rise in the price of gold.

The Chancellor as I foresaw was pretty peeved by David Serpell's note on bank rate but agreed reluctantly not to cut it and at same time said he must have better reasons for not doing so this week. But since Bill Martin put up the US rate on Friday he was saved from looking foolish and presumably will now pipe down till next month. The Building Societies put up their rates on the very day US rate was increased so we had an ideal alibi and yet press was told that we didn't really approve of action by building societies.

[42] Paul Samuelson – American economist; Professor of Economics, MIT.

I see, too, that Chancellor's words on unemployment are already being quoted against us. Increase last month too big to be laughed off and he knows quite well that we think trend has changed: so he has started down the primrose path.

Haven't seen him since the Budget i.e. over 1 month ago.

Thursday, 25 April   The most interesting thing Morse told me about the Washington meeting was that William and H. Lever talked all the way across the Atlantic. M. Posner said that William kept him amused on the outward journey. Yet the day before he left I can remember thinking how exhausted William looked and how his eyes closed as Nicky and I argued over the case for an immediate rise in the price of gold (partly perhaps because he switches off where he judges no point of substance arises but I thought there was more to it than boredom). On the Sunday he had been roused at 7.15 by Denis' telephone call after our meeting with the Chancellor. So he had had a long and pretty exhausting day.

J.M. also said that the Canadians had been very sad at being left out as they had as much as anyone at stake. He agreed that Ansiaux had played a leading part. In fact until then he had felt that Ansiaux never measured up to his reputation (via Roy Bridge) from the early fifties and put this down to his car accident. But at Washington he had risen to the occasion and put his views very clearly and fairly, trying also to be fair to the French. Carli had also been active. Yet I thought he was less openly pro-British than Ansiaux and decidedly less so than Blessing (with his Unilever past). C. could remain very quiet and say nothing at all if not interested – he did so for entire sessions at Basle. But if interested he talked well and forcefully in mixed academic/central banking style. Holtrop talked far too much and had made it difficult to get business done – his successor was much better.

J. said that Washington had been quite unlike a typical Basle meeting because the Governors had taken up positions that had due regard to their government's interests and views and had behaved much more in the manner of Treasury officials. It was wrong therefore for William to feel that for once he had been allowed to see how the central bankers did their work.

Another remark of his in the car interested me. I said that the Chancellor had been near to overruling the Governor on a cut in bank rate. J. pointed out that it was the bank's rate and therefore could not be changed without their agreement. I said that this was going too far. He then said that both sides had a veto on moving and that it was usually the Bank that wanted to move. I had to agree that I couldn't recall a specific case where the Bank had been pushed into cutting the rate against its will (or even into increasing it when it didn't accept the need to do so). But there have been times when it was clearly for the Chancellor to say what he wanted and I was not conscious that the Bank regarded its active agreement as indispensable to a move.

Lunch with C. Dow. Happy in his work. He agreed that we should try to get Getzwold or Emminger to act as Chairman of EPC. E. might succeed Blessing but he felt that he was regarded by Germans as "too clever". I've usually been told that they regarded him as a dangerous radical. Apparently yesterday

Schiller didn't even try to keep open possibility of emergency action to expand German economy but accepted that there would be no slowing down. E. was ready with counter-arguments he didn't have to produce.

A curiously inconclusive meeting at what may be a very critical stage for the dollar. If we get through to the June meeting without a crisis I'll be happy. But if the US does vote substantial cuts in expenditure and no increase in taxes we may get by until then.

Tuesday, 30 April   Chancellor this morning discussed economic situation. Obviously vague about departmental responsibilities since he hesitated about asking Roy Workman to open. He seemed to visualise worst outcome and want to plan for it and I had to say that it was a bit early to assume failure of devaluation. Tried to confine discussion to UK but of course this is to exclude some of the more important contingencies for which planning is really needed. It is natural to be troubled by rise in imports and fear that the spending spree is still going on but it doesn't help to assemble 7 or 8 advisers (including four economists) with no prepared paper and ask them for considered views when some don't even know the facts and the Board of Trade has a long paper on the stocks. As for unemployment, Chancellor is now being pursued by his own statements and is probably disproportionately worried.

When we turned to external account, Chancellor said that he now doubted whether we should see *any* reflux.

Sam Goldman now off to Bologna so anything on finance will be further delayed.

Robert Hall discussed with me the whereabouts of records and pointed out that up to 1959 policy minutes were on non-registered files and often destroyed. Nobody could find record of pre-devaluation discussions and when Plowden was asked about them he was told that there was no record of his (or Robert's) participation. But fortunately Robert kept his own papers. The *minutes* of the Budget C. were not kept nor other papers in form of personal comments and minutes. The records of 1955 Budget discussions in particular were defective. The rule was to keep on registered files only what you needed in self-defence, and this didn't arise in discussions on general policy.

Ned Dunnett spoke at Helsby dinner in favour of "visitors" to Departments on mediaeval college pattern. The life of a permanent secretary was a lonely one since they couldn't discuss their subordinates with anyone and even on other things had no one to confide in. In a very large department like Defence the Permanent Secretary could not know what went on down the line or have a chance to meet even his under-secretaries. How could he promote them with any genuine knowledge?

Wednesday, 15 May   Chancellor had a meeting on gold etc. early in the week at which little emerged. I took the opportunity to rub in: (a) that the Germans now had the initiative and their reactions were not necessarily to be explained in terms of the US balance of payments, (b) that interest rate relationships had changed to the advantage of the US balance of payments but not so as to give us any elbow room with our own interest rates.

Nicky drew a wonderful picture of the European currencies floating against the dollar but pegged (each of them) on the mark, with the German authorities operating in the market to smooth the fluctuations on $/Dm rate. He agreed that what was the "logical" solution did not always commend itself to those in high places! Nicky also said to me later à propos of investment grants that he recognised that corporation tax did not work so as to stimulate investment but for this reason he now favoured leaving investment grants alone. It was better to have a higher rate of profits tax and let this be offset by investment grants. My own view would be the opposite and I said so today at Donald's meeting of Economic Advisers. Nicky doesn't take any account of the high proportion of investment grants that goes to a small groups of capital-intensive industries and the consequent penalisation of profit-making firms in other industries. He argues that profits reflect luck anyhow and that in macro-economic terms profits are governed by investment so that the profits of clothing firms are linked with the level of investment in the steel industry. He also argues that there is a high correlation between the rate of growth of assets and the rate of return on assets and that investment grants put money into the hands of the growing firms and so give them extra momentum.

I talked to Douglas Allen on Wednesday morning about staff and he told me that N.K. had offered to help part-time after October (he has also been thinking of going to Barbara Castle if the Chancellor doesn't want him). D. spoke to the Chancellor who was quite firm (and no doubt relished the idea of N. attaching himself to Barbara). So that is one fixed point. D. said that he wanted to leave open as long as possible the question of my successor and I saw the force of this, especially when he went on to say that Donald might go to Cabinet Office or come to Treasury. On Thursday, however, Austin Robinson told me confidentially that D. was supported for the Oxford Chair (though he did not apply) and that he would be likely to take it. Neither Douglas nor Austin dissented when I said that Berrill and Posner would presumably be back in Cambridge by mid-1969 so that the way was open for a new structure from then on.

At the Trial of the Pyx lunch I sat next Harold Hartley[43] who must be roughly 90. He looked remarkedly spry, except that he could hardly stand up (he succeeded in doing so for one toast), couldn't manoeuvre his food very skilfully and had a hearing aid that didn't work and seemed to keep buzzing. He talked throughout the lunch and being deaf was largely beyond prompting. First he told me when I asked if he was still interested in power problems that he was a consultant to C.E.G.B. He had launched BOAC and BEA, reorganised the gas industry before the war, and worked on the L.M.S. for nearly 10 years with Stamp. He recalled how the Foreign Office had reacted "within an hour" to his information about the intentions of TWA to fly on our routes to Italy: they set up Alitalia immediately and it remained the crack Italian line. Then he had

---

[43] Sir Harold Hartley – Scientist and businessman.

been summoned once with Stamp by De Valera to Dublin. De V. told them on arrival of a deal in which Cunliffe Owen had been engaged to take over commercial flights to UK (with a reciprocal UK engagement). "I ought not to have let that tobacco chap get away with it" said De V. "I want you to have the business and share it with *our* people". He refused to go into details and switched to philosophy and mathematics. But the outcome was Aer Lingus and an eventual purchase for BOAC of Constellations and other planes that were sold for sterling at a good price (Hartley could have paid a higher price in £s on Australian account as he had an offer in his pocket).

He married a daughter of A.L. Smith and could quote Compton Mackenzie's "Memoirs" on the subject. Ezra Pound had lain on the floor looking at her and saying to her unbelievingly "Can something so wonderful as that be married to a *chemist*?" H. knew Yeats well and has a lot of his correspondence (if he could find it).

I asked him why he didn't let somebody tape record him but he said that he was "like the prince" and made a gesture to show he always wrote things out longhand. That very day he had had a letter from Prince Philip written over Luxor, giving his address in Australia, and had cabled back.

He also had a collection of books on chemistry which he had collected since his student days at Oxford, including a copy of "The Skeptical Chymist" which cost him £1 and a unique copy of the lecture given in 1860 by Cannezaro that had laid the basis for the Periodic Table of Atomic Weights by Mendelyev who was in the audience. He had bought this in 1893 when his tutor had given him a German bookseller's circular in which it was on offer. I think he got it for about 1d.

He spoke also of an American chemical engineer who in the First World War had been able to produce TNT at 9s. a lb. when we were importing it at 10s. a lb. I mentioned Nobel and Hartley waved him aside as someone who was not in the same class. (K.G. – ?)

Austin Robinson at lunch yesterday lamented the number of people in White-hall who had to be "squared" before anything was agreed. He also said that only about $7\frac{1}{2}$ m. tons of coal could be produced on terms competitive with tax-free oil. But he found Richard Kahn beginning to act as an apologist for the N.C.B. – R. was "not a quantitative economist" and was too much influenced by arguments about the social cost of closing pits when we were really planning for 25 years ahead and a new generation of miners.

Cecil King let off his little bomb last night and didn't realise that he would have to resign from the Court of the Bank of England. It is obvious that King had been preparing this move for some time and his piece had been seen earlier in the day by others before it appeared in this morning's *Daily Mirror*.[44]

---

[44] Cecil King, a nephew of Lords Northcliffe and Rothermere, and Chairman of the International Publishing Corporation, the largest newspaper, magazine and book publishing business in the world, attacked the Prime Minister and the government (which he had previously supported) in the *Daily Mirror* on 10 May and resigned simultaneously his Directorship of the Bank of England. On 30 May he was dismissed from his posts as Chairman and Director of the I.P.C.

The local election results can hardly be a great surprise but they may have contributed to today's reaction in exchange markets. Why there should have been speculation on a revaluation of the mark *this* week, not *last* week I can't imagine.

Washington, Saturday, 18 May   Left on Wednesday with Mary for Puerto Rico [American Bankers Association Conference] via New York and Washington. Dined with Pat and E. Loftus[45] on Wednesday night.

Thursday. Called at Fed. George Garvy started at once on the change in the US psychology. Four political murders in a few years: a President, the leader of the "Nazis", two negro leaders, one of the violents (Malcolm X), one of the moderates (King). A violent, troubled society. The US had misjudged the trends in the world and found itself tied up in a small corner of S.E. Asia to the neglect of Europe. Even in Asia it was Japan with which the US had to deal but the Japanese were already finding their own way knowing that they could not depend on the US for the next 100 years. There was no leadership in Europe except de Gaulle who, however one might regard him, had often been right. The Scandinavians were disappointing and there was no obvious bridge to E. Europe.

Yet big changes were in progress. It was the insiders, the men brought up or trained in Russia itself like Dubcek[46] who were working the revolution. He fully expected to see the same thing eventually in Russia itself. The intellectuals there had guarded fiercely their independence of mind and it might yet be as if the things of the past generation had never been. In Italy Fascism had left no trace anywhere in the Italian culture.

Then he switched to H. Wilson. Why didn't he resign and let the Tories come in for six years? This might save the party but staying on would surely make matters worse. Here I disagreed: the Labour Party couldn't run away a third time and all the courage H.W. had shown would go for nothing if he resigned in a state of demoralisation.

We talked of the young and George spoke of their alienation from business. They now thought of the Harvard Business School as the lowest form of career and this was something new in US whatever our experience in UK. Americans travelled in Europe and saw other things in life than those they were brought up to – not just a small èlite but a great mass of Americans wanting a more relaxed life. And so we came back to the changes in values in America and the disquiet it provoked.

With MacLaury[47] I talked about the UK and S. Africa. He spoke of a capital inflow of $70m a month but later withdrew this figure. The Fed. are anxious to see S. Africa sell gold and can't see how they can avoid it much longer.

Alan Holmes was immersed in the market, the rise in gold, weakening of £, disorderly conditions in the discount market following the report that Congress

---

[45] Pat Loftus was Deputy Head of the Statistics Division of the UN in New York.

[46] Dubcek – Czech President during the Soviet invasion of 1968.

[47] Bruce MacLaury – Director, Brookings Institution, Washington.

might not pass the tax increase. Bill rate is up to 5.80% and public bodies are borrowing long term at as much as 8%. The Treasury issued 7 year bonds at 6% (the ceiling only applies over 7 years) and 15 (?) months paper also at 6%. Both issues successful but now at discount.

With Rivel and company at Chase Manhattan we got onto the international aspects. John Wilson thought a change in exchange rates ultimately desirable and Youngdahl said that if US balance was in surplus again we wouldn't need SDR's. He said he knew the Middle West and that opinion there was now more and more "unsold" on internationalism and increasingly isolationist. The foreign aid bill had little support. The US felt its first obligation was to its domestic problems – the cities etc., etc. – and was disenchanted with its world role.

Rivel agreed on the danger of a collapse of the Euro-dollar market if the gold price went on rising and a stampede into marks began. Y. kept interjecting that this or that would be the time to buy bonds e.g. if there were a "real" slump. They were all for the tax bill and couldn't see that it mattered whether expenditure was cut by $6b or $4b. Nobody could tell to within $2b and a new President could undo what L.B.J. did. He would need to make it clear that he didn't propose to exercise his veto.

Yesterday I began by calling on Deming with Evan Maude. He was engaged with Fowler for some time before we saw him and obviously in the middle of a flap. He told us that on a head count they thought that they could get the tax bill but that it wouldn't be introduced until after Memorial Day – probably June 4. We then had a long discussion on monetary policy and the movement in rates. His fear was that there would be a ratchet effect as savings rates were jacked up and that it would be more difficult to get rates down thereafter. I asked about the two-tier gold market and he saw no reason why it should not go on indefinitely. Carli thought so and Tungeler[48] had spoken of a further two years at least. There had been some gold sales to fringe countries – Ireland, for example (and he added that if the independence movement in Scotland was successful that would no doubt be another demand to meet), Malaysia, Lebanon (!), and even Italy for reasons associated with the elections. But the total was small and raised no real threat. I did not ask how the US deficit was to be financed without some gold sales.

He also expressed confidence that SDR's would be issued in sufficiently big amounts. The talk in London a year ago had been of $1b and now $1 1/2 – $2b was "in the ball park". I expressed some scepticism. He then cited Ansiaux as a supporter of the need for substantial issues of SDRs and Carli as very much of that opinion. The Central Bankers had been shaken by events after the November devaluation and had changed their views greatly. Emminger was in agreement but he could not say what the others in Germany thought. Already they were within sight of the necessary governmental ratification since in many countries it was a central bank matter not requiring legislation: but by number they were a long way short of the 64 countries that had to approve.

---

[48] Johannes Tungeler – 1946–53 with Bank Deutsche Länder; from 1953 with the Bundesbank.

Okun was obviously worried quite as much by the danger of getting the tax bill *plus* the expenditure cuts as by the thought of getting neither. He added up the "fiscal drag" of $10-12b, the $10b in taxes, and the cut of $6b in expenditure to conjure up a picture of an economy running down, and although he didn't give me the GNP figures, he obviously thought of, at best, a slow expansion once the bill was through, *provided* the defence figures were to be relied on. But in the past they had not proved so. (Later Geoffrey Bell showed me the NIF tables, borrowed from Jaszi,[49] on a promise to tear them up. Even on a high expenditure figure the expansion from Q2 was of the order of 1–1$\frac{1}{2}$% p.a. only.)

We discussed forecasting methods and were joined by Duesenberry,[50] who said the first thing was to make sure that your staff did what you asked them, not something else that they had thought up. They did not present a series of alternative forecasts but commented on their main forecast and the risks of error. They did however experiment with alternative policy outcomes and used computers to get a quick view of how for example different government expenditures affected GNP. They also had some handy desk calculators that could do elementary regressions. They agreed that oversophistication in some directions didn't make up for haziness over key items and that we had a special problem on exports which was less important in US. The idea that the visible balance might be easier to predict than exports and imports separately also struck them as reasonable.

When I asked about the flow of funds etc. they said they could find little evidence of a liquidity effect except on housing. Here the financial constraints provided a better indicator than any other although the April figure for starts was out of line with the predictions. They used formalised relationships for things like consumption, stockbuilding, etc. but used survey data mainly for business investment, subject to adjustment in the light of price and profits behaviour. Profits they found to be best explained by reference to activity, *not* incomes and prices. The purely formal models yielded very odd results.

I said our forecasts were in effect plans since the Government would be held to them. D. pointed out that although the US government didn't have the same powers they had other problems in the independent existence of the Fed. and the ostensible need to forecast how the Fed. would behave (just as the Fed. could say it had to predict how the US government would behave).

Ray Goldsmith talked to me at length about US politics and said that if Rockefeller got the Rep. nomination he would almost certainly be elected. But Nixon would get the nomination unless the Republicans felt he had no chance against the Democratic candidate.

At lunch I asked Brill[51] what use was made of the flow of funds analysis. He said that in recent years they had concluded that it was a mistake to try to justify decisions by bringing in the whole accountancy matrix. This just left the Board

[49] George Jaszi – American statistician, US Dept. of Commerce.
[50] James Duesenberry – Professor of Economics, Harvard Unversity.
[51] Daniel Brill – Economist and statistician with the Federal Reserve Board.

cold. But it was useful to go through the process of working out the matrix in order to see how changes in the money supply etc. might operate. The analysis, i.e., provided a background and could be used when specific decisions had to be taken.

Evan Maude and I saw Frank Southard[52] at 4 p.m. and discussed the gold situation. He obviously did not regard the two tier arrangement as a durable one but thought the US was doing "a good Canute job". The S. Africans could sell gold to the Fund without limit at $35 an oz. (or slightly less) so that they could preserve access to officials channels. The IMF in turn could turn over dollars in exchange out of it existing $ holdings or raise other currencies in exchange for gold: the final outcome would be very little different from an outright sale by the South Africans to one of the main central banks. He had suggested that the South Africans should hold newly mined gold in a separate account and treat transfers to their reserve as irreversible. Gold could then flow into the central bank circuit but not out again. According to IMF the South Africans would have to sell $500m in gold this year (against $1.1b normally) but the South Africans themselves put the figure at $750 m.

Friday, 24 May   Returning from Dorado Beach, Puerto Rico via New York. On Thursday I talked to Emminger about the French attitude before devaluation. He said that on the Monday he had to be at a meeting of the Monetary Committee of the Six. They had already had discussions among themselves and agreed on a procedure. To their surprise when Larre arrived he started by announcing that he was instructed to protest both on the procedure and on the substance (involving acceptance of a devaluation of up to 15%). On the first point Emminger had asked why the French should want a meeting of Ministers which could hardly be kept secret and would be certain to start off speculation. Had Larre or his Minister ever read the conclusions of the Council of Ministers which specified the procedure to be followed and was based on this consideration? (The answer is that nobody in the French team survived from that occasion in the new administration.) As for substance what *had* French Ministers been saying throughout the year about the need for an adjustment in the pound sterling? Larre argued that his Ministers had been misunderstood and had said nothing implying a need to devalue the pound.

The meeting reassembled later and was the stormiest Emminger remembered in EEC with shouting that got louder and angrier. Eventually after midnight they broke up and told Sir Denis Rickett that five of them could accept the British proposal but the French would not (as D. had in fact expected). The French did in the end get their meeting of Ministers – on Sunday night after devaluation had already been announced. Brunet, to the amusement of the others, suggested that if it was not too late the British should be urged not to devalue but to institute import controls. Emminger commented that the whole episode showed the Mercantilism of the French and their mortal fear of competition from outside. He didn't think that the French would contemplate a change in their parity with

[52] Frank Southard – American economist, Vice Pres. of IBRD.

the rest of EEC. In fact, their exports to other EEC countries had risen more than Germany's or Italy's since 1958.

Emminger said that he personally launched his first memo on the revaluation of the DM in October 1959 when he had seen that increasing orders for machine tools came faster from abroad while domestic orders were recovering. Today he was being told that none of the German manufacturers of machinery was as yet feeling any effect of increased competition from the UK.

He also argued that the recession had raised productivity fast in Germany. There was more cutting out of unprofitable lines, more co-operation by the Unions in introducing new practice.

Sunday, 9 June   I have now been back for a fortnight crammed with incident. Reading for a D. Litt. – demonstration against Bagrit. Silver wedding celebration next day with all children and lots of relatives. Assassination of Kennedy on 5 June (first heard of it from liftman on my way in). Peerage for Tommy announced yesterday. Meanwhile Nicky in hospital for wisdom teeth removal

When we got back, Chancellor was in throes of papers on public expenditure and furious to find that borrowing requirement had risen to £750m without any indication to him that this had happened. He has since told IMF (Goode) that he won't let borrowing requirement stay there and will cut it down (I believe to about £500m though I don't believe this to be possible).

Douglas Allen told me that the tighter credit squeeze had been decided on when the advice reaching him and the Governor was against it.[53] I don't know whether the Governor approved but Egerton told me at lunch that the City felt disenchanted with him because he didn't stand up for their interests. This feeling went further back but had been inflamed by the credit episode (on which they were not consulted because the Chancellor wanted something to offset the effects of the NIESR forecast and q.r. proposal). Of course the City has no idea what the present state of the reserves is even if it doesn't believe the official figures. Egerton said it was accepted that next Governor would have to come from outside the Bank and that John Stevens would be high in the running.

Haven't so much as set eyes on Chancellor since my return: nor, for that matter, any other Treasury minister.

Tuesday, 18 June   The May trade figures became available on Tuesday last week, the day before I left for The Hague, and showed to our consternation no change on April. N.K. came to see me that evening to insist that action of some kind was necessary. He favoured import deposits and I saw some advantage in this: indeed I had urged before going off to Puerto Rico that we should have

[53] On 23 May the Bank of England tightened credit by imposing a ceiling on bank loans to the private sector (including export credit) limiting the increase above November 1967 to 4 per cent. This followed the issue earlier in May of the National Institute *Economic Review* forecasting a current account deficit in 1969 of £365 million and recommending that preparations be made for the introduction of quotas on imports in case such restrictions were needed, which seemed to the Institute very likely.

another look at the scheme and in the meantime F. Figgures had prepared a hostile report (which I haven't seen).

Thinking it over that evening I decided that a surcharge for six months was preferable and told others this next day including M.P. and Donald (who said that Peter Shore had come up with a very similar idea – a descending surcharge). N.K. prepared a memo which all of us signed and we then discussed it briefly with Douglas before M.P. and I left for Heathrow. It said that "serious consideration" should be given to a surcharge and outlined the advantages. I had asked if I could tackle Emminger, van L. and others privately in The Hague when I saw Douglas earlier in the day but we agreed this was not possible – indeed I couldn't give them the figures for May.

Yesterday the Chancellor had a meeting with us and the Bank. I had concluded in favour of a 5% surcharge in July if the figures were bad again, arguing that nobody would expect a 5% devaluation while the effect on stockbuilding might be considerable. But the Chancellor began by telling us that on Thursday he had told his colleagues what the Economic Advisers had urged but they had concluded that a scheme of import deposits was preferable if anything was to be done and that nothing should be done in June. The Bank (Morse) were fairly calm about the prospects for the next fortnight but I pointed out that the market would go through the same train of thought as us and get excited about the *June* figures. As N.K. said, people might *assume* that the Government would restrict imports and act accordingly (I said just this to him last Tuesday).

It became clear that Sam, N.K. and the Bank were all in agreement *for* prior deposits (if anything), Harold Lever against both schemes, supported by Douglas who felt that if the news was very bad neither scheme would be enough and, if it weren't too bad, would dish our chances of financial support. F.F. rubbed in possible US reactions but the Chancellor said that Deming had as good as said that *domestic* pressures for protection were what really mattered in US. Morse said we couldn't move while the Basle negotiations were still on and we hadn't yet got our $1,400m from IMF. The Chancellor had hoped to reach a decision between the two contingency schemes but deferred it because it was plain that there were some big snags in prior deposits (e.g. staff of over 200 had to be set aside *now* to get scheme off the ground in a month: surcharge needs only 4-7 days). Consultation not easy to arrange and impossible unless we were ready to go. Talk would get around if we approached A, then B, etc. Chancellor spoke of talking to Blessing who is notoriously insecure.

Today we had a meeting with Sam on a paper prepared by the Bank and covered by Lovell/Radice. This made the scheme more plausible: 25% deposit for 6 months on T.I.C. [Temporary Import Charge] goods with, say, £250 m. of deposits and a cut in imports by perhaps 10%. We agreed that the deposit should be higher in the early stages and left the issue of coverage for later examination. N.K. thought that industry was highly liquid (citing Ray Goldsmith[54] on difference from other countries) with £20,000 m. of deposits held by independent

---

[54] Ray Goldsmith – American economist working at OECD Development Centre in mid-1950's.

and commercial companies so that £250 or £370 m. of deposits would have a limited effect (and could be undone easily enough). But the Bank and I doubted whether surplus liquidity was on this scale. N.K. recalled controversy in 1966 over SET and felt that we had been unnecessarily alarmed at that time. Why did we worry so much about the effect of a small cut in liquidity and yet think a lot more had no effect?

Rupert Raw thought (M.P. says) that the Central Banks would not think too badly of a surcharge along lines suggested. He told me that the Dutch had made a drawing specially to avoid paying gold as indeed the French have too.

Thursday, 20 June   A second meeting with Chancellor at which there was a more coherent and rational discussion of import deposits. Agreed to start contingency plan for earmarking of staff and printing of forms. Meeting followed one yesterday morning with Douglas and in the afternoon with Customs plus another this morning held by Sam and taken up very largely by him and N.K. who can both be highly voluble. D. made it clear that he was against both schemes because they would damage confidence and be interpreted as implying a failure of strategy. If we had to move at all we'd have to do something still more drastic involving a new approach. In this I agree. The mere issue of lower figures of imports would do little good if no one could say with any great assurance that the eventual level, after the removal of the scheme, would be lower than now. Harold Lever made much the same point. It is also pretty clear that the Customs can't be ready even in four weeks, that there will be major anomalies, and that we couldn't announce the scheme any later than 11 July so that there would be a week or more in which imports would accelerate. About 10% of imports come by air.

There is also a controversy on liquidity with the Bank prepared to consider a scheme curtailing this by £350–400m but very doubtful about a substantially higher figure. Yet if scheme has to have a wide coverage a high deposit rate (say 50%) implies far more tie-up of cash than £350m. The coverage point was brought out by D. yesterday morning (I had put it more vaguely the previous day but everybody was too engrossed with rates of deposit). I regard both schemes as dead.

Monday, 24 June   Deep gloom. The forecasts are taking shape and show as usual a poor outlook tomorrow and a bright future thereafter. Bigger deficit than last year but a surplus emerging in 1969 and reaching fair proportions by the end of the year.

N.K. expressed strongly the view that imports must be inflated by stockbuilding and probably had been all through 1967. But Jim Shepherd said that even if stock figures were adjusted upwards they would still be inconsistent with this view. He thought some revision of his equations inevitable and this pointed to a sustained increased in import propensities.

Tuesday, 25 June   We have revised downwards our balance of payments forecast for 1968 by no less than £600 m. of which £400m represents imports.

Of course if we believe this we can hardly go on as we are. But I can't see why we have to add £266m or 10% to the forecast (c.i.f.) for industrial materials made as recently as March.

Most serious business at present is over the import deposits scheme. We had two hours today in Sam's room and very tiresome it was. Sam prolix, N.K. straying over the whole subject when everybody wanted to get to the end of a limited exercise, Frank Figgures fuming, and the Bank keeping quiet but making their points effectively. Frank thought N. "intolerable" and said so, but he also tried to tell S. how to conduct the meeting and this didn't really help. N. wants us to begin by trying to save £100m. in imports a month and then decide how to do it. But of course if that were the idea we wouldn't start from import deposits and say "no change in strategy".

Saturday, 29 June   The end of June is a good time to take stock. When I went off to Puerto Rico I was chiefly afraid of the US dithering over their Budget and although I was prepared for two months' bad trade figures I didn't doubt that things would soon swing round. I told a French banker who was sceptical that we had six weeks (i.e. to 11 July) to show that we were on the way up but I was hopeful that by mid-July there would be some firm evidence. In the US the news when I arrived was bad because the Bill had just been set back. But I had little doubt that it would eventually pass: it was simply that any delay, any bad news might push us over. At least we had had no major strikes or outrageous settlements.

Yesterday N.K. said that foreign bankers wouldn't hold it as other than common sense if we acted to restrict imports. He didn't want us to float with no reserves and a huge deficit. We *had* to act and if it misfired, then we might have to float but at least with less danger of excessive imports. The bankers would lend us more to save the rate if we were cutting our deficit and could show that in time devaluation at the existing rate would be sustainable. How could we risk relying on foreign speculators to pay for our imports? Of course, it was mad not to have floated in November – everybody agreed that this was a major error (he quoted Milton Gilbert) – and he had spent the past few years pleading that we should be ready to do this as the only safe course of action. He had warned the Chancellor of the risks of a fixed rate. But the Bank had carried the day. The whole speech was a powerful one, laced with the usual quota of "It is ri*di*culous", but prevented me from getting him to address himself to the *diagnosis* of current imports and the likelihood that they might begin to subside.

We then went off to a Budget C. meeting – now once again rechristened at Douglas' suggestion and after lunch to yet another meeting on forecasting methods under Donald.

At 3.45 the Chancellor held his meeting ostensibly to discuss consumer spending. But of course we didn't get round to that. I had sent him a minute on Thursday evening on the new forecasts and he asked me to speak on them. He then commented: (a) that it showed how little faith one could put in forecasts, (b) that they showed what a mistake it was to delay the Budget until March instead of having it in February as he had wanted, (c) that the need to wait for the forecasts which was urged on him in January had ended in more being done than the forecasts indicated as necessary so that the delay had been pointless, and (d) that we must have forecasts at shorter intervals so as to avoid such shocks.

Then he produced the bit of good news left with him by the Governor: that the sum of the identified deficit and the balancing item in Q2 was only £0–50m Since Maurice Allen had spoken to me about this and shown that it all hung on a big swing in the balancing item and perhaps some dying down in capital outflow, I felt obliged to pour a large dose of cold water on it and urged that we shouldn't fool ourselves that things were improving in Q2 and pin our faith on a sustained positive balancing item. I was surprised to find the Chancellor a little obstinate on this and Douglas supporting him on the grounds that nobody could have foretold the outcome. The Chancellor is thinking of releasing the news early but of course he'll be laughed at if the trade figures are bad.

I warned him that the figures might well be bad and that we could hardly refrain from acting if they were. I repeated some of N.K.'s arguments. He wondered if I had any reason for expecting bad figures and seemed comforted that the forecast showed a decline in imports in Q3. So far as action was concerned he was quite clear that he had to get the Basle arrangement settled: were the Central Bankers making any new difficulties? He was told "No" and I pointed out that my fears arose out of the current gossip among *private* bankers on the continent that we would devalue again by September. He also ruled out further deflation because he could not hope to carry his colleagues. I repeated Fred's point that we could use monetary policy more firmly (in 1955 a 10% reduction was asked for in advances) but he was clear that we couldn't tighten credit again in July after what happened a month ago. The import savings associated with deflation could only amount to 20–25% of the deflation.

Douglas said that if the situation called for stronger measures than import deposits it would prove to have been a mistake to use this measure first particularly since it would be calculated to precipitate, not avoid a crisis. I retorted that we couldn't refrain from taking steps that might save the rate because we should then have difficulty in preparing an adequate package. It was worth something to get imports under control *before* we floated. M.P. was obviously not anxious to get the Chancellor to make promises to act and felt that the forecast might be too pessimistic.

As we came out Fred asked bitterly why they should feel so let down by the forecasts. Hadn't they had the figures of a monthly £80–90m visible deficit for some months and why couldn't they draw the same conclusions as the forecasters?[55] Forecasts were merely a way of organising current information so as to throw light on the future. I said that monthly forecasts would *not* have revealed the true prospects since they would give free rein to timid imaginations.

[55] The monthly trade figures fluctuated widely and gave no indication of the underlying trend. The balance of visible trade (excluding imports of military aircraft) moved from –£50 million in June to –£80 million in July and down to –£28 million in August. It had, as Fred said, averaged over –£80 million in the three months February to April. By the final quarter of 1968 the monthly average was –£35 million.

Only a major forecasting exercise really got people down to working out the full implications of what was going on.

Later I called on Douglas to tell him why I had agreed to a more limited coverage for the import deposits scheme (I thought 50% more important than the need to cover crude materials even if, as now transpired, the volume of imports had risen quite steeply). I said we had been little at cross purposes on the scheme because I had changed my mind and now thought it something we ought to do if the figures were bad. I had previously agreed that it would either be too little or force us into doing a lot more. D. pointed out (a) that the City would be likely to take a very hostile view, partly because of political differences and the scheme could be made to seem rather ridiculous and ill-thought out à la SET (S. America etc.); (b) that we had lost $170m that day so that a saving of £200m was nothing in comparison with the loss we would suffer if confidence was affected. But he didn't rule it out. Deming when consulted in general terms about import restriction had not thought that people expected it of us but had also said that the US would not react and this had now been confirmed by further soundings in the Department of Commerce.

The Chancellor also asked about France. What would we do if France devalued this week-end? He didn't think they would but that might be a reason for supposing the contrary. We couldn't afford to let another $1,000m ooze away. We agreed that the Bank would have to close the UK market and give up supporting sterling elsewhere i.e. we would have to float. But nobody spoke of blocking or of other measures. It was disconcerting that it should be left to the Chancellor to pose the question and to find that we hadn't given the matter a thought.

Monday, 1 July   Lunch with Keyser Ullmann: nearly all young men, younger than Edward du Cann[56] and confident of future disaster, but less clear what they wanted to do. Change the government or at least the P.M.; cut government expenditure; deflate; and then presumably hope for the best although that's just what they feared *this* government might do.

I had just come from 3/4 hour meeting with the Chancellor on import deposits. The Financial Secretary showed us a memo. full of the dangers of the scheme and suggesting alternative possibilities very vaguely. These came down to credit restriction by banks, not Customs, and stopping prepayment for imports. But he then spoke of a continuing scheme of 20% deposits if we had to face a prolonged deficit. Sam spoke at length and Douglas hardly at all. Financial Secretary wanted Bank to say by how much interest rates would rise: he visualised confusion at the docks, a housing crisis, etc. and nobody could deny that there might be serious dislocation. There would have to be some if the scheme were to bite. Chancellor said it was like hire purchase – as it was – and asked why Financial Secretary thought it would have three times effect of Budget on money supply. Some confusion between monetary and demand

---

[56] Edward du Cann – Con. Econ. Sec. to Treasury, 1962–63; Minister of State, Board of Trade, 1963–64.

effects – Financial Secretary, Harold Lever, talking about £500m Budget and £600m in six months from deposit scheme. I had to contradict Maurice Parsons again – this time I hope rightly – about the course of consumer spending which we think has fallen quite a lot even if the level now forecast is higher than in April. It emerged that we *didn't* need to agree on coverage and rate just yet.

Chancellor was very good in handling discussion and got the points very quickly. At the end he asked if the scheme could be a bridge to q.r.'s or whether a surcharge was preferable. Sam rambled and Douglas put the question again. Jasper Hollom spoke up for a surcharge on the grounds that if q.r.'s were feared people would pay very high rates for money to furnish deposits: a gilt edged and highly profitable investment. Talked afterwards to Financial Secretary who has in mind special difficulties of import merchant (Berrill had already made the point to us on steel).

Du Cann agreed at lunch that money was getting tight. (As H. Lever said, Rolls Royce loan at 8¼% stands at a discount). Yet none of the group spoke up for credit restriction. They believed that what had to be changed was inflationary psychology, distrust of currency and consequent rush into goods (and equities?).

Long meeting at 4 on import forecast which left me persuaded that we have swung much too far and that imports *will* react if no fresh crisis. We had to go without tea – a thing unheard of in Whitehall – for lack of a messenger to make it.

Donald tried to argue that change in imports was really proportionate to change in final sales but this seems *too* exaggerated when in fact the excess of imports over forecasts is roughly equal to excess of consumption and GDP is only slightly over. It seems to me inconceivable that the stock figures can be right (although *total* stocks may have fallen). Car stocks are well down, for example, but imported car stocks are said to be up.

Tuesday, 2 July   Sam goes off to Rome tomorrow to brief Italians for Basle. Today we were both at a long meeting with Douglas on gold, the dollar, etc. at which D. suggested that the most likely development was a steady growth of import restrictions. Then Sam and I went to see Financial Secretary and agreed that perhaps, after all, if we had to have a contingency plan it should be with a low deposit rate and a wide coverage to bring a mild degree of deflation concentrated on imports and lasting a year.

When I got Alan Neale to see me at 3.00 however he would have no truck with less than 50% and T.I.C. I spoke to Wilfred Morton to make sure that he could handle a second contingency plan. But when I saw Douglas and F.F. in the evening, D. was quite clear that 25% was too weak to do the job. However he agreed that the paper for the Chancellor should mention this alternative and should also raise q.r.'s to which he now turns more and more. But of course if you accept his premises *no* scheme of prior deposits is really worthwhile, and it hardly matters what Wilfred works on. If a scheme that bites severely on imports is advanced it is sure to have the wrong effect on confidence; while if it bites mildly it can be dismissed as not sufficient.

D. had a point when he said that the new style scheme couldn't be squared with the new forecasts. But neither he nor I think the forecasts reliable. Of course I've now dithered so much on all this that I've argued in turn for a surcharge, a 50% deposit scheme and a 25% deposit scheme and have also been against *any* deposit scheme. I never expected to spend so long on a type of device that I took for granted to be inappropriate to use in the UK. Yet we're so anxious to find *some* line of action if the figures are bad (or worse) that we have to agonise over alternative versions of a rather hopeless proposition.

Lunch yesterday with Roger Opie who described how the voting went on the Bank merger case. The banks concerned made a very bad impression and the Governor had to retract at various points. He rested his argument mainly on the international aspect on which we were never asked our opinion. Sam had taken no action on Radice's minute so I made sure today that Douglas and Robert A. were aware of what was in train and asked A. Neale to let us have the timetable. We agreed that the fact that the majority was against might prove sufficient if the Chancellor wanted to stop the merger even if he had no statutory powers.

Sunday, 7 July   Glasgow for SSRC conference in Q.M. Hall.

Donald Robertson discussed Donovan Report and need for large additional resources for wage negotiation if company bargaining is to be effective. He said that railway settlement was one he had set aside because had he given that award it would have been referred to NBPI – in fact he was told so at the time when he contemplated it. Now there will have to be a fresh deal (and wage increase) on productivity and ASLEB will not qualify so that either it makes them strike or else it fails to satisfy NUR.

On Thursday elected President of R.E.S. Aubrey Jones gave a lamentable address full of howlers, the gist of which was that traditional instruments for regulating the economy were losing potency, it was consequently very important to make use of new ones like incomes policy. He would not say whether sanctions should be used to back it but implied that privately he thought so, i.e. the government can't do the job but *I* can provided you give me the necessary powers! He also wanted references to the Board to be more carefully and coherently selected and suggested using a C.E.A. for the purpose to co-ordinate different departments. In Glasgow it was put to me that recent Board Reports have been increasingly sloppy and that A.J. could give them more personal attention.

Friday: long meeting with Donald MacD., J. Jukes and Co. on forecasts (other Treasury advisers away). I found a message saying Burke T. had stopped circulation of E.F. Report and then let *us* have copies marked Top Secret. We had to withdraw drafts from "peripheral" departments and suspend circulation of Annexes. Meeting of E.F. cancelled. Ministers clearly in a funk and not just fed up with forecasts.

In the afternoon of Thursday we had meeting with Chancellor at which he seemed to incline against prior deposits and trust to luck. W. Morton told him that exports in June were as high as in May with fewer working days and everybody fell to calculating how large an increase this would yield on an adjusted basis, the Chancellor saying at one point that we must be in surplus. Two hours later figures came round showing tiddly rise of £9m. W. also hinted that imports might be down because of the go-slow holding up arrival of documents – this apart from Kennedy Round effects. We have a week to make up our minds whether to go ahead or not with scheme.

Saturday, 13 July   A quiet week. When I got back from Glasgow I went into the office in search of the trade figures. The outcome was suspiciously good as I told M. Posner at lunch at the canteen (he had come up for the day, his wife having conveniently given birth the previous day). Curious, however, that a deficit of £50m should be thought unbelievably good when it exceeds the 1964 average!

Chancellor at Misc. 205 repeated his strictures on forecasts (but quite dispassionately). Unfortunately this means that forecasts remain in quarantine and we can't get on with preparing for IMF. They were getting very worried and are sending Goode to head Mission, threatening to make it "formal".

At Garden Party on Thursday I saw P.M., Reggie M., and Joe Grimmond in turn. P.M. said they had thought up a "really lovely one" for me: economists are to say what should be done with SSRC.

We had a long meeting on Friday on the bank merger with Jasper Hollom representing the Bank. Treasury is solid against it and Board of Trade also but Bank is pro. We don't know what Ministers think but given the majority vote they will probably accept that they should come down against and revert to previous régime of informal veto. Likely that if they do, people will find it hard to understand the Nat. Prov./Westminster merger.

Sunday 21 July   Still fairly quiet. Mainly getting Monthly Report off, preparing for Paris, etc. The forecasts have at last been released to a pruned EF circulation but the accumulation of Top Secret papers about the forecasts is now increasingly awkward. The P.M. held out after the Chancellor had written but he seems unaware that LCES will issue on Monday or Tuesday a forecast of +£100m for 1969 balance of payments. It was expected on Friday but now is likely just on the eve of WP No. 3 and IMF visit.

I called on Burke Trend earlier in the week and found him in his panelled room.

Ministers had been very confused by the Public Expenditure decisions and Crosland had broken out at the last meeting when the Chief Secretary had sought to explain the increase in Misc. Services in terms of some errors in the original figures and re-classification. Why should they cut schoolbuilding or road construction to meet the mistakes of some statistician? Then there had been the philosophical problem that for example the nationalised industries were outside PESC while other forms of capital expenditure were in. I didn't add that shortfalls and overspends made nonsense of much of what they did and that they were trying to decide how to save what no decision taken now might affect at all. So we will be asked to look again at the accountancy, the statistics, the philosophy etc. while the IMF hammers away at the borrowing requirement.

Tommy made his maiden speech on Tuesday and by a curious irony it fell to Lionel to congratulate him. Peter Davies heard it and thought that it came over quite well (it reads well) but the press said it was over their Lordships' heads and too fast. I gather that T. was quite white with nervous excitement. Rowley C. said he made his maiden speech on Egypt and that he had to speak in 1956 in the Debate on the Address again on Egypt – when Suez made it an unexpectedly difficult assignment. He agreed that nearly every speaker was very tense in delivering his maiden speech.

Lionel took the opportunity of bowing to those "great and good men" the Governor and ex-Governor of the Bank of England, so T. got his money's worth.

Monday, 29 July   Most of last week in Paris for EPC/WP3. I recorded on Saturday a full report on OECD. There was a fairly brief discussion on Wednesday which was badly mis-reported especially in *Financial Times* and *Guardian*.

It was quite an interesting meeting. For example, nobody referred to the LCES forecast of the balance of payments although Emminger said that it didn't help when "a well-known British research institute" claimed that the dollar was seriously overvalued (there were headlines in the German press based on a paragraph in the LCES). Emminger told me that he had been very interested in my forecast of a £500m surplus next year (I said "in the course of the year" and took steps to remove the ambiguity in WP3) and was unaware that our borrowing requirement differed from the £364m in the Estimates. The Dutch were particularly suspicious and Kessler raised the whole problem of UK prospects in WP3 without making any very clear point – and certainly none that he could not have raised just as easily in EPC. Why they should think anything for the worse has occurred since the Hague meeting I can't imagine. But the Fund Staff's May report has obviously made a highly unfavourable impression.

Larre made one very boring speech that might as well have gone back to Clovis for all it had to do with the future of the French economy. At WP3 he launched an attack on the leaks in the Anglo-Saxon press (his figure for the deficit was what chiefly worried him). But he is notoriously one of the chief sinners and the Secretariat thought him the source of much that got out this time too. Later he made a silly speech about SDR's.

I ought also to mention some bright speeches by Ossola who attacked the French import restrictions soundly as not in keeping with the rest of their policy. "Inappropriate" was his word till the French demurred and he explained that he was not "an authority on diplomatic language". He also echoed Larre's dictum from an earlier meeting that "candour among friends is a duty" – and presumably also a pleasure.

Today I gave a general presentation to the IMF and then went off for lunch at the Bank. The Governor and M.P. talked to me about B.R. which I had gathered from Sam the Governor wants to cut by $1/2\%$. It has to be this week because a week later people will think it reflects inside knowledge of the trade figures and a week later still may be too late. I was very critical because I doubted whether other bankers would see it in the light he did as quite compatible with at least as much restraint as before. Stopper, after all, said the market recovery was a near miracle but reflected expectations not performance. Why couldn't we wait a couple of months? Etc., etc. Sam agrees but I'm told the Chancellor is of the Governor's way of thinking and the Governor said Douglas Allen was too. On the other hand, Jeremy Morse and Jasper Hollom are not. It also looks a little unseemly to me to be in such a hurry to squeeze through a reduction after one set of good trade figures.

The Governor has written to the Chancellor stressing the need for restraint but I haven't seen the letter. He is quite right to fear some impulse to reflate and Ministers are already talking of plans to mitigate unemployment this winter.

At the reception for the IMF Brian Rose asked me how far the forecasts reflected a more cautious temper brought on by bad news for 5 months. He judged that the Budget hadn't had time to affect imports till June and in the aeroplane before he saw our forecasts thought that the surplus for next year might be put at £350m, not £265m or even £150m. As I told Jeremy Morse and Getzwold at Le Bourget it's rather comforting to think that for once we may have been too cautious in our forecasts. A great many people are now beginning to think that the change in the visible balance will come sooner than we are predicting.

Dick Goode asked us (a) why consumption shouldn't be brought back to where we originally forecast and (b) how we viewed the balance of payments forecast – as satisfactory or not and with what degree of confidence. I think they are half-inclined to believe that we are over-doing caution. But I doubt whether Goode will encourage the Governor tomorrow to cut bank rate this week! And Bill Martin may also have shown only moderate enthusiasm although it would suit the Fed. The Governor and Deputy both said that money was coming in now (which I heard from Rupert) and that the American banks were not pulling out Euro-dollars (of which I'm less certain). At least we're ending July with a surplus and that would have seemed almost incredible a month ago when we lost $200m in a single day. The figures will be out on Friday (and so justify a cut in bank rate).

Tuesday, 30 July   Quiet: no sign of IMF. R. Armstrong told me that the Chancellor's attitude to a bank rate change was governed by the greater ease (politically) of getting it down now. It might be thought in September that it was a reaction to high unemployment. This stands my line of argument on its head but doesn't take account of the advantages of waiting at least for one more good figure (say, another fortnight). Chancellor is seeing Stopper on Friday but that will be too late.

Jordan Moss[57] says Crossman has got his 1963 Brains Trust together: T.B.,

[57] N Jordan Moss Asst. Sec., Treasury, 1956–68; Under-Sec., 1968–71; Counsellor, UK Perm. Delegation to OECD, Paris, 1963–64.

N.K., Abel-Smith[58] and Titmuss[59]. But they don't agree, T.B. has nothing constructive to say and N.K. says it's all eyewash. To which Crossman replied that of course it's all eyewash (earnings related pensions) but none the less important. They are arguing about funding, on which I thought we'd said the last word in 1953.[60] You can't use the Budget to balance the economy and run a fund within the surplus tied in any meaningful way to Social Security. Funds and "pay as you go" don't marry; and the forcing of growth by higher investment need have little to do with pensions.

Stephen Wilson[61] says that the biographer of Herbert Morrison has come in search of papers. What went to Chester[62] at Nuffield was what remained after he had destroyed nearly everything under pressure from his second wife: she made him keep his invitation cards to the Palace. The P.M. didn't want a history of external economic policy and preferred a history of the exit from India as the greatest achievement of the first Labour Government. Colonial Office and Comm. Office didn't much like it. In the end there won't be a history but six volumes of documents edited by Mansergh. The external economic policy idea is not dead but still needs Privy Council approval. So Richard Sayers may not have to wait three years this time as he did in 1945 when he was first sounded about a Financial History of the War, with Wilfred King as the only other runner (Wilfrid was never told).[63]

Wednesday, 31 July   So ends July: with sterling high and disbelief that now at last we may have found relief. No crisis and Harold's prestige recovering. Yet in the first six months we lost over £1,000m spot and in the second quarter the short term capital outflow was not far short of £300m. The diversification of sterling went on apace and the rundown in sterling liabilities more than accounts for the capital outflow since devaluation: in fact more sterling money is coming back. Kuwait alone has withdrawn half her gross liabilities of a year ago and drew £75m in June alone.

Bill Nield said that two years in the Cabinet Office had taught him that if Ministers saw unemployment over 2% they would always find that more compelling than the state of the balance of payments. Peter Shore was very worried, in spite of frequent sessions, by the unemployment figures in MTAC and had

[58] Brian Abel-Smith – Prof. of Social Administration, LSE, 1965–91; Special Adviser to the Sec. of State for Social Services, 1968–70; 1974–78.

[59] R Titmuss – Prof. of Social Administration, LSE, 1950–73; Dep. Chm., Supplementary Benefits Commission, 1965–73.

[60] The reference is to the Report of the Committee on Economic and Financial Problems of the Provision for Old Age (Cmnd 9333) to which I wrote an (unpublished) appendix attacking the proposal to fund State pensions. It was withdrawn when the chairman, after Treasury advice, abandoned the idea.

[61] S S Wilson – Min. of Transport, 1929–47; Keeper of the Public Records, 1960–64; Historical Section, Cabinet Office, 1964–77.

[62] D N Chester – Former member of Economic Section; Warden of Nuffield College, Oxford.

[63] When Richard Sayers was unable to undertake a history of external economic policy, the job was ultimately undertaken by Professor Leslie Pressnell.

pointed out that there would be an election on this basis with unemployment still over 2%, which they just couldn't stand. The Chancellor, I judge, thinks differently but he knows that his power rests on continuing balance of payments difficulties and however much he fears bad figures he must also fear that they become too good. A marked improvement in the next two months would make things awkward for him at the Party Conference.

Douglas Allen at an earlier meeting spoke of the need for "seasonally adjusted Ministers" – in reference to their proneness at this time of year to inflate and take the edge off winter unemployment.

Thursday, 1 August   No cut in bank rate. Governor told Chancellor he had decided against even before adverse judgment (predictable) of Dick Goode. This was because the inflow of funds has dried up and the US won't cut their discount rate for at least a fortnight. So they will now think again in the middle of the month. As the Chancellor will be away let's hope the figures are either very good or rather poor. On the whole I would almost prefer the latter, given the way opinion may swing.

It's interesting all the same that the responsible press commentators are all advising the Government to stick to its guns and not reflate. (P. Jay, Trethowan,[64] Sam B., etc.). Their influence as always is considerable even if they really speak only for themselves; but the lobbies are still more powerful, once organized, and unemployment is a powerful organizer of lobbies.

Directorate – mainly on Basle. I said my piece about the threefold increase in tap stock prices and found little support, Sam being strongly pro-Bank in the interests of orderly markets and Robert Armstrong also unsympathetic. The Governor told me on Monday he was not anxious to get long rates down but I can't see the recent handling of the gilt-edged market as entirely consistent with this (i.e. *after* the original damper when the price of tap stock was lowered).

Raphael told me that William's "circus" after devaluation didn't extend beyond P.J. and S.B./Freddie Fisher with an occasional bringing in of the *Daily Telegraph*. It's quite clear that Denis knew nothing at all about it and of course I learned only by accident.

Export price index jumped in June. This may yet cause trouble. Unemployment figures in August will be well up – the Chancellor no doubt had this in mind over bank rate.

Lunch at the Reform with Sam, David Hubback, Dick Goode and Co. No indication what they will recommend but probably tightening of money supply – they are thinking of a *rise* in interest rates.

Long meeting with Donald and Co. on SSRC finance. We foresee surplus of social scientists with post-graduate degrees and little of real value to do.

Interchange of minutes with W.G. on the devaluation package. He established to my satisfaction that we had given ample warning of the need to announce

[64] Ian Trethowan – Polit. editor, ITV, 1958–63; joined BBC 1963 as commentator on current affairs; Man. Dir., BBC Radio, 1969–75; BBC TV, 1976–77; Dir. Gen., BBC, 1977–82.

measures *at once* on the full scale even if they didn't take full effect at once. We had visualised the importance of confidence in the new rate as well as the political difficulty of taking action later and W. argued strongly that the economic difficulties *were* the psychological and political consequences of not taking sufficiently resolute action at the start. He agreed however that we hadn't fully appreciated, after the initial mistake, how serious was the inflationary virus.

Tuesday, 6 August   I had lunch on Friday with Freddie Fisher at Oxford and Cambridge Club. He pressed me to write what I knew even if it were locked up for 30 years. He would like to know what advice the Treasury gave over hire purchase last autumn.

At Nita Maton's[65] cocktail party I met Leak[66] for the first time for over 20 years and he didn't recognise me. He lives for his grandchildren, gardening and bowling. He thought his promotion to Assistant Secretary with responsibility for the Statistics Division a bit of luck. Flux was away in The Hague (about 1933) – for the World Economic Conference I thought he said but that was in London – and somebody had to prepare a memo. quickly on the balance of payments for Stamp's E.A.C. Leak said he could do it and was so successful that he was put in charge of the Statistics Division.

The IMF saw the Chancellor this afternoon and there was probably no real disagreement. Essentially they are inclined to think that our policies are working better than we allow but they reserve judgment and intend us therefore to keep firmly to those policies and if they are not having the promised results (e.g. on consumption or credit) to reinforce them.

Thursday, 8 August   The most important point made by Dick Goode was that Q2 private credit to residents and non-residents went up by nearly £500m and the government's financing requirements were £500m so that in spite of a deficit of about this size, the money supply *also* increased by £500m. Not much of a liquidity squeeze!

The July import figures came in last night and were a decided shock since they were up to £670m (including US aircraft) – an all-time record; and in spite of a rise in exports by £18m the deficit will be about £80m on the month after £50m last month. It may console the Chancellor and the President of the Board of Trade that taking June/July together this is a reduction on previous high figures but it won't look that way to the world and we'll be lucky to get through to September (with the Chancellor in Cyprus!). I had persuaded myself that we might get within striking distance of £50m because of the way ships and aircraft have fluctuated and thought –£70m about the worst we might have to face. It certainly won't help the IMF to establish that we erred on the safe side in our forecasts. The N.I.E.S.R. have still to deliver *their* forecast but Jim

---

[65] J N (Nita) Maton – Dep. Dir. of Statistics, Board of Trade till 1967.

[66] H Leak and A W Flux – In the first half of this century, the Board of Trade appointed four successive Directors of Statistics who appeared to have links with water supply: Flux, Fountain, Plummer and Leak.

Ball will put the 1969 surplus at £250m on Sunday. (Current account only as it transpired).

Monday, 12 August   Robin Armstrong told me today that the Governor was still hoping to get bank rate down. He took a "very relaxed view" of the probable market reaction to the trade figures. Sam reminded me that the opposition to a cut had come in part from within the Bank (Jasper H. or Jeremy Morse).

The real difficulty about the trade figures is that they effectively dispel the illusion that the Budget will now have the same effect externally as it had domestically on consumption. Slow and steady it must be when the world expects something more dramatic.

The Chancellor apparently took some comfort from the thought that if we had to have a bad month it had better be now. Exactly what I had concluded!

Thursday, 15 August   Market took the trade figures very calmly and so did gilt-edged market. But second thoughts will no doubt set in and in August reactions may be sluggish. Already, after hours, rumours of an intensification of credit squeeze about which Sam B. rang me up. Sam G. had had the Governor to see him and a statement will have to be issued. I expect it's all due to leakage of what the Governor told the Clearing Banks, and I told Sam B. that the existing policy would be quite tough enough if we could stick to it.

What concerns me is the gilt-edged market where we are liable to generate still more liquidity by taking in stock and finding the IMF coming down on us for repeating the familiar cycle.

I had a long meeting today on reporting trends in money supply and think that we may have arrived at a more illuminating way of analysing the figures – rather à la Goode.

The Chancellor seems willing to allow token expansion in development areas as price of rest of his policy. But the papers will alert everybody to the fact that it can be no more than token so there is little gain presentationally.

All this came up nearly a month ago at the Permanent Secretary's meeting when Tony Part argued for winter help and Steve told him not to be silly and offer Ministers needless encouragement to inflate.

The swing in the gilt-edged market will cause trouble if the Bank of England was behind the hints over the past few days that bank rate might yet come down soon in spite of the trade figures. It looks like inspired comment, quite inconsistent with tighter money whatever the Governor may think.

Monday, 19 August   Lunch with John Cooper of Schroder's. He says they are advising clients to invoice in dollars. This may not cost us foreign exchange at once but it leads to accumulation of dollar instead of sterling balances (as in the diamond market) and of course puts us at the mercy of foreign financing. So far the Bundesbank will pick up the bills via swaps with the commercial banks and it works out cheaper than sterling financing while also freeing clients from effects of the squeeze. The Bundesbank will even finance sterling bills if one end of the transaction is in Germany. Cooper was very surprised at market reaction to Basle and thought dollar invoicing would be more important. But he would be a lot more surprised if he knew that Basle isn't yet "in the bag" and that we continue to have difficulties with Kuwait, Singapore and Australia. F. Figgures not back yet.

On Friday the Clearing Banks took strong exception to a possible statement by the Bank of England on credit restriction and none will be issued. It happens that nobody has taken much interest since Sam Britttan's article in the *Financial Times* (based on his conversation with me) but it was quite a fair piece and didn't talk of any *letter* to the Clearers. In fact I was at pains to emphasise that Gov. and Banks were in constant touch. And apparently both sides pretty touchy.

Saturday, 14 September   Before I went off $3\frac{1}{2}$ weeks ago to the Solway I had a quick word with Sam G. about the gilt-edged market. He explained that the Bank was unwilling to hold the price steady because to do so would bring dealings to a stop. The market would suspect that the Bank knew more than they would say and that in holding down long rates they were acting with this knowledge. Buying would therefore be discouraged. The absence of movement in prices would also make against dealings on any scale. I said that I could see the force of preserving an active market and letting market pressures register in price movements in ordinary circumstances. But these were not ordinary circumstances. We knew that long rates were high and so did the market. We could encourage the market to take advantage of a temporary bargain and it would pay us to do so because we badly wanted to tighten liquidity. We ought not to yield to short-term pressures that were very easily reversed as soon as bad news came along but should remember that, whatever the immediate suspicions of the market, the level of prices for gilt-edged had an independent influence on holdings that we could not ignore. If the Bank merely wanted orderly dealings let them make sure that they had an ample range and supply of tap stocks.

S. was not convinced and obviously doubtful whether the Bank would take heed of this advice but promised to discuss it with them. He was on leave this week i.e. from Monday when I got back.

Meanwhile we had a run on the pound because of rumours about a revaluation of the DM, and of pressure by the UK authorities in Basle and London on the Germans. Of course, there is no truth at all in this, as both O'Brien and Schiller have said publicly. But it all looked like an inspired leak in the British press.

I pointed out to Baffi in Montreal that in time the British press would tumble to the (larger) Italian surplus and he said that he had warned Carli of this already and advised him that it was a further reason for standing firm on the DM.

It is true however that the Basle negotiations were difficult and are still unfinished. The press on Monday again made a hash of it (especially Peter Jay) with stories that it had all been H. Lever's doing (making clear that there had been a Ministerial leak and from what source) and that it meant the dissolution of the sterling area. Frank F. had so much trouble in Australia that in the end Leslie O'B. had to go out (this news did *not* leak). In the case of Malaysia and Singapore the difficulties are not yet resolved. We think that S. was cheating and the P.M. had to communicate with Lee over the head of his Finance Minister. With Kuwait the agreement is informal.

Returning to London I found Harry and Elizabeth Johnson at the airport and motored back with them. Liz J. said that she had found quite a lot of Keynes' minutes on Treasury files at the P.R.O. It was not true that his black box held everything from W.W.I. Indeed, much was not very intelligible without access to the files.

Lunch later with Duesenberry en route to Ditchley. He reminded me of the remarks by Myrdal[67] at Ulricehamn about Lundberg's openmindedness. M. compared him to the man asked by a lady to help him with her zip. "Certainly. Do you want it pulled up or down?" He also said that if US activity continued to rise as in Q3 there would be mass conversion to Friedman[68] (since the money supply was expanding but taxation was intended to damp down activity) but he felt pretty sure that there would be a change before long.

On the whole a quiet week at the office. Michael P. went off to a conference in Italy but Donald was back by Wednesday and so was Nicky. Much debate has gone on about contingency planning but I didn't attend any of the Chancellor's meetings. On Thursday I saw Tony Crosland in the Foreign Office quadrangle after SEP and he said to me as he got into his car. "There is a great hate in the Board of Trade against the Treasury for changing their minds in August over Misc. 205". I said "People are always in favour of getting somebody else to do the controlling" and he agreed. The fact is that we are now chary of using import deposits (except Nicky who is worried at the new enthusiasm for import quotas) because we can't calculate their effect; we regard a surcharge as a better run-in over the first two months; and we now see ways of using Customs Officers to handle the immediate administrative problem of issuing quota where this seemed an almost insuperable problem before.

But I take none of this very seriously. I fully expected a reaction in the deficit to under £50m and it is in fact £30m although some at least of this reduction is suspect (e.g. imports of ships delivered abroad are nil against £12m in July). This gives us a breathing space and I can't believe that will get such a big reaction in September as to revive talk of quotas.

N.K. however buttonholed me on Wednesday after a long meeting on a national minimum wage (all of us were strongly against this: if it is effective it will be very expensive, especially if combined with equal pay; and if, as is more probable, it is ineffective because differentials re-establish themselves it will produce the worst form of inflation).

N. wanted a floating rate rather than quotas. I said that this would be madness in the next month or two since it would inflate our import bill without adding to exports; and in the longer run I was not convinced that devaluation had failed. N. agreed that he had in mind action at least 2–3 months away and that it would be difficult to go for a floating rate if either (a) things now got rapidly better or

[67] Gunnar Myrdal – Swedish economist and politician; Exec. Sec., UNECE, 1947–57; Prof. of International Economy, Stockholm Univ., 1960–67.

[68] Milton Friedman – Prof. of Economics, Univ. of Chicago, 1968–83; an early monetarist.

(b) we had sudden deterioration. I couldn't visualise the circumstances he had in mind in which it would be appropriate to float (perhaps a marked check to exports) and reminded him that three months ago he had argued that we couldn't *afford* the current level of imports so that it would be natural to cut imports first before floating.

N. thought that the rate wouldn't go below about 2.20 except briefly. I said this seemed optimistic. If we failed to hold the present rate why should holders of sterling think that a further small reduction in the rate would be so different. Wouldn't there be a strong desire to get out of sterling, guarantees or no guarantees?

Earlier I had said it would be a mistake to float just as soon as the Basle agreement was signed.[69] N. didn't like this: he had been told earlier to wait *until* it was signed, and now he was told that it was still the wrong time to float. The agreement safeguarded our right to let the pound float (this is news to me). In any event he was worried by the drift of contingency planning. Quotas were a cul-de-sac and would be resented abroad. At least import deposits were aimed at the excess of liquidity from which we suffered.

The Treasury seems rather listless at present – partly the effect of the holidays and the season of the year, but also a sense of waiting for things to happen. There is a growing interest in monetary affairs and the battles over public expenditure are still continuing or in the offing. But not much is going on that is really new.

Two items, however, are worth mentioning. The Select Committee on Nationalised Industries has reported, arousing nostalgia in John Hunt. They speak à propos of Power of the wisdom of talking to the organ-grinder (Treasury) rather than his monkey (M. of P.). It could be more happily put. They also make no bones about who was right on the electricity programme cuts. But they have gone overboard for a single Minister of Nationalised Industries when what is wanted is an enlarged P.E. Division of the Treasury.

Then we had the merger of English Electricity and GEC/AEI, without reference to the Monopolies Commission. This is bound to make some people ask what mergers *are* to be referred in future and gives the IRC powers hitherto thought to have rested with the Monopolies Commission.

Sunday, 15 September   I went in pouring rain to fetch Walter Heller from Carlton Tower for lunch. He stayed till about 4.30 and spoke with his usual fluency. At lunch he reminded me of some of my maxims (though I think he invented them) at the conference at Ulricehamn in 1967 in honour of Professor Eric Luneberg: "Never underestimate the power of a platitude". "Never give a figure *and* a date – only one or the other".

---

[69] In October 1968, after consultations extending over the previous three months, the BIS and twelve members of the OECD (the Basle Group) agreed to make available for the next three to five years a facility for $2000 million to cover any prospective rundown in the sterling balances held by members of the sterling area. This was on condition that the United Kingdom and sterling area countries would make a contribution to the facility. The agreement followed earlier arrangements by the same group from 1966 onwards to offset fluctuations in sterling balances.

He said that over the past year he has frequently been rung up by the press to ask when he is taking over from Joe Fowler and that *Life* had a team of photographers ready to take off till he told them not to waste their time. When he saw the President with Hubert Humphrey[70] not long ago the President said (to his surprise) that for the past year he had wanted to get Walter as his next Secretary of the Treasury and he could think of no-one better qualified for the job. L.B.J. did in fact press Kermit Gordon to take it before going to Joe Fowler but Kermit, in spite of Walter's support for the idea, felt that this was not what he was cut out for. As head of the Bureau of the Budget his authority was clear cut and there was none of the in-fighting that a Secretary of the Treasury or a Chairman of the Council of Economic Advisers had to be prepared for. Of course he might have to appeal to the President for support if his ruling was challenged and as Kermit Gordon once told me he could not go too often or he would forfeit his moral independence (and his hope of effective support). But this was a different situation from the usual dogfights involving Congress and a group of different agencies.

Walter was also enthusiatic about H.H.H. He had an encyclopaedic mind and was better informed about a wider range of problems than almost any other man in the United States. He could revise drafts on economic issues without making nonsense of them, e.g. he had gone over 16 draft answers for *Fortune* with Walter, 14 on economic issues, and made useful amendments. But he didn't duck any of them when he had this option. He felt constrained to take a stand on more issues than he need. When he got off the plane on a visit to de Gaulle in Paris he was handed a script for a toast and rejected it at once. He said: "You don't tell de Gaulle when he is your host how often the United States has helped him. You remind him how often France has helped the United States, however difficult you find it to think of examples", and he therefore gave the State Department a series of items to check on from Lafayette onwards. At the lunch party he had de Gaulle in tears. Similarly in visiting NATO, OECD, etc. he spoke most effectively, rejecting his written briefs and handing them over to his hosts at the end as a supplement.

Walter said that if Nixon[71] was elected, as now seemed likely, McCracken[72] was the probable Chairman of the Council and was the most reasonable of the candidates. Burns[73] and Saulnier[74] had never hit it off, and Burns had advised Nixon against Saulnier. If H. was elected, Okun would probably stay. Nixon might pick Nelson Rockefeller[75] as Secretary of State. But according to Walter,

[70] Hubert Humphrey – American Senator, 1949–64; Vice Pres. of USA, 1965–69.

[71] Richard Nixon – Vice Pres. of USA, 1953–61; President, 1969–74; granted Pres. Pardon by Pres. Ford after Watergate.

[72] Paul McCracken – Member, US Council of Economic Advisers, Washington, 1956–59; Chm., 1969–72.

[73] Arthur F Burns – Prof.of Economics, Columbia Univ., 1944–69; Pres. Nat. Bureau of Econ. Research, 1957–67; Chm., Fed. Reserve Board, 1970–78.

[74] Raymond J Saulnier – Consultant to Council of Econ. Advisers, Washington, 1953–55, Chm. 1957–60.

[75] Nelson Rockefeller American public servant and politician; Governor, New York

both Nixon and H. were thinking of David Rockefeller as Secretary of the Treasury (if Humphrey didn't ask Walter himself, of which there was a fair chance).

Walter also spoke rather slightingly of McCarthy[76] whom he regarded as an adornment of the Senate but lacking the necessary range to be a Vice President. He had imagined in 1964 that L.B.J. was going to nominate him Vice President and felt let down when H.H.H. was nominated. But this showed how little he understood of politics since it was never "on" and L.B.J. was given to these "games". McCarthy, travelling in the plane with Walter, had suggested that employment could be increased by giving tax concessions in favour of expenditure on domestic servants, etc., and reinforced this by pointing out that it would be a popular move. Not the idea of a man of principle. Walter thought him a one-issue man and hoped that he would in due course support H.H. But he had asked for time, feeling that to throw his weight behind H.H. so soon would be resented by his young supporters.

Walter added that H.H. in his acceptance speech had put in something in the first five minutes to defend the action of the police and it was only later, and misjudging the electoral position, that he had spoken in a different sense. His reference to legislative joy and happiness was a direct "quote" from McCarthy.

Walter spoke of his book which was now recommended student reading in over 200 colleges and selling well. He thought it important to write at once while the material was fresh and regarded lectures as perhaps the best form although he proposed to rewrite the book now that it had caught on.

Monday, 16 September   Little or nothing to do. Left the office by 6.15 which is almost a record. There is a curious listlessness as if there ought to be a crisis and in fact there is none. In fact for the first time for ages it is possible to sit down and ask what we should be doing instead of struggling to keep the in-tray from piling up too high. Nevertheless there will be at least 7 meetings this week of SEPO(A) on agriculture and Peter Baldwin feels that there are plenty of crises on public expenditure: only "when you try to put your foot down it goes through the floor".

Sunday, 22 September   The *Economist* came down against the $\frac{1}{2}$% cut in bank rate while most of the press agitated for another $\frac{1}{2}$%. The IMF and the Fed. were also reported to be hostile. I was far from enthusiastic but was told by Sam Goldman on Tuesday that it was all settled. No official news reached me, nor M.P.

Busy with Monthly Report which I put in on Thursday after discussing a draft with MacDougall. He, as usual, went carefully over the short-term macro parts and had nothing to say on industry so that in the end I had to draft a few platitudes without even submitting them to him for discussion.

State, 1958–73; Vice Pres. of USA, 1974–77.

[76] E J McCarthy – American politician; Senator from Minnesota, 1954–70; Presidential candidate, 1976.

On Friday the running forecast arrived on my desk and showed unemployment likely to reach 3% by the end of next year, without any corresponding improvement in the trade balance. The Chancellor was away so I held up all copies to go outside Treasury except Donald's. Frank Cassell[77] also sent me a note on imports for the Chancellor but we are obviously not much wiser about the underlying trend.

Tuesday, 24 September   I got as far as shaking hands with the Chancellor yesterday at the Commonwealth Officials reception but haven't set eyes on him for ages. Nicky took me with M.P. in his car to Lancaster House and I found them walking away while I was trapped in the back. M.P. had seen the Chancellor who expostulated with him on his cheerfulness and then made the same kind of criticisms as Michael of the running forecast, i.e. how could we reconcile ourselves to 3% unemployment and would it really be 3%? Robert Armstrong says Chancellor has no faith at all in the forecasts but worries about them.

Tonight N.K. took me to Indian High Commissioner's reception for Morarji Desai[78]. He said he kept being invited to lecture abroad or by Marshall Society, etc., etc. and tended to say (like me) "not now, next year" and then got caught by the obligations he had taken on a year ago. The *Review of Economic Studies*, Marshall Society and others wanted him to reminisce, not on their early history, but on his life in the Treasury. "Apart from the fact that I like my colleagues in the Treasury", he said, "I can't tell them that I was in favour of devaluation all along and they weren't. I can't just tell them that decisions are not taken rationally. What *can* I say?" So I promised to let him have my lecture as a pump-primer. He said that one thing that struck him was that it was very much the same inside as outside in the sense that you had the same information but a little earlier and still had to make up your mind.

Yesterday at yet another meeting on National Minimum Wage he arrived late and then monopolised the meeting with a flow of criticisms of the draft (to K. Berrill's disgust), some of them quite new and all very ingenious. They implied a far more favourable view of the proposals so we naturally asked if he had changed his mind. But he said "No. I just want to get the intellectual basis of it right even if I disagree on other grounds". M.P. said he was half persuaded by N.K. What was wrong? N. said he preferred to rely on SET to get higher productivity and on family allowances to deal with poverty. He accepted that there was a *risk* of more rapid inflation if we adopted a N.M.W. but didn't like assertions that the wage-profile had remained unchanged over 80 years and that in the United States and elsewhere the introduction of N.M.W. had caused differentials to be re-established. Inflation went on as before so that they re-emerged: that was all. And earlier he quoted Shove's review of Hicks on monopsonistic exploitation.

[77] Frank Cassell – Dep. Editor, *The Banker* 1958–65; Econ. Adviser, Treasury, 1965–68; Senior Econ. Adviser, 1968–74.

[78] Morarji Desai – Finance Minister, India, 1958–63; Dep. Prime Minister and Minister of Finance, 1967–69.

Tonight Jha[79] told me that in the I.C.S. starting salaries for administrators were 350 rupees per month compared with 400 when he started and top salaries 3,500 compared with 4,000. Throughout the public sector – including the nationalised industries – this was so. But outside firms wouldn't dream of paying such low rates. In real value the contraction was enormous. For Ministers the rate under the British had been 6,000 per month and now it was 2,000; but with house, car, etc. it was more reasonable. Our devaluation was "the immaculate deception".

Reggie Maudling and Jim Callaghan were both there together and spoke to M. Desai to be photographed in a group. They took no notice of me but Jim Callaghan embraced N.K. warmly, kissing him on both cheeks! Donald MacD. told me later of the conversation between R.M. and J.C. It started with R.M. asking how J. liked the Home Office after the Treasury. He said it was a great improvement. If you wanted something done you could get it done whereas in the Treasury if you wanted to get the economy to go somewhere it never did. "You should pick on the Home Office if you get back" he told Reggie, "not the Treasury". Reggie protested he rather liked the Treasury. "Of course", he murmured, "I left you with rather a difficult position to handle"; and he didn't ask if J.C. wasn't cooking up trouble in the Home Office.

Friday, 27 September   I have at last got off to William Armstrong a memo on conjunctural policy which I promised him for the week-end (for his Stamp Lecture). I tried to get agreement to the circulation of the running forecast, first to other ministers, then at least to the Prime Minister, but the Chancellor doesn't want it to go to the Prime Minister even until he gets back from Canada. This means that the Prime Minister will make his speeches to the Party Conference without knowing what our conclusions are. I made a mild protest to Robert Armstrong and to Douglas Allen but the fact is that the Chancellor was chiefly concerned to know whether he would be speaking at Blackpool and couldn't give his mind to forecasts. He also, as Douglas pointed out, is preoccupied with the way immediately ahead and not much interested yet in the shape of 1969. He told R.A. "I'd be more interested if I believed the figures". But of course *this* forecast is much like its predecessor and the facts have tended to bear that one out. For the first time since the Chancellor took office events are not too different from our expectations as reflected in the forecasts.

Tuesday, 1 October   Yesterday I went to a dinner in honour of Lord Crowther at the Dorchester and saw again Barbara Jackson,[80] Pat Norton,[81] Donald McLachlan[82] and a whole lot of my contemporaries of 1946. I had a chance to talk to all

---

[79] L K Jha – Sec., Indian Ministry of Finance, 1960–64; Sec. to Prime Minister, 1964–67; Governor, Reserve Bank of India, 1967–70.

[80] Barbara (Ward) Jackson – Asst. Editor, *The Economist* 1939–57; Visiting Scholar, Harvard Univ., 1957–68.

[81] Pat Norton – Staff of *The Economist*.

[82] Donald McLachlan – Asst. Editor, *The Economist* 1947–54; Dep. Editor, *Daily Telegraph* 1954–60; Editor, *Sunday Telegraph* 1961–66.

sorts of people including Alastair Burnet, John Midgley[83] and George Steiner[84]. The latter I congratulated on his TV appearance with a psychiatrist to discuss violence but he soon became absorbed with his former lady boss of 1952-56 – "the best time of my life". Then, when I did catch his attention he launched out on the virtues of computers and the M.I.T., the need to copy the Americans and Russians in teaching computer languages in school, the lack of even a score of politicians who understood the possibilities of the computer and its impact on political life, etc., etc.

I asked Paul Bareau why the English press (and especially *The Times*) was making such a fool of itself over Milton Friedman and he said he understood it must all be Treasury inspired. I laughed at this and said we could hardly have put Peter Jay up to publishing an article appealing to the Treasury for help in refuting Milton Friedman.

William Armstrong asked me at lunch why P.J. was plugging the money supply but I couldn't enlighten him. He has no car but doesn't feel the need of one and doubts whether he will ever feel it now.

Sam Goldman has sent over a note of the latest meeting of the Strengers group (a good example of the inner, inner circle) at which they discussed French devaluation. Deming said it was unlikely till the spring but as they have lost about half their reserves (i.e. over $3b but including swap facilities) and are still losing at up to $100m a week (chickenfeed to us!) they *may* act earlier. Emminger thought that Germany would be consulted. They all agreed to Deming's proposition (put as a question) that it would be a good thing from the international point of view, if the French devaluation was accompanied by an upvaluation of the Dm and perhaps also the lira. Sam put the UK view that if the Germans did *not* move and the dollar and the pound were still in trouble, the net effect would be to cause a flight from both currencies. This, he thought, impressed Emminger.

Our losses in the first week of September, when the last flight into Dm took place, were £100m which, however bad, was small by past standards. In fact, Q3 was a vast improvement on Q1 and Q2 and left us nearly in balance on monetary movements.[85]

Sunday, 6 October   My last interview was with M.P. who told me that the q.r. scheme couldn't be introduced till December because of a muddle between the Board of Trade and Customs and that it was lucky the export figures were so good. We discussed "accompanying measures" but it struck me as something for the file. The Board of Trade insist that they can't extend the coverage and that semis can be dealt with only through centralised buying as in wartime. Bretherton points out that controls lead to excess stocks. And in any event it's

---

[83] John Midgley – American correspondent of *The Economist*.

[84] George Steiner – American writer and scholar; *The Economist* 1952–56; Princeton Univ., 1956–60; Fellow of Churchill College, Cambridge, 1961–69.

[85] In the third quarter, a relatively small current account deficit of £60 million was fully covered by an inflow of capital.

very hard to see how we justify introducing q.r.'s in *November* after refraining from using them for the really critical year. If we *did*, everybody would be very worried about the pound and would expect us to deflate even if there were no economic case for it.

By now things look a great deal better than at any time this year. We should have good trade figures and may be fairly near balance i.e. closer to our Budget forecast than we had hoped. Unemployment can't be falling without some good reason and it doesn't look as if consumption alone can account for it, since retail sales are still within the broad limits of our forecast. Perhaps for this reason my mind doesn't turn now to Treasury affairs but begins to dwell on what to do next year.

Monday, 7 October   At lunch on Friday I discussed with Raymond Bell and Jack Rampton[86] the withdrawal of the Civil Service into its shell since the war. They agreed that there was very little contact with business and that the main reason was the high cost. If few younger members joined clubs this was because they had to count the pennies: even the failure to buy a daily paper recently reported of some of the entrants of '56 could be put down to this. Before the war, a young man would celebrate his promotion to Principal by joining a club; and some joined earlier. But how could they afford to even eat there if they joined? They couldn't claim entertaining a business guest as an expense whereas in business there was no such difficulty. An American who joined a business after a spell in the diplomatic service went on tour in Europe and turned in a large expense account on his return with some hesitation only to be called upon to explain why it wasn't three times as big. Jack Rampton said he reckoned that his salary in Malaya was the equivalent in English terms of about £9,000 a year.

In other words, high taxation has bitten on the civil service but not to the same extent on businessmen who can charge many things to expenses including car, house, lunch, etc. The civil servant can't readily invite a business colleague to lunch without people looking askance at the transaction: not for Lynskey type reasons but because it is unheard of. It thus rests with business to do all the inviting and this creates a sense of dependence and a lack of real intimacy.

I asked Jack how it was possible to make appointments sensibly to the Boards of public corporations in such a state of ignorance and he readily agreed that it was a great handicap. I was reminded of my encounter with Helsby when I proposed Chapman[87] and others for the Arbitration Court and nobody knew anything about my suggested candidates.

Today with Bob Painter[88] and Nick Jordan Moss we discussed the flair some people have for seeing a business deal. Bob quoted his "library fag" – a man

---

[86] Jack Rampton Under-Sec., Treasury, 1964–68; Dep. Sec., Min. of Technology, 1968–70; Dep. Sec., Dept. of Trade and Industry, 1970–72.

[87] J H Chapman – Glasgow contemporary employed by G Colman Ltd; killed in mountaineering accident.

[88] Robert Painter – in 1968 Asst. Sec. in Home Finance Division, Treasury.

who barely escaped being thrown out as unfit for public school education – as a man who was now the biggest turkey breeder in Europe and had just sold turkey incubators of his own invention to the Russians on a grand scale. He then cited the man who made bowl fires by using waste circles of metal stamped out in some other factory and then, when faced with no demand, adapted them by fitting infrared centres and selling them to chicken farmers. Nick spoke of White's and the atmosphere in the bar where they all knew a thing or two about where to sell this or that. One man who was with the partisans in the war picked up commissions on the basis that he would be seeing Tito[89] next week – and he would – and had got to hear in time of a big refrigeration contract that was likely to go to Hall's. By timely representations to Hall's he collected his 2% commission on the deal (presumably at least £1m) and so earned enough to see him through for a month or two.

Chancellor and Douglas still away and not expected till Thursday or Friday.

Sunday, 13 October Olympic games on T.V. Rhodesian talks broke down. Stock exchange slump.

Whitehall D.C. on Thursday at Athenaeum. Usual attack over failure to "face reality" which came down in the end to the difficulty of getting spares for British cars abroad. Contrasts drawn with willingness of foreigners (e.g. in Germany) to put great efforts into export as if our exports had been a source of profit to the exporters on the same scale. Maurice P. also insisted on consumer boom lying behind imports both in Q1 and since. Nobody took seriously possibility that we would have a surplus at rate of £500m by end of 1969 and there were laughs at idea that this differed from £500m *in* 1969.[90] Gordon Richardson as we left said to me: "I can't see how we can get through 1969 without import restrictions" (meaning quotas). General tendency also to think industrial investment would never revive: yet next day we published figures showing expectation of 15% increase next year (and *The Times* put this as an aside in a final sentence concentrating on probable fall *this* year when it is nearly over already). Yet I expect that if we avoid an engineering strike (which troubled Leslie Rowan) opinion will swing round very fast.

From our point of view difficult to see what is happening. We have GDP either -2%, -1/2% or 0% in Q1; unemployment falling when everybody thinks that productivity is shooting up and employment figures show unexpected falls in keeping with this but not with unemployment.

Chancellor held meeting on q.r.'s etc. on Friday but as usual nobody invited me and I thought it as well to stay away in any event.

Douglas says my successor can't be decided till P.M. pronounces and W.A. hasn't put question yet to P.M. The fact that Burke Trend is away may make it

---

[89] Tito – President of Republic of Yugoslavia.

[90] The current account of the balance of payments nevertheless was in surplus from Q1 1969 onwards and the surplus in the second half of the year was at £680 million a year. Similarly manufacturing investment grew steadily at about 7 per cent per annum from 1967 to 1970 and was at an all-time high in 1970.

easier as B.'s ideas of Cabinet Office organisation might conflict. We agreed that the Chancellor should carry on without any major move although he spoke to D. on way to United States about possible hire purchase and D. advised him to hold that in reserve in case q.r.'s were used. The retail sales figures for August clearly rattled a lot of people. Some of those in Cabinet probably looking for signs that strategy is a failure.

We still haven't sent Running Forecast to anybody except P.M. and to him only on Wednesday. Even President hasn't had it.

Chancellor very firm in United States on possibility of additional military expenditure. Warned that United States might be restrictionist on imports. Australians suggested they would prefer U.K. to limit imports rather than capital exports.

Wednesday, 16 October   IMF seminar began.[91] Quite a good discussion: in low key and leading on from questions of mechanism to presentation and thence to policy presumptions in relation to the impact of balance of payments deficits on the money supply and on economic activity. Nicky arrived in the afternoon and we went over a good deal of the same ground twice but perhaps it was worth it.

I had to crowd in other urgent jobs and then go off with Douglas Allen to IMTA dinner where I sat next E. Compton [the first Ombudsman] and John Stewart from Glasgow (President of Scots CA's). Edmund told me of his enquiries into GPO prodding DES to recover licences from students for radios (without legal authority) and then refusing to refund even when DES carried it up to Ministerial level. For him question is whether he can disclose that DES put up this fight inside or whether that is bad form. Also he got from Short[92] personally the reasons why he decided to go ahead when even his Department didn't know, Short being constitutionally incapable of telling people why he decides this way or that. E. agreed we needed more open discussion but pointed out that Ministers were shot at if officials talked, e.g. his investigation as Comptroller into aircraft cases led to attacks by Labour on Amery. A case he is investigating now is in the P.M.'s constituency and everybody else knew this although he hadn't known.

On the academics he agreed that they looked at other countries and drew false comparisons especially on factual points and especially in relation to France. Droit administratif, etc. written up when the number of cases under Conseil d'état was only 20,000 p.a. M.P.'s letters alone number 250,000. The Inland Revenue deals with at least 20,000 cases a year, etc., etc. You get effective appeal procedures where they are least needed. The celebrated case of the mistress/Secretary of the Mayor of a town in Corsica suing for arrears of salary

[91] An IMF team led by Jacques Polak [Jacques Polak – Asst. Director/Director, Research Dept., IMF, 1947–80.] engaged in a discussion of fundamental issues of monetary and financial policy with the Treasury and the Bank for two long sessions.

[92] Edward Short – Parliamentary Sec. to the Treasury and Govt. Chief Whip, 1964–66; Postmaster General, 1966–68; Sec. of State for Education and Science, 1968–70.

(?) took seven years to settle and most other cases just as long. But tell this to the Professors and they ignore it.

Peru (where he was born). His opposite number as Comptroller showing him over the building showed him on one floor a crowd outside a guichet and said "Voila les declamations!", explaining that he couldn't run his system of Exchequer without declamations! He had a staff of over 600 or 10 times as many as E.

Spoke yesterday at No. 11 to Chancellor for half an hour on the economic situation. He is too optimistic about balance of payments and keeps thinking that we are in balance already or very nearly so when in fact the third quarter deficit was probably £120 m. on current account and we were just lucky on long-term capital inflow. He was quite meticulous on the trade deficit figures, quoting 27 and 29 when I said twice 30.[93] I said he might want to consider hire purchase if there was an engineers' strike and he agreed that temporary, swingeing credit restrictions might well be in order. He was also concerned about consumption and I pointed out that we were probably above 1967 II in the third quarter instead of 2% down. On the whole he let me talk and didn't say a great deal about the way he was thinking but seemed to agree that we had to sweat it out.

N.K. denounced recent Treasury appointments to me this afternoon – with some justification. Odd to move S.G. to Public Expenditure after over 20 years on finance and just as David Serpall was getting equipped to do the job. Ken B. would be much better and so for that matter would Bryan Hopkin who presumably wasn't even considered. I wonder who really decided it all – presumably William?

Racine, Wisconsin, Tuesday, 22 October   Kenneth Younger[94] made some interesting remarks to me on the bus back from Wingspread to Racine. He had had intimate contact with Harold Wilson over 15 years and never heard him make an original remark. Lacked imagination and creativeness, for all his powers of memory and cleverness. In fact a bit of a twirp. Never voted once for him as leader of party in Shadow Cabinet (in fact I think he said member of S.C.). Then on Suez he said that Eden[95] must have been using drugs. Very anxious to be liked and almost deferential to members of Opposition Front Bench. But in Suez Debates arrogant and quite unlike himself. Israeli Ambassador, asked to lunch with him some days before Suez, couldn't get a word in; Eden spoke throughout and took four double whiskies before lunch. K.Y. blamed Macmillan for letting Eden go through with it: he was "first in, first out". A gambler. Selwyn's role was more understandable. He came straight off aeroplane from United

---

[93] The Chancellor was nearer the mark than I was. The seasonally adjusted current deficit is now estimated at £20 million in the third quarter. At the time the uncorrected deficit was £80 million. It is, however, true that there was an exceptional inflow of long-term capital estimated at £182 million.

[94] Kenneth Younger Parliamentary Sec., Home Office, 1947–50; Minister of State, 1950–51; Director, RIIA, 1959–71.

[95] Anthony Eden Foreign Sec., 1940–45, 1951–55; Prime Minister, 1955–57.

States to the Cabinet to find that Eden had made up his mind already. Then he was hustled off after lunch to catch another plane to Paris to talk to Guy Mollet[96]. With Eden it wasn't obsession with oil but with appeasement that was his undoing because circumstances were quite different: Nasser[97] wasn't Hitler.

There had been long discussion earlier on Suez and Coral Bell[98] quoted Dulles'[99] reported remark in hospital "Why didn't you go through with it?" Would United States have felt differently if we had? The reply to this by Bob Bowie[100] was that Eisenhower felt cheated and that United States had S. Korea and Taiwan at back of their mind and felt that if they let us go through with Egypt they would be in impossible position in Far East.

On Selwyn, who was his Brigadier in Germany in 1945 after starting from Territorials, K.Y. said he was a man he could respect without particularly liking: chip on his shoulder came out in dealings with subordinates. But he was undoubtedly able and had good judgment. He succeeded K.Y. as Minister of State at Foreign Office and told him it was last thing he expected (he had expected Financial Secretary of Treasury or Solicitor General) since he spoke no foreign language, had never attended a debate on foreign affairs, and had visited very few foreign countries. Yet he had to leave in three days for United Nations to lead UK Delegation for next three months. K.Y. thought he might yet be Lord Chancellor.

Sunday, 27 October   I left for Racine, Wisconsin on Monday, getting there about 8 p.m. with Peter Jay and David Howell[101]. On Tuesday Wallace[102] was billed to speak at, of all places, Racine so the discussions at Wingspread on Anglo-American relations were suspended to give us a taste of American politics. Wallace is, as Patrick O'Donovan reports in *The Observer*, a short and handsome gangster with a smile like another man's snarl. He was at pains to show that he commanded negro support in Alabama and that his wife did, too. He made much of the need for an "open housing" law and the need to allow citizens to carry guns since (a) a man should be free to sell his house to somebody of his own choosing and (b) if peaceful citizens had no guns the thugs would soon make use of theirs.

The whole proceedings seemed to me very restrained and there wasn't the least sign of scuffling, or violence, or even barracking of the type to be expected in England. The one thing that impressed me was when he dwelt on the way

---

[96] Guy Mollet Sec. Gen. of the French Socialist Party, 1946–49; member of various French Cabinets in 1950's and 1960's.

[97] Nasser – President of Egyptian Republic.

[98] Coral Bell – American writer on international relations.

[99] John Foster Dulles – US Sec. of State, 1953–59.

[100] Robert Bowie – Prof. of Law, Harvard Univ., 1945–55; Asst. Sec. of State for Policy Planning, 1955–57; Counsellor, Dept. of State, 1966–68.

[101] David Howell – Economic Section, Treasury, 1959–60; Chm., Bow Group, 1961–62; Editor *Crossbow* 1962–64; Parliamentary Sec., Civil Service Dept., 1970–72.

[102] George Wallace – American lawyer and politician; Governor of Alabama, 1963–67; Presidential candidate, 1968.

the newspapers reported him as saying what people wanted to hear. There was no doubt that what he had to say was what many people wanted to hear. But it came over without any great rhetoric or passion, in great volume certainly (the decibels of the amplification were too much for me) but no high eloquence, just a straightforward talk laced with rather cheap repartees such as any small-town politician might use. He seemed to be a rather ordinary, vulgar little man who would have been more at home as a bookie or an auctioneer.

Monday, 28 October   Buffet supper at 86 Eaton Square chez Harold and Diane Lever. All the aspiring Socialists and their wives seemed to be there swilling vast quantities of champagne in the atmosphere of an 18th century or 19th century political salon: Peter Shore, Jack Diamond, John Stonehouse, John Freeman,[103] and quantities of M.P.s as well as Weinstock[104] (who came up in the lift with us), Bagrit and other tycoons. Mary Wilson. Michael Foot, Rees Mogg, Peter Jay, Sam Brittan, etc., etc. Fortunately we entered with Jack Diamond and soon got talking to Douglas Allen and his wife, Peter Jay, then Elwyn Jones,[105] and finally Rees Mogg.

I found R.M. as smug as ever and lacking in humour. He was very pleased with Frances so I did nothing to upset him. But he was full of the virtues of being agriculturally self-sufficient so as to make ourselves less exposed to the risks of exporting. I assumed he must have a stake in farming and Mary confirmed this on the basis of her talk with Mrs. R.M. who is 29 and has three kids. He thought that Labour had a chance of retaining power (for "13 years of misrule") if they went to the country by October 1969 but that they might wait too long and would find their chances slipping thereafter. Kennedy had been worth 30 seats to Labour in 1964 and Nixon might have the same value to the Tories in 1970 but probably not by October 1969. He seemed sure that Nixon would win and judged that H. wouldn't carry any states that didn't border on the Atlantic. He had really no chance of Ohio, for example.

The Tories had the advantage of Enoch Powell since the racial issue worked to their advantage and they could disclaim Powell without losing the votes of his supporters. Never before in his lifetime had dockers marched behind Tory banners and it was an advantage that Heath could exploit that working class thinking now entertained some elements of Tory philosophy (i.e. xenophobia?).

Weinstock did not strike me as a particularly daemonic type. He was cross with the wage settlement for raising women's wages and with the employers for making a fuss over the skilled men when their earnings already exceeded the minimum of £19 (or even £20).

I found that the Chancellor had put in a paper early last week (not copied to me – or to anyone (?!) suggesting tighter hire purchase not later than October 25 i.e. last Friday.[106] This had been resisted and the Treasury forecasts quoted

---

[103] John Freeman – Editor, *New Statesman* 1951–58, 1961–65; Dep. Ed., 1958–60; British High Commissioner in India, 1965–68; Brit. Ambassador to US, 1969–71.

[104] Lord Weinstock – Man. Dir., Gen. Electric Co. plc since 1963.

[105] Elwyn Jones (later Lord) – Attorney General, 1964–70; Lord Chancellor, 1974–79.

[106] Consumer spending rose by 3 per cent in 1968 – well above the original post-

against him; he was asked to provide the latest forecast – still taking shape – for tomorrow's meeting of SEP and the Board of Trade are urging on their Minister that the regulator is preferable to hire purchase. In this we agree. I had drawn Fred's attention before leaving for the United States to the high level of car output in September and the figures have just been published. But it looks to me as if somebody close to the Chancellor may have been talking to the press which is strongly urging restrictions on demand. The Chancellor no doubt has in mind an increase in taxation in the next Budget but he will find this hard to fix if the surplus is as big as we now expect. On the other hand, if he uses hire purchase now there is no guarantee he won't have to raise taxes in a month – as was pointed out to him by other Ministers. All this should come up tomorrow at the Budget Committee.

Wednesday, 30 October   Chancellor's proposals for tightening hire purchase were considered yesterday by Misc. 205 without decision and then finally accepted at Cabinet. Apparently Dowler and Harris[107] were in despair over resistance to proposals and talked to M. Posner about resignation (i.e. by the Chancellor). This seemed crazy to us since effect of tightening hire purchase is marginal unless there are immediate gains in car exports. George Harriman[108] was reported in *The Times* in this sense and must have made up some Ministers' minds for them but the industry thinks otherwise and John Boreham[109] says export markets are not denied supplies. This was what was said in January and was plainly untrue. I think it probably untrue now, i.e. I suspect that H. is right. But that still leaves me thinking the whole thing pretty marginal and rather sorry that the Chancellor wouldn't look at the p.t. regulator (which we preferred).

M.P. said that Chancellor had been angry at S. Brittan's piece in *Financial Times* predicting what the Chancellor had in mind just when he did have it in mind: Chancellor felt he should have had this article as a minute from his own staff. But as I was in the United States, Fred in Paris, and only A. Roy left how could we have supplied it, even if we happened to agree (as we didn't). At least we had put the possibility to him. I raised it as a possible reaction to an engineers' strike and he was obviously taken with the idea. Douglas warned him earlier that he might need to keep hire purchase in reserve in case we used more drastic measures to help balance of payments. Probably he has been itching to do for a month. He asked for a paper (from D. Wass![110]) just before I left for

devaluation plan. This and pressure from OECD may have influenced the Chancellor in arguing for hire purchase restrictions but the end of October, with no particular piece of bad news, seemed a rather curious time for the move.

[107] J H Harris – Spec. Asst. to Home Secretary, 1967; to Chancellor, 1968–69.

[108] George Harriman – Man. Dir., Austin Motor Co.

[109] John Boreham – CSO, 1958–63; Chief Statistician, General Register Office, 1963–67; Director of Economics and Statistics, Min. of Technology, 1967–71.

[110] Douglas Wass – Private Sec. to Chancellor, 1959–61; to Chief Sec., 1961–62; Asst. Sec., Treasury, 1962–68; Treasury rep. in Washington, 1965–67; Under-Sec., 1968–70.

the United States, to outline pros and cons and this was duly submitted early last week after a meeting with Douglas on Monday. Then the Chancellor put in a paper (this time it was drafted by D.W.) urging hire purchase restrictions on his colleagues and it was resisted. He must have squared the P.M. but P. Shore was against.

What one couldn't tell all week was how far the press was egged on by Roy and how far he was responding to press agitation. He wanted to get it all fixed by last Friday so as not to find the week-end press agitating for what would be better done first. He is also against tax increases at this stage but not necessarily next April. No doubt the important thing is to show that the government has a grip on the economy and this is why the Labour poll is improving.

Budget Committee yesterday unexciting. Goodbye to Alec Johnston. Later I took the chair at Tuesday Club for Ian Mikardo on nationalisation. He didn't speak a word of English till he was 6 and took up consultancy well before the war when Urwick Orr and Bedaux (AIC) were almost the only consultants in the United Kingdom. He was impressed by what a relative from the United States told him about the work done by consultants but really sparked only when he saw three successive vans/tricycles from a laundry company deliver parcels to the same address.

On nationalisation he was not very revealing. Chief Secretary afterwards said nine facts out of ten were wrong. He would like more direct Ministerial responsibility but seemed to have only a vague idea of what went to the running of an industry by a government department. However, we exchanged reminiscences of the Nuffield Conference in 1947 at which I first met him (and Jim Callaghan) and he recalled particularly Lord Evershed's strictures on "general directions".

Today Douglas Allen had a meeting on the Plan Document and explained to Bill Nield that it was far too much like earlier Plan Documents. You had to be ready to contemplate how wrong things might go and say what sort of response you would make. But what could we say about our obligation to repay £1,000m next year out of a small surplus, not yet achieved? The TUC wanted a Plan (and others too) for purposes of armtwisting: getting short-run decisions that we wouldn't otherwise take. But the document as it stood had no message for what we should do to get through next year or so and was far too precise (and optimistic) about the more distant future. Otto C. argued that industry would not be interested in the document and this was hotly disputed by Bill Nield who quoted his industrial advisers.

Thursday, 31 October   British Academy – Court of Gov. of LSE – farewell party at No. 11 to Robert Armstrong – farewell dinner at Rule's to Michael Young.

At the first, Lionel commented on Ely's decision to have an orthodox funeral and on the gruesome character of the Jewish funeral service. He also waxed hot on the silliness of the junior staff who sided with the students and later in the day he presided over the Court at LSE in his usual Johnsonian style. We had a draft to approve on our future attitude to "misconduct". Frank Lee commented on its rhetoric and this got toned down. Maudling felt it smacked too much of legal opinion and others said that it was too negative and minatory. But there was general agreement that a line should be drawn and penalties exacted if it were crossed. Adams expected an immediate confrontation at the Union meeting tomorrow followed by a sit-in and agreed that we should probably not be able to identify the real leaders of the "rebellion". Lord Tangley[111] was only just able to bring himself to accept the document, which would be represented as a second defeat for the Governors, if it represented a firm warning of action next time. Tom Marshall[112] abstained but took a long time to say so. No indication of real dissent.

At lunch I said to Peter Thornton[113] and Bill Hughes[114] that Maudling hadn't tried to monkey with the press and they laughed, recalling incidents in the late fifties over the removal of import restrictions when Frank Lee had made it clear that it would be idle to put the leak procedure into effect.

Friday, 1 November   Sam G. told me that the hire purchase leak occurred in the *Sketch* on Monday and was the work of the motoring correspondent who had scored a similar success before and appeared to have a good contact in Mintech. Barbara Castle had opposed the measure but was borne down by the P.M., Chancellor and President (who however favoured purchase tax).

Roy Allen told me that 30/40 of the LSE staff were "rebels" (out of 300/400) and he and Dick Lipsey[115] agreed that it was an illusion that the "revolt" was the work of a few very clever "agitators". Both were in agreement with the Governors' statement but expected a strong reaction from a large proportion of the students.

Robert Hall endorsed the restrictions on hire purchase. He said that at any level of unemployment higher than 2% (or even 1.3%) nobody would ever declare that they wanted higher unemployment and no Minister would have been willing to restrict demand in his time at the present level of unemployment (reached twice before 1960- in 1952/53 and 1958/9). He agreed however that the unemployment figures were now accompanied by complaints of labour shortage not heard at similar levels in the fifties.

Roger Thatcher said that we are now spending twice as much per unemployed man as five years ago (including redundancy payments etc.). This increase in hush money is clearly having its effect.

Sunday, 3 November   Sam G. told me that D.A. is very worried about the Chancellor's tendency to discuss policy with his little "Court" (Harris and Dowler)

---

[111] Lord Tangley – Lawyer and businessman; Chm., Royal Commission on Trade Unions and Employee Associations, 1965–68.

[112] T H Marshall – Prof. of Sociology, LSE, 1954–56; Director, Social Services Dept., UNESCO, 1956–60.

[113] Peter Thornton – Asst. Under-Sec. of State, DEA, 1964–67; Under-Sec., 19667– 70; Dep. Sec., Cabinet Office, 1970–73.

[114] William Hughes – Second Sec., Board of Trade, 1963–70; Dep. Sec., Dept. of Trade and Industry, 1970–71.

[115] Richard Lipsey – Prof. of Economics, LSE, 1961–63; Univ. of Essex, 1963–70.

and then call together officials briefly to hear judgment before he invites them to give evidence. Maybe Sam exaggerates. But I told him that I had a similar preoccupation. It may be that the Economic Section was brought in to the discussion of hire purchase and that Andrew Roy was the only available man at the critical time. But the Chancellor (and his staff) made no effort to see that I was consulted (or even informed) on my return from the United States. The circulation of SEP papers is an added source of difficulty and I don't even discover whether a paper has been circulated till long after.

For example, my Monthly Economic Report came back to me on Thursday although prepared before I left for the United States. Here there were good reasons for withholding it which I had discussed with Peter Thornton: that Barbara would demand a full-scale debate on economic policy if it went round. But I was unaware that it had been withheld. And in any event Ministers are now in the absurd position that they have taken a major decision of short-term policy on the one occasion when they had *no* monthly economic report; and are demanding to be provided with the *short-term* forecast before deciding on *medium-term* strategy (public expenditure in 1970/71) just at the point in time when they already have a *medium-term* projection (the plan documents)!

The government are in trouble with the car manufacturers because Crosland speaks of car sales in seasonally adjusted terms while they have no s.a. figures. The government doesn't publish its s.a. series and has itself to blame for the confusion.

Our November forecast is now in draft. It brings out how little progress we have made in the past 18 months. Consumption has absorbed most of the increase in output since 1967 I and the balance of trade shows no switch of resources in its favour since then (indeed a little the other way). The £500m surplus is as far away as ever and likely I fear to remain so, although it would need six years of it to pay off our debts. Instead we ran a £500m deficit in the first 6 months of this year. For the moment everything seems fairly stable but the public is not used to "long hard slogs" and grasps at straws. The most we can hope for is that we start the year in approximate balance: but the forecast is not likely to be favourable.

Monday, 4 November   Today I was inducted as Master. I raced from a Treasury meeting on the forecast to the Royal Commonwealth Institute in Northumberland Avenue and got there ahead of the Visitor – the Bishop of Liverpool.

Ian Bancroft told me on the way home that the Ministry of Defence takes the lead on most important defence/foreign policy issues, so that Healey is not completely excluded from the post he covets. The Foreign Office are inclined to take bold initiatives on matters not within their competence and without real understanding. They wanted us for example to make an offer to the Dutch (over the deal on tanks which ultimately went to the Germans) to buy some Fokker Friendships without being able to say what we should do with them if we did. They also wanted to make the concession of single frequency landing in Hong Kong to K.L.M. as if this would dispose the Dutch to change a publicly stated decision on tanks. I talked to Shonfield at SSRC about his enquiry into Foreign

Office staffing and he had obviously been struck by the same superficiality of approach.

Ian said that the Cabinet Office took the chair at the Defence Review Working Party and that it was the calibre of the Ministry of Defence members that put them in the lead.

I find that we do publish s.a. figures of car registration but in *Economic Trends* not in the *Monthly Digest*. Nobody seems to be aware of this.

Wednesday, 6 November   Nixon elected. David Hubback told me the result at 6.30 p.m. although Harris was pretty sure of it at 3.

Lunch with Milton Gilbert. He doubted whether Emminger had any chance of succeeding Blessing on two grounds: first, he showed no real independence and stuck too closely to the party line or got back into line too quickly; second, Blessing disagreed with most of what he said. These two things didn't seem altogether consistent. On the first M. mentioned that E. had no need to speak so often or try to be so much the spokesman. On the second he recalled a discussion between Zylkstra and Blessing in which Z. complained bitterly of a *Times* leader in which after expressing a minor difference of view with E., the writer went on to speak of a plot in which the Bank of England was a participant involving the Dutch and Germans (I can't now recall the details). Z. expostulated with B. on Emminger and B. said there was an old tradition in the Bundesbank that all members of the Board could speak in public without reference to their colleagues. "But E. doesn't speak for the Board. I make the policy, not E. I don't read all he writes- I couldn't". M. agreed that E. was nevertheless an outstanding economist and referred particularly to his Chairmanship of the Group of Ten although he emphasised that there was no "E plan".

M. also spoke of Sergent[116] destroying his career by taking sides while Sec-Gen. of the OEEC over the EFTA/EEC dispute. This experience convinced him of the difficulty of having an active Sec-Gen. so long as there was no role for him of speaking on behalf of all the members (as had happened over the Marshall Plan and liberalisation). He also doubted whether "the continentals" would support "another Frenchman" (de Lattre[117]) for the post since there was already a Frenchman in IMF and BIS.

We had a long and useful discussion of monetary policy in which he put a view not unlike Polak's but more forceful and clearly.

P.E. Club: Harry Johnson on a Wealth Tax. Paul Bareau told me of the conversation between Keynes and Niemeyer after N. left the Treasury for the Bank. "Have they made you a Director?". "No; but I have a key to the Directors' lavatory". "Ah! That must be the thin edge of the wedge, I suppose".

Peter Vinter told me last week that when Nicky came to say goodbye he said: "When I came to the Treasury I thought Ministers were my friends and officials my opponents. Now I have come to realise that it is officials who are my friends and the real trouble is with Ministers".

---

[116] Réné Sergent – Sec. Gen. of OEEC, 1955.

[117] André de Lattre – French representative at WP No. 3.

Friday, 8 November   The trade figures arrived last night and I saw them on my return from the Council meeting of the RES (my first in the Chair). They are a great deal worse than seemed likely although Donald MacD. had already pointed out to me the possibility of –70, given the normal month to month variations. I had a long talk with Michael P. and we both felt that they might precipitate drastic action. The government was bound to wish to retain the initiative and be seen to do so: how then could it avoid reacting to such an apparent change for the worse. M. wanted credit restriction plus the regulator plus q.r.'s plus perhaps import deposits – half in jest but half seriously.

Earlier we had a meeting of Directorate at which it was agreed that I should let the Chancellor know at once what the forecasts looked like (this reached him ahead of the import figures) and put the P.M. on warning. We will have a meeting of economists on Tuesday on a note which I will draft, interpreting the situation in the light of the forecasts but we will hold up circulation of the forecasts till the P.M. agrees to their circulation so as to avoid a July-type freeze. It is amusing that even Douglas twits me with reluctance to publish our forecasts when even Ministers can't be allowed to see them and we have to arrange in advance what is to be disclosed to the IMF.

The Plan is also to be redrafted and presumably will omit public expenditure details although these are in fact the rationale of the whole operation. Once the government explains the basis of *its* decisions, industry can make its own plans (whether they add up or don't) without necessarily believing all that the government says.

W.A. this morning gave us an account of the structure of the United States civil service which made it very apparent that the Fulton C. did a pretty sloppy job and recommended a uniform grading structure without taking in how different things were in the United Kingdom. The Americans have classes only in the sense that people doing a defined job constitute a class (Stenographers Grade 2). People in an occupational group are in a "series" and each job in the series is defined at great length in books covering hundreds of pages. Thus a generalist administrative class would be fitted into the grading structure only if cut up into a collection of series with carefully defined job descriptions for each post. Mobility does *not* arise because of the grading structure but because of advertising and freedom for all to apply. Moreover the pay of a given series may be slid up or down a little in relation to the grades concerned if the market rates are out of line: the minimum can go up for any post to the maximum for the grade. There are no less than 50,000 people on exceptional rates out of 1.2m civil servants. All this simplifies training because this is done by series and on a specialised basis. But it complicates the selection of "managers"; and in scientific establishments there is provision for the designation of some scientists to administrative roles i.e. out of series.

I had the impression that William had used his time to great advantage in the United States and Canada.

Monday, 11 November   Week-end spent on memo on forecasts which now show no surplus next year, and very little in early 1970.

Harold Cameron called at 5.30 and recalled watching the deals in New York in November 1967 when it was obvious that the United States companies were covering their British assets and some purely speculative deals were going through. In January 1968 he described his talk with Lou Rasminsky[118] who thought that he could leave the forward rate to take the strain but didn't appreciate that it would fall on the spot through hedging or that the total he might have to take might run to $20b. On the Friday when he saw Lou, the Bank of Canada had in fact to meet withdrawals of $80m in one day. The United States companies in fact learned from years of forward covering of the pound the technique they used this spring on the Canadian $.

Wednesday, 13 November   Afternoon in the Hague to hear Sydney Caine. Host of familiar faces. Dined with van Lennep and Robert Hall discussing probable direction of United States economic policy (Deming and Fowler had just been over). We all agreed that there would be little change in spite of what George Moore[119] told van Lennep in Japan: that he had persuaded Nixon to drop controls on export of capital. Robert said Nixon would hurry to occupy the middle ground, knowing how much support he could lose over the next four years. He would also, now he was elected, pay little regard to what previous advisers had told him.

R. said that Hauge[120] was brought to Eisenhower's attention, when on the *Business World*, as a speech-writer (by the editor). He got on well with Arthur Burns and as Saulnier was weak, dominated him. The Committee of Four consisted of Martin, Burns, Hauge, and the Secretary of the Treasury, who found that they simply had to have a common line. There was no Chairman. Van Lennep suggested that Ellsworth might serve in the White House.

Edith Penrose[121] maintained that crude oil was so superabundant that some Arab countries would have a strong temptation to make concessions to oil companies to get them to use their crude. We talked to Fellowes who is Co-ordinator of Public Relations in Shell about tactics in dealing with Arab countries and prospect of Russian hegemony in which E. did not believe.

Yesterday busy on paper for Chancellor on the forecasts. The outlook is not good and today's trade figures may start real trouble especially if National Institute now extrapolates them in *its* forecast.

Barbara C. has sent round a paper on incomes policy inviting the Chancellor to say what importance he attaches to incomes policy i.e. to stand up and give her public backing. This is quite the other way round from past exchanges with the Ministry of Labour.

---

[118] Louis Rasminsky - Dep. Governor of the Bank of Canada, 1956–61; Governor, 1961–73.

[119] George Moore - American banker; Pres., First National City Bank of New York, 1959–67; Chm., 1967–70.

[120] Gabriel Hauge – American economist; Asst. to Pres. for Economic Affairs, 1953–58; Dir., Manufacturers' Trust Co. from 1958, Chm. from 1963.

[121] Edith Penrose – American economist specialising in energy studies; Reader in Economics, Univ. of London, 1960–64; Head of Dept. of Economics, SOAS, 1964–79.

Harry J. told me on the plane that not a week passed but he wrote an article: indeed he had no lunch because he was writing one (for a newspaper). He gives 30 lectures a year at LSE plus Seminar of 1½ hours a week plus supervisions (and he tries to spend a lot of time with students) plus 12 lectures on the theory of tariffs. He visits about a dozen universities in a term to lecture, some as far away as Durham. I asked how he ever read anything. He said learning was subject to inc. returns. One got through work more quickly and with less effort as one went on.

Sunday, 17 November

There had been fears earlier in the year of a franc devaluation (entry for 29 June 1968) and of its likely side-effects on sterling. The franc continued in a precarious state and at the beginning of October (entry for 1 October) it was agreed by an influential group that if a French devaluation occurred it would be best if it was accompanied by an upvaluation of the Dm and perhaps also of the lira. The pressure became acute in mid-November and the Ministerial Group of Ten arranged to meet in Bonn with leading central bankers on 20 November to discuss what should be done. The leading European exchange markets remained closed from 20–22 November while the meeting was in progress.

The sterling crisis that ensued was perhaps the most palpitating of all. There was a serious risk of a fresh devaluation of the pound. The Chancellor, faced with bad trade figures for October, gloomy forecasts, and heavy losses of foreign exchange, decided to take precautionary measures and submitted a set of fresh restrictive proposals for Cabinet approval. In a kind of last fling, he brought the 10 per cent 'regulator' into operation, limited private sector credit still further and introduced import deposits of 50 per cent of the value of imported goods, repayable after six months, on about one-third of total imports. These measures were announced over a year after devaluation, on Friday 22 November, and were the last set of deflationary measures to be taken before it began to be apparent that the devaluation was succeeding.

The French, who were anxious to accompany a devaluation of the franc with an appreciation of the mark (or a movement in some other currency) took no decision even when the Group of Ten undertook to provide them with a £2,000 million standby. Two days later, however, on 22 November, it was announced, to the astonishment of Europe, that there would be no devaluation – a decision clearly taken by General de Gaulle in person.

Sunday, 17 November   The franc/mark storm blew up as the week-end approached and I made sure that we had plans ready although I'm not sure whether they are the right ones, since they seem remarkably like the ones we had in July. Apparently we'd float for a day or two to see whether the United States would rally round.

I had an hour with the Chancellor and D.A. on Thursday to go over the forecasts. We touched policy only rather gingerly. Chancellor was clear that if he had to take fiscal action it would help if he could check capital outflow simultaneously. But D. pointed out that this really meant, not Australia, but the whole sterling area, since otherwise we should be faced with leaks. It was agreed that my Economic Advisor's paper should go to Misc. 205 for meeting on Tuesday, not to SEP, because this would mean telling Ministers on SEP what the forecast was.

We had a meeting on Friday with D. to discuss handling of forecasts and D. said we should look at situation over period up to and including Budget and decide on the appropriate scale of action. It emerged that the change on current account next year was only –£40m, mainly in first six months and this strengthens my view that we should exclude immediate action of a drastic character to limit imports. D. told the Chancellor yesterday that he had thought of £300m in additional taxation in the Budget. He also made it pretty clear that he didn't much like q.r.'s especially if we were short of capacity.

On Friday evening we had a party for Otto Clarke, Frank Figgures, the Elkins,[122] and Wynne Godley. W. said that he gave up a professional career as an oboeist because of the agonies he went through before performances. Public speaking was as nothing to the strain of appearing public on a platform although for some reason there was no interference with the physical difficulty – which is very real – of playing the oboe. Many great players apparently go through hell and are never satisfied that they have performed satisfactorily. Nor does it get easier with time.

Otto argued strongly that civil servants didn't know how to write a brief: they gave testimony. It took a journalist to consider for whom he was writing and adapt his brief to the audience. When Heathcoat Amory was in the Treasury he told Otto that he was the only man whose briefs he could use in Cabinet. Frank demurred and said that the civil servant had the great advantage that he knew precisely for whom he was writing while academics (and perhaps even journalists) did not. If a Minister changed, the style of briefs changed; and certainly there were some briefs that would just not get written for one Minister that would be offered to another. You had to know on what days a Ministers would read a longer brief and when it had to be very short. Besides, as I pointed out, most of what went to a Minister was not to arm him for war in the Cabinet but to inform him either about the economy (as essential background) or get his agreement to the line being taken by officials or to documents that would commit him.

Otto and Frank agreed that H. Amory had the merit of modesty and readiness to listen. Roy does read what he is given but I have been told that on public expenditure he had felt that he needed a more concrete reply to the objections made in Cabinet.

Monday, 18 November   Douglas Allen was rung up thrice yesterday from Basle by the Governor on an open line and asked us all to get to his office by 9.30. The story emerged bit by bit, first from him, then from F. Figgures

[122] A.B. Elkin – Legal adviser to OEEC in the 1950's.

who spoke to Roy Bridge and finally from the Governor himself at a meeting shortly after 4 with the Chancellor. The French (Brunet) took the line that they were not prepared to borrow their way out of their difficulties like us, that the General was prepared to eat his words on devaluation, and that they proposed to move unilaterally by 15% unless the Germans were prepared to go part of the way to meet them. They were quite co-operative within the limits of what were obviously instructions and exposed their position in some detail. Blessing said that he was prepared to recommend outright a 5% revaluation to his Government but was entirely silent on a $7\frac{1}{2} / 7\frac{1}{2}$ proposal and advised that a 10% revaluation of the Dm was out of the question. He was seeing Schiller in the afternoon and Kiesinger[123] at 6. Couve was to broadcast at 8 on some prearranged questions. The Governor said that the French were speaking of a move within a week and that it was unlikely that they would move tonight. The Germans had a Bank Holiday on Wednesday and for this reason a joint move on Tuesday night seemed possible and desirable. He expected Brunet to tell him tonight if the French were going to close their markets tomorrow. If they did we should close ours and support the pound in New York and elsewhere pending a clarification of German intentions. He had left the others in no doubt that we should be obliged to float if the Dm stayed put and that this was his professional opinion not what his political masters were threatening. The Governor argued that if the French and Germans both moved we should not then do "frightful things" since this would be a breach of faith. But he agreed when I pressed him, that this did not cover import deposits nor even perhaps q.r.'s, although this would be much more distasteful: he was thinking primarily of floating. He wanted us to be prepared to use foreign exchange to avoid floating on Tuesday and Wednesday if the French moved tonight. We felt that we had to support the rate until we were sure that the Germans couldn't be prevailed on to move even by 5%. But I was not very happy, seeing that the Governor had made clear to Blessing that we would have little choice.

To go back to 9.30. Michael Posner thought that we might use the opportunity to go down by 5% and I had a sneaking inclination to do this which, when I talked to Fred, he shared. But the immediate effect would be to aggravate the deficit and the reaction might be to make people think it only a first instalment. So when we saw the Chancellor at 11 we came down against it and so did he. We also were now inclined to favour tighter credit this week instead of delaying. The Chancellor was half-inclined to go for import deposits because he felt that to deflate without some direct action in imports would be politically inacceptable. (He was quite clear that deflation by January was necessary.) In fact he said that he had concluded over the week-end that he would have to use some form of import restriction this winter. I queried this, pointing out that on current account we were much where we had expected in July and that we might make people worry about our intentions on the rate. By the afternoon the Chancellor was doubtful about import deposits and more than half against them

---

[123] Kurt George Kiesinger – 1949–1958 and 1969–19809 Member of the Bundestag; 1958–1966 Minister of Baden-Wurtemburg; 1966–69 Federal Chancellor.

while I was half in favour. Douglas said that he feared a shambles and none of us could guarantee to avoid it or estimate the value to the balance of payments. Frank F. said it would be no bigger shambles this week than any other week.

In between I spoke to Fred and A. Roy and they made it clear that we could expect little real help from the Governor's credit proposals since we were already taking credit for £75m reduction in banks' credit to persons this winter and the £200m cut in the ceiling would be largely offset by £700m or more extra fixed rate credit for exports. They agreed that we should use the regulator 100% now and I put this to the Chancellor in the afternoon as the most important weapon and one capable of improving the balance of payments in a year by £100m p.a.

We also had a discussion of bank rate. Both Michael Posner and I favoured an increase in the morning but the Chancellor changed his mind and in the afternoon the Governor agreed with him while D. said he didn't feel strongly. The Governor agreed that we should aim to jack up long rates to an attractive level so that the market stopped sagging but felt that this could be done without raising bank rate.

D. insisted at our earlier meeting that if we got a Dm rate that looked stable even till the next German election, this would make it unnecessary for us to change our rate. He and the Chancellor were obviously against q.r.'s, half implicitly only, but by throwing all the emphasis on import deposits (which D. also is against – he wants deflation alone).

There was a lot of debate on timing and the Chancellor was attracted to immediate action this week all along the line. On this D. felt that if he really wanted to do import deposits he'd have to wait and so ought to leave over the regulator to have a makeweight.

At 8.20 I went to listen to Couve who was eloquent but never so much as mentioned the rate – an omission that listeners couldn't fail to notice. He concentrated on the obvious war-cry of speculation coupled with the "malady" of the international financial system and then switched to the need for budgetary equilibrium e.g. smaller deficits in the nationalised industries. All rounded off with confident assertions that France disposed of all the means necessary for support of the franc.

Hotel Bristol, Paris, Tuesday, 19 November   What is it like to be at the eye of a hurricane or in a boat accelerating as it nears Niagara? I suppose that if there were lots of ordinary things and people around to occupy one's thoughts, it might pass almost unnoticed. At any rate it seems hard to believe that within a couple of days we may be floating and that, apart from some words from the Governor to Blessing and from the Chancellor to Schiller, we've been powerless to intervene. In retrospect I should have laid heavy odds against a franc devaluation this week (although I knew that a contingency plan was needed): Jeremy Morse asked on Thursday or Friday "Why are we wasting time on all this? There isn't the faintest chance of the French moving". Yesterday Réné Larre told van Lennep that he could rest assured that no devaluation was contemplated and we had to ring through to Basle to make sure that the French position was unchanged. Today Emminger is reported to have said that the

Bundesbank had lost the battle and that the most we could hope for was some adjustment in the turnover tax to favour imports.

The Chancellor comes out rather well. He said yesterday that he had read through all the papers about import deposits over the week-end and last night he reflected at length on the matter (no doubt after dinner with the French Ambassador), concluding in favour of using the device on three grounds: (a) that apart from presentational advantages there was the solid support of a united Cabinet to be won; (b) that there would be a prolonged controversy in the press over any failure to restrict imports directly when he was deflating and he ran the risk of having to do in December what had been repudiated as unthinkable a couple of weeks before; (c) there might well be forestalling based on the expectation of direct limitation of imports. Nevertheless he was confident that he could carry the Cabinet without import deposits if this seemed right: the P.M. was half against and so was Crosland. The Chancellor gave everyone a chance to give his views and his own interventions were clear and calm, not intended to shut out contrary opinions or leave open what had to be decided at once.

We started the day well, with no market pressure and the knowledge that our fears of yesterday had not been fulfilled. But the news from Washington showed insufficient realisation of the urgency or of the weakness of our position. Rostow spoke to the Ambassador of "over-reacting". Deming talked to Sam from Bonn of a Group of Ten Meeting "at the end of the week". It was agreed that Sam should go to Bonn and contact the Americans: he hoped to get away by 2 p.m. but the earliest plane was 4.30. So an RAF plane was procured and he left from Gatwick after meeting up with his passport (which had been taken by despatch rider from his home to Heathrow and then on to Gatwick: Douglas reminded him as he was about to leave the Chancellor's room of the need for a passport and took some pleasure in doing so after Sam's confidence that he could get to Bonn by early afternoon). Unfortunately the plane was diverted and he had to land miles from Bonn (just as Deming and Fowler last night had to land at Wiesbaden and were then lost by their chauffeur on the way to Bonn).

In addition, Raymond Bell will leave for Vienna for the EFTA meeting in case Crosland can't go: in any event he may not much like dining on Thursday night in Vienna and keeping mum on import deposits which we would announce on Friday morning if possible.

One great difficulty lay in the Governor's confrontation with the Banks at 4.30 as we had to decide whether to retain the credit squeeze proposals and add on import deposits. If we did, the Banks would need to be told today and since, I believe, this has now been done, the die is cast. Let's hope that the security is better than it was last week when the banks leaked to Peter Jay the substance of the Governor's memo.

I left Fred and the others working out the economic consequences of the package but ignorant of an indispensable piece of the jigsaw: namely, the rate. We may now, as the Chancellor pointed out, have to move before the French, who could hang on until the end of the week. God knows what they have been losing – we lost $155m by 4.30 today and two or three days like that are just not endurable, especially as there is sure to be escalation. Maybe the closing of the German market tomorrow will precipitate things: but, if so, the French will move 15% and that will presumably close the door to a change in the Dm.

The P.M. seems to have had some last minute idea of applying the scarce currency clause but that mouse won't run.

Paris, Wednesday, 20 November   EPC preceded by a press conference at Embassy at 9.15 – the small hours for most of those who came. I gathered that Group of 10 were meeting at 4 p.m. in Bonn and later M.P. wired that Douglas had gone with Chancellor.

Doubtful at first if meeting would take place and at the end Sec. General insisted on adjournment for 10 minutes telling us that we must meet tomorrow because public opinion would be affronted if we did not! He refused to listen to argument but I was glad to hear another Dane, Schmidt,[124] say that some of us had other work and that he had been recalled to his capital. Dane cut Dane!

We discussed United States and United Kingdom with the usual forays by Kessler into monetary policy and theory. Then the Austrians explained why they had to refrain from budget deficits whatever the economic logic; and the Swiss took exception to the views of the Secretary on their "unduly high current surplus".

When at last we escaped into Okun's farewell party I found that neither he nor any of the Americans knew anything of what took place at Basle so that they expected Bonn to yield a package of $2b for the French and couldn't see why anyone should talk about floating. Bob Roosa was there and discussed his recent paper, arguing that he had found new reasons why floating would be impossible for the United States in the importance of the capital balance, and the high gross inflow into the United States.

Andy Brimmer explained to me the historical work he had done on the F.R.B.'s power to "rule and determine the rate". It was exercised once only – in July 1927 and resulted in the virtual dismissal of the Governor by Coolidge. The effort to rule on the rate was not the first: an earlier attempt was frustrated over lunch when an opponent persuaded one of the members of the Board to change his mind. Even in July 1927 the majority in favour was only 4:3. It all originated in a visit by Norman to Strong[125] and in the conviction by Strong that he ought to raise rates in the United States as a contribution to the problems in Europe (the logic is obscure and Andy said it was "subtle"). The Chicago Reserve Bank refused five times, being then under the domination of the Chairman of Marshall Field and operating in the atmosphere generated by the *Chicago Tribune*. The Chicago Bank persisted even when the unprecedented step was taken of circulating the minutes of the F.R. Board. Since 1955 there have been 26 increases in rate of which about half originated in New York (in 1927 all the members were from the Eastern seaboard) and the lag till all Banks brought the

[124] Erik Schmidt – Head of Danish Ministry of Finance and rep. at meetings of WP No. 3.
[125] Governor Strong Governor of the Federal Reserve Bank of New York in the 1920's.

increase into operation extended up to 39 days.

Andy Brimmer also spoke of development of market in Fed. Funds via brokers until there is now something very like our old discount market i.e. a buffer between the Central Bank and member banks, handling "reserve money" i.e. relending excess reserves.

Friday, 22 November   De Gaulle's 78th birthday.

I got back by Golden Arrow at 8.30 p.m. last night after the meeting of W.P. 3 had been cancelled. Dined with M.P. at my club and found as I expected no sign of any real profit from the Bonn Conference. It was called by Schiller for obscure reasons and much against our inclination since a Conference that resulted in nothing and was billed as the biggest thing since Bretton Woods could do a lot of harm. I redrafted some passages of the Chancellor's speech but as the new draft never reached him this was largely a waste of time. Michael and I pressed Frank, who was enjoying himself as Director and Computer and Communications Network all in one, on the danger of waiting for a communiqué that might never appear. But Frank explained that Barbara and Co. wouldn't stand for the package divorced from its international context: they regarded that as "a different scenario", in the Treasury jargon that even Barbara now speaks.

I went off home at 11.30 p.m. to get back by 8.30 for one of Frank's round-ups. But it became clear that nothing definite was known, there were unlimited possibilities of things coming unstuck, and little could be done. Frank came and went and put 14 questions for us to answer that had come from the Chancellor via David Dowler in Bonn. We reassembled at 12 noon and the picture changed from minute to minute. The Parliamentary Committee met at 9 and apparently agreed. The Cabinet, meeting at 9.30, was still in session. But the P.M. would not allow the telegrams about the measures to be released nor let Tony Crosland be allowed to tell EFTA even though he was on the point of leaving his colleagues in Vienna without uttering a word. We didn't know whether the Cabinet would agree on the measures, nor who would sign the Regulator Order, nor when the Chancellor would leave Bonn, nor when a communique would be issued (if at all), nor who would make a statement in the House, nor indeed whether we could count on a statement before the week-end.

Some of this comprehensive uncertainty was dissipated by 12.30. It was agreed between the Chancellor and P.M. that the President should be allowed to tell EFTA and the Chancellor should give the Group of 10 an outline before leaving. If he got back in time he would speak; if not, the P.M. The statement would be made about 4 (it was in the end at 3.49) if the communiqué was out. If it was not out, a statement should be issued in writing from No. 10 in the course of the evening. The Chancellor was reported to have left Bonn about 12.30 but this probably meant the city, not the airport which is 45 min. away. The Governor and Douglas were staying to deal with the communiqué. (Neither was seen in the Treasury on Friday.)

I went off to lunch and Ronnie Mackintosh[126] told me that the Chancellor

---

[126] Ronald Mackintosh – Dep. Sec., DEA, 1966–68; Cabinet Office, 1968–70.

had come in for some considerable criticism at the Parliamentary Committee and Cabinet. If he had thought that the measures would go through *without* I.D.'s he had misjudged the situation. Nobody at Cabinet seemed to understand import deposits – neither the President nor the Chancellor being present. Most of the objections were probably on purchase tax (especially on cars), as M.P. told me on Thursday night (Wedgy Benn and Co.). Ronnie thought that the Cabinet would have preferred the P.M. to make the statement but this was obviously not the P.M.'s preference.

There were some efforts to get wider coverage for the scheme. T.B. rang up M.P. on this and apparently Peter Shore on Thursday was on the same tack although his Department had participated fully in discussions of the scheme. M.P. was also rung up by N.K. lamenting that his favourite nostrum (floating) was not to be adopted and harking back to 1931 ("before you were born, Michael" – which is not quite true) and the recovery in sterling from the trough. M.P. is thought by the Section to share N.K.'s preference so it is a little piquant to have him defending the fixed rate *against* N.K. (it shows how even one's colleagues can get it wrong).

We went over through the rain at 3.30 to the Chancellor's room at the House of Commons and found the Chancellor already there. There was no chance of altering the speech (except for one word) so all our briefs were wasted; but it did embody bits of the passages I drafted, with some characteristic revisions (for the better, I hasten to add). The Chancellor went off almost at once to see the P.M. and was soon on his feet. He seemed pretty much as usual in spite of the lack of rest and constant strain. I don't know when he recorded the 9 p.m. broadcast.

I then went to the City Editors Conference at which Sydney Gampell asked whether something lay behind the phrase about "sterling parity" reminding us of the same phrase in 1955 when widening of margins was under discussion. We were pressed on the economic effects and it was clear that the Chancellor's inclusion of the "$\frac{1}{2}$% of GDP" in the speech hadn't really helped to convey what we expected (similarly with Peter Jay's article this morning). As we left, Wilsher asked me if I thought de Gaulle would devalue and I told him that he was always capable of changing his mind.

Frank had a final meeting and it was agreed that Ryrie should come in to cover possible announcement of franc devaluation. F.F. sketched possible statement and we were told that 11.1% was the general expectation. (Later $12\frac{1}{2}$% was rumoured but without any apparent foundation.) Ronnie Mackintosh raised question what we did if no devaluation and this was left aside: nobody took it very seriously although it was recognised as a possibility.

I learned at the press conference for first time that all goods in ships already entered would escape 50% deposit. It was still in doubt all day, however, whether it was allowed to borrow 50% deposit abroad or take credit for this. Board of Trade were against and M.P. and I for. (M.P. rang me on Saturday to say he had settled it.)

So on Friday night there was a universal expectation that franc would be devalued and some bewilderment that conference should have gone on so long for so little.

Saturday, 23 November   But on Saturday night General announced he would *not* devalue: universal "stupefaction". I suppose that he couldn't resist one last try after all the press speculation just to show that he could rise above compulsions of opinion and speculation. Now Larre proves right: and those who told me in the Muette that it would end with a $2b package for France and no devaluation have also proved right. Those who knew least (Okun, Roosa and Co.) guessed right! What have the French gained? A small concession by the Germans and a demonstration that the mark will not be revalued: but not enough to restore confidence in the Franc. We for our part have gained by putting policy in a firmer light and are now less vulnerable: perhaps just in time. But the Labour Party has taken a knock and this will have to be the last shock if they are to hold together.

Frances says that the French Unions were threatening to demand a 10% rise if the franc was devalued by 10%.

Monday, 25 November   Much argument about handling of gilt-edged market. M.P. had rung me about this on Saturday night from York and I spoke to Sam G. about it. We had also had some discussion on Friday and Freddie Fisher asked me what we proposed to do at the press conference. When I got in I had a message to see M.P. who was with F.F. in a meeting so we had a chance to raise the matter and agreed that it would be a mistake to take in any large quantity of stock. At that point the market was quiet. Later, after my harangue of the IMF, M.P. spoke to me again about a rather unsatisfactory account by Robert Armstrong of his exchanges with the Bank. So I went to talk to Douglas and found him in agreement that rates should rise. I pointed out that debt management had become "an affair of the Bank" and monetary policy almost "an affair of the Treasury" – an extraordinary situation. D. thought that probably William had had such close contacts with the Bank through Leslie O'B. that no formal discussions had ever been necessary. He agreed that I should put in a minute to get things started and I did so at once. Fortunately – perhaps because "our man on *The Times*" wrote such a "good" leader on Saturday – the gilt-edged market wasn't too depressed, and little support was needed.

The IMF raised the issue in the morning themselves and at lunch Wynne spoke to me about the inevitable effect of a squeeze getting on for £1,000m by next March. Maurice Allen said that Charles Goodhart had signalised his arrival in the Bank by a minute on gilt-edged. In the Tube Frank Cassell also picked on this issue to put to me, pointing out at the same time that import deposits in reverse would be the very devil. So we'll have to get it thoroughly aired.

D. told me a little of Bonn which had been very frustrating. Schiller was a hopeless chairman and went on repeating the same things. The German machine was so inefficient that we were powerless to call off the meeting when we tried to do so (realising its uselessness once the German measures were announced): it had already been announced on German T.V. before the Germans could cancel it. Sam in Bonn had to be told from London what had been released to the press in Bonn (e.g. when he rang about the meeting he was unaware what the German measures were). The German press was told first of things that other countries were asked to keep strictly secret. Larre tried to do a deal first with Douglas, and then with S.G. and Harold Lever, to get somebody to move with the franc. He proposed to D. that France and United Kingdom should devalue by say 5% while Germany, Italy and Netherlands should revalue. Then, to S.G., he suggested (after D. had advised him that his proposal was not acceptable) that France and United Kingdom should "move together", either up or down! The Germans might have been persuaded to move if they were not alone and there was some chance that Italians might have agreed to a small revaluation. But neither France no Germany liked moving on their own.

Frances mentioned that Malraux,[127] Faure[128] and perhaps Débré, were in favour of not devaluing the franc.

Chancellor's speech too much of the usual slapstick but I gather from Ryrie that he easily got the better of Heath.

Tuesday, 26 November Dinner at Senate House after William's Stamp Memorial Lecture. The lecture was immeasurably better than the draft and obviously represented a lot of hard work. Nicky said the idea of starting from the Employment Policy White Paper was his and William agreed that until he got this idea he didn't see clearly how to proceed.

Nicky wanted to know how markets had been today – he told Mary that he misses the gossip frightfully. He was amused to see the French use his proposal to Callaghan in 1964 in order to avoid devaluation. But as they have $27\frac{1}{2}\%$ payroll tax and large TVA they have far more room for manoeuvre in juggling costs falling on exports.

Peter Menzies[129] told me that ICI were afraid their profits (which were above even their expectations) would incite big wage claims but he didn't disagree that the higher profits were needed to cover additional investment. Two years ago they had been in bad liquidity trouble but investment in his view was a function of consumer demand and he was paid to ensure that liquidity didn't get in the way. All this came up when Eddie Playfair asked me what had happened to open market operations and I emphasised that bank credit was a small element in total capital liabilities of industry.

Ronnie Tress[130] said that Plowden (not mentioned by William) was first public acknowledgement that public investment should not be used as a regulator. But he agreed that there had been much earlier appreciation of the need for a longer time horizon.

[127] André Malraux – Minister of State for Cultural Affairs in French Govt., 1960–69.
[128] Edgar Faure French lawyer and politician; Prime Minister, 1952 and 1955–56; Minister of Finance, 1953–54 and 1958; Minister of Agriculture, 1966–68; Minister of Education, 1968–69.
[129] Peter Menzies – Director, ICI, 1965–72; Dep. Chm., 1967–72.
[130] Ronald Tress – Prof. of Political Economy, Bristol Univ., 1951–68; National Incomes Commission, 1963–65; Chm., S.W. Economic Planning Council, 1965–68.

I have a vivid picture of Nicky shambling bareheaded along Whitehall, umbrella in hand as if he were going to a funeral, on Friday night as I left the Treasury. He told me tonight that he had probably just come from a $3\frac{1}{2}$ hr meeting on earnings-related pensions. He finds it hard work to do all his teaching in Cambridge, attend Faculty meetings, seminars, etc. and put in two days in Whitehall.

Thursday, 28 November   Freddie F. told me that after the World Bank meeting he had a long talk with Deming who spent the first half an hour explaining how the Fund was now doing the right thing about South African gold: then suddenly switched to a widening of the exchange points as the next step in United States policy. Freddie said he was astonished to hear the No. 2 man in the Treasury speak so openly to a journalist he hardly knew. He thought that there might be a fresh crisis before Nixon's inauguration on rumours that he might go for wider bands or an increase in the gold price. I told him that this might only provoke N. to take a position in public in favour of the status quo. F. also thought that we couldn't get to our balance of payments target without a further increase in taxation or cut in public expenditure but that the P.M. wouldn't stand for yet another tax increase.

At dinner tonight Bill Harcourt, who was in Paris last Friday, said that Couve had told journalists that the franc would be devalued but that the formal announcement would come later. He could think of no similar case in which a P.M. had made such a statement and then had to retract it.

Last night Mrs Norman Butler told me a little of Rab who she said was reduced to a kind of computer through separation from his parents in India. This left him with a chronic sense of isolation and uncertainty. When she visited him at Trinity he asked her (his cousin): "How do you think I'm doing as Master?" (a question that I had in fact just asked of her).

Sunday, 1 December   Nicky complains of low blood pressure. This accounts for his embarrassing tendency to close his eyes and go to sleep in the middle of a meeting: only, unlike me, he hears all that goes on and can join in at once when he is roused as happened at Ulricehamn after my talk. It seems to me significant that his questions to me on Tuesday started with: "How much did we lose yesterday?' It might be the epitaph for the sixties.

The Times on Monday attacked the Chancellor for failing to act in time; and although this is unfair it does bring out once again the need to be ahead of events (if your colleagues will let you). Before this crisis I was well aware that the government ran the risk of seeming to have to react to events rather than dominate them. But how could this be avoided without courting disaster? By q.r.'s? Or by floating? Surely that would be worse than reacting after? It is true that the package gave an impression of firm government that was deceptive because nobody knows what import deposits will do. But perhaps the regulator could have been used earlier? Well, we favoured that and the Chancellor thought the political risks too great. I'm not convinced that a major error was involved even though we barely made it; just as I'm not convinced that the failure to use the regulator in January was a major error even if the press is united in thinking so. The error was not to do it in November.

Yet when I think back I'm conscious how rarely I personally have gone to the Chancellor to say: Do this or −...The reason lies largely in my ambiguous position since 1964. In that year the assessments were clearly written in the forecasts − it should not have been necessary to speak. But I regret that I did not speak unambiguously: I assumed that it was for William to do so but I think now that I was wrong. I did speak up in July 1966 and in October 1967. But too often I have waited for the Chancellor to propose and not come forward with my own suggestions for action. The moral seems to me to be that anyone in my job needs clear instructions from above as to what is expected of him and a clearer line to the Chancellor than I have had since 1964. Or perhaps that we need to avoid the brinkmanship that puts us constantly on the verge of disaster and leaves us without reserves. Even the lesser evil is now invariably frightful and almost as bad as the worst we can imagine! I suppose that 1963 was really my biggest mistake of all and set us out on a road we ought never to have followed.

I talked to Dick Goode on Friday night at the IMF party and he seemed remarkably optimistic. He agreed that part of this was diplomacy but he genuinely felt that we ought now to see a big improvement in our position. I am increasingly sceptical. There are few signs that industry is gaining ground abroad on any scale, with the obvious exception of motor cars and some bits of engineering. In chemicals, textiles, steel etc. the balance of trade is less favourable in real terms than a year ago and is not likely to get any better. There seem to be supply constraints, in spite of quite moderate expansion over the past year.

Dick told me of Senator Taft's remark to him about 1947. "I find that economists aren't really much help to me. They can tell me the direction in which things are going to move but I usually know that already. What I want to know is how far and that they can't tell me".

Brian Rose was enthusiastic about the IMF Seminar because the dangers he foresaw didn't materialise: a public disagreement between Fund and Government and an open disagreement, with some unpleasantness, between Bank and Treasury during the meeting. We talked about shifts in the party line à la Russe and how institutions came to adopt fresh policies. I assured him that the Seminar had exercised a real influence because, as he had concluded, it had started trains of thought that were still moving. He was scathing about Nicky who had talked excessively and made Polak see red: but he felt that Nicky's presence had been a bond of union for those who couldn't stand his lengthy interjections.

The papers are still full of the events in Bonn and after. I wish they would show a little more understanding of the German outlook. Of course the Germans behaved very badly and the British were completely misrepresented (nobody drags an Ambassador out of bed in his dinner jacket). At least Roy has kept mum and quoted only Schiller's admonition to secrecy, instead of expressing justifiable resentment. But the press seems to be behaving towards the Germans in just the way they attribute to the civil service and the government.

Sam B. volunteered to go to Bonn and was off on Thursday morning at 8. Frances says he created quite a scene at Schiller's press conference by asking in English, at the end of a string of questions in German, why on earth the Conference had ever been called.

The P.M. is said to have gone out of his way to be nice to the German Ambassador when they met at the Palace last week. So Michael Halls told me on Friday.

Monday, 2 December   Budget Committee: so large we could hardly get round D.'s table and Frank Figgures had to sit in an armchair until Fred Atkinson and A. Lovell[131] left. I found to my surprise that I am now the oldest member, A. Johnston having left. Tony Part, Bill Nield attended for first time and A. France for the second. The level of discussion seemed to me pretty low. Bill Nield complained to me afterwards that Tony P. talked too much – as indeed he did – but none of the non-Treasury participants had much grasp of the issues. Their general line was to argue for taking no risks – as if we could avoid risks of all sorts – but without any agreement on the taxes they would put up (direct or indirect) or what might be done with monetary policy or by revamping expenditure. F.F. came nearest the issues when he suggested off-loading on to the consumer from state subsidies (but he chose agriculture on which there are endless papers). T. Part started on confidence and Douglas pointed out that there are 6 different ways in which the government can affect business confidence (e.g. if it expands demand or makes prices rise or fails to get out of debt) and they are usually irreconcilable.

My thesis was that we should look at 1970/71 not 1969 and be prepared to cut public expenditure then rather than raise taxes in 1969. There is probably little to be gained by trying to press still harder on personal consumption now since the forecast swing in the balance of payments is about as large as logistical factors (i.e. the sluggishness of the economy) will permit. If we ask what has gone wrong this time it is that the swing in the balance of payments hasn't taken place because imports have risen with exports; and the buoyancy of the economy has been maintained by high stockbuilding and unexpectedly high consumption. If next year neither of these is there to produce expansion and the balance of payments changes as slowly as this year we'll have a major row because unemployment will rise steeply.

There *should* have been no shortage of resources this year to slow down the swing. But are we wrong? At first it looked as if high imports were temporary and caused by stockbuilding. Then we thought the propensity to import might have risen. But now a more appalling idea is about. What if there are capacity constraints so that we can't push up exports without dragging up imports too in most industries? I've hinted at this for at least two months and now there is some evidence it may be true. Of course, it's possible that the capacity limitations are temporary and will pass and in most of the engineering industry they don't exist. But we would be wise to exercise a little caution in planning

---

[131] A.Lovell – Principal, Home Finance Division, Treasury.

for a swing of £1,000m in the current account between 1968 and 1969 II.[132]
The surplus on current account now forecast for the end of next year seems as
high as we are likely ever to attain with a devaluation to 2.40 (indeed perhaps
higher) and exceeds anything reached in my lifetime. If we got there on current
account we wouldn't need to fear very much for our capital account: we could
borrow long term to fund some at least of our debts. The real doubt is whether
import deposits will have anything like the effect on visible trade that we are
assuming.

Wednesday, 4 December   Permanent Secretary meeting – all chairs filled in
D.'s room (probably 20 people at least). D. gave us an excellent account of
the way the crisis blew up and developed: starting with the forecasts/bad trade
figures/speculation on the franc and mark; going to Basle; and winding up in
Bonn. He made it clear that we thought we had a firm assurance on Tuesday
night that the New York market would be shut, but on Wednesday found that it
was in fact open, that pressure on the pound continued there, and that it would
probably have made little difference if London had stayed open too. In fact
we *couldn't* re-open without any communiqué and yet the fact that London,
Paris and Bonn were all shut pointed to the possibility that all three currencies
would be re-aligned. At the week-end we were more jittery than I had gathered
about how things would go on the Monday. Over the month we lost £300m,
with Friday, Monday and Tuesday the big days: quite as much as in March in
fact. None of this seems to have come back: but things may change yet. The
trade figures plus the Q3 balance of payments should help to put things in better
perspective.

   Schiller apparently floated the idea of a re-alignment of currencies a year
hence. But this would simply prolong the uncertainty and both the Chancellor
and Carli spoke against.

   There is no doubt that Customs have made a frightful hash of the Import
Deposits bill. Nobody in the Treasury had heard of the proposal to give an
exemption for imports embodied in exports until the press conference and how
this could go forward without challenge baffles my understanding. (Customs is
very badly run at the top level in my view – neither Wilfred Morton nor Arthur
Taylor[133] has the least grasp of economics). In addition piles of amendments
have been drafted for a bill drafted a year ago. I suppose that things get too
stale to be taken critically as A. Neale points out.

   Tonight I went to P. Bareau's cocktail party and entered to the sound of
halting French as someone tried to explain import deposits in words of one
syllable for lack of familiarity with words of two. It turned out to be Enoch
Powell addressing M. de Juniac of the Banque de Paris et des Pays Bas. I had a
word with him as he left saying that I had understood him "même en français"
on which he switched at once to German.

[132] The swing in the current balance, as officially estimated, is now put at £915 million
and was carried a good deal further in 1970-71.
[133] Arthur Taylor – Under-Sec., Treasury, 1957–63; Commissioner of Customs and
Excise, 1963–65; Dep. Chm., 1965–70.

It is ironic that in this sluggish economy we manage to have production held up by a shortage of brakes (Girling's)!

T.V. programme showed Chancellor confronting East Anglia students nearly all of whom seemed to hold strong left wing views and to be more interested in Biafra than anything else. I thought that he showed to great advantage although he must have been armed by Mrs. Castle at Misc. 205 yesterday or SEP today. For he kept insisting how public expenditure had increased – every major service by 50% since 1964 – when his whole struggle in Cabinet has been to contain this. He was depressed yesterday I gather after Misc. 205 because his colleagues took pride in this increase as their one big achievement and didn't seem to mind high taxes. It's only the P.M. and the Chancellor who see the electoral drawbacks of high taxes while the others think first of the party, not of electoral defeat. They don't see that they haven't really cut public expenditure because it grows all the time without fresh decisions and still faster because decision are taken that imply higher expenditure without the same struggle as accompanies a cut.

Thursday, 5 December   Douglas told me on Tuesday evening that Donald would be succeeding me: P.M. had agreed. Tonight I had a long talk with Donald about the job and the problems of staffing. He said rather sadly as he left that on all previous occasions he had been starting something new: for the first time he was taking over a going concern. I replied that I had had quite a lot of experience taking over jobs from him!

I emphasised that A. Roy and P. Brown had long experience and shouldn't be lightly passed over in favour of somebody junior unless he was outstanding.

Mary took me to Thai Embassy cocktail party where we talked to George Thomson and his wife. George remarked à propos of Chancellor's talk on T.V. that young people now were very exercised over the things like Biafra and Rhodesia that we couldn't control and far less over the things within this country for which the government had to take responsibility. The loss of the Empire had reacted in all sorts of ways on the prevailing outlook and we were perhaps not always aware of this factor in the background.

Long debate with S.G. on a proposal of his for setting up an authoritative forecasting body to take some of the odium off government. Rather à la C. Dow 1963. I decided that this provided a good subject for my R.E.S. Presidential Address. Sam was not in the least moved by my arguments so perhaps anything I write will pass equally unnoticed. But a little attempt at education might help.

At Paul Bareau's last night, a Mr Robert Gordon said that when he sold his family house in Ulster to the local authority, 300 rifles were found in a secret cache, all greased and ready for use. The bolts had been surrendered long ago but "they" had duplicates and triplicates. In any event advantage had been taken of war-time to trade up into Tommy guns etc. especially when there were US troops around. Ulster was armed to the teeth. As for Paisley, he was the creation of British T.V.: had he been given no publicity he would have ceased to matter. Now the bands parading every July 12, which were having difficulty in recruiting, found lots of willing recruits.

Wednesday, 11 December   Just back from my last trip to Paris for WP3: a sad occasion as it concluded nearly 20 years of association with OEEC/OECD. I find that Hella Pick again reports me as saying that we would have a surplus of £500m next year – what is one to do? She clearly had a garbled account of what went on and learned nothing from her last efforts to report the proceedings from Paris by hearsay. No wonder "bitter remarks" were made about the British press by British (as well as German) representatives!

We had as usual a long hearing for although I got my exposé, over in 10/15 minutes last night, the discussion went on till after 12 this morning chiefly because everybody was interested in analysing the effects of our Import Deposits scheme. I told Kessler that we had spent a full day with the IMF on the effects on the money supply of a capital inflow but this didn't prevent him from assuming, supported by de Stryker and Ossola, that we might use the money to bid up the price of gilt-edged.

We went off on Monday with the knowledge that by Thursday things would look better. The export figures were available on Wednesday night and by Friday night we knew that the deficit was of the order of 15/20 i.e. we swung from 25 over 40 to 25 under 40 but at least we're beginning to get people to think in terms of the 3 months' moving average. On Monday morning we had a talk on the Governor's letter on the gilt-edged market. I argued for a big trade-off between purchases and drops in the price with a view to getting to an $8\frac{1}{2}\%$ basis by Thursday if possible so that we could be in an advantageous position to maintain the squeeze. I could see that we might generate too much alarm and that we ought not to demoralize the market but short of that, there was everything to be said for a decisive move continuing last week's trend. The Chancellor apparently had thought independently of a rise in bank rate as I also suggested after the meeting but this was subject to discussion with the Governor. In Paris it emerged that the Bank had squeezed the bears yesterday in the foreign exchange market and this naturally was interpreted as an indication that trade figures would be good. (I have some reservations about this sort of intervention but on the whole I think it has some advantages: perhaps we were losing too heavily to wait till Thursday – I don't know).

I picked up some gossip about Bonn. Emminger has kept a diary and proposes to write within next five years consulting me to make sure that he has got it right. Lou Rasminsky going back on the plane said that he couldn't remember as badly managed a Conference with the exception of Savannah. He and Brunet were pushed out and had to sit on a bench awaiting news. So was Barre, who took it ill. "Goodbye, Mr Barre" said Schiller. "We don't need you". Ossola said that Strauss[134] remained in the meeting with about 40 other Germans ("a claque" he said) and addressed them as if still in the Bundesrat without much understanding. Schiller obviously wanted him there. Ossola had suggested earlier to S. that the meeting should be confined to the Six with consultation with the Americans (already on the spot) and with a British representative.

[134] Franz Josef Strauss – dep.chm. 1953, chm. 1961 C.S.U.; Federal Min. of Finance, 1966–69.

When consulted by S. about the French intentions he told him, although he had been at Basle, that he did not think that the French would devalue and he was astonished to hear Ortoli[135] announce that this was the firm intention of the French government. When Jenkins spoke up to enquire what the Governors had agreed to be desirable, S. began by waving aside what the bankers thought, saying it was for governments to decide and then brought pressure on Blessing to make statements in line with the position he (S.) was taking. He also insisted that Ossola sat next to him, separating him from Blessing.

Soames[136] told us that Débré was a 20% devaluer but that if this was ruled out he would go for a rise in the price of gold. The French would now try to get somebody else to move with them and keep close to the Americans so as to aim at a general realignment. They would not go for a 20% devaluation because as R. Raw said it would be regarded as damaging the whole structure and bring them discredit. Moreover according to R. it would not bring French money back so long as there were doubts about the solidarity of the régime. Soames called the German ambassador in Paris a shit and referred to a conversation in which he had said while Bonn was in progress that the probable outcome was that the Dm would not be revalued but the franc and the pound would be devalued. This remark caused Débré who overheard it to write a letter to Schiller expressing indignation at the German attitude.

R. Raw said that at the Cabinet meeting on devaluation the General had asked each Minister in turn for his view, starting with Jeanneney[137]. There was a small majority against and it was left to the General to decide. Couve stayed behind to talk it over with him before a final decision was taken. The unions would probably have taken a stronger line against the government if it had devalued.

Much talk of students again. The Japanese were particularly worried because the students had nothing constructive to say and seemed to want to destroy the whole system. Emminger said the German universities were turning out far too many sociologists and politologists with half-baked theories of society and politics and little practical sense or experience. He reminded us that Cohn Bendit[138] had been described as The Adjustment Process in person and that he was now in Germany. This was exactly what I had been discussing with C. before lunch and we had agreed that perhaps after a time he might have some effect! I gathered also that the French government was relieved that Cohn Bendit got his degree since this would help to keep him from returning to France (where he is not allowed).

R. spoke of the new French measures on forward dealings as savage. They

---

[135] François Ortoli – French economist, Dir. of Cabinet to Prime Minister, 1962–66; Commissioner Gen. of the Econ., 1966–67; Minister of Works, 1967–68; of Education, 1968; of Finance, 1968–69.

[136] Christopher Soames – Cons. Sec. of State for War, 1958–60; Minister of Agriculture, Fisheries and Food, 1960–64; Ambassador to France, 1968–72.

[137] Jean-Marcel Jeanneney – Prof. of Economics at Grenoble and Paris Universities between 1937 and 1980; Minister of Industry, 1959–62; Minister of Social Affairs, 1966–68.

[138] Cohn Bendit – A prominent figure in the student disturbances in Paris in 1968.

confine forward cover to one month and will oblige French exporters to repatriate large funds. They are already doing so on a big scale but are hoping to get some relaxation before Friday by which date all outstanding forward contracts have to be renegotiated. The French at Basle spoke of their subsidised export credit as a "sottise de premiere ordre" since it led exports to give maximum credit to their suppliers, cash the certificates and so get money very cheaply. The amount involved could be up to $1b.

Frank Figgures now takes over WP3 and of course his connection with OEEC is even longer than mine. Fred Deming said farewell as I did. All the others except Emminger are comparative newcomers. I suppose that I shall chiefly remember Ossola's picture of door-to-door propaganda among the peasants of Calabria to sell them Mutual Fund Certificates and of the helplessness of exchange control regulations to stop it.

Thursday, 12 December   Douglas had a meeting at 3 on the Budget judgment, preparatory to B.C. on Monday. He said he didn't want to argue but simply to get clear what the various views were. Everybody wants to cut consumption next year and even M.P. had swung over to a hawkish view. But I entered a mild dissent. I think that the balance of payments will be slower to improve than we forecast, that the gain from general deflation will be small – certainly in comparison with the cost in output and social friction – and that it would be far better to aim at a bigger cut in public expenditure in 1970/71, however difficult at this stage. But Fred took the other view and wrote off cuts in investment grants as unlikely to be of much effect. My view is that we may find local bottle-necks in capacity pushing up imports or else limiting exports and that, given time, these will sort themselves out. But in that event why not let cut in consumption stretch out too? This is what happened this year and it didn't really make a critical difference to balance of payments. Douglas suggested that we could get an increase in tax this year that we wouldn't get next year; but I'm not convinced that in 1970 we'll have a great shortage of capacity to handle external balance.

I found to my surprise that bank rate was not increased because Governor argued Chancellor out of it. In addition Bank let gilt-edged bounce back up so that we've lost a lot of ground and will have to do the job all over again. They still think in tactical terms and assume that present level of gilt-edged will be found attractive. But we have the whole of the credit squeeze to come.

In Paris few people seemed to expect much from our import deposits scheme and they were therefore more interested in monetary implications. But in London there is still a school of thought expecting quite an impact on imports.

Sunday, 15 December   On Friday I gave the Ec. Section a long lecture on its history, accomplishments and future: my swan song and inevitably a sad one. I at times have the feeling that all will go well once I go and that the disasters of the last 7½ years will appear in retrospect as my doing as if I were a kind of economic hoodoo.

Bill Hood,[139] discussing the power of Central Banks, agreed that it rested ultimately on competence although it might have to be backed up by a threat of resignation from the Governor. In the Bank of Canada the outside Directors take no part in framing policy but chiefly advise on matters of housekeeping or indicate likely market reactions. The Bank is more likely to work closely with the Ministry of Finance because it is a government creation and has no independent tradition. Nor is it likely to act as spokesman for the business or financial community. Lou Rasminsky has a considerable reputation in Canada now and in any conflict with Government, this would count.

Frances came to dinner and I chaffed her about the leader on Monday asking who was to head the Coalition Government. Getzwold had agreed in Paris that both *The Times* and *The Economist* seemed to have taken leave of their senses. (Emminger also said that *The Times* reported an inflow of $300m into Germany when this was quite untrue since there had been only a very short flurry after the report of the Wise Men.)

The papers have now swung right round after the trade figures and are far too complacent: except *The Economist* which still clamours for a floating pound (why now and not in November 1967?), the withdrawal of the Government Broker from the gilt-edged market, and a wage freeze.

Finally I must record Trudeau's[140] bon mot: "Vive le franc libre".

Monday, 16 December   My last B.C. meeting, entirely on submission to Chancellor, a thing normally sent by the Chairman at his own discretion and formerly covering an Assessment by the Chief Economist. Most of the talking was done by the non-Treasury members, especially Part and Nield, who were technically among the least sophisticated. They all wanted to put up taxes in the next Budget either (*quia impossibile*) because they don't think taxes really cut demand and didn't work this year or because you can't go wrong putting up taxes if you're in deficit.

Bill Nield gave us an account of Chequers. The Chancellor apparently excelled himself and made a deep impression. They were all impressed by a story of Robens about a miner who turned up for work after six months' unemployment and explained his absence by pointing out that he had drawn £800 in redundancy pay and a further £17 a week in national insurance and supplementary benefits. This disposed them to agree that the unemployment figures were not a good guide to the tightness of the labour market and that it was better to concentrate on Scotland, Wales and the North as individual regions. They also accepted that it was better to go slowly till they had put the external deficit behind them rather than rush into an unsustainable expansion. (I look forward to the TUC *Economic Review* to see how much of this is incorporated.) Bill said he was astonished to see the degree of agreement reached. Of course, they are all very keen to increase industrial investment and it was this that made Bill

---

[139] William Hood – Canadian representative at WP No. 3.

[140] Pierre Trudeau – Parliamentary Sec. to P.M. of Canada, 1966–67; Minister of Justice, 1967–68; Prime Minister of Canada, April 1968.

and Tony Part keenest to "make room" by stamping on consumption.

Douglas pointed out that if it were necessary to take direct action in imports some accompanying measures would be required and that this might make it preferable to keep tax increases back to make up the package.

Wednesday, 18 December   Lunch yesterday with Bob Bethke on a very wet day. He was full of reasons why the Fed. would not put up the discount rate. But of course they did. I thought that with unemployment down to 3.3% and not much sign of rapid slowing down, Bill Martin would play safe but agreed that perhaps he might wait a month if the Open Market Comm. met on 14 January, well before the inauguration. It must look like a vote of no confidence in fiscal policy but if the choice lay between December and January I suppose there was a lot to be said for acting at once. Perhaps it will allow us (or force us) to follow suit.

Meanwhile Kennedy has started a run into gold and we will soon see whether that can be handled as easily as I have been assured (e.g. by Rupert Raw).

Donald lamented today about P. Shore's inability to make up his mind. He (Donald) has had 50 letters of congratulation in the past month and the P.M. has been delaying an announcement until P.S. is satisfied. (He has had the whole issue to settle for two months.) P.S. isn't happy to take Bryan Hopkin who said on Monday that he was a candidate after being asked on Friday. But where will he find a man of B.'s standing to come to a job with so limited a future? P.S. is also holding up all the I.R.C. appointments till he gets back from his illness although they have to be made by the end of the year.

Thursday, 19 December   Lunch with Tom Wilson,[141] trying to get him to think well of appointment as Secretary of Royal Economic Society and a Cambridge Fellowship. Bryan Hopkin already committed to DEA. Yet Donald tells me tonight that Peter Shore, now back, still is reluctant to take him.

Saw W.A. before my departure and went over the main points I had to make about the Government Ec. Service. It was only at 9 p.m. when talking to Keeling[142] that I remembered we hadn't discussed the C.A.S. and my proposal to convert it to a new Brookings.

N.I.E.S.R. party. The entire contribution of British industry (and the press) to the finances of the Institute last year was about £13,000. Joan Robinson[143] was there looking very lined in the face, pasty and suddenly old. I talked to Freddy Fisher, Nevin,[144] Liz Johnson,[145] Zwegintsov, Mrs Solow[146] and (at

---

[141] Tom Wilson – Prof. of Political Economy, University of Glasgow, 19 – .

[142] Desmond Keeling – Director, Centre for Admin. Studies, 1963–65; Under-Sec., Treasury and Director of Training, 1963–68.

[143] Joan Robinson – Cambridge economist; should have been awarded Nobel Prize.

[144] Edward Nevin – Professor of Economics, University Coll., Swansea from 1968.

[145] Elizabeth Johnson – Wife of Professor Harry Johnson, LSE, and editor of Keynes' Collected Writings.

[146] Mrs Solow – Wife of Professor Robert Solow, MIT.

some length) Jeremy Bray. Maurice Allen exuded doom. I was leaving "just in time". The Governor was about to write to the Chancellor (after the New Year) and he would be doing the drafting. Things might go better for a time next year, but there were the import deposits to repay and everything would slip back. I expostulated on the grounds that a big visible improvement seems highly likely over the next six months but Maurice said he would take me on when I came to the Bank on 30 December. I don't quite see what in particular is troubling him unless it is our first glimpse of 1970 and he neglects what *could* be favourable trends abroad (French costs rising, Germany unemployment low and falling, United States unemployment down to 3.3%, Italy and Japan trying to keep up a fast rate of expansion).

Freddy Fisher thought that we would either have a really big improvement soon or else we would have very little improvement. He didn't think that things would go on as before with a gradual decline in the deficit. (But of course it hasn't been gradual: the visible deficit was over £80m a month in the Spring and now it is down to £40m)

Sunday, 28 December   Claus Moser[147] came to ask what he should do about staying at CSO after his three years were up. I suggested that LSE *might* give him two more but he is doubtful. He likes the CSO and might yet elect to stay on unless something else in London came up. Bryan has agreed to go to DEA and on Monday I heard at last that Donald's appointment has now been agreed. Bryan told me that the press release would be dated 31 Dec.! He had worked out for himself that there was a Ministerial disagreement. What he will make of planning, regulation, industry and nationalisation, I don't know. But I should certainly expect that he and Peter Shore will find little in common.

Last night we went out to a party at Phil Kaiser's. I ran into P. Gordon Walker in plum smoking jacket in the hall. He reminded me of my dictum at Chequers that it was hardest of all to forecast where you are now and went on to say that planning was impossible. The information necessary for it was never up-to-date and never could be and the coordination involved in planning took time so that it was impossible to assemble, use, and communicate information with the speed that planning (in some unspecified sense) required. It might have been John Jewkes speaking!

Tuesday, 30 December   People keep asking me if I'm looking forward to Oxford, perhaps out of envy – or at least they profess envy. But of course one usually goes into the future crabwise, looking backwards or sideways and not much concerned about what lies ahead. I have so many things to clear up, apart altogether from Christmas and the hope of some leave, that I have little time to think of what life will be like except in terms of carpets, curtains, wallpaper, etc. I have to busy myself rejecting invitations to speak or write or serve on committees till I can see whether any leisure remains. Above all I feel myself

---

[147] Claus Moser – Professor of Social Statistics, LSE, 1961–70; Statist. Adviser, Robbins Cttee., 1961–64; Director, CSO from 1967.

going through a long post mortem of my spell at the Treasury, speculating on what might have been or what possible justification there may be for what I did or neglected to do: lost in a kind of inner confessional, conducted in the middle of periodic dips into minutes written years ago. In particular I have been looking at my minute on devaluation of 4 February 1963 and my later MSS note to William in July 1965. They stand up rather well in retrospect.

I reckon that since I joined the Treasury in June 1961 I must have written (or dictated) 4,500 minutes in all, which (at, say, 400 words on the average) implies a total output in written form of about 2 m. words. Most of it of course is of no continuing interest but here and there are papers that are not without some merit.

Lunch at Bank of England. I talked first to Leslie who was also in reminiscent mood. He said that in Tuesday he would complete the first half of his term of office. He had begun by putting up bank rate to 7% in his first week, beating Rowley by a week and had seen the July package take shape in his first month. He thought, looking back, that it would have been better to devalue earlier: but not in July 1966 – the wrong attitude was then still prevalent and it would have been treated as an easy way out. Even in November 1967 Jim Callaghan had still been woefully weak (as I could confirm). The Party in fact had not learned what was involved by July 1966 or even later. Perhaps April 1967 would have been the right time to devalue: or a couple of months later when war broke out in the Middle East. At least I did meditate devaluation at the end of April (not a renewed bid to get into Europe!) but how could the Government have justified so sudden a change of front? I still think late September would have been right, and that it was possible to see then that it was right. (The Governor had in mind that in April we had cleared up our debts – but of course not the IMF debt).

We talked about the contrast with 1949 and agreed that it was curious how little there was to show for a 15% devaluation and a very large budgetary shift. Somebody would explain it all one day! Meanwhile if we did get into substantial surplus we would probably be able to count on some agreement to funding part at least of our debts.

Earlier the Governor suggested that the mistake we made after the war was to accept the United States loan on their terms and then find it frittered away because of our efforts to meet these terms. This is not quite how I should regard the 1947 experience.

We had an agreeable lunch with a full attendance. As we came in, we found Rupert Raw alone and he began discussing our meeting with Soames. It was some time before I realised that this had nothing to do with the Forsyte Saga and was a reference to our conversation in the Paris Embassy. Conversation was rather halting at times but once we got on to the subject of Cunliffe,[148] Keynes, etc. it livened up. The Governor said he was "an optimistic fatalist" when I asked about prospects for 1969. But Maurice Allen didn't seize the occasion to spread gloom. Instead we moved on to the familiar theme of British engineers,

[148] Lord Cunliffe – Governor of the Bank of England, 1913–18.

the lack of public esteem for their work, and the over-manning of their products when a genuine advance in technique occurred. The dockers provided the most lurid examples as usual.

It emerged that Richard Sayers is to take five years over his history of the Bank so that there isn't much chance of his doing a study of external economic policy since the war for H.M.G.

Thursday, 1 January 1969   Of the candidates for the Governorship of the Banque de France, Bloch-Lainé[149] was said by Rupert Raw to be the most likely rather than Wormser and Alphand[150]. The Governor said that Bill Martin would retire in 1970 and that his appointment couldn't be extended. I asked if Congress didn't have the power to authorise extension and the Governor said presumably Congress could do anything but he regarded this as hardly worth a thought. Rupert said that the Governor of the Banque de France had no contract and was in fact a tenant-at-will who could be removed at any time so that there was no fixed point at which a successor to Brunet had to be found.

These Bank lunches are rather splendid affairs. A round table is reserved for Governors, Directors and guests plus Advisers if there is room. But there is a second table – oblong – that can be brought into use on busy days. Each regular diner has a silver napkin ring, with a number, made from the badges used 1 1/2 centuries ago by Bank messengers. Other silver dates as near to 1694 as possible. Sherry and claret are served, with a liqueur if desired: cigars and cigarettes at the end of the meal. All the food is on the side and doesn't need to be brought in. There are three uniformed waiters to serve, the chief waiter in black with white tie. The food is excellent and there is normally a choice of three main dishes plus soup, sweet and cheese. Fruit in season. I suppose that the round table seats 10: we were 8 and this left not much room. The evening paper is usually on the table when you come in, i.e. at about 1.30 p.m.

Yesterday passed uneventfully. A long lunch with Ash Wheatcroft,[151] mainly on the possibility of joining the Board of Urwick Orr. A couple of hours in the morning with Donald and before that with Douglas Allen and Second Sec-retaries. My party in the evening was not very heavily attended but Chancellor and Financial Secretary came: no speeches but quite gay. I told the Chancellor as he left that now he had got rid of me, things couldn't fail to go much better. Earlier he asked me if I could remember a year when things went better than I had expected at the beginning and I hazarded 1963. He seemed to take it for granted that it never happened! But he was ready to accept that perhaps things might now improve gradually.

W. Armstrong and Douglas, Sam and Frank F. all came but Ken B. was in Switzerland and M.P. in York. Remarkably little was drunk. We went out later

---

[149] François Bloch-Lainé – Dir. Gen., Caisse des Dépots, 1953–67; member of Council of Bank of France, 1947–67.

[150] H.Alphand – Head of the French Foreign Office.

[151] G.S.A. Wheatcroft – Professor of Employment Law, Univ. of London, 1959–68; First Editor, *British Tax Review*, 1956–71.

to a midnight party and came back to find the children's party at its height. But I went to bed with a sense of unfinished business: in the literal sense I had still books and papers to move and letters to reply to and minutes to write. All of which have occupied me today so that I've had no feeling at all of being "out" of the Treasury. Indeed I was there for over 2 hours packing up. But by tomorrow night we'll be in Bosham and then I'll know that I've crossed the line between official and academic life.

Index

Public sector survey group 82
Public sector tenders, holiday in 67
Public Works Loan Board (PWLB)
159, 254

QUANT, Mary 193
Quantitative import restrictions
(q.r's) 27, 36, 56, 74, 77, 172,
220, 230–1, 257, 262, 327–30

RADCLIFFE, Lord 103
RADICE, I.L. 23, 50, 295, 306, 312
RAE, John 78
RAISMAN, Sir Jeremy 220
RAMPTON, Jack 328
RAND, Mary 193
RAO, V.K.R.V. 231
RAPHAEL, Chaim 12, 149, 176,
211, 250, 258, 317
RASMINSKY, L. 340, 356, 359
RAW, Rupert 75, 77, 120–1, 216,
256, 281–3, 307, 315, 357, 360–3
RAWLINSON, Anthony 77, 79,
287, 295
REDDAWAY, W.B. 113, 203, 231,
236, 261, 265
Reddaway Enquiry into effects of
SET 236, 265
REES, Albert 137
REES-MOGG, W. 6, 140, 220, 333
Reflation, danger of 29, 32, 77,
159–67; in 1967 196, 198, 224
Regional Employment Premium
(REP) 196, 206–7, 215
Regional Policy 32, 175, 195, 203
Regulator, tax 67, 92, 93–8, 115,
131, 147
REID, Sir E. 180
REILLY, Sir P. 91
REIRSON, Roy 30–1, 280
RENDALL, P.S. 215
Rent Act 136
Reorganisation Finance Commis-
sions (RFC's) 77
Reserve Currencies 23, 33, 89, 223,
249
Restrictive practices 113, 195, 262
Restrictive Trade Practices Act 56
REY, Jean 211–2, 257
REYNOLDS, Prof. Lloyd 251
Rhodesia 91, 98; reserve losses 84

RICHARDSON, Gordon 3, 5, 13,
22, 24, 329
Richard Thomas Ltd., 22
RICKETT, Sir Denis 11, 16–17, 21,
26, 35, 38, 40, 53, 57–8, 64–5,
74–6, 79–84, 91–4, 99, 100, 122,
126, 140, 144, 151, 158, 165,
178–9, 184, 188, 195–7, 204–5,
215–6, 223, 228, 233–7, 243–52,
256–9, 266–74, 279–89, 292,
297, 304, 317
RIPPON, Geoffrey 290
RIVEL (Chase Manhattan Bank)
206, 302
ROBARTS, D.J. 69
ROBBINS, Lord 118, 160, 184–5,
359
ROBERTS, Prof. Ben 137, 164
ROBERTSON, Prof. D.J. 295, 312
ROBINSON, Austin 283, 299–300
ROBINSON, Joan 274, 300
ROBINSON, Kenneth 143
ROBLIN, D. 263
ROLL, Sir Eric 2–32 *passim*; 38,
43, 58, 63, 70–99, 110–38, 282,
286–7, 290
ROOSA, R.V. 158, 266, 286, 346,
349
Roosa bonds 173, 203
ROOTHAM, Jasper 59, 271
ROSE, Brian 55, 316, 352
ROSE, Harold 290
ROSENSTEIN RODAN, Paul
107–8
ROSS, William 73
ROSTOW, Eugene 188
ROSTOW, Walt 147, 154, 188, 202,
345
ROTHSCHILD, Lord 215
ROWAN, Sir Leslie 19, 22, 94,
165, 219, 329
ROY, Andrew 7, 182, 334, 337,
344
Royal Commission on Taxation 263
R.T.Z. Ltd. 203
RUEFF, Jacques 78, 177
RUMBOLD, Sir Algernon 81
RYRIE, W.S. 192, 348, 350

SALISBURY, Lord 180
SAMUELSON, Paul 296